A DESCRIPTIVE CATALOGUE

OF THE

MEDIEVAL AND RENAISSANCE MANUSCRIPTS

OF THE

UNIVERSITY OF NOTRE DAME

AND

SAINT MARY'S COLLEGE

A DESCRIPTIVE CATALOGUE

of the

MEDIEVAL AND RENAISSANCE MANUSCRIPTS

of the

UNIVERSITY OF NOTRE DAME

and

SAINT MARY'S COLLEGE

DAVID T. GURA

University of Notre Dame Press
Notre Dame, Indiana

Published by the University of Notre Dame Press
Notre Dame, Indiana 46556
www.undpress.nd.edu

Manufactured in the United States of America

Library of Congress Cataloging-in-Publication Data

Names: Gura, David Turco, author.
Title: A descriptive catalogue of the medieval and Renaissance manuscripts of the University of Notre Dame and Saint Mary's College / David T. Gura.
Description: Notre Dame, Indiana : University of Notre Dame Press, 2016. | Includes bibliographical references and index.
Identifiers: LCCN 2016032984 (print) | LCCN 2016042351 (ebook) | ISBN 9780268100605 (hardcover) | ISBN 0268100608 (hardcover) | ISBN 9780268100629 (pdf)
Subjects: LCSH: University of Notre Dame. Library—Catalogs. | Snite Museum of Art—Catalogs. | Cushwa-Leighton Library—Catalogs. | Manuscripts, Medieval—Indiana—Notre Dame—Catalogs. | Manuscripts, Renaissance—Indiana—Notre Dame—Catalogs. | BISAC: REFERENCE / Catalogs. | LITERARY CRITICISM / Renaissance. | LANGUAGE ARTS & DISCIPLINES / Library & Information Science / Cataloging & Classification.
Classification: LCC Z6621. U6646 G87 2016 (print) | LCC Z6621. U6646 (ebook) | DDC 011/.31—dc23
LC record available at https://lccn.loc.gov/2016032984

∞ *This paper meets the requirements of ANSI/NISO Z39.48-1992 (Permanence of Paper).*

In memoriam

Olivia Remie Constable (1960–2014)

Contents

Preface and Acknowledgments

When I first arrived at the University of Notre Dame, my initial task as Curator of Ancient and Medieval Manuscripts was to develop a new shelfmark system for perpetual use. It quickly became apparent that the value of this collection for both teaching and research was not well known within the university community and was virtually unkown outside of it. I began the present project in the Fall of 2010, namely, to update and correct the previous catalogue by J. Corbett, and to describe all the materials acquired since . . . but the manuscripts kept coming. Many of the "new" manuscripts were acquired to increase the collection's breadth and for pedagogical purposes, especially in support of new courses in paleography and codicology that I developed at the suggestion of the late Olivia Remie Constable, then the Robert M. Conway Director of the Medieval Institute, and with the support of Louis E. Jordan, who was head of Rare Books and Special Collections. Other manuscripts were selected in consultation with Margot Fassler and Peter Jeffery for the Sacred Music Program. The spirit of inquiry and the newly found "manuscript mania" at Notre Dame led me to search for manuscripts beyond the Hesburgh Library. Those held by the Snite Museum of Art and Saint Mary's College, once known to only a select few and never described, are now widely accessible for the first time. David Ganz once told me that a man could spend his entire life writing a manuscript catalogue. I now understand what he meant. Anyone who has done a similar project knows well that two sets of eyes are better than one, and in this regard I owe thanks to many people.

Foremost, I wish to thank all those in the University of Notre Dame and Saint Mary's College communities who supported this project, contributed funds for the acquisition of manuscripts, shared their opinions, and brought their classes into the Rare Book Room (in alphabetical order): Prof. Chris Abram, Roberta Baranowski, Tracy Bergstrom, Prof. Alexander Blachly, Prof. W. Martin Bloomer, Prof. Maureen Boulton, Prof. Calvin Bower, Prof. Theodore Cachey, Rebecca Ceravolo, Aedín Ní Bhróithe Clements, Prof. Shawn Colberg,

Prof. Olivia Remie Constable, Dr. Rebecca DeBoer, Lorenzo Dell'Oso, Sue Donovan, Dr. David Dressing, Prof. Rev. Michael Driscoll, Liz Dube, Prof. Stephen Dumont, Prof. Kent Emery, Jr., Prof. Margot Fassler, Laura Fuderer, Dr. David Ganz, Prof. Bernd Goering, Prof. Rev. Msgr. Michael Heintz, Prof. Dan Hobbins, Jill Hobgood, Bob Hohl, Harv Humphrey, Dr. Andrew J. M. Irving, Prof. Peter Jeffrey, Prof. C. J. Jones, Dr. Louis E. Jordan, Prof. Danielle Joyner, John Kovacs, Alan Krieger, Dr. Stephen Little, Natasha Lyandres, Kitty Marschal, Prof. Elizabeth Mazurek, Prof. Vittorio Montemaggi, Prof. Hildegund Müller, Prof. Amy Mulligan, Prof. Susan Omer, Dr. Dianne Phillips, Prof. Charles M. Rosenberg, George Rugg, Prof. Katy Schlegel, Dr. Julia Schneider, Robert Simon, Dr. Marina Smyth, Dr. Cheryl Snay, Marsha Stevenson, David Sullivan, Dr. Julie Tanaka, Sara Weber, and Stephen Wrinn. I also thank Therese Bauters, Monica Crabtree, and Laura Sill in the Acquisitions Department of the Hesburgh Library for their adept handling of all the fiscal complications of the manuscript acquisition process, and my curatorial assistants (past and present) Wesley Wood and Brendan Coyne for their willingness to complete a variety of tasks. I owe a special thanks to Diane Parr Walker, the Edward H. Arnold University Librarian of the Hesburgh Library, Chuck Loving, the director of the Snite Museum of Art, and Janet Fore, the director of the Cushwa-Leighton Library at Saint Mary's College, for their enthusiastic support of my research and continued use of the collections.

I also express my gratitude to the following archivists, curators, professors, librarians, and friends for allowing me access to their collections, sharing information, and checking the shelfmarks of their fragments: Prof. Alison Altstatt (University of Northern Iowa), Dr. Pablo Alvarez (University of Michigan), Dott.ssa Agnese Bellieni (Università Cattolica del Sacro Cuore), Randolph Boyd (Chapman University), Laura Fleischmann (Albright-Knox Art Gallery), Kathryn Floyd (Geneva College), don Federico Gallo (Biblioteca Ambrosiana), Glynnis Gilbert (Tampa-Hillsborough County Public Library), Stephen Grinch (Otterbein University),Will Hansen (Newberry Library), Elizabeth Hays (Lima Public Library), Prof. Greg Hays (University of Virginia), Stevie Horn (University of Saskatchewan), Prof. Eric Johnson (The Ohio State University), Heather Kendall (Phoenix Public Library), Peter Kidd, Prof. Erik Kwakkel (Leiden University), Dr. Susan L'Engle (St. Louis University), Anna Morton (University of North Carolina at Chapel Hill), Timothy Murray (University of Delaware), Dr. Paul S. Needham (Princeton University), Dr. Cillian O'Hogan (British Library), Dr. Emily Peters (RISD Museum), Catie Polack (Licking County Library), Prof. Susan Rankin (University of Cambridge), Sr. Ruthagnes, O. S. F. (Sisters of St. Francis of Perpetual Adoration), Dr. William P. Stoneman (Harvard University), Dr. Jill Unkel (Chester Beatty Library), Ed Vermue (Oberlin College), Dr. Richard Virr (McGill University), and Brandon Wason (Emory University).

To Prof. Frank T. Coulson for teaching me that a paleographer must be able to read all hands, to Prof. Albert Derolez for teaching me the skills of analytical manuscript description, to Prof. Scott Gwara for his numerous insightful and unparalleled observations, and to my research assistant Halle McGuire Hobbins for her diligence: *gratias uobis ago maximas.*

Last, but not least, I thank my family for their encouragement, my young son, Samson Desiderius, for teaching me the value of perspective, and my loving wife, Alisa, for her patience, support, and her understanding that sometimes I just think about manuscripts.

Discipulis praesentibus et futuris: haec manuscripta uobis sunt.

D. T. G.
Scribebam Nostrae Dominae Indianensis,
mense Martis anno Domini MMXVI
Deo gratias.

Plates

Plates 1–8 follow the introduction, beginning on p. 52.

Manuscripts

Manuscripts by Repository with Short Description

University of Notre Dame, Hesburgh Library

cod. Lat. a. 1	Book of Hours, use of Sarum. Low Countries, s. xv^{2}.
cod. Lat. a. 2	Book of Hours, use of Rome. Low Countries, s. xv^{2}.
cod. Lat. a. 3	Book of Hours, use of Sarum. England, s. xv.
cod. Lat. a. 4	Statuta Angliae. England, s. xiv^{2}.
cod. Lat. a. 5	Peter Riga, *Aurora.* France s. xiii^{1}.
cod. Lat. a. 6	Book of Hours, use of Rome. Low Countries, s. xv^{2}.
cod. Lat. a. 7	Ferial Psalter. Low Countries, s. xv^{2}.
cod. Lat. a. 8	Book of Hours, use of Paris. France, s. xv.
cod. Lat. a. 9	Book of Hours, use of Rouen. France, s. xv^{2}.
cod. Lat. a. 10	Jerome, *Interpretationes*; anon. liturgical commentary. England, s. xiii^{2}.
cod. Lat. a. 11	Gregory the Great, *Dialogi* (Lib. II); lauda. Italy, s. xv^{1}.
cod. Lat. a. 12	Office of the Dead (Dominican). Germany, s. xv^{2}.
cod. Lat. a. 13	Bible fragment (Esther, Job, Psalms). France, s. xiii^{2}.
cod. Lat. a. 14	Calendar (Bruges). Low Countries, s. xv^{2}.
cod. Lat. a. 15	Book of Hours, use of Bourges and Paris. France, s. xv^{2}.
cod. Lat. a. 16	Book of Hours, use of Rome. Low Countries, s. xv^{2}.
cod. Lat. b. 1	Psalter (Dominican). Germany, s. xv^{2}.
cod. Lat. b. 2	Psalter (Dominican). Germany, s. xv^{1}–xv^{2}.
cod. Lat. b. 3	*Facetus* (*cum nihil utilius*). France, s. xiv^{2}.
cod. Lat. b. 4	Psalter and Diurnal (Carthusian). France, s. xiii^{2}.
cod. Lat. b. 5	Nicholas de Byard, Humbert of Romans, Ps.-Bernard. France, s. xiii^{ex}/xiv^{in}.

cod. Lat. b. 6	Ascetic and devotional treatises. France, s. xv^{2}.
cod. Lat. b. 7	Bible. Bohemia, s. xv^{1}.
cod. Lat. b. 8	Alan of Lille, *Liber parabolarum*. Low Countries, s. xv^{2}.
cod. Lat. b. 9	Peraldus, *Summa de uitiis*. Italy, s. xiv^{1}.
cod. Lat. b. 10	Two humanist miscellanies. Italy, s. xv^{2}.
cod. Lat. b. 11	Philip the Chancellor, sermons. France, s. xiii.
cod. Lat. b. 12	Florilegium. Bohemia, s. xv^{2}.
cod. Lat. b. 13	Missal (Coutances). France, s. xiii^{2}.
cod. Lat. b. 14	Sermon collection. Germany, s. xvi^{in}.
cod. Lat. b. 15	Antiphonary. Switzerland or Germany, s. xvi^{1}.
cod. Lat. c. 1	Nicholas of Pelhřimov, *Scriptum super quattuor euangelia*. Bohemia, s. xv.
cod. Lat. c. 2	Gradual (Franciscan). Italy, s. xvi^{1}.
cod. Lat. c. 3	Gradual (Franciscan). Italy, s. xvi^{1}.
cod. Lat. c. 4	Peter Comestor, *Historia scholastica*. France, s. xiii^{1}.
cod. Lat. c. 5	Nicholas of Osimo, *Suppl. summae pisanellae*. Italy, s. xv^{2}.
cod. Lat. c. 6	Peter Riga, *Aurora*. Iberia, s. xiii^{1}.
cod. Lat. c. 7	Augustine, *Rectractationes*; *De doctrina christiana*. England, s. xv^{2}.
cod. Lat. c. 8	Rule of the Compagnia Ambrosiana. Italy, s. xv^{ex}–xvi.
cod. Lat. c. 9	Francesco da Fiesso, *De uisitatione* and prefaces by Giovanni Agostino Folperti. Italy, s. xvi^{1}.
cod. Lat. c. 10	Zanobi Acciaiuoli (tr.), Olympiodorus, *In Ecclesiasten*. Italy, s. xvi^{1}.
cod. Lat. c. 11	Humanist miscellany. Italy, s. xv^{2}.
cod. Lat. c. 12	Pontifical. France, s. xiv^{2}.
cod. Lat. c. 13	Missal. Spain, s. xiv.
cod. Lat. c. 14	Gradual. Southern Germany or Austria, s. xiv^{1}.
cod. Lat. c. 15	Gradual. France, s. xiii^{2}.
cod. Lat. d. 1	Sermons of Peregrinus of Opole; texts of Narcissus Herzburg, Nicolaus von Dinkelsbühl, Peter Reicher of Pirchenwart, Thomas Ebendorfer. Germany or Austria, s. xv.
cod. Lat. d. 2	Cyprian and Ps.-Cyprian, works. Southern France, s. xv^{2}.
cod. Lat. d. 3	Martin of Troppau, Geoffrey of Monmouth, Ps.-Methodius; genealogical chronicle. England, s. xv^{1}.
cod. Lat. d. 4	Walter Burley, commentary on *Ars uetus*. Italy, s. xv.
cod. Lat. d. 5	Boethius, *De consolatione philosophiae*; works of Filippo da Strada. Italy. s. xv^{2}.
cod. Lat. d. 6	Piccolomini, works; various epistolary extracts. Austria or Bohemia, s. xv^{2}.
cod. Lat. e. 1	Boniface VIII, *Liber sextus*. Southern France or Italy, s. xiv.
cod. Lat. e. 2	Buridan, *Quaestiones* on Aristotle's *Ethics*. Italy, s. xv.

cod. Lat. e. 3	Paulus de Liazariis, *Lectura super Clementinis*. Italy, s. xiv^{2}.
cod. Lat. e. 4	Psalter. England, s. xiv^{2}.
MS Eng. d. 1	*A Mirror to Devout People* (*Speculum deuotorum*). England, s. xv^{1}.
MS Fr. c. 1	*Le Sacre de Claude de France*. France, s. xvi^{1}.
MS Fr. c. 2	Cuvelier, *Chanson de Bertrand du Guesclin*. France, s. xv^{2}.
MS Fr. d. 1	*Roman de la Rose*. France, s. xv^{2}.
MS Ger. a. 1	Prayerbook. Germany, s. xv^{ex}.
MS Ital. b. 1	Italian poetry. Italy, s. xvi^{1}.
MS Ital. b. 2	Catherine of Siena, *Letters*; Ugo Panziera, *Trattati spirituali*; Feo Belcari, *Laude*. Italy, s. xv^{2}.
MS Ital. d. 1	Henry Suso, *Horologium sapientiae* (in Italian). Italy, s. xv^{2}.
Frag. I. 1	Prayerbook [leaf]. Low Countries, s. xv^{2}.
Frag. I. 2	Book of Hours (Geert Groote) [leaf]. Low Countries, s. xv^{2}.
Frag. I. 3	Miniature; Forgery from Philip Duschnes [withdrawn].
Frag. I. 4	Psalter [6 leaves]. Spain, s. xvi.
Frag. I. 5	Book of Hours or Psalter [leaf]. Low Countries, s. xv^{2}.
Frag. I. 6	Evangeliary [leaf]. Southern France, s. xv^{2}.
Frag. I. 7	Pocket Bible [leaf]. France, s. xiii^{2}.
Frag. I. 8	Book of Hours [leaf]. France, s. xv^{2}.
Frag. I. 9	Book of Hours [leaf]. France, s. xv^{2}.
Frag. I. 10	Book of Hours [leaf]. France, s. xv^{1}.
Frag. I. 11	Simon of Cremona, sermons [leaf]. Germany, s. xv^{2}.
Frag. I. 12	Psalter [leaf]. Low Countries, s. xiii.
Frag. I. 13	Gradual, Temporale [binding fragment]. Austria, Germany, or Bohemia, s. xii^{1}.
Frag. I. 14	Isidore of Seville, *Origines* [2 leaves]. France, s. xii^{ex}.
Frag. I. 15	Evangeliary [leaf]. Eastern Mediterranean (Crete), s. xii.
Frag. I. 16	Missal [binding fragments]. England, s. xiv^{2}.
Frag. I. 17	Breviary, Sanctorale. England, s. xiii^{2}/xiv^{1}.
Frag. I. 18	Missale [binding fragment]. Germany, s. xiii^{in}.
Frag. I. 19	John Chrysostom (sp.), *Homilia in sanctum Mattheum* [binding fragments]. England, s. xv^{1}.
Frag. I. 20	Book of Hours [3 leaves]. Low Countries, s. xv^{2}.
Frag. I. 21	Glossed Bible (2 Par.) [leaf]. France, s. xii^{2}.
Frag. I. 22	Mass book [binding fragment]. Germany, s. xi^{ex}.
Frag. I. 23	Unidentified binding fragment. France, s. xiv^{in}.
Frag. I. 24	Breviary [binding fragment]. Southern France (?), s. xv.
Frag. I. 25	Breviary [binding fragment]. England, s. xii^{2}.
Frag. I. 26	Jerome, *Commentarii in Ezechielem* [binding fragments]. England, s. xii.

Frag. I. 27	Office book [binding fragment]. Southern Italy (Benevento), s. xii^{ex}.
Frag. I. 28	Mass book [binding fragments]. Italy, s. xi^{ex}.
Frag. I. 29	Gradual [binding fragment]. Germany, s. xiii^{1}.
Frag. I. 30	Breviary [binding fragment]. Austria or Germany, s. xiii^{in}.
Frag. I. 31	Giles of Rome, *Quaestiones*. France, s. xiv^{1}.
Frag. I. 32	Gregory the Great, *Homiliae in Ezechielem prophetam* [leaf]. Italy, s. xiii^{2}.
Frag. I. 33	Calendar [leaf]. France, s. xv^{2}.
Frag. I. 34	Bible [leaf]. France, s. xiii^{2}.
Frag. I. 35	Ovid, *Metamorphoses* [binding fragment]. France, s. xiii.
Frag. I. 36	Psalter-Hours [leaf]. Low Countries, s. xiii^{2}.
Frag. II. 1	Atlantic Bible [leaf]. Italy, s. xii^{1}.
Frag. II. 2	Antiphonary, Temporale [leaf]. Italy, s. xv.
Frag. II. 3	Gradual [binding fragment]. Italy, s. xv.
Frag. II. 4	Calendar (Carthusian) [6 leaves]. Spain, s. xvi^{1}.
Frag. II. 5	Missal [binding fragment]. France or Low Countries, s. xv^{2}.
Frag. III. 1	Book of Hours, use of Vannes and Rennes [92 leaves]. France, s. xv.
Frag. V. 1	Antiphonary, Sanctorale [leaf]. Italy, s. xvi^{in}.
Frag. V. 2	Gradual, Sanctorale [leaf]. Spain, xvi.
Frag. V. 3	Antiphonary, Temporale [binding fragment]. Italy, s. xiii^{1}.
Constable MS 1	Book of Hours [leaf]. Low Countries, s. xv^{2}.
Constable MS 2	Book of Hours [leaf]. Low Countries, s. xv^{2}.
Constable MS 3	Bible [leaf]. France, s. xiv^{1}.
Constable MS 4	Processional [leaf]. England, s. xiii^{1}.
Constable MS 5	Gregory the Great, *Dialogi* [binding fragment]. Italy, s. xii^{2}.
Constable MS 6	*Authenticum* [leaf]. Italy, s. xiv^{1}.
Constable MS 7	Lectionary or Breviary [binding fragment]. Spain, s. xiii^{in}.
Constable MS 8	Bible [leaf]. Low Countries, s. xiv^{in}.
Constable MS 9	Atlantic Bible [binding fragments]. Italy, s. xii^{1}.

University of Notre Dame, Snite Museum of Art

Acc. 1967.19	Book of Hours (Geert Groote) [leaf]. Low Countries, s. xv^{2}.
Acc. 1967.20.4	Book of Hours [leaf]. Italy, s. xv^{2}.
Acc. 1972.34	Book of Hours (Geert Groote) [leaf]. Low Countries, s. xv^{2}.
Acc. 1973.51	Psalter [leaf]. France, s. xiii^{ex}.
Acc. 1973.55	Book of Hours, use of Sarum [leaf]. Low Countries, s. xv.
Acc. 1974.28	Antiphonary, Temporale [leaf]. Italy, s. xv.
Acc. 1974.29	Antiphonary, Sanctorale [leaf]. Italy, s. xv^{2}.
Acc. 1974.30	Book of Hours [leaf]. France, s. xv^{2}.

Acc. 1974.31	Book of Hours [leaf]. Low Countries, s. xv^{2}.
Acc. 1974.32	Book of Hours [leaf]. France, s. xv^{2}.
Acc. 1974.33	Book of Hours [leaf]. France, s. xv^{2}.
Acc. 1975.43	Bible [leaf]. Southern France, s. xiii^{ex}.
Acc. 1975.56	Book of Hours [leaf]. France, s. xv^{2}.
Acc. 1975.57	Bible [leaf]. Southern France, s. xiii^{ex}.
Acc. 1978.28	Calendar (Parisian; use of Rome) [6 leaves]. France, s. xv^{ex}.
Acc. 1980.58.4	Antiphonary, Temporale [leaf]. Southern France, s. xv^{ex}.
Acc. 1980.58.5	Antiphonary, Temporale [leaf]. Italy, s. xv^{2}.
Acc. 1984.3.1	Gradual, Temporale [leaf]. Spain, s. xvi.
Acc. 1984.3.2	Antiphonary, Sanctorale [leaf]. Italy, s. xiv.
Acc. 1984.3.3	Antiphonary, Sanctorale [leaf]. Germany or Low Countries, s. xvi^{in}.
Acc. 1984.3.4	Antiphonary, Sanctorale [6 leaves]. Spain, s. xvi^{2}.
Acc. 1984.3.6	Confessional. Italy, s. xv^{2}.
Acc. 1984.3.7	Antiphonary, Temporale [leaf]. Spain, s. xvi^{2}.
Acc. 1985.25	*Meditationes uitae Christi* (Italian; 'short version'). Italy, s. xiv^{2}.
Acc. 1989.20.1	Miniature of St. Agatha [cutting]. Low Countries, s. xv^{2}.
Acc. 1989.20.2	Bible [leaf]. France, s. xiii^{2}.
Acc. 1989.20.3	Bible [leaf]. France, s. xiii^{2}.
Acc. 1989.20.4	Book of Hours ("Ghistelles Hours") [leaf]. Low Countries, s. xiv^{in}.
Acc. 1989.20.5	Bible [binding fragment]. England, s. xiii^{2}.
Acc. 1989.20.6	Book of Hours [leaf]. France or Flanders, s. xiv^{2}.
Acc. 1989.20.7	Master of Monza (attr.), Three saints [cutting]. Italy, s. xiii^{2}.
Acc. 1996.48	Antiphonary, Sanctorale [leaf]. Low Countries, s. xv^{2}.
Acc. 2015.37	Psalter [leaf]. Low Countries, s. xv^{2}.

Saint Mary's College, Cushwa-Leighton Library

MS 1	Peter Lombard, *Sentences* (Lib. IV); excerpts of Rather of Verona and Adalgerus; selections of Burchard of Worms, *Decretum.* Germany, s. xii^{ex}–xiii^{2}.
MS 2	Thomas Aquinas, *De ente et essentia*; Aristoteles Latinus, *De longitudine*, *Analytica priora*; sermon collection. France and England, s. xiii^{ex}–xiv^{in}.
MS 3	Book of Hours, use of Amiens. Northern France, s. xv^{2}.
MS 4	Antiphonary, Temporale [2 leaves]. Italy, s. xiv^{2}.
MS 5	Gradual, Temporale [2 leaves]. Italy, s. xv^{2}.
MS 6	Gradual, Temporale [leaf]. Spain, s. xvi.
MS 7	Antiphonary, Sanctorale [leaf]. Spain, s. xvi^{in}.

MS 8	Gradual, Common of saints [leaf]. Spain, s. xvi.
MS 9	Gradual, Sanctorale [leaf]. Spain, s. xvi.
MS 10	Gradual, Common of saints [leaf]. Spain, s. xvi.

Manuscripts by Century

Manuscripts containing contents that span multiple centuries are repeated in each category.

S. XI

Frag. I. 22
Frag. I. 28

S. XII

Frag. I. 13
Frag. I. 14
Frag. I. 15
Frag. I. 21
Frag. I. 25
Frag. I. 26
Frag. I. 27
Frag. II. 1
Constable MS 5
Constable MS 9
MS 1 (Saint Mary's)

S. XIII

cod. Lat. a. 5
cod. Lat. a. 10
cod. Lat. a. 13
cod. Lat. b. 4
cod. Lat. b. 5
cod. Lat. b. 11
cod. Lat. b. 13
cod. Lat. c. 4
cod. Lat. c. 6
cod. Lat. c. 15
Frag. I. 7
Frag. I. 12
Frag. I. 17
Frag. I. 18
Frag. I. 29
Frag. I. 30
Frag. I. 32
Frag. I. 34
Frag. I. 35
Frag. I. 36
Frag. V. 3
Constable MS 4
Constable MS 7
Acc. 1973.51
Acc. 1975.43
Acc. 1975.57
Acc. 1989.20.2
Acc. 1989.20.3
Acc. 1989.20.5
Acc. 1989.20.7
MS 1 (Saint Mary's)
MS 2 (Saint Mary's)

S. XIV

cod. Lat. a. 4	cod. Lat. e. 3	Constable MS 8
cod. Lat. b. 3	cod. Lat. e. 4	Acc. 1984.3.2
cod. Lat. b. 5	Frag. I. 16	Acc. 1985.25
cod. Lat. b. 9	Frag. I. 17	Acc. 1989.20.4
cod. Lat. c. 12	Frag. I. 23	Acc. 1989.20.6
cod. Lat. c. 13	Frag. I. 31	MS 2 (Saint Mary's)
cod. Lat. c. 14	Constable MS 3	MS 4 (Saint Mary's)
cod. Lat. e. 1	Constable MS 6	

S. XV

cod. Lat. a. 1	cod. Lat. d. 2	Frag. II. 3
cod. Lat. a. 2	cod. Lat. d. 3	Frag. II. 5
cod. Lat. a. 3	cod. Lat. d. 4	Frag. III. 1
cod. Lat. a. 6	cod. Lat. d. 5	Constable MS 1
cod. Lat. a. 7	cod. Lat. d. 6	Constable MS 2
cod. Lat. a. 8	cod. Lat. e. 2	Acc. 1967.19
cod. Lat. a. 9	MS Eng. d. 1	Acc. 1967.20.4
cod. Lat. a. 11	MS Fr. c. 2	Acc. 1972.34
cod. Lat. a. 12	MS Fr. d. 1	Acc. 1973.55
cod. Lat. a. 14	MS Ger. a. 1	Acc. 1974.28
cod. Lat. a. 15	MS Ital. b. 2	Acc. 1974.29
cod. Lat. a. 16	MS Ital. d. 1	Acc. 1974.30
cod. Lat. b. 1	Frag. I. 1	Acc. 1974.31
cod. Lat. b. 2	Frag. I. 2	Acc. 1974.32
cod. Lat. b. 6	Frag. I. 5	Acc. 1974.33
cod. Lat. b. 7	Frag. I. 6	Acc. 1975.56
cod. Lat. b. 8	Frag. I. 8	Acc. 1978.28
cod. Lat. b. 10	Frag. I. 9	Acc. 1980.58.4
cod. Lat. b. 12	Frag. I. 10	Acc. 1980.58.5
cod. Lat. c. 1	Frag. I. 11	Acc. 1984.3.6
cod. Lat. c. 5	Frag. I. 19	Acc. 1989.20.1
cod. Lat. c. 7	Frag. I. 20	Acc. 1996.48
cod. Lat. c. 8	Frag. I. 24	Acc. 2015.37
cod. Lat. c. 11	Frag. I. 33	MS 3 (Saint Mary's)
cod. Lat. d. 1	Frag. II. 2	MS 5 (Saint Mary's)

S. XVI

cod. Lat. b. 14
cod. Lat. b. 15
cod. Lat. c. 2
cod. Lat. c. 3
cod. Lat. c. 8
cod. Lat. c. 9
cod. Lat. c. 10
MS Fr. c. 1
MS Ital. b. 1
Frag. I. 4
Frag. II. 4
Frag. V. 1
Frag. V. 2
Acc. 1984.3.1
Acc. 1984.3.3
Acc. 1984.3.4
Acc. 1984.3.7
MS 6 (Saint Mary's)
MS 7 (Saint Mary's)
MS 8 (Saint Mary's)
MS 9 (Saint Mary's)
MS 10 (Saint Mary's)

Manuscripts by Country or Region

Austria or Bohemia

cod. Lat. d. 6

Austria, Germany, or Bohemia

Frag. I. 13

Bohemia

cod. Lat. b. 7
cod. Lat. b. 12
cod. Lat. c. 1

Eastern Mediterranean

Frag. I. 15

England

cod. Lat. a. 3
cod. Lat. a. 4
cod. Lat. a. 10
cod. Lat. c. 7
cod. Lat. d. 3
cod. Lat. e. 4
MS Eng. d. 1
Frag. I. 16
Frag. I. 17
Frag. I. 19
Frag. I. 25
Frag. I. 26
Constable MS 4
Acc. 1989.20.5
MS 2 (Saint Mary's)

France

cod. Lat. a. 5
cod. Lat. a. 8
cod. Lat. a. 9
cod. Lat. a. 13
cod. Lat. a. 15
cod. Lat. b. 3
cod. Lat. b. 4
cod. Lat. b. 5
cod. Lat. b. 6
cod. Lat. b. 11
cod. Lat. b. 13
cod. Lat. c. 4
cod. Lat. c. 12
cod. Lat. c. 15
cod. Lat. d. 2
MS Fr. c. 1
MS Fr. c. 2
MS Fr. d. 1
Frag. I. 6
Frag. I. 7
Frag. I. 8
Frag. I. 9
Frag. I. 10
Frag. I. 14
Frag. I. 21
Frag. I. 23
Frag. I. 24
Frag. I. 31
Frag. I. 33
Frag. I. 34
Frag. I. 35
Frag. III. 1
Constable MS 3
Acc. 1973.51
Acc. 1974.30
Acc. 1974.32
Acc. 1974.33
Acc. 1975.43
Acc. 1975.56
Acc. 1975.57
Acc. 1978.28
Acc. 1980.58.4
Acc. 1989.20.2
Acc. 1989.20.3
MS 2 (Saint Mary's)
MS 3 (Saint Mary's)

France or Italy

cod. Lat. e. 1

France or Low Countries

Frag. II. 5
Acc. 1989.20.6

Germany

cod. Lat. a. 12
cod. Lat. b. 1
cod. Lat. b. 2
cod. Lat. b. 14
MS Ger. a. 1
Frag. I. 11
Frag. I. 18
Frag. I. 22
Frag. I. 29
MS 1 (Saint Mary's)

Germany or Austria

cod. Lat. c. 14
cod. Lat. d. 1
Frag. I. 30

Germany or Low Countries

Acc. 1984.3.3

Iberia (Spain or Portugal)

cod. Lat. c. 6
cod. Lat. c. 13
Frag. I. 4
Frag. II. 4
Frag. V. 2
Constable MS 7
Acc. 1984.3.1
Acc. 1984.3.4
Acc. 1984.3.7
MS 6 (Saint Mary's)
MS 7 (Saint Mary's)
MS 8 (Saint Mary's)
MS 9 (Saint Mary's)
MS 10 (Saint Mary's)

Italy

cod. Lat. a. 11
cod. Lat. b. 9
cod. Lat. b. 10
cod. Lat. c. 2
cod. Lat. c. 3
cod. Lat. c. 5
cod. Lat. c. 8
cod. Lat. c. 9
cod. Lat. c. 10
cod. Lat. c. 11
cod. Lat. d. 4
cod. Lat. d. 5
cod. Lat. e. 2
cod. Lat. e. 3
MS Ital. b. 1
MS Ital. b. 2
MS Ital. d. 1
Frag. I. 27
Frag. I. 28
Frag. I. 32
Frag. II. 1
Frag. II. 2
Frag. II. 3
Frag. V. 1
Frag. V. 3
Constable MS 5
Constable MS 6
Constable MS 9
Acc. 1967.20.4
Acc. 1974.28
Acc. 1974.29
Acc. 1980.58.5
Acc. 1984.3.2
Acc. 1984.3.6
Acc. 1985.25
Acc. 1989.20.7
MS 4 (Saint Mary's)
MS 5 (Saint Mary's)

Low Countries

cod. Lat. a. 1
cod. Lat. a. 2
cod. Lat. a. 6
cod. Lat. a. 7
cod. Lat. a. 14
cod. Lat. a. 16
cod. Lat. b. 8
Frag. I. 1
Frag. I. 2
Frag. I. 5
Frag. I. 12
Frag. I. 20
Frag. I. 36
Constable MS 1
Constable MS 2
Constable MS 8
Acc. 1967.19
Acc. 1972.34
Acc. 1973.55
Acc. 1974.31
Acc. 1989.20.1
Acc. 1989.20.4
Acc. 1996.48
Acc. 2015.37

Switzerland or Germany

cod. Lat. b. 15

Manuscripts by Language

Manuscripts containing multiple languages are repeated in each category. For manuscripts in the Hesburgh Library, the dominant language corresponds to the manuscript's fond.

Dutch

Frag. I. 1
Frag. I. 2
Acc. 1967.19
Acc. 1972.34
Acc. 1974.31

English

cod. Lat. a. 13
MS Eng. d. 1

French

cod. Lat. a. 4
cod. Lat. a. 8
cod. Lat. a. 9
cod. Lat. b. 4
cod. Lat. b. 14
cod. Lat. b. 15
MS Fr. c. 1
MS Fr. c. 2
MS Fr. d. 1
Frag. I. 20
Frag. I. 33
Acc. 1975.56
Acc. 1978.28
MS 3 (Saint Mary's)

German

cod. Lat. a. 12
cod. Lat. b. 1
cod. Lat. b. 2
cod. Lat. d. 1
MS Ger. a. 1

Greek

cod. Lat. b. 10
cod. Lat. c. 11
Frag. I. 15
Frag. I. 26 (one word in Greek)

Italian

cod. Lat. a. 11	cod. Lat. d. 5	MS Ital. d. 1
cod. Lat. b. 10	MS Ital. b. 1	Acc. 1984.3.6
cod. Lat. c. 8	MS Ital. b. 2	Acc. 1985.25

Latin

cod. Lat. a. 1	cod. Lat. c. 3	Frag. I. 11
cod. Lat. a. 2	cod. Lat. c. 4	Frag. I. 12
cod. Lat. a. 3	cod. Lat. c. 5	Frag. I. 13
cod. Lat. a. 4	cod. Lat. c. 6	Frag. I. 14
cod. Lat. a. 5	cod. Lat. c. 7	Frag. I. 16
cod. Lat. a. 6	cod. Lat. c. 8	Frag. I. 17
cod. Lat. a. 7	cod. Lat. c. 9	Frag. I. 18
cod. Lat. a. 8	cod. Lat. c. 10	Frag. I. 19
cod. Lat. a. 9	cod. Lat. c. 11	Frag. I. 20
cod. Lat. a. 10	cod. Lat. c. 12	Frag. I. 21
cod. Lat. a. 11	cod. Lat. c. 13	Frag. I. 22
cod. Lat. a. 12	cod. Lat. c. 14	Frag. I. 23
cod. Lat. a. 13	cod. Lat. c. 15	Frag. I. 24
cod. Lat. a. 14	cod. Lat. d. 1	Frag. I. 25
cod. Lat. a. 15	cod. Lat. d. 2	Frag. I. 26
cod. Lat. a. 16	cod. Lat. d. 3	Frag. I. 27
cod. Lat. b. 1	cod. Lat. d. 4	Frag. I. 28
cod. Lat. b. 2	cod. Lat. d. 5	Frag. I. 29
cod. Lat. b. 3	cod. Lat. d. 6	Frag. I. 30
cod. Lat. b. 4	cod. Lat. e. 1	Frag. I. 31
cod. Lat. b. 5	cod. Lat. e. 2	Frag. I. 32
cod. Lat. b. 6	cod. Lat. e. 3	Frag. I. 34
cod. Lat. b. 7	cod. Lat. e. 4	Frag. I. 35
cod. Lat. b. 8	MS Eng. d. 1	Frag. I. 36
cod. Lat. b. 9	MS Fr. c. 1	Frag. II. 1
cod. Lat. b. 10	MS Ital. d. 1	Frag. II. 2
cod. Lat. b. 11	Frag. I. 4	Frag. II. 3
cod. Lat. b. 12	Frag. I. 5	Frag. II. 4
cod. Lat. b. 13	Frag. I. 6	Frag. II. 5
cod. Lat. b. 14	Frag. I. 7	Frag. III. 1
cod. Lat. b. 15	Frag. I. 8	Frag. V. 1
cod. Lat. c. 1	Frag. I. 9	Frag. V. 2
cod. Lat. c. 2	Frag. I. 10	Frag. V. 3

Latin *(continued)*

Constable MS 1
Constable MS 2
Constable MS 3
Constable MS 4
Constable MS 5
Constable MS 6
Constable MS 7
Constable MS 8
Constable MS 9
Acc. 1967.20.4
Acc. 1973.51
Acc. 1973.55
Acc. 1974.28
Acc. 1974.29
Acc. 1974.30
Acc. 1974.32
Acc. 1974.33
Acc. 1975.43
Acc. 1975.57
Acc. 1980.58.4
Acc. 1980.58.5
Acc. 1984.3.1
Acc. 1984.3.2
Acc. 1984.3.3
Acc. 1984.3.4
Acc. 1984.3.7
Acc. 1989.20.2
Acc. 1989.20.3
Acc. 1989.20.4
Acc. 1989.20.5
Acc. 1989.20.6
Acc. 1989.20.7
Acc. 1996.48
Acc. 2015.37
MS 1 (Saint Mary's)
MS 2 (Saint Mary's)
MS 3 (Saint Mary's)
MS 4 (Saint Mary's)
MS 5 (Saint Mary's)
MS 6 (Saint Mary's)
MS 7 (Saint Mary's)
MS 8 (Saint Mary's)
MS 9 (Saint Mary's)
MS 10 (Saint Mary's)

Abbreviations

The following abbreviations are used for works cited in select fields of the catalogue, such as brief bibliography, edition statements, or other areas within the manuscript descriptions. The works also appear in the bibliography, with the exception of the multi-volume series *AH*, *AL*, *DSAM*, *PG*, *PL*, and *SR*.

AH	Clemens Blume and Guido Maria Dreves, eds. *Analecta hymnica medii aevi* 1–55. Leipzig: Fues's Verlag (R. Reisland), 1886–1922.
AL	J. Brams et al., eds. *Aristoteles Latinus*. Leiden: Brill, 1961–.
Baldwyne 1	Peter Northeast, *Wills of the Archdeaconry of Sudbury, 1439–1474. Wills from the Register 'Baldwyne', Part I: 1439–1461*. Suffolk Records Society 44. Woodbridge: Boydell Press, 2001.
Baldwyne 2	Peter Northeast and Heather Falvey, *Wills of the Archdeaconry of Sudbury, 1439–1474. Wills from the Register 'Baldwyne', Part II: 1461–1474*. Suffolk Records Society 53. Woodbridge: Boydell Press, 2010.
Bertalot, *Initia*	Ludwig Bertalot and Ursula Jaitner-Hahner, *Initia humanistica Latina: Initienverzeichnis lateinicher Prosa und Poesie aus der Zeit des 14 bis 16.* 1–2.2. Tübingen: M. Niemeyer, 1985–2004.
BHL	[Bollandists], *Bibliotheca Hagiographica Latina* 1–2. Brussels: Socii Bollandiani, 1898–1901. *Novum Supplementum* by Henryk Fros. Brussels: Société des Bollandistes, 1986.
Bloomfield	Morton W. Bloomfield, Bertrand Georges Guyot, Donald Roy Howard, and Thyra B. Kabelao, *Incipits of Latin Works on the Virtues and*

Vices, 1100–1500 A.D., Including a Section of Incipits of Works on the Pater Noster. Cambridge, MA: Mediaeval Academy of America, 1979. Supplement: Richard Newhauser and István Pieter Bejczy, *A Supplement to Morton W. Bloomfield et al., 'Incipits of Latin Works on the Virtues and Vices, 1100–1500 A.D.'* Instrumenta Patristica et Mediaevalia 50. Turnhout: Brepols, 2008.

BRIQUET — Charles-Moïse Briquet, *Les filigranes: Dictionnaire historique des marques du papier dès leur apparition vers 1282 jusqu'en 1600; A Facsimile of the 1907 Edition with Supplementary Material* 1–4, ed. Alan Stevenson, 3rd ed. Amsterdam: The Paper Publications Society, 1968.

BRUYLANTS — Placide Bruylants, *Les Oraisons du Missel Romain: Texte et Histoire* 1–2. Louvain: Centre de Documentation et d'information Liturgiques, 1952; repr. 1965.

CCCOGD — Giuseppe Alberigo, Adolf Martin Ritter, et al., eds. *Conciliorum oecumenicorum generaliumque decreta: Editio critica.* Corpus Christianorum 1–3. Turnhout: Brepols, 2006–2013.

CIC — Emil Friedberg, *Corpus Iuris Canonici* 1–2. Graz: Akad. Druck- und Verl.-Anst, 1959.

CO — Edmund Eugène Moeller, Jean-Marie Clément, and Bertrand Coppieters 't Wallant, eds. *Corpus orationum.* Corpus Christianorum Series Latina 160 et al. Turnhout: Brepols, 1992–2004.

COLOPHONS — Saint-Benoît de Port-Valais (Bénedictins de Bouveret), *Colophons de manuscrits occidentaux des origines au XVIe siècle* 1–6. Fribourg: Suisse, Editions universitaires, 1965–1982.

CORBETT — James A. Corbett, *Catalogue of the Medieval & Renaissance Manuscripts of the University of Notre Dame.* Notre Dame, IN: University of Notre Dame Press, 1978.

COTTINEAU — Laurent Henri Cottineau, *Répertoire topo-bibliographique des abbayes et prieurés* 1–3. Mâcon: Protat frères, 1934–1970.

CPL — Eligius Dekkers and Emil Gaar, eds. *Clavis patrum latinorum: Qua in corpus christianorum edendum optimas quasque scriptorum recensiones a Tertulliano ad Bedam.* Corpus Christianorum Series Latina. 3rd ed. Steenbrugge: In Abbatia Sancti Petri, 1995.

de la Mare, *Lyell* Albinia C. de la Mare, *Catalogue of the Collection of Medieval Manuscripts Bequeathed to the Bodleian Library Oxford by James P. R. Lyell.* Oxford: Clarendon Press, 1971.

de Ricci Seymour de Ricci and William Jerome Wilson, *Census of Medieval and Renaissance Manuscripts in the United States and Canada* 1–3. New York: H. W. Wilson, 1935, 1937, 1940.

Derolez Albert Derolez, *Codicologie des manuscrits en écriture humanistique sur parchemin* 1–2. Mitteilung-Kommission für Humanismusforschung 4. Turnhout: Brepols, 1984.

DSAM Marcel Viller et al., eds. *Dictionnaire de spiritualité, ascétique et mystique, doctrine et histoire* 1–17. Paris: G. Beauchesen et ses fils, 1932–1995.

Faye and Bond Christopher Urdahl Faye and William Henry Bond, *Supplement to the Census of Medieval and Renaissance Manuscripts in the United States and Canada.* New York: Bibliographical Society of America, 1962.

HE Christopher Wordsworth, *Horae Eboracenses: The Prymer or Hours of the Blessed Virgin Mary According to the Use of the Illustrious Church of York; with Other Devotions as They Were Used by the Lay-Folk in the Northern Province in the XVth and XVIth Centuries.* Publications of the Surtees Society 132. Durham: Andrews and Co., 1920.

Heawood Edward Heawood, *Watermarks Mainly of the 17th and 18th Centuries.* Monumenta chartae papyraceae historiam illustrantia 1. Culver City: Krown and Spellman, 2003.

Hoskins Edgar Hoskins, *Horae Beatae Mariae Virginis or Sarum and York Primers with Kindred Books and the Primers of the Reformed Roman Use Together with an Introduction.* London: Longmans, Green, and Co., 1901.

IPMEP Robert E. Lewis, N. F. Blake, and A. S. G. Edwards, *Index of Printed Middle English Prose.* New York: Garland, 1985.

Iter Paul Oskar Kristeller, *Iter Italicum: A Finding List of Uncatalogued or Incompletely Catalogued Humanist Manuscripts of the Renaissance in Italian and Other Libraries* 1–6. London: Warburg Institute; Leiden: Brill, 1963–1993.

KAEPPELI — Thomas Kaeppeli and Emilio Panella, *Scriptores Ordinis Praedicatorum Medii Aevi* 1–4. Rome: Ad. S. Sabinae; Istituto storico domenicano, 1970–1993.

LEROQUAIS — Victor Leroquais, *Les Livres d'heures manuscrits de la Bibliothèque Nationale* 1–2. Paris: Protat frères, 1927. *Supplement aux Livres d'heures manuscrits de la Bibliothèque Nationale.* Mâcon: Protat frères, 1943.

LEROQUAIS, *Psautiers* — Victor Leroquais, *Les Psautiers manuscrits des bibliothèques publiques de France* 1–2. Mâcon: Protat frères, 1940–1941.

MANIPULUS FLORUM — Craig L. Nighman, The Electronic *Manipulus florum* Project. http://web.wlu.ca/history/cnighman/index.html. 2001–2013.

MANSI — Giovan Domenico Mansi et al., *Sacrorum conciliorum nova et amplissima collectio* 1–54. Paris: H. Welter, 1901–1927.

MEARNS — James Mearns, *The Canticles of the Christian Church, Eastern and Western, in Early and Medieval Times.* Cambridge: Cambridge University Press, 1914.

MEERMAN — Gerard Meerman and Johan Meerman, *Bibliotheca Meermanniana; sive, Catalogus librorum impressorum et codicum manuscriptorum, quos maximam partem collegerunt viri nobilissimi Gerardus et Joannes Meerman; morte dereliquit Joannes Meerman, toparcha in Dalem et Vuren, etc. etc. Quorum publica fiet auctio die VIII sqq. junii, anni MDCCCXXIV Hagae Comitum in aedibus defuncti . . . Per bibliopolas S. et J. Luchtmans, Lugduno-Batavos, fratres Van Cleef, Haganos et Amstelodamenses, et B. Scheurleer, Haganum* 1–4. Hagae Comitum, 1824.

MOHAN — Gaudens Eugene Mohan, "Initia operum Franciscalium (XIII–XV S.)." *Franciscan Studies* 35 (1975): i, iii, v–ix, 1–92; 36 (1976): 92–177; 37 (1977): 178–375; 38 (1978): 375–498.

MONE — Franz Joseph Mone, *Lateinische Hymnen des Mittelalters* 1–3. Aalen: Scientia, 1964.

MUNBY — Alan Noel Latimer Munby, volumes in the series Phillipps Studies 1–5 (see bibliography for volume titles). Cambridge: Cambridge University Press, 1951–1960.

Ottosen — Knud Ottosen, *The Responsories and Versicles of the Latin Office of the Dead*. Aarhus: Aarhus University Press, 1993.

PG — Jacques-Paul Migne, ed. *Patrologia graeca.*

Phillipps — Thomas Phillipps, *Catalogus librorum manuscriptorum in bibliotheca D. Thomae Phillipps, BT. impressum Typis Moedio-Montanis 1837–1871.* Reprinted as *The Phillipps Manuscripts* with an introduction by A. N. L. Munby. London: Holland Press, 1968.

Piccard — Gerhard Piccard, *Wasserzeichenkartei im Hauptstaatsarchiv Stuttgart.* Stuttgart: Kohlhammer, 1961–1997.

PL — Jacques-Paul Migne, ed. *Patrologia latina.*

RH — Ulysse Chevalier, *Repertorium hymnologicum* 1–6. Subsidia hagiographica 4. Louvain: Lefever, 1892–1912; Brussels: s.n., 1920–1921.

SB — Francis Procter and Christopher Wordsworth, *Breviarium ad usum insignis ecclesiae Sarum* 1–3. Cambridge, 1879–1886; repr. Farmborough, Hants: Gregg, 1970.

SBO — Jean Leclercq, Charles H. Talbot, and Henri Rochais, *Sancti Bernardi Opera* 1–9. Rome: Editiones Cistercienses, 1957–1977.

Schneyer — Johannes Baptist Schneyer, *Repertorium der lateinischen Sermones des Mittelalters für die Zeit von 1150–1350* 1–11. Beiträge zur Geschichte der Philosophie und Theologie des Mittelalters, Bd. 43. Münster: Aschendorffsche Verlagsbuchhandlung, 1973–1990.

Sharpe — Richard Sharpe, *A Handlist of the Latin Writers of Great Britain and Ireland before 1540, with Additions and Corrections.* Publications of the *Journal of Medieval Latin* 1. Turnhout: Brepols, 2001.

Sonet/Sinclair/Rézeau — Jean Sonet, *Répertoire d'incipit de prières en ancien français.* Geneva: Librairie Droz, 1956.
Keith Val Sinclair, *Prières en ancien français. Nouvelles réferences, renseignements complémentaires, indications bibliographiques, corrections et tables des articles du 'Répertoire' de Sonet.* Hamden, CT: Archon Books, 1978.

Keith Val Sinclair, *Prières en ancien français. Additions et corrections aux articles 1–2374 du 'Répertoire de Sonet.* Capricornia 7. Townsville, Queensland: Department of Modern Languages, James Cook University of North Queensland, 1987.
Pierre Rézeau, *Répertoire d'incipit des prières français à la fin du moyen âge. Addenda et corrigenda aux répertoires de Sonet et Sinclair nouveaux incipit.* Geneva: Librairie Droz, 1986.

SR — *Statutes of the Realm.* London: G. Eyre and A. Strahan, 1810–1828.

STEGMÜLLER — Friedrich Stegmüller (8–11 with N. Reinhardt), *Repertorium Biblicum Medii Aevi* 1–11. Madrid: s.n., 1950–1980.

WALTHER, *Initia* — Hans Walther, *Initia carminum ac versuum medii aevi posterioris latinorum.* Carmina medii aevi posterioris latina 1. Göttingen: Vandenhoeck and Ruprecht, 1969.

WALTHER, *Proverbia* — Hans Walther, *Proverbia sententiaeque latinitatis medii aevi. Lateinische Sprichworter und Sentenzen des Mittelalters in alphabetischer Anordnung.* Carmina medii aevi posterioris latina 2. Göttingen: Vandenhoeck and Ruprecht, 1963–1967.

WILMART — André Wilmart, *Auteurs spirituels et textes dévots du moyen âge latin: Études d'histoire littéraire.* Paris: Bloud and Gay, 1932.

Introduction

Criteria for Selection

This catalogue describes the 288 medieval and Renaissance manuscripts (69 codices and 219 fragments from 86 parent manuscripts) held by repositories in Notre Dame, Indiana. Bound manuscripts, individual leaves, cuttings, and extracted binding fragments written in Western historical Latin scripts are included (and a single twelfth-century leaf in Greek). Charters and other documentary materials, letters, and fragments still in book bindings are excluded. The chronological limit begins with the late eleventh century, the date of the earliest fragment, and continues through the first half of the sixteenth century. With these limitations, the catalogue contains all codices, leaves, and fragments written in Pregothic, Gothic, and Humanistic scripts held by the University of Notre Dame and Saint Mary's College.

Formation of the Collections and Fonds in Use

1. University of Notre Dame, Hesburgh Library

At the time of de Ricci's and Wilson's *Census*, three medieval manuscripts were recorded at the University of Notre Dame[1] (codd. Lat. b. 1, Lat. b. 2, and Lat. d. 1), though a fourth manuscript (cod. Lat. b. 10) lay hidden in the Library's "Treasure Room," listed as a printed book. The first two manuscripts are Dominican psalters from the collection of General Rush C. Hawkins (1831–1920), which were sold by G. A. Leavitt and Co. in 1887 and presumably then to the university by D. G. Francis. The third codex (cod. Lat. d. 1), a large volume of sermons and theological texts, was acquired by Msgr. Andrew Arnold Lambing (1842–1918)

1. Seymour de Ricci and William Jerome Wilson, *Census of Medieval and Renaissance Manuscripts in the United States and Canada* 1–3 (New York: H. W. Wilson, 1935, 1937, 1940), 1:714, nos. 1–3.

in 1874 and donated to the university prior to the *Census*. The unknown fourth manuscript (cod. Lat. b. 10), two humanist miscellanies bound together, was given to the university in 1922 by Henry Stoy Rigden, who acquired it in 1918.

The collection's growth would remain dormant until Rev. Paul E. Beichner, C.S.C., began work on his critical edition of Peter Riga's *Aurora* in the 1950s.[2] In support of Beichner's edition, the university acquired two thirteenth-century copies of the work, one French (cod. Lat. a. 5), the other Iberian (cod. Lat. c. 6). By the time of Faye and Bond's supplement to the *Census* in 1962,[3] the Treasure Room now housed a total of eight medieval manuscripts in addition to other rare materials. The collection was under the supervision of librarian and classicist Dr. Francis D. Lazenby, who had been appointed curator of the Treasure Room in 1955.[4] In addition to the two copies of the *Aurora*, the collection now included a richly illuminated Flemish book of hours (cod. Lat. a. 1), a fourteenth-century courtly poem, *Facetus* (cod. Lat. b. 3), and the university's first dated manuscript: a Bible written at Blatná in 1417 according to its colophon (cod. Lat. b. 7), which was donated by Rev. Urban de Hasque (1875–1954). Records are scant, but at least forty-eight manuscripts spanning the thirteenth through eighteenth century were ordered by Lazenby in consultation with other members of the faculty between 1959 and 1968. This period of robust acquisition occurred when Rt. Rev. Astrik L. Gabriel, O. Praem. (1907–2005), was director of the Medieval Institute (1952–1975). Canon Gabriel, himself a collector of rare imprints and manuscripts, advocated for the expansion of the collection and even purchased a few manuscripts independently. The manuscripts were generally theological, scholastic, or philosophical works but included the odd legal and liturgical book.

The first catalogue was written by Prof. James A. Corbett (1908–1989) and published by the University of Notre Dame Press in 1978.[5] Corbett's scope included codices up to 1750[6] and lists sixty-four manuscripts. Of these entries, only thirty-nine date before the mid-sixteenth century, and the other twenty-five manuscripts range from the seventeenth to nineteenth century. Corbett's catalogue includes basic information, but mainly transcribes incipits and explicits, and aims to identify texts. No information regarding codicological

2. Paul E. Beichner, *Aurora Petri Rigae Biblia Versificata: A Verse Commentary on the Bible* 1–2 (Notre Dame, IN: University of Notre Dame Press, 1965).

3. Christopher Urdahl Faye and William Henry Bond, *Supplement to the Census of Medieval and Renaissance Manuscripts in the United States and Canada* (New York: Bibliographical Society of America, 1962), 186–187, nos. 4–8.

4. Marina Smyth, "The Medieval Institute Library: A Brief History," in *What Is Written Remains: Historical Essays on the Libraries of Notre Dame*, ed. Maureen Gleason and Katharina J. Blackstead (Notre Dame, IN: University of Notre Dame Press, 1994), 218.

5. James A. Corbett, *Catalogue of the Medieval & Renaissance Manuscripts of the University of Notre Dame* (Notre Dame, IN: University of Notre Dame Press, 1978); first reviewed by Marie-Thérèse d'Alverny, "Review of *Catalogue of the Medieval and Renaissance Manuscripts of the University of Notre Dame*, by James A. Corbett," *Scriptorium* 35 (1981): 106–108.

6. Corbett, *Catalogue*, preface (unnumbered page).

features is provided, with the exception of writing support, general measurements, bindings, and the occasional mention of a catchword. Treatment and classification of script types and hands are not included, nor are localizations or origins advanced for most manuscripts. Many entries suffer from transcription errors, misidentification, and lack of bibliography.

After Corbett's catalogue, medieval manuscript acquisitions at Notre Dame all but ceased. Between 1978 and 2000 only three manuscripts—all of English origin—were acquired: an illuminated psalter (cod. Lat. e. 4), once owned by William Morris at Kelmscott House; a book of hours (cod. Lat. a. 3); and a Middle English *Mirror to Devout People* (*Speculum deuotorum*), owned by John Scrope and Elizabeth Chaworth (MS Eng. d. 1), from the collection of William Foyle.

Regular acquisitions resumed during the period of 2010–2015, in which twenty-two codices were purchased. Ten were neumed liturgical manuscripts spanning the thirteenth through the sixteenth century, acquired in support of the university's Sacred Music Program: a diurnal (cod. Lat. b. 4), a gradual in two volumes (codd. Lat. c. 2 and Lat. c. 3), two missals (codd. Lat. b. 13 and Lat. c. 13), a pontifical (cod. Lat. c. 12), two graduals (codd. Lat. c. 14 and Lat. c. 15), an antiphonary (cod. Lat. b. 15), and an Office of the Dead (cod. Lat. a. 12).

At the behest of Prof. Olivia Remie Constable (1960–2014), the Robert M. Conway Director of the Medieval Institute from 2008 to 2014, and with encouragement from Dr. Louis E. Jordan, head of Rare Books and Special Collections from 1992 to 2012, advanced courses in Latin paleography and Western codicology were developed. In support of these courses, twelve other codices and a substantial number of fragments were acquired at the curator's selection through collaboration with several librarians. These manuscripts were for pedagogical purposes, to enhance the collection's breadth and provide specimens of script types and codicological features by region and period.

The shelfmarks used between 1978 and 2010 were assigned by Corbett and vaguely continue the numbers given in the *Census* and its supplement (nos. 1–8); Corbett claims that the numbers generally represented the order in which the manuscripts were acquired.[7] Provenance research on the collection now shows that this is not accurate. There were also shelfmark inconsistences beginning as early as 1951. For example, Corbett in 1951[8] identifies "MS 2" as de Ricci no. 1, but in Beichner's edition,[9] "MS 2" is the "MS 5" of Corbett in his 1978 catalogue.[10] Thus, depending on the source, "MS 2" could be one of three manuscripts: two different psalters from Germany of the fifteenth century, or a thirteenth-century *Aurora* from France.

In August 2010, all manuscripts later than the first half of the sixteenth century were moved to the proper fonds within the early modern and modern manuscript collections.

7. Corbett, *Catalogue*, preface (unnumbered page).
8. James A. Corbett, "Two German Dominican Psalters," *Mediaeval Studies* 13 (1951): 247–252.
9. Beichner, *Aurora Petri Rigae Biblia Versificata*, 1:lii, 2.
10. Corbett, *Catalogue*, 5–8.

The medieval and Renaissance manuscripts were left with nonsequential and duplicate numbers. A shelfmark system for perpetual use was developed that could be browsed and expanded easily and that maximized the limited vault storage space available at the time.

The medieval and Renaissance manuscript books residing in the Hesburgh Library's Department of Rare Books and Special Collections are organized in the following way: format, language, height, shelf number. The bulk of the collection is formed by the fifty-six bound manuscripts written in Latin, which are organized into the larger fond *codices Latini*. Each manuscript carries the prefix "cod. Lat." The remaining eight manuscripts written in various vernaculars are ordered according to language, carrying the prefix "MS" followed by Eng. (English), Fr. (French), Ger. (Germanic languages), or Ital. (Italian). All manuscripts are then arranged by height ascending (including enclosure), which is indicated by the following letters:

a 0–7 inches
b 7.5–9.75 inches
c 9.75–12.5 inches
d 12.5–15.5 inches
e Flat storage

Thus, cod. Lat. a. 12 = codex Latinus, up to seven inches in height, twelfth on the "A" shelf, and cod. Lat. e. 2 = codex Latinus, stored flat, second on "E" shelf. MS Eng. d. 1 = English bound manuscript, up to 15.5 inches in height, first on the vernacular "D" shelf.

Fragments, leaves, and unbound quires are organized into the larger fond *Fragments*. Each manuscript carries the prefix "Frag." followed by a Roman numeral corresponding to the enclosure's location, and Arabic numerals corresponding to the folder's number within the box (e.g., Frag. I. 19, Frag. V. 3). Each new shelfmark is assigned on the basis of a unique parent manuscript and does not correspond to the number of items. For example, Frag. III. 1 contains 92 leaves from one parent manuscript.

In August 2015, fifteen manuscripts from the personal collection of Prof. Giles Constable were donated to the university in memory of his daughter, Prof. Olivia Remie Constable. The small collection consists of five leaves, four binding fragments, and five documents spanning the twelfth through sixteenth century. All items from the donation occupy their own fond "Constable Manuscripts" and are numbered sequentially (e.g., Constable MS 1, Constable MS 2, etc.). Constable MSS 1–9 consist of ten fragments from nine parent manuscripts, which are described in this catalogue. The remaining items are documents and are thus excluded.

2. University of Notre Dame, Snite Museum of Art

The collection of the Snite Museum of Art comprises thirty-three manuscripts, of which most are single illuminated leaves and fragments. The first leaf, a fragment of a book of hours in the translation of Geert Groote (Acc. 1967.19), was purchased for the museum (then called the "University Art Gallery") in November 1966 (accessioned 1967) by Rev. Anthony J. Lauck, C.S.C., from London Grafica Arts, Inc. (Detroit, MI). The museum purchased fourteen leaves between 1967 and 1975 from dealers and select biblioclasts such as Ferdinand Roten Galleries, Matthias Komor, Walter Schatzki, and Philip Duschnes. The bulk of these leaves was acquired in 1974 using the Charles A. Wightman Purchase Fund, which was constituted from the monies gained through the auction of deaccessioned items from the Wightman family. The remaining eighteen manuscripts were donations between 1978 and 1989, since the purchasing of medieval manuscripts is usually done by the Hesburgh Library. In 1978, noted cellist and art collector Janós Scholz (1903–1993) donated a richly illuminated French calendar (ca. 1490–1500). Sixteen manuscripts were the property of Chicago-based artist, calligrapher, and collector Everett McNear (1904–1984). McNear donated several items prior to his death in 1984, and his wife, Ann Katherine McNear (1902?–1994), donated the remaining manuscripts in 1985 and 1989 in his memory. A leaf from an antiphonary (Acc. 1996.48) was donated in 1996 by Dr. Dean A. Porter, who was formerly the museum's director. A psalter leaf (Acc. 2015.37), the most recent accession, was discovered in the museum's "Teaching Collection" in the summer of 2015 and is hitherto unpublished.

The manuscripts are organized by the museum's regular convention for acquisitions: Acc. (prefix), year of accession, and gift number. For example, the fourteenth-century illuminated *Meditationes uitae Christi* (Acc. 1985.25) was the twenty-fifth gift of 1985, but the fifteenth-century confessional (Acc. 1984.3.6) was the sixth item given by Everett McNear, the museum's third donor in 1984.

3. Saint Mary's College, Cushwa-Leighton Library

Ten medieval manuscripts held by Saint Mary's College are housed in the Cushwa-Leighton Library. The dates and precise circumstances of the acquisitions by Saint Mary's College remain unknown. A note on the flyleaf of a thirteenth-century manuscript containing book 4 of Peter Lombard's *Sentences*, extracts of Burchard of Worms, and other texts (MS 1) records an accession date of October 1962. The college's second manuscript (MS 2), containing some works of Aquinas, Aristoteles Latinus, and others, arrived with MS 1. Both were offered together for sale with a price in Reichsmarks by Emil Hirsch (1866–1954). Hirsch was forbidden to work as a rare book dealer under the Nazi regime and operated in exile.[11] The modern provenance of the third manuscript, a book of hours from Amiens (MS 3), is even less clear than the previous two. Clear ownership can be ascribed to the Grisel family,

11. Ernst Fischer, *Verleger, Buchhändler & Antiquare aus Deutschland und Österreich in der Emigration nach 1933: Ein biographisches Handbuch* (Stuttgart: Verband Deutscher Antiquare e.V., 2011), 139–140.

nobility in Fay-lès-Hornoy (now Thieulloy-l'Abbaye) from the late fifteenth through early seventeenth century, but nothing subsequent is known.[12] Nine leaves (MSS 4–10) from six parent manuscripts are considered to be unrecorded gifts from alumnae over the years by the library staff (MSS 4, 5, 6, 9, and 10 are framed). All of the leaves were cut from music manuscripts written in Italy and the Iberian Peninsula from the fourteenth through the sixteenth century (three leaves from two antiphonaries, and six leaves from five graduals).

The three codices (MSS 1–3) were catalogued at one point with the Library of Congress scheme with the dates 1200, 1300, and 1561 (also thought to be an imprint). The manuscripts were known only to some of the staff in the college's library, and had never been examined by specialists or published. The rediscovery of the "Saint Mary's Three" occurred in the spring semester of 2011. A small handwritten note in the lower margin of the Medieval Institute's copy of de Ricci's *Census* made mention of Msgr. A. A. Lambing of Pittsburgh (the donor of Hesburgh Library, cod. Lat. d. 1). The note read, "St. Mary's has a ms. w. Lambing's ex libris." As it turns out, the note actually refers to an early imprint once owned by Lambing, but it allowed the manuscripts to be rediscovered. The manuscripts were then loaned to the Hesburgh Library for conservation treatment, analytical description, and digitization.

In consultation with Bob Hohl and Jill Hobgood, librarians and curators of the Rare Book Collection at Saint Mary's, it was determined that a general shelfmark system was best since the college does not actively acquire medieval manuscripts. The medieval manuscripts held by the Cushwa-Leighton Library are designated as MS 1 through MS 10.

Overview of the Collection

1. Books of Hours and Devotional Texts

The collection's nine books of hours represent a diverse selection of uses, textual arrangements, illuminations, and centers of production. The assortment of calendars is especially diverse. All nine manuscripts were made in France or the Low Countries during the fifteenth century, with the exception of one English example. One manuscript is a representative specimen of Parisian production and content (cod. Lat. a. 8). It characteristically contains the Hours of the Virgin and the Office of the Dead in the use of Paris. The Litany, preceded by the French prayers *Doulce Dame* and *Doulz Dieu*, is general and features saints common to Parisian groups of *horae* like Denis, Ivo, Fiacre, and Geneviève. The calendar, written in French, is typical of the Parisian model, which was used widely in and outside of Paris. A codex of split use (cod. Lat. a. 15) shows the wide dissemination of the use of Paris in other locations. The Hours of the Virgin are for the use of Paris, but the calendar is dis-

12. David T. Gura, "A Hitherto Unknown Book of Hours from the *Amiénois*: Notre Dame, Saint Mary's College, Cushwa-Leighton Library, MS 3 (or the Le Féron-Grisel Hours)," *Manuscripta* 56 (2012): 227–268.

tinctly that of Bourges. Numerous saints and feasts particular to Bourges and its suffragan dioceses are featured prominently, including Ursin, William of Bourges, Sulpicius Severus, Austregisilius, and the translation of St. Stephen. Like the majority of books of hours in the collection, the two codices exemplify the effects of modern biblioclasty on illuminated manuscripts. All miniatures were excised from cod. Lat. a. 15, and only four remain in cod. Lat. a. 8. These miniatures are not of exceptional quality and are badly damaged—two features that allowed them to escape the biblioclast's razorblade. Both manuscripts were then bound haphazardly in the modern era and are completely out of order.

Specimens of Flemish books of hours made for export are represented in four manuscripts. One small codex attests to the demand of the English market for books of hours (cod. Lat. a. 1). The manuscript contains the Hours of the Virgin and the Office of the Dead for the use of Sarum, as well as the artificialized Sarum calendar.[13] The calendar features typical English saints, such as Dunstan, Aldhelm, Swithun, Cuthburga, Cuthbert, and Hugh of Lincoln. However, the names and dates are extremely corrupt, typical of an origin in Flanders.[14] The manuscript contains twenty-eight miniatures painted in demi-grisaille technique, including the full Passion Cycle, miniatures for each suffrage, and iconography common to most introductory miniatures. A single leaf (Acc. 1973.55) also provides a textual snapshot of the antiphons, capitulum, and hymn for Lauds in the use of Sarum from a Flemish-made book of hours. All the miniatures as well as those in another specimen (cod. Lat. a. 2) are painted on the verso of singletons, which were then inserted into the manuscripts—a practice illustrative of Flemish production. A single cutting of St. Agatha with her attributes (Acc. 1989.20.1) exemplifies the same technique, though nothing of its parent manuscript is known.

Three codices (codd. Lat. a. 2, Lat. a. 6, and Lat. a. 16) were made at Bruges for the use of Rome and display other Flemish features. Each contains a minimalist calendar redacted from a Bruges model in order to appear as general as possible. Certain saints' feasts, grades, and positions within the Litany betray their origins in the Low Countries: Basil, Donatian, Amalberga, Bavo, and the translation of St. Thomas, to name a few. Similar features are also seen in a single calendar (cod. Lat. a. 14), which was removed from a book of hours likely made somewhere between Tournai and Cambrai. Five full-color miniatures remain in cod. Lat. a. 2, but all have been excised from codd. Lat. a. 6 and Lat. a. 16. The borders in cod. Lat. a. 6, however, are identical to another book of hours connected to the so-called "Master of the Dresden Prayerbook,"[15] and, along with the miniature of St. Jerome in cod. Lat. a. 1, provide examples of reverse-traced illuminations and the use of pattern books. The four

13. The manuscript was first described in James A. Corbett, "A Fifteenth Century Book of Hours of Salisbury," *Ephemerides Liturgicae* 71 (1957): 293–307.

14. Nigel Morgan, "The Introduction of the Sarum Calendar into the Dioceses of England in the Thirteenth Century," in *Thirteenth Century England VIII: Proceedings of the Durham Conference 1999*, ed. Michael Prestwich, Richard Britnell, and Robin Frame (Woodbridge: Boydell Press, 2001), 185, n. 25.

15. The manuscript, now in a private collection, is described in Roger S. Wieck with Sandra Hindman and Ariane Bergeron-Foote, *Picturing Piety: The Book of Hours*, Les Enluminures Catalogue 13 (London: Paul Holberton Pub. for Les Enluminures, 2007), 198–204.

Flemish books of hours also exhibit a selection of texts not commonly found in manuscripts produced in France: the Fifteen O's of St. Bridget, Seven Last Words of Christ, Mass of the Virgin, the Gradual Psalms, Commendation of Souls, and the Psalter of Jerome in the normal and variant forms.[16] Two leaves also from Bruges (Constable MSS 1 and 2) provide specimens of the use of Southern Textualis in Flemish books of hours, as exemplified in cod. Lat. a. 6.

The collection also contains books of hours produced in other notable centers in the *Amiénois* and the *Rouenais*. Saint Mary's MS 3 contains the Hours of the Virgin and Office of the Dead for the use of Amiens. The composite calendar is written in French with Picardisms, and deviates little from the Amiens model compiled by Susie Nash.[17] Like the calendar, the Litany features the major saints of the diocese, most notably Firmin the Martyr, Firmin the Confessor, and Fuscian. Though all miniatures have been removed, the remaining border decorations are characteristic of the types compiled by Nash from Amiens.[18] The manuscript also provides the collection's sole example of a *livre de raison*.[19] The birth of one Jehenne Le Féron on July 6, 1478, is recorded, and further annotations reveal that book passed from one family to another with Jehenne's marriage to Jean Grisel,[20] the seigneur du Fay, ca. 1507. The *livre de raison* is written in the autograph of Jean's descendant, François Grisel, who continues the entries through 1586. The manuscript remained in the possession of the Grisel family in Fay-lès-Hornoy (now Thieulloy-l'Abbaye) in Picardie at least until the early seventeenth century.

The use of Rouen is represented in one codex (cod. Lat. a. 9) and three fragments (Frag. I. 33, Acc. 1975.56, and Acc. 1978.28). Cod. Lat. a. 9 provides examples of the Hours of the Virgin and Office of the Dead, and the calendar and Litany evidence saints such as Austreberte, Mellon, Romain, and "Nigaise" (complete with the *Rouenais* spelling). Four miniatures with characteristic Rouen-style border arrangements also remain in the codex. Frag. I. 33, featuring a miniature of courting and hawking, is another example of the characteristic layout of a calendar from Rouen. The calendar is not composite and imitates the triple grading system to create a deluxe aesthetic with gold, blue, and red inks. The leaf also includes the translation of St. Ouen (May 5). Two other fragments attest to the widespread use of Parisian model calendars during the fifteenth century. Similar in layout, Acc. 1975.56 incorporates miniatures of a man warming himself by the fire and the Zodiac sign Pisces

16. Many of these are discussed with respect to their English contexts in Nigel Morgan, "English Books of Hours," in *Books of Hours Reconsidered*, ed. Sandra Hindman and James H. Marrow (Turnhout: Harvey Miller, 2013), 78–87.

17. Susie Nash, *Between France and Flanders: Manuscript Illumination in Amiens* (London: The British Library and University of Toronto Press, 1999), 405–408; Gura, "A Hitherto Unknown Fifteenth-Century Book of Hours," 238–241.

18. Nash, *Between France and Flanders*, 253, identifies five border types.

19. On this practice, see Virginia Reinburg, *French Books of Hours: Making an Archive of Prayer, c. 1400–1600* (Cambridge: Cambridge University Press, 2012), 62–70.

20. Gura, "A Hitherto Unknown Fifteenth-Century Book of Hours," 252–254.

for February. The fragment contains notable variants of the "P-Group" of Parisian calendars, datable to the 1460s. Acc. 1978.28 is a complete calendar and contains sixty-six of the principal variants of the "T-Group" of Parisian calendars based on du Pré and Verard, which were in use between 1490 and 1500.[21] Its deluxe miniatures depict the monthly labors and Zodiac signs.

Cod. Lat. a. 3 is an example of a simple book of hours produced in England, and the contemporary binding consigns its contents to an early stage of their compilation. Though no calendar or Office of the Dead is contained in cod. Lat. a. 3, the Hours of the Virgin are for the use of Sarum, and the Litany includes some English saints in common with that of cod. Lat. a. 1: Swithun, Birinus, and Edith. Contemporary provenance can also be ascribed to the area of Sudbury and ownership to one John Mekylwode, who has written his name twice in the manuscript. Mekylwode was active in Stowmarket, Fornham, and likely Wyverstone from at least 1441 until his death in 1462. His will was proved at Stowmarket on October 13 of the same year.[22]

Perhaps the most diverse example is a fragmentary Breton book of hours (Frag. III. 1), of which 92 of the 129 leaves are in the Hesburgh Library. The manuscript was formerly part of the great Bergendal Collection (*olim* MS 8) of Toronto entrepreneur Joseph Pope before it was sold at auction and broken. The calendar is historiated with the monthly labors, and its entries are for the use of Vannes.[23] Emphatic feasts celebrate the ordination of its founding saint and first bishop, St. Padarn, and the deposition of his relics. Numerous other Breton, Welsh, Cornish, and Irish saints also occur in the calendar and Litany, including Gildas, Winwaloe, Karanteg, Ivo of Kermartin, Maude, Gudwal, Meriadeg, Bili, Turiaw, Samson, William of Saint-Brieuc, Gwenhael, Malo, Columbanus, Corentin, and Guigner among many others. The Hours of the Virgin are for the use of Rennes, but the Office of the Dead is the artificially produced "Short Office Five," commonly found in books of hours.[24] Twenty-two of the thirty full-color illuminations have been recovered. The miniatures are painted in a rustic style and introduce each canonical hour of the Hours of the Virgin, Hours of the Cross, and Hours of the Holy Spirit, as well as saints' suffrages and other texts [**PLATE 1**].

Though all books of hours in the collection are primarily in Latin, the Dutch tradition of Geert Groote is represented in select fragments, which show not only the orthographical vagaries of the vernacular but also the range and styles of manuscript illumination in the Low Countries. The characteristic penwork of Delft (Frag. I. 2), well executed Dutch

21. Erik Drigsdahl, "The Composite Paris Calendar 1330–1530," CHD: Center for Håndskriftstudier i Danmark, at http://manuscripts.org.uk/chd.dk/cals/pariscal.html.

22. Peter Northeast, *Wills of the Archdeaconry of Sudbury, 1439–1474. Wills from the Register 'Baldwyne', Part I: 1439–1461*, Suffolk Records Society 44 (Suffolk: Boydell Press, 2001), 40–41, n. 103.

23. For example, compare to the calendar in København, Kongelige Bibliothek, Thott 114 8o, of which a transcription made by Drigsdahl is accessable at http://manuscripts.org.uk/chd.dk/cals/th114kal.html.

24. Knud Ottosen, *The Responsories and Versicles of the Latin Office of the Dead* (Aarhus: Aarhus University Press, 1993), 365.

dentelles (Acc. 1967.19), and illumination similar to manuscripts made near Arnhem (Acc. 1972.34) are represented. Two other modestly illuminated leaves from other devotional traditions in Dutch increase the collection's breadth (Frag. I. 1 and Acc. 1974.31).

Other fragmentary leaves, mainly French or Flemish, in the collection provide didactic examples of various features: extravagant piece borders (Frag. I. 20), the use of Bastarda as opposed to Textualis (Frag. I. 8), gold acanthus borders (Frag. I. 9), trompe l'oeil initials (Acc. 1974.30 and 1974.32), earlier borders solely of black and gold rinceaux (Frag. I. 10), and artificial capitalis as a display script (Acc. 1974.33). A single leaf (Acc. 1967.20.4) acts as the collection's sole specimen of an Italian book of hours. Rare examples of fourteenth-century illuminated books of hours are represented by two leaves (Acc. 1989.20.4 and 1989.20.6), of which the former (Acc. 1989.20.4), from the so-called "Ghistelles Hours," is among the earliest known specimens of Flemish *horae*.

In addition to books of hours, there are manuscripts containing a wide variety of devotional works. An illuminated prayerbook (MS Ger. a. 1) from the Niederrhein provides a sample of northern devotional texts circulating near the end of the fifteenth century. Written in Middle Low German on mixed quires of parchment and paper, the manuscript contains three Gospel Harmonies,[25] Jordan of Quedlinburg's *Sixty-five Articles of the Passion of Christ*,[26] Henry Suso's *Hundred Articles of the Passion of Christ*,[27] and several prayers and texts attributed to Bernard of Clairvaux. A fifteenth-century manuscript made for Elizabeth Chaworth/Scrope (MS Eng. d. 1) contains a copy of the Middle English devotional work *A Mirror to Devout People*, composed by a Carthusian at the Sheen Charterhouse.[28] Similarly, a fourteenth-century manuscript of the "short version" of *Meditationes uitae Christi* (Acc. 1985.25), written in Italian, contains a cycle of forty-eight illuminations from Bologna.[29] Other examples show a demand for mystic and devotional texts in fifteenth-century Italy, such as the letters of Catherine of Siena, Ugo Panziera's *Trattati spirituali* (MS Ital. b. 2), and translations of Henry Suso's *Horologium sapientiae*, Office of Eternal Wisdom, and meditations on the passion of Christ (MS Ital. d. 1).

25. On the first two, see J. Deschamps, "De verspreiding van Johan Scutkens vertaling van het Niewe Testament en de Oudtestamentische perikopen," *Nederlands Archeif voor Kergeschiedenis* n.s. 51 (1975/1976): 159–179, esp. 169–177.

26. J. M. Willmeumier-Schalij, "De LXV artikelen van de Passie van Jordanus van Quedlinburg in middelnederlandse handschriften," *Ons Geestelijk Erf* 53 (1979): 15–35.

27. On the text and its translations and reception, see José van Aelst, *Passie voor het Lijden: De Hundert Betrachtungen und Begehrungen van Henricus Suso en de oudste drie bewerkingen uit de Nederlanden* (Leuven: Peeters, 2005); and van Aelst, *Vruchten van de passie: De laatmiddeleeuwse passieliteratuur verkend aan de hand van Suso's Honderd artikelen*, Middeleeuwse studies en bronnen 129 (Hilversum: Verloren, 2011).

28. Paul J. Patterson, *A Mirror to Devout People* (*Speculum devotorum*), Early English Text Society o.s. 346 (Oxford: Oxford University Press, forthcoming); also Patterson, "Myrror to devout people (*Speculum devotorum*): An Edition with Commentary," Ph.D. diss., University of Notre Dame, 2006.

29. The illuminations are treated in detail in Dianne Phillips, "The *Meditations on the Life of Christ*: An Illuminated Fourteenth-Century Italian Manuscript at the University of Notre Dame," in *The Text in the Community: Essays on Medieval Works, Manuscripts, Authors, and Readers*, ed. Jill Mann and Maura Nolan (Notre Dame, IN: University of Notre Dame Press, 2006), 237–281.

Further tracts in Latin by Jean Gerson, Pierre d'Ailly, Gerard van Vliederhoven, Anselm, Ekbert of Schönau, Pseudo-Augustine, Bernard of Clairvaux, Arnulfus de Boeriis, Bonaventure, and Ludolph of Saxony were compiled in a fifteenth-century manuscript probably intended for devotional education (cod. Lat. b. 6). The manuscript likely originates from northern France, but the Low Countries cannot be ruled out completely, and there are similarities to popular texts of the *Devotio Moderna*.[30] In addition to the numerous tracts, the codex also contains two florilegia. The first provides brief extracts of Saints John Chrysostom, Jerome, Gregory, Isidore of Seville, Bernard, Cyprian, Ambrose, and Augustine, and the second contains over one hundred verse selections, beginning with Richard of Wetheringsett's *Summa "Qui bene presunt."*

The specialized practices of the Compagnia Ambrosiana of Milan are seen in an interesting manuscript copied ca. 1500 (cod. Lat. c. 8). The codex contains the Society's Rule, various meditative texts, and a number of commemorations in Latin and Italian. Many excerpts dealing with the life of St. Ambrose, (pseudo) epistolary extracts, and selections of his *De officiis* are mixed among the other devotional texts. The Office for St. Ambrose has also been added to the final leaves, along with an obituary for Giovanni Marco de Capponi, who died on March 17, 1550, which states that he was the founder of the Compagnia and the compiler of its Rule.

2. Bibles, Biblical Texts, and Patristics

The only complete Bible (cod. Lat. b. 7) in the collection was written at Blatná (present-day Czech Republic) and completed on October 30, 1417, according to its colophon (the feast of St. Victorinus of Pettau is usually celebrated on November 3, to which the nearest Saturday in 1417 was October 30). The manuscript contains the Old and New Testaments with fifty-six prologues, a Psalter, the *Interpretation of Hebrew Names* attributed to Langton, and other accessory texts. Script and decoration are representative of the Bohemian and Germanic traditions, of which the locus of production is a definitive confluence. A fragmentary pocket Bible (cod. Lat. a. 13) provides an example of the Parisian tradition of the thirteenth century. The manuscript is decorated but not historiated, and the remaining texts consist of Esther (incomplete), Job with two prologues, and Psalms. Cod. Lat. a. 13 also contains contemporary marginal glossing in Latin, and several instances of English translations written during the fourteenth century. Examples of twelfth-century formats include leaves and fragments from two Atlantic Bibles written in Italy ca. 1140 (Frag. I. 1, Constable MS 9) and from a glossed Bible of the Abbey of Saint-Oyan de Joux (Condat)/Saint-Claude written ca. 1175 (Frag. I. 21). Three illuminated leaves ca. 1250 supplement the Parisian tradition in cod. Lat. a. 13 with standard subject matter, such as the Head of God and Gideon in

30. Many of the texts present are discussed in Nikolaus Staubach, "*Memores Pristinae Perfectionis: The Importance of the Church Fathers for the Devotio Moderna*," in *The Reception of the Church Fathers in the West: From the Carolingians to the Maurists* 1, ed. Irena Dorota Backus (Leiden: Brill, 1997), 405–471.

mail (Acc. 1989.20.2), attendants bringing Abishag to David (Acc. 1989.20.3), and Moses leading men (Frag. I. 34). The historiated initials of three leaves were illuminated in the innovative style of the Dominican Painter.[31] The parent manuscript was Sir Alfred Chester Beatty's MS W.116, a Bible broken in 1969 by Folio Fine Art (London) and disseminated. Two further leaves from the other so-called "Chester Beatty Bible" are also held. Beatty's MS W.173 (*olim* Phillipps MS 2506) was written and illuminated in the Bordeaux region at the onset of the fourteenth century. Acc. 1975.43 features a large initial depicting the Tree of Jesse, which begins the Gospel of Matthew, and Acc. 1975.57 shows Jeremiah in lamentation. Two other examples of scriptural biblioclasty (Constable MSS 3 and 8) both originate from parent manuscripts broken by Otto F. Ege for his portfolios *Leaves from Famous Bibles, Nine Centuries, 1121 A.D.–1935 A.D.* The first is a leaf from a fourteenth-century French Bible containing part of Ezekiel (Constable MS 3). The other leaf (Constable MS 8) is a fragment of the *Interpretation of Hebrew Names* from a large Flemish Lectern Bible written during the early fourteenth century. This is also the collection's sole example of a three-column layout for text. A former binding fragment of two conjugate leaves (Acc. 1989.20.5) is the only witness in the collection to Bible production in England. The fragment consists of the end of Wisdom and the beginning of Sirach with both prologues.

Three manuscripts of biblical paraphrase and interpretation copied during the thirteenth century augment the scriptural holdings. Codd. Lat. a. 5 and Lat. c. 6 are copies of Peter Riga's verse paraphrase and commentary, the *Aurora*. The former codex, produced in France, was posited by Beichner to represent a stage of Riga's text between the second and third medieval editions.[32] The small-format manuscript bears ownership marks of the Jesuit Collège-Agen, to which it was donated in 1599. The latter, written in the Iberian Peninsula, contains Riga's third edition and some accretions from the first redaction of Aegidius of Paris, which are copied sparsely in the margins.[33] Cod. Lat. c. 6 also provides a most illustrious example of Iberian Southern Textualis in its early phase, which incorporates features that may indicate a Portuguese scribe. A copy of Peter Comestor's *Historia scholastica* (cod. Lat. c. 4), written in France, is mostly complete (ending imperfectly in 2 Maccabees). The first folio contains marginal glosses in a scholastic presentation, including Isidore of Seville's definition of history copied in the lower margin: "Historia est narratio rei gestae per quam ea quae in praeterito facta sunt dignoscuntur" (History is the narration of a deed through which the things that happened in the past are distinguished).[34]

31. Robert Branner, *Manuscript Painting in Paris during the Reign of Saint Louis: A Study of Styles* (Berkeley: University of California Press, 1977), 118–122.

32. Beichner, *Aurora Petri Rigae Biblia Versificata*, 1:lii.

33. On Aegidius's revisions, see Greti Dinkova-Bruun, "*Corrector Ultimus*: Aegidius of Paris and Peter Riga's *Aurora*," in *Modes of Authorship in the Middle Ages*, ed. Slavica Rancovi, Papers in Mediaeval Studies 22 (Toronto: Pontifical Institute of Mediaeval Studies, 2012), 172–189, esp. 185–189.

34. *Origines* 1.41.1.

A few manuscripts spanning the twelfth through fifteenth century constitute the patristic holdings. Complete works of Boethius and Saints Cyprian, Jerome, Augustine, Gregory the Great, and Ambrose are represented, and selections of Origen, John Chrysostom, Isidore of Seville, and Cassiodorus are contained in excerpts and fragments.

Several works of St. Cyprian (and Pseudo-Cyprian) are copied in a deluxe manuscript of the fifteenth century from southern France (cod. Lat. d. 2). The codex contains sixty-eight of the letters and eleven treatises copied roughly in chronological order: *Ad Donatum, De habitu uirginum, De lapsis, De ecclesiae catholicae unitate, De dominica oratione, De opere et eleemosynis, De mortalitate, Ad Demetrianum, De bono patientiae, De zelo et liuore*, and *Ad Fortunatum*. Eight spurious works, consisting of *Quod idola dii non sint, De laude martirii, Aduersus Iudaeos, De aleatoribus, De montibus Sina et Sion, Ad Vigilium, Exhortatio ad poenitentiam*,[35] and the Irish text *De duodecim abusiuis saeculi*,[36] are also found in the manuscript. Nine additional brief excerpts of St. Cyprian and Pseudo-Cyprian are among the vast tome of epistolary extracts found in cod. Lat. d. 6, a fifteenth-century codex.

Two manuscripts, both copied in England, contain the works of St. Jerome. A manuscript of the *Interpretationes nominum hebraicorum* (cod. Lat. a. 10) of the thirteenth century lacks the preface but is otherwise complete. Two binding fragments from the same folio of *Comentarii in Ezechielem* (Frag. I. 26) fit together to create a contiguous text. Copied ca. 1150 in English Praegothica, Frag. I. 26 also provides a single word in Greek: στήριγμα (foundation). Excerpts of Pseudo-Jerome's *Regula monachorum* followed by Pseudo-Cyril of Jerusalem's *Epistola de miraculis Hieronymi* (cod. Lat. b. 6) and Pseudo-Jerome's poem *Quindecim signa ante diem iudicii* (cod. Lat. e. 3) are also attested in the collection.

St. Augustine's *De doctrina christiana* and *Retractationes* II.4 are the entirety of a single volume (cod. Lat. c. 7). The manuscript was copied in England during the fifteenth century in a script that shows clearly the influence of European Cursiva on Anglicana. The *Manuale* and *Speculum peccatoris* attributed to Pseudo-Augustine are also found in the aforementioned miscellany of devotional treatises (cod. Lat. b. 6).

A small-format manuscript (cod. Lat. a. 11), only 103 mm in height, contains the second book of St. Gregory the Great's *Dialogi* and an Italian *lauda*. The volume, written in Italy, is dated November 29, 1431, by its anonymous Benedictine scribe. A twelfth-century binding fragment also from Italy (Constable MS 5) contains part of the third book. Twenty-four excerpts from St. Gregory's *Registrum Epistolarum* are among the epistolary extracts in cod.

35. See Laetitia Ciccolini, "Un florilège biblique mis sous le nom de Cyprien de Carthage: L'*Exhortatio de paenitentia* (*CPL* 65)," *Recherches Augustiniennes et Patristiques* 36 (2011): 89–138.

36. See Aidan Breen, "*De XII abusiuis*: Text and Transmission," in *Ireland and Europe in the Early Middle Ages: Texts and Transmission*, ed. Próinséas Ní Chatháin and Michael Richter (Dublin: Four Courts Press, 2002), 78–94; see also Mary Clayton, "*De Duodecim abusiuis*, Lordship and Kingship in Anglo-Saxon England," in *Saints and Scholars: New Perspectives on Anglo-Saxon Literature and Culture in Honour of Hugh Magennis*, ed. Stuart McWilliams (Woodbridge: Boydell and Brewer, 2012), 141–163.

Lat. d. 6. A leaf containing the fourth homily from the first book of the *Homiliae in Ezechielem prophetam* (Frag. I. 32) is an Italian product of the late thirteenth century. Written in Semitextualis and in a small format, the manuscript was likely used as a preaching aid.

The complete text of St. Ambrose's *De bono mortis*, selections of Cassiodorus's *Expositio psalmorum*, and a brief excerpt of Origen's *Commentary on Romans* in the Latin translation of Rufinus of Aquileia are among the varied contents of a lengthy humanist miscellany (cod. Lat. b. 10), and *De consolatione philosophiae* of Boethius is copied in another (cod. Lat. d. 5).[37] Two binding fragments (Frag. I. 19) from a Latin manuscript copied in England during the early fifteenth century contain portions of the ninth *Homilia in sanctum Mattheum* attributed to St. John Chrysostom. Conjugate leaves (Frag. I. 14), also extracted from a former book binding, consist of portions of Isidore of Seville's *Origines* (or *Etymologiae*). The text is written in a French Praegothica during the end of the twelfth century, and vestiges of the hierarchy of script are seen in the Uncial forms used in the opening word of *Origines* 12.1.

3. Liturgical and Music Manuscripts

The collection is richest in liturgical and music manuscripts spanning the late eleventh through the sixteenth century. Office and Mass books of Augustinian, Carthusian, Dominican, Franciscan, and other uses from Austria, England, France, Germany, Italy, and Spain provide a breadth unparalleled in the other holdings described in this catalogue. The majority of these are neumed manuscripts using four-line staves, but diverse systems of musical notation are found among select leaves and fragments.

Five complete psalters provide a varied selection of production and use. Two neumed psalters (codd. Lat. b. 1 and Lat. b. 2) are Dominican manuscripts used by the nuns of the Katharinenkloster in Nuremberg.[38] Textual evidence can generally date the copying of cod. Lat. b. 2 before 1456 and cod. Lat. b. 1 afterward, based on the appearance of Vincent of Ferrer and the feast of the Transfiguration in the calendars, litanies, and collects. The calendars of both psalters clearly express Dominican features, including the liturgical grade *totum duplex*, and contain numerous feasts particular to the order: those of Saints Thomas Aquinas

37. A detailed discussion of both codices follows in section 7 on Italian Humanism, below.

38. The manuscripts were first published by Corbett, "Two German Dominican Psalters." On the convent's library, see Karin Schneider, "Die Bibliothek des Katharinenklosters in Nürnberg und die städtische Gesellschaft," in *Studien zum städtischen Bildungswesen des späten Mittelalters und der frühen Neuzeit*, ed. Bernd Moeller, Hans Patze, and Karl Stackmann (Göttingen: Vandenhoeck and Ruprecht, 1983), 70–82; and Walter Fries, "Kirche und Kloster zu St. Katharina in Nürnberg," *Mitteilungen des Vereins für Geschichte der Stadt Nürnberg* 25 (1924): 47–57; also Marie-Luise Ehrenschwendtner, "A Library Collected by and for the Use of Nuns: St Catherine's Convent, Nuremberg," in *Women and the Book: Assessing the Visual Evidence*, ed. Jane H. M. Taylor and Lesley Smith (Toronto: British Library and University of Toronto Press, 1996), 123–132. On the saint and convent in the city, see Anne Simon, *The Cult of Saint Katherine of Alexandria in Late-Medieval Nuremberg* (Burlington, VT: Ashgate, 2012).

(translation, feast, octave), Vincent of Ferrer (feast and octave), Peter Martyr (feast and translation), and Dominic (translation, feast, and octave), as well as the *anniuersarium patrum et matrum, anniuersarium in cimiteriis nostris sepultorum,* and *anniuersarium familiarum et benefactorum ordinis.* Furthermore, the calendars have entries suggesting that they were copied for the diocese of Bamberg: Saints Erhard, Kunigunde (translation and feast), Ulric, Sebald, Wenceslas, Otto, Katherine, and Conrad. The Litanies are similarly full of Dominican and Bamberger saints. The curious practice of doubling certain saints in the Litany is represented in both manuscripts, which double the patron of the order, St. Dominic, and patroness of the convent, St. Katherine.

A ferial psalter (cod. Lat. a. 7) used by those living under the Augustinian rule was produced ca. 1460–1480 near Arnhem. Although the psalter is not neumed, it provides rich examples of border decoration and initials by the so-called "Masters of Margriet Uutenham."[39] The Office for the Dead is for the use of Utrecht and, similar to that of Windesheim, contains both a major and minor office. According to older auction descriptions, a calendar once began the volume but has since been removed. A thirteenth-century leaf (Frag. I. 12), from a manuscript broken by Otto F. Ege,[40] provides an earlier example from the Low Countries. Though later corrections are added in Anglicana, all decoration, including the lone dentelle initial, versals, and line fillers, is without doubt Flemish.[41]

Borders and historiated initials typical of the "International Gothic" style are found in a psalter copied in England in the second half of the fourteenth century (cod. Lat. e. 4). Characteristically, the iconographic program used in the division of psalms mainly depicts David either with harp, playing bells, or in abstract poses, but other initials are historiated with Jonah and the whale, a choir singing, and God, the Father and Son. Feasts of English and Anglo-Saxon saints fill the calendar, including those of Wulfstan, Edward, Cuthbert, Richard of Chichester, Augustine of Canterbury, Edmund, Dunstan, Aldhelm, Swithun, Edith, Bathild, Kenelm, Oswald, and Cuthburga. Perhaps the calendar's most interesting features are those which attest to the English Reformation's attempts to censor the Catholic Church. The feast of St. Thomas Becket, the translation of his relics, and all instances of the word *papa* (pope) have been thoroughly erased [**PLATE 2**].

Examples of continental illumination are seen among other psalter fragments from France (Acc. 1973.51) and a newly discovered fragment probably from the Low Countries (Acc. 2015.37). Acc. 1973.51 is a leaf from a psalter once thought to be at the Benedictine

39. Henri L. M. Defoer, "The Artists of the East Netherlands, ca. 1460–1480," in *The Golden Age of Dutch Manuscript Painting*, ed. James H. Marrow et al. (New York: G. Braziller, 1990), 250–252; Ines Dickmann, "Das Stundenbuch der Sophia van Bylant und die Meister der Margriet Uutenham," in *Das Stundenbuch der Sophia van Bylant*, ed. Rainer Budde and Roland Krischel (Cologne: Wallraf Richartz Museum, 2001), 177–186; cf. table on 206–207 and plates on 208–216.

40. Scott Gwara, *Otto Ege's Manuscripts* (Cayce, SC: De Brailes, 2013), *Handlist* no. 125.

41. See Kerstin Carlvant, *Manuscript Painting in Thirteenth-Century Flanders* (Turnhout: Harvey Miller, 2012).

Abbey of St. Peter and St. Hilda in Whitby,[42] but this provenance has been challenged lately.[43] The psalter's illustration program is recognizable by its use of birds: one is perched on the opening initial of each psalm.[44]

The oldest psalter in the collection, copied in France near the end of the thirteenth century, forms part of a composite manuscript (cod. Lat. b. 4). Among its varied contents, the codex contains a calendar, a neumed diurnal, a neumed hymnal, and numerous other texts. The calendar, Office of the Virgin, and Office of the Dead are for Carthusian use, as are later additions to the Litany and Sanctorale. Copious annotations, additions, and corrections throughout the volume show at least four centuries of continued use. Notable examples are found in the manuscript's calendar and Sanctorale. The feast on December 8, formerly known to the Carthusians as the "Sanctification of the Virgin," was changed in 1341 to the "Conception of the Virgin,"[45] and corrections by a contemporary hand reflect this change [**PLATE 3**]. Similarly, when the feast of St. Ursula and the Eleven Thousand Virgins was introduced to the order in 1352, contemporary additions were likewise present, and the feast of St. Hugh of Lincoln was regraded in the calendar to reflect its solemnization in 1339.[46] A Parisian locale is more than probable, and the Charterhouse of Vauvert near Paris (Chartreuse de Vauvert-lès-Paris) is the most likely candidate. Particular additions for St. Louis, the founder, occur frequently, and an obit on January 29 for the "*comitissa de blois*" is probably Jeanne de Châtillon (1253–1291), who was a benefactor to the charterhouse.[47] Due to its earlier date and the order's overall attitude of "Be a Saint rather than be called one,"[48] very few Carthusian saints appear in the calendar and Sanctorale. Saints Hugh of Grenoble and Hugh of Lincoln are the two most recognizable entries. Another calendar (Frag. II. 4), removed from a Carthusian manuscript, shares many of the same characteristics. Copied in

42. See Neil R. Ker and Andrew G. Watson, ed. *Medieval Libraries of Great Britain, A List of Surviving Books: Supplement to the Second Edition*, Royal Historical Society Guides and Handbooks 15 (London: Royal Historical Society, 1987), 68; and Toshiyuki Takamiya, "A Handlist of Western Medieval Manuscripts in the Takamiya Collection," in *The Medieval Book: Glosses from Friends and Colleagues of Christopher de Hamel*, ed. James H. Marrow, Richard A. Linenthal, and William Noel (Houten: Hes & De Graaf, 2010), 435.

43. Nigel Morgan, ed., *English Monastic Litanies of the Saints after 1100*, vol. 2, *Pontefract-York*, Henry Bradshaw Society 120 (London: Boydell Press, 2013), 28–29.

44. For example, see the thirty leaves in Cambridge, Harvard University, Houghton Library, MS Lat 394.

45. Jacques Hourlier and Benoît du Moustier, "Le Calendrier cartusien," *Études grégoriennes* 2 (1957): 160–161.

46. Ibid., 160; see also Julian M. Luxford, "The Commemoration of Foundation at English Charterhouses," in *Self-Representation of Medieval Religious Communities*, ed. Anne Müller and Karen Stöber (Berlin: LIT, 2009), 292.

47. Henri Platelle, *Présence de l'au-delà: Une vision médiévale du monde* (Villeneuve d'Acqu: Presses universitaires du Septentrion, 2004), 283–285; p. 284 details her donation for fourteen new *celules* and their upkeep. See also Raoul de Sceaux, "Étude sur la chartreuse de Vauvert-lès-Paris," *Le amis de saint François* 71 (1955): 14–32.

48. A Carthusian monk, *Carthusian Saints*, Carthusian Booklets Series, no. 8 (Arlington, VT: Charterhouse of the Transfiguration, 2006), 5.

Spain during the sixteenth century, Frag. II. 4 includes the feast of the order's founder, St. Bruno (October 6), and, like cod. Lat. b. 4, the two Hughs and the Feast of the Relics (November 8). Since Bruno was declared a saint by equipollent canonization in 1510 by Pope Leo X, a *terminus post quem* is established.[49] The feast of St. Illdefonso of Toledo (January 23) and the Iberian forms in the well-executed Southern Textualis also reinforce a Spanish location.

A third Dominican manuscript, a neumed Office of the Dead (cod. Lat. a. 12), contains several features similar to the two psalters discussed above, codd. Lat. b. 1 and Lat. b. 2. Also copied in Germany during the fifteenth century, the small codex was modified for use in the diocese of Bamberg. In addition to Dominican saints Peter Martyr, Dominic (doubled), Thomas Aquinas, Vincent of Ferrer (added), and Catherine of Siena, a later hand adds Henry, Louis, Sebald, Anne, Barbara, Ursula, Kunigunde, and Elizabeth. In fact, the collects following its Litany are nearly identical to those found in the psalters. Evidence of continued use and modification after 1523 is also seen in a prayer written on an inserted leaf, which invokes St. Antoninus among the other Dominican saints. The manuscript was also used by nuns, which can be seen in marginal comments introducing morphological variants for the feminine gender of nouns and substantive adjectives.

The collection's only antiphonary (cod. Lat. b. 15) was copied on paper during the sixteenth century in either Switzerland or Germany. There is no Temporale, and its Sanctorale is incomplete, beginning imperfectly in July. Several hands write in the manuscript, but the scripts are artificial and poorly imitative of their medieval exemplars. Several leaves copied in the fifteenth and sixteenth century represent varied aesthetic and geographical presentations. Six specimens of the fourteenth through fifteenth century from Italy and southern France consist of various fragments from the Temporale and Sanctorale (Frag. II. 2, Acc. 1974.28, 1974.29, 1980.58.4, 1980.58.5, and 1984.3.2). The leaves have four-line staves traced in red ink and illuminated initials and border sprays characteristic of Italy. One fragmentary bifolium (Frag. V. 3) is an Italian example from the thirteenth century. The four-line staves are ruled with hard-point technique, and C is traced in yellow ink and F in red ink.[50] Northern examples are represented sparsely by two leaves: a fifteenth-century fragment from the Low Countries (Acc. 1996.48) consists of part of the Office of St. Katherine, and a leaf from Germany copied during the sixteenth century (Acc. 1984.3.3) depicts St. Mary Magdalene in a decorated initial. Most of the antiphonary fragments are of Spanish origin, but there are a few Italian examples. Two conjugate leaves (Saint Mary's MS 4), which constituted the inner bifolium of their former quire, were copied in Italy during the fourteenth century and contain four-line staves. A leaf from the Office for St. Clement (Saint Mary's MS 7), also with four-line staves, contains the decoration and script illustrious of the Iberian Peninsula

49. A Carthusian monk, *Carthusian Saints*, 21.

50. On the use of red and yellow inks for staves in the thirteenth century, see John Haines, "The Origins of the Musical Staff," *The Musical Quarterly* 91 (2008): 357–359.

ca. 1500. The remaining leaves, some quite large, are from the sixteenth century, and the chant is written on five-line staves (Acc. 1984.3.4 and 1984.3.7).

Two neumed missals and three fragments diversify the liturgical and musical content. One missal was copied during the thirteenth century for use in Coutances (cod. Lat. b. 13). It is likely that the missal was used in the southeastern part of the Cotentin Peninsula, which extends into the English Channel. Obituaries recorded in the calendar indicate numerous persons from Lingreville, Bricqueville-sur-Mer, and Bréhal, as well as one from Tribehou to the north. The surnames "De Alnetis" and "Lamaignen" occur most frequently. The incomplete calendar contains May through December but features many feasts related to the diocese, especially those of Laudus, Rumpharius, Marculf, Magloire, and the Feast of the Relics in Coutances. Others feasts include Petroc, Euverte, Floscellus, Mellon, Nigaise, Ouen, Philibert of Jumièges, Romain, Taurin, Vigor, Wandregisil, and the translation of the Crown of Thorns. Additions throughout the codex provide evidence of continued use from the thirteenth through fifteenth century. Some even situate the artifact within its geographical and historical milieu. For example, a note records that after a synod in 1285, the prayers on the first folio (now f. 6r) are to be said for obtaining victory in Aragon and Valencia. The note then chronicles the departure of a certain knight, Lord William, from Bricqueville-sur-Mer and that of Philip III (or IV) and his army from Saint-Denis. Many of the later additions include prayers and masses for saints popular in England, such as Etheldreda, Dunstan, Anne, and Thomas Becket, as well as the mass prayers from the Trental of St. Gregory.[51] These texts were written by several hands in Anglicana, and reflect the Anglo-Norman character of the region. The missal also contains a number of votive and requiem masses, followed by four litanies and the mass for Corpus Christi.

The second missal (cod. Lat. c. 13) was copied in Spain in the fourteenth century. It lacks a calendar, and the Temporale and Sanctorale are not complete. Though neumed, many of the four-line staves throughout the manuscript remain blank, while others have musical notation that postdates the medieval period. Additions are sparse, of which the most notable is the feast of Corpus Christi. The final portion of the codex consists of sixty-eight votive and requiem masses. The intentions of the masses range from individuals such as priests, pilgrims, and sailors to moral matters such as the temptation of the flesh and remission of sin. Others are intended for specific daily concerns, for example, inclement weather or drought.

Binding fragments of the thirteenth through fifteenth century provide examples of three missals copied in England (Frag. I. 16), Germany (Frag. I. 18), and northern France or perhaps the Low Countries (Frag. II. 5). Of these fragments, two (Frag. I. 16 and Frag. I. 18) were at one time in bindings of imprints already in the collection, and one (Frag. II. 5) was donated anonymously.

51. On these, see Richard Pfaff, "The English Devotion of St. Gregory's Trental," *Speculum* 49 (1974): 75–90, esp. 82–84.

The gradual is represented by four codices and nine fragments. The systems of musical notation among the codices vary distinctly and exemplify different specimens. For example, a gradual copied in France or by a French scribe during the thirteenth century (cod. Lat. c. 15) contains four-line staves in which C and F are also marked with yellow and red inks. Although there is no calendar and much of the manuscript is incomplete, thirty-nine sequences remain. Much of the manuscript's content, especially its sequences, have a very Germanic quality and are deserving of further musicological study. A distinctly German or Austrian gradual was copied in the fourteenth century (cod. Lat. c. 14), likely for Augustinian use. The musical notation is Hufnagelschrift, characteristic of Germanic regions. Over forty-five sequences and a number of Alleluia melodies and verses are also included. The collection's third gradual is bound in two separate volumes (codd. Lat. c. 2 and Lat. c. 3). Both volumes were copied in Italy during the sixteenth century in a later Italian Rotunda, and all neumes are written on four-line staves traced in red ink. Each volume also contains ownership marks of the convent of the Annunciata in Ventimiglia, which became an observant house in 1509,[52] though 1503 has also been suggested.[53] Among the contents of the first volume (cod. Lat. c. 2) are the Temporale, ordinary chants, and six sequences. Franciscan saints Bonaventure, Francis, Anthony, Bernadine, Catherine of Siena, and Clare are found in the Litany. The second volume (cod. Lat. c. 3) supplies more ordinary chants, the Sanctorale, a few votive masses, ten sequences (three for St. Francis), and eight Marian antiphons. Within the Sanctorale are celebrations for Saints Bernadine, Anthony, Clare, and Francis, and for the Transfiguration and Stigmata. The initials painted throughout both volumes are late Italian examples of the littera duplex and flourished styles, often deviating from the standard types by adding gold and bianchi girari interiors. The bindings, by John Ramage (1836–1891), provide the collection's only examples of gilt binders' stamps on their front turn-ins. An earlier example of a mass book is a fragment from the twelfth century, likely copied in Austria, Germany, or Bohemia (Frag. I. 13). The former piece of spine lining contains part of the Temporale for Sundays after Pentecost, and adiastematic neumes are written above the text. A similar fragment (Frag. I. 29) also uses adiastematic neumes. Copied in the thirteenth century, Frag. I. 29 contains portions of the *Credo* and *Sanctus* as well as *Sanctus* and *Agnus* tropes.

As seen among the collection's antiphonaries, many of the gradual leaves are from Italian and Spanish parent manuscripts. An Italian specimen of the fifteenth century (Frag. II. 3) was formerly a book binding. Donated by a local convent, the leaf contains a small section of the Common of the saints for martyrs. A similar Italian example (Saint Mary's MS 5) is a bifolium containing portions of the Temporale and Sanctorale near Christmas. The remaining leaves are Spanish examples copied during the sixteenth century, using five-line

52. John Richard Humpidge Moorman, *Medieval Franciscan Houses* (St. Bonaventure, NY: The Franciscan Institute, 1983), 504.

53. Girolamo Rossi, *Storia della città di Ventimiglia* (Oneglia: G. Ghilini, 1886), 189.

staves: two from the Temporale (Acc. 1984.3.1 and Saint Mary's MS 6) and four from the Sanctorale (Frag. V. 2, Saint Mary's MSS 8, 9, and 10).

The collection also includes a neumed pontifical (cod. Lat. c. 12), which was copied in southern France during the second half of the fourteenth century. The text is that of Durand, but the manuscript is incomplete. Decoration is quite modest and consists only of littera duplex, flourished, and plain initials in red and blue ink. Most of the cadels within the staves feature pen and ink drawings, which depict faces and grotesques. One of the rarer features is seen in the section for the dedication of a church, in which the Greek alphabet is written in its entirety [**PLATE 4**]. Also for use by a bishop, but not liturgical, is Francesco da Fiesso's treatise on episcopal visits to cloisters, *De uisitatione*. The text is present in a Renaissance manuscript (cod. Lat. c. 9), written on paper in a script under the influence of Humanistic Cursive. This particular copy contains a dedicatory preface to Filippo Arrivabene, archbishop of Monemvasia, which is dated Cremona, May 10, 1529. *De uisitatione* is divided into thirty chapters on visitation and includes the types of questions the bishop should ask. There are also sections on the Articles of Faith and the sacraments.

The remaining fragments contain representative samples of types of liturgical books, some with musical notation, which are not represented among the codices. These include Mass books similar to sacramentaries and plenary missals (Frag. I. 22 and Frag. I. 28), as well as breviaries (Frag. I. 17, Frag. I. 24, Frag. I. 25, Frag. I. 30), evangeliaries (Frag. I. 6), and lectionaries (Constable MS 7). A leaf (Constable MS 4) from a processional, which was included in Otto F. Ege's *Fifty Original Leaves from Medieval Manuscripts* portfolio, has now been shown to be from Wilton Abbey.[54] The fragments span the late eleventh through fifteenth century and originate from various regions of Italy, England, Germany, and France. The earliest fragments are two sequential leaves copied in Italy near the close of the eleventh century (Frag. I. 28). Adiastematic neumes have been added above chanted portions during the first week of Lent. A fragment of an Office book copied in the Benevento (Frag. I. 27) near the end of the twelfth century contains a portion of St. Gregory the Great's *Homiliae in Euangelia* and neumed antiphons for the Epiphany. The manuscript is written in the region's characteristic script, Beneventan Minuscule,[55] and provides a rare paleographical specimen. Also of note is the collection's only Greek manuscript (Frag. I. 15). The leaf, which contains three Gospel readings, was copied during the twelfth century in the eastern Mediterranean, likely Crete.

4. Philosophy, Theology, and Scholasticism

Apart from those already mentioned, several manuscripts provide varied examples of philosophical, theological, and scholastic texts, treatises, and methods. The earliest examples in the

54. Alison Altstatt, "Re-membering the Wilton Processional," *Notes: The Quarterly Journal of the Music Library Association* 72.4 (June 2016): 690–732. I am grateful to Alison Altstatt of the University of Northern Iowa School of Music for sharing her research on this manuscript.

55. For this particular fragment, see Virginia Brown, "A Second New List of Beneventan Manuscripts (V)," *Mediaeval Studies* 70 (2008): 309, 327.

collection of Aristotelian and Thomistic texts are contained in one manuscript (Saint Mary's MS 2), which was copied at the close of the thirteenth century. The scribe who copied Thomas Aquinas's *De ente et essentia* and the accompanying glosses dates the text December 10, 1299 [**PLATE 5**]. Latin versions of Aristotle's *De longitudine et breuitate uitae* and a glossed *Analytica priora*, which contains diagrams of three syllogisms, follow the text of Aquinas.

Two manuscripts illustrate the structure of the medieval *quaestio* and provide very different physical examples of the ways in which *quaestiones* circulated. A single quire copied in Italy in the early fourteenth century contains five *quaestiones* by Giles of Rome (Frag. I. 31), of which three were previously unknown.[56] Although mildly disturbed, the manuscript still retains the unbound form in which it circulated within the medieval university. The manuscript is undecorated, and the emphasis is clearly on the text. There are a high number of corrections by the text hand and others, using diverse techniques such as erasures, strikes, transformations, expuncti, and marginal additions with *signes-de-renvoi*. A manuscript of John Buridan's *Quaestiones supra decem libros Ethicorum Aristotelis ad Nicomachum*[57] (cod. Lat. e. 2) provides a distinctly different form. The manuscript, copied in Italy on paper during the fifteenth century, is a large format codex (431 mm in height). Its first folio is richly illuminated with three unidentified heraldic marks in the lower margin and contains a historiated initial depicting either Buridan, Aristotle, or perhaps the owner. Lemmata are underlined in red ink, and paraph (i.e., pilcrow) marks in both red and blue show the mixture of decoration and utilitarian aesthetic. Despite a rather deluxe presentation in its first few folios, the remainder of the manuscript is undecorated. However, the most interesting feature of the codex is the circumstances of its production. The professional scribe, who copied the entire manuscript, appends a telling distich for his patron: "The end of my course is here, I seek the wages for my work/If you don't pay, tomorrow you will be less inclined."

Other examples of logic are found among a few manuscripts. Another Italian manuscript copied during the fifteenth century (cod. Lat. d. 4) contains Walter Burley's commentary on the *Ars uetus*, or Old Logic.[58] Burley's expositions on Porphyry's *Isagoge* and Aristotle's *Categoriae*, which is incomplete, are accompanied by minimal glossing. The *Termini naturales* of William of Heytesbury,[59] here attributed to Walter Burley, and an incomplete

56. I owe many thanks to Prof. Stephen Dumont of the Department of Philosophy, University of Notre Dame, for sharing his identification of the *quaestiones* and his forthcoming research: "New Questions by Giles of Rome (I): The Intention and Remission of Forms."

57. The text is printed in *Questiones Ioannis buridani super decem libros ethicorum aristotelis ad nicomachum* (Paris, 1513; repr. Frankfurt-am-Main, 1968); see Jack Zupko, *John Buridan: Portrait of a Fourteenth-Century Arts Master* (Notre Dame, IN: University of Notre Dame Press, 2003), 227–242; and generally Gyula Klima, *John Buridan* (Oxford: Oxford University Press, 2009).

58. See Mischa von Perger, "Walter Burley's *Expositio vetus super librum Porphyrii*: An Edition," *Franciscan Studies* 59 (2001): 237–238.

59. Andrea Tabarroni, "A Note on a Short Treatise Attributed to Ockham: The 'Super terminos naturales,'" *Franciscan Studies* 44 (1984): 329–349; on William's life and works, see James A. Weisheipl, "Ockham and Some Mertonians," *Mediaeval Studies* 30 (1968): 195–199; and Weisheipl, "Repertorium Mertonense," *Mediaeval Studies* 31 (1969): 212–216.

text of Albert of Saxony's *Tractatus proportionum* are both Italian Humanist examples copied in one manuscript (cod. Lat. c. 11). Two geometric diagrams are also traced in the margins of Albert's *Tractatus.*

In stark contrast to the other manuscripts of this category is a particular theological volume. The heretical writings of the Taborite bishop Nicholas of Pelhřimov,[60] known as "Biskupec" ("the little bishop"), are contained in a manuscript copied in Bohemia (cod. Lat. c. 1). The codex is the first part of Nicholas Biskupec's long commentary on the Gospels, *Scriptum super quattuor euangelia*, and is dated July 15, 1435, by its scribe. The contemporary binding is labeled *prima pars* and contains a possible former shelf number; perhaps the other volumes are still extant.

5. Sermons, Summae, and Preaching

Sermons composed by a wide range of authors, a few *summae*, and other preaching materials constitute the collection's holdings related to pastoral care. The earliest sermons are those of Philip the Chancellor (cod. Lat. b. 11), contained in a manuscript copied in France during the thirteenth century. Ninety-two sermons, primarily on the Psalms, are written in a highly abbreviated Northern Textualis and occupy sixty folios, which are now disbound. Many of the lemmata and pericopes are underlined in red or black ink, and an alphabetical index is written on the last five folios.

The sermons of Peregrinus of Opole are the most numerous and concentrated example.[61] Sixty-four sermons, *Sermones de tempore*, and forty-nine sermons, *Sermones de sanctis*, are collected in a large paper codex (cod. Lat. d. 1), which was likely compiled in either southern Germany or Austria in the fifteenth century. Following Peregrinus's sermons *de tempore* are ten additional sermons. Of the four that are unattributed, three are extant in other manuscripts, and the final six sermons are those of Antonius Azaro de Parma. Similarly, another eleven unattributed sermons follow the sermons *de sanctis* of Peregrinus. Topics include the Circumcision, Epiphany, and Saints Blaise, Ulrich, Stephen, Afra, and Giles. In addition to sermon material, the manuscript also incudes tracts such as *De passione* of Narcissus Hertz de Berching,[62] *De poenitentia* of Peter Reicher of

60. See František Michálek Bartoš, "Postila Mikuláš Biskupce na evangelní harmonii," *asopis Musea Království českého* 93 (1919): 174–176, and Amedeo Molnár, "De divisione Scripture sacre multiplici Nicolaus Biskupec de Pelh imov," *Communio Viatorum* 13 (1970): 154–170; also Thomas A. Fudge, "Crime, Punishment and Pacifism in the Thought of Bishop Mikuláš of Pelh imov, 1420–1452," in *Bohemian Reformation and Religious Practice* 3 (2000): 69–103. For the full bibliography: Pavel Spunar, *Repertorium auctorum Bohemorum provectum idearum post Universitatem Pragensem conditam illustrans. Tomus II*, Studia Copernicana 35 (Wrocław: Institutum Ossolinianum, 1995).

61. Critically edited in Ryszard Tatarzyński, *Peregrini de Opole Sermones de tempore et de sanctis*, Studia Przegladu tomistycznego 1 (Warsaw: Institutum Thomisticum PP. Dominicanorum Varsaviensium, 1997).

62. See Alois Madre, *Nikolaus von Dinkelsbühl: Leben und Schriften. Ein Beitrag zur theologischen Literaturgeschichte*, Beiträge zur Geschichte der Philosophie und Theologie des Mittelalters 40.4 (Münster: Äschendorffsche Verlagsbuchhandlung, 1965), 308–309.

Pirchenwart,[63] excerpts of the *Legenda aurea*, Jacque de Nouvion's *Disputatio cum Hussitis*, and various texts attributed to Nicolaus von Dinkelsbühl. The final text is a lengthy sermon by Thomas Ebendorfer de Haselbach.[64]

The remaining sermons in the collection provide examples of use, compilation, and production. For example, ten sermons have been copied between the two Aristotelian texts in Saint Mary's MS 2. Whether these anonymous sermons, mainly for the Common of saints, were preached both within and outside the university community remains unknown. However, their presence among philosophical and scholastic texts illustrates the scope of personalization and customization a manuscript may have, whether as a model, *uademecum*, or schoolbook. Likewise, a small number of sermons of Bernard of Clairvaux are excerpted and interspersed among other texts in a florilegium (cod. Lat. b. 12) and epistolary compilation (cod. Lat. d. 6).

A mixture of Latin and the vernacular in preaching can be seen in two manuscripts. In the aforementioned manuscript (cod. Lat. d. 5), written by Filippo da Strada, a Dominican in Venice, are no fewer than six sermons. Sermons on virginity, marriage, St. Cyprian, and specifically for the marriage of Sebastian Erizzi and Cipriana Trevisan are in Italian, whereas others are composed by the preacher in Latin. Thirteen anonymous sermons are found in a small paper manuscript copied ca. 1500 in Germany (cod. Lat. b. 14). These sermons for Easter, Pentecost, Corpus Christi, the Assumption, Nativity, and Purification were once part of a larger volume. The first two contain substantial sections in German, which alternate with those in Latin.

A single leaf (Frag. I. 11) contains a fragment of the sermons of Simon of Cremona. The parent manuscript was broken ca. 1926 by the "Foliophiles Inc.," and leaves were disseminated widely in portfolios in the 1960s by Alfred W. Stites. The manuscript, though broken, is especially significant because its bold Cursiva is the hand of a known scribe. The sermons were copied by Caspar Misnensis, a Carthusian scribe, at the Charterhouse of Buxheim in 1434.[65] Caspar's hand is also known in two other manuscripts both dated the following year.[66]

Other texts, particularly *summae*, supplementary treatises, and other preaching aids written by members of the Dominican and Franciscan orders, provide a sample of the tools

63. Ibid., 230–232.

64. Alphons Lhotsky, *Thomas Ebendorfer: Ein österreichischer Geschichtsschreiber, Theologe und Diplomat des 15. Jahrhunderts*, Schriften der Monumenta Germaniae historica 15 (Stuttgart: Anton Hiersemann, 1957), 78, no. 56.

65. Bénedictins de Bouveret, *Colophons de manuscrits occidentaux des origines au XVIe siècle* (Fribourg: Suisse Editions universitaires, 1965–1982), 2: nos. 4840–4842.

66. München, Bayerische Staatsbibliothek, Clm 4402, f. 109, and Augsburg, Universitätsbibliothek, Cod. II.1.2o 15, f. 218vb. For Clm 4402, see Karl Halm, Georg von Laubmann, and Wilhelm Meyer, *Catalogus Codicum Latinorum Bibliothecae Regiae Monacensis* 1.2 (Munich: Bibliotecae Regiae, 1894), 189; and Bénedictins de Bouveret, *Colophons* 2: no. 4840; for Cod. II.1.2o 15, see Günter Hägele, *Lateinische mittelalterliche Handschriften in Folio der Universitätsbibliothek Augsburg* (Wiesbaden: Harrassowitz, 1996), 1:131–132.

available for preachers and confessors alike. For example, consider a manuscript of the *Summa de uitiis* of William Peraldus, a French Dominican, which was copied in Italy during the fourteenth century (cod. Lat. b. 9). The work contains nine treatises—on vices, gluttony, lust, avarice, sloth, pride, envy, wrath, and the sin of the tongue—which are indicative of the texts in demand after the Fourth Lateran Council.[67] Peraldus's *Summa* was one of the most popular resources for preachers and confessors in their pastoral work.[68] In the codex, the treatises are preceded by a table of contents occupying the first eight folios. The table shows the medieval divisions of the treatises, which were also subdivided into parts and chapters. For example, in the fourth treatise, dealing with avarice, Part I addresses what makes us detest avarice, and chapter 4 discusses how avarice is a grave spiritual illness, possibly the worst, and can be shown in twelve ways. The manuscript's decoration serves its functional purposes and employs initials no higher than littera duplex and flourished types. By no means ostentatious, the decorator adds the occasional zoomorphic motif among the flourishes.

A fifteenth-century copy of Nicholas of Osimo's *Supplementum summae Pisanellae* (cod. Lat. c. 5), also made in Italy, shows the presence of canon law among pastoral manuscripts. Nicholas[69] was a Franciscan who enlarged and expanded a previous work, the *Summa de casibus conscientiae*, by the Dominican canonist Bartholomew of San Concordio, which, in turn, was an adaptation of John of Freiburg's *Summa confessorum*.[70] Like Bartholomew's text, also known as the *Summa Pisana* or *Summa Pisanella*, Nicholas's *Supplementum* was a confessor's manual.[71] The contents are arranged alphabetically and deliver an exposition of canon law and moral precepts for use by confessors. Adding to the manual's utilitarian purpose are indices of subjects and the rubrics for both civil and canon law. The *Supplementum* also features a layout particular to itself, which differentiates Nicholas's additions from the text of Bartholomew. An initial **A** signals the beginning of an added section, and a **B** marks its conclusion and where Bartholomew's *Summa* resumes.[72] Decoration

67. Richard Newhauser, *The Treatise on Vices and Virtues in Latin and the Vernacular*, Typologie des Sources du Moyen Âge Occidental 68 (Turnhout: Brepols, 1993), 127.

68. Siegfried Wenzel, "The Continuing Life of William Peraldus's 'Summa vitiorum,'" in *Ad litteram: Authoritative Texts and Their Medieval Readers*, ed. Mark D. Jordan and Kent Emery, Jr. (Notre Dame, IN: University of Notre Dame Press, 1992), 135–163; Newhauser, *The Treatise on Vices and Virtues*, 127–230; also Silvana Vecchio (trans. Helen Took), "The Seven Deadly Sins between Pastoral Care and Scholastic Theology: The *Summa de vitiis* by John of Rupella," in *In the Garden of Evil: The Vices and Culture in the Middle Ages*, ed. Richard Newhauser (Toronto: Pontifical Institute of Mediaeval Studies, 2005), 104–127, esp. 109; and Mark D. Jordan, *The Invention of Sodomy in Christian Theology* (Chicago: University of Chicago Press, 1998), 110.

69. See Umberto Picciafuoco, *Fr. Nicolò da Osimo, 1370?–1453: Vita, opere, spiritualità* (Monteprandone: Officine Grafiche Anxanum, 1980).

70. Pierre Michaud-Quantin, *Sommes de casuistique et manuels de confession au Moyen Âge (XII–XVI siècles)* (Louvain: Nauwelaerts, 1962), 60–66.

71. Thomas N. Tentler, *Sin and Confession on the Eve of the Reformation* (Princeton, NJ: Princeton University Press, 1977), 33–34.

72. Michaud-Quantin, *Sommes de casuistique et manuels*, 63.

in the manuscript is more functional than anything else, and, like cod. Lat. b. 9, zoomorphic motifs appear sparingly.

A confessional of the fifteenth century copied in northern Italy (Acc. 1984.3.6) stands in contrast to the *Pisanellae* of cod. Lat. c. 5. The small paper codex is only eleven folios, folded in quarto, and likely is a portion of a larger volume. The text of the confessional is mostly in Italian with Latin prayers, but its decoration is more deluxe than the others. A gold-painted initial with bianchi girari and borders with blues, greens, purples, and more bianchi girari frame the text on the first folio.

Another composite manuscript, copied in southern France ca. 1300, contains different preaching aids (cod. Lat. b. 5). Most of the codex is an alphabetical compendium of what Kaske succinctly describes as "fundamental abstract concepts (e.g. *abstinentia*, *patientia*, etc.) rather than the symbolic meanings of concrete biblical images."[73] The *Summa de abstinentia* is ascribed with some hesitation to Nicholas de Byard.[74] Byard's *Summa* also circulated as the *Dictionarius pauperum* and *Tractatus de uitiis et uirtutibus*. Within the same codex is the tract *De dono timoris*, by Humbert of Romans, who was formerly the fifth Master General of the Dominican Order.[75] The work is a collection of *exempla*, or stories used to make a moral point, which were intended for preachers to use in the preparation of sermons.[76] A preacher would select an example that conveyed the values or behaviors he wanted to illustrate, or combat, in his sermon. All of the *exempla* in Humbert's collection relate to the gift of fear, and the tract helps a preacher choose, use, and modify the *exempla*.[77] The final text in the manuscript is the *Meditationes* of Pseudo-Bernard of Clairvaux. The tract highlights inner spirituality, and the various titles under which it circulated include *De interiori homine* and *Meditationes piissimae de cognitione humanae conditionis*. Unlike the previous texts, the *Meditationes* was not a preaching aid but rather one recommended for the formation of novices.[78] Dominican ownership (ca. 1500) can be confirmed by the mark of one Andreas Praedicator. Later marks show that manuscript was in the convent of San Paolo in Brindisi (Apulia) in 1597.

Extracts of Saints Augustine, Gregory the Great, Pseudo-Chrysostom, and Bernard of Clairvaux are found in a small florilegium (cod. Lat. b. 12). The manuscript is a single paper quaternion folded in quarto, which was copied in Bohemia during the fifteenth century.

73. Robert Kaske with Arthur Groos and Michael W. Twomey, *Medieval Christian Literary Imagery: A Guide to Interpretation* (Toronto: University of Toronto Press, 1988), 37, no. 7.

74. Marian Michèle Mulchahey, *"First the Bow Is Bent in Study": Dominican Education before 1350* (Toronto: Pontifical Institute of Mediaeval Studies, 1998), 518–520, and Kaske, *Medieval Christian Literary Imagery*, 37; and also Louis Jacque Bataillon, "The Tradition of Nicholas of Biard's Distinctiones," *Viator* 25 (1994): 245–288. Bataillon implies that Nicholas was a Dominican on 245.

75. See Mulchahey, *"First the Bow Is Bent in Study,"* 460–462.

76. On *exempla* in general, see ibid., 414–419; 414, n. 42 contains a fuller bibliography; see 458–472 for collections of *exempla*.

77. Ibid. 462.

78. Ibid., 110–112.

The florilegium was no doubt a preaching aid, and its compiler made use of Thomas of Ireland's *Manipulus florum*.[79] The *Manipulus* consists of approximately 6,000 extracts from patristic and classical authors, which were gathered under 266 topics in alphabetical order.[80] The topics included many abstractions, such as friendship, lust, piety, and grace, around which sermons could be composed. The manuscript concludes with a descriptive account of Rome's topography and buildings followed by a list of churches and several indulgences, which could have been used as a pilgrim's guide.

While not explicitly designed as a preaching aid,[81] the *Legenda aurea* of Iacobus de Voragine is best mentioned here. Various manuscripts in the collection include extracts of the *Legenda*, which shows a tradition of multifaceted usage. For example, the section *De nomine* for St. Ambrose is excerpted in the *Compagnia Ambrosiana* manuscript (cod. Lat. c. 8), and portions on St. Peter's Chair are copied at the end of the psalter with Latin and French prayers (cod. Lat. b. 4). Five chapters from the *Legenda*[82] dealing with the division of the liturgical year are also interspersed with sermons and sermon material (cod. Lat. d. 1). This last occurrence is more harmonious with the *Legenda*'s ability to function in a similar manner as *exempla.*

6. Historiography and Epistolography

Several historical (and not so historical) texts ranging from the extremely popular to the little known are present in four codices. A volume written and compiled in England during the fifteenth century (cod. Lat. d. 3) provides four diverse examples of content and layout. The manuscript contains a portion of Martin of Troppau's *Chronicon pontificum et imperatorum*.[83] The chronicle presents the popes and emperors in fifty-year increments using a customized parallel layout. The two columns use succession diagrams of yellow and green lines with red and black roundels, and red Arabic numerals indicate precise years. Some roundels are modified to accommodate emphatic or unusual features. For example, entries for Christ and Augustus, who begin the line of popes and emperors, are larger and more ornate than the

79. Richard H. Rouse and Mary A. Rouse, *Preachers, Florilegia, and Sermons: Studies on the Manipulus florum of Thomas of Ireland* (Toronto: Pontifical Institute of Mediaeval Studies, 1979), 188–197; see 197–207 for the use of the *Manipulus* within other florilegia.

80. Ibid., 117. All of the 266 topics have been edited by Chris L. Nighman in the online Electronic *Manipulus florum* Project, http://web.wlu.ca/history/cnighman/.

81. On this concept, see Mulchahey, *"First the Bow Is Bent in Study,"* 465–466, especially n. 200.

82. Chapters 31–34 address *Septuagesima*, *Sexagesima*, and *Quadragesima*, and chapter 35 the *rationes de quattuor temporibus.*

83. Edited in Ludwig Weiland, "Martini Oppaviensis chronicon pontificum et imperatorum," *Monumenta Germaniae Historica Scriptores* 22 (1872): 377–475; see also Wolfgang-Valentin Ikas, *Martin von Troppau (Martinus Polonus), O.P. (1278) in England: Überlieferungs- und wirkungsgeschichtliche Studien zu dessen Papst- und Kaiserchronik*, Wissensliteratur im Mittelalter 40 (Wiesbaden: Reichert, 2002), 195–198; and Wolfgang-Valentin Ikas, "Martinus Polonus' Chronicle of the Popes and Emporers: A Medieval Best-Seller and Its Neglected Influence on Medieval English Chroniclers," *The English Historical Review* 116 (2001): 327–341.

others. Likewise, the entry for Romulus and Remus uses two conjoined circles to illustrate that they were twins. As a historical text, Martin's *Chronicon* enjoyed great popularity and circulated widely. The number of manuscripts is perhaps only rivaled by the *Historia scholastica* of Peter Comestor,[84] and the work was translated into several vernaculars, including non-Western languages.[85] Two interesting features allow this copy of the *Chronicon* to stand out from others. First are the remnants of the Protestant censorship of Henry VIII: as in cod. Lat. e. 4, forms of the word *papa* (pope) have been erased from the chronicle (some more vigorously than others). Secondly, the chronicle has been modified to extend the range of dates. Martin's third recension of the work ends in 1277 with the advent of the papacy of Nicholas III, but cod. Lat. d. 3 continues from 1277 to 1415, ending with the deposition of Antipope John XXIII.[86] The full text of Geoffrey of Monmouth's (now) pseudo-historiographical work, *Historia regum Britanniae*, also known as *De gestis Britonum*,[87] is copied by another hand following Martin's *Chronicon*. The text also incorporates Geoffrey's other work, the *Prophetiae Merlini*, which is a collection of prophecies attributed to the wizard Merlin. Three other short texts, which can precede the *Historia*, are transmitted in cod. Lat. d. 3. The first of these, *Ab origine mundi*, which occurs only in four manuscripts,[88] recounts an alternative founding myth of Albion by women, the Albina story.[89] The other two texts also provide prefatory matter on the Trojans, since the founding myth begins with Brutus, the great-grandson of

84. Ikas, "Martinus Polonus' Chronicle," 331, but cf. 331, n. 4.

85. The Middle English translation is critically edited in Dan Embree, *The Chronicles of Rome: An Edition of the Middle English "Chronicle of Popes and Emperors" and "The Lollard Chronicle,"* Medieval Chronicles 1 (Woodbridge: Boydell Press, 1999); and from a single manuscript in Embree, "The Fragmentary Chronicle in British Library, Additional MS 37049," *Manuscripta* 37 (1993): 193–200; on the others, see Ikas, "Martinus Polonus' Chronicle," 332, and 332, n. 2 on the Greek, Armenian, and Persian translations.

86. On these, see Wolfgang-Valentin Ikas, *Fortsetzungen zur Papst- und Kaiserchronik Martins von Troppau aus England*, Monumenta Germaniae historica, Scriptores rerum Germanicarum 19 (Hannover: Hahnsche Buchhandlung, 2004), 53–56; the additions are critically edited on 280–289. See also Ikas, *Martin von Troppau*, 18–19, 21, 195–198, 203; and Julia C. Crick, *The Historia Regum Britannie of Geoffrey of Monmouth IV: Dissemination and Reception in the Later Middle Ages* (Cambridge: D. S. Brewer, 1991), 57–58.

87. Critically edited with an English translation in Michael D. Reeve and Neil Wright, *Geoffrey of Monmouth: The History of the Kings of Britain. An Edition and Translation of De gestis Britonum [Historia regum Britannie]*, Arthurian Studies 69 (Woodbridge: Boydell Press, 2007).

88. James P. Carley and Julia Crick, "Constructing Albion's Past: an Annotated Edition of *De Origine Gigantum*," *Arthurian Literature* 13 (1995): 41–114; the manuscripts are listed on 50; and Crick, *The Historia Regum Britannie of Geoffrey of Monmouth IV*, 22.

89. On the Albina story, see Lesley Johnson, "Return to Albion," *Arthurian Literature* 13 (1995): 19–40; on the Latin versions, see Carley and Crick, "Constructing Albion's Past," 48–54; Jeffrey Jerome Cohen, *Of Giants: Sex, Monsters, and the Middle Ages* (Minneapolis: University of Minnesota Press, 1999), 47–60; and Jocelyn Wogan-Browne, "Mother or Stepmother to History? Joan de Mohun and Her Chronicle," in *Motherhood, Religion, and Society in Medieval Europe, 400–1400: Essays Presented to Henrietta Leyser*, ed. Conrad Leyser and Lesley Smith (Surrey: Ashgate, 2011), 305–316; and for a succinct overview, see Christopher Baswell, "England's Antiquities: Middle English Literature and the Classical Past," in *A Companion to Medieval English Literature and Culture, c.1350–c.1500*, ed. Peter Brown (Chichester: Wiley-Blackwell, 2009), 242–243.

Aeneas: a Trojan genealogy,[90] followed by an excerpt of Dares the Phrygian's *De excidio Troiae historia*.[91] The manuscript contains a longer eschatological text, a Latin translation of Pseudo-Methodius's *Apokalypsis*,[92] and a short excerpt from the fifth book of Bede's *Historia ecclesiastica gentis Anglorum*, both of which also circulated with Geoffrey's *Historia*.[93] The remainder of the codex contains an unidentified genealogical chronicle, which begins imperfectly with Noah and ends during the reign of Henry V. The chronicle is especially noteworthy for its innovative use of layout. Genealogical relationships are illustrated using a complex series of diagrams comprised of roundels and lines in red ink. The *mise-en-page* for the diagrams dominates the page, the text is written in various configurations, and formalized columns are not always distinguished [**PLATE 6**]. The text of the chronicle copied as a codex seems to survive uniquely in cod. Lat. d. 3, but close parallels and verbatim sections appear in a genealogical roll in Aberystwyth.[94] Taken as a whole, the manuscript reflects a historical compilation for an educational purpose. The four scribal bookhands also provide illustrative examples of English Cursiva and Anglicana during the fifteenth century. Though the manuscript's provenance from the sixteenth through twentieth century is well documented, its contemporary usage is not known. It is tempting to think the codex at one time belonged to a Benedictine house, especially given the presence of Martin's *Chronicon*.[95]

No fewer than forty separate texts are contained in a large paper manuscript copied in Austria or Bohemia during the fifteenth century (cod. Lat. d. 6). The contents are a mixture of historiographical and epistolographical texts, with greater emphasis placed on the latter. The codex begins with the *Historia bohemica* written by Aeneas Siluius Piccolomini shortly before he became Pope Pius II.[96] Piccolomini's work is a geo-historical account of Bohemia, including its pagan prehistory, which employs philological and etymological techniques representative of the period's humanistic activities. The *Historia bohemica* is also seen as an ecumenical effort that later created a cultural communality after Bohemia was divided by religious conflict,[97] particularly by the Hussites. Several other texts and speeches from the

90. Crick, *The Historia Regum Britannie of Geoffrey of Monmouth IV*, 43–44.

91. Ibid., 35–39; the Latin text is edited in Ferdinand Meister, *Daretis Phrygii de excidio Troiae historia* (Leipzig: Teubner, 1991).

92. On the text's popularity after the Norman Conquest, see Stephen Pelle, "The *Revelationes* of Pseudo-Methodius and 'Concerning the Coming of Antichrist' in British Library MS Cotton Vespasian D. XIV," *Notes and Queries* 56 (2009): 324–330; cf. the Latin text in cod. Lat. d. 3 with that edited in W. J. Aerts and G. A. A. Kortekaas, *Die Apokalypse des Pseudo-Methodius: Die ältesten griechischen und lateinischen Übersetzungen*, Corpus Scriptorum Christianorum Orientalium 569 (Leuven: Peeters, 1998).

93. For the *Apokalypsis*, see Crick, *The Historia Regum Britannie of Geoffrey of Monmouth IV*, 58–59, and 33–35 for Bede.

94. Aberystwyth, National Library of Wales, Roll 55. An edition of the text is currently in progress.

95. Ikas, "Martinus Polonus' Chronicle," 334.

96. Critically edited in Joseph Hejnic and Hans Rothe, *Aeneas Silvius Piccolomini. Historia Bohemica 1: Historisch-kritische Ausgabe des lateinischen Textes* (Cologne: Bölau, 2005).

97. This view is put forth by Alfred Thomas, *Prague Palimpsest: Writing Memory, and the City* (Chicago: University of Chicago Press, 2010), 27–28.

Council of Basel (1431–1449) by Nicholas de Tudeschis,[98] Gerhardus Landrianus, Guiliano Cesarini, Lodovico Pontano,[99] and Augustinus Iauriensis immediately follow Piccolomini's *Historia* and his *Bulla de profectione in Turcos*. However, the manuscript's dominant focus clearly is epistolography. Over 124 letters and epistolary extracts, some as short as six words, are culled from the corpus of Piccolomini, Cyprian, Gregory, Bernard of Clairvaux, Abelard and Heloise, and others. Many may be used formulaically or provide sententious examples for someone learning to draft a proper letter. Other examples are excerpted from the prefaces of Greek to Latin translations of the works of Plutarch, Pseudo-Plato, and Xenophon by Guarino Veronese and Leonardo Bruni. The compilers of the epistolary excerpts had access to many of the texts in their entirety, which is evidenced by comments such as "obmisi quasi dimidiam" following the explicits. Of its contemporary use, ownership marks provide the names of a certain Iohannes Andrea of Neisse and Jos. Czeyskendorff of Krakow, without dates. In 1484 the codex was given to one Martin Leheure by Nicholas Halbendorff and Martin Kwinesye, and by 1493 the volume was at a church in Reichenbach.[100] Its contemporary binding still contains the hasp and part of a chain.

An account in French of Claude de France's entry to Paris in 1517 for her coronation is copied in a parchment codex (MS Fr. c. 1). The author of what is known as *Le Sacre Couronnement et Entrée de Madame Claude Royne de France fille du Roy Loys XII et de Madame Anne de Bretaigne* is anonymous, but the text is similar to that of Pierre Gringore, who also described the pageant.[101] This anonymous version, known in six other manuscripts,[102] details various parts of the ceremony including the costume worn and descriptions of the scenes depicted in the entry theaters.[103] Most of the known manuscripts are richly illuminated

98. Nicholas de Tudeschis' *Quoniam ueritas uerborum* is edited in Hermann Herre and Ludwig Quidde, *Deutsche Reichstagsakten unter Kaiser Friedrich III. Abt. 1441–1442* (Stuttgart: Perthes, 1928), 440–538.

99. Thomas Woelki, *Lodovico Pontano (ca. 1409–1439). Eine Juristenkarriere an Universität, Fürstenhof, Kurie und Konzil*, Education and Society in the Middle Ages and Renaissance 38 (Leiden: Brill, 2011); Pontano's *Praesens citatio* is edited on 548–576, and *Primum diligenter* on 577–635.

100. On the provenance, see David E. Luscombe, "Excerpts from the Letter Collection of Heloise and Abelard in Notre Dame (Indiana) MS 30," in *Pascua Mediaevalia*, ed. R. Lievens, E. Van Mingroot, and W. Verbeke (Leuven: Leuven University Press, 1983), 537–538.

101. Both accounts are edited in Cynthia J. Brown, *Pierre Gringoire, Les Entrées Royales a Paris de Marie d'Angleterre (1514) et Claude de France (1517)*, Textes Littéraires Francais (Geneva: Libraire Droz, 2005); see Appendix IV, 273–313, for this text, but MS Fr. c. 1 is not mentioned. The text was also printed in Théodore Godefroy, *Le ceremonies observées en France aux sacres & couronnemens de roys, & reynes, & de quelques anciens ducs de Normandie, d'Aquitaine, & de Bretagne: comme aussi à leurs entrées solennelles: et à celles d'aucuns dauphins, gouuerneurs de prouinces, & autres seigneurs, dans diuerses villes du du royaume* 1 (Paris: Sébastien Cramoisy and Gabriel Cramoisy, 1649), 472–486.

102. First listed in Gordon Kipling, *Enter the King: Theatre, Liturgy, and Ritual in the Medieval Civic Triumph* (Oxford: Clarendon Press, 1998), 69, n. 45; MS Fr. c. 1 is also not known.

103. On these, see Cynthia J. Brown, *The Queen's Library: Image-Making at the Court of Anne of Brittany, 1477–1514*, Material Texts (Philadelphia: University of Pennsylvania Press, 2011), 54–62.

with miniatures featuring representations of these *tableaux vivants*. For example, a Tree of Jesse design depicting Claude's ancestry is among the most well known.[104] However, all miniatures have been removed from MS Fr. c. 1, but stubs remain where they were likely inserted.

7. Italian Humanism

Two codices in the collection particularly embody the concept of the humanist miscellany, both in their scripts and in their selection of texts. The earlier of the two (cod. Lat. c. 11) evidences the humanistic return to the classical world and the desire for Greek literature. The first text is a life of the poet Homer by Pietro Perleone (Petrus Parleo),[105] which is preceded by a dedicatory epistle. The dedication quickly began to circulate independently of Perleone's *Vita Homeri* and attach itself to other works. In the eighteenth century this aspect of the textual transmission led the *Vita* to be misattributed to Pier Candido Decembrio.[106] Perleone's Latin text incorporates minimal Greek in the form of etymology and glossing. For example, on the poet's name, Perleone capitalizes on the idea that Homer was blind and etymologizes "Homer" using the articular infinitive ἀπὸ τοῦ μὴ ὁρᾶν ("from *not seeing*"). Two Latin translations of Greek texts are also found in the manuscript. The first is the *Vita Camilli* translated by Ognibene da Lonigo,[107] which was dedicated to Gianfrancesco Gonzaga. The second is Guarino Veronese's translation of Pseudo-Plutarch's

104. C. Brown, *The Queen's Library*, 57, fig. 9, features a plate from the anonymous version; for Gringore's design and a plate, see Kipling, *Enter the King*, 69–71.

105. On Perleone, see Margaret L. King, *Venetian Humanism in an Age of Patrician Dominance* (Princeton, NJ: Princeton University Press, 1986), 416–417; King, *The Death of the Child Valerio Marcello* (Chicago: University of Chicago Press, 1994), 24–59, esp. 26–27 and 38–43, 163, 299, 302–303; Anthony F. D'Elia, "Marriage, Sexual Pleasure, and Learned Brides in the Wedding Orations of Fifteenth-Century Italy," *Renaissance Quarterly* 55, no. 2 (2002): 380–410; D'Elia, "Genealogy and the Limits of Panegyric: Turks and Huns in Fifteenth-Century Epithalamia," *The Sixteenth Century Journal* 34 (2003): 979, n. 30; and D'Elia, "Heroic Insubordination in the Army of Sigismundo Malatesta: Petrus Parleo's *Pro Milite*, Machiavelli and the Uses of Cicero and Livy," in *Humanism and Creativity in the Renaissance. Essays in Honor of Ronald G. Witt*, ed. Christopher S. Celenza and Kenneth Gouwens, Brill's Studies in Intellectual History 136 (Leiden: Brill, 2006), 31–60; also Patricia H. Labalme, *Bernardo Giustiniani: A Venetian of the Quattrocento*, Uomini e Dottrine 13 (Rome: Edizione di Storia e Letteratura, 1969), 65–68, 74, 98–99, 103, 254, 321; Lucia Gualdo Rosa, "Niccolò Loschi e Pietro Perleone e le traduzioni dell'orazione pseudo isocrata 'A Demonico,'" *Atti dell'istituto veneto di scienze lettere e arti* 131 (1972–1973): 825–856.

106. The misattribution seems to originate with Bandini's description of Firenze, Biblioteca Medicea Laurenziana, Plut. 63.30; see Angelo Maria Bandini, *Catalogus codicum latinorum Bibliothecae Mediceae Laurentianae* (Florence: s.n., 1774–1777) 2:702, col. 2; James Hankins, *Plato in the Italian Renaissance* 1–2, Columbia Studies in the Classical Tradition 17 (Leiden: Brill, 1990; repr., 1992), 2:415–417, clarifies authorship, and nn. 4 and 5 list other manuscripts of Perleone's *Vita Homeri.*

107. Edited in Marianne Pade, *The Reception of Plutarch's Lives in Fifteenth-Century Italy* 1–2, Renaessance studier 14 (Copenhagen: Museum Tusculanum Press, 2007), 2:53–54; see also 1:229–230 and 2:230.

Parallela minora.[108] A *Vergiliana Panegyris* on Carlos of Viana written by Angelo Decembrio[109] is copied between the Plutarchian texts. The final contents, already discussed above, are William of Heytesbury's *Termini naturales* and one folio of Albert of Saxony's *Tractatus proportionum.*[110]

The fullest selection of texts and themes is seen in a manuscript comprising two miscellanies bound together, but written by the same hand (cod. Lat. b. 10). The manuscript was copied ca. 1490, likely within the circle of Pomponio Leto. The first portion is a mixture of classical, patristic, and scientific texts. An interest in the topography of the ancient world is evident among a few of the opening selections. Foremost is a copy of the *Curiosum Vrbis Romae*, also known as the *Regionary Catalogues*,[111] a fourth-century list of monuments, buildings, and other landmarks in Rome. As is common, the rubric misattributes authorship to Sextus Rufus, an error that seems to begin with Flavio Biondo.[112] Immediately following are excerpts of Pausanias's *Description of Greece.* The selections are drawn from the first two books (1.1.4–2.23.4), and are partial translations and summaries in Latin. Greek occurs in the rubrics and in the marginal scholia. Latin excerpts of varying lengths from eight books of Philostratus's *Vita Apollonii* follow the text of Pausanias, and the translator remains unidentified. Two folios provide evidence of textual criticism, or at least a lecture, dealing predominantly with the first decade of Livy's *Ab Vrbe Condita.* The textual annotations of Marcantonio Coccio Sabellico[113] are copied for books 1–3, 5–6, 8, 10, and 21 of Livy.

108. Edited in Francesca Bonanno, *Plutarco Parallella minora: Traduzione latina di Guarino Veronese* (Messina: Centro interdipartimentale di studi umanistici, 2008), 75–92, which is also the major study; additionally see Giovanna Pace, "Osservazioni sulla tecnica versoria di Guarino Guarini: Il caso dei *Parallela minora*," in *Ecos de Plutarco en Europa: De Fortuna Plutarchi Studia Selecta*, ed. Rosa Maria Aguilar and Ignacio R. Alfageme (Madrid: Servicio de Publicaciones de la Universidad Complutense, 2006), 207–232; and in the same volume, Paola Volpe Cacciatore, "Guarino Guarini traduttore di Plutarco," 261–268.

109. Edited in Michael D. Reeve, "The Rediscovery of Classical Texts in the Renaissance," in *Itinerari dei Testi Antichi*, ed. Oronzo Pecere, Saggi di Storia Antica 3 (Rome: "L'Erma" di Bretschneider 1991), 115–157.

110. The latter is edited in Hubertus Lambertus Ludovicus Busard, *Der Tractatus proportionum von Albert von Sachsen*, Österreichische Akademie der Wissenschaften, Mathematisch–naturwissenschaftliche Klasse, Denkschriften 116.2 (Vienna: Springer in Komm., 1971), 57–72; for Albert's life and a chronology, see Benoît Patar, *La Physique de Bruges de Buridan et Le Traité du Ciel d'Albert de Saxe* 1–2 (Longueuil: Presses philosophiques, 2001), 1:76–82.

111. Edited in Roberto Valentini and Giuseppe Zucchetti, *Codice Topographico della città di Roma* (Rome: Tipgrafio del Senato, 1940–1953), 1:89–164; see also Arvast Nordh, *Libellus de regionibus urbis Romae; Notitia urbis Romae regionum XIV*, Skrifter utgivna av Svenska institut i Rom 8 (Lund: C.W.K. Gleerup, 1949); Henri Jordan, *Topographie der Stadt Rom im Alterthum* 2 (Berlin: Weidmannsche Buchhandlung, 1871–1907), 539–574; and Lawrence Richardson, *A New Topographical Dictionary of Ancient Rome* (Baltimore: Johns Hopkins University Press, 1992), xx.

112. Elmer Truesdell Merrill, "The Date of *Notitia* and *Curiosum*," *Classical Philology* 1 (1906): 133–144.

113. Carlo Dionisotti, *Gli umanisti e il volgare fra quattro e cinquecento* (Florence: Le Monnier, 1968), 83–97; Felix Gilbert, "Biondo, Sabellico, and the Beginnings of Venetian Official Historiography," in *Florilegium Historiale: Essays Presented to Wallace K. Ferguson*, ed. J. G. Rowe and W. H. Stockdale (Toronto:

Other texts include Pseudo-Messalla's *De Augusti progenie*[114] and Pseudo-Seneca's *De uerborum copia*,[115] as well as the texts of Origen, Cassiodorus, and Ambrose previously mentioned. The strongest emphasis in this first portion of the manuscript is on scientific and alchemical texts. In succession are copied the *Compendium aureum* of Alexius Africanus,[116] *De uirtutibus herbarum* of (Pseudo-)Thessalus of Tralles[117] in Latin, *Liber de uinis* of Arnau de Villanova,[118] *Ars operatiua medica* of Pseudo-Ramon Llull,[119] and twelve recipes in Latin and Italian. The second portion of the miscellany contains more classical texts and two commentaries, which echo the compiler's interests in rhetoric, Roman topography, and the classical tradition. Of these texts, some remained in relative obscurity during the Middle Ages but were brought to the fore by early Humanists and influential Renaissance figures such as Petrarch and Poggio Bracciolini. Perhaps the most intriguing of these in cod. Lat. b. 10 is Petronius's *Satyricon*, one of the few surviving examples of the Roman novel.[120] The

---

University of Toronto Press, 1971), 275–293; and also Ruth Chavasse, "The *studia humanitatis* and the Making of a Humanist Career: Marcantonio Sabellico's Exploitation of the Humanist Literary Genres," *Renaissance Studies* 17 (2003): 27–38.

114. Henri Jordan, "Über das Buch Origo Gentis Romanae," *Hermes* 3 (1869): 389–428.

115. J. Fohlen, "Un apocryphe de Sénèque mal connu: Le *De verborum copia*," *Mediaeval Studies* 42 (1980): 139–211.

116. Louis Delatte, *Textes Latins et vieux Français relatifs aux Cyranides: La traduction latine du XIIe siècle. Le Compendium aureum. Le de XV stellis d'Hermes. Le Livre de secrez de nature*, Bibliothèque de la Faculté de Philosophie et Lettres de l'Université de Liège 93 (Paris: Faculté de philosophie et lettres, 1942), 213–233; Willy L. Braekman, "A Treatise on the Planetary Herbs Found by Alexius Africanus in the Tomb of Kyranos," *Würzburger medizinhistorische Mitteilungen* 8 (1990): 161–192; David Bain, "Grelot and *The Compendium aureum*," *Eikasmos* 12 (2001): 346–352; Francis J. Carmody, *Arabic Astronomical and Astrological Sciences in Latin Translation: A Critical Bibliography* (Berkeley: University of California Press, 1956), 57; Linda Ehrsam Voigts, "Plants and Planets: Linking the Vegetable with the Celestial in Late Medieval Texts," in *Health and Healing from the Medieval Garden*, ed. Peter Dendle and Alain Touwaide (Woodbridge: Boydell Press, 2008), 29–59.

117. David Pingree, "Thessalus Astrologus," in *Catalogus translationum et commentariorum: Mediaeval and Renaissance Latin Translations and Commentaries; Annotated Lists and Guides* 3, ed. F. Edward Cranz, assoc. ed. Paul Oskar Kristeller (Washington, DC: Catholic University of America Press, 1976), 83–86; and Pingree, "Thessalus Astrologus: Addenda," in *Catalogus translationum et commentariorum* 7, ed. Virginia Brown, assoc. eds. Paul Oskar Kristeller and F. Edward Cranz (Washington, DC: Catholic University of America Press, 1992), 330–332.

118. Michael McVaugh, "Chemical Medicine in the Medical Writings of Arnau de Vilanova," in *Actes de la II Trobada Internacional d'estudis sobre Arnau de Vilanova*, ed. Josep Perarnau, Trebalis de la Secció de Filosofia i Ciències Socials 30 (Barcelona: Institut d'Estudis Catalans, 2005), 239–267; and in the same volume, Michela Pereira, "Maestro di segreti caposcuola contestato? Presenza di Arnaldo da Villanova e di temi della medicina arnaldiana in alcuni testi alchemici pseudo-lulliani," 381–412.

119. Michela Pereira, *The Alchemical Corpus Attributed to Raymond Lull*, Warburg Institute Surveys and Texts 18 (London: The Warburg Institute, University of London, 1989), 66, no. I.6.

120. The manuscript was first discussed in T. Wade Richardson, "A New Renaissance Petronius Manuscript: Indiana Notre Dame 58," *Scriptorium* 38 (1984): 89–100. The text is edited in Giulio Vannini, *Petronii Arbitri Satyricon 100–115: Edizione critica e commento*, Beiträge zur Altertumskunde 281 (Berlin: De Gruyter, 2010); and previously in Konrad Müller, *Petronius Satyricon Reliquiae* (Leipzig: Teubner, 1995); see viii–x of Müller's edition and 42–43 of Vannini.

text had only been "rediscovered" by Poggio Bracciolini in 1420, and most other witnesses ultimately derive from his own copy made in 1423.[121] The *Satyricon* was later known for its depictions of debauchery and Roman sexuality. Also copied is *De fluminibus* by Vibius Sequester, a compilation of geographical place-names used by Roman poets. The work is comprised of seven alphabetical lists of rivers, water sources, lakes, forests, swamps, mountains, and peoples. Sources are usually Virgil, Ovid, Lucan, and Silius Italicus, but others are used, including Cornelius Gallus, whose works survive in only ten lines.[122] The famous pentameter "uno tellures amne diuidit duas" (divides two lands with one river)[123] was the only line of Gallus known until the discovery of the papyrus in Qaṣr Ibrîm in 1978.[124] Petrarch once owned a manuscript containing *De fluminibus*, from which all Italian copies of the Renaissance are thought to descend.[125] Another rare text copied after that of Vibius Sequester also reflects this great age of textual rediscovery. Suetonius's *De grammaticis et rhetoribus*,[126] which gives accounts of Roman teachers of grammar and rhetoric, was part of his larger *De uiris illustribus*. The text survived in a single ninth-century manuscript along with Tacitus's minor works.[127] *De grammaticis et rhetoribus* was known to Poggio

121. For an overview of the tradition, see M. D. Reeve, "Petronius," in *Texts and Transmission: A Survey of the Latin Classics*, ed. L. D. Reynolds (Oxford: Clarendon Press, 1983), 295–300; see also Albinia C. de la Mare, "The Return of Petronius to Italy," in *Medieval Learning and Literature: Essays Presented to Richard William Hunt*, ed. Jonathan James Graham Alexander and Margaret T. Gibson (Oxford: Clarendon Press, 1976), 220–254. On the work's later reception, see Anthony Grafton, *Bring out Your Dead: The Past as Revelation* (Cambridge, MA: Harvard University Press, 2001), 208–224; and Corinna Onelli, "Freedom and Censorship: Petronius' *Satyricon* in Seventeenth-Century Italy," *Classical Receptions Journal* 6 (2014): 104–130.

122. On Gallus, his text, and commentary, see Edward Courtney, *The Fragmentary Latin Poets* (Oxford: Clarendon Press, 1993), 259–270; Adrian S. Hollis, *Fragments of Roman Poetry, c.60 BC–AD 20* (Oxford: Oxford University Press, 2007), 218–252; and generally, Emmanuelle Raymond, "Caius Cornelius Gallus: 'The inventor of Latin love elegy,'" in *The Cambridge Companion to Latin Love Elegy*, ed. Thea S. Thorsen (Cambridge: Cambridge University Press, 2013), 59–67.

123. Vib. Sequest. 1.74; critically edited in Remo Gelsomino, *Vibius Sequester* (Leipzig: Teubner, 1967).

124. Cairo, Egyptian Museum, P. Qaṣr Ibrîm 78-3-11/1 (LI/2); first published by R. D. Anderson, P. J. Parsons, and R. G. M. Nisbet, "Elegaics by Gallus from Qasr Ibrîm," *Journal of Roman Studies* 69 (1979): 125–155; for the papyrus more recently, see Mario Capasso, *Il ritorno di Cornelio Gallo: Il papiro di Qaṣr Ibrîm venticinque anni dopi* (Naples: Graus, 2003); for a full bibliography, see Paolo Gagliardi, "Plakato iudice te: Per la lettura dei vv. 8–9 del papiro di Gallo," *Zeitschrift für Papyrologie und Epigraphik* 176 (2011): 82, n. 1; on the fragment as a modern forgery, see Franz Brunhölzl, "Der sogenannte Galluspapyrus von Kasr Ibrim," *Codices Manuscripti* 10 (1984): 33–40; see also Guglielmo Ballaira, *Esempi di scrittura latina dell' età romana* 1 (Turin: Edizioni dell' Orso, 1993), 31–42.

125. Richard H. Rouse, "Vibius Sequester," in *Texts and Transmission*, ed. Reynolds, 292.

126. Critically edited in Robert A. Kaster, *C. Suetonius Tranquillus: De Grammaticis et Rhetoribus* (Oxford: Clarendon Press, 1995). The text of Suetonius in cod. Lat. b. 10 (*olim* MS 58) was first studied by Marvin L. Colker, "Two Manuscripts of Suetonius' *De Grammaticis et Rhetoribus*," *Manuscripta* 27 (1983): 165–169.

127. For the textual tradition, see Robert A. Kaster, *Studies on the Text of Suetonius "De Grammaticis et Rhetoribus"* (Atlanta: Scholar's Press, 1992), and Kaster's introduction in *C. Suetonius Tranquillus: De Grammaticis et Rhetoribus*; also Michael Winterbottom, "Suetonius, *De grammaticis et rhetoribus*," in *Texts and Transmission*, ed. Reynolds, 404–405.

ca. 1425, brought to Rome by Enoch of Ascoli in 1455, and disseminated more broadly after his death.[128]

The manuscript concludes with excerpts from the first book of Symmachus's letters and two commentaries. The letters, not printed until 1503, are exemplary for their style in late antique epistolography.[129] Their presence in this compilation reflects the compiler's interest in style and even rhetoric. The commentaries, one on Cicero's *Paradoxa Stoicorum* and the other on Statius's *Siluae*, are copied in succession. Both of the works commented upon also enjoyed renewed circulation during the Renaissance: the *Paradoxa* through Poggio in 1417 and more widely from Guarino ca. 1430,[130] and the *Siluae* also through Poggio, but disseminated after 1453.[131] Both commentaries are transmitted in *catena* format, that is, lemmata and gloss without text, and likely represent an oral lecture.[132] The Ciceronian commentary begins much like a medieval *accessus* and adopts similar approaches. For example, the opening gloss addresses the *titulus operis* (title of the work), and incorporates grammatical and etymological expositions in both Greek and Latin. The commentary on Statius is incomplete, but provides quotations from Domizio Calderini (1446–1478) and Angelo Poliziano (1454–1494),[133] both of whom were among the *Pomponiani* and had previously commented on the work.[134]

A manuscript previously mentioned (cod. Lat. d. 5) contains, in addition to Boethius's *De consolatione*, numerous original works of Filippo da Strada (Philippus Ligurensis) copied in Venice in the late fifteenth century.[135] Texts including verses, sonnets, and commen-

128. Kaster, *Studies on the Text of Suetonius*, 2; and Kaster, *C. Suetonius Tranquillus, De Grammaticis et Rhetoribus*, liv.

129. Michele R. Salzman, *The Letters of Symmachus. Book I* (Atlanta: Society of Biblical Literature, 2011), lxvii–lxviii.

130. Rouse, "Cicero, *De natura deorum, de diuinitate, Timaeus, De fato, Topica, Paradoxa Stoicorum, Academica priora, De legibus*," in *Texts and Transmission*, ed. Reynolds, 124–130.

131. Michael D. Reeve, "Statius, *Siluae*," in *Texts and Transmission*, ed. Reynolds, 397–399.

132. On the term and format, see John O. Ward, "From Marginal Gloss to *Catena* Commentary: The Eleventh-Century Origins of a Rhetorical Teaching Tradition in the Medieval West," *Parergon* 13 (1996): 109–120. For the later use and resurgence of the format among humanists, see David T. Gura, "From the *Orléanais* to Pistoia: The Survival of the *Catena* Commentary," *Manuscripta* 54 (2010): 171–188.

133. On this commentary, see Richardson, "A New Renaissance Petronius Manuscript," 91; and Harald Anderson, *The Manuscripts of Statius* 1–3 (Arlington, VA: s.n., 2009), 1:267–268; the quotation from Polizano is disputed on 268.

134. Reeve, "Statius, *Siluae*," in *Texts and Transmission*, ed. Reynolds, 398. Of great use is the online resource Reportorium Pomponianum, http://www.repertoriumpomponianum.it; see also Giancarlo Abbamonte, "Naples—A Poets' City: Attitudes towards Statius and Virgil in the Fifteenth Century," in *Remembering Parthenope: The Reception of Classical Naples from Antiquity to the Present*, ed. Jessica Hughes and Claudio Buongiovanni (Oxford: Oxford University Press, 2015), 185–186.

135. The identification of Filippo da Strada as author was made by Lorenzo Dell'Oso; see his two unpublished theses: "Tra le carte del MS. Lat. D 5 della Hesburgh Library *(U. Of Notre Dame)*: Una silloge quattrocentesca inedita di versi volgari. Ricognizione filologica, edizione fototipica, diplomatico-interpretativa e critica," Tesi di Laurea magistrale, Università degli Studi di Pavia, 2013; and "Litre De

tary in Latin and Italian are written in the Dominican friar's autograph throughout the entire manuscript.[136] Several of Filippo's literary compositions are a reaction against the new culture of print,[137] as well as a longer running verse commentary in the lower margins of *De consolatione*.[138] The codex also contains a few liturgical texts, nuptial blessings, and sermons used by Filippo in a pastoral capacity, as well as a calendar. The calendar is graded sparsely (e.g., *duplex maius*), but points toward Venetian use and includes celebrations for Saints Hyginus, John Chrysostom, Geminiano, Mark (translation and apparition), Faustinus and Jovita, Ercolano of Perugia, Vincent Ferrer, Monica (translation), Isidore of Chios (procession and feast), George, Bernardine (translation and feast), Francis (translation and feast), Secundus of Asti, Anthony of Padua, Transfiguration, Clare, Moses, and Magnus of Oderzo; it also includes the dedication of the basilica St. John Lateran I (here, *dedicatio basilice saluatoris et theodori*), the dedication of the basilica of Saints Peter and Paul, and the feast of Lucia. Many of Filippo's writings are copied over a period of time, and as space on the page became limited, he had to innovate. No fewer than ten of his compositions are written with the page inverted, and many others are scrawled in the margins of the calendar and in all available space on the flyleaves.

A later manuscript of the Renaissance also provides evidence of the translation of non-Latin sources. Copied in the early sixteenth century (cod. Lat. c. 10), the codex contains the commentary of Olympiodorus on *Ecclesiastes* as it survives in the Latin translation of Zanobi Acciaiuoli (1461–1519). Zanobi, a Dominican, was a librarian and translator during the papacy of Leo X. He was appointed prefect of the Vatican Library in 1518. The manuscript also contains Zanobi's prefatory epistle, in which he dedicates the work to Guillaume Briçonnet (c. 1472–1534).[139] This copy of the text itself is unremarkable, but its paper quires provide an example of the Arabic technique of board-ruling, which enjoyed a resurgence in many Italian manuscripts of the fifteenth and sixteenth century.

Stampa Son Caliginose: The Role of Filippo Da Strada (1450–1505) in the Debate of Printing in Renaissance Italy," M.A. thesis, University of Notre Dame, 2015. Authorship was previously attributed to "Phillipus Iadrensis" in a "dealer blurb" written for H. P. Kraus by Ives in 1943 to sell the manuscript: Samuel A. Ives, *Philippus Iadrensis, a Hitherto Unknown Poet of the Renaissance: A Contribution to Italian Literary History*, Rare Books: Notes on the History of Old Books and Manuscripts 2.2. Published for the Friends and Clients of H. P. Kraus (New York: H. P. Kraus, 1943).

136. On the autograph, see Dell'Oso, "Tra le carte del MS. Lat. D 5 della Hesburgh Library," 44–49; and Lorenzo Dell'Oso, "Un domenicano contra la stampa: Nuove acquisizioni al *corpus* di Filippo da Strada," *Tipofilologia* 7 (2014): 69–99. Dell'Oso edits several of the Italian texts in his theses and article.

137. Dell'Oso, "Un domenicano contra la stampa," 70–75.

138. A small section of Filippo's Latin texts is edited in Anthony P. McDonald, "Between Philosophy and the Muse: A Fifteenth Century Versification of Boethius's *Consolatio Philosophiae*," M.A. thesis, University of Notre Dame, 2013; see the prologue on 45–49 and the introduction with excerpts from book 1 on 50–54. The identity of the author was not known to McDonald.

139. See Eugene F. Rice, Jr., *The Prefatory Epistles of Jacques Lefèvre d'Etaples and Related Texts* (New York: Columbia University Press, 1972), 285–287.

8. Law

A small group of legal manuscripts provides examples both within and external to university settings. Of the manuscripts, three codices contain canon law and its interpretation (codd. Lat. e. 1, Lat. e. 3, and Saint Mary's MS 1), one provides English statutes (cod. Lat. a. 4), and a leaf and two flyleaves are the only examples of civil law (Constable MS 6 and cod. Lat. c. 6). The *Liber sextus* (cod. Lat. e. 1) of Pope Boniface VIII, framed by the *Glossa aurea* of Iohannes Monachus (Jean Lemoine), illustrates the synergistic *mise-en-page* typical of law and gloss. The large codex was copied in southern France or Italy during the fourteenth century. In addition to numerous glosses and annotations throughout, a contemporaneous user has quickly copied a portion of the *Declaratio arboris consanguinitatis* of Iohannes Andreae (Giovanni d'Andrea) on a flyleaf. Another codex of the same stature and with a nearly identical binding (cod. Lat. e. 3) provides the *Lectura super Clementinis* of Paulus de Liazariis. The fourteenth-century codex originates from Bologna and preserves eight pecia marks used in the university's system of copying [**PLATE 7**]. Two historiated initials featuring canonists are painted in the Bolognese style and begin each half of the lectura. *Repetitiones* by de Liazariis and Iohannes Calderinus have been added by contemporary hands not only in Rotunda, but also in Italian Cursiva Antiquior. A composite manuscript (Saint Mary's MS 1) contains selections of the *Decretum* of Burchard of Worms copied during the thirteenth century in Germany. All the selections are from book 19, which contains the penitential also called the *Corrector*. The book was often transmitted separately from the rest of *Decretum* as a didactic work, but the possibility of actual pastoral use remains.[140] The presence of portions of the fourth book of Peter Lombard's *Sentences*, which also addresses penance, points toward classroom use.[141]

A small book containing a number of Statuta Angliae copied in England during the fourteenth century (cod. Lat. a. 4) may have belonged to a clerk or secretary. In addition to Magna Carta and Carta de Foresta, over thirty-four Statutes of the Realm in Latin and Anglo-Norman French are written by two hands, which are among the collection's earliest examples of Anglicana. Justinian's *Digesta* is represented by the two fragments which were used as flyleaves in the aforementioned copy of Peter Riga's *Aurora* (cod. Lat. c. 6). The excerpted collection of Justinian's *Nouellae*, which circulated in the Latin West as the *Authenticum* or *Liber authenticorum*, is represented by a single fourteenth-century fragment from Italy (Constable MS 6). The leaf follows the format in which the *Nouellae* were

140. Ludger Körntgen, "Canon Law and the Practice of Penance: Burchard of Worms's Penitential," *Early Medieval Europe* 14 (2006): 103–117; see also Atria A. Larson, *Masters of Penance: Gratian and the Development of Penitential Thought and Law in the Twelfth Century* (Washington, DC: Catholic University of America Press, 2014), 9–11; and Greta Austin, *Shaping Church Law around the Year 1000: The Decretum of Burchard of Worms* (Burlington, VT: Ashgate, 2009), 230–233.

141. On Peter Lombard's use of Gratian, see Larson, *Masters of Penance*, 315–342, and the appendix on 507–510.

grouped into nine *collationes* with *tituli* and further subdivisions.[142] After the leaf was extracted from its parent manuscript it was folded into a document folio, the leather cord of which is still attached.

9. School Texts

In addition to aforementioned texts such as the *Aurora* and *Historia scholastica*, which were used within cathedral schools and medieval universities, there are examples of medieval texts which began to enter the so-called "Liber Catonianus"[143] in the fourteenth century. Two of the eight *Auctores octo morales*, a collection of school texts that endured through the mid-sixteenth century,[144] are represented: Alan of Lille's[145] *Liber parabolarum* (cod. Lat. b. 8) and the anonymous *Facetus* (cod. Lat. b. 3). The collection's *Liber parabolarum* is a paper manuscript folded in quarto of just sixteen folios, which was copied during the fifteenth century in the Low Countries. The small codex contains the Latin version,[146] written in Semihybrida. Alan's *Liber parabolarum*, also known as the *Doctrinale minus*, draws heavily on classical literature and scripture as it conveys moral maxims from its comparisons.[147] The complete work consists of six chapters containing a total of 365 distichs; cod. Lat. b. 8 ends imperfectly at VI.6.[148]

A text similar in use and popularity was the *Facetus*, a Latin poem on manners and morals. The author of the 136 rhymed hexameters is not known, but the poem is often attributed to a certain "Magister Iohannes," who is falsely conflated with John of Garland. The *Facetus* circulated in two separate versions, which were distinguished by their opening variants. The collection's copy (cod. Lat. b. 3), written near the end of the fourteenth

142. On these and their citation formats, see James A. Brundage, *Medieval Canon Law* (New York: Routledge, 1995), 204–205; and Kenneth Pennington, "Roman and Secular Law," in *Medieval Latin: An Introduction and Bibliographical Guide*, ed. Frank Anthony Carl Mantello and A. G. Rigg (Washington, DC: Catholic University of America Press, 1996), 255–257.

143. Changes to the "Liber Catonianus" during the thirteenth and fourteenth century in England are discussed in Tony Hunt, *Teaching and Learning Latin in Thirteenth-Century England* 1–3 (Cambridge: D. S. Brewer, 1991), 1:70–75.

144. Jan M. Ziolkowski, "Mastering Authors and Authoring Masters in the Long Twelfth Century," in *Latinitas Perennis I: The Continuity of Latin Literature*, ed. Wim Verbaal et al. (Leiden: Brill, 2007), 114.

145. See Marie-Thérèse d'Alverny, *Alain de Lille: Textes Inédits*, Études de philosophie médiévale 52 (Paris: Librairie philosophique J. Vrin, 1965), 51–52; also Guy Raynaud de Lage, *Alain de Lille: Poete du XIIe siècle*, Publications de l'Institut d'études médiévales 12 (Montréal: Institut d'études médiévales, 1951), 15–17.

146. Tony Hunt, *Les Paraboles Maistre Alain en Françoys*, Modern Humanities Resarch Association Critical Texts 2 (London: Modern Humanities Research Association, 2005), 153–178, contains the Latin version, though not critically edited; the French translation is edited on 51–117; for the Latin text critically edited, see Oronzo Limone, *Liber parabolarum: Una raccolta di aforismi* (Galatina: Congedo, 1993).

147. For an example, see Nicholas Orme, *Medieval Schools: From Roman Britain to Renaissance England* (New Haven: Yale University Press, 2006), 102.

148. Hunt, *Les Paraboles Maistre Alain en Françoys*, 1–2.

century in France, consists of the "cum nihil utilius" version.[149] The manuscript is a small parchment sexternion, whose outer bifolium served as the wrapper and preserves the way in which it circulated within the classroom. Like Alan's *Liber parabolarum*, the *Facetus* was also translated into the vernacular, and the two often circulated together.[150]

10. Vernacular Poetry

Five manuscripts contain French and Italian poetry from different medieval genres that enjoyed great popularity in the vernacular. Among those represented are the *chanson de geste*, romance, *lauda*, and sonnet. The first of these, the *chanson de geste*, is seen in a manuscript of Cuvelier's *Chanson de Bertrand du Guesclin*,[151] which was copied in France on May 28, 1464, according to its colophon (MS Fr. c. 2). The poem is an epic verse chronicle recounting the life of the Breton hero Bertrand du Guesclin (1323–1380).[152] The version transmitted in MS Fr. c. 2 is shortened and heavily interpolated,[153] and the manuscript exemplifies a lower level of production. The paper quires folded in folio are gathered irregularly in quires of eight and nine bifolia, and decoration is minimal and unpracticed.

The widely disseminated French poem, the dual-authored *Roman de la Rose* of Guillaume de Lorris and Jean de Meun,[154] is the collection's only example of medieval romance (MS Fr. d. 1). At its most basic level, the poem is a love story told through an allegorical dream, which contains forays into various topics including psychology, sexuality, history, and philosophy.[155] The parchment codex, in contrast to MS Fr. c. 2, was produced at a higher level, although it is not as deluxe as many other manuscripts of the

149. Both versions of the Latin text and and French translations are edited in Joseph Morawski, *Le Facet en françoys: Edition critique des cinq traductions des deux Facetus latins avec introduction, notes et glossaire* (Poznan: Gebethnera i Wolffa, 1923); cod. Lat. b. 3 contains two final lines not in Morawski's edition.

150. On the German translation, see Michael Baldzuhn, *Schulbücher im Trivium des Mittelalters und der Frühen Neuzeit* 1–2 (Berlin: De Gruyter, 2009), 2:996–1015; German translations edited in Carl Schroeder, "Der deutsche Facetus," *Palaestra* 6 (1911): 1–30; see also Hunt, *Teaching and Learning Latin*, 1:76.

151. The major study and critical edition is Jean-Claude Faucon, *Le chanson de Bertrand du Guesclin de Cuevelier* 1–3 (Toulouse: Éditions universitaires du Sud, 1990–1991).

152. On the poem's influence, see Richard Vernier, "The Afterlife of a Hero: Bertrand du Guesclin Imagined," in *The Hundred Years War (Part II): Different Vistas*, ed. L. J. Andrew Villalon and Donald J. Kagay (Leiden: Brill, 2007), 329–345; a summary of the chronicle is provided on 218–220 of Maureen Boulton, "The Knight and The Rose: French Manuscripts in the Notre Dame Library," in *The Text in the Community*, ed. Mann and Nolan, 217–236.

153. On the text, see Faucon, *Le chanson*, 2:445–96, and 3:312, 327–328, 339–348 (*siglum G*); also Boulton, "The Knight and the Rose," 222–224.

154. Edited in Daniel Poirion, *Le Roman de la Rose*, Texte intégral 270 (Paris: Garnier-Flammarion, 1974).

155. A succinct overview of the poem and its treatment to date is given in Jonathan Morton, "Le Roman de la rose," *French Studies* 69 (2015): 79–86.

poem.[156] In MS Fr. d. 1, one historiated initial featuring a dedication scene of the two authors begins the text,[157] which is accompanied by a single bracket border of acanthus [**PLATE 8**]. The choice of script is a Southern Textualis of French variety, which is of a higher quality than the Bastarda used in MS Fr. c. 2. The first folio contains a contemporary painted armorial, which also points toward Norman ownership.[158]

Four manuscripts of the fifteenth and sixteenth century contain examples of the Italian genres, the *lauda* and the sonnet. In most of the examples, the poems accompany devotional and even patristic texts: an anonymous Italian poem, *Donna de paradiso*, similar to that of Iacopone da Todi, follows the text of Gregory the Great (cod. Lat. a. 11); two poems of Feo Belcari, *Venga ciascun devoto ed umil core* and *I' son l'Arcangel Rafael di dio*,[159] occur among the letters of Catherine of Siena and a spiritual treatise (MS Ital. b. 2); and the aforementioned works of Filippo da Strada are in his manuscript of Boethius (cod. Lat. d. 5). A small parchment codex of nineteen folios copied during the sixteenth century consists solely of sonnets and other poetry (MS Ital. b. 1). Sixteen sonnets and one *capitolo* of Serafino Aquilano[160] occupy most of the manuscript, but a few poems by Iacopo Sannazaro,[161] Iacopo Corsi,[162] and Giovan Francesco Caracciolo[163] are positioned between Serafino's sonnets.

11. Miniatures

Various aspects of illumination and other forms of decoration have been discussed already in relation to particular manuscripts. However, there is value in a brief discussion of miniatures for the reader interested foremost in miniature painting. The collection's strength by far lies in its northern examples, of which specimens from France and the Low Countries are the most numerous. Miniatures occur most frequently among the

156. See the Roman de la Rose Digital Library Project, http://romandelarose.org, which currently contains over 130 manuscripts.

157. Boulton, "The Knight and the Rose," 225.

158. Boulton, ibid., 226, identifies the arms as belonging to the Norman family Fraidel.

159. The texts are edited in Stefano Cremonini, "Per l'edizione delle laude di Feo Belcari," Ph.D. diss., Università degli Studi di Bologna, 2006.

160. Edited in Antonio Rossi, *Serafino Aquilano: Sonetti e altre rime*, Biblioteca del Cinquecento 119 (Rome: Bulzoni, 2005).

161. *Sonetto* 100 is edited in Alfredo Mauro, *Iacobo Sannazaro: Opere Volgari*, Scrittori d'Italia 220 (Bari: Laterza, 1961), 212–216.

162. On the two poems, see Dino S. Cervigni, "Inediti di Jacopo Corsi e del Sannazaro in un ms. della University of Notre Dame," *Studi e problemi di critica testuale* 19 (1979): 25–31; edition on 29.

163. See Marco Santagata, "Nota su un sonetto attribuito al Sannazaro," *Studi e problemi di crictica testuale* 20 (1980): 25–27; *Argo* 11 is edited in Barbara Giovanazzi, "Per l'edizione degli *Amori* e di *Argo* di Giovan Francesco Caracciolo," Tesi Dott. (Università degli Studi di Trento, 2009), 477.

devotional manuscripts, especially books of hours of the fifteenth century.[164] Within these are examples of the characteristic illuminations that introduce the different canonical hours and other devotional texts in a book of hours. A complete Passion Cycle introducing the Hours of the Virgin survives in a Flemish book of hours made for export to England (cod. Lat. a. 1). All of the manuscript's twenty-eight miniatures were painted using a demi-grisaille technique on the versos of leaves later inserted. The lengthy section of saints' suffrages contains miniatures of John the Baptist, John the Evangelist, Saints Christopher, George, Thomas Becket, Anne, Mary Magdalene, Katherine, Barbara, and Margaret, and the Trinity. Other representative images found in the manuscript are Christ as *Saluator mundi*, Adam, Eve, and the serpent, David in penance, the raising of Lazarus, two angels (*commendatio animarum*), and St. Jerome as cardinal. This last image, at least, is likely a reverse tracing since it appears to show St. Jerome with a pen in the left hand and a knife in the right. Five full-color miniatures painted in Bruges remain in a book of hours made for the use of Rome (cod. Lat. a. 2). Of these, a miniature of the Annunciation is the only remnant of the Infancy Cycle in the collection's manuscripts from the Low Countries. The manuscript also contains images of the Crucifixion, Virgin and Child, Last Judgment, and a funeral scene. The remaining miniatures from the Low Countries consist of a cutting of St. Agatha (Acc. 1989.20.1) from Bruges, and an initial historiated with an unidentified saint painted near Arnhem (Acc. 1972.34).

Although fragmentary, contrasting French examples of illuminations from Brittany, Paris, and Rouen also occur. Produced near Rennes for the use of Vannes, Frag. III. 1 contains twenty-two full-color miniatures painted in a rusticated style common to many Breton books of hours. In its complete state this manuscript contained full expressions of the Infancy and Passion Cycles, split among the canonical hours for the Hours of the Virgin, Hours of the Cross, and Hours of the Holy Spirit. Still surviving from the Infancy Cycle are miniatures of the Nativity, Annunciation to the shepherds, Flight into Egypt, and the Presentation in the Temple. From the Passion Cycle remain miniatures of Christ before Pilate, the Mocking of Christ, the Flagellation, Christ carrying the Cross, Christ nailed to the Cross, Crucifixion, Expiration on the Cross, Deposition, Pietà, Entombment, and another unidentified scene. Among the surviving saints' suffrages of Frag. III. 1 are miniatures depicting Peter Martyr, Francis, and John the Apostle, each complete with several iconographical attributes. Three miniatures without text also survive: the Three Living and Three Dead, Mary Magdalene, and two unidentified saints. Five badly damaged miniatures remain in the collection's only Parisian book of hours (cod. Lat. a. 8), which depict the Annunciation, King David, a funeral scene, and the Mass of St. Gregory. Likewise, four miniatures remain in cod. Lat. a. 9, which is the collection's sole example of a book of hours produced and illuminated in Rouen. This manuscript also used the Infancy Cycle to introduce the Hours of the Virgin, of

164. Historiated Parisian Bible leaves of the thirteenth century by the Dominican Painter (Acc. 1989.20.2, 1989.20.3, and Frag. I. 34) and others produced in Bordeaux ca. 1300 (Acc. 1975.43 and 1975.57) are discussed in section 2 above, "Bibles, Biblical Texts and Patristics."

which the Annunciation and Nativity scenes are still present. Similarly, historiated calendars with monthly labors (Frag. III. 1, Frag. I. 33) and the Zodiac (Acc. 1975.56 and 1978.28) also provide examples of Breton, *Rouenais*, and Parisian miniature painting.

The concentration of Italian miniatures is second to that of the northern examples. The most numerous are those found in a fourteenth-century copy of the *Meditationes uitae Christi* (Acc. 1985.25). These forty-eight miniatures, which constitute a vast program of illustration, have been attributed by Dianne Phillips to the circle of Stefano Azzi in Bologna.[165] Also of great significance is a small cutting (Acc. 1989.20.7) from an exceptionally early illuminated manuscript of the *Legenda aurea*. The fragment, depicting three tonsured saints, was formerly in the collection of Robert Forrer (1866–1947) along with ten others,[166] and at least twenty-one different cuttings from the parent manuscript are known. The artist, once thought to be Spanish, has been identified correctly as the Master of Monza.[167] This particular cutting contains a fragment of the end of chapter 129 and the beginning of 130, on Saints Protus and Hyacinthus.

Utility of the Collection

The collection has broad utility in the realms of teaching, research, and public outreach. Primarily, the collection is well-suited for pedagogy for students of all levels. For example, the Curator of Ancient and Medieval Manuscripts teaches yearly over one hundred general sessions to undergraduates in courses from the departments of Music, Theology, Classics, Art History, Irish Languages and Literatures, Italian, and Liberal Studies (to name only a few) at the University of Notre Dame and Saint Mary's College. In these sessions, particular aspects of the physical manuscript are used to illustrate themes in courses as specific as book production in Gothic Paris, and as general as the art of the medieval codex. Undergraduates are afforded *in situ* time with the manuscripts. Advanced, graduate level courses in Latin paleography and Western codicology for the Medieval Institute are also supported by the collection, as well as specific seminar projects from other departments, which include exercises such as localizing liturgical and martyrological calendars to a diocese, or indexing chant for electronic databases such as CANTUS.[168]

165. Phillips, "The *Meditations on the Life of Christ*," 243.

166. Robert Forrer, *Unedierte Federzeichnungen Miniaturen und Initialen des Mittelalters* 1 (Strassburg: Schlesier and Schweikhardt, 1902), 15, and tables VI–VIII.

167. See Giovanni Valagussa, "Santi lombardi di fine Duecento," in *Scritti per l'Istituto Germanico di Storia dell'Arte de Firenze*, ed. Cristina Acidini Luchinat et al. (Florence: Casa Editrice Le Lettre, 1997), 23–34; Filippo Todini, ed., *Miniature: La Spezia, Museo civico Amedeo Lia* (Cinisello Balsamo: Silvana editoriale, 1996), 291–294; and Gaudenz Freuler, *Italian Miniatures from the Twelfth to the Sixteenth Centuries* (Cinisello Balsamo: Silvana editoriale, 2013), 427–431.

168. Cantus: A Database for Ecclesiastical Chant. www.cantusdatabase.org.

The collection also supports undergraduate and graduate student research, in which items from the collection are not merely incorporated but serve as the main topic of research. Theses have ranged from editions of unedited texts to iconographic studies. Professional scholars also make great use of the collection for their various research programs, the citations of which are meticulously noted in the entries for each manuscript. However, most of the collection's research value has been obscured by its lack of accessibility and the absence of critical bibliographical study. It is the author's hope that the publication of this catalogue will lead to further research on the collection at all levels.

In recent years, manuscripts in the collection have also featured prominently in public exhibitions and other forms of outreach. For example, an exhibit on sacred music was accompanied by performances of chant from the collection's manuscripts.[169] Other exhibitions on the reconstruction of a Breton book of hours broken in 2011 have highlighted the issues of biblioclasty, provided didactic programming locally, and received international attention.[170]

Method of Citation

The manuscripts in this catalogue should be cited using the following formula: city, institution, repository, fond, and shelfmark. The full formula should be used upon first mention, and subsequent references may use short forms. The following provide examples of the full citation for each possible repository and fond:

Notre Dame, Univ. Notre Dame, Hesburgh Library, cod. Lat. b. 4
Notre Dame, Univ. Notre Dame, Hesburgh Library, MS Eng. d. 1
Notre Dame, Univ. Notre Dame, Hesburgh Library, Frag. I. 14
Notre Dame, Univ. Notre Dame, Hesburgh Library, Constable MS 6
Notre Dame, Univ. Notre Dame, Snite Museum of Art, Acc. 1985.25
Notre Dame, Saint Mary's College, Cushwa-Leighton Library, MS 3

169. David T. Gura with audio by Alexander Blachly, "Sacred Music at Notre Dame: The Voice of the Text," Department of Rare Books and Special Collections, Hesburgh Library, University of Notre Dame, February 2–August 3, 2015; see Carol C. Bradley, "A Collaborative Study of Medieval Manuscripts and Sacred Music," in *NDWorks* 12.11, June 2015, 4–5.

170. David T. Gura, "Hour By Hour: Reconstructing a Medieval Breton Prayerbook," Snite Museum of Art, University of Notre Dame, January 18–March 16, 2015; see "A Broken Book of Hours—Saving a Medieval Manuscript," medievalists.net, April 8, 2015, http://www.medievalists.net/2015/04/08/a-broken-book-of-hours-saving-a-medieval-manuscript/; also David T. Gura, "Hour By Hour: Reconstructing a Medieval Breton Prayerbook," Department of Rare Books and Special Collections, University of Notre Dame, January 10–August 19, 2013; see Carol C. Bradley, "Reconstructing a Broken Book," *NDWorks* 11.1, July 25, 2013, 1; and Ben Mauk, "Scattered Leaves," *The New Yorker*, January 6, 2014, http://www.newyorker.com/currency-tag/scattered-leaves.

Format of Entries

The conventions listed below appear for each manuscript only when applicable. For example, if a manuscript does not contain paper, the Bibliographical Format and Watermarks fields are omitted.

Origin: This field contains the country or region and date(s) of origin. Concerning country or region, attributions are general and are based on a study of the manuscript (e.g., northern France, Italy, Low Countries, etc.). Dates most often are given within one-half of a saeculum: s. xiv^{1} = before 1350; s. xiv^{2} = after 1350. When the date can be narrowed further, N. R. Ker's method to denote the beginning, middle, end, or turn of a century is used: s. xiv^{in}, s. xiv, s. xiv^{ex}, s. xiv/xv.[171] Manuscripts which have material spanning different centuries are dated with a range: s. xiii^{2}–xv^{1} = contents span the second half of the thirteenth through the first half of the fifteenth century. If the place of origin and/or date can be determined more specifically, either by localizable and datable features or by the presence of a colophon, the information is given in parentheses: e.g., (dated Blatná, 30 October 1417),[172] (dated 29 November 1431),[173] (Nuremberg?, *post* 1456).[174]

Content Overview: A brief description of the contents of the manuscript is given. This is not the complete listing of contents but includes general information: e.g., ascetic and devotional treatises, Bible, sermon collection. Liturgical manuscripts are described by type: e.g., psalter, missal, gradual, etc. Books of hours include the use(s) if known: e.g., Book of Hours, use of Sarum. When specific authors and works are listed, the normative forms are used: e.g., Augustine, *De doctrina christiana*; Pietro Perleone, *Vita Homeri*; Petronius, *Satyricon.*

Following the general overview of the contents, other summary information is listed: language(s), material, number of flyleaves and folio count, dimensions of the page (H x W), brief description of foliation, and other anomalous information (e.g., material of flyleaves, blank folios, post-medieval title pages, etc.).

Collation: The collation statement is given using a numeric formula: small Roman numerals indicate flyleaves, quires are indicated by Arabic numerals, leaves indicating quire form with additions and subtractions are given in superscript. Thus: i +1$^{10-1}$ + 2–28^{10} + 29$^{8-1}$ +i indicates one flyleaf in the front, quire 1 is a quinion lacking one leaf, quires 2–28 are quinions with ten leaves, and quire 29 is a quaternion lacking one leaf followed by one rear flyleaf. Detailed descriptive information is given in the **Quires** field.

171. Neil R. Ker, *Medieval Manuscripts in British Libraries* 1 (Oxford: Clarendon Press, 1969), vii.
172. Hesburgh Library, cod. Lat. b. 7.
173. Hesburgh Library, cod. Lat. a. 11.
174. Hesburgh Library, cod. Lat. b. 1.

Bibliographical Format: This field is appropriate only for manuscripts with paper quires,[175] or those which contain mixed quires.[176] The position of watermarks and chain-lines is used to determine the folding of the paper. The following abbreviations are used:

2°	Folio
4°	Quarto
8°	Octavo

Quires: The collation statement is explained in detail with attention to the normal and aberrant quire forms. Missing leaves are listed by position in the quire form, and added leaves by folio number. Quire forms occurring most commonly are:

I^{2}	Bifolium	(one bifolium, two leaves)
II^{4}	Binion	(two bifolia, four leaves)
III^{6}	Ternion	(three bifolia, six leaves)
IV^{8}	Quaternion	(four bifolia, eight leaves)
V^{10}	Quinion	(five bifolia, ten leaves)
VI^{12}	Sexternion	(six bifolia, twelve leaves)

For parchment quires, it is not always possible to discern the flesh side of the animal's skin from the hair side. When possible, the side of the animal's skin that faces outward in the quire's current state is specified using the following:

H/H	Hair sides out
F/F	Flesh sides out
H/F	Hair side out for first leaf, flesh side for last leaf in the quire
F/H	Flesh side out for first leaf, hair side for last leaf in the quire

Also indicated is whether the quires obey Gregory's Rule[177] of "like facing like" (i.e., flesh on flesh, hair on hair). The disposition of the material, damage, and trimming are discussed.

Quire Marks: Quire marks refer specifically to Roman numerals used as cardinals or ordinals on the final verso of a given quire. The position of the quire mark on the page is specified.

175. Hesburgh Library, codd. Lat. b. 8, Lat. b. 10, Lat. b. 12, Lat. b. 14, Lat. b. 15, Lat. c. 1, Lat. c. 9, Lat. c. 10, Lat. c. 11, Lat. d. 1, Lat. d. 4, Lat. d. 6, Lat. e. 2, MSS Fr. c. 2, Ger. a. 1, Ital. b. 2, Ital. d. 1, Frag. I. 11; and Snite Museum of Art, Acc. 1984.3.6.

176. Hesburgh Library, codd. Lat. d. 2 and Lat. d. 3.

177. See Albert Derolez, *The Palaeography of Gothic Manuscript Books From the Twelfth to the Early Sixteenth Century* (Cambridge: Cambridge University Press, 2003), 33, n. 9.

Catchwords: The orientation of the catchword (i.e., horizontal or vertical) is followed by its position on the final verso of a given quire. Whether or not catchwords correspond to the first word of the following gathering is indicated.

Signatures: Signatures are combinations of letters, numbers, and other symbols, including the *ad hoc* type, which usually occur only on the rectos for the first half of a gathering.[178]

Foliation: This field is used only when the foliation of a particular manuscript deserves a more detailed description. This is often the case when multiple systems of foliation are present, including medieval and modern sets.

Watermarks: The number of total occurrences and the different watermarks are listed. Distinct watermarks are numbered individually (**A**, **B**, **C**, etc.) and followed by descriptive type and motifs (e.g., letter P, bull's head, scales, etc.). The locations of the watermarks are given by quire and folio number, but by bifolia when folded in quarto (e.g., ff. 3/8, 11/20). Each entry is then followed by the appropriate reference number to Briquet,[179] Piccard,[180] Heawood,[181] or other work when applicable.[182] The locations and dates given by Briquet or Piccard follow each entry in parentheses, but these are purely for reference.

As it is rare to find an exact match, most references are preceded by "cf."; however, when the reference seems identical, the phrase "corresponds closely to" is used. There are few occurrences among these manuscripts in which no likeness remotely close to the watermark can be found. In these situations, the approximate dimensions of the watermark (H x W), the distance between the chainlines in millimeters, and a brief description of the motif's separative features are provided in lieu of a reference number. For the nine manuscripts with more than two watermarks, a corresponding table shows the full distribution and bibliographical references for all watermarks contained (see Appendix 3, Tables).

Layout: All information concerning the *mise-en-page* is gathered in this field. Distinct ruling patterns are distinguished based on a combined analysis of layout, measurements,

178. See Hesburgh Library, cod. Lat. b. 4 as an example of multiple systems of signatures used within a single manuscript.

179. Charles-Moïse Briquet, *Les filigranes: Dictionnaire historique des marques du papier dès leur apparition vers 1282 jusqu'en 1600; A Facsimile of the 1907 Edition with Supplementary Material* 1–4, 3rd ed., ed. Alan Stevenson (Amsterdam: Paper Publications Society, 1968).

180. Gerhard Piccard, *Wasserzeichenkartei im Hauptstaatsarchiv Stuttgart* (Stuttgart: Kohlhammer, 1961–1997); now available online at http://www.piccard-online.de.

181. Edward Heawood, *Watermarks Mainly of the 17th and 18th Centuries*, Monumenta chartae papyraceae historiam illustrantia 1 (Culver City: Krown and Spellman, 2003).

182. E.g., Vladimir Mosin, *Anchor Watermarks*, Chartae Papyraceae Historiam Illustrata XIII (Amsterdam: Paper Publications Society Labarre Foundation, 1973).

and pricking patterns.[183] For each distinct ruling pattern, scale images are provided and patterns are numbered (**A**, **B**, **C**, etc.).[184] When there are aberrations or variations within the same pattern, these are numbered (**A1**, **A2**).[185] Folio references are followed by the technique (i.e., hard-point, lead, crayon, ink, frame-ruling, board, rake-ruling, or "combined"), dimensions of the ruling (H x W) and intercolumnia (if multiple columns), and number of lines per page. Below the summary of the layout is a detailed discussion of the ruling and pricking patterns, techniques, use of the ruling, and whether the writing is "above top line" or "below top line."[186] For Humanistic manuscripts written on parchment, a reference number to a pattern in Derolez's study is also provided.[187]

SCRIPT: Most of the manuscripts described in this catalogue are written in forms of Gothic script. To identify, classify, and describe these scripts requires precision, objectivity, and unambiguous terminology. Thus, Albert Derolez's refinement and expansion of Lieftink's system is used to describe all Gothic scripts in this volume. Levels of execution (Formata, Libraria, Currens) are assigned to specimens where possible. Humanistic minuscule and cursive are described as such, and later scripts are described generally and dated to the appropriate century. When multiple hands occur in a manuscript, they are numbered (e.g., M1, M2, M3), and discussed individually.

DECORATION: This field may consist of up to four subfields (numbered **I–IV**): RUBRICATION, INITIALS, LINE FILLERS, and BORDERS & FRAMES. Miniatures are treated separately in the **MINIATURES** field.

> **I.** RUBRICATION: Rubrics, tituli, running titles, chapter numbers, letter heightening, and paraph marks are described in this subfield. The presence of guide letters, words, and numerals is also noted.
>
> **II.** INITIALS: Initial types and their functioning hierarchy are listed. The majority of the painted initials in this catalogue are late medieval and Renaissance types, and the need for clear and concise terminology is important. To avoid ambiguity and over-description,

183. See Hesburgh Library, cod. Lat. c. 6, in which pattern **C** uses the pricking pattern of **A**, then modifies it with a single pricking to create two columns. However, in the same manuscript, pattern **D** is traced identically to **C**, but uses a different pricking pattern.

184. The presentation of the information in this field is much informed by Nash's innovative approach to the descriptions of manuscripts in *Between France and Flanders*.

185. For example, in Hesburgh Library, cod. Lat. b. 4, cf. patterns **A1** and **A2**, and **C1** and **C2**.

186. See Neil R. Ker, "From 'Above Top Line' to 'Below Top Line': A Change in Scribal Practice," *Celtica* 5 (1960): 13–16.

187. Albert Derolez, *Codicologie des manuscrits en écriture humanistique sur parchemin* 1–2, Mitteilung-Kommission für Humanismusforschung 4 (Turnhout: Brepols, 1984).

this catalogue uses the distinct types as classified by Derolez.[188] Brown's "decorated initial" is added for those which do not conform to the normal types.[189] The late medieval and Renaissance types in this catalogue are:

Historiated
Decorated
Foliate
Dentelle
Flourished
Trompe l'oeil
Plain
Cadel

Each type is discussed separately in order of hierarchy, and is numbered (A, B, C, etc.). Sizes and placement configurations are described according to Gumbert's categories.[190] Folio references to specific initials are provided when appropriate, especially for those at the top of the hierarchy in a given manuscript.

III. Line Fillers: All styles of line fillers are described in this field.

IV. Borders & Frames: Border arrangements and frames, like ruling patterns, are presented with scale images and numbered (A, B, C, etc.).[191] However, to avoid confusion, letters will begin where those for ruling patterns stop (i.e., there will never be two As in a description where one is a ruling pattern and the other is a border arrangement). Late medieval border arrangements for books of hours and other manuscripts similarly produced are classified according to Farquhar.[192]

Diagrams: This field is used to describe diagrams (e.g., proportions, syllogisms) and note their positions.[193]

188. Derolez, *The Palaeography of Gothic Manuscript Books*, 40–42; for an earlier use of similar terms, see James Douglas Farquhar, "The Manuscript as a Book," 68–69, in Sandra Hindman and James Douglas Farquhar, *Pen to Press: Illustrated Manuscripts and Printed Books in the First Century of Printing* (College Park, MD: Art Department, University of Maryland, 1977), which attributes the terms to Martinus Joseph Schretlen, *Dutch and Flemish Woodcuts of the Fifteenth Century* (New York, 1925; repr. New York: Hacker Art Books, 1969), 36.

189. Michelle P. Brown, *Understanding Illuminated Manuscripts: A Guide to Technical Terms* (Los Angeles: Getty Publications, 1994), 47.

190. J. P. Gumbert, "Times and Places for Initials," *Quaerendo* 39 (2009): 304–327.

191. As with ruling patterns, the graphical presentation of this material is much informed by Nash, *Between France and Flanders*.

192. Farquhar, "The Manuscript as a Book," 73–74.

193. Hesburgh Library, codd. Lat. b. 10, Lat. c. 11, Lat. d. 3; Saint Mary's College, MS 2.

Miniatures: The number of miniatures, locations, and a brief description of each are listed. This field also specifies if the pictures are inserted or normal, and if the picture is on the recto or verso of the folio.

Calendar: If a manuscript contains a calendar,[194] its codicological features are described in this field: whether one page is used per month or two, the colors, and whether Roman time is marked. If two pages are used per month, "recto/verso" or "verso/recto" is specified to indicate a month's placement. All other information will appear in the Layout and Contents fields.

Music & Staves: The number of lines, color of the staves, total height in millimeters, and a description of the neumes are provided for manuscripts containing music.[195]

Contents: The majority of manuscripts in this catalogue do not require specialized treatment in an analytical description of the contents. Texts are numbered (1, 2, 3, etc.) in the order in which they occur in the manuscript and subdivided when necessary (e.g., 1.1, 1.2). Every effort has been made to identify accurately each text and author (or attributed author). Authors and texts are listed using the normative forms as already specified in the Content Overview. Rubrics and "medieval titles" are not used as the title's entry. As happens, some texts do not have a known author or translator (or even plausible attributions), and in these instances the author entry reads "Anonymous." The basic descriptive information of rubric, incipit, explicit, and colophon (authorial or scribal) suffices for most entries. These, along with folio references in square brackets (e.g., [f. 22v]), are transcribed in the following fields, separated by a semicolon:

RUB.	Rubric
INC.	Incipit
EXPL.	Explicit
AUTH. COLOPHON	Authorial colophon which circulates with the text and forms part of the textual tradition.[196]
SCRIBAL COLOPHON	Colophon added by scribe which is not inherently part of the textual tradition of a work.[197]

194. Hesburgh Library, codd. Lat. a. 1, Lat. a. 2, Lat. a. 3, Lat. a. 6, Lat. a. 8, Lat. a. 9, Lat. a. 14, Lat. a. 15, Lat. a. 16, Lat. b. 1, Lat. b. 2, Lat. b. 4, Lat. b. 13, Lat. d. 5, Lat. e. 4, Frag. I. 33, Frag. II. 4, Frag. III. 1; Snite Museum of Art, Acc. 1975.56, 1978.28; Saint Mary's College, MS 3.

195. Hesburgh Library, codd. Lat. a. 12, Lat. b. 1, Lat. b. 2, Lat. b. 4, Lat. b. 13, Lat. c. 2, Lat. c. 3, Lat. c. 12, Lat. c. 13, Lat. c. 14, Lat. c. 15; Snite Museum of Art, Acc. 1974.28, 1974.29, 1980.58.4, 1980.58.5, 1984.3.1, 1984.3.2, 1984.3.3, 1984.3.6, 1984.3.7, 1996.48; Saint Mary's College, MSS 4, 5, 6, 7, 8, 9, and 10.

196. For example, Hesburgh Library, cod. Lat. c. 5.

197. For example, Hesburgh Library, codd. Lat. a. 11, Lat. b. 5, Lat. b. 6, Lat. b. 7, Lat. b. 9, Lat. c. 1, Lat. e. 2, and, ambiguously, Lat. c. 11; Saint Mary's College, MS 2. Generally, see Louis Jordan, "Problems of

In transcriptions all abbreviations are expanded silently, and the orthography of each manuscript is preserved; capitalization, however, is not introduced. Transcriptions of Latin texts use lower-case **u**, upper-case **V**, and **i** not **j** (except with numerals occurring within the text, which are employed selectively in instances where corrections, additions, and erasures were made, and in the expansion of select abbreviations). Comments of a text-critical or descriptive nature are in italics within square brackets (e.g., [*sic*]). Instances where text in the manuscript is omitted, supplied, illegible, or lost are indicated using the following:

< > Text omitted by scribe or lost and supplied.
( ) Text supplied from the expansion of an abbreviation (Massai).
*** Illegible or lacuna.

Descriptive or bibliographical comments follow each entry in smaller type. These may discuss details of the entry in this particular context, or note other important information. When possible, the following subfields are provided after the comments:

EDITION: Edited versions of the text are listed here, though not every text that appears in this catalogue has been edited. Incunabular editions are cited only when no other editions are known.

BIBLIOGRAPHY: This subfield provides a select bibliography for a particular text or item. It is not inclusive nor reflective of all scholarship on a given topic, but is intended as a good beginning point for further inquiry. This includes references to incipitaria, repertoires, and the like (e.g., Bloomfield, Kaeppeli, Stegmüller).

Where appropriate, bibliographic references are also provided in square brackets within the text field. For example, a collection of ten prayers may be a single content item in a manuscript, but different bibliographic references may accompany the text describing each individual prayer.

The only complete Bible in the collection[198] is presented similarly to Ker's arrangement,[199] in which, following a list of the order of books, the incipits are provided for the prologues with references to Stegmüller.[200]

Interpreting Dated Colophons Based on the Examples from the Biblioteca Ambrosiana," in *Scribi e colofoni: Le sottoscrizioni di copisti dalle orgini all'avvento dalla stampa. Atti del seminario di Erice X Colloquio del Comité international de paléographie latine (23–28 ottobre 1993)*, ed. Ema Condello and Giuseppe De Gregorio (Spoleto: Centro italiano di studi sull'alto Medioevo, 1993), 367–384.

198. Hesburgh Library, cod. Lat. b. 7.

199. Ker, *Medieval Manuscripts in British Libraries*, 1:vii–viii and 1:96–97.

200. Friedrich Stegmüller (8–11 with N. Reinhardt), *Repertorium Biblicum Medii Aevi* 1–11 (Madrid: s.n., 1950–1980).

The textual contents of books of hours, liturgical, and other devotional manuscripts are difficult to describe accurately using general fields. Thus, entries for these types forgo the general *incipit* and *explicit* fields, and include more substantive textual descriptions. The aim is to bring any unique and identifying features to the fore for further comparison or consultation. Textual information for books of hours is collected according to Erik Drigsdahl's method of "CHD Tests."[201] The following abbreviations may occur in the descriptions of books of hours and liturgical manuscripts:

ANT.	Antiphona
ANT. SUP. BEN.	Antiphona super Benedictus
ANT. SUP. MAGNIF.	Antiphona super Magnificat
ANT. SUP. NUNC DIM.	Antiphona super Nunc dimittis
CAP.	Capitulum
HYM.	Hymnus
INV.	Invitatorium
LECT. I	Lectio prima
OR.	Oratio
PS(S).	Psalmus/psalmi
R.	Responsum/responsorium
V.	Versus/uersiculus

Similarly, the Office of the Dead is described by the sequence of its responsories using the numbers found in Ottosen.[202] Calendars and litanies use the normative forms of saints' names, and Latin forms are given in parentheses when necessary. Noteworthy or uncommon saints are listed along with their position, date, or grade. For books of hours and other manuscripts produced in a similar manner, all martyrs, confessors, and virgins present in the litany are listed in order of occurrence for comparative purposes.[203]

The subdivision of all contents of books of hours, liturgical, and devotional manuscripts attempts to follow the hierarchy of initials of the manuscript as closely as possible while maintaining accuracy.

Binding: Bindings are described in brief terms, but more details are provided if the binding is medieval, or noteworthy for provenance information. The general terms used correspond to J. Greenfield's glossary and M. Brown's *Guide*.[204]

201. Drigsdhal, CHD: Center for Håndskriftstudier i Danmark, http://manuscripts.org.uk/chd.dk/, and http://manuscripts.org.uk/chd.dk/use/index.html.

202. Ottosen, *The Responsories and Versicles.*

203. The presentation of the litany is also informed by Nash, *Between France and Flanders.*

204. Jane Greenfield, *ABC of Bookbinding: A Unique Glossary with Over 700 Illustrations for Collectors and Librarians* (New Castle, DE: Oak Knoll Press, 1998); M. Brown, *Understanding Illuminated Manuscripts*, esp. the diagrams on 6–7.

Owners & Provenance: Previous owners are listed chronologically with dates when possible. Booksellers with location are listed as possessors, but not auction houses. If the year and source of the acquisition are known, they will conclude the field. Citations and references to dealer and auction catalogues appear in the Sales & Catalogues subfield.

> Sales & Catalogues: This subfield lists bookseller and auction catalogue references in short form. For bookseller catalogues: name, catalogue number, entry number (e.g., B. Rosenthal, Cat. 1, no. 41). For auction catalogues: house, date, month, year, lot number (e.g. Sotheby's, 22 July 1918, lot 531). An essential tool for tracking down many catalogue references is the Schoenberg Database of Manuscripts,[205] without which much would be untraceable. All references have been checked against the actual catalogues, but, in the few instances where a catalogue is unobtainable, the entries are marked: (unverified).

Most of the fragments described in this catalogue are the results of modern biblioclasty. The dispersal of leaves from broken manuscripts is as rapid and vast as is their ability to vanish into collections, private and public alike. To this end, great effort has been made to provide a comprehensive list of locations, shelfmarks, citations, and contents (where appropriate) of all discoverable leaves from the parent manuscripts.

Former Shelfmark: All former shelfmarks are listed in chronological order. The full shelfmark is given if all particulars are known. However, former shelfmarks for the manuscripts of the University of Notre Dame and Saint Mary's College are listed in short form: e.g., MS 5 (Notre Dame).

Bibliography: Citations are limited to those which mention specific aspects of a particular manuscript or the manuscript as a whole. Citations include previous catalogue entries, descriptions, and references in *conspectus siglorum* of critical editions. Bibliographical citations are in author-date format.

Arrangement of Entries

The entries are first arranged by institution and repository: University of Notre Dame, Hesburgh Library (232 items; 64 codices, 168 fragments from 52 parent mss.), Snite Museum of Art (44 items; 2 codices, 42 fragments from 28 parent mss.), and Saint Mary's College, Cushwa-Leighton Library (12 items; 3 codices, 9 fragments from 7 parent manuscripts). The manuscripts in the Hesburgh Library are arranged alphabetically by fonds and shelfmarks: *codices Latini* are followed by the vernacular manuscripts, and then all fragments concluding with the Constable manuscripts. All manuscripts in the Snite Museum of Art and the Cushwa-Leighton Library are listed numerically by their respective systems.

205. Schoenberg Database of Manuscripts, dla.library.upenn.edu/dla/schoenberg/index.html.

PLATE 1. University of Notre Dame, Hesburgh Library, Frag. III. 1, f. 47r. Miniature of St. Francis from a Breton book of hours (use of Vannes and Rennes).

PLATE 2. University of Notre Dame, Hesburgh Library, cod. Lat. e. 4, f. 1r (detail). Erasure of *pape* in the calendar of an English psalter.

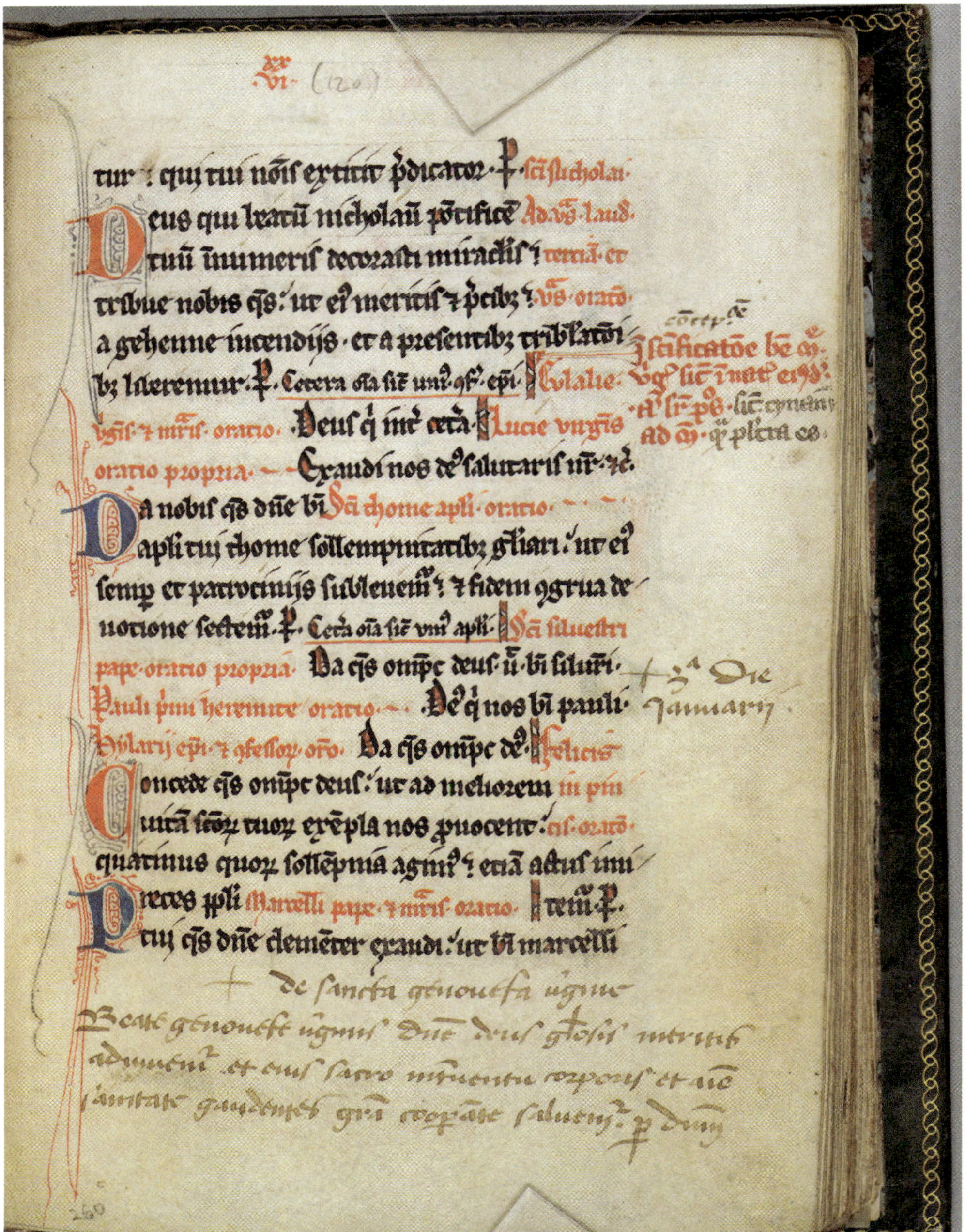

PLATE 3. University of Notre Dame, Hesburgh Library, cod. Lat. b. 4, f. 260r. Correction of the feast of the "Sanctification of the Virgin" to the "Conception of the Virgin" in a Carthusian diurnal ca. 1341.

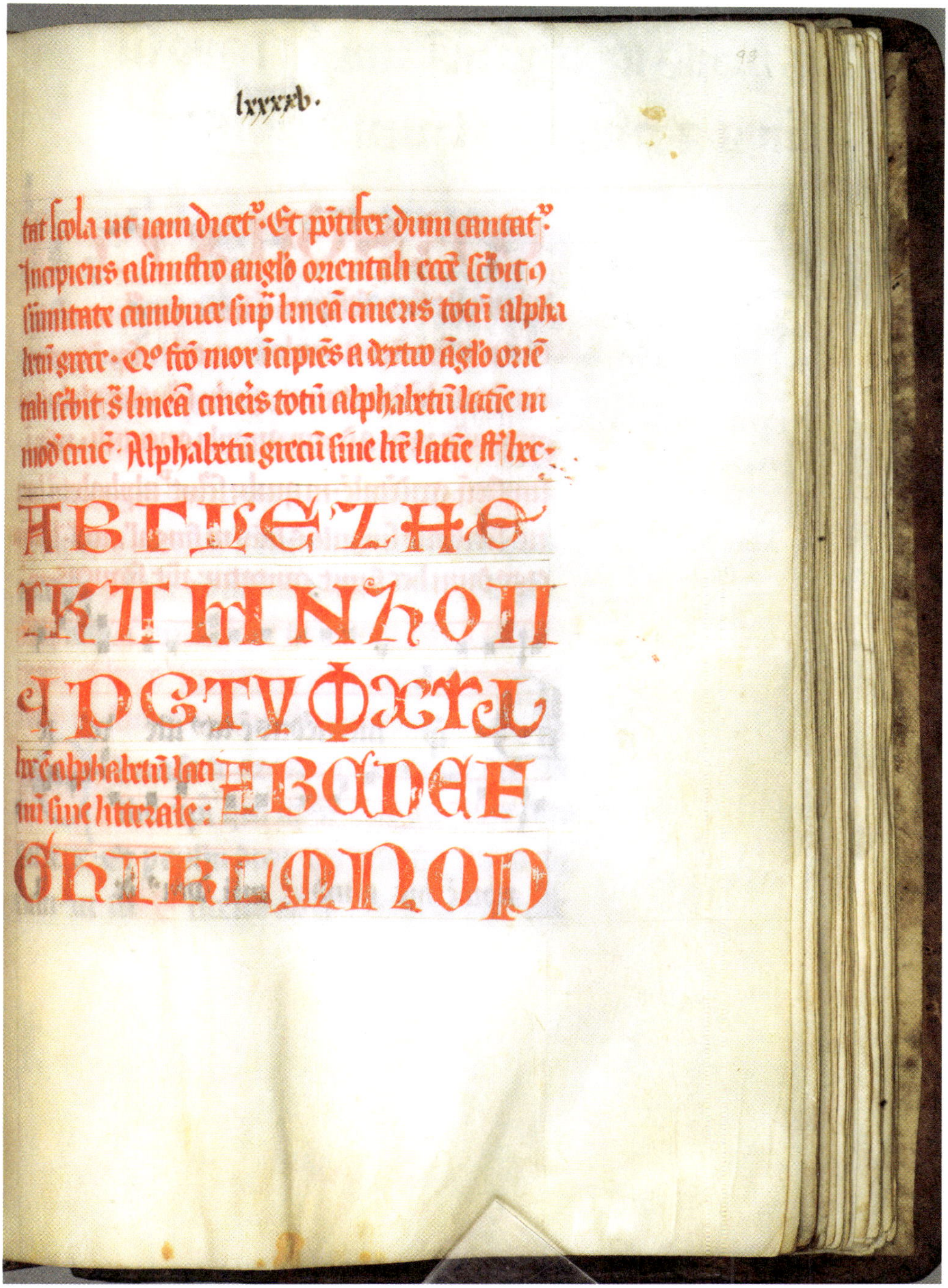

PLATE 4. University of Notre Dame, Hesburgh Library, cod. Lat. c. 12, f. 95r. Greek alphabet for the dedication of a church as it appears in a fourteenth-century pontifical.

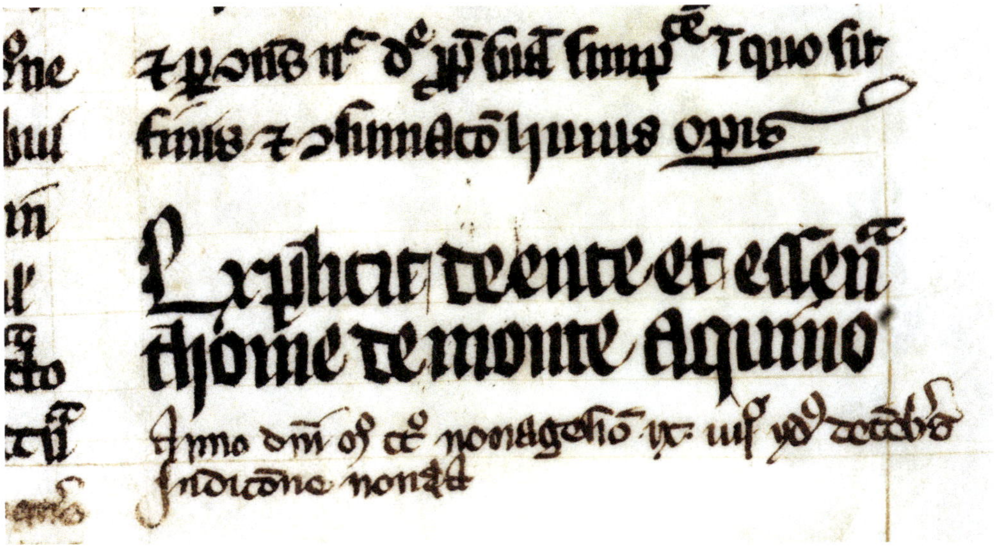

PLATE 5. Saint Mary's College, Cushwa-Leighton Library, MS 2, f. 6r (detail). Colophon dated 1299 in the glosses to the *De ente et essentia* of St. Thomas Aquinas.

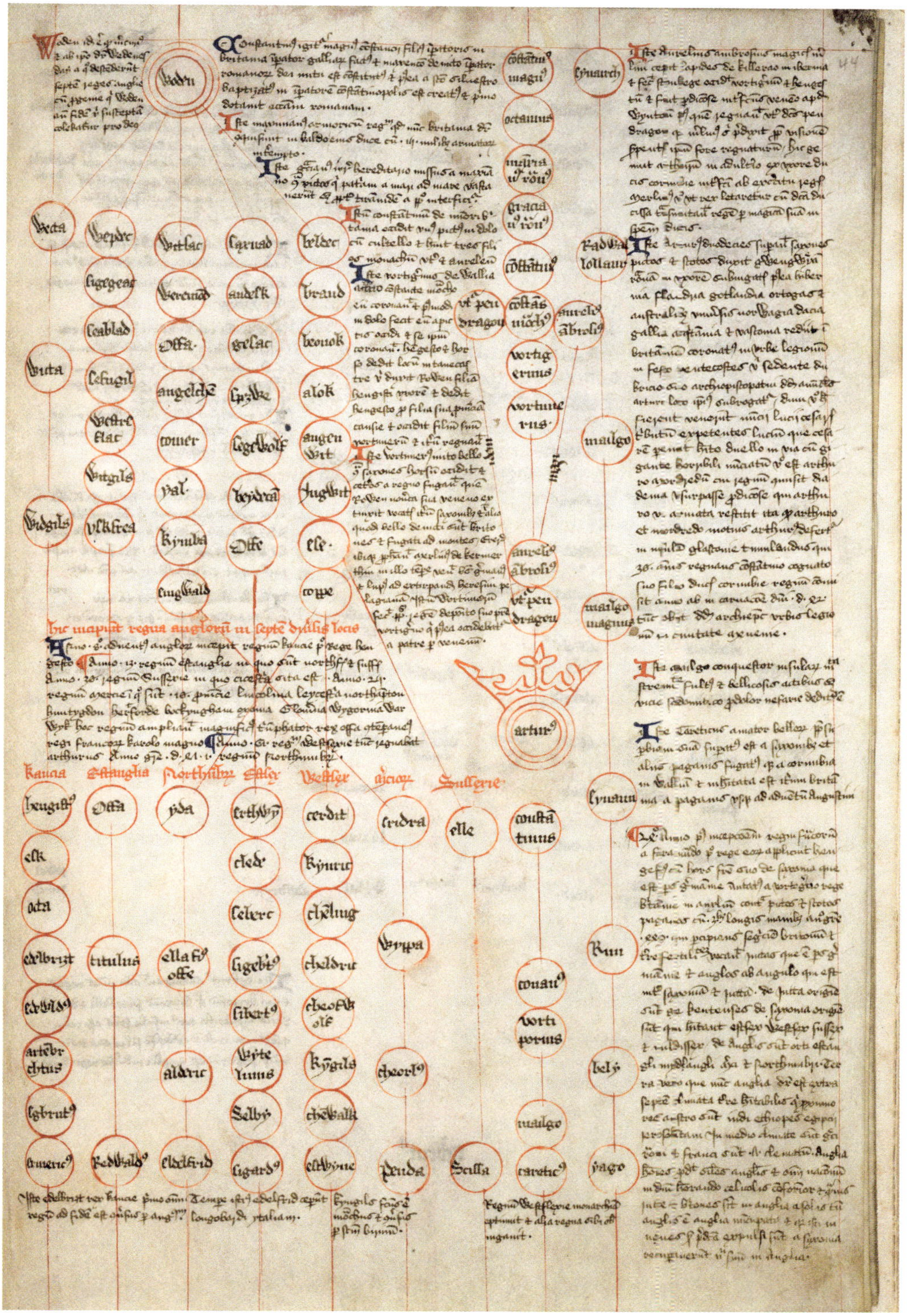

PLATE 6. University of Notre Dame, Hesburgh Library, cod. Lat. d. 3, f. 44r. The complex *mise-en-page* of an English genealogical chronicle. The roundel featuring King Arthur is crowned.

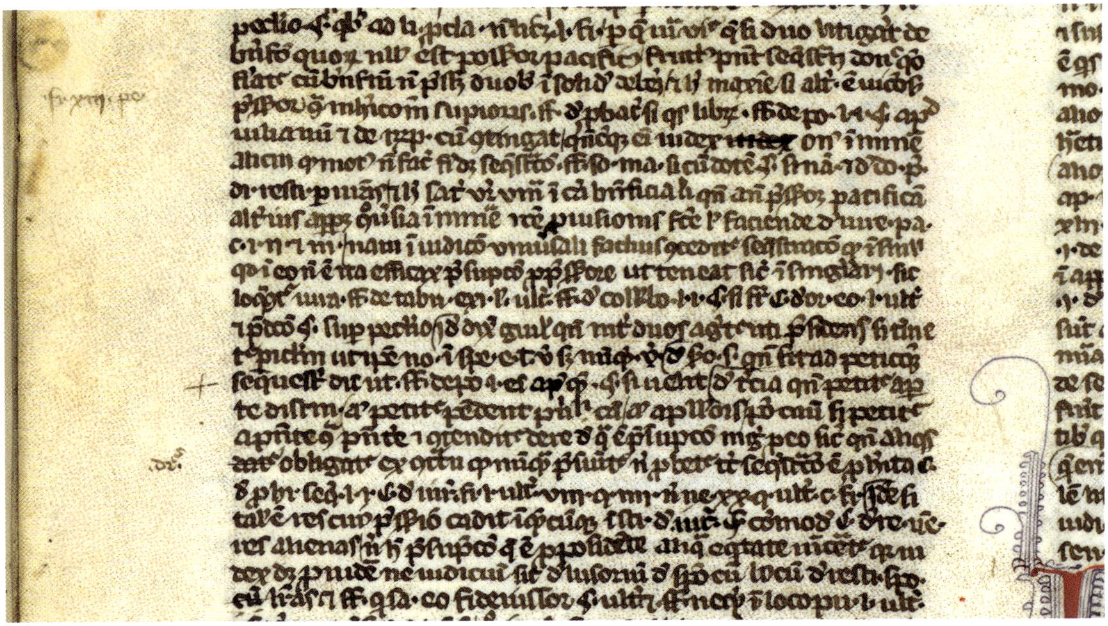

PLATE 7. University of Notre Dame, Hesburgh Library, cod. Lat. e. 3, f. 18r (detail). Pecia mark (top left) from a university manuscript containing a *lectura* of Paulus de Liazariis.

PLATE 8. University of Notre Dame, Hesburgh Library, MS Fr. d. 1, f. 1r. Presentation miniature in the *Roman de la Rose.*

Catalogue

University of Notre Dame, Hesburgh Library

cod. Lat. a. 1

Origin: Low Countries, s. xv^2 (Flanders; for the English market).
Content Overview: Book of Hours, use of Sarum.

In Latin, on parchment; v +236 ff. +v; generally 88 x 66 mm (page) [see Layout for ruling]; three sets of foliation with Arabic numerals [see Foliation].

Collation: v +1–2^6 +3^{8+1} +4^{8+6} +5^{8+5} +6–7^{8+1} +8^8 +9–11^{8+2} +12–14^{8+1} +15^{2+1} +16^{8+1} +17^8 +18^{8+1} +19–21^8 +22^{8+1} +23^8 +24^{6+2} +25^{8+1} +26^8 +27^{6+2} +28^2 +v

Quires: Parchment quaternions are the predominant quire forms; ternions used for the calendar in quires 1–2; miniatures were executed on singletons with stubs then inserted [see Miniatures] into existing gatherings. Quires 15, 24, and 27 are irregular. Quire 15 is a bifolium with one singleton added (f. 134); quire 24 is a ternion with an inserted miniature and another singleton glued to it containing the corresponding border (ff. 208–209); quire 27 is a ternion with a singleton with stub (f. 229) and another singleton (f. 234) added.

Quire Marks: Arabic numerals in brown ink are written in the lower center margin of ff. 1r (2), 7r (3), 13r (4), 22r (5), 36r (6), 49r (7), 58r (8), 75r (9). The numerals were added after miniatures were inserted (e.g., f. 49r). The numbers do not correspond with the current quire structure of the manuscript.

Foliation: Three sets of foliation occur in the manuscript. Set 1: Arabic numerals in modern pencil; upper right margin. Set 2: Arabic numerals in modern pencil; adjusts by one digit (e.g., Set 1, f. 153 = Set 2, f. 154). Set 2 writes over or attempts to alter the final digit of Set 1 but does not erase. Set 2 does not span the entire manuscript; begins on f. 152, but often obscured by Set 3. Set 3: Arabic numerals in modern blue ink; often written over previous pencil foliations. Set 3 does not span the entire manuscript, but only ff. 1–4, 26, 28, 30, 32, 34, 36, 37, 39, 41, 42, 44, 45, 47, 49, 51–59, 61–77, 79–83, 85–87, 89–91, 93, 106, 108–119, 121–124, 126–135, 137–151, 156–158, 160, 189, 191, 207, 216–217, 219, 234–235, and flyleaves viii, ix, x as ff. 239–241. The foliation of Sets 2 and 3 includes the final flyleaves.

Layout:

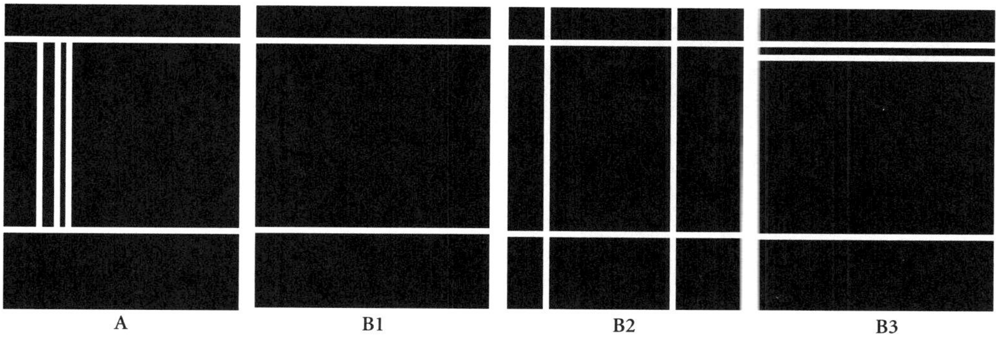

A ff. 1r–12v. Red ink; 55 x 38 mm; cols. 5/3/20 mm; 17 lines.
B ff. 13r–236v. Red ink; 55 x 35 mm; 17 lines.

Patterns **A** and **B** are traced irregularly in red ink; the text frame is inconsistent in horizontal dimensions and often asymmetrical; writing below top line; prickings visible on some folios. Pattern **A** has three calendric columns (5/3/20 mm); pattern **B** has a single column. Pattern **B** is traced aberrantly producing three variant forms (**B1–B3**): verticals absent and have no traces regardless of technique (**B1**); verticals or partial verticals traced lightly in red ink or lead (**B2**); an additional horizontal in the upper margin (**B3**). **B3** occurs on a single bifolium only (ff. 196/199); manuscript likely ruled by the bifolium. The inserted miniatures contain no ruling.

Script: A single hand of the fifteenth century (M1) writes all texts in Northern Textualis Formata with brown ink. The script is executed somewhat rapidly; both forms of two-compartment **a** are used; inconsistent treatment of ascenders and descenders.

Decoration:
I. Rubrication: Rubrics in red ink (faded); letter heightening of majuscules in yellow ink.
II. Initials: Foliate, dentelle, and flourished initials occur in hierarchy.
a. Foliate initials (5 line square inset) in demi-grisaille and gold with white and gray penwork begin the major sections of the text.
b. Dentelle initials (3 line square inset) occur in the calendar and throughout the texts (2 line square inset).
c. Flourished initials (1 line versals) in blue with red penwork and gold with blue penwork alternate throughout the texts.
III. Line Fillers: Line fillers in red and blue ink are found in the Litany on ff. 149r–154v. Spaces for unexecuted line fillers are reserved throughout the manuscript.

IV. Borders & Frames:

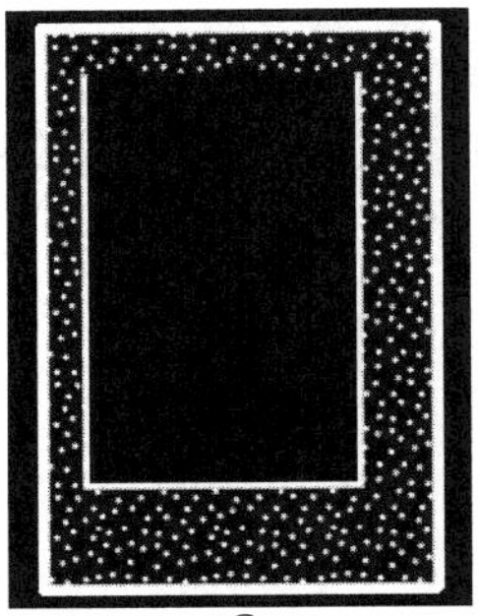

C

D

Text folios facing each miniature contain functional four-margins borders (C); borders comprised of acanthus and vegetal motifs. The palette is mainly grisaille with yellow and gold adding white and gray penwork. Area to be decorated is frame-ruled in black ink; text frames within **C** are contained by double bars in three-margins type; gold outer, and gray and white inner are outlined in black; text written first, often interrupting the bars or obscured by them. Foliate initials are either completely inside the double bars or extend into the border. Folios with **C** do not have bounding lines or through lines, but are ruled for text lines. Borders on folios with miniatures (**D**) have the same composition as C; miniature frames are arch-topped (**D**), contained by double bars colored as above; no ruling.

Miniatures: Twenty-eight demi-grisaille miniatures are painted on the verso of inserted leaves; rectos are blank, pointing toward Flemish origin; all miniatures enclosed by arch-topped frames; many damaged, especially the faces. Miniatures are: Christ as *saluator mundi* (f. 13v); Trinity (f. 23v); John the Baptist (f. 26v); John the Evangelist (f. 28v); Christopher (f. 30v); George (f. 32v); Thomas Becket (f. 34v); Anne (37v); Mary Magdalene (f. 39v); Katherine (f. 42v); Barbara (f. 45v); Margaret (f. 47v); Agony in the garden (f. 49v); Betrayal (f. 59v); Christ before Pilate (f. 77v); Flagellation (f. 83v); Christ carrying the Cross (f. 87v); Crucifixion (f. 91v); Deposition (f. 95v); Entombment (f. 99v); Crowned Virgin and Child, one angel (f. 106v); the Virgin (f. 119v); Adam, Eve, serpent, tree (f. 124v); David in penance (f. 135v); Raising of Lazarus (f. 158v); two angels carrying two souls to heaven (*commendatio animarum*) (f. 189v); Man of Sorrows with *Arma Christi* (f. 209v); Jerome as cardinal writing with left hand (f. 217v), likely from a reversed tracing.

Calendar: Two pages per month; recto/verso; not composite; dominical letter **a** in red ink; Roman time not marked.

Contents:

1. Calendar (constructed Sarum)—ff. 1r–12v.

Written in black ink with graded feasts in red; several feasts with significance in England appear: Edward the Martyr, Richard of Chichester [*ut uid.*], Alphege, John of Beverly [*ut uid.*], Dunstan,

Aldhelm, Gildard, translation of Edward, Swithun, Cuthburga, Giles, translation of Cuthbert, Lambert, Gereon, translation of Wulfram, Hugh of Lincoln, "Little" Hugh of Lincoln [*ut uid.*], Elisabeth of Hungary, Thomas Becket. The corruption of names and dates is consistent with an origin in Flanders (see MORGAN 2001, 185 n. 25). Orthographical forms of important saints and dates as they appear in the manuscript are: *edwardi regis* (Mar. 18); *riti episcopi* (Apr. 3, Apr. 18); *alphegi episcopi* (Apr. 21); *beuerlachi martiris* (Apr. 30); *dustani episcopi* (May 19); *adelini episcopi* (May 26); *gildardi episcopi* (Jun. 8); *translacio sancti edwardi* (Jun. 21); *eligii episcopi* (Jun. 25; red); *swichini martiris* (Jul. 10); *cutburge uirginis* (Aug. 31); *translacio cutberti* (Sept. 4); *lamberti episcopi* (Sept. 17); *uulfranni episcopi* (Oct. 15); *hugonis martiris* (Nov. 14); *hugonis episcopi* (Nov. 18); *elysabeth uidue* (Nov. 20); *eligii episcopi* (Dec. 1; red); *richi episcopi* (Dec. 10); *sancti thome ponthifex* (Dec. 29; red). CORBETT no. 4, p. 32 has hypercorrected some dates, recorded others inaccurately, and switched some saints and dates.

2. Fifteen *Orationes* (the 15 O's of St. Bridget)—ff. 14r–22v.

RUB.: incipiunt quindecim orationes secundum passionem christi crucis; INC.: [f. 14r] o domine ihesu christe eterna dulcedo te amantium . . .; EXPL.: [f. 22v] . . . et conuersacio mea tibi placita et accepta ac finis uite mee ita laudabilis amen [*HE* 76–80].

The fifteenth *oratio* omits "ut post huius uite terminum te merear laudare cum omnibus sanctis tuis in eternum"; see LEROQUAIS 2:98–99.

3. Commemorations—ff. 24r–48v.

Each commemoration begins on a recto with full borders and foliate initial, and is preceded by a miniature on the facing verso.

3.1. Trinity—ff. 24r–25v. RUB.: ad honorem sancte trinitatis; INC.: domine deus omnipotens pater et filius et spiritus sanctus da michi famulo tuo .n. uictoriam . . . libera me famulum tuum .n. de omnibus inimicis meis . . .; EXPL.: [f. 25r] . . . ut non timeam quid faciat michi homo; OR.: libera me domine ihesu christe fili dei uiui qui in cruce suspensus fuisti . . . et ab omnibus periculis libera me domine qui uiuis et regnas deus per omnia secula seculorum amen [HOSKINS 116–117; DE LA MARE, *Lyell*, 373, no. 88].

3.2. John the Baptist—f. 27r–v. RUB.: ad honorem sancti iohannis baptiste; INC.: gaude iohannes baptista qui in maternali cista sanctus uere extitisti . . . [*AH* 29: no. 208]; OR.: beate iohannes baptista christi precursor atque preco redemptoris nostri porrige . . . et ad lucem celestis gaudii perducas per christum dominum.

3.3. John the Evangelist—f. 29r–v. RUB.: ad honorem sancti iohanni [*sic*] euwangeliste [*sic*]; INC.: gaude pater uia morum felix euuangeliorum sidus fulgens radio . . . [*AH* 29: no. 210]; OR.: ecclesiam tuam quesumus domine benignus illustra . . . perueniat sempiterna per christum dominum nostrum amen [*CO* 2416c].

3.4. Christopher—f. 31r–v. RUB.: ad honorem sancti christoforis [*sic*] martiris; INC.: o sancte christofore martir ihesu christi qui pro christi nomine penas pertulisti . . . [*AH*

46: no. 207]; OR.: concede quesumus omnipotens deus ut qui beati christofori martiris tui memoriam . . . quem ipse meruit in humeris suis portare [*HE* 133].

3.5. George—f. 33r–v. RUB.: ad honorem sancti georgii martiris; INC.: georgi martir inclite te decet laus et gloria predotatum milicia . . . [*HE* 131; cf. *AH* 33: no. 97]; OR.: omnipotens sempiterne deus qui deprecantium uoces benignus exaudis . . . ualeant precedere digneris per christum dominum nostrum amen [Hoskins 113].

3.6. Thomas Becket—ff. 35r–36v. RUB.: ad honorem beati thome episcopi; INC.: gaude lux londoniarum thoma tutor animarum dei prouidencia . . . [*AH* 29: no. 167]; OR.: deus qui beatum thomam martirem tuum atque pontificem die martis . . . ut ad celi gaudia possimus peruenire per christum dominum nostrum amen.

3.7. Anne—f. 38r–v. RUB.: ad honorem beate anne; INC.: gaude felix anna que concepisti prolem que erat paritura mundi saluatorem . . . [cf. *AH* 46: no. 188]; OR.: domine ihesu christe qui beate anne tantam gratiam donare dignatus es . . . ad gaudia celorum perducas per [cf. *CO* 1366b].

3.8. Mary Magdelene—ff. 40r–41r. RUB.: ad honorem beate marie magdelene; INC.: gaude pia magdalena spes salutis uite uena lapsorum fiducia . . .; OR.: deus qui beate marie magdalene penitenciam ita tibi gratam placitam . . . propiciacionis tue clementiam senciamus per christum dominum nostrum amen [*CO* 1370].

3.9. Katherine—ff. 43r–44r. RUB.: ad honorem beate katherine; INC.: gaude uirgo katherina per quam doctores lux diuina traxit ab erroribus . . . [*AH* 29: no. 216; cf. no. 217]; ANT.: facque tibi presentamus laudes ut post gaudeamus in celesti lumine amen; OR.: deus qui beatam katherinam uirginem et martirem tuam gloriosis miraculis . . . ut sue pie conuersacionis proficiamus exemplo per christum dominum nostrum amen.

3.10. Barbara—f. 46r–v. RUB.: ad honorem beate barbare uirginis; INC.: gaude barbara regina summa pollens in doctrina angeli misterio . . . [*AH* 29: no. 180]; OR.: omnipotens sempiterne deus trina et una inseparabilis maiestas . . . promeruit specialiter impetrare per christum.

3.11. Margaret—f. 48r–v. RUB.: ad honorem beate margarete; INC.: gaude uirgo gloriosa margareta preciosa rubricata sanguine . . . [*AH* 29: no. 221]; OR.: indulgenciam nobis domine beata margareta uirgo et martir imploret . . . et merito castitatis et tue professione uirtutis per christum dominum nostrum amen [cf. *CO* 3125b].

4. Hours of the Virgin, use of Sarum; commemorations (*ad laudes*); Short Hours of the Cross (intercalated); *Salue Regina* with verses—ff. 50r–105v.

The Short Hours of the Cross are intercalated with the Hours of the Virgin followed by *Salue Regina* with verses. The intercalated material is described separately after the *Horae BMV*; commemorations, Short Hours of the Cross, and *Salue Regina* are neither mentioned nor recorded in Corbett 1957 and Corbett [1978].

4.1. Hours of the Virgin, use of Sarum—ff. 50r–68v, 78r–82r, 88r–90v, 92r–94v, 96r–98r, 100r–103v.

RUB.: incipiunt hore beate marie secundum usum sarum.

4.1.1. Matins—ff. 50r–58v. RUB.: ad matutinum; INV.: aue maria . . .; HYM.: quem terra ponthus . . .; ANT. PS. 8: benedicta tu; LECT. I: sancta maria uirgo . . .; R. I.: sancta et immaculata . . .

4.1.2. Lauds—ff. 60r–68v. RUB.: ad laudes; PSS.: 92, 99, 66, Benedicite, 148, 149, 150; ANT.: o admirabile; CAP.: maria uirgo semper letare . . .; HYM.: o gloriosa domina . . .; ANT. SUP. BEN.: o gloriosa.

4.1.3. Prime—ff. 78r–82r. RUB.: ad primam.; PSS.: 53, 116, 117; HYM.: ueni creator spiritus . . .; ANT.: o admirabile . . .; CAP.: in omnibus requiem . . .; R.: aue maria . . .; V.: benedicta tu . . .

4.1.4. Terce—ff. 84r–86v. RUB.: ad terciam; PSS.: 119, 120, 121; HYM.: ueni creator spiritus me; ANT.: quando natus es; CAP.: ab inicio et ante . . .; R.: sancta dei genitrix . . .; V.: intercede pro nobis . . .

4.1.5. Sext—ff. 88r–90v. RUB.: ad sextam; PSS.: 122, 123, 124; ANT.: rubum quem uiderat; CAP.: et sic in syon . . .; R.: post partum uirgo . . .; V.: dei genitrix intercede . . .

4.1.6. None—ff. 92r–94v. RUB.: ad nonam; PSS.: 125, 126, 127; ANT.: germinauit; CAP.: et radicaui in populo . . .; R.: speciosa facta es . . .; V.: in deliciis tuis . . .; V.: dignare me laudare . . .

4.1.7. Vespers—ff. 96r–98r. RUB.: ad uesperas; PSS.: 121, 122, 123, 124, 125; ANT.: post partum; CAP.: beata es maria . . .; HYM.: aue maris stella . . .; ANT. SUP. MAGNIF.: sancta maria.

4.1.8. Compline—ff. 100r–103v. RUB.: ad completorium; PSS.: 12, 42, 128, 130; ANT.: cum iocunditate; CAP.: sicut cinamonum [*sic*] et balsamum . . .; HYM.: uirgo singularis . . .; ANT. SUP. NUNC DIM.: glorificamus te.

4.2. Commemorations (*ad laudes*)—ff. 69r–75v.

4.2.1. Holy Spirit—f. 69r. RUB.: memoria de sancto spiritu; ANT.: ueni sancte spiritus . . .; OR.: deus qui corda fidelium . . . semper consolacione gaudere per [*CO* 1666].

4.2.2. Holy Cross—f. 69r–v. RUB.: memoria de sancta cruce; ANT.: libera nos salua nos . . .; OR.: omnipotens sempiterne deus qui dedisti nobis famulis tuis . . . firmitate ab omnibus semper muniamur aduersis per eundem christum dominum nostrum [*CO* 3920].

4.2.3. Holy Cross—ff. 69v–70r. RUB.: memoria de sancta cruce; ANT.: nos autem gloriari oportet . . .; OR.: deus qui sanctam crucem tuam ascendisti . . . et confortare digneris qui uiuis et regis.

4.2.4. Michael—f. 70r–v. RUB.: memoria de sancto michaele; ANT.: michael archangele ueni . . .; OR.: deus qui miro ordine angelorum . . . uita nostra muniatur per xpristum [*sic*] dominum nostrum amen. [*CO* 1798].

4.2.5. John the Baptist—ff. 70v–71r. RUB.: memoria de sancto iohanne baptista; ANT.: inter natos mulierum . . .; OR.: perpetuis nos quesumus domine sancti iohannis baptiste tuere . . . attolle suffragiis per christum [*CO* 4222b].

4.2.6. Peter and Paul—f. 71r–v. RUB.: memoria de sancto petro et paulo; ANT.: petrus apostolus et paulus doctor . . .; OR.: deus cuius dextera beatum petrum apostolum . . . eternitatis gloriam consequamur per [*CO* 1158b].

4.2.7. Andrew—f. 71v. RUB.: memoria de sancto andrea; ANT.: andreas christi famulus dignus dei . . .; OR.: maiestatem tuam domine suppliciter . . . apud te sit pro nobis perpetuus intercessor per christum dominum [*CO* 3290b].

4.2.8. Laurence—ff. 71v–72r. RUB.: memoria de sancto laurencio; ANT.: laurencius bonum opus operatus est . . .; OR.: da nobis quesumus omnipotens deus uiciorum nostrorum . . . tormentorum suorum incendia superare per christum dominum nostrum [*CO* 960].

4.2.9. Stephan—f. 72r–v. RUB.: memoria de sancto stephano; ANT.: stephanus uidit celos apertos uidit et introiuit . . .; OR.: da nobis quesumus domine imitari . . . pro suis persecutoribus exorare dominum nostrum ihesum christum filium tuum amen [*CO* 939].

4.2.10. Thomas—ff. 72v–73r. RUB.: memoria de sancto thoma; ANT.: tu per thome sanguinem quem pro te impendit . . .; OR.: deus pro cuius ecclesia gloriosus pontifex thomas . . . peticionis sue salutarem consequantur effectum per [*CO* 1315].

4.2.11. Nicholas—f. 73r–v. RUB.: memoria de sancto nycholao; ANT.: beatus nycholaus adhuc puerulus . . .; OR.: deus qui beatum nicholaum pium pontificem tuum . . . a gehenne incendiis liberemur per christum dominum [*CO* 1463].

4.2.12. Mary Magdalene—ff. 73v–74r. RUB.: memoria de sancta maria magdalena; ANT.: maria unxit pedes ihesu et extersit capillis capitis . . .; OR.: largire nobis clementissime pater . . . sempiternam impetret beatitudinem per christum dominum [*CO* 3231].

4.2.13. Katherine—f. 74r–v. RUB.: memoria de sancta katherina; ANT.: uirgo sancta katherina grecie gemma . . .; OR.: omnipotens sempiterne deus qui gloriose uirginis . . . ubi uisionis tue claritatem mereamur intueri per christum [*CO* 3916].

4.2.14. Margaret—f. 74v. RUB.: memoria de sancta margareta; ANT.: erat autem margareta annorum quindecim . . .; OR.: deus qui beatam margaretam uirginem ad celos per palmam . . . exempla sequentes ad te pertingere mereamur [*CO* 1384a].

4.2.15. All Saints—ff. 74v–75r. RUB.: memoria de omnibus sanctis; ANT.: omnes sancti et electi dei nostri memoramur . . .; OR.: omnium sanctorum tuorum quesumus domine intercessione placatus . . . nobis tribue et remedia sempiterna concede per [*CO* 4102].

4.2.16. Peace—ff. 75r–v. RUB.: memoria pro sancta pace; ANT.: da pacem domine in diebus nostris . . .; OR.: deus a quo sancta desideria recta consilia et iusta sunt opera . . . sint tua protectione tranquilla per christum dominum nostrum [*CO* 1088a].

4.3. Short Hours of the Cross (intercalated)—ff. 75v–76v, 82r–v, 86v, 90v, 94v, 98r–v, 103v–104r.

Matins, ff. 75v–76v; Prime, f. 82r–v; Terce, f. 86v; Sext, f. 90v; None, f. 94v; Vespers, f. 98r–v; Compline, ff. 103v–104r; *Recommendatio*, f. 104r. Each stanza concludes with the usual verse, response, and prayer, which are written fully at Matins; all other repetitions are given in cue form. For the hymns see *AH* 30: no. 13.

4.4. *Salue Regina* with verses—ff. 104r–105v.

RUB.: salutacio ad uirginem mariam; INC.: salue regina misericordie . . . post hoc exilium ostende. o clemens o pia o dulcis maria; V.: uirgo mater ecclesie . . .; RUB.: o clemens; V.:

uirgo clemens uirgo pia uirgo dulcis . . .; RUB.: o pia; V.: funde preces tuo nato . . .; RUB.: o dulcis; V.: gloriosa dei mater . . .; RUB.: o mitis; V.: dele culpas miserorum . . .; RUB.: maria; V.: et nos soluat a peccatis . . .; RUB.: o clemens o pia o dulcis o mitis; V.: aue maria . . .; R.: benedicta tu . . .; OR.: omnipotens sempiterne deus qui gloriose uirginis . . . et a morte perpetua liberemur per christum dominum nostrum amen.

EDITION: *HE* 63; cf. LITTLEHALES 1897, lviii–lix.

5. Ps.-Bonaventure, farced *Salue Regina*—ff. 107r–112v.

RUB.: has uideas laudes qui sacra uirgine gaudes et uenerando piam studeas laudare mariam uirginis intacte dum ueneris ante figuram pretereundo caue ne taceatur aue inuenies ueniam sic salutando mariam salue; INC.: [f. 107r] salue uirgo uirginum stella matutina sordidorum . . . [*RH* 18318]; OR.: [f. 112v] deus qui de beate marie uirginis utero uerbum tuum . . . apud te intercessionibus adiuuemur per eundem christum [*CO* 1518].

A verse and response precede the prayer on f. 112v.

6. *O intemerata* and *Obsecro te* (masculine forms)—ff. 112v–118v.

6.1. *O intemerata*—ff. 112v–115r. RUB.: alia oracio de eadem; INC.: o intemerata . . . michi peccatori . . . ego miserrimus peccator . . . michi peccatori . . .; EXPL.: . . . benignissimus paraclitus qui cum patre uiuis et regnas deus per omnia secula seculorum amen [cf. WILMART, 494–495].

6.2. *Obsecro te*—ff. 115r–118v. INC.: obsecro te domina . . . ego sum facturus locuturus aut cogitaturus . . . michi famulo tuo . . .; EXPL.: . . . audi et exaudi me dulcissima maria mater dei et misericordie amen. [cf. LEROQUAIS 2:346–347].

7. Phillipe de Grève, Seven Joys of the Virgin—ff. 120r–123v.

RUB.: quicumque hec septem gaudia in honore beate marie uirginis semel audit dixerit centum dies indulgenciarum obtinebit a domino papa clemente qui hec septem gaudia proprio stilo composuit; INC.: [f. 120r] uirgo templum trinitatis deus summe bonitatis et misericordie . . .; EXPL.: [f. 123v] . . . o maria tota munda a peccatis nos emunda per hec septem gaudia et fecunda nos fecunda et due tecum ad iocunda paradisi gloria amen.

EDITION: MONE 2: no. 457.
BIBLIOGRAPHY: *RH* 21889; MONE 2: no. 457; WALTHER, *Initia* 20561, cf. 20560; WILMART, 329 n. 1 (cites MONE 2: no. 457 as no. 165).

8. Jean of Limoges (attr.), *De passione Christi*—ff. 125r–129r.

RUB.: ad salutandum ymaginem christe; INC.: omnibus consideratis paradisus uoluptatis es ihesu piissime . . .; EXPL.: [f. 128r] . . . ad hunc cetum quem christus eripuit amen; kyrielyson . . .; pater noster; et ne nos; V.: christus factus est . . .; V.: ora pro nobis sancta dei genitrix . . .; v.: ualde honorandus est beatus iohannes euwangelista [*sic*] . . .; or.: [f. 128v] omnipotens sempiterne deus qui unigenitum filium tuum . . . a peccatorum nostrorum nexibus adiuuemur per eundem.

Edition: *AH* 31:87–88 [*sine rubricis*]; Horváth 1932, 3:111–115.
Bibliography: *RH* 14081; Walther, *Initia* 13294; Wilmart, 584 n. 527 (cited as *AH* 52:133 and repeated in Corbett 1957, 304 and Corbett [1978], 41).

9. Seven Last Words of Christ—ff. 129r–131r.

rub.: oracio de septem uerbis christi; inc.: [f. 129r] domine ihesu christe qui septem uerba die ultima uite tue in cruce pendens dixisti . . .; expl.: [f. 131r] . . . in regno meo epulari iocundari et commorari per infinita secula seculorum amen.

The prayer is often attributed to Bede. See *HE* 140–142 for the Sarum variants.

Edition: *HE* 140–142; Leroquais 2:342.

10. *Precor te*—ff. 131r–132r.

rub.: alia oratio de eodem; inc.: [f. 131r] precor te piissime domine ihesu christe propter eximiam caritatem . . .; expl.: [f. 132r] . . . propter magnam misericordiam tuam michi tribuere digneris amen [Leroquais 2:100; Wilmart, 378 n. 12].

11. Eucharistic Prayers—ff. 132r–134v.

11.1. ff. 132r–133r. rub.: salutaciones ad sanctum sacramentum; inc.: aue domine ihesu christe uerbum patris filius uirginis agnus dei . . . pax dulcedo requies nostra uita perhennis amen [Wilmart, 377 n. 1, 412; *HE* 70].

11.2. f. 133r. inc.: aue principium nostre creationis aue precium nostre redemptionis . . . uere cognoscere et te feliciter accipere merear amen [*RH* 2059; Wilmart, 23 n. 2, 366, 377 n. 1].

11.3. f. 133r–v. inc.: aue uerum corpus natum de maria uirgine uere passum immolatum . . . mortis in examine o clemens o pie o dulcis ihesu fili marie [*AH* 54: no. 164; Wilmart, 373–76, 379 n. 1; *HE* 70; Walther, *Initia* 1996].

11.4. f. 133v. inc.: aue caro christi cara immolata crucis ara redemptoris hosti a morte tua . . . luce clara tecum frui gloria amen [Wilmart, 366, 379 n. 1; cf. *RH* 1710].

11.5 ff. 133v–134r. inc.: anima christi sanctifica me corpus christi salua me . . . ut cum angelis laudem te in secula seculorum amen [*RH* 1090; Leroquais 2:340; Wilmart, 377 n. 1].

11.6. f. 134r–v. rub.: cuilibet dicenti hanc oracionem inter eleuationem corporis christi et tercium agnus dei dominus papa bonifacius sextus concessit duo milia annorum indulgenciarum ad supplicationem philippi regis francie. inc.: domine ihesu christe qui sacratissimam carnem tuam et preciosissimum sanguinem tuum . . . ab omnibus inmundaciis mentis et corporis et ab uniuersis malis nunc et in euum amen. [*HE* 72; Wilmart, 378 n. 10].

12. Penitential Psalms—ff. 136r–146r.

13. Gradual Psalms—ff. 146v–149r.

The first twelve psalms are given in cue form only; last three written *in toto*.

14. Litany and Collects—ff. 149r–157v.

rub.: incipiunt letanie omnium sanctorum.

14.1. Litany—ff. 149r–156r.

Includes Cedda (*cedda*), Gildard (*ghildarde*), Medard (*medarde*), Aubin (*albine*), Swithun (*swichine*), Birinus(?) (*urine* [*sic*]; cf. *HE* 92 n. 13), Edith (*editha*), Afra (*affra*).

14.2. Collects—ff. 156r–157v.

14.2.1. f. 156r. inc.: deus cui proprium est misereri semper et parcere . . . miseratio tue pietatis absoluat [*CO* 1143].

14.2.2. f. 156r. rub.: oratio; inc.: exaudi quesumus domine supplicum preces . . . indulgenciam tribuas benignus et pacem [*CO* 2541].

14.2.3. f. 156r–v. inc.: omnipotens sempiterne deus qui facis mirabilia magna solus pretende super famulos tuos pontifices nostros et super cunctas congregaciones illis commissas . . . rorem tue benedictionis infunde [*CO* 3938c].

14.2.4. f. 156v. rub.: oracio; inc.: deus qui caritatis dona per gratiam . . . tota dilectione proficiat [*sic*] [*CO* 1483].

14.2.5. f. 156v. inc.: ineffabilem misericordiam tuam quesumus domine clementer . . . pro hiis meremur benignus eripias [*CO* 3129].

14.2.6. f. 156v. rub.: alia collecta; inc.: fidelium deus omnium conditor et redemptor . . . piis supplicationibus consequantur [*CO* 2684b].

14.2.7. ff. 156v–157r. inc.: pietate tua quesumus domine nostrorum solue uincula . . . et inimicis nostris ueram caritatem per [*CO* 4227].

15. Office for the Dead, use of Sarum—ff. 159r–188v.

Ottosen nos. 14-72-24, 32-57-28, 68-82-38.

16. Commendation of souls—ff. 190r–207v.

rub.: incipiunt comendationes [*sic*] animarum; inc.: [f. 190r] beati inmaculati in uia qui ambulant in lege domini . . .; or.: [f. 206r] tibi domine commendamus animam famuli tui .n. et animas famulorum famularumque tuarum . . . misericordissime pietatis absterge per christum dominum nostrum [*CO* 5884]; or.: [f. 206v] misericordiam tuam domine sancte pater omnipotens sempiterne deus pietatis affectu . . . contemplacionis tue perpetuo sacientur per dominum. requisescant in pace amen.

Ps 118 divided into sections followed by the *Kyrie* and *Pater noster*; Ps 138 followed by [f. 206r] *a porta inferi . . . credo uidere bona domini . . . requiescant in pace amen . . . domine exaudi oracionem meam et clamor meus. HE* 111–114 provides a base text with notes and textual variations, though it is not the exact version contained here.

17. Psalms of the Passion—ff. 209r–215v.

RUB.: incipiunt psalmi de passione.

Pss 21–30.6; Pss 21, 25, 27, 28, and 30.2–6 written in full; Pss 22–24, 26, and 29 in cue form only. Those written in full begin with a dentelle initial (2 line square inset); cues begin with a flourished initial (1 line versal); see *HE* 114–115.

18. Psalter of St. Jerome (with prefatory rubric and prayers)—ff. 215v–234v.

18.1. Prefatory Rubric and Prayer—ff. 215v–216v. RUB.: beatus uero iheronimus in hoc modo psaltherium istud disposuit sicut angelus domini docuit cum per spiritum sanctum porro propter hoc abbreuiatum est quod hii qui sollitudinem huius seculi habent uel homines qui in infirmitatibus iacent aut qui inter longinquum agunt seu qui naufragio nauigant aut qui bellum commissuri sunt contra hostes seu qui militant contra inuidiam diabolorum aut quod uotum uouerit deo cantare integrum psaltherium et non possunt uel qui ieiunant et ieiunio fortiter debilitantur et qui festa uel sollempnia non custodiunt et minime possunt cantare magnum psaltherium et qui animas suas saluas uolunt facere secundum misericordiam dei et uiam eternam uolunt habere assidue cantent hoc psaltherium et possidebunt regnum eternum amen [cf. LEROQUAIS 2:89]; OR.: suscipere digneris domine deus omnipotens istos psalmos consecratos quos ego indignus decantare cupio . . . pro me misero famulo tuo . . . ad ueram penitenciam faciendam omnium peccatorum nostrorum.

18.2. Psalter of St. Jerome and Prayer—ff. 218r–234v. RUB.: incipit psaltherium sancti iheronimi; INC.: uerba mea auribus percipe domine intellige . . .; EXPL.: . . . ne reminiscaris domine delicta nostra uel parentum nostrorum neque uindictam sumas de peccatis nostris. OR.: omnipotens sempiterne deus clementiam tuam suppliciter deprecor ut me famulum tuum . . . et defunctis proficiat sempiternam amen.

EDITION: *HE* 115–122.
BIBLIOGRAPHY: *HE* 115–122.

Binding: s. xvii/xviii; tightback; brown leather over pasteboard; gilt tooled; marbled pastedowns and endpapers.

Owners & Provenance: James Bohn (London, bookseller; 1803–1880); Robert Biddulph Philipps, esq. of Longworth (1798–1864); Bernard Quaritch (1952): donated to the university by a certain Walter L. Darling of Chicago, IL, ca. 1957 according to Corbett. No university records can be found to confirm Darling's donation. Robert Biddulph Philipps indicates that he acquired the manuscript from Bohn in 1845 (or at least Bohn described it then).

Sales & Catalogues: Quaritch, Cat. 699, no. 82.

Former Shelfmark: MS 4 (Notre Dame).

Bibliography: Corbett 1957; Faye and Bond, 186, no. 4; Corbett no. 4; D'Alverny 1981, 106; Gibson 1993, 12–13, 72–73, 100; Boulton 2003, 227 n. 21.

cod. Lat. a. 2

Origin: Low Countries, s. xv² (Bruges).
Content Overview: Book of Hours, use of Rome.

In Latin, on parchment; i +185 ff. +i; generally 110 x 75 mm (page) [see Layout for ruling]; foliated in modern pencil in lower inner margin; front flyleaf is a miniature, approx. s. xviii; ff. 79v, 138v blank but ruled.

Collation: i $+1^{12}$ $+2^{8+2}$ $+3^{8}$ $+4^{8+1}$ $+5-13^{8}$ $+14^{4}$ $+15^{8+1}$ $+16^{8}$ $+17^{8+1}$ $+18-22^{8}$ $+23^{4}$ +i

Quires: Parchment quaternions, F/F, are the predominant quire forms. Quire 1 is a sexternion, F/F; quires 14 and 23 are binions; all quires obey Gregory's Rule. Miniatures were painted on versos of singletons and inserted into the quaternions with the stubs [see Miniatures]. At least eight miniatures may have been removed: between ff. 52 and 53; between ff. 64 and 65; between ff. 69 and 70; between ff. 74 and 75; before f. 80; between ff. 84 and 85; between ff. 92 and 93; between ff. 98 and 99.

Layout:

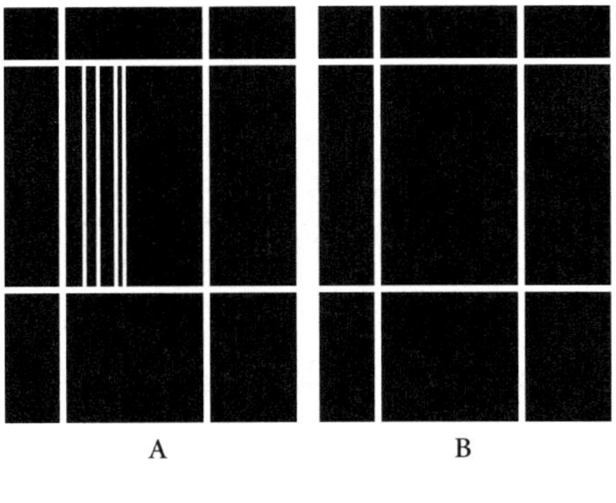

A ff. 1r–12v. Rose ink; 60 x 36 mm; cols. 5.5/3/4/.5/24 mm; 17 lines.
B ff. 13r–185v (except miniature folios). Rose ink; 59–60 x 36 mm; 17 lines.

Pattern B is traced throughout the manuscript in rose ink; single column; writing below top line. Additional verticals in rose ink create Pattern A for the calendar (ff. 1r–12v); four calendric columns (5.5/3/4/.5/24 mm; superfluous vertical, .5 mm in width, traced between cols. 3 and 4); writing below top line. Miniature folios contain no ruling (ff. 13, 21, 33, 116, 139).

Script: A single hand (M1) writes all text in Northern Textualis Formata of the fifteenth century (s. xv^{2}). M1 writes with visible rapidity and displays a marked forking of ascenders and use of decorative hairlines.

Decoration:

I. Rubrication: Rubrics in rose ink; letter heightening of majuscules and cadels in yellow ink.

II. Initials: Foliate, dentelle, and flourished initials occur in hierarchy.

a. Foliate initials (6 line square inset) are painted blue and deep rose; each initial is framed by a contrasting color which alternates (blue/deep rose); vegetal motifs contrast color of initial; leaves are a mixture of both colors.

b. Dentelle initials (2–4 line square inset) are painted throughout the manuscript.

c. Flourished initials (1 line versals) in blue ink with red penwork and gold with blue penwork alternate throughout the text.

III. Line Fillers: Line fillers in gold and blue ink, primarily in the Litany (ff. 128r–133r).

IV. Borders & Frames:

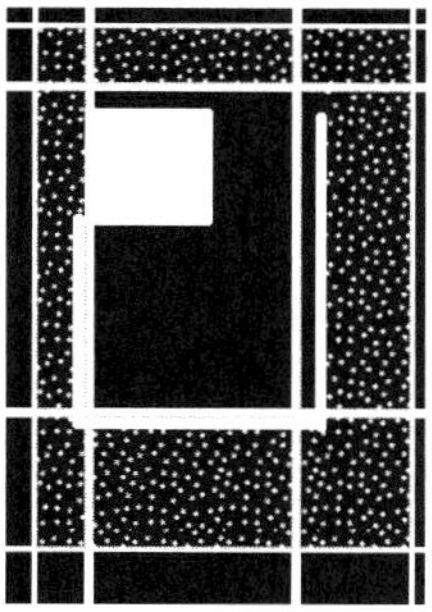

C

D

Text folios facing miniatures contain functional four-margins borders (C); borders comprised of acanthus and vegetal motifs with occasional inhabitants and black and gold rinceaux. The palette is mainly blues, light greens and pinks, golden yellow, and minimal orange. Inhabitants include a cock (f. 14r), a peacock (f. 34r), and a bird (f. 117r). Area to be decorated is defined by lead; text frames within C contained by double baguettes in dentelle style of the three-margins type outlined in black. Acanthus sprays from the outer right baguette in three different configurations: upper and lower; upper, middle, and lower; upper only. Borders on miniature folios (D) have the same composition as C without the integral sprays; f. 33v contains a Roman urn with flowers. Miniatures are enclosed in arch-topped frames (D) contained by double baguettes colored as above. Miniatures are painted on the verso of unruled folios and inserted by stubs into the quires [see Miniatures].

Miniatures: Five arch-topped miniatures remain; painted on the verso, pointing toward Flemish production: Crucifixion (f. 13v); Virgin and Child (f. 21v); Annunciation (f. 33v); Last Judgment (f. 116v); funeral scene (f. 139v).

Calendar: Two pages per month, recto/verso; not composite; dominical letter **a** in rose ink; Roman time marked in blue and gold.

Contents:

1. Calendar (redacted from a Bruges model)—ff. 1r–12v.

The calendar is not composite, but 133 days are filled. There is a strong connection to the dioceses of Tournai and Cambrai as well as elements specific to Bruges. This is likely a redaction of a composite calendar. Several notable feasts pointing toward the southern Netherlands and Flanders are present with the addition of a few English and Welsh saints. It is not improbable that a calendar for the English market, in part, furnished (or contaminated) the model, though localization to Bruges is sufficient.

Written in black ink with graded feasts in rose; notable feasts include: Brigid (Feb. 1), Amand (Feb. 6; rose), Milburga (Feb. 23), Gertrude (Mar. 17), David of Wales (Mar. 1), Waleric (Apr. 1), Brendan (May 17), Helen (May 21), Second Translation of Eligius (Jun. 25; rose), Translation of St. Thomas (Jul. 3; rose), Translation of Thomas Becket (Jul. 7), Magnus (Aug. 19), Bertin (Sept. 5), Gorgonius (Sept. 9), Lambert (Sept. 17), Remigius and Bavo (Oct. 1; rose), Donatian (Oct. 14; rose), Quentin (Oct. 31), Leonard (Nov. 6), Livinius (Nov. 12), Malo (Nov. 15), and Eligius (Dec. 1; rose).

2. Short Hours of the Cross—ff. 14r–20v.

Matins, ff. 14r–15r; Prime, ff. 15r–16r; Terce, f. 16r–v; Sext, ff. 16v–17v; None, ff. 17v–18v; Vespers, ff. 18v–19v; Compline, ff. 19v–20r; *recommendatio*, f. 20v. Each stanza concludes with the usual verse, response, and prayer which are written fully for all hours. For the hymns see *AH* 30: no. 13.

3. Mass of the Virgin—ff. 22r–27v.

rub.: incipit missa beate marie uirginis; **inc.**: introibo ad altare dei ad deum qui letificat . . .

4. Gospel Lessons—ff. 28r–32v.

Standard readings from John (ff. 28r–29r), Luke (ff. 29r–30v), Matthew (ff. 30v–32r), and Mark (f. 32r–v).

5. Hours of the Virgin, use of Rome; *Salue Regina*—ff. 34r–98v.

5.1. Hours of the Virgin, use of Rome—ff. 34r–97v.

rub.: incipiunt hore beate marie uirginis secundum consuetudinem romane ecclesie.

5.1.1. Matins—ff. 34r–52v. **inv.**: aue maria . . .; **hym.**: quem terra ponthus . . .; **ant. ps. 8**: benedicta tu; **lect. i**: in omnibus requiem . . .; **r. i.**: sancta et immaculata . . .

5.1.2. Lauds—ff. 53r–64v. **rub.**: ad laudes de sancta maria; **pss.**: 92, 99, 62, 66, Benedicite, 148, 149, 150; **ant.**: assumpta est maria; **cap.**: uiderunt eam filie syon . . .; **hym.**: o gloriosa domina . . .; **ant. sup. ben.**: beata dei genitrix.

5.1.3. Prime—ff. 65r–69v. **RUB.**: ad primam; **PSS.**: 53, 84, 116; **HYM** : memento salutis auctor . . .; **ANT.**: assumpta est maria; **CAP.**: que est ista . . .; **R.**: dignare me . . .; **V**: da michi uirtutem . . .

5.1.4. Terce—ff. 70r–74v. **RUB.**: ad terciam; **PSS.**: 119, 120, 121; **HYM.**: memento salutis auctor . . .; **ANT.**: maria uirgo assumpta; **CAP.**: et sic in syon . . .; **R.**: diffusa est . . .; **V**: propterea benedixit . . .

5.1.5. Sext—ff. 75r–79r. **RUB.**: ad sextam; **PSS.**: 122, 123, 124; **HYM.**: memento salutis auctor . . .; **ANT.**: in odorem; **CAP.**: et radicaui . . .; **R.**: benedicta tu . . .; **V**: et benedictus fructus . . .

5.1.6. None—ff. 80r–84v. **RUB.**: ad nonam; **PSS.**:125, 126, 127; **HYM.**: memento salutis auctor . . .; **ANT.**: pulchra es . . .; **CAP.**: in plateis sicut cynamomum . . .; **R.**: post partum . . .; **V**: dei genitrix . . .

5.1.7. Vespers—ff. 85r–92v. **RUB.**: ad uesperas; **PSS.**: 109, 112, 121, 126, 147; **ANT.**: dum esset; **CAP.**: ab initio et ante . . .; **HYM.**: aue maris stella . . .; **ANT. SUP. MAGNIF.**: beata mater.

5.1.8. Compline—ff. 93r–97v. **RUB.**: ad completorium; **PSS.**: 128, 129, 130; **HYM.**: memento salutis auctor . . .; **CAP.**: ego mater pulchre . . .; **ANT. SUP. NUNC DIM.**: sub tuum.

5.2. *Salue Regina*—ff. 97v–98v.

RUB.: antiphona de sancta maria; **INC.**: salue regina misericordie . . . post hoc exilium ostende. o clemens o pia o dulcis maria; **V.**: aue maria . . .; **R.**: benedicta tu . . .; **OR.**: omnipotens sempiterne deus qui gloriose uirginis . . . et a morte perpetua liberemur per eundem christum dominum nostrum. amen.

6. Office of the Virgin for Advent—ff. 99r–111v.

7. *Obsecro te* (masculine forms)—ff. 112r–115v.

RUB.: oracio ad mariam uirginem; **INC.**: [f. 112r] obsecro te domina . . . ego sum facturus locuturus aut cogitaturus . . . michi famulo tuo . . .; **EXPL.**: [f. 115v] . . . audi et exaudi me dulcissima maria mater dei et misericordie amen [cf. LEROQUAIS 2:346–347].

8. Penitential Psalms, Litany, and Collects—ff. 117r–138r.

8.1. Penitential Psalms—ff. 117r–127v.

8.2. Litany—ff. 127v–134r.

Martyrs: Stephan, Linus, Cletus, Clement, Cornelius, Cyprian, Laurence, George, Vincent, Fabian, Sebastian, John, Paul, Cosma, Damian, Gervais, Prothais, Lupus, Victor (*cum soc.*), Nichase (*cum soc.*), Quentin (*cum soc.*), Eustace (*cum soc.*), Maurice (*cum soc.*), Denis (*cum soc.*), Donatus, Erasmus (Elmo), Blaise. *Confessors*: Silvester, Leo, Gregory, Ambrose, Jerome, Augustine, Anthony, Nicholas, Martin, Leonard, Bernard, Francis, Louis, Eligius, Giles, Dominic. *Virgins*: Mary Magdalene, Mary of Egypt, Felicitas, Perpetua, Agatha, Agnes, Clare, Anna, Amalberga, Margaret, Barbara, Katherine, Julian, Elizabeth, Ursula, Martha.

8.3. Collects—ff. 134r–138r.

8.3.1. Votive prayers—ff. 134r–135r. RUB.: preces; INC.: saluos fac seruos tuos et ancillas tuas . . . et clamor meus ad te ueniat.

8.3.2. f. 135r–v. RUB.: oratio; INC.: deus cui proprium est misereri et parcere . . . miseratio tue pietatis absoluat per [*CO* 1143].

8.3.3. f. 135v. RUB.: oratio; INC.: exaudi quesumus domine supplicum preces . . . tribuas benignus et pacem [*CO* 2541].

8.3.4. f. 135v. RUB.: oratio; INC.: ineffabilem nobis domine misericordiam tuam . . . pro hiis mereamur eripias per christum [*CO* 3129].

8.3.5. f. 136r. RUB.: oratio; INC.: deus qui culpa offenderis . . . qui pro peccatis nostris mereamur auerte per [*CO* 1511].

8.3.6. f. 136r. RUB.: oratio; INC.: omnipotens sempiterne deus miserere famulo tuo ministro nostro . . . et tota uirtute perficiat per christum dominum [*CO* 3859].

8.3.7. f. 136v. RUB.: oratio; INC.: deus a quo sancta desideria recta consilia . . . tempora sint tua protectione tranquilla [*CO* 1088a].

8.3.8. f. 136v. RUB.: oratio; INC.: ure igne sancti spiritus renes nostros . . . et mundo corde placeamus [*CO* 6025].

8.3.9. ff. 136v–137r. RUB.: oratio; INC.: fidelium deus omnium conditor . . . piis supplicationibus consequantur per christum [*CO* 2684b].

8.3.10. f. 137r. RUB.: oratio; INC.: actiones nostras quesumus domine . . . et per te cepte finiantur per [*CO* 74].

8.3.11. ff. 137r–138r. RUB.: oratio; INC.: omnipotens sempiterne deus qui uiuorum dominaris . . . suorum ueniam consequamur . . . per omnia secula seculorum [*CO* 4064].

9. Office for the Dead, use of Rome—ff. 140r–185r.

OTTOSEN nos. 14-72-24, 46-32-57, 68-28-38.

BINDING: s. xix; tightly bound in black leather; blind tooled; metal studs; two metal clasps; rear cover detached.

OWNERS & PROVENANCE: Acquired by the university from H. P. Kraus; date of acquisition unknown.

SALES & CATALOGUES: H. P. Kraus, Cat. 115, no. 20.

FORMER SHELFMARK: MS 35 (Notre Dame).

BIBLIOGRAPHY: CORBETT no. 35; D'ALVERNY 1981, 106; BOULTON 2003, 227 n. 21.

cod. Lat. a. 3

Origin: England, s. xv.
Content Overview: Book of Hours, use of Sarum.

In Latin, on parchment; ii +80 ff.; generally 110 x 80 mm (page) [see Layout for ruling]; foliated with Arabic numerals in modern pencil.

Collation: ii $+1–3^{8}$ $+4^{1+1+1+8-1}$ $+5^{8}$ $+6^{8-2}$ $+7^{8-1}$ $+8–9^{8}$ $+10^{8+2}$

Quires: Parchment quaternions are the normal quire forms; flyleaves I and II are a bifolium. Quire 4 is comprised of three singletons (ff. 25, 26, 27) bound with a quaternion lacking its first leaf [see Contents 2.2.6]. Quire 6 lacks the third and fifth leaves. Quire 7 lacks the third leaf. Quire 10 is a quaternion inserted into a bifolium comprising f. 72 and the rear pastedown. Quires 1–3 are misbound; the correct sequence is 3–1–2 (Matins begin on f. 17r and conclude on f. 4v) [see Contents 2.1].

Layout:

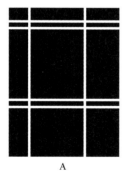

A

A ff. 1r–80v (except f. 72). Ink; 62–65 x 39–40 mm; 13 lines.

Pattern A is traced in brown ink (f. 72 is unruled); single column of text; writing below top line. Prickings are visible in the outer right margins of some folios.

Script: A total of four distinct hands (M1–M4) can be identified. M1 and M2 are scribal bookhands. M2 writes the chief contents of the manuscript (ff. 1r–79r) in a distinctly

English variety of Northern Textualis Formata of the fifteenth century. Representative English features of script for the period abound; M2 displays a preference for box-**a** except after combinations of **c**, **e**, **f**, **g**, **r**, **t**, **x** (similar to Oeser's fourth variant; see Derolez 2003b, 85). M1 writes the text on flyleaves Iv–IIv (Ps 118) and on ff. 79r–80r (*pietate tua quesumus* . . .) in an English variety of Northern Textualis of the same period. Hands M3 and M4 write additional material: M3 writes on f. 52r [see Contents 3], beginning in Textualis executed at a low level and then switching mid-word (*precepisti*, line 3) to Cursiva with a strong Bastarda influence; M3 also adds *oremus* in the upper margin on f. 28r. M4 is the autograph of a John Mekylwode (fl. s. xv), who was active in Suffolk, particularly the Archdeaconry of Sudbury, Fornham St. Martins, and Wyverstone [see Owners & Provenance]. Mekylwode writes his name, an alphabet, 'pen trials' (f. 80v), and other text throughout the manuscript (e.g., flyleaves I–IIr, ff. 72r–v).

Decoration:

I. Rubrication: Rubrics in red ink; letter heightening of majuscules in red ink of different composition.

II. Initials: Dentelle, flourished, and plain initials occur in hierarchy.

a. Dentelle style initials (4–5 line square inset) of low quality are painted on ff. 17r, 42r (unfinished), and 53r (with marginal spray); initials are badly worn and soiled.

b. Flourished initials (2 line square inset) run throughout the manuscript. All flourished initials are blue with red penwork; typical of English production, there is no alternation of the flourished initials.

c. Plain initials (1 line versals) in red and blue ink alternate throughout the manuscript; guide letters remain on flyleaves I–II.

III. Line Fillers: A line filler of low execution in red and black ink occurs on f. 26r.

Contents:

1. Psalm 118 [incomplete]—flyleaves Iv–IIv

inc.: [Iv] <r>etribue seruo tuo uiuifica me . . .; expl.: . . . [IIv] <u>iam iniquitatis amoue a me et de lege tua mi<serere>.

The text is written by M1; spaces for initials and guide letters remain.

2. Hours of the Virgin, use of Sarum; commemorations (*ad laudes*); Short Hours of the Cross (intercalated); *Salue Regina* with verses—ff. 1r–52r.

Since the manuscript has been bound out of order, the text begins imperfectly: inc.: [f. 1r] -pere [*sc.* capere] non poterant tuo gremio contulisti . . .; the description below is presented in order of sense, and the intercalated material is described separately after the *Horae BMV*. This section of the manuscript is mutilated and several texts are incomplete.

2.1. Hours of the Virgin, use of Sarum—ff. 17r–24v, 1r–16v, 30v–50v.

The hymn of Prime (*ueni creator spiritus . . .*) differs from those of the short hours (*memento salutis*). Compline begins and ends imperfectly: INC.: [f. 47r] <conuerte nos> deus salutaris noster et auerte iram tuam a nobis . . .; EXPL.: [f. 50r] . . . graciam tuam quesumus domine mentibus nostris infunde ut qui angel<o>.

RUB.: in honore sancte marie uirginis.

2.1.1. Matins—ff. 17r–24v, 1r–4v. INV.: aue maria . . .; HYM.: quem terra pontus . . .; ANT. PS. 8: benedicta tu; LECT. I: sancta maria uirgo . . .; R. I: sancta et inmaculata . . .

2.1.2. Lauds—ff. 4v–16v. PSS.: 92, 99, 62, 66, Benedicite, 148, 149, 150; ANT.: o admirabile; CAP.: maria uirgo semper letare . . .; HYM.: o gloriosa domina . . .; ANT. SUP. BEN.: o gloriosa dei.

2.1.3. Prime—ff. 30v–35v. RUB.: <ad> primam; PSS.: 53, 116, 117; HYM.: ueni creator spiritus . . .; ANT.: o admirabile; CAP.: in omnibus requiem . . .; R.: aue maria . . .; V.: benedicta tu . . .;

2.1.4. Terce—ff. 36r–39r. RUB.: ad tertiam; PSS.: 119, 120, 121; HYM.: memento salutis; ANT.: quando; CAP.: ab inicio et ante . . .; R.: sancta dei genitrix . . .; V.: intercede pro nobis . . .

2.1.5. Sext—ff. 39v–42r. RUB.: ad sextam; PSS.: 122, 123, 124; ANT.: rubum; CAP.: et sic in syon . . .; R.: post partum uirgo . . .; V.: dei genitrix intercede . . .

2.1.6. None—ff. 42v–45v. RUB.: ad nonam; PSS.: 125, 126, 127; ANT.: germinauit; CAP.: et radicaui in populo . . .; R.: speciosa facta es . . .; V.: in deliciis tuis . . .; V.: dignare me laudare . . .

2.1.7. Vespers [incomplete]—f. 46r–v; RUB.: [f. 45v] ad uesperas; *** HYM.: -reis profer lumen cecis mala . . . [*sc.* aue maris stella]; ANT. SUP. MAGNIF.: sancta.

2.1.8. Compline [incomplete]—ff. 47r–50v. PSS.: 12, 42, 128, 130; ANT.: cum iocunditate; CAP.: sicut synamomum et balsamum . . .; HYM.: uirgo singularis; ANT. SUP. NUNC DIM.: [*null.*].

2.2. Commemorations (*ad laudes*)—ff. 16v, 25r–29v.

Martin is the only named saint in the commemorations; all others are general (e.g., apostles, martyrs, confessors).

2.2.1. Holy Spirit—ff. 16v, 25r. ANT.: ueni sancte spiritus . . .; OR.: deus qui corda fidelium . . . semper consolacione gaudere [*CO* 1666].

2.2.2. Martin—f. 25r–v. ANT.: o martine o pie quam gaudere . . .; OR.: deus qui conspicis quia ex nulla nostra uirtute . . . pontificis contra omnia aduersa muniamur per christum dominum nostrum amen [*CO* 1497a].

2.2.3. Angels—f. 26r–v. RUB.: [f. 25v] de angelis; ANT.: factum est silencium celo . . .; OR.: deus qui miro ordine angelorum . . . uita nostra muniatur per christum dominum nostrum [*CO* 1798].

2.2.4. Apostles—ff. 26v–27r. RUB.: de apostolis; ANT.: tractent enim nos in conciliis et in synagogis . . .; OR.: quesumus omnipotens deus ut beati .n. .n. apostoli tui tuum nobis implorent auxilium . . . etiam periculis eruamur per christum [cf. *CO* 474b].
2.2.5. Martyrs—f. 27r–v. RUB.: de martiribus; ANT.: lauerunt stolas suas et candidas eas fecerunt . . .; OR.: omnipotens sempiterne deus da nobis sanctorum martirum tuorum .n. ita digne . . . afficiamur gaudiis sempiternis per [*CO* 3822].
2.2.6. Confessors [incomplete]—f. 27v. RUB.: de confessoribus; ANT.: sint lumbi uestri precincti et lucerne ardentes in manibus uestris . . .
2.2.7. Relics—f. 28r–v. ANT.: corpora sanctorum in pace sepulta sunt . . .; OR.: propiciare quesumus nobis domine famulis tuis . . . muniamur aduersis per christum [*CO* 4703a].
2.2.8. All Saints [incomplete]—f. 28v. RUB.: de omnibus sanctis; ANT.: omnes electi dei nostri memoramini ante deum ut uestris . . .; OR.: omnium sanctorum tuorum quesumus domine intercessione placatus . . . et remedia sempiterna concede per [cf. *CO* 5308].
2.2.9. Peace—f. 29r–v. RUB.: de pace; ANT.: da pacem domine . . .; OR.: deus a quo sancta desideria recta consilia iusta sunt opera . . . sint tua proteccione tranquilla [*CO* 1088a].

2.3. Short Hours of the Cross (intercalated) [incomplete]—ff. 29v–30v, 35v–36r, 39r–v, 42r–v, 45v.

Matins, ff. 29v–30v; Prime, ff. 35v–36r; Terce, f. 39r–v; Sext, f. 42r–v; None, f. 45v. Verses, responses, and prayers written fully at Matins (incomplete due to mutilation of f. 30). All other repetitions are given in cue form. For the hymns see *AH* 30: no. 13. Vespers, Compline, and the *recommendatio* are lacking.

2.4. *Salue Regina* with verses [incomplete]—ff. 51r–52r.
INC.: dulcis o maria exaudi preces omnium ad te pie clamancium; o pie. V.: funde preces . . .; o mitis. V.: gloriosa dei mater . . .; o pulcra. V.: dele culpas . . .; o dulcis. s. maria . . .; OR.: omnipotens sempiterne deus qui gloriose uirginis . . . et a morte perpetua et subitanca et inprouisa liberemur et ad gaudia eterna perducans per.

The end of the prayer is a variant compared to the Sarum "norm" (cf. LITTLEHALES 1897, lviii–lix).

EDITION: cf. *HE* 63.

3. Prayer from the Office for the Dead (*oratio pro patribus et matribus*)—f. 52r

INC.: [f. 52r] deus qui nos patrem et matrem honerare [*sic*] precepisti miserere quesumus clementer animabus patrum et matrum nostrorum eorumque omnia peccata dimitte nosque eos in eterne claritatis gaudio fac uidere per christum dominum nostrum [*CO* 1903].

The prayer has been added by M3 [see SCRIPT].

4. Penitential Psalms, Gradual Psalms, Litany, and Collects—ff. 53r–80r.

4.1. Penitential Psalms—ff. 53r–65v.

Psalms are written *in toto*; no introductory rubric.

4.2. Gradual Psalms—ff. 65v–69r.

The first twelve psalms are given in cue form only; last three written *in toto*.

4.3. Litany—ff. 69r–77r.

Martyrs: Stephen, Linus, Cletus, Clement, Fabian, Sebastian, Cosma, Damian, Primus, Felician, Denis (*cum soc.*), Victor (*cum soc.*); *Confessors*: Silvester, Leo, Jerome, Augustine, Isidore, Julian, Gildard, Medard, Aubin, Eusebius, Swithun, Birinus; *Virgins*: Mary Magdelene, Mary of Egypt, Magaret, Scholastica, Petronilla, Genevieve, Praxedes, Soteris, Prisca, Tecla, Afra, Edith.

The Litany is one of the "Sarum Lenten litanies" (see Pfaff 2009, 430–434). The invocation of saints is identical to those listed for *Feria secunda in Quadregesima* in the Sarum Breviary of 1531 (see *SB* 2:251). The collects are those found in *SB* 2:254–255 (see also *HE* 97 n. 9); 4.4.7 was written by M1, but the others by M2.

4.4. Collects—ff. 77r–80r.

4.4.1. f. 77r–v. inc.: deus cui proprium est misereri semper et parcere . . . miseratio tue pietatis absoluat per christum dominum [*CO* 1143].

4.4.2. ff. 77v–78r. inc.: omnipotens sempiterne deus qui facis mirabilia magna solus pretende super famulos tuos et super cunctas congregaciones illis commissas . . . perpetuum eis rorem tue benedicionis infunde [*CO* 3938c].

4.4.3. f. 78r. inc.: deus qui caritatis dona per gratiam . . . tota dilectione perficiat [*CO* 1483].

4.4.4. f. 78v. rub.: require istam orationem sequentem ad matutinas [*oratio* on f. 29r–v]. oratio; inc.: deus a quo sancta desideria [*CO* 1088a].

4.4.5. f. 78v. inc.: ineffabilem misericordiam tuam quesumus domine clementer . . . pro hiis meremur benignus eripias [*CO* 3129].

4.4.6. ff. 78v–79r. inc.: fidelium deus omnium conditor . . . piis supplicationibus consequantur [*CO* 2684b].

4.4.7. ff. 79r–80r. inc.: pietate tua quesumus domine nostrorum solue uincula . . . et omnibus fidelibus defunctis in terra uiuentium uitam et requiem eternam concede per eundem christum dominum nostrum amen [*CO* 4227].

Binding: s. xv^2; tawed skin over boards; leather strap (detached) with metal snap; likely a girdle binding due to the presence of yaps.

Owners & Provenance: A John Mekylwode has written his name on ff. 72v and 80v. John Mekylwode is mentioned in wills and probates contained in the Register Baldwyne, which localizes him to the archdeaconry of Sudbury. He was active in Stowmarket, Fornham, and likely Wyverstone from at least 1441 until his death in 1462. A Henry Awnselme of

Wyverstone names Mekylwode as his brother in his will on 15 February 1461/62 (Baldwyne 1:488, no. 1402, and repeated 490, no. 1408). Mekylwode's own probate (*var.* Mekylwoode) does not give a place of residence, but was proved at Stowmarket on 13 October 1462, and his wife Isabel was the executrix (Baldwyne 2:81, no. 140). In addition to Henry, Mekylwode also served as an executor for William Knotyng of Stowmarket in February of 1441 (Baldwyne 1:40–41, no. 103). Date and source of acquisition by the university are unknown.

Former Shelfmark: MS 66 (Notre Dame).

cod. Lat. a. 4

Origin: England, s. xiv^{2}.
Content Overview: Statuta Angliae.

In Latin and French (one line of English), on parchment; ii +168 ff. +ii; generally 140 x 105 mm (page) [see Layout for ruling]; medieval flyleaves are numbered as ff. 1 and 168, text begins on f. 2r; foliated in modern pencil; ff. 131v–133v, 155v blank.

Collation: iii +1^{10} +2^{8-2} +3^{8-1} +4–8^{8} +9–12^{12} +13^{10} +14^{12} +15^{14} +16^{10} +17^{10-1} +iii

Quires: The manuscript is structured irregularly using a variety of parchment quire forms. Quires 1, 13, 16, and 17 are quinions, F/F. Quires 2–8 are quaternions, F/F. Quires 9–12 and 14 are sexternions, F/F. Quire 15 is comprised of seven bifolia, F/F. Quire 2 lacks the fourth and fifth leaves; quire 3 lacks the first leaf; quire 17 lacks the tenth leaf.

Catchwords: Horizontal catchwords in the lower right margins except quires 2, 14–17; catchword for quire 11 (f. 99v) rubbed out; all correspond.

Layout:

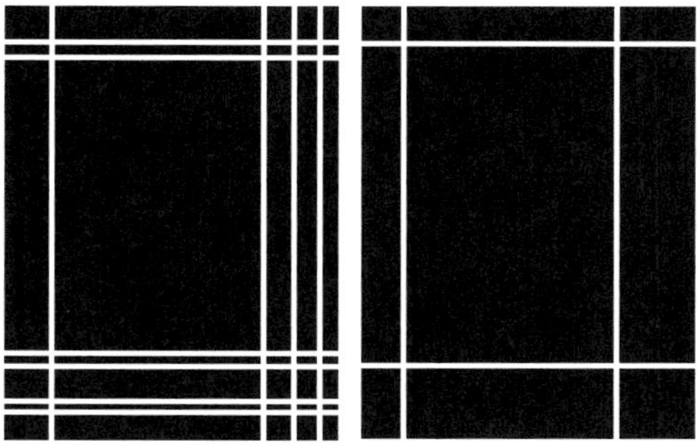

A B

A ff. 2r–148r. Combined technique; 105 x 72 mm; 21–26 lines.
B ff. 149r–167v. Combined technique; 109 x 67 mm; 19–21 lines.

Pattern A is traced on ff. 2r–148r in lead and brown crayon in variable forms; single column; writing below top line; prickings for vertical bounding lines occasionally visible. Pattern A is faded and disrupted by trimming throughout to various degrees. Pattern **B** is traced in brown crayon and ink on ff. 149r–167v; single column; writing below top line; prickings visible often at the intersection of vertical and horizontal bounding points.

Script: Three scribal bookhands (M1–M3) write Anglicana (Cursiva Antiquior) in brown ink. Three divisions of labor appear: M1 writes ff. 2r–148r, M2 writes 149r–155r, and M3 writes 156r–167v. A later addition (s. xv) in Anglicana is written in black ink on f. 148r by M4; another addition written by M5 in Anglicana (s. xv) in black ink on f. 135v (in English).

Decoration:

I. Rubrication: Rubrics in brown ink by respective text hands in larger script; paraph marks alternate in red and blue ink throughout the manuscript (red ink only on ff. 156r–160r).

II. Initials: Flourished and plain initials occur outside hierarchy.

a. Flourished initials (2–3 lines square inset) divide instruments, chapters, and tracts alternating in red and blue with contrasting penwork up to f. 141r; another flourished initial (5 line square inset) by a different painter in red ink with brown penwork on f. 149r.

b. Plain initials (2 line square inset) in red ink are painted on ff. 157r–165r.

Contents:

1. Magna Carta—ff. 2r–9v.

In Latin; 25 Edward I; *SR* 1: charters, 33–36.

2. Carta de Foresta—ff. 10r–14r.

In Latin; 25 Edward I; *SR* 1:120–124.

3. Provisions of Merton—ff. 14r–17v.

In Latin; 20 Henry III; *SR* 1:1–4.

4. Statute of Marlborough—ff. 17v–26v.

In Latin; 52 Henry III; *SR* 1:19–25.

5. Statute of Gloucester—ff. 27r–33r.

In French; 6 Edward I; *SR* 1:45–50; cf. Contents 21, and Sutherland 1963, 190.

6. Exposition of the Statute of Gloucester—f. 33r.

In Latin; 6 Edward I; *SR* 1:50.

7. Statute for religious men—ff. 33r–34r.

In Latin; 7 Edward I; *SR* 1:51.

8. *Quia Emptores*—ff. 34r–35v.

In French; 18 Edward I; *SR* 1:106.

9. Statutes of Westminster the First—ff. 35v–54v.

In French; 3 Edward I; *SR* 1:26–39.

10. Statutes of Westminster the Second—ff. 55r–92r.

In Latin; 13 Edward I; *SR* 1:71–95.

11. Lists of chapters—ff. 92v–97r.

Magna Carta (ff. 92v–93r); *Stat. Westm. prim.* (ff. 93r–94r); *Stat. Westm. sec.* (ff. 94r–95v); Provisions of Merton (ff. 95v); Statute of Marlborough (ff. 96r–v); *Stat. Glouc.* (ff. 96v–97r).

12. Statute of merchants—ff. 97r–100r.

In French; 13 Edward I; *SR* 1:53–54.

13. Statute of Winchester—ff. 100v–104v.

In French; 13 Edward I; *SR* 1:96–98.

14. Statute for religious men—ff. 104v–105v.

In Latin; 7 Edward I; *SR* 1:51.

15. Statute of Waste—ff. 105v–107r.

In Latin; 20 Edward I; *SR*: 1:109–110.

16. Statute of Champerty—f. 107r–v.

In French; *SR*: 1:216 [see Contents 16].

17. Statute concerning conspirators—ff. 107v–108r.

In Latin; here, presented as a separate instrument; *SR*: 1:216 [see Contents 15].

18. Provision for the day in leap year—f. 108r–v.

In Latin; 40 Henry III; *SR* 1:7.

19. Articles on the charters—ff. 108v–114v.

In French; 28 Edward I; cf. *SR* 1:136–141.

20. Statute of persons to be put in assizes and juries—ff. 114v–115v.

In Latin; 21 Edward I; *SR* 1:113.

21. Statute of Gloucester—ff. 115v–119r.

In Latin; see SUTHERLAND 1963, 190–193 for text and brief introduction; cf. CONTENTS 5.

22. Statutes of Exeter—ff. 119r–122r.

In French; *SR* 1:210–212.

23. Statutes of the Exchequer—ff. 122r–127v.

In French; *SR* 1:197–198.

24. Statute of fines—ff. 128r–131r.

In Latin; 27 Edward I; *SR* 1:126–130, but lacking the preamble (text begins at *SR* 1:128).

25. Assize of bread and ale [incomplete]—f. 134r–v.

In Latin; *SR* 1:199–200.

26. Carta Mercatoria—ff. 135r–141r.

In Latin; Carta Mercatoria of 1303; see GRAS 1918, 259–264 for text.

27. Various—ff. 141r–148r.

INC.: [f. 141r] sictum [*sic*] est de magna carta statuta de mertone statutum de marlberge gloucestri primis et de ultimis statutibus westmonasterii una cum capitulis nunc dicendum est de eorum notabilitatibus dampna in triplo in uasto . . .; EXPL.: [f. 148r] . . . congnoscere [*sic*] non obstante regia prohibicione si porrgatur [*sic*].

Includes the following as underlined headings: dampna grauia (f. 142r); prisona unius anni (f. 142r–v); prisona duorum annorum (ff. 142v–143r); prisona trium annorum (f. 143r); prisona quadraginta dierum (f. 143r); prisona dimidii anni (f. 143r–v); prisona iterata et uoluntaria (ff. 143v–144r); secta regis (f. 144r–v); in quibus casibus procedendum est ad iudicium post magnam districtionem (f. 144v); in quibus casibus procedendum ad inquisitionem post magnam districtionem (ff. 144v–146v); regia prohibicio (sub hac forma layci . . .) (ff. 146v–147r) preceding the Statute of Circumspecte Agatis, see *SR* 1:101; Statute of Circumspecte Agatis (ff. 147r–148r), *SR* 1:101–102, 13 Edward I; Statute of Breaking Prisons (f. 148r) added in black ink by a later hand [see SCRIPT], *SR* 1:113, 23 Edward I (1 Edw. 2 stat. 2).

28. Statutes of Westminster (*4 Edw. 3*)—ff. 149r–155r.

In French; 4 Edward III; *SR* 1:261–265.

29. Statute of Ireland concerning coparceners—ff. 156r–157r.

In Latin; 20 Henry III; *SR* 1:5.

30. Statute concerning Bakers, etc.—ff. 157r–159v.

In Latin; *SR* 1:202–204 [see CONTENTS 34].

31. *De diuisione denariorum*—f. 159v.

In Latin; *SR* 1:204.

32. Statute concerning the selling of flour—f. 160r–v.

In Latin; here, presented as a separate instrument, but often included with the *Stat. de Pistor. etc.* [see CONTENTS 30]; *SR* 1:204 n. 15.

33. Statute concerning Wards and Reliefs—ff. 160v–161v.

In French; *SR* 1:228.

34. *Tractatus de antiquo dominico corone*—ff. 161v–162v.

INC.: [f. 161v] licet in antiquo dominico corone non currat aliud breue nisi paruum de recto clausum . . .; EXPL.: [f. 162v] . . . nisi forte ius habuit in aliqua cote secundum consuetudinem maneri et cetera.

HARWOOD 1866, xviii–xix contains the Latin text and attributes it to Anger de Ripon.

35. *Modus diuersarum settarum et diuersorum presbyterum* [*ut uid.*]—ff. 162v–165r.

INC.: [f. 162v] en plee de terre adeprimes uue essoign et primes ueue de terre . . .; EXPL.: [f. 165r] . . . ou il perdera grenoses issues de iour en iour taunt que il uiegne et cetera.

36. View of Frankpledge—ff. 165r–167r.

In French; *SR* 1:246.

37. Statute of Gavelet in London—f. 167r–v.

In Latin; *SR* 1:222.

BINDING: s. xviii–xix; white leather (possibly pigskin) over boards; gilt spine title.

OWNERS & PROVENANCE: Henry Faryndon (s. xv/xvi); Willyam Maule (*fort.* s. xvi); John Prinn (1686–1743); Quaritch (1962); date and source of acquisition by the university are unknown.

SALES & CATALOGUES: Sotheby's, 27 February 1962, lot 487; Quaritch, Cat. 833, no. 18.

FORMER SHELFMARKS: Prinn Library, Stat. E. i; MS 25 (Notre Dame).

BIBLIOGRAPHY: CORBETT no. 25; BAKER 1985, no. 160.

cod. Lat. a. 5

Origin: France, s. xiii^{1}.
Content Overview: Peter Riga, *Aurora.*

In Latin, on parchment; ii +178 ff. +ii; generally 157 x 98 mm (page) [see Layout for ruling]; paper flyleaves; foliated in modern pencil with Arabic numerals.

Collation: ii $+1\text{–}19^{8} +20^{10} +21\text{–}22^{8}$ +ii

Quires: Parchment quaternions, H/H, are the normal forms; quire 20 is a quinion, H/H; all quires obey Gregory's Rule. The parchment is not well scraped; many hair sides are distinctive in their abundance of black hair; numerous imperfections and end cuts visible (e.g., ff. 14, 15, 58, 110, 111). The manuscript has been trimmed; fire damage is present on ff. 1–2.

Catchwords: Horizontal catchwords in black ink are centered in the lower margin (except quire 22); stylized with red ink; all correspond.

Layout:

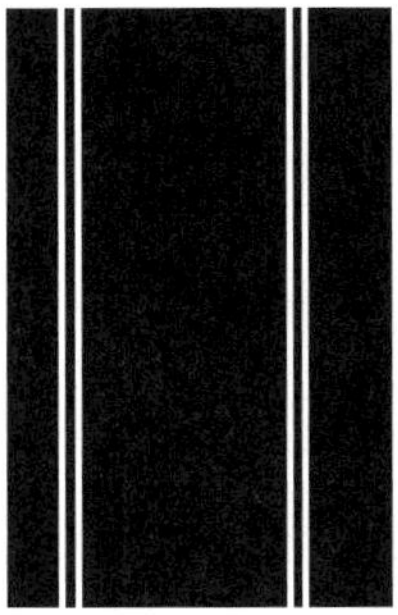
A1

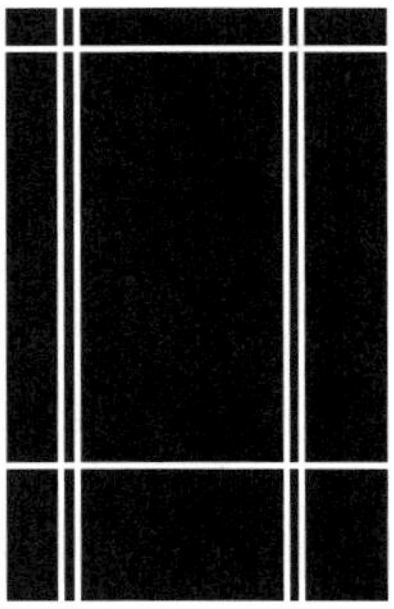
A2

A ff. 1r–178v. Lead; 110 x 57 mm; 39 lines.

Pattern **A** is traced in lead; single column; writing above top line; prickings visible in upper and lower margins for vertical bounding lines, and in the right margin for horizontals. Double verticals to the left encapsulate the majuscule beginning each line of verse. Horizontals are often traced so lightly, the page appears as **A1**; when traced with more pressure, **A2** is visible. Ink dots are drawn for each line along the inner vertical bounding line on the right. In the *Actus Apostolorum* section (ff. 165r–178v) the final letter for each rhyming hexameter is placed between the right verticals and connected with red lines.

Script: The text is written in a rapid Northern Textualis of the thirteenth century. A later hand (s. xvi^{ex}) adds ownership marks and acquisition information of the Jesuit Collège-Agen on ff. 1r and 2r [see Owners & Provenance].

Decoration:
I. Rubrication: Rubrics and *tituli* in red ink; majuscules in red ink on ff. 1r–2r.
II. Initials: Flourished and plain initials occur in hierarchy.
a. Flourished initials (3–4 line square inset) in red and blue ink with contrasting penwork occur on ff. 1r–v, 2r, 23r, 59v, 63r, 70v, 71v, 79r, 91r, 97v, 108r, 110v, 114r, 120r, 139v, 159r, 165r. Initials with descenders are often 4+2 line stepped insets (e.g., f. 2r); overflow occurs with ascenders and descenders. Flourished initials begin major divisions of the work.
b. Plain initials (2–3 line square inset; 1 line versals) alternate in red and blue ink throughout the manuscript. Initials with descenders are often 2+3 line stepped insets (e.g., f. 34r), or 1+2 line stepped insets (e.g., ff. 26r, 39v); forms of **l** are 1 line standing with overflow (e.g., ff. 8r, 49r); forms of **i** may be 3–4 square insets (e.g., f. 15v) or 5 line square insets taken up 1 line (e.g., f. 137r). Plain initials are also used as versals (e.g., f. 90v; variants as 1+2 line stepped insets also occur).

Contents:

1. Peter Riga, *Aurora*—ff. 1v–178v.

Beichner 1965, 1:lii posits that the text of this manuscript represents a stage between the second and third medieval editions of the *Aurora*, or an incomplete copy of the third edition.

Order of books: "A Teachers Preface" [Beichner 1965, 1:4–7]; "Peter Riga's Preface" [Beichner 1965, 1:7–8]; Gn; Ex; Lv; Nm; Dt; Ios; Idc; Rt; 1–4 Rg (3 and 4 undivided); Tb; Dn; Idt; Esr (explicit rubric for 4 Rg); 1–2 Mcc; Prol. to Gospels; Gospels; *Recapitulationes*; Act.

Edition: Beichner 1965.
Bibliography: Beichner 1965; Stegmüller 6823–6825; Dinkova-Bruun 2007; Dinkova-Bruun 2011; Dinkova-Bruun 2012, esp. 185–189.

Binding: The manuscript is now detached from its binding; s. xvii; calf; blind tooled; three raised bands.

Owners & Provenance: Bernard Carles of Toulouse (fl. 1599); Jesuit Collège-Agen (Lot-et-Garonne); Paris, Collège de Clermont (Collège Louis-le-Grand); Gerard Meerman

(1722–1771); John Meerman; Sir Thomas Phillipps (1792–1872); W. J. Leighton (ca. 1912). Acquired by the university in August 1954 from B. Rosenthal in support of Beichner's then in-progress critical edition.

Two ownership marks name the Jesuit Collège-Agen (Lot-et-Garonne) as the owner beginning in 1599 (ff. 1r, 2r). The manuscript was donated to the college by a certain Bernard Carles of Toulouse: *dono datus collegio Aginnensi societatis Iesu a Bernardo Carles bibliopola Tolos. 1599* (f. 2r); the bookseller has not been identified further (see Corbett [1978], 50). According to Meerman's note as well as Saugrain 1764, 134, no. 402, the manuscript was at Valliscaulium (Val-des-Choux), though this cannot be substantiated. Meerman, 4:92, no. 539 and Saugrain 1764, 134, no. 402 also specify 174 folios rather than 178. However, Phillipps' catalogue states that Phillipps MS 1726 and Meerman, 4:92, no. 539 are the same manuscript (Phillipps no. 1726); neither Phillipps number nor ownership mark appear in the manuscript. Temple Scott states explicitly that Phillipps' *Aurora* contained the ownership marks mentioned above, and transcribes them (see Scott 1897, no. 4044). Further ownership and provenance marks have been erased on flyleaf I and f. 178v.

Sales & Catalogues: Luchtmans, Van Cleef, Schurbeer, 8 June 1824, lot 539; Quaritch, Cat. 164, no. 132; Sotheby's, 10 June 1896, lot 114; Quaritch, Cat. 211, no. 26; Sotheby's, 11 December 1903, lot 594; Leighton 1912, no. 245; Sotheby's, 27 October 1919, lot 2605; Maggs Bros., Cat. 395, no. 74; ibid., Cat. 404, no. 7; J. Rosenthal, Cat. 90, no. 178; L'Art Ancien, Cat. 37, no. 14; B. Rosenthal, Cat. 1, no. 78.

Former Shelfmarks: Paris, Collège de Clermont, no. 402 (Saugrain 1764); Phillipps MS 1726; MS 5 (Notre Dame), which Beichner cites as MS 2, though it does not correspond to Corbett, De Ricci, or Faye and Bond.

Bibliography: Scott 1897, no. 4044; Phillipps no. 1726; Munby 3:25–26, 144, 148; Beichner 1956, 143 n. 29; Faye and Bond, 186, no. 5; Beichner 1965, lii; Corbett no. 5; D'Alverny 1981, 106; Lapidge 2006, 32–33, 40 n. 72; Nolan 2006, 2.

cod. Lat. a. 6

Origin: Low Countries, s. xv[2] (Bruges).
Content Overview: Book of Hours, use of Rome.

In Latin, on parchment; ii +162 ff. +i; generally 86 x 63 mm (page) [see Layout for ruling]; ff. 1–2 were previously flyleaves; f. 1 formerly a pastedown; calendar begins on f. 3r; foliated in Arabic numerals with modern pencil; a folio was skipped between ff. 81 and 82, resulting in (now) f. 81a; ff. 1v–2v, 82v, 161v, 162r–v blank but ruled.

Collation: iv $+1^{4-1}$ $+2^{8-1}$ $+3^{8}$ $+4^{6}$ $+5^{8}$ $+6^{6}$ $+7–8^{8}$ $+9^{8-2}$ $+10–11^{8}$ $+12^{6-1}$ $+13–19^{8}$ $+20^{4}$ $+21^{6}$ $+22^{6}$ $+23^{8-2+2}$ +i

Quires: Parchment quaternions, F/F, are the predominant quire forms, though ternions and binions are also used. Quires 1 and 2 comprising the calendar are a binion followed by a quaternion; this irregular structure is present in another book of hours produced in the same workshop (see Wieck 2007, 201 for his collation of Paris, *Les Enluminures*, BOH 24) [see Borders & Frames]. Quire 1 lacks the first leaf; quire 2 lacks the fifth; quire 9 lacks the second and third leaves; quire 12 lacks the first leaf. Quire 23 (ff. 155–162) is structured irregularly and contains additional content: a bifolium (ff. 160–161) has been inserted asymmetrically between ff. 159 and 162, which is part of a quaternion that lacks the first leaf, and the last leaf was canceled; text of quire 23 is now incomplete. At least thirteen miniatures were inserted and later removed: before f. 13; between ff. 16 and 17; before f. 21; before f. 27; between ff. 45 and 46; between ff. 59 and 60; between ff. 63 and 64; between ff. 67 and 68; between 71 and 72; before f. 83; between ff. 91 and 92; between ff. 110 and 111.

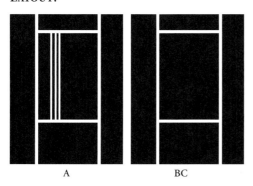

Layout:

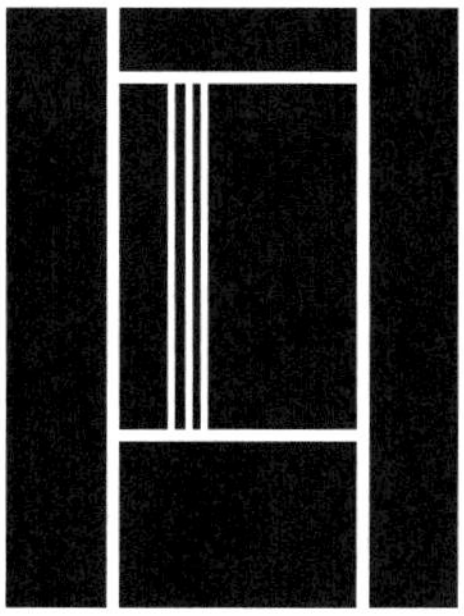
A

BC

A ff. 3r–12v. Black and rose ink; cols. 8/3/1/22 mm; 51 x 35 mm; 16 lines.
B ff. 13r–20v. Rose ink; 51 x 35 mm; 16 lines.
C ff. 1r–2v, 21r–162v. Black ink; 51 x 35 mm; 16 lines.

Pattern **C** is the normal pattern traced in black ink throughout the manuscript; single column; writing below top line; ink has faded to varying degrees. Pattern **A** used for the calendar adds three verticals in rose ink to **C** to create four calendric columns (8/3/1/22 mm). Pattern **B** is traced in rose ink on ff. 13r–20v; single column; writing below top line; Contents 2 and 3 align with **B**. Prickings for vertical bounding lines occasionally are visible in the upper and lower margins; most lost due to trimming.

Script: Two scribal bookhands (M1–M2) write all texts in the manuscript. M1 writes a Southern Textualis Formata (Rotunda) of the Flemish variety on ff. 1r–154v. M2 writes text on ff. 155r–161r rapidly in a Semitextualis by a Northern hand (M2), admitting occasional cursive forms for **g**.

Decoration:
I. Rubrication: Rubrics in red ink added by M1.
II. Initials: Foliate and dentelle initials occur in hierarchy.
a. Foliate initials (5 line square inset) in blue with white penwork, and tendrils in blue and red with white penwork begin the major sections of the text.
b. Dentelle initials (2 line square inset; 1 line versals) run throughout the texts in a hierarchical fashion with alternating backgrounds of red or blue. When the 2 line type is in the left margin, floral sprays form piece borders.
III. Line Fillers: Line fillers of the dentelle style occur in the Litany on ff. 104r–107r.
IV. Borders & Frames:

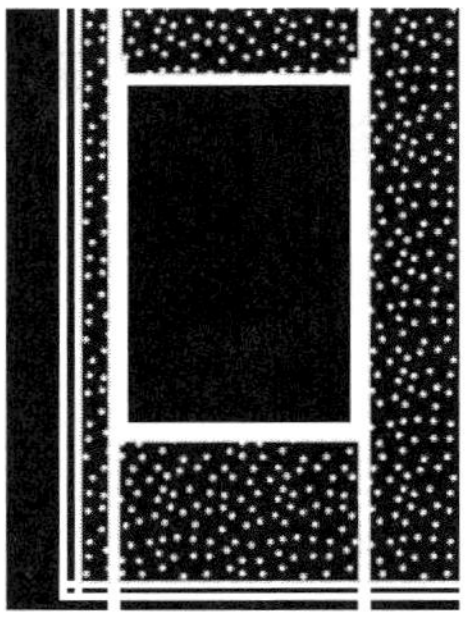

D

Four-margins functional borders (**D**) are painted on folios beginning major texts. Area to be decorated is frame-ruled in light red ink with double lines; text frames contained by a single bar three-margins type of gold outlined in black. Borders are acanthus and floral motifs with black and gold rinceaux inhabited by numerous creatures; palette is comprised of mainly blues and gold for the acanthus with some dark red; floral motifs in reds, lilac, dark pink, light greens with some purple. Creatures include butterflies, snails, an owl, various birds, a monkey, and a peacock. All creatures are executed in a dark brown color, but the peacock is blue, green, gold, brown, black, and red. Foliate initials extend beyond text frame into the border. All decoration, color selection, and patterns for the inhabited borders are identical to those found in another book of hours described in Wieck 2007, 198–204 (no. 20; Paris, *Les Enluminures*, BOH 24) attributed to the workshop of the so-called Master of the Dresden Prayerbook. Wieck 2007, 198 states that the leaves "were illuminated by an artist who trained under (or was at least heavily influenced) by the Master of the Dresden Prayerbook."

Miniatures: Miniatures have been excised, but were inserted with the illustrations on the verso; at least thirteen miniatures have been excised.

Calendar: Two pages per month; recto/verso; not composite; lacking January and September; leaf added for January; dominical letter **a** in red ink; Roman time not marked.

Contents:

1. Calendar (minimalist; Bruges model)—ff. 1r–12v.

Minimal calendar based on one from Bruges, but redacted thoroughly to appear general. The translation of St. Thomas (Jul. 3) is graded in red ink, which is a Bruges idiosyncrasy. Basil (Jun. 14; red) and Donatian (Oct. 14) are two other popular Bruges feasts which appear. Bernardino of Siena appears supporting a *post* 1450 date.

2. Hours of the Cross—ff. 13r–16v.

Matins, ff. 13r–14r; Prime, f. 14r–v; Terce, ff. 14v–15r; Sext, f. 15r–v; None, f. 15v; Vespers, ff. 15v–16r; Compline, f. 16r–v; *recommendatio*, f. 16v. Each stanza concludes with the usual verse, response, and prayer, which are written fully at Matins and Prime. All other repetitions are given in cue form. For the hymns see *AH* 30: no. 13.

3. Hours of the Holy Spirit—ff. 17r–20v.

Matins, f. 17r–v; Prime, ff. 17v–18r; Terce, f. 18r–v; Sext, ff. 18v–19r; None, f. 19r; Vespers, f. 19v; Compline, ff. 19v–20r; *recommendatio*, f. 20r–v. Each stanza concludes with the usual verse and prayer, which are written fully at Matins (verse fully at Prime). Other repetitions are given in cue form.

4. Mass of the Virgin—ff. 21r–26v.

rub.: incipit missa beate marie uirginis; **inc.**: [f. 21r] introitus. salue sancta parens . . .

Text lacks *introibo ad altare dei* . . . and *confiteor deo celi et beate marie uirgini et omnibus sanctis* . . . which usually precede the introit.

5. Hours of the Virgin, use of Rome [incomplete]; *Salue Regina*—ff. 27r–82v.

The *Horae* are followed by *Salue Regina*; seasonal variants with rubrics appear throughout; Prime and Compline are incomplete.

5.1. Hours of the Virgin, use of Rome [incomplete]—ff. 27r–81Ar.
RUB.: incipiunt hore beate marie uirginis secundum usum romanum.

5.1.1. Matins—ff. 27r–45v. RUB.: ad matutinas; INV.: aue maria . . .; HYM.: quem terra pontus . . .; ANT. PS. 8: benedicta tu; LECT. I: in omnibus requiem . . .; R. I.: sancta et immaculata . . .

5.1.2. Lauds—ff. 46r–57r. RUB.: ad laudes; PSS.: 92, 99, 62, 66, Benedicite, 148, 149, 150; ANT.: assumpta; CAP.: uiderunt eam filie syon . . .; HYM.: o gloriosa domina . . .; ANT. SUP. BEN.: beata.

5.1.3. Prime [incomplete]—ff. 58r–59v. PSS.: 84, 116; CAP.: que est ista . . .; R.: dignare me . . .

5.1.4. Terce—ff. 60r–63v. RUB.: ad terciam; PSS.: 119, 120, 121; HYM.: memento salutis auctor . . .; ANT.: maria uirgo; CAP.: et sic in syon . . .; R.: diffusa est . . .; V: propterea benedixit . . .

5.1.5. Sext—ff. 64r–67v. RUB.: ad sextam; PSS.: 122, 123, 124; HYM.: memento salutis auctor . . .; ANT.: in odorem; CAP.: et radicaui . . .; R.: benedicta tu . . .

5.1.6. None—ff. 68r–71v. RUB.: ad nonam; PSS.:125, 126, 127; HYM.: memento salutis auctor . . .; ANT.: pulcra; CAP.: in platheis sicut cinamomum . . .; R.: post partum . . .

5.1.7. Vespers—ff. 72r–78v. RUB.: ad uesperas; PSS.: 109, 112, 121, 126, 147; ANT.: dum esset; CAP.: ab initio et ante . . .; HYM.: aue maris stella . . .; ANT. SUP. MAGNIF.: beata mater.

5.1.8. Compline [incomplete]—ff. 79r–81Ar. PSS.: 129, 130; HYM.: memento salutis auctor . . .; CAP.: ego mater pulcre . . .; ANT. SUP. NUNC DIM.: sub tuum.

5.2. *Salue Regina*—ff. 81Ar–82r.
RUB.: ad salutantum [*sic*] uirginem mariam; INC.: salue regina misericordie . . . post hoc exilium ostende. o clemens o pia o dulcis uirgo maria; V.: aue maria . . .; R.: benedicta tu . . .; OR. omnipotens sempiterne deus qui gloriose uirginis . . . et a morte perpetua liberemur per christum dominum nostrum. amen.

6. Office of the Virgin for Advent—ff. 83r–91v.

7. Penitential Psalms, Litany, and Collects—ff. 92r–110v

7.1. Penitential Psalms—ff. 92r–103v.

7.2. Litany—ff. 103v–108r.

Martyrs: Stephan, Laurence, Vincent, Fabian, Sebastian, John, Cosma, Damian, Gervais, Protais, Christopher. *Confessors*: Silvester, Gregory, Ambrose, Jerome, Augustine, Leonard, Bernard, Francis, Dominic. *Virgins et al.*: Mary Magdalene, Mary of Egypt, Anna, Agatha, Claire, Margaret, Barbara, Katherine, Elizabeth, Ursula, Martha.

7.3. Collects—ff. 109r–110v.

7.3.1 f. 109r–v. RUB.: oratio; INC.: deus cui proprium est misereri semper et parcere . . . miseratio tue pietatis absolua [*sic*] [*CO* 1143].

7.3.2. f. 109v. RUB.: oratio; INC.: exaudi quesumus domine supplicium preces . . . indulgentiam tribuas benignus et pacem [*CO* 2541].

7.3.3. f. 109v. RUB.: oratio; INC.: ineffabilem nobis domine misericordiam tuam clementer . . . quas pro hiis meremur eripias [*CO* 3129].

7.3.4. ff. 109v–110r. RUB.: oratio; INC.: deus qui culpa offenderis penitenti amplacaris preces . . . qui pro peccatis nostris meremur auerte [*CO* 1511].

7.3.5. f. 110r. RUB.: oratio; INC.: actiones nostras quesumus domine aspirando perueniet . . . a te semper incipiant et per te cepta finiatur [*CO* 74]

7.3.6. f. 110r–v. RUB.: oratio; INC.: omnipotens deus qui uiuorum dominaris . . . delictorum suorum ueniam consequantur per christum [*CO* 4064].

8. Office for the Dead, use of Rome—ff. 111r–142v.

OTTOSEN nos. 14-72-24, 46-32-57, 68-28-38.

9. "Variant" Psalter of St. Jerome [incomplete]—ff. 143r–151v.

RUB.: incipit psalterium sancti iheronimi; INC.: [f. 143r] beatifica domine peccatricem animam meam et concede michi . . .; EXPL.: [f. 151v] . . . me de tenerbis et umbra mortis.

The *incipit* appears to be a variant of *Letifica domine peccatricem animam meam* (see LEROQUAIS, *Psautiers* 2:227), which is found in San Marino, Huntington Library, HM 1180, ff. 79–86v. The *beatifica* variant is also found in Firenze, Biblioteca Riccardiana, Ricc. 379/3; Palermo, Biblioteca centrale, MS liturg. I. A. 14 and MS liturg. I. A. 17; Roma, Biblioteca Casanatense, MS 501; and the manuscript described in WIECK 2007 (now in a private collection, USA).

10. *Obsecro te* [incomplete]—ff. 152r–154v.

INC.: [f. 152r] . . . mater orphanorum consolatio desolatorum . . . ego sum facturus locuturus aut cogitaturus . . . et michi indigna [*sic*] famula [*sic*] tua [*sic*] .n. impetres . . .; EXPL.: [f. 154v] . . . uitam honestam et honorabilem michi tribuat et uictoriam [cf. LEROQUAIS 2:346–347].

Both masculine and feminine forms are used; the feminine forms are syntactically incorrect.

11. Ps.-Augustine, *Oratio* [incomplete]—ff. 155r–161r.

INC.: [f. 155r] <mun>dum peccata relaxare afflictos redimere in carcere positos soluere . . .; EXPL.: [f. 161r] . . . et uerum me perducere digneris qui uiuis et regnas in secula seculorum. amen.

Masculine forms are used throughout the prayer on ff. 155r, 157r–v, 159v, 160r–v; onomastic cues in red ink.

Binding: s. xix; calf over pasteboard; blind tooled; gilt spine.

Owners & Provenance: A 'joannes carrere clericus' (Jean Carrère?) has written his name on f. 1r. (s. xvii?); an ownership mark of a 'Benoit a Bulan' is written on ff. 146v–147r. Acquired from King Alfred's Notebook (Cayce, SC) by the university in August 2011.

Sales & Catalogues: King Alfred's Notebook, *Enchiridion* 5 (Suppl.), no. 1; ibid., *Enchiridion* 6, no. 1.

cod. Lat. a. 7

Origin: Low Countries, s. xv^2 (Arnhem).
Content Overview: Ferial Psalter; Offices of the Dead (use of Utrecht); hymns.

In Latin, on parchment; 101 ff.; generally 175 x 122 mm (page) [see Layout]; foliated in modern pencil with Arabic numerals; f. 1 blank.

Collation: 1^{10} +2–5^{10} +6^{10-1} +7–9^{10} +10^{10+2}

Quires: Quinions, F/F, are the normal quire forms. Quire 1 contains a constructed bifolium: f. 2 is a singleton pasted to the stub on f. 9. Quire 6 lacks the second leaf, which contained the initial and border decoration beginning Saturday's psalm; some transfer from the gold rinceaux visible on f. 51v [see Borders & Frames]. Quire 10 is a quinion with two leaves added as a constructed bifolium: ff. 100 and 101 are singletons without stubs which are joined by a parchment reinforcement strip pasted to f. 99v. The manuscript has been trimmed for rebinding.

Catchwords: Horizontal catchwords are partially visible in the lower right margins of quires 3–9; all are partially trimmed; those for quires 3–5 and 6–9 correspond.

Layout:

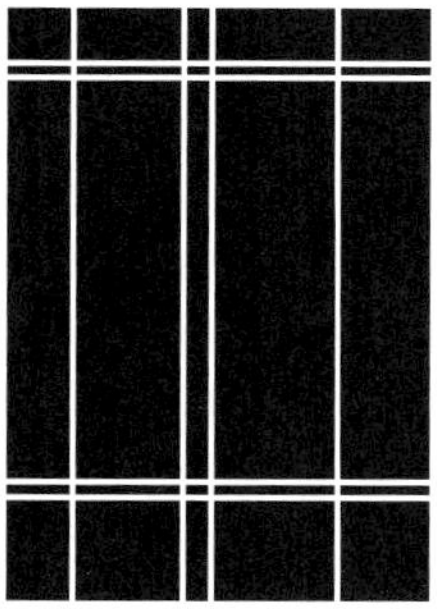

A

A ff. 1r–101v. Ink; 122 x 76 mm; intercol. 8 mm; 28 lines.

Pattern **A** is traced in brown ink; two columns of text (intercol. 8 mm); writing below top line; prickings for vertical bounding lines and horizontal through lines are visible in the upper, lower, and outer margins. Pricking pattern in the right margin is atypical, suggesting rake-ruling: four prickings between the horizontal through lines are spaced 8/8/9 lines. The ruling of the excised ownership marks on f. 1r and 101v has been retraced in black ink [see OWNERS & PROVENANCE].

SCRIPT: A single hand (M1) writes texts and rubrics in a well-executed Northern Textualis Formata of the late fifteenth century; box-**a** used exclusively. Corrections abound: erasures (e.g., ff. 63r[b], 80v[a]), cross-outs in red ink (e.g., f. 10r[b]); interlinear additions and corrections (e.g., f. 17r[a]); marginal additions using *signes-de-renvoi* often stylized in red or blue (e.g., ff. 11v[a], 32r[b], 53v[b], 58v[a], 64v[a], 89r[b]); some corrections were first crossed out in red ink, then erased (e.g., ff. 63r[b], 86v[a]); some additions by M1 in the lower margins are ruled below the text frame (e.g., ff. 58v[a], 90v). Further additions and corrections are added by M2 in left margin of f. 64r[a] in Hybrida Currens, and by M3 in lower margins on ff. 84r[b] and 84v[a–b] in Hybrida Libraria (M1 appears to correct only in Northern Textualis).

DECORATION:

I. RUBRICATION: Rubrics in red ink; letter heightening in red ink; some responsories underlined in red ink (e.g., ff. 49r[a], 80v[a]).

II. INITIALS: Foliate, littera duplex, flourished, and plain initials occur in hierarchy.

A. Foliate initials with floral sprays are used for the major division of the psalms (standing initial approx. 8 lines, f. 2r[a]; 6 line square insets, ff. 15r[b], 22r[a], 29r[a], 35r[b], 44v[b], 69v[a]), and the beginning of the hymnal (6 line square inset, f. 92v[a]); an excised leaf between ff. 51 and 52 contained a foliate initial and border [see BORDERS & FRAMES].

B. Littera duplex initials (5 line square insets) occur at the beginning of Pss 21 (f. 13r[a]) and 51 (f. 28r[a]).

C. Flourished initials (2–4 line square insets; hanging initial **i**s) in red and blue ink with contrasting penwork in red or purplish blue and extensive white penwork occur throughout ff. 60v–97r; those on ff. 75r[b] and 79r[b] incorporate a gold dot; green dots occasionally used. Initials 4 lines in size begin the following sections: Ps 53 (f. 60v[b]), and the major and minor Offices of the Dead (ff. 85v[a] and 90v[a]). Initials 3 lines in size begin hymns for Terce (f. 65r[b]), Sext (f. 66v[a]), None (f. 68r[a]), and Compline (f. 79r[b] with gold dot and green ink); psalms for Vespers (ff. 71r[a], 71v[b], 72v[b], 73v[a], 75r[b] with gold dot and green ink, and 77r[b]); *preces* for Matins and Vespers (f. 81r[a]); Litany (f. 82r[a]); hymns for Vespers in the Octave of Easter and the Assumption (ff. 93r[b] and 97r[b]). An initial 2 lines in size begins the hymn on the feast of Augustine (f. 97r[b]). A few plain initials incorporate the same extensive white penwork as the others without the flourishing (e.g., ff. 60v[a], 96r[b], 98v[a]); the same occurs on f. 36v[a], but white penwork has been painted over with blue.

D. Plain initials (1–2 line square indent; occasional hanging initial **i**s; 1 line versals) in red and blue ink alternate throughout the texts; psalms and hymns begin with initials of the 2 line size.

III. Borders & Frames:

A variety of border arrangements occur in conjunction with the foliate initials on ff. 2r, 15r, 22r, 29r, 35r, 44v, 69v, and 92v. Partial borders and floral sprays; darker palette of blues, reds, pinks, and purples with greens; white highlights on all decorative elements; rinceaux is gold and often terminates into petals and floral motifs. Rosettes and blue and pink knots on gold in the borders of f. 2r; borders on f. 69v with gold rinceaux and clover; dark green, pink, blue, and red acanthus leaves in the lower margin. All border decoration and initials resemble the style of the so-called Masters of Margriet Uutenham; consistent with this style, the manuscript contains no historiation or miniatures (see Defoer 1990, 244–245, 250–252; and Dickmann 2001). According to Defoer 1990, this style of decoration can be localized to the region of Arnhem, ca. 1460–1480; cf. table in Budde and Krischel 2001, 206–207 and plates on pp. 208–216.

Calendar: Excised according to prior description [see Ownership & Provenance].

Contents:

1. Ferial Psalter—ff. 2r^{a}–82r^{a}.

Eight-part division of the psalms with invitatories, antiphons, versicles, etc.: Sunday (ff. 2r^{a}–12v^{b}), feria secunda (ff. 15r^{a}–22r^{a}), feria tertia (ff. 22r^{a}–29r^{a}), feria quarta (ff. 29r^{a}–35r^{b}), feria quinta (ff. 35r^{b}–44v^{a}), feria sexta (ff. 44v^{a}–51v^{b}); Saturday (ff. 51v^{b}–60v^{b}) is incomplete and Ps 101 begins imperfectly on f. 52r^{a}; Vespers (ff. 69v^{a}–79r^{b}). Canticles are not included in a separate section; *Te deum* (f. 10r^{a}); *Benedicite omnia* (f. 11v^{a}); *Quicumque uult* (f. 62r^{b}); *Magnificat* (f. 79r^{a}); *Nunc dimittis* (f. 80r^{a}). Prime (ff. 13r^{a}–15r^{a}; 60v^{a}–65r^{b}), Terce (ff. f. 65r^{b}–66v^{a}), Sext (ff. 66v^{a}–68r^{a}), None (ff. 68r^{a}–69r^{b}), Compline (ff. 79r^{b}–81r^{a}). Lesser hours dispersed throughout Ps 118, six stanzas each (first four in Prime); variant prayers (ff. 81r^{a}–82r^{a}).

2. Litany, Collects, and Votive Prayers—ff. 82r^{a}–85v^{b}

Saluator mundi precedes the Litany as an antiphon for the seven psalms on f. 82r^{a}.

2.1. Litany—ff. 82r^{a}–83v^{b}

Localization to the Diocese of Utrecht is possible: Poncian and Lambert among the martyrs; Martin, Remigius, Wilibrord, Lebuinus, Radbodus, Seruatius, Odulphus among confessors; Agnes, Anastasia, Walburgis, Ghertrud, Margaret, Kathrine, Barbara, and Ursula among the virgins. Martin, Augustine, and Seruatius are emphasized with a majuscule heightened in red ink.

2.2. Collects and Votive prayers—ff. 83v^{b}–85v^{a}.

2.2.1. ff. 83v^{b}–84r^{a}. inc.: miserere nobis domine miserere nobis miseris misericors trinitas . . . ab omni malo preterito presenti et futuro [*PL* 101.591].

2.2.2. f. 84r^{a-b}. inc.: libera nos de morte ad uitam de tenebris ad lucem . . . habere mereamur apud [-d] dominum nostrum in celis [*PL* 101.591].

2.2.3. f. 84r^{b}. inc.: maiestati tue nos quesumus domine omnium sanctorum supplicacio . . . offendimus iustorum precibus expiemur [*CO* 3297a].

2.2.4. f. 84r^{b}–84v^{a}. INC.: preces nostras quesumus domine memor fragilitatis . . . et plenitudinem eternorum largiris [*CO* 4620].

2.2.5. f. 84v^{a-b}. INC.: omnipotens sempiterne deus pater indulgenciarum . . . habere mereamur in hoc seculo et uitam eternam in futuro.

2.2.6. f. 84v^{b}. INC.: deus infinite misericordie et maiestatis immense . . . celeri consequantur effectu [*CO* 1257].

2.2.7. ff. 84v^{b}–85r^{a}. INC.: indulgenciam et remissionem omni peccatorum . . . gratiam sancti spiritus tribuat nobis pius pater et immors dominus amen.

2.2.8. f. 85r^{a}. INC.: exaudi quesumus domine supplicum preces . . . indulgenciam tribuas benignus et pacem [*CO* 2541].

2.2.9. f. 85r^{a}. INC.: deus cui proprium est misereri semper et parcere . . . constringit miseracio tue pietatis absoluat [*CO* 1143].

2.2.10. f. 85r^{a}. INC.: ineffabilem [-misericordiam] misericordiam tuam nobis domine . . . quas pro hiis meremur eripias per dominum nostrum [BRUYLANTS 2:648; *CO* 3129].

2.2.11. f. 85r^{b}. RUB. [f. 85r^{a}]: pro infirmo collecta; INC.: deus infirmitatis humane singulare presidium . . . incolumis presentari mereatur [BRUYLANTS 2:234; *CO* 1259].

2.2.12. f. 85r^{b}. RUB.: pro in tribuacione constitutis; INC.: rege quesumus domine famulos tuos et intercedentibus omnibus sanctis tuis gratie tue . . . et sempiternis gaudeant institutis [*CO* 5023].

2.2.13. f. 85r^{b}. RUB.: pro amico temptato; INC.: omnipotens mitissime deus respice propitius preces nostras . . . dignum fieri habitaculum mereatur [BRUYLANTS 2:753; *CO* 3780].

2.2.14. f. 85r^{b}–v^{a}. RUB.: pro iter agentibus; INC.: adesto domine supplicacionibus uestris et uiam famulorum tuorum . . . tuo spirito protegantur auxilio [BRUYLANTS 2:30; *CO* 151].

2.2.15. f. 85v^{a}. RUB.: pro inimicis; INC.: deus pacis caritatisque amator da . . . nosque ab insidiis eorum potenter eripias [BRUYLANTS 2:241; *CO* 1293].

2.2.16. f. 85v^{a}. RUB.: pro familiaribus; INC.: deus qui caritatis dona per gratiam sancti spiritus . . . et que tibi placita sunt tota dilectione perficiant per. [*CO* 1483].

3. Office of the Dead, use of Utrecht—ff. 85v^{a}–92r^{b}.

The major and minor Offices for the Dead both appear to follow the use of Utrecht with one aberration (see below).

3.1. Major office, use of Utrecht—ff. 85v^{a}–90v^{a}.

OTTOSEN nos. 25-44-47, 138-93-83, 39-79-38. The ninth reading is 1 Cor 15.19–31 (*fratres si in hac uita . . .*), which distinguishes the Utrecht series from that of Windesheim according to OTTOSEN, 70. In position seven, R 39 deviates from the Utrecht series recorded by Ottosen (*libera eas* [sic] *domine de penis inferni*) in lieu of R 40 (see OTTOSEN, 345; in the numerical listing of responsories, R 39 is indicated as not used). Collects follow on ff. 89r^{a}–90v^{a}.

3.2. Minor office, use of Utrecht—ff. 90v[a]–92r[b].

OTTOSEN nos. 14-72-24, 68-57-82, 93-58-29. R 93 in position seven and R 29 in position nine are consistent with the use of Utrecht; according to OTTOSEN, 282, the Windesheim series replaces R 93 with R 32 and deletes R 29. Collects follow on ff. 91v[b]–92r[b].

4. Hymns—ff. 92v[a]–101r[a].

Various hymns for seasonal variations, propers, commons, a *commemoratio* to the Virgin on Saturdays, and the dedication of a church.

4.1. Seasonal Variations—ff. 92r[b]–93v[a].

4.1.1. f. 92r[b]. RUB.: sequens ymnus dicitur sabbato et dominicis post octauam trinitatis usque ad kalendarium augusti quando dicitur historia de sapientia ad uesperas et post libros sapientie sabbato ad uesperas usque ad festum michaelis; [f. 92v[a]] de sancta trinitate ymnus; INC.: o lux beata trinitas et principalis unitas . . . [*AH* 51: no. 40].

4.1.2. f. 92v[a–b]. RUB.: post michaelis usque ad aduentum sabbatis ad uesperas et post octauas epyphanie usque ad septuagesimam ymnus; INC.: deus creator omnium poli rectorque . . . [*AH* 50: no. 7].

4.1.3. ff. 92v[b]–93r[a]. RUB.: dominicis post ocatuas epyphanie et post libros sapientie ad uesperas hymnus; INC.: lucis creator optime lucem dierum proferens . . . [*AH* 51: no. 34].

4.1.4. f. 93r[a]. RUB.: post octauas pentecoste usque ad michaelis a completorio ymnus; INC.: te lucis ante terminum rerum creator . . . [*AH* 51: no. 44].

4.1.5. f. 93r[b]. RUB.: a festo michaelis usque ad aduentum domini ad completorium ymnus; INC.: ihesu saluator seculi uerbum patris altissimi . . . [*AH* 14a: no. 125].

4.1.6. f. 93r[b]–93v[a]. RUB.: in octaua pasche ad uesperas hymnus; INC.: ad cenam agni prouidi . . . [*AH* 27: no. 36]; RUB. [f. 93v[a]]: ad completorium ymnus; INC.: o uere digna hostia . . . [*AH* 12: no. 92].

4.2. Proper—ff. 93v[a]–99v[a].

Includes John the Baptist, Peter and Paul, Mary Magdalene, Laurence, Augustine, Michael, Martin, and Katherine. The hymn on the feast of Augustine is emphasized by a 2 line square inset flourished initial [see DECORATION].

4.2.1. Ascension—ff. 93v[a]–94r[a]. RUB.: in ascensione domini ymnus; INC.: festum nunc celebre . . . [*AH* 51: no. 50, 143]; RUB. [f. 94r[a]]: ad completorium; INC.: ihesu nostra redempcio amor . . . [*AH* 2: no. 49].

4.2.2. Exaltation of the Cross—f. 94r[a–b]. RUB.: de sancta cruce ymnus; INC.: salue crux sancta salue mundi . . . [*AH* 54: no. 6].

4.2.3. Ascension—f. 94r[b]–v[a]. RUB.: in die ascensionis ymnus; INC.: uita sanctorum decus angelorum uita . . . [*AH* 51: no. 85].

4.2.4. Pentecost—ff. 94v^{a}–95r^{a}. RUB.: in festo penthecoste; INC.: ueni creator spiritus . . . [*AH* 21: no. 73]; RUB. [f. 94v^{b}]: feria quarta quinta et sexta ad completorium; INC.: beata nobis gaudia anni reduxit orbita . . . [*AH* 4: no. 195].

4.2.5. Corpus Christi—f. 95r^{a-b}. RUB.: in festo sacramenti ymnus; INC.: pange lingua gloriosi corporis . . . [*AH* 50: no. 386].

4.2.6. John the Baptist—f. 95r^{b}–v^{b}. RUB.: in festo iohannis baptiste; INC.: ut queant laxis resonare fibris . . . [*AH* 50: no. 96]; RUB. [f. 95v^{b}]: ad completorium; INC.: preco preclarus sacer . . .

4.2.7. Peter and Paul—ff. 95v^{b}–96r^{a}. RUB.: in festo petri et pauli; INC.: aurea luce et decore roseo lux lucis . . . [*AH* 51: no. 118].

4.2.8. Visitation—f. 96r^{b}–v^{a}. RUB.: in festo uisitationis beate et cetera; INC.: in mariam uite uiam matrem ueram . . . [*AH* 52: no. 42]; RUB.: ad completorium; INC.: o christi mater celica . . . [*AH* 52: no. 43; *RH* 12792].

4.2.9. Mary Magdalene—f. 96v^{a-b}. RUB.: in festo marie magdalene; INC.: uotiua cunctis orbita lucis . . . [*AH* 51: no. 175].

4.2.10. Transfiguration—f. 96v^{b}. RUB.: in festo transfiguracionis christi; INC.: o nata lux de lumine ihesu redeptor [*sic*] seculi . . . [*AH* 51: no. 99].

4.2.11. Laurence—f. 97r^{a}. RUB. [f. 96v^{b}]: in festo laurentii ymnus; INC.: en martiris laurencii armata pugnauit fides . . . [*AH* 50: no. 33]; RUB.: ad completorium; INC.: conscendat usque sydera celique pulset . . . [*AH* 50: no. 227].

4.2.12. Assumption—f. 97r^{b}. RUB.: in festo assumpcionis beate marie; INC.: o quam gloriosa luce choruscas stirpis . . . [*AH* 51: no. 126].

4.2.13. Augustine—f. 97r^{b}–v^{b}. RUB.: in festo beatissimi patris augustini ad uesperas hymnus; INC.: magne pater augustine preces nostras suscipe . . . [*AH* 52: no. 117]; RUB.: ad completorium; INC.: celi ciues applaudite et uos fratres . . . [*AH* 52: no. 118].

4.2.14. Nativity—ff. 97v^{b}–98r^{a}. RUB.: in natiuitate beate marie; INC.: maria mater domini eterni patris filii fer opem . . . [*AH* 4: no. 68].

4.2.15. Michael—f. 98r^{a}–v^{a}. RUB.: in die michaelis ymnus; INC.: christe sanctorum decus angelorum auctor . . . [*AH* 50: no. 146]; RUB. [f. 98r^{b}]: ad completorium; INC.: tibi christe splendor patris uita ac uirtus . . . [*AH* 50: no. 156].

4.2.16. All Saints—f. 98v^{a}. RUB.: in festo omnium sanctorum ymnus; INC.: ihesu saluator seculi redemptis ope subueni . . . [*AH* 51: no. 130].

4.2.17. Martin—ff. 98v^{a}–99r^{a}. RUB.: de sancto martino ymnus; INC.: fratres unanimes federe . . . [*AH* 50: no. 154]; RUB. [f. 99r^{a}]: ad completorium; INC.: en gratulemur spiritu uoti colentes debita hec festaque . . . [*AH* 4: no. 387].

4.2.18. Katherine—f. 99r^{a}–v^{a}. RUB.: in festo katherine ymnus; INC.: katherine collaudemus uirtutem insignia cordis . . . [*AH* 52: no. 245].

4.3. Common—ff. 99v^{a}–100r^{b}.

4.3.1. Apostles—f. 99v^{a-b}. RUB.: de apostolis ad uesperas; INC.: exultet celum laudibus . . . [*AH* 51: no. 108].

4.3.2. Martyr—f. 99v^b. RUB.: de uno martire ymnus; INC.: martir dei qui unicum patris sequendo filium . . . [*AH* 51: no. 113].
4.3.3. Martyrs—ff. 99v^b–100r^a. RUB.: de martiribus ymnus; INC.: rex gloriose martirum corona . . . [*AH* 51: no. 112].
4.3.4. Confessor—f. 100r^a. RUB.: de uno confessore; INC.: iste confessor domini sacratus festa plebs . . . [*AH* 51: no. 118].
4.3.5. Virgins—f. 100r^{a-b}. RUB.: de uirginibus ymnus; INC.: ihesu corona uirginum quem mater illa concepit . . . [*AH* 2: no. 104].

4.4. Saturday Commemoration of the Virgin—f. 100r^b–v^a. RUB.: in conmemoracione beate marie sabbatis; INC.: aue maris stella dei mater . . . [*AH* 51: no. 140]; RUB. [f. 100v^a]: ad completorium; INC.: fit porta christi peruia referta plena gratia transit . . . [cf. *AH* 52: no. 53].

4.5. Church dedication—ff. 100v^a–101r^a. RUB.: in dedicacione ecclesie ymnus; INC.: urbs beata iherusalem dicta pacis uisio . . . [*AH* 51: no. 102].

Binding: s. xix; aquamarine velvet over pasteboards; front board loose.

Owners & Provenance: Unidentified British dealer catalogue entry pasted to inside front cover describing the manuscript as a "Psalterium Davidis, cum calendrio" for a price of £6.15s. Dealer marks and a price code in pencil written on the front pastedown. Acquired from King Alfred's Notebook (Cayce, SC) by the university in November 2011.

Sales & Catalogues: King Alfred's Notebook, *Enchiridion* 7, no. 1.

cod. Lat. a. 8

Origin: France, s. xv.
Content Overview: Book of Hours, use of Paris.

In Latin and French, on parchment; vi +119 ff. +vi; generally 140 x 105 mm (page) [see Layout for ruling]; foliated in modern pencil with Arabic numerals; ff. 82r–v, 111v blank (f. 82r ruled).

Collation: vi $+1^{12}$ $+2–3^{8}$ $+4^{4}$ $+5–8^{8}$ $+9^{2}$ $+10–15^{2}$ $+16^{4}$ $+17^{8}$ $+18^{2}$ $+ 19^{4}$ $+20^{6+1}$ $+21^{2+1}$ $+22^{4+1}$ +vi

Quires: Original collation has been disturbed and quires have been regathered during modern rebinding; many bifolia were replaced in a seemingly random order. The collation statement refers to the current state of the manuscript. Originially, a sexternion, F/F, was used for the calendar; quaternions, F/F, were the normal quire forms.

Layout:

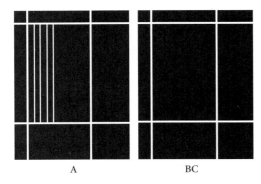

A BC

- A ff. 1r–12v. Ink; 94 x 58 mm; cols. 6.5/6/6/6/34 mm; 17 lines.
- B [see below] Ink; 92–93 x 60 mm; 17 lines.
- C [see below] Rose ink; 92–93 x 60 mm; 17 lines.

Pattern **A** is traced in brown ink on ff. 1r–12v; five calendric columns (6.5/6/6/6/34 mm); writing below top line. Pattern **B** is traced in brown ink on ff. 41r–48v, 81r–82r, 79r–80v, 13r–20v, 13r–20v, 33r–40v, 97r–104v, 83r–86v, 69r–70v, 21r–28v, 74r–v, 117r–v, 112r–114v,

119r–v, 116r–v, 73r–v, 49r–56v, 57r–64v, 87r–94v; single column; writing below top line. Pattern C is traced in rose ink on ff. 65r–68v, 75r–78v, 105r–111r, 71r–72v, 115r–v, 118r–v, 29r–32v; single column; writing below top line; no prickings are visible for any patterns.

Script: All texts are written in Northern Textualis Formata of the fifteenth century seemingly by a single hand (M1).

Decoration:
I. Rubrication: Rubrics in red ink; letter heightening of majuscles in red ink.
II. Initials: Foliate, dentelle, and plain initials occur loosely in hierarchy.
a. One foliate initial (4 line square inset) is painted on f. 13r; interior excised.
b. Dentelle initials (2–4 line square inset) are used to begin and divide major texts.
c. Plain initials (2–6 line square inset; 1 line versals) alternate in red and blue ink throughout the text; larger-sized initials used in the Litany only.
III. Line Fillers: Line fillers in red, and red and blue ink.
IV. Borders & Frames:

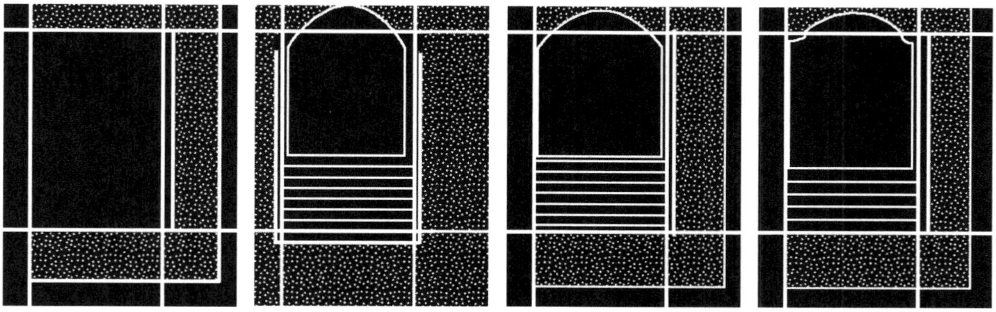

D E F G

Text folios contain functional three-margins-outer borders (D) on ff. 33r, 40v, 45r, 48r, 68r, 69r, 70v, 71v, 75v, 101r, 104r, and 108v; the borders of D are comprised of black and gold rinceaux with floral motifs in orange, blue, pink, and green; frames in D use a single dentelle style baguette in the outer margin; area to be decorated is outlined in lead. Miniature folios contain three different border and frame combinations. Four-margins border (E) is painted on f. 13r comprised of black and gold rinceaux, acanthus leaves in blue, gold, and red, and vegetal motifs in red, pink, green, and gold; miniature frame in E is arch-topped contained by dentelle style frame with six lines of text below; outer frame in E in three-margins configuration colored as above, spraying from initial. Three-margins-outer borders on ff. 21r and 32v (F) painted as D; miniature frames in F are arch-topped contained as above with six lines of text below (different than E); other frames as in D. Three-margins-outer borders on ff. 116r and 118v (G) painted as D; miniature frames in G are arch-topped with recesses contained as above with five lines of text below; remaining frames as in D.

Miniatures: Annunciation (f. 13r); King David with harp (f. 21r); funeral scene (f. 32v); Crucifixion (f. 116r); Mass of St. Gregory (f. 118v); most are damaged and worn.

Calendar: Two pages per month; recto/verso; composite; dominical letter a in red ink; Roman time without numerals marked in red and black ink.

Contents:

Contents are listed in contextual order with folio numbers; a list of the contents by present codicological unit with sequential folio numbers follows the description.

1. Calendar (Paris)—ff. 1r–12v.

Composite calendar in French with graded feasts in red ink; saints and grading are typical of the Parisian model calendar; of note is the *Rouennais* form 'Nigaise' (Nov. 17).

2. Gospel Lessons—ff. 41r–45r.

The four standard lessons occur with rubrics: John (ff. 41r–v; *oratio* f. 42r), Luke (ff. 42r–43r), Matthew (ff. 43r–44v), Mark (ff. 44v–45r).

3. *Obsecro te* (masculine forms)—ff. 45r–48r.

rub.: de beata maria oratio; **inc.**: [f. 45r] obsecro te domina . . . ego sum facturus locuturus aut cogitaturus . . . et mihi famulo . . .; **expl.**: [f. 48r] . . . audi et exaudi me dulcissima uirgo maria mater dei et misericordie amen [cf. Leroquais 2:346–347].

4. *O Intemerata*—ff. 48r–v, 81r–v, 79r–80v.

rub.: de beata maria; **inc.**: [f. 48r] o intemerata . . .; **expl.**: [f. 80v] . . . cum sanctis et electis suis uitam et requiem sempiternam amen [cf. Wilmart, 494–495].

5. Hours of the Virgin, use of Paris—ff. 13r–20v, 33r–40v, 97r–104v, 83r–84v, 69r–v, 95r–96v, 70r–v, 85r–86v, 65r–66v, 75r–78v, 67r–v.

5.1. Matins—ff. 13r–20v, 33r. **inv.**: aue maria . . .; **hym.**: quam glorifica luce . . .; **ant. ps. 8**: exaltata es; **lect. i**: surge beatissima uirgo maria . . .; **r. i.**: beata es uirgo maria . . .

5.2. Lauds—ff. 33r–40v. **rub.**: in laudibus; **pss.**: 92, 99, 62, 66, Benedicite, 148, 149, 150; **ant.**: benedicta tu; **cap.**: te laudent angeli . . .; **hym.**: uirgo dei genitrix . . .; **ant. sup. ben.**: hec est regina.

5.3. Prime—ff. 40v, 97r–101r. **rub.**: ad primam; **pss.**: 1, 2, 5; **hym.**: ueni creator spiritus . . .; **ant.**: benedicta tu; **cap.**: felix namque es . . .; **r.**: diffusa est gracia . . .; **v.**: propterea benedixit te . . .

5.4. Terce—ff. 101r–104r. **rub.**: ad terciam; **pss.**: 119, 120, 121; **hym.**: ueni creator spiritus . . .; **ant.**: dignare me; **cap.**: paradisi porta per euam . . .; **r.**: specie tua . . .; **v.**: intende prospere procede . . .

5.5. Sext—ff. 104r–v, 83r–84v, 69r. RUB.: ad sextam; PSS.: 122, 123, 124; ANT.: post partum; CAP.: gaude maria uirgo . . .; R.: adiuuabit eam deus . . .; V.: deus in medio eius . . .

5.6. None—ff. 69r–v, 95r–96v, 70r. RUB.: ad sextam [*sic*] ; PSS.: 125, 126, 127; ANT.: sicut lilium; CAP.: per te dei genitrix . . .; R.: elegit eam deus . . .; V.: et habitare eam . . .; V.: post partum uirgo . . .

5.7. Vespers—ff. 70v, 85r–86v, 65r–66v, 75r–v. RUB.: [f. 70r] ad uesperas; PSS.: 121, 122, 123, 124, 125; ANT.: beatam me dicent; CAP.: beata es uirgo maria . . .; HYM.: aue maris stella . . .; ANT. SUP. MAGNIF.: sancta maria.

5.8. Compline—ff. 75v–78v, 67r–v. RUB.: ad completorium; PSS.: 12, 42, 128, 130; ANT.: sancta dei genitrix; HYM.: uirgo dei genitrix . . .; CAP.: sicut cynamomum et balsamon . . .; V.: ecce ancilla domini . . .; ANT. SUP. NUNC DIM.: cum iocunditate.

6. The Fifteen Joys of the Virgin (*Doulce Dame*)—ff. 68r–v, 105r–108v.

INC.: [f. 68r] douce dame de misericorde mere de pitie fontaine de tous . . .; EXPL.: [f. 108v] . . . de dieu soit fecte amen. aue maria gracia plena dominus [SONET/SINCLAIR/RÉZEAU 458].

7. Seven Requests to our Lord (*Doulz Dieu*)—ff. 108v–111r.

RUB.: les .v. ioys nostre dame [*sic*]; INC.: [f. 108v] douls dieux douls peres sainte trinite ung seulz dieu . . .; EXPL.: [f. 111r] . . . que uray confes puisse mourir amen. pater noster. aue maria [SONET/SINCLAIR/RÉZEAU 504].

8. Penitential Psalms, Litany, and Collects—ff. 21r–28v, 74r–v, 117r–v, 112r–114v, 119r–v.

8.1. Penitential Psalms—ff. 21r–28v, 74r–v, 117r–v.

8.2. Litany—ff. 117v, 112r–114v, 119r.

Martyrs: Stephen, Clement, Laurence, Vincent, George, Denis (*cum soc.*), Fabian, Sebastian, Christopher; *Confessors*: Silvester, Leo, Ivo, Hilary, Lazarus, Fiacre, Landegar, Louis, Germain, Benedict, Anthony, Augustine; *Virgins*: Mary Magdalene, Anna, Martha, Avia, Agatha, Margaret, Genevieve, Katherine, Fides, Spes, Caritas.

8.3. Collects—f. 119r–v.

8.3.1. INC.: deus cui proprium est misereri semper et parcere . . . miseratio tue pietatis absoluat [*CO* 1143].

8.3.2. RUB.: oratio; INC.: fidelium deus omnium conditor . . . piis supplicacionibus consequantur qui uiuis et regnas deus per omnia secula seculorum amen [*CO* 2684b].

9. Hours of the Cross—ff. 116r–v, 73r–v, 71r–v, 118r.

Matins, ff. 116r–v, 73r; Prime, f. 73r–v; Terce, f. 73v; Sext, ff. 73v, 71r; None, f. 71r; Vespers, f. 71r–v; Compline, ff. 71v, 118r; *recommendatio*, f. 118r. Each stanza concludes with the usual verse, response, and prayer which are written fully for Matins; all other repetitions are given in cue form. For the hymns see *AH* 30: no. 13.

10. Hours of the Holy Spirit—ff. 118v, 29r–32r.

Matins, ff. 118v, 29r–v; Prime, ff. 29v–30r; Terce, f. 30r; Sext, f. 30r–v; None, ff. 30v–31r; Vespers, f. 31r–v; Compline, ff. 31v–32r; *recommendatio*, f. 32r.

11. Office of the Dead, use of Paris—ff. 32v, 115r–v, 72r–v, 49r–64v, 87r–94v.

Ottosen nos. 72-14-32, 57-24-68, 28-46-38.

Binding: s. xix; stiff vellum over pasteboards; gilt tooled; marbled endpapers and pastedowns; rebacked.

Owners & Provenance: Acquired by the university in March 2013.

Sales & Catalogues: Bonhams, 10 October 2012, lot 2009.

Contents by Present Codicological Unit:

1. Quire 1 (VI^{12})—ff. 1r–12v.

Calendar. Ruling pattern **A**.

2. Quire 2 (IV^{8})—ff. 13r–20v.

inc.: [f. 13r] domine labia mea aperies et os meum annunciabit laudem . . .; expl.: [f. 20v] . . . fiat misericordia tua domine super nos quem ad modum sperauimus.

Matins *BMV*. Ruling pattern **B**.

3. Quire 3 (IV^{8})—ff. 21r–28v.

inc.: [f. 21r] domine ne in furore tuo arguas me neque in ira tua corripias me miserere . . .; expl.: [f. 28v] . . . si iniquitates obseruaueris domine.

Penitential Psalms. Ruling pattern **B**.

4. Quire 4 (II^{4})—ff. 29r–32v.

inc.: [f. 29r] -de domine ad adiuuandum me festina . . . expl.: [f. 32v] . . . quia inclinauit aurem suam michi et in diebus.

Hours of the Holy Spirit (ff. 29r–32r); Office of the Dead (f. 32v). Ruling pattern **C**.

5. Quire 5 (IV^{8})—ff. 33r–40v.

inc.: [f. 33r] in te in te domine speram non confundar in eternum . . .; expl.: [f. 40v] . . . deus in adiutorium meum intende domine.

Matins *BMV* (f. 33r); Lauds *BMV* (ff. 33r–40v); Prime *BMV* (f. 40v). Ruling pattern **B**.

6. Quire 6 (IV^8)—ff. 41r–48v.

INC.: [f. 41] secundum iohannem in principio erat uerbum et uerbum erat apud deum . . .; **EXPL.**: [f. 48v] . . . quem adoro qui sacratissimam carnem conprecio- [*sic*].

Gospel lessons (ff. 41r–45r); *Obsecro te* (ff. 45r–48r); *O intemerata* (f. 48r). Ruling pattern **B.**

7. Quire 7 (IV^8)—ff. 49r–56v.

INC.: [f. 49r] -pter legem tuam sustinui te domine . . .; **EXPL.**: [f. 56v] . . . parce michi domine nichil enim sunt dies mei quid.

Office of the Dead. Ruling pattern **B.**

8. Quire 8 (IV^8)—ff. 57r–64v.

INC.: [57r] est homo quia magnificans eum aut quid apponis erga eum cor tuum . . .; **EXPL.**: [64v] . . . domine deus meus clamaui ad te et sana-.

Office of the Dead. Ruling Pattern **B.**

9. Quire 9 (II^4)—ff. 65r–68v.

INC.: [f. 65r] nostrum et linga [*sic*] nostra in exultatcione . . .; **EXPL.**: [f. 68v] . . . douce dame pries luy que il ueulle uenir en mon cuer espirituellement aue maria gracia plena dominus tecum.

Vespers *BMV* (ff. 65r–66v); Compline *BMV* (f. 67r–v); *Doulce Dame* (f. 68r–v). Ruling pattern **C.**

10. Quire 10 (I^2)—ff. 69r–70v.

INC.: [f. 69r] concede misericors deus fragilitati nostre presidium ut qui sancte dei genitricis . . .; **EXPL.**: [f. 70v] . . . illuc enim ascenderunt tribus tribus domini testimonium israel.

Sext *BMV* (f. 69r); None *BMV* (ff. 69r–v, 70r); Vespers *BMV* (f. 70r–v). Ruling pattern **B.**

11. Quire 11 (I^2)—ff. 71r–72v.

INC.: [f. 71r] pendens deputatus pre tormentis siciens felle saturatus agnus crimen diluit sic ludificatus . . .; **EXPL.**: [f. 72v] . . . quia apud te propiciacio est pro.

Hours of the Cross (f. 71r–v); Office of the Dead (f. 72r–v). Ruling pattern **C.**

12. Quire 12 (I^2)—ff. 73r–74v.

INC.: [f. 73r] inter iudicium tuum et animam meam nunc et in hora mortis mee . . .; **EXPL.**: [f. 74v] . . . uelociter ex [*sic*] me domine defecit.

Hours of the Cross (f. 73r–v); Penitential Psalms (f. 74r–v). Ruling pattern **B.**

13. Quire 13 (II⁴)—ff. 75r–78v.

INC.: [f. 75r] -foue flebiles ora pro populo interueni pro clero intercede pro deuoto femineo sexu . . .; EXPL.: [f. 78v] . . . lumen ad reuelacionem gencium et gloriam plebis tue israel gloria patri et filio.

Vespers *BMV* (f. 75r–v); Compline *BMV* (ff. 75v–78v). Ruling pattern **C**.

14. Quire 14 (I²)—ff. 79r–80v.

INC.: [f. 79r] per que ei displicui tribuans michi ueram humilitatem ueram mansuetudinem . . .; EXPL.: [f. 80v] . . . cum sanctis et electis suis uitam et requiam sempiternam amen.

O intemerata. Ruling pattern **B**.

15. Quire 15 (I²)—ff. 81r–82v.

INC.: [f. 81r] -sissimo sanguine suo ipse dat cotidie fidelibus suis sub forma panis . . .; EXPL.: [f. 81v] . . . precibus et meritis tuis absoluat me ab omnibus peccatis meis.

O intemerata (f. 81r–v); f. 82r–v blank. Ruling pattern **B**.

16. Quire 16 (II⁴)—ff. 83r–86v.

INC.: [f. 83r] oculi ancille in manibus domine sue ita oculi nostri ad dominum deum nostrum donec miseratur nostri . . .; EXPL.: [f. 86v] . . . iunc [*sic*] repletum est gaudio os.

Sext *BMV* (ff. 83r–84v); Vespers *BMV* (ff. 85r–86v). Ruling pattern **B**.

17. Quire 17 (IV⁸)—ff. 87r–94v.

INC.: [f. 87r] -sti me domine eduxisti ab inferno animam meam saluasti me a descendentibus in lacum . . .; EXPL.: [f. 94v] . . . dum ueneris iudicare seculum per ignem. sequitur antiphona. requiem.

Office of the Dead. Ruling pattern **B**.

18. Quire 18 (I²)—ff. 95r–96v.

INC.: [f. 95r] in conuertendo dominus captiuitatem syon facti sumus sicut consolati . . .; EXPL.: [f. 96v] . . . domine exaudi orationem et clamor meus ad te ueniat oremus.

None *BMV*. Ruling pattern **B**.

19. Quire 19 (IV⁸)—ff. 97r–104v.

INC.: [f. 97r] ad adiuuandum me festina gloria patri et filio sicut erat in principio. hympnus. ueni creator spiritus . . .; EXPL.: [f. 104v] . . . ecce sicut oculi seruorum in manibus dominorum suorum sicut.

Prime *BMV* (ff. 97r–101r); Terce *BMV* (ff. 101r–104r); Sext *BMV* (f. 104r–v). Ruling pattern **B**.

20. Quire 20 (III^{6+1})—ff. 105r–111v.

INC.: [f. 105r] e tres douce dame pour ycelle grant ioie que uous eustes quant uous alastes . . .; EXPL.: [f. 111r] . . . que uray confes puisse mourir amen. pater noster aue maria.

Doulce Dame (ff. 105r–108v); *Doulz Dieu* (ff. 108v–111r); f. 111v blank. Ruling pattern **C**.

21. Quire 21 (I^{2+1})—ff. 112r–114v.

INC.: [f. 112r] -tor mundi deus ora spiritus sancte deus ora . . .; EXPL.: [f. 114v] . . . agnus dei qui tollis peccata mundi mise-.

Litany. Ruling pattern **B**.

22. Quire 22 (II^{4+1})—ff. 115r–119v.

INC.: [f. 115r] meis inuocabo circumdederunt me dolores mortis et pericula inferni . . .; EXPL.: [f. 119v] . . . qui uiuis et regnas deus per omnia secula seculorum amen.

Office of the Dead (f. 115r–v); Penitential Psalms (f. 117r–v); Litany (ff. 117v, 119r); collects (f. 119r–v); Hours of the Cross (ff. 116r–v, 118r); Hours of the Holy Spirit (f. 118v). Ruling pattern C (ff. 115r–v, 116r–v, 118r–v); ruling pattern **B** (ff. 117r–v, 119r–v).

cod. Lat. a. 9

Origin: France, s. xv^2 (Rouen?).
Content Overview: Book of Hours, use of Rouen.

In Latin and French, on parchment; i +100 ff. +i; generally 167 x 114 mm (page) [see Layout for ruling]; foliated in modern pencil with Arabic numerals in the lower right margin; f. 1 is the second flyleaf (medieval parchment).

Collation: $ii +1^{12} +2^{8} +3^{2} +4–7^{8} +8–9^{3-1} +10^{2} +11–13^{8} +14^{4+1} +i$

Quires: Parchment quaternions, F/F, are the normal quire forms. Quire 1 is a sexternion, F/F; bifolia are used for quires 3 and 10; quire 14 is a binion with a singleton added via reinforcement strip. Quires 8 and 9 are quaternions each lacking a leaf. Markings in light brown ink which appear in the lower right corners of ff. 17r and 63r are likely the remnants of *ad hoc* signatures, but are trimmed.

Layout:

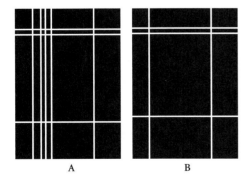

A B

A ff. 2r–13v. Red ink; 96 x 67 mm; cols. 9/5/6/46 mm; 16 lines.
B ff. 13r–99v. Red ink; 96 x 66 mm; 16 lines.

Pattern **A** is traced in red ink on ff. 2r–13v; four calendric columns (9/5/6/46 mm); writing below top line. Pattern **B** is traced in red ink on ff. 13r–99v; single column; writing below top line; prickings for vertical bounding lines visible in the upper and lower margins of most folios.

Script: The manuscript is written in Northern Textualis Formata of the fifteenth century, seemingly by a single hand (M1). A contemporary hand, M2, writes the text of *Stabat mater dolorosa* in Cursiva Formata (Bastarda) on f. 100r–v [see Contents 12].

Decoration:

I. Rubrication: Rubrics in red ink; letter heightening of majuscules in yellow ink (ff. 14r–100r).

II. Initials: Foliate and dentelle initials occur in hierarchy.

a. Foliate initials (3 line square inset) begin major sections of the text on ff. 18r, 21r, 24r, 32r, 42r, 45v, 47v, 49v, 51v, 53r, 67v, 72r, 94r, 99v; all letter forms are in blues with white penwork and inner vegetal motifs in blues and reds.

b. Dentelle initials (2 line square inset; 1 line versals) occur throughout the manuscript.

III. Line Fillers: Line fillers of the dentelle type occur throughout the manuscript; occasionally unfinished (e.g., f. 24r).

IV. Borders & Frames:

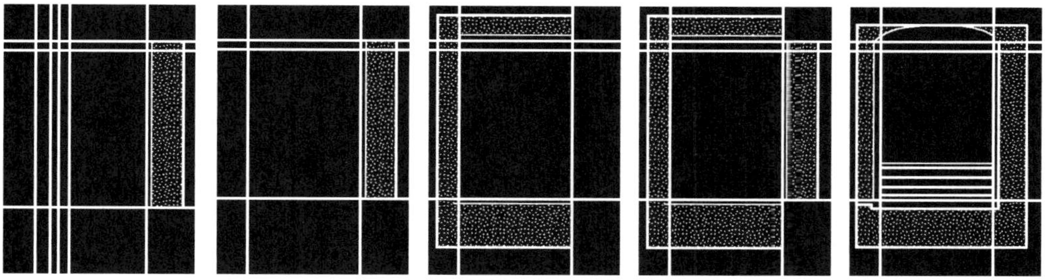

C1 C2 D D2 E

Three types of borders in black and gold rinceaux with florals and strawberries in greens, blues, oranges, and reds are painted on most text folios. The area to be decorated is frame-ruled in red and/or orange ink after ruling patterns were executed. Decorative outer borders are painted on the rectos of the calendar (C1) and on the rectos and versos of most folios throughout the manuscript (C2); some folios have no borders. Functional three-margins-left borders (D) appear on ff. 18r, 21r, 47v, 49v, 51v, 94r, and 99v. A functional three-margins-left border with a decorative outer border (D2) appears on f. 32r. Frames in D2 and D3 are double dentelle-style baguettes on the left. Miniature folios (E) have functional four-margins borders frame-ruled in both red and black ink; borders contain acanthus leaves in blues and yellows with orange; strawberries, grapes, and floral and vegetal motifs in greens, reds, blues, and purples occur with stippling in black ink. Patterns are outlined: hearts (f. 24r), circles (f. 42r), squares (f. 67v), and rectangular lines (f. 72r); all miniatures contained in arch-topped frames outlined in gold above three lines of text. Border arrangements are typical of Rouen.

Miniatures: Four arch-topped miniatures remain: Annunciation (f. 24r); Nativity (f. 42r); Crucifixion (f. 67v); funeral scene (f. 72r). The two missing folios likely contained miniatures to introduce the Penitential Psalms (quire 8) and the Hours of the Cross (quire 9).

Calendar: Two pages per month, recto/verso; not composite; some entries excised [see Contents 1]; dominical letter **a** in dentelle style; Roman time without numerals marked in red and blue ink.

Contents:

1. Calendar (Rouen)—ff. 2r–13v.

Non-composite calendar in French with entries alternating in red and blue and graded feasts in gold; these features point toward Rouen as a place of production. Of the saints listed several are significant to Rouen, and some maintain spellings of the *Rouennais*: Sever (Feb. 1), Aubert (Feb. 9), Godard (Jun. 8), translation of Ursin (Jun. 12), Marciel (Jul. 3; gold), translation (?) of Cler (Jul. 16 [*sic*]), Victor (Jul. 21), Sauveur (Aug. 6; gold), Nigaise (Oct. 11), Michiel (Oct. 16), Mellon (Oct. 22), Romain (Oct. 23; gold), Malo (Nov. 15), Ursin (Dec. 30). Some entries have been cut out of the calendar intentionally: Jun. 10/Jun. 26, Oct. 9/Oct. 28, Nov. 14/Nov. 30.

2. Gospel Lessons—ff. 14r–18r.

The four standard lessons occur with rubrics: John (ff. 14r–15r), Luke (ff. 15r–16r), Mark (ff. 16r–17v), Matthew (ff. 17v–18r).

3. *Obsecro te* (masculine forms)—ff. 18r–21r.

rub.: oroison moult deuote de nostre dame; inc.: [f. 18r] obsecro te domina . . . ego sum facturus locuturus . . . aut cogitaturus . . . michi famulo tuo . . .; expl.: [f. 21r] . . . audi et exaudi me dulcissima uirgo maria mater dei et misericordie amen [cf. Leroquais 2:346–347].

4. *O intemerata* (masculine forms)—ff. 21r–23v.

rub.: aultre oroison de nostre dame fort deuote. inc.: [f. 21r] o intemerata . . . michi peccatori miserrimo . . .; expl.: [f. 23v] . . . cum electis et sanctis suis uitam et leticiam sempiternam amen [cf. Wilmart, 494–495].

5. Hours of the Virgin, use of Rouen; commemorations (*ad laudes*)—ff. 24r–55v.

5.1. Hours of the Virgin, use of Rouen—ff. 24r–55v.

5.1.1. Matins—ff. 24r–32r. inv.: aue maria . . .; hym.: quem terra ponthus . . .; ant. ps. 8: benedicta; lect. i: sancta maria uirgo uirginum . . .; r. i.: beata es uirgo maria . . .

5.1.2. Lauds—ff. 32r–40r. rub.: in laudibus; pss.: 92, 99, 62, 66, Benedicite, 148–149, 150; ant.: assumpta est; cap.: in omnibus requiem . . .; hym.: o gloriosa domina . . .; ant. sup. ben.: o gloriosa dei.

5.1.3. Prime—ff. 42r–45v. pss.: 1, 2, 5, 116; hym.: ueni creator spiritus . . .; ant.: maria uirgo; cap.: per te dei genitrix . . .; r.: aue maria . . .; v.: benedicta tu . . .

5.1.4. Terce—ff. 45v–47v. pss.: 119, 120, 121; hym.: ueni creator spiritus; ant.: in odorem; cap.: ab inicio et ante . . .; r.: sancta dei genitrix . . .; v.: interce [*sic*] pro nobis . . .

5.1.5. Sext—ff. 47v–49v. RUB.: ad sextam; PSS.: 122, 123, 124; ANT.: benedicta; CAP.: et sic in syon . . .; R.: post partum uirgo . . .; V.: dei genitrix . . .

5.1.6. None—ff. 49v–51v. RUB.: ad nonam; PSS.: 125, 126, 127; ANT.: pulcra es; CAP.: et radicaui . . .; R.: speciosa facta es . . .; V.: in deliciis tuis . . .; V.: dignare me laudare . . .

5.1.7. Vespers—ff. 51v–52v. PSS.: 121, 122, 123, 124, 125; ANT.: beata mater; CAP.: beata es uirgo maria . . .; HYM.: aue maris stella . . .; ANT. SUP. MAGNIF.: sancta maria.

5.1.8. Compline—ff. 53r–55v. PSS.: 12, 42, 128, 130; ANT.: cum iocunditate; CAP.: sicut synamomum et . . .; HYM.: uirgo singularis; V.: ecce ancilla . . .; ANT. SUP. NUNC DIM.: ecce completa.

5.2. Commemorations (*ad laudes*)—ff. 40r–41v.

5.2.1. Holy Spirit—f. 39v. ANT.: ueni sancte spiritus..; OR.: deus qui corda fidelium sancti spiritus . . . et de eius semper consolatione gaudere per christum [*CO* 1666].

5.2.2. Nicholas—ff. 39v–40r. ANT.: beatus nicholaus adhuc puerilus . . .; OR.: deus qui beatum nicolaum pontificem tuum . . . a iehenne incendiis liberemur per christum [*CO* 1463].

5.2.3. James—f. 40r. ANT.: sanctissime apostole christi iacobe sedule . . .; OR.: esto domine plebi tue sanctificator . . . ut beati apostoli iacobi . . . et secura deseruiat per christum [*CO* 2445d].

5.2.4. Margaret—f. 40r–v. RUB.: memore de saincte marguerite; ANT.: erat autem margareta annorum . . .; OR.: deus qui beatam uirginem margaretam . . . ad te peruenire mereamur per christum [*CO* 1384a].

5.2.5. Katherine—ff. 40v–41r. RUB.: memore de saincte katherine; ANT.: uirgo sancta katherina grecie gemma . . .; OR.: deus qui dedisti legem moysi . . . corpus beate katherine uirginis et martiris tue . . . ad montem qui christus est ualeamus peruenire per christum [*CO* 1521].

5.2.6. Peace—f. 41r–v. RUB.: memore la paix; ANT.: da pacem domine in diebus . . .; OR.: deus a quo sancta desideria recta consilia et iusta sunt . . . tempora sint tua protectione transquila [*sic*] per dominum nostrum . . . secula seculorum amen benedicamus domino deo gratias [*CO* 1088a].

6. Penitential Psalms, Litany, and Collects—ff. 56r–67r.

6.1. Penitential Psalms [incomplete]—ff. 56r–64r.

Psalm 6 begins imperfectly on f. 56r.

6.2. Litany (Rouen)—ff. 64r–67r.

The litany is general, but some saints significant to Rouen appear: Nigaise, Mellon, Romain, and Austreberte. *Martyrs*: Stephan, Laurence, Vincent, Fabian, Sebastian, Denis (*cum soc.*), Nigaise (*cum soc.*), George, Christopher; *Confessors*: Silvester, Gregory, Martin, Mellon, Romain, Augustine, Nicholas, Benedict, Bernard, Anthony; *Virgins*: Anna, Mary Magdalene, Barbara, Katherine, Margaret, Quiteria, Apollonia, Agatha, Austreberte.

6.3. Collects—ff. 67r.

6.3.1. INC.: deus cui proprium est misereri semper et parcere . . . miseratio tue pietatis absoluat per christum [*CO* 1143].

6.3.2. RUB.: oratio; INC.: fidelium deus omnium conditor . . . piis supplicationibus consequantur qui uiuis et regnas deus per omnia secula seculorum amen [*CO* 2684b].

7. Hours of the Cross [incomplete]—ff. 67r–69v.

Matins, f. 67r–v; Prime, f. 68v; Terce, ff. 68v–69r; Sext, f. 69r; None, f. 69r; Vespers, f. 69r–v; Compline, ff. 69v–70r; *recommendatio*, f. 69v [incomplete]. Each stanza concludes with the usual verse, response, and prayer which are written fully for Matins; all other repetitions are given in cue form. For the hymns see *AH* 30: no. 13.

8. Hours of the Holy Spirit [incomplete]—ff. 70r–71v.

The Hours of the Holy Spirit begin imperfectly; Matins, f. 70r; Prime, f. 70r–v; Terce, f. 70v; Sext, ff. 70v–71r; None, f. 71r; Vespers f. 71r; Compline, f. 71r–v; *recommendatio*, f. 71v. Antiphon, verse, response, and prayer are written fully for Matins; all other repetitions are given in cue form.

9. Office of the Dead, use of Rouen—ff. 72r–94r.

Ottosen nos. 14-72-24, 32-57-40, 68-82-38.

10. The Fifteen Joys of the Virgin (*Doulce Dame*)—ff. 94r–99v.

RUB.: cy ensienuent les quinze ioies de nostre dame; INC.: [f. 94r] doulce dame de misericorde mere de pitie fontaine de tous . . .; EXPL.: [f. 99v] . . . et pour les trespasses quil aient pardon et repos amen [Sonet/Sinclair/Rézeau 458].

11. Seven Requests to our Lord (*Doulz Dieu*)—ff. 99v–100r.

RUB.: cy ensienuent les .vij. requestes que leu doibt faire adieu; INC.: [f. 99v] douls dieu douls pere sainte trinite ung dieu . . .; EXPL.: [f. 100r] . . . mon amee fille huy seras aueque moy en paradis amen [Sonet/Sinclair/Rézeau 504].

12. *Stabat mater*—ff. 100r–v^{b}.

INC.: [f. 100r] <s>tabat mater dolorosa iuxta crucem lacrimosa dum pendebat filius . . .; EXPL.: [f. 100v^{b}] . . . quando corpus morietur fac ut anima donetur paradisi gaudia amen.

The text is added by M2 [see Script].

Binding: s. xix; stiff vellum over pasteboards; green leather title piece; gilt tooled.

Owners & Provenance: The ownership mark (s. xix) of a "monseigneur(?) of Notre-Dame de Charité" appears in the lower margin of f. 2r. Acquired from Bonhams (London, Knightsbridge) by the university in March 2013.

Sales & Catalogues: Bonhams 1793, 19 March 2013 (Auction 20751), lot 46.

cod. Lat. a. 10

Origin: England, s. xiii².
Content Overview: Jerome, *Interpretationes nominum hebraicorum*; liturgical commentary [anonymous].

In Latin, on parchment; iv +136 ff. +iv; 144 x 108 mm (page) [see Layout for ruling]; foliated with Arabic numerals in modern pencil (f. 94 *bis*; now f. 94a); flyleaves i, ii, vii, viii, modern paper; flyleaves iii, iv, v, vi, paper (earlier); f. 68v blank but ruled.

Collation: iv $+15^{12}$ $+6^{12-4}$ $+7–11^{12}$ $+12^{12-4}$ +iv

Quires: Sexternions are the predominant quire forms, indicative of the thirteenth century. No quire marks or catchwords remain; the manuscript has been trimmed on all three sides. Quires 6 (ff. 61–68) and 12 (ff. 128–135), the final quires of each text [see Contents 1 and 2], are sexternions with the last four leaves canceled; no text is lost.

Layout:

A

A ff. 1r–61v. Lead and crayon; 121–124 x 79 mm; 23 lines.

Pattern **A** is traced throughout the entire manuscript in lead with the occasional use of brown crayon (e.g., f. 135r); single column of text; written below top line; few prickings remain due to trimming; superfluous double horizontal through lines appear consistently in the pattern.

Script: Text is written by a single hand, M1, in Northern Textualis of the thirteenth century in brown ink; corrections abound in varying techniques (e.g., f. 78r): erasures, corrections in the margins added with lead and ink using *signes-de-renvoi*, and those added above the text appear as interlinear glosses. Additional material has been added in the lower margin of f. 130r; the script displays some documentary influence in the use of *litterae elongatae*, and the typical bifurcation associated with Anglicana in the first line.

Decoration:

I. Rubrication: Rubrics in red ink on ff. 1–68v; spaces reserved for rubrics on ff. 69–135 and guide words in lead remain in most instances. Paraph marks in red and blue ink alternate through ff. 69–135.

II. Initials: Littera duplex, flourished, and plain initials occur in hierarchy; guide letters in brown ink visible in many sections.

a. One littera duplex initial (4 line square inset) occurs on f. 1r.

b. Flourished initials (2 line square inset) in blue and red ink with contrasting penwork alternate throughout the manuscript.

c. Plain initials (1 line versals) in red and blue ink alternate; occasionally on ff. 69–136 these plain initials are flourished with a single line in the contrasting color (more akin to heightening).

Contents:

1. Jerome, *Interpretationes nominum hebraicorum*—ff. 1r–68r.

rub.: incipiunt interpretationes hebraicorum nominum secundum ieronimum. de libro genesis; inc.: [f. 1r] athiopiam [*sic*] tenebras uel caliginem assiriorum dirigencium . . .; expl.: [f. 68r] . . . sathane transgressori siue aduersario symeon audienti tristiciam sodoma pecori tacenti.

Text lacks the preface.

Edition: De Lagarde 1959; *PL* 23.771–858.
Bibliography: Stegmüller 3305; *CPL* 1961, no. 581.

2. Liturgical commentary [anonymous]—ff. 69r–135v.

inc.: [f. 69r] locorum que orationi sunt dicata alia sunt sacra alia sancta alia religiosa . . .; expl.: [f. 135v] . . . si secus est resonent eadem psallentis in ore principio mensis prima feria propriore.

Author is unknown and commentary is unedited.

Binding: s. xix; brown sheepskin over boards; blind tooled; marbled pastedowns and flyleaves; spine with gilt title; boards extremely bowed.

Owners & Provenance: Erased ownership mark of a Thomas [***] Belcher (1822) on f. 135v; bookplate of Francis Edward Freeland (d. 23 February 1843), presumably of Chichester; Bernard Quaritch, Ltd (1899); Wigan Public Library (October 1899–1992?), purchase note by Henry Tennyson Folkard on flyleaf Iv. Acquired from Les Enluminures (Chicago, IL) by the university in April 2013.

Sales & Catalogues: Quaritch, Cat. 193, no. 140; Bonhams, October 2, 2012 [Auction 20412], lot 110.

Former Shelfmark: Wigan, Wigan Public Library, 36.646.

Bibliography: Folkard 1900, 4:1649; Folkard 1902, 5:1861; Ker 1969–2002, 4:571.

cod. Lat. a. 11

ORIGIN: Italy, s. xv^1 (dated 29 November 1431).
CONTENT OVERVIEW: Gregory the Great, *Dialogi* (Lib. II); Anon., *Donna de paradiso.*

In Latin and Italian, on parchment; i +48 ff. +i; generally, 103 x 75 mm (page) [see LAYOUT for ruling]; flyleaves i and ii, modern paper; medieval and modern foliation [see FOLIATION]; f. 48v blank.

COLLATION: i $+1^{10-2}$ $+2-5^{10}$ +1

QUIRES: Quinions, F/F, are the normal quire forms, typical of Italian production in the fifteenth century. Quire 1 lacks its first bifolium. The parchment is stained.

CATCHWORDS: Horizontal catchwords centered in the lower margins of quires 2–4; catchwords are stylized and heightened in yellow in the Italian fashion; all correspond.

FOLIATION: Medieval foliation with Roman numerals in red ink in upper margin; modern foliation in pencil with Arabic numerals; f. 1 (modern) = f. lx (medieval).

LAYOUT:

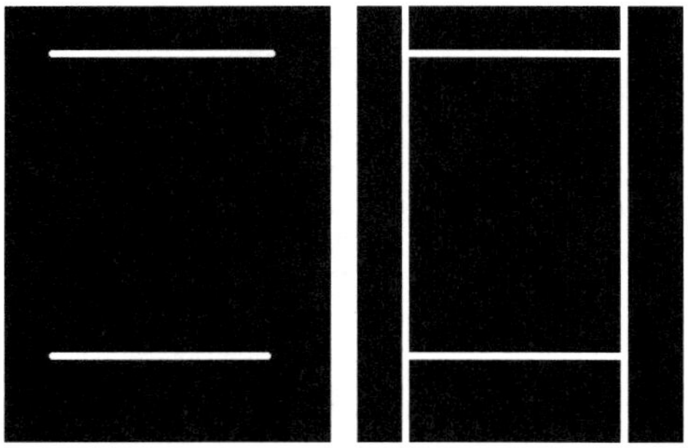

A1 A2

A ff. 1r–48v. Ink; 68 x 50 mm; 20 lines.

Pattern A is traced in brown ink; single column; writing below top line. Prickings are visible in the upper and lower margins for vertical bounding lines; verticals are often untraced or faded completely, resulting in **A1**. Single vertical bounding lines traced lightly in ink (or lead) are visible on some folios (e.g., ff. 9r, 17r, 31r), which are represented in **A2**.

Script: A single hand (M1) writes the text of the *Dialogi* (ff. 1r–42v) in Southern Textualis Formata (Rotunda). The vernacular quatrains (ff. 43r–48r) are written by M1 in Semitextualis. A few corrections in the margins and annotations are added by a second hand (M2) under the influence of Humanistic script (e.g., ff. 42r, 48r).

Decoration:

I. Rubrication: Rubrics, names of interlocutors, scribal colophon, paraph marks, and medieval foliation written in red ink; letter heightening of majuscules, cadels, and catchwords in yellow ink.

II. Initials: Flourished initials and one plain initial occur.

a. Flourished initials (1–2 line square inset) in red and blue ink alternate throughout the *Dialogi* (ff. 1r–42v); blue initials have contrasting penwork in red ink; flourishing of red initials traced lightly in washed-out brown ink, perhaps blue; occasional heightening in yellow (e.g., 4r).

b. One plain initial in red ink occurs only on f. 43r; heightened in yellow ink.

Contents:

1. Gregory the Great, *Dialogi* (Lib. II)—ff. 1r–42v.

inc.: [f. 1r] [Prologue] in qua prius conuersatus fuerat preest. [Lib. II] hic itaque cum iam relictis litterarum studiis petere deserta decreuisset . . .; expl.: [f. 42v] . . . loquendi uires interim per silencium reparemus. scribal colophon: [f. 42v] explicit secundus liber dyalogorum beati gregorii pape urbis rome de uita et miraculis beatissimi patris benedicti abbatis anno domini .m.cccc.xxxj. die undetricensimo mensis nouembris hora .xij. ante diem.

The text contains Book 2 only, beginning imperfectly with the end of the Prologue.

Edition: De Vogüé 1978–1980; Simonetti and Pricoco 2005–2006.
Bibliography: Castaldi 2003; Boccini 2006.

2. Anon., *Donna de paradiso*—ff. 43r–48r.

rub.: in cena domini per tres dies laude; inc.: [f. 43r] donna de lo paradiso lo to figlolo le sy e preso yhesu christo beato anccori donna non demorare . . .; expl.: [f. 48r] . . . fyglolo cum madre in uno tracto. deo gratias amen donna de lo paradiso et cetera.

The poem is written in quatrains; authorship is uncertain; cf. Iacopone da Todi, *Laude*, 70.

Binding: s. xx; brown leather; blind tooled; three raised bands.

Owners & Provenance: Laucournet (2000); Les Enluminures. According to Laucournet's description (pasted to inside front cover), the manuscript was at one time in the Abbey of Santa Giustina in Padua. There are no ownership marks to corroborate this; the colophon indicates the manuscript was copied by one living according to the Benedictine Rule. The library of Santa Giustina was dissolved by Napoleon in 1810. Acquired from Les Enluminures (Chicago, IL) by the university in August 2013.

Sales & Catalogues: Laucournet, 16 November 2000, lot 23.

cod. Lat. a. 12

Origin: Germany, s. xv^2.
Content Overview: Office of the Dead (use of the Dominicans), neumed; Penitential Psalms; Litany.

In Latin with some German, on parchment; ii +82 ff. +vi; generally 132 x 113 mm (page) [see Layout for ruling]; flyleaves i and iii, paper; flyleaf ii, medieval parchment; flyleaves iv–viii, modern paper.

Collation: ii +1–9^8 +10^{8+2} +vi

Quires: Parchment quaternions, F/F, are the normal quire forms; quire 10 has a quarter-leaf (f. 80) and singleton (f. 82), both with stubs added, and does not obey Gregory's Rule; flyleaf II originally pasted to f. 1r. The parchment is thick and well scraped; imperfection visible on f. 22 (lacking stitching). The manuscript has been trimmed on all three sides.

Layout:

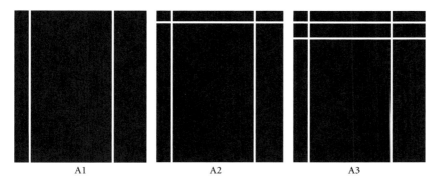

A1 A2 A3

A ff. 1r–79v, 81r–82v. Combined technique; 107 x 69 mm; 15 lines.

Pattern **A** is traced in three variant forms with combined technique (**A1–A3**); single column/full-music layout; writing below top line. **A1** is the basic pattern with vertical bounding lines traced in brown ink; horizontals of **A1** are traced lightly in lead or dark crayon, though barely visible (e.g., f. 8r). **A2** occurs only when staves are drawn at the top of the page: the top horizontal line is traced in red ink through both verticals and becomes the first staff line [see Music & Staves]. Single prickings are visible in the outer margins; double prickings for the first and third line create Pattern **A3**, which is visible on certain folios (e.g., ff. 69r, 70r); prickings for verticals lost due to trimming. The quarter-sheet inserted into quire 10 (now f. 80) is not traced on the recto; pattern on f. 80v is smaller, but imitative of **A3**.

Script: A single hand (M1) writes the text on ff. 1r–79v and 81r–82r in Northern Textualis Formata of the fifteenth century. Regionally, the script of M1 is representative of German types (s. xv²) in overall appearance and style of abbreviations ('zigzag' forms, etc.). Substantial additions in Northern Textualis (s. xv²) have also been made by a number of hands: M2 on flyleaf IIr and f. 82v [see Contents 1.1, 4]; M3 on flyleaf IIv and f. 60r–v [see Contents 1.2, 2.2.1–2]; M4 on flyleaf IIv and f. 82r [see Contents 1.3, 1.4, 3.3.11]; M5 on f. 60v [see Contents 2.2.3]; M6 on ff. 74v–75r and f. 80v [see Contents 3.2, 3.3.5]. A later hand, M7 (s. xvi¹), adds text in Hybrida Libraria on f. 80r [see Contents 3.3.4]. Marginal additions on ff. 44r, 58v, 59r in Northern Textualis by M1 and Semihybrida by M8. A seventeenth-century hand writes in German and Latin on front pastedown and flyleaves Ir–v, IIIr–v; a modern hand writes in German on flyleaves IV–VIII; later corrections written in the margins on ff. 26r and 29r.

Decoration:

I. Rubrication: Rubrics in red ink written by their respective text hands; letter heightening of majuscules and cadels in red ink.

II. Initials: Flourished and plain initials occur in hierarchy; cadels in music only.

a. Flourished initials (4 line square inset) in blue with purple penwork and white stylization occur on ff. 1r and 60v; another (3 line square inset) in blue with red penwork and white stylization occurs on f. 8r.

b. Plain initials (2 line square inset; 1 line versals) alternate in red and blue throughout the manuscript. Corrected initials are drawn in black (e.g., f. 64v).

c. Cadels (approx. 2 line square inset) in black ink with red heightening occur only within staves in music sections.

Music & Staves: Four-line staves drawn in red ink; 11 mm; square neumes in black ink. Staves drawn at the top of the page, the first line extends beyond the vertical bounding lines [see Layout].

Contents:

1. Additions—flyleaf IIr–v.

Additions written by M2 (1.1), M3 (1.2), and M4 (1.3, 1.4) [see Script]; 1.3 and 1.4 use the feminine forms (though the participle in 1.4 is masculine).

1.1. flyleaf IIr. inc.: magnificat animam meam dominum . . . abraham et semini eius in secula.

1.2. flyleaf IIv. RUB.: für lebend und für toten oracio; INC.: omnipotens sempiterne deus qui uiuorum dominaris . . . delictorum suorum ueniam et gaudia consequi mereantur eterna [cf. *CO* 4064].

1.3. flyleaf IIv. INC.: <a>bsolue quesumus domine animam famule ab omni uinculo . . . resuscitata respiret [cf. *CO* 16].

1.4. flyleaf IIv. INC.: <a>bsolue quesumus animas famularum tuarum ab omni uinculo . . . resuscitati respirent [cf. *CO* 16].

2. Office of the Dead, use of the Dominicans; neumed—ff. 1r–60r.

OTTOSEN nos. 14-72-24, 32-57-28, 68-46-38.

2.1. Votive prayers—ff. 58r–60r.

Marginal comments in Latin and German with *signes-de-renvoi* on ff. 58v–59r by M1 and M8 [see SCRIPT]; comments specify morphological variations for gender and number of nouns and adjectives; explicit of 2.1.7 completed in the right margin by M5.

2.1.1. f. 58r–v. RUB.: pro episcopo defuncto oratio; INC.: deus qui inter apostolicos sacerdotes famulum tuum episcopum pontificali . . . ut eorum quoque perpetuo aggregetur consorcio per [*CO* 1757b].

2.1.2. f. 58v. RUB.: pro uiro defuncto oratio; INC.: inclina domine aurem tuam ad preces nostras . . . et sanctorum tuorum iubeas esse consortem [*CO* 3116b].

2.1.3. ff. 58v–59r. RUB.: pro femina defuncta oratio; INC.: quesumus domine pro tua pietate . . . in eterne saluacionis partem restitue pro dominum [*CO* 4843].

2.1.4. f. 59r. RUB.: in anniuersario oratio; INC.: deus indulgenciarum domine da animabus fidelium tuorum . . . quietis beatitudinem luminis claritatem per [*CO* 1251].

2.1.5. f. 59r–v. RUB.: pro fratribus et sororibus oratio; INC.: deus uenie largitor et humane salutis actor . . . ad perpetue beatitudinis consorcium peruenire concedas per [*CO* 2205].

2.1.6. f. 59v. RUB.: pro parentibus oratio; INC.: deus qui nos patrem et matrem honorare precepisti . . . nosque eos in eterne claritatis gaudio fac uidere [cf. *HE* p. 111].

2.1.7. f. 60r. RUB. [f. 59v]: pro cunctis fidelibus defunctis oratio; INC.: fidelium deus omnium conditor et redemptor animabus . . . piis supplicacionibus consequantur qui uiuis et regnas cum [*CO* 2684b] deo patre in unitate spiritus sancti deus per omnia secula seculorum [*in dex. marg. add.* M5].

2.2. Added Prayers—f. 60r.

Additional prayers written by M3 (2.2.1, 2.2.1) and M5 (2.2.3) [see SCRIPT]; 2.2.3 is incomplete due to trimming.

2.2.1 RUB.: dis ist für alle ellend selen oratio; INC.: largire piissime deus animabus . . . misericordie tue recipiant adiumentum.

2.2.2. RUB.: fil man und uil frawen oratio; INC.: absolue quesumus domine animas famulorum famularumque tuarum . . . ut in resurrectionis gloria inter sanctos tuos resuscitati respirent.
2.2.3. INC.: deus in cuius miseratione anime fidelium requiescunt famulis et famulabus tuis omnibus [incomplete].

3. Penitential Psalms, Litany, and Collects—ff. 60v–82r

3.1. Penitential Psalms—ff. 60v–72v.

The antiphon *Ne reminiscaris domine* has interlinear glosses written by M3 for the appropriate forms of *meus*, *-a*, *-um* above those of *noster*, *-tra*, *-trum*.

3.2. Litany (Dominican)—ff. 72v–79r.

The litany contains several Dominican saints: Peter Martyr, Dominic (doubled), Thomas Aquinas, Vincent of Ferrer (added), and Catherine of Siena. Later additions by M6 supply regional saints, particularly the diocese of Bamberg: Henry, Louis, Sebald, Anne, Barbara, Ursula, Kunigunde, and Elizabeth of Hungary. M6 has also made erasures and corrected Anthony and Bernard, who were reversed, and Margaret.

3.3. Collects—ff. 79v–82r.

Dominican saints named in six of the prayers: Dominic (3.3.2), Peter Martyr (3.3.3), and Thomas Aquinas (3.3.6). A prayer mentioning Peter Martyr, Thomas Aquinas, Vincent of Ferrer, Antoninus, and Catherine of Siena (3.3.4) occurs on the inserted quarter-leaf f. 80r written by M7; Antoninus was canonized in 1523. A prayer to Vincent of Ferrer (3.3.5) was added by M6. The remainder of the page is filled by another prayer (3.3.11) written by M4. The collects are nearly identical to those found in codd. Lat. b. 1, Lat. b. 2, and Claremont, Claremont Colleges, Honnold/Mudd Library, Crispin 8 and Crispin 9 (see DUTSCHKE ET AL. 1986, 24–36).

3.3.1. f. 79v. RUB. [f. 79r]: oremus; INC.: protege domine famulos tuos subsidiis pacis . . . a cunctis hostibus redde securos per [*CO* 4756b].
3.3.2. f. 79v. RUB.: alia oratio; INC.: concede quesumus omnipotens deus ut qui peccatorum . . . beati dominici confessoris tui patrocinio subleuemur per [*CO* 766].
3.3.3. ff. 79v, 81r. RUB.: alia oratio; INC.: preces quas tibi domine offerimus intercedente beato petro martyre . . . sub tua protectione custodi per [*CO* 4625].
3.3.4. f. 80r. concede quesumus omnipotens deus ut ad meliorem uitam sanctorum tuorum petri thome uincencii anthoninii et katherine . . . comemoracionem agimus eciam actus imitemur per [cf. *CO* 749].
3.3.5. f. 80v. deus qui gentium multitudinem mira beati uincencii confessoris tui . . . habere mereamur in celis amen.
3.3.6. f. 81r. RUB.: oratio; INC.: deus qui ecclesiam tuam mira beati thome confessoris tui erudicione . . . et que egit imitacione complere per [cf. *CO* 1566].

3.3.7. f. 81r. RUB.: oratio; INC.: ineffabilem misericordiam tuam domine nobis clementer ... quas pro hiis meremur eripias per [*CO* 3129].

3.3.8. f. 81r–v. RUB.: oratio; INC.: pretende domine famulis et famulabus tuis dexteram celestis ... que digne postulant assequantur per [*CO* 4587a].

3.3.9. f. 81v. RUB.: oratio; INC.: ecclesie tue domine preces placatus admitte ut destructis aduersitatibus ... ac dirige in uiam salutis eterne per [*CO* 2404b].

3.3.10. ff. 81v–82r. RUB.: oratio; INC.: deus a quo sancta desideria recta consilia et iusta sunt opera ... sint tua protectione tranquilla per christum [*CO* 1088a].

3.3.11. f. 82r. INC.: <c>oncede quesumus omnipotens deus ut intercessio nos sancte dei genitricis semperque uirginis marie ... merita recolimus patrocinia senciamus per eundem [*CO* 752a, *recensio longa*].

4. Benedictus dominus deus [incomplete]—f. 82v.

INC.: [f. 82v] benedictus dominus deus israel ...; EXPL.: ... in tenebris in umbra mortis sedent.

The text is written by M2 [see SCRIPT].

BINDING: s. xvii/xviii; brown leather over boards; sewn on four cords; blind tooled; remnants of leather straps on lower board; metal pins on upper; edges dyed red; bookmark tabs of pink and white leather affixed to the edges (e.g., ff. 8, 19, 46).

OWNERS & PROVENANCE: Alberta von Herzen Jesu (3 July 1822); acquired from Les Enluminures (Chicago, IL) by the university in August 2013.

FORMER SHELFMARK: KI. Cc.36 (modern pencil, unknown).

cod. Lat. a. 13

Origin: France, s. xiii^{2}.
Content Overview: Pocket Bible (fragmentary) with glosses: Esther (incomplete); Job; Psalms.

In Latin with some English, on parchment; i + 31 ff. +1; generally 150 x 101 mm (page) [see Layout for ruling]; paper flyleaves (s. xvi^{2}?) with watermark visible on front pastedown and flyleaf i; f. 31v blank but ruled.

Quires: Collation has been disturbed when the fragment was rebound; parchment sexternions were the normal quire forms; no quire marks, catchwords, or signatures remain. The parchment is very thin and well scraped; the manuscript has been trimmed on all three sides for rebinding.

Layout:

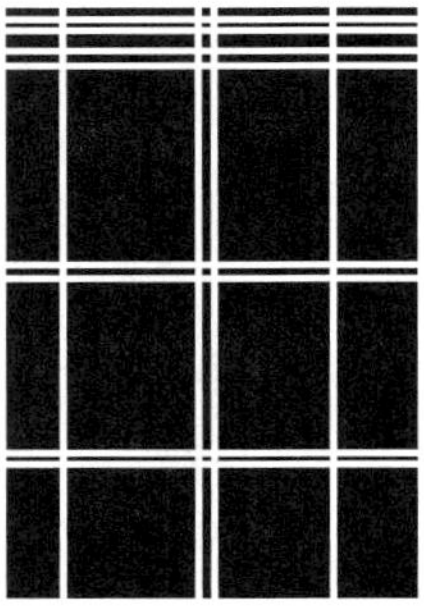

A

A ff. 1r–31v. Lead; 105 x 66 mm (intercol. 4 mm); 43 lines.

Pattern A is traced in lead on ff. 1r–31v; two columns (intercol. 4 mm); writing below top line; prickings in the upper and lower margins for vertical bounding lines; uppermost horizontals used to display book name; superfluous double horizontals through the middle of the page.

Script: A single hand (M1) writes the biblical texts in Northern Textualis of the thirteenth century. Interlinear and marginal glosses are added by four hands (M2–M5): M2 writes glosses in Latin in Anglicana (Cursiva Antiquior) of the late thirteenth century; M3 writes sparsely in English in Anglicana of the fourteenth century, mainly in the upper and lower margins; M4 writes Latin glosses in Cursiva Antiquior, but does not exhibit the particular features of Anglicana (e.g., f. 6r); M5 writes Latin glosses in a rapid Northern Textualis (e.g., f. 12r).

Decoration:

I. Rubrication: Rubrics in red ink through ff. 12r–14v only; indents reserved in the rest of the fragment; letter heightening of majuscules in red ink; paraph marks in red and blue ink.

II. Initials: Decorated, flourished, and plain initials occur in hierarchy.

a. Decorated initials (5–7 line square inset) in pink, green, and blue typical of the thirteenth century mark the beginning of prologues, books, and division of psalms. Many initials incorporate grotesques and bestial figures. Initials 7 lines in height occur on ff. 2r[b] (Iob), 12r[b] (Psalms), and 19v[a] (Ps 13); 6 lines on ff. 15v[a] (Ps 26), 17v[b] (Ps 38), and 21v[b] (Ps 68); 5 lines on ff. 1v[a] (prologue to Iob), 2r[a] (ibid.), 26v[a] (Ps 95), and 29r[a] (Ps 109, etc.); 4 lines on f. 24r[b] (Ps 80) [see Contents 3].

b. Flourished initials (1–2 line square indent) in red and blue ink with contrasting penwork occur in the texts; some of the 1 line size have later flourishing.

c. Plain initials (1 line versals) alternate in red and blue throughout the text.

Contents:

1. Esther [incomplete]—f. 1r[a]–v[a].

inc.: [f. 1r[a]] populos urbes atque prouincias quocumque regis iussa ueniebant . . .; expl.: [f. 1v[a]] . . . que ad pacem sui seminis pertinerent.

The text begins imperfectly at Est 8.17.

2. Iob with prologues—ff. 1v[a]–12r[a].

2.1. Prologue—ff. 1v[a]–2r[a]. inc.: cogor per singulos scripture diuine libros . . .; expl.: . . . et studiosum se magis quam maliuolum probet [Stegmüller 344].

2.2. Prologue—f. 2r[a–b]. inc.: sicut [*sic*] fiscellam iunco texerem aut palmarum folia conplicarem . . .; expl.: . . . magis utile quid ex otio meo ecclesiis christi euenturum ratus quam ex aliorum negocio [Stegmüller 357].

2.3. Iob—ff. 2r[b]–12r[a]. inc.: uir erat in terra hus nomine iob . . .; expl.: . . . usque ad quartam generationem et mortuus est senex et plenus dierum.

3. Psalms—ff. 12r[b]–31r[b].

inc.: [f. 12r[b]] beatus uir qui non abiit consilio impiorum . . .; expl.: [f. 31r[b]] . . . omnis spiritus laudet dominum.

Division of psalms: Pss 1, 13, 26, 38, 68, 95, and 109; Ps. 109 and the following are given by cue. The six canticles with ferial days and references are listed after the psalms conclude by M2 on f. 31r.

Binding: non-contemporary (s. xx?); brown leather over binder's board; blind tooled; re-backed.

Owners & Provenance: Acquired from King Alfred's Notebook (Cayce, SC) by the university in August 2013. The parent manuscript was an imperfect Bible of 294 folios containing Esther 5.4 through Apocalypse 15.6, which was sold by Dominic Winter in June 2013 (lot 351). The Bible contained the ownership marks of Thomas Martin (1697–1771) of Palgrave, a bookplate of a Thomas Barber of Norfolk, and an inscription of an Emily Bagot. The manuscript was subsequently broken up and sold in small portions, of which 75 leaves were listed on eBay on 17 December 2013.

Sales & Catalogues: Dominic Winter, 19–20 June 2013, lot 351 (parent manuscript).

cod. Lat. a. 14

Origin: Low Countries, s. xv^2 (Bruges).
Content Overview: Calendar.

In Latin, on parchment; 6 ff.; generally 160 x 113 mm (page) [see Layout for ruling].

Collation: i +1^6 +i

Quires: A ternion, F/F, comprises the manuscript; obeys Gregory's Rule.

Layout:

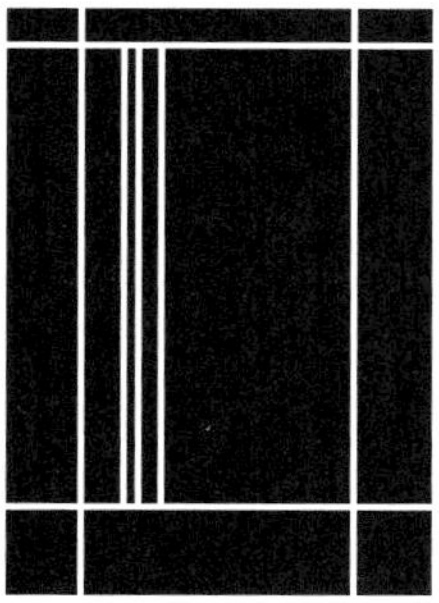

A

A ff. 1r–6v. Ink; 126 x 72 mm; cols. 11/4/6/51 mm; 32 lines.

Pattern **A** is traced in brown ink; four calendric columns (11/4/6/51 mm); writing below top line; no prickings are visible.

Script: A single hand (M1) writes all text in Northern Textualis Formata; script is executed rapidly; frequent use of **w**.

Decoration:
I. Rubrication: Graded feasts in red ink; letter heightening of majuscules in red ink.
II. Initials: Dentelle initials occur in hierarchy.
a. Dentelle initials (2 lines square inset) begin each month (**kl**) with alternating grounds.

Calendar: one page per month; dominical letter **a** in red ink; Roman time not marked.

Contents:

1. Calendar (Bruges).

Minimalist calendar written in black ink with graded feasts in red ink; the calendar is the use of Tournai in a redacted form; likely made in Bruges during the mid-fifteenth century. The feast of Alban as protomartyr (Jun. 22) may show the influence of a Sarum calendar made for export in the same location. Feasts include: translation of Thomas (Jul. 3; red), translation of Donatian (Aug. 8), Remigius (Oct. 1; red), Donatian (Oct. 14), Hubert (Nov. 3), Martin (Nov. 11; red), Liuinus of Ghent (Nov. 12).

Binding: s. xxi (2011); modern marbled paper over pasteboard; acid-free flyleaves.

Owners & Provenance: Acquired from King Alfred's Notebook (Cayce, SC) by the university in July 2012.

Sales & Catalogues: King Alfred's Notebook, *Enchiridion* 8, no. 4; ibid., *Enchiridion* 9, no. 4; ibid., *Enchiridion* 10, no. 6.

cod. Lat. a. 15

Origin: France, s. xv^2.
Content Overview: Book of Hours, use of Bourges and Paris.

In Latin, on parchment; ii +109 ff. +i; generally 95 x 70 mm (page) [see Layout for ruling]; foliated in modern pencil with Arabic numerals; f. 109 blank but ruled.

Collation: ii $+1–2^{6} +3^{4-1} +4^{4} +5^{8-3} +6–7^{8} +8^{4} +9^{8-1} +10^{8-1} +11^{6} +12–15^{8} +16^{6} +17^{2} +18^{4+1}$ +i

Quires: Parchment quaternions, F/F, are the predominant quire forms used for quires 5–8, 9–10, and 12–15; all quires obey Gregory's Rule unless specified otherwise. Quires 1–2, 11, and 16 are ternions, F/F; the bifolia for quires 1–2 are constructed from singletons and paste. Quire 3 is a binion, F/H, with the last leaf canceled; binions are also used for quires 4 (H/H; constructed bifolia) and 8 (F/F); quire 18 is a binion, F/F, with one leaf added to the end of the quire; quire 18 does not obey Gregory's Rule with its addition. Quire 5 is a quaternion lacking the first three leaves (H/F). Quires 9–10 are quaternions, F/F, which do not obey Gregory's Rule: quire 9 lacks the seventh leaf; quire 10 lacks the sixth. Quire 17 is a bifolium, H/H, inserted in reverse and inverted in a later binding [see Catchwords]; the correct textual order following f. 102v (quire 16) is ff. 104r–v, 103r–v (quire 17), 105r, etc. (quire 18) [see Contents 10].

Catchwords: Two sets of horizontal catchwords are present. Catchwords written in the lower right margin for quires 5–6, 9–11, 13–17 are written by the main hand, M3 [see Script]; all correspond. Other catchwords are written within quire 5 (f. 23v) and for the misbound quire 17 (f. 104v) [see Quires] by a sixteenth-century hand; added catchword on f. 23v corresponds to keep the singleton in order; catchword, "meum," on f. 104v artificially corresponds (ff. 103r, 104r, and 105r all begin with "meum").

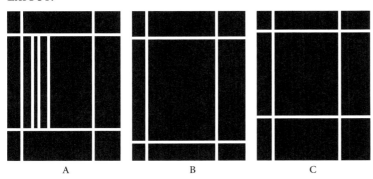

Layout:

A

B

C

A ff. 1r–12v. Rose ink; 62 x 44 mm; cols. 6.5/4/6/28 mm; 17 lines.
B ff. 13r–19v. Rose ink; 66 x 43 mm; 14 lines.
C ff. 20r–108v. Rose ink; 54 x 41 mm; 15 lines.

Pattern **A** is traced in rose ink on ff. 1r–12v for the calendar; four calendric columns (6.5/4/6/28 mm); writing below top line; no prickings are visible. Pattern **B** is traced in rose ink on ff. 13r–19v; single column; writing below top line; prickings occasionally visible in the upper margin for single vertical bounding lines. Pattern **C** is traced in rose ink on ff. 20r–108v; single column; writing below top line; prickings visible in the upper and lower margin for vertical bounding lines and in the outer margin for all horizontals.

SCRIPT: Three scribal bookhands can be distinguished (M1–M3). M1 writes the text of the calendar (ff. 1r–12v) in Northern Textualis Formata [see CONTENTS 1]. M2 writes the inserted Gospel lessons (ff. 13r–19v) in Northern Textualis Formata [see CONTENTS 2]. M3 writes the remainder of the manuscript (ff. 20r–108v) in Cursiva Formata (Bastarda) of the French variety. A late fifteenth-century hand, M4, completes the prayer *Ecclesiam tuam* after the cue on f. 65v in Cursiva Formata (Bastarda).

DECORATION:
I. RUBRICATION: Rubrics in red ink; letter heightening of majuscules in yellow ink (ff. 20r–108v).
II. INITIALS: Dentelle and plain initials occur in hierarchy, which has been disturbed.
A. Dentelle initials (2–3 line square inset; 1 line versals) occur from two different manuscripts; dentelles of the 2–3 line size are painted on ff. 1r–12v and ff. 13r–19v. Many dentelles of the 1–2 line size on ff. 20r–108v were cut from the same manuscript as ff. 13r–19v, and pasted throughout the text; most do not correspond to the text and some are inserted horizontally. Dentelles on ff. 20r–108v original to that section are of the 2–3 line size and begin major divisions of text, corresponding to the borders [see DECORATION IV].
B. Plain initials (2 line square inset; 1 line versals) alternate in red and blue ink on ff. 20r–108v.
III. LINE FILLERS: Arabesque line fillers occur in red and blue ink.
IV. BORDERS & FRAMES:

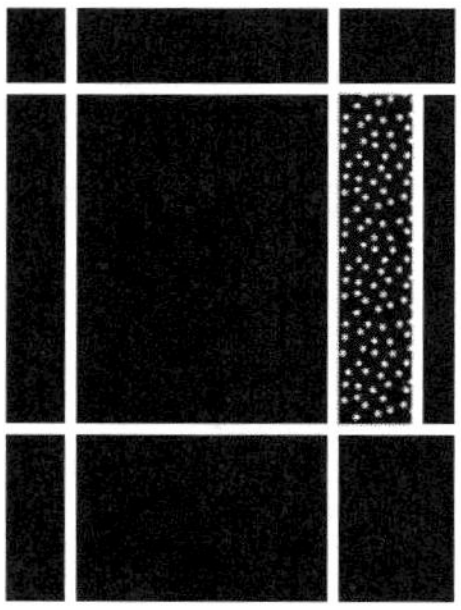

D

Functional outer borders (D) comprised of yellow, blue, and gold acanthus, floral motifs, strawberries, and black and gold rinceaux occur on ff. 30r, 44v, 53v, 59r, 73r, 90r, 93r, 96r; area to be decorated is defined in rose ink; folios with borders begin the major divisions of canonical hours and other texts. A section of the border from a now missing folio was cut and pasted onto f. 31v as a piece border; non-functional [see Decoration II.a]

Calendar: two pages per month; recto/verso; Roman time marked without numerals in black and red ink.

Contents:

1. Calendar (use of Bourges)—ff. 1r–12v.

Martyrological calendar with 146 days filled in black and red ink; graded feasts in red ink. The calendar is clearly for the use of Bourges and includes other saints particular to its suffrain dioceses and southern France. Significant feasts include: the Octave of Ursin (Jan. 5), William of Bourges (Jan. 10; red), Hilary, bishop of Poitiers (Jan. 13), Bonitus, bishop of Arvernae (Jan. 15), Sulpicius (Jan. 17; red), Sulpicius Severus (Jan. 29), Généford (Feb. 25), dedication of the church of Bourges (May 5), translation of William of Bourges (May 7; red), Austregisilius (May 20), Genulph, bishop of Cahors (Jun. 20), Iterius, bishop of Nevers (Jun. 25), liberation of Jerusalem (Jul. 15; red), Transfiguration (Aug. 6; red), Privat, bishop of Mende (Aug. 21), Lupus (Sept. 1), Euverte (Sept. 8), Marianus, monk (Sept. 19), Silvain (Sept. 22), Gerald (Oct. 13), Ambrose, bishop of Cahors (Oct. 16), Caprasius (Oct. 20), translation of Ursin (Sept. 11), Veranus, bishop of Cavillon (Nov. 12), translation of Stephen (Nov. 18; red), James the Hermit (Nov. 19), Eusicius (Nov. 27), Valerie at Limoges (Dec. 10), Lazarus, bishop of Marseilles (Dec. 17), and Ursin, bishop of Bourges (Dec. 29; red) displaces Thomas Becket (Dec. 30).

2. Gospel Lessons—ff. 13r–19v.

Standard readings with rubrics: John (ff. 13r–14v), Luke (ff. 14v–16r), Matthew (ff. 16v–18r), Mark (ff. 18v–19v); text written by M2.

3. Hours of the Virgin, use of Paris [incomplete]—ff. 20r–40v, 45r–v.

3.1. Matins [incomplete]—ff. 20v–30r. **hym.:** o quam glorifica luce . . .; **ant. ps. 8:** benedicta tu; **lect. i:** surge beatissima uirgo . . .; **r. i:** beata es uirgo maria . . .

3.2. Lauds—ff. 30r–40r, 45r–v. **rub.:** in laud(ibus); **pss.:** 92, 99, 62, 66, Benedicite, 148, 149, 150; **ant.:** benedicta tu . . .; **cap.:** te laudant angeli . . .; **hym.:** uirgo dei genitrix . . .; **ant. sup. ben.:** hec est regina . . .

Gospel lessons [see Contents 4] are inserted before the final collects of Lauds. The Hours of the Virgin resume with Prime following the collects of Lauds on f. 45v [see Contents 5].

4. Gospel Lessons [incomplete]—ff. 41r–44v.

Standard readings with rubrics: Luke (ff. 41r–42r), Matthew (ff. 42r–44r), and Mark (f. 44r–v); John is missing; text written by M3.

5. Hours of the Virgin, use of Paris [incomplete]—ff. 45v–65v.

5.1. Prime [incomplete]—ff. 45v–50v. PSS.: 1, 2, 5; HYM.: ueni creator spiritus . . .; ANT.: benedicta tu; CAP.: felix namque es . . .; R.: diffusa est . . .; V.: propterea benedixit . . .

5.2. Terce [incomplete]—ff. 51r–53v. PSS.: 119.5–7, 120, 121; ANT.: dignare me laudare . . .; CAP.: paradisi porta . . .; R.: specie tua . . .; V.: intende prospere . . .

5.3. Sext [incomplete]—ff. 53v–56v. RUB.: non(a) [*sic*]; PSS.: 122, 123, 124; HYM.: ueni creator; ANT.: post partum . . .; CAP.: gaude maria uirgo . . .; R.: adiuuabit eam . . .; V.: deus in medio . . .

5.4. None [incomplete]—ff. 57r–59v. PSS.: 125.6, 126, 127; ANT.: sicut lilium . . .; CAP.: per te dei genitrix; R.: elegit eam . . .; V.: et habitare . . .; V.: post partum . . .

5.5. Vespers [incomplete]—ff. 59v–61v. PSS.: 121, 122, 123, 124, 125; ANT.: beatam me; CAP.: beata es uirgo maria . . .; HYM.: aue maris stella . . .; ANT. SUP. MAGNIF.: sancta maria.

5.6. Compline [incomplete]—ff. 62r– 65v. PSS.: 42, 128, 130; ANT.: sancta dei genitrix . . .; HYM.: uirgo dei genitrix . . .; CAP.: sicut cynamomum et balsamum . . .; V.: ecce ancilla domini; ANT. SUP. NUN. DIM.: cum iocunditate.

6. *Obescro te* and *O intemerata* (masculine forms)—ff. 66r–72v.

6.1. *Obsecro te*—ff. 66r–70r. RUB.: [f. 65v] oratio deuota ad nostram dominam; INC.: obsecro te domina . . . ego sum facturus locuturus aut cogitaturus . . . michi famulo tuo . . .; EXPL.: . . . audi et exaudi me dulcissima uirgo maria mater dei et misericordie amen [cf. LEROQUAIS 2:346–347].

6.2. *O intemerata*—ff. 70r–72v. INC.: o intemerata . . . michi miserrimo peccatori . . . ego miserrimus peccator . . .; EXPL.: . . . paraclitus gratiarum dator qui cum pater et filio uiuit et regnat deus per omnia secula seculorum amen [cf. WILMART, 494–495].

7. Penitential Psalms, Litany, and Collects—ff. 73r–90r.

7.1. Penitential Psalms—ff. 73r–86r.

7.2. Litany—ff. 86r–89r.

Martyrs: Stephen, Linus, Cletus, Clement, Laurence, Vincent, Fabian, Sebastian; *Confessors*: Martin, Silvester, Nicholas, Martin, Germain, Ambrose, Augustine, Jerome, Maurus, Fiacre; *Virgins*: Mary Magdalene, Anne, Katherine, Margaret, Felicity, Agatha, Agnes, Lucia, Genevieve, Fides, Spes, Caritas, Neomadia (Neosnadia).

7.3. Collects—ff. 89v–90r.

7.3.1. INC.: deus cui proprium est misereri semper et parcere . . . miseracio tue pietatis absoluat per dominum [*CO* 1143].

7.3.2. INC.: fidelium deus omnium conditor . . . piis supplicacionibus consequantur qui uiuis et regnas deus [*CO* 2684b].

8. Hours of the Cross—ff. 90r–93r.

Matins, ff. 90r–91r; Prime, f. 91r; Terce, f. 91v; Sext, ff. 91v–92r; None, f. 92r; Vespers, f. 92r–v; Compline, f. 92v; *recommendatio*, ff. 92v–93r. Each stanza concludes with the usual verse, response, and prayer, which are written fully for Matins; all other repetitions are given in cue form. For the hymns see *AH* 30: no. 13.

9. Hours of the Holy Spirit—ff. 93r–96r.

Matins, ff. 93r–94r; Prime, f. 94r; Terce, f. 94r–v; Sext, f. 94v; None, f. 95r; Vespers, f. 95r–v; Compline, f. 95v; *recommendatio*, ff. 95v–96r. Antiphon, verse, response, and prayer are written fully for Matins; all other repetitions are given in cue form.

10. Office of the Dead (Short Office Fourteen)—ff. 96r–108v.

Ottosen nos. 72-14-38. The section is misbound [see Quires] and ends imperfectly in Lauds; textual order after f. 102v: ff. 104r–v, 103r–v, 105r, etc.

Binding: s. xxi; brown leather; gilt tooled; gilt spine; rebound in 2015; edges dyed red. Front and rear boards from the previous binding (s. xviii–xix) are brown leather over pasteboard with paper pastedowns.

Owners & Provenance: The ownership mark of a Daniel Hazard (fl. s. xix?) is written in black and red ink on the inner board of the previous binding; Israel Burr Perlman (1886–1953) of Chicago, IL, purchased the manuscript from Sotheby's in 1930; acquired from King Alfred's Notebook (Cayce, SC) by the university in April 2015.

Sales & Catalogues: Sotheby's, 29 July 1930, lot 277; DuMouchelles, 16 January 2015, lot 10005.

cod. Lat. a. 16

Origin: Low Countries, s. xv^2.
Content Overview: Book of Hours, use of Rome.

In Latin, on parchment; i +113 ff.; generally 101 x 70 mm (page) [see Layout for ruling]; foliated in modern pencil with Arabic numerals; f. 15v blank but ruled.

Collation: i $+1^{12-1}$ $+2^{8-2}$ $+3^{8}$ $+4^{8-1}$ $+5-6^{8}$ $+7^{6-1}$ $+8^{8-1+1}$ $+9^{8}$ $+10^{6}$ $+11^{8-1}$ $+12^{4}$ $+13^{8-1}$ $+14^{2+1+1+1}$ $+15^{6}$ $+16^{6-1}$ $+17^{4}$

Quires: Original collation has been disturbed and some quires have been regathered; texts are not bound in order. The collation statement reflects the current arrangement of the manuscript. Originally, a sexternion, F/F, comprised the calendar; quaternions, F/F, were the normal quire forms. Folios containing decoration have been excised; the remnants of a bifolium which contained border decoration are two stubs now sewn into quire 2 as a reinforcement between ff. 13v/14r and 15v/16r; border decoration is visible on the verso of the stub between ff. 15v/16r. Many quires are lacking leaves: quire 2 lacks the first and sixth; quire 4 lacks the fifth; quire 7 lacks the first; quire 11 lacks the third; quire 13 lacks the first; and quire 16 lacks the third. Quire 8 is a quaternion lacking its final leaf with a singleton (f. 61) pasted to f. 60v resulting in F/H. Quire 14 is disturbed by rebinding and sewing, but appears to be one bifolium (ff. 94/98) with three singletons (ff. 95–97).

Layout:

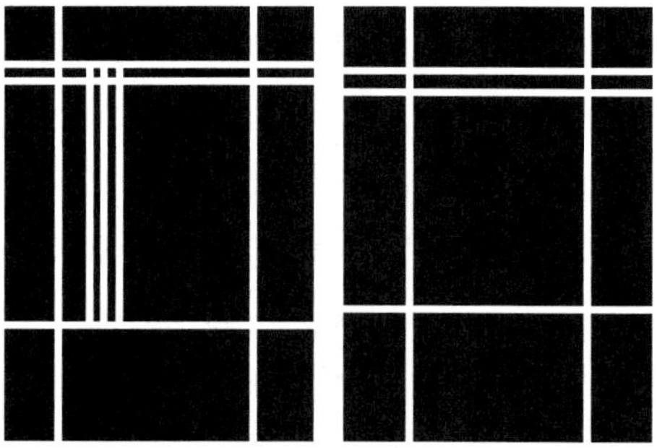

A B

A ff. 1r–11v. Rose ink; 60 x 44 mm; cols. 7/3/4/30 mm; 17 lines.
B ff. 12r–113v. Rose ink; 55 x 40 mm; 13 lines.

Pattern **A** is traced in rose ink on ff. 1r–11v; four calendric columns (7/3/4/30 mm); writing below top line; no prickings are visible. Pattern **B** is traced in rose ink on ff. 12r–113v; single column; writing below top line; prickings occasionally visible in the lower margin for vertical bounding lines.

Script: A single hand (M1) writes all text in Northern Textualis Formata.

Decoration:
I. Rubrication: Rubrics in red ink; letter heightening of majuscules in red ink.
II. Initials: Dentelle and flourished initials occur in hierarchy.
a. Dentelle initials (2 line square inset; hanging **is**) on alternating grounds mark textual divisions throughout the manuscript; dentelles also occur in the calendar (**kl**).
b. Flourished initials (1 line versals) in blue ink with red penwork and gold with blue penwork alternate throughout the manuscript.
III. Line Fillers: Arabesque line fillers in red and blue ink occur within the Litany on ff. 77v–81r.

Calendar: Two pages per month; recto/verso; dominical letter **a** in red ink; Roman time without numerals marked in red and blue ink.

Contents:
Contents are listed in contextual order with folio numbers; a list of the contents by present codicological unit with sequential folio numbers follows the description.

1. Calendar (minimalist)—ff. 1r–11v.

Minimalist calendar redacted to appear as general as possible; graded feasts in red ink; calendar is badly damaged; February mostly torn away and March missing completely. The exemplar was likely from Tournai; the feast of Remigius and Bavo (Oct. 1) remains graded in red ink; Bavo and Remigius also appear in the Litany among the confessors [see Contents 7.2].

2. Hours of the Cross [incomplete]—ff. 12r–15r.

Matins (*oratio* only), f. 12r–v; Prime, ff. 12v–13r; Terce, f. 13r; Sext, f. 13r–v; None, ff. 13v–14r; Vespers, f. 14r; Compline, f. 14v–r; *recommendatio*, f. 15r. Each stanza concludes with the usual verse, response, and prayer, which are written fully for all hours. For the hymns see *AH* 30: no. 13.

3. Mass of the Virgin [incomplete]—ff. 16r–22r.

inc.: [f. 16r] christus sine macula ad uitam eternam . . .; expl.: [f. 22r] . . . ad resurrectionis gloriam perducamur per dominum nostrum ihesum christum filium tuum qui tecum uiuit et regnat in unitate spiritus sancti deus per omnia secula seculorum amen [*CO* 2748].

The text begins imperfectly.

4. Gospel Lessons—ff. 22r–28v.

Standard readings with rubrics: John (ff. 22r–23v), Luke (ff. 23v–25v), Matthew (ff. 25v–27v), Mark (ff. 27v–28v).

5. Added Prayer—f. 29r.

INC.: [f. 29r] <d>eus cui omne cor patet . . .; EXPL.: [f. 29r] . . . et digne laudare mereamur per dominum [*CO* 1135].

6. Hours of the Virgin, use of Rome [incomplete]—ff. 30r–61v, 107r–109v, 99r–104v, 94r–98v.

6.1. Matins [incomplete]—ff. 30r–48v. HYM.: quem terra pontus . . .; ANT. PS. 8: benedicta; LECT. I: in omnibus requiem; R. I: sancta et immaculata.

6.2. Lauds [incomplete]—ff. 49r–60v. PSS.: 92.3–5, 99, 62, 66, Benedicite [incomplete], 148.6–14, 149, 150; ANT.: assumpta est . . .; CAP.: uiderunt eam filie syon . . .; HYM.: o gloriosa domina . . .; ANT. SUP. BEN.: beata dei.

6.3. Prime [incomplete]—ff. 61r–v, 105r–106v. PSS.: 54.5–9, 84, 116; ANT.: assumpta es . . .; CAP.: que est ista . . .; R.: dignare me . . .

6.4. Terce [incomplete]—ff. 107r–109v. PSS.: 119.6–7, 120, 121; ANT.: maria uirgo assumpta est . . .; CAP.: et sic in syon . . .; R.: diffusa est . . .

6.5. Sext [incomplete]—ff. 99r–100v. PSS.: 123.2–8, 124; ANT.: in odorem . . .; CAP.: et radicaui . . .; R.: benedicta tu.

6.6. None [incomplete]—ff. 101r–102v. PSS.: 125.6, 126, 127; ANT.: pulcra es . . .; CAP.: in plateis sicut . . .; R.: post partum . . .

6.7. Vespers [incomplete]—ff. 103r–104v, 94r–96v. PSS.: 109.3–7, 112, 121, 126, 147; ANT.: dum esset; CAP.: ab inicio ante . . .; HYM.: aue maris stella . . .; ANT. SUP. MAGNIF.: beata mater.

6.8. Compline [incomplete]—ff. 97r–98v. PSS.: 128.7–8, 129, 130; HYM.: memento salutis auctor; CAP.: ego mater pulcre . . .; ANT. SUP. NUN. DIM.: sub tuum.

7. Penitential Psalms, Litany, and Collects [incomplete]—ff. 87r–92v, 83r–86v, 76r–82v.

7.1. Penitential Psalms [incomplete]—ff. 87r–92v, 83r–86v, 76r–77r.

7.2. Litany [incomplete]—ff. 77r–82r.

Martyrs: Cornelius, Cyprian, Laurence, Vincent, Piatus, Denis (*cum soc.*), Maurice, Nicaise, Quintin, Sebastian, Christopher, Thomas; *Confessors*: Silvester, Gregory, Hilary, Martin, Nicholas, Augustine, Ambrose, Jerome, Benedict, Bavo, Eloy, Giles, Anthony, Remigius, Germain, Vedast, Amand, Medard, Bernard, Severin; *Virgins*: Mary Magdalene, Mary of Egypt, Felicity, Martha, Agatha, Agnes, Margaret, Christina, Katherine, Tecle, Petronelle, Brigid, Barbara, Juliana, Elizabeth, Apollonia, Lucia.

7.3. Collects—f. 82r–v.

7.3.1. f. 82r. RUB.: oratio; INC.: exaudi quesumus domine supplicum preces . . . indulgenciam tribuas benignus et pacem [*CO* 2541].

7.3.2. f. 82r–v. RUB.: oratio; INC.: fidelium deus omnium conditor . . . piis supplicationibus consequantur per dominum nostrum ihesum christum filium tuum qui tecum uiuit et regnat in unitate spiritus sancti deus per omnia secula seculorum amen [*CO* 2684b].

8. Office of the Dead (Short Office Five) [incomplete]—ff. 70r–75v, 62r–69v, 110r–113v.

OTTOSEN nos. 14-72-38.

BINDING: s. xix/xx; brown leather over pasteboard; blind tooled; sewn on three cords; marbled pastedown and flyleaf; boards detached; only the rear board remains.

OWNERS & PROVENANCE: Acquired from ElevenEleven Books (Clarkson, NY) by the university in May 2015.

CONTENTS BY PRESENT CODICOLOGICAL UNIT:

1. Quire 1 (VI^{12-1})—ff. 1r–11v.

Calendar.

2. Quire 2 (V^{10-4})—ff. 12r–17v.

RUB.: oratio; INC.: [f. 12r] domine ihesu christe fili dei uiui pone passionem crucem . . .; EXPL.: [f. 17v] . . . a presenti liberari tristicia et eterna perfrui leticia per christum dominum nostrum amen. lectio [*rub.*].

Hours of the Cross (ff. 12r–15r); Mass of the Virgin (ff. 16r–17v).

3. Quire 3 (IV^{8})—ff. 18r–25v.

RUB.: libri sapiencie.; INC.: [f. 18r] in inicio et ante secula creata sum . . .; EXPL.: [f. 25v] . . . ubi est qui natus est rex iudeorum uidimus.

Mass of the Virgin (ff. 18r–22r); Gospel lessons (ff. 22r–25v).

4. Quire 4 (IV^{8-1})—ff. 26r–32v.

INC.: [f. 26r] enim stellam stellam [*sic*] eius in oriente et uenimus . . .; EXPL.: [f. 32v] . . . omnia subiecisti sub pedibus eius.

Gospel lessons (ff. 26r–28v); added prayer (f. 29r); Matins *BMV* (ff. 30r–32v).

5. Quire 5 (IV^{8})—ff. 33r–40v.

INC.: [f. 33r] oues et boues uniuersas insuper et pecora campi . . .; EXPL.: [f. 40v] . . . dominus narrabit in scriptu-.

Matins *BMV*.

6. Quire 6 (IV^{8})—ff. 41r–48v.

INC.: [f. 41r] -ris populorum principium horum qui fuerunt in ea . . .; EXPL.: [f. 48v] . . . patrem inmense maiestatis uenerandum tuum.

Matins *BMV*.

7. Quire 7 (III^{6-1})—ff. 49r–53v.

INC.: [f. 49r] es eleuauerunt flumina domine eleuauerunt flumina uocem suam . . .; EXPL.: [f. 53v] . . . benedicite spiritus et anime iustorum domino benedicite sancti et humiles corde domine benedicite.

Lauds *BMV*.

8. Quire 8 (IV^{8-1+1})—ff. 54r–61v.

INC.: [f. 54r] -ceptum posuit et non preteribit . . .; EXPL.: [f. 61v] . . . aut extendas iram tuam a generatione in generacionem.

Lauds *BMV* (ff. 54r–60v); Prime *BMV* (f. 61r–v).

9. Quire 9 (IV^{8})—ff. 62r–69v.

INC.: [f. 62r] propter hanc in altum regredere dominus iudicat populos . . .; EXPL.: [f. 69v] . . . et conuoluta est a me quasi tabernaculum pas-.

Office of the Dead.

10. Quire 10 (III^{6})—ff. 70r–75v.

INC.: [f. 70r] in regione uiuorum. antiphona. heu me. ad dominum cum tribularer . . .; EXPL.: [f. 75v] . . . conuertere domine et eripe animam meam quoniam non.

Office of the Dead.

11. Quire 11 (IV^{8-1})—ff. 76r–82v.

INC.: [f. 76r] mortuos seculi et anxiatus est super me spiritus meus . . .; EXPL.: [f. 82v] . . . piis supplicationibus consequantur per dominum nostrum ihesum christum filium tuum qui tecum uiuit et regnat in unitate spiritus sancti deus per omnia secula seculorum amen.

Penitential Psalms (ff. 76r–77r); Litany and collects (ff. 77r–82v).

12. Quire 12 (II^{4})—ff. 83r–86v.

INC.: [f. 83r] -ris sacrificium deo spiritus contribulatus cor contritum et humilitatem . . .; EXPL.: [f. 86v] . . . si iniquitates obseruaueris domine domine quis sustinebit quia.

Penitential Psalms.

13. Quire 13 (IV$^{8-1}$)—ff. 87r–93v.

INC.: [f. 87r] inter omnes inimicos meos discedite a me . . .; EXPL.: [f. 93v] . . . sacrificium dedissem utique holocaustis non delectabe-.

Penitential Psalms.

14. Quire 14 (II$^{2+1+1+1}$)—ff. 94r–98v.

INC.: [f. 94r] lauda deum tuum syon quoniam confortauit seras . . .; EXPL.: [f. 98v] . . . domine intercessio gloriosa nos protegat et.

Vespers *BMV* (ff. 94r–96v); Compline *BMV* (ff. 97r–98v).

15. Quire 15 (III^{6})—ff. 99r–104v.

INC.: [f. 99r] homines uiuos forte uiuos deglutiscent nos . . .; EXPL.: [f. 104v] . . . lauda iherusalem dominum.

Sext *BMV* (ff. 99r–100v); None *BMV* (ff. 101r–102v); Vespers *BMV* (ff 103r–104v).

16. Quire 16 (III$^{6-1}$)—ff. 105r–109v.

INC.: [f. 105r] deus tu conuersus uiuificabis nos et plebs tua letabitur in te . . .; EXPL.: [f. 109v] . . . et pacem tuam ut supra. benedicamus domino. deo gracias.

Prime *BMV* (ff. 105r–106v); Terce *BMV* (ff. 107r–109v).

17. Quire 17 (II^{4})—ff. 110r–113v.

INC.: [f. 110r] -torum precisa est uelut a texente uita mea . . .; EXPL.: [f. 113v] . . . absoluti tecum sine fine letentu<r> per. fidelium deus omnium et cetera.

Office of the Dead.

cod. Lat. b. 1

Origin: Southern Germany, s. xv^2 (Nuremberg?, *post* 1456).
Content Overview: Psalter, neumed (Dominican).

In Latin with some German, on parchment; i + 212 ff. +i; generally 163 x 122 mm (page) [see Layout for ruling]; foliated in modern pencil with Arabic numerals; leather and metal finger tabs attached throughout; flyleaves, medieval parchment; f. 212v blank.

Collation: i $+1^{6}$ $+2{-}6^{10}$ $+7^{10+1}$ $+8{-}9^{10}$ $+10^{10-1}$ $+11{-}21^{10}$ $+22^{6}$ +i

Quires: Parchment quinions, F/F, are the normal quire forms. Quires 1 and 22 are ternions. Quire 7 contains a partial leaf (f. 57) pasted to f. 58r (asymmetrical insertion). Quire 10 lacks the sixth leaf (stub remains on f. 92). Medieval parchment flyleaves are singletons with stubs added to quires 1 and 22 (not reflected in collation statement).

Catchwords: Horizontal catchwords in the lower right margin for quires 2–21; all correspond. Catchwords in Northern Textualis except that for quire 15 (f. 146v) which is written in Hybrida or Cursiva (single compartment **a**; not enough other letter forms present to classify properly).

Layout:

A1 A2 B1 B2 C

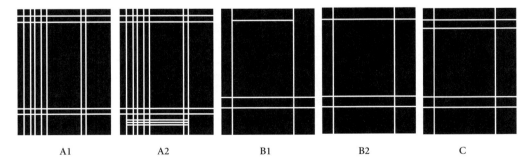

A ff. 1r–6v. Ink; 126 x 86 mm; cols. 9/5/8/7.5/51/7 mm; 32 lines.
B ff. 7r–176v. Ink; 116 x 76 mm; 18 lines.
C ff. 177r–212r. Ink; 111 x 73 mm; 18 lines.

Pattern **A** is traced lightly in brown ink on ff. 1r–6v; six calendric columns (9/5/8/7.5/51/7 mm); writing below top line; double prickings in the upper and lower margins for vertical bounding lines and calendric columns (recto and verso); single prickings in the outer margin for text lines, ruled individually. A variant pattern (**A2**) occurs on ff. 1r and 2r; **A2** contains four additional lines per page in the lower margin for two lines of German text [see Contents 1]. Patterns **B** (ff. 7r–176v, with variants) and **C** (ff. 177r–212r) are traced in brown ink; single column; writing below top line. Shifts between **B1** (ff. 7r–60v, 65r–67v, 70r/75v) and **B2** (ff. 61r–64v, 68r–69v, 70v/75r, 76r–176v) occur in quires 7 and 8: **B2** is traced on final two bifolia of quire 7 (ff. 61r–64v); **B1** is traced on the conjugate ff. 70r/75v (third bifolium in quire 8), but **B2** is traced on the conjugate ff. 70v/75r. **B1** contains an atypical pricking pattern in the outer margin which suggests rake-ruling: every four lines from the headline followed by two additional pricks. **B2** exhibits the same pricking pattern until f. 92, where there are prickings for each line (ruled individually). Pattern **C** begins with quire 19; **C** uses the same pricking pattern as **B2** for individual ruling, but dimensions are smaller.

Script: Three scribal bookhands (M1–M3) write all texts in Northern Textualis Formata with clear Germanic features. The script is extremely black in appearance with some fading. Plentiful corrections by erasures (e.g., ff. 23v, 165v) and cross-outs in red ink (e.g., f. 94r); additions with red *signes-de-renvoi* (e.g., ff. 40v, 82v, 95r, 112r, 125v) by text hands, and black by others (e.g., ff. 7v, 76v, 185v). M1 writes the calendar on ff. 1r–6v in Northern Textualis Formata; M1 exhibits a forking of ascenders similar to M2, but the script is overall less formal with less angularity. M2 writes all text on ff. 7r–171r in Northern Textualis Formata (Quadrata); M2 displays a distinctive use of hairlines, both integral and superfluous; two graphs for the **con** abbreviation are in use (e.g., f. 114v), though preference is for the Germanic form. M2 is also prone to heavy forking of truncated ascenders. M3 writes the text beginning on the bottom of f. 171r through f. 212r in Northern Textualis Formata (Quadrata). M3 uses hairlines more sparingly (almost always superfluous); ascenders are not truncated as M2 and do not display forking. M3 marks the majority of **i**s with a hairline; exclusive use of the Germanic form for the **con** abbreviation. A fourth hand (M4) corrects sections of the manuscript usually by erasure; M4 writes Northern Textualis in dark black ink (e.g., ff. 82v, 170v, 176v, 196v, 202v, 210r–v, 211v). Addition in the lower margin of f. 76v in Hybrida (*fort.* M1); addition in margins of ff. 7v and 112r in Cursiva. A later hand (s. xvi) adds ferial information in the margins (e.g., f. 164v).

Decoration: Stylized *litterae elongatae* occur on ff. 171v–211r in conjunction with M3.

I. Rubrication: Rubrics in red ink; letter heightening of majuscules and cadels in red ink.

II. Initials: Various types of initials occur in hierarchy; many do not conform properly to the usual types.

a. One foliate style initial (7 line square inset) begins Ps 1 (f. 8r); blue with pink interior and gold penwork; some spray into inner margin [see Borders & Frames].

B. One dentelle style initial (4 line square inset) begins Ps 109 (f. 137v); low level of execution: gold with blue interior and white penwork; red flourished background with sprays and gold dots into outer and lower margins.

C. Littera duplex style initials (3–4 line square inset) occur. Three line size initials: gold and blue with red flourishing begins Ps 26 (f. 34r); blue and red with red flourishing begins Ps 52 (f. 65r). Four line size: blue, red, and white with red flourishing begins Ps 68 (f. 81r); gold and blue with red flourishing begins Ps 80 (f. 101r); blue and red with red flourishing begins Ps 97 (f. 118v). All flourishing sprays into margins for border effects [see BORDERS & FRAMES].

D. Flourished type initials (2–3 line square inset) in red and blue ink are used sparsely; low-level flourishing in contrasting color and minimal penwork (e.g., ff. 27r, 44r, 145r, 145v); contrasting colors often removed (e.g., f. 31v).

E. Plain initials (1–3 line square inset; occasional hanging initial **i**) in red and blue ink alternate throughout the manuscript (red only for calendar). Those 3 lines in height begin the invitatory (f. 7r), some hymns, antiphons, and a canticle, though not used consistently. Initials 2 lines in height begin psalms (except those of the major divisions), canticles, hymns, capitula, and other divisions (e.g., Litany, f. 197v; prayers, ff. 202r–203r). One line versals are used throughout all texts without musical notation. Numerous plain initials incorporate border sprays similar to flourished types (e.g., ff. 31r, 36v, 54v); guide letters visible in the bodies of all sizes.

F. Cadels in black and red ink with green, yellow, and pink washes occur in initial position of all antiphons within staves. Most contain human and animal grotesques (e.g., ff. 48v, 136v) and other zoomorphic motifs (e.g., butterfly, f. 33v; bird, f. 152v). The cadels are 4 staves and 1 text line in height (approx. three lines of text) with marginal extensions and sprays depending on position [see BORDERS & FRAMES].

III. LINE FILLERS: Rectangular line fillers of black and red stippling occur sparsely (e.g., ff. 7v, 169r).

IV. BORDERS & FRAMES: Partial acanthus borders in upper, inner, and lower margins of f. 8r; green, dark yellow, pink, and gold. Red penwork and gold dots (grotesque on f. 65r); borders similar to three-margins left style on ff. 34r, 65r, 81r, 101r, 118v. Cadel sprays extend into partial borders with penwork and occasional acanthus leaves.

CALENDAR: One month per page; dominical letter **a** in red ink; Roman time marked in red ink.

MUSIC & STAVES: Four-line staves in red ink, ruled individually [see LAYOUT]; 12 mm; square neumes in black ink; blank staves on f. 19r.

CONTENTS:

1. Calendar (Dominican)—ff. 1r–6v.

Liturgical calendar in black and red ink. Several feasts indicate Dominican use and permit a localization to a Dominican house in the diocese of Bamberg, likely the Katharinenkloster in Nuremberg: Erhard (Jan. 8), translation of Thomas Aquinas (Jan. 28; red; totum duplex), *anniuersarium patrum et matrum* (Feb. 4), Kunigunde (Mar. 3; red; simplex), Thomas Aquinas (Mar. 7; red; totum duplex), octave of Thomas Aquinas (Mar. 14; memorie), Gertrude (Mar. 17), Vincent of Ferrer (Apr. 5; red; totum duplex), octave of Vincent of Ferrer (Apr. 12; memorie), Adalbert (Apr. 24; 3 lectiones), Peter Martyr (Apr. 29; red; totum duplex), translation of Peter Martyr (May 7; red; totum duplex), Apparition of St. Michael (May 8; totum duplex), translation of Dominic (May 24; red; totum duplex), Ulric (Jul. 4), *anniuersarium in cimiteriis nostris sepultorum* (Jul. 12), Henry (Jul. 13; red; simplex), Margaret (Jul. 14; red; simplex), Dominic (Aug. 5; red; totum duplex), Transfiguration (Aug. 6; totum duplex), octave of Dominic (Aug. 12; simplex), Sebald (Aug. 19; red; simplex), *anniuersarium familiarum et benefactorum ordinis* (Sept. 5), translation of Kunigunde (Sept. 9; red; simplex), Wenceslas (Sept. 28; 3 lectiones), Michael (Sept. 29; red; totum duplex), Otto (Sept. 30; red), octave of Michael (Oct. 6; memorie), *anniuersarium omnium fratrum et sororum ordinis nostri* (Oct. 10), Katherine (Nov. 25; red; totum duplex), Conrad (Nov. 26); cf. calendars in cod. Lat. b. 2, and San Marino, Huntington Library, HM 25771. German text about the Golden Numbers added in the lower margin for January (f. 1r) and March (f. 2r).

2. Psalter, neumed—ff. 7r–185r.

The invitatory *Venite exultemus* and hymn *Nocte surgentes* on f. 7r; neumed. Eight-part division of psalms marked by initials in hierarchy: Pss 1 (f. 8r), 26 (f. 34r), 52 (f. 65r), 68 (f. 81r), 80 (f. 101r), 97 (f. 118v), and 109 (f. 137v); the psalter includes noted antiphons, hymns, etc.

3. Canticles—ff. 185v–197v.

Six ferial canticles; *Benedicite omnia* (f. 193r), *Te deum* (f. 194r), *Benedictus dominus deus* (f. 195r), *Quicumque uult* (f. 195v).

4. Litany and Collects—ff. 197v–203r.

4.1. Litany (Dominican)—ff. 197v–202r.

The Litany prominently features Dominican saints and others pointing toward Nuremberg; notable saints include: Peter Martyr, Dominic (doubled), Thomas Aquinas, Vincent of Ferrer, Henry, Sebald, Katherine (doubled), Margaret, Ursula, Kunigunde. Erasures on ff. 199r and 200r for the doubles of Dominic and Katherine.

4.2. Collects—ff. 202r–203r.

Identical to those found in Claremont, Claremont Colleges, Honnold/Mudd Library, Crispin 8 and Crispin 9 (see Dutschke et al. 1986, 24–36). Dominican saints are named in four of the prayers: Dominic (4.2.2), Peter Martyr (4.2.3), Thomas Aquinas (4.2.4), and Vincent of Ferrer (4.2.5).

4.2.1. f. 202r. rub.: oratio; inc.: protege domine famulos tuos subsidiis pacis . . . a cunctis hostibus redde securos per [*CO* 4756b].

4.2.2. f. 202r. rub.: oratio; inc.: concede quesumus omnipotens deus ut qui peccatorum . . . beati dominici confessoris tui patrocinio subleuemur [*CO* 766].

4.2.3. f. 202r. RUB.: oratio; INC.: preces quas tibi domine offerimus intercedente beato petro martyre . . . sub tua protectione custodi [*CO* 4625].

4.2.4. f. 202r. INC.: deus qui ecclesiam tuam mira [*corr.*] beati thome confessoris tui erudicione . . . et que egit imitatione complere [cf. *CO* 1566].

4.2.5. f. 202r–v. RUB.: oratio; INC.: deus qui gencium multitudinem mira beati uincencii confessoris tui . . . in terris premiatorem habere [*corr.*] mereamur in celis per.

4.2.6. f. 202v. INC.: ineffabilem misericordiam tuam domine nobis clementer . . . pro hiis meremur eripias per [*CO* 3129].

4.2.7. f. 202v. RUB.: oratio; INC.: pretende domine famulis et famulabus tuis dexteram celestis . . . que digne postulant assequantur per [*CO* 4587a].

4.2.8. ff. 202v–203r. INC.: ecclesie tue domine preces placatus admitte ut destructis aduersitatibus . . . ac derige in uiam salutis eterne per [*CO* 2404b].

4.2.9. f. 203r. INC.: deus a quo sancta desideria recta consilia et iusta sunt opera . . . sint tua protectione tranquilla [*CO* 1088a].

5. Seasonal Variations—ff. 203r–212r.

5.1. Advent—ff. 203r–205r.

Includes antiphons, chapter, hymns (*Verbum supernum; Vox clara*), etc.

5.2. Septuagesima—f. 205v.

Verse and hymn (*Sum<m>i largitor*).

5.3. Quadragesima—ff. 205v–207r.

Verses, chapters, hymn (*Iam Christe soi*), etc.

5.4. Passion Sunday—ff. 207v–208v.

Antiphons and verses.

5.5. Easter—ff. 209r–212r.

Antiphons; invitatory; verses; hymns (*Pange lingua gloriosi*; *Lustra sex*; *Aurora lucis*; *Sermone blando*).

BINDING: s. xv; red pigskin over boards; blind tooled or stamped; sewn on four double cords; metal pins on upper board; one leather strap remains; leather and metal finger tabs in pink, green, and white throughout; binding is partly detached.

OWNERS & PROVENANCE: Sister Maria Agness Hueberin, O.P. (ca. 1600); General Rush C. Hawkins (1831–1920), on whom see STILLWELL 1923; D. G. Francis Bookseller (label on pastedown); acquired by the university sometime after the 1887 Hawkins sale, but prior to 1935 as evidenced by entry in DE RICCI.

Sales & Catalogues: George A. Leavitt & Co., March 21–25, 1887, lot 1562.

Former Shelfmarks: MS 1 (Notre Dame).

Bibliography: De Ricci 1:714, no. 1; Corbett 1951 (misidentified as De Ricci 1:714, no. 2); Corbett no. 1; D'Alverny 1981, 106; Emery, Jr. and L. Jordan 1998, 500.

cod. Lat. b. 2

Origin: Southern Germany, s. xv^{1}–xv^{2} (Nuremburg, additions *post* 1456).
Content Overview: Psalter, neumed (Dominican).

In Latin with some German, on parchment; 223 ff.; generally 157 x 110 mm (page) [see Layout for ruling]; foliated in modern pencil with Arabic numerals; metal finger tabs attached throughout.

Collation: 1–18^{8} +19^{6} +20–27^{8} + 28^{6} +29^{4+1}

Quires: Quaternions, H/H, are the predominant quire forms; ternions comprise quires 19 and 28; quire 29 is a binion with a singleton attached asymmetrically by its stub (f. 223). The first leaf of quire 1's quaternion is the front pastedown; the last leaf of quire 29's binion is the rear pastedown. Parchment is well scraped and of a high quality; the manuscript has been trimmed.

Catchwords: Horizontal catchwords in the lower right margin for quires 2–13 and 15–27; all legible catchwords correspond; others are fragmentary due to trimming; catchwords are written in Cursiva.

Layout:

A

B

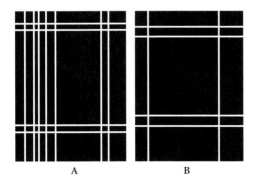

A ff. 1r–6v. Ink; 115 x 87 mm; cols. 9/5/7.5/9/47/8 mm; 30 lines.
B ff. 7r–223v. Ink; 103–106 x 70–71 mm; 18 lines.

Pattern **A** is traced in brown ink on ff. 1r–6v; six calendric columns (9/5/7.5/9/47/8 mm); writing above top line; prickings visible in the upper and lower margins for vertical bounding lines and calendric columns (recto and verso). Pattern **B** is traced in brown ink on ff. 7r–223v; single column of text; writing below top line; prickings visible for vertical bounding lines and horizontal through lines. **B** displays pricking in the outer margin for text lines ruled individually.

Script: Two scribal bookhands (M1–M2) write all texts in Northern Textualis Formata of the fifteenth century. M1 writes ff. 1r–219v with minimal use of hairlines, and regular forking of ascenders; M1 displays a consistent use of a Cursiva **g** form (single-horned). M2 writes ff. 220r–223v in Northern Textualis Formata (Quadrata); quadrangles are prominent; superfluous hairlines occur. The script of M2 conveys a more formal presentation than that of M1. A third hand of the fifteenth century (M3) adds the translation of St. Martin to the calendar on f. 4r in a watery brown ink. M3 writes either Cursiva or Hybrida (not enough letter forms present to classify properly). A later hand of the sixteenth century (M4) labels ferial days in the margins in both Latin and German (e.g., ff. 149r, 164r, 180v).

Decoration:

I. Rubrication: Rubrics in red ink added by respective text hand; letter heightening of majuscules and cadels in red ink.

II. Initials: Flourished, plain, and cadel initials occur in hierarchy; some do not conform strictly to the usual types.

a. Flourished type initials (2–9 line square inset) divide major sections of the manuscript. Initials on ff. 7r, 37v, 54v, 70v, 86v, 106v, and 127r in red and blue ink with contrasting interior penwork; outer flourishing in yellow and purple, often with sprays and extensions into margins; all inhabited by white grotesque creatures in typical Nuremberg style (except f. 86v, vine-stems). Initials on ff. 32r, 125r, 144v, 180r, 187r are quartered in red and blue ink with contrasting interior penwork; outer flourishing and grotesques as above. Initials 7–9 lines in height mark the typical eight-part divisions: Pss 1 (f. 8r), 26 (f. 37v), 38 (f. 54v), 52 (f. 70v), 68 (f. 86v), 80 (f. 106v), 97 (f. 125r), 109 (f. 144v). Smaller types 4–6 lines in height emphasize psalms included in the ten-part division and beyond: Pss 21 (f. 32r), 51 (f. 68v), 101 (f. 127r), and 142 (f. 180r); a single 2 line initial in red ink with yellow flourishing and white grotesques is used for Ps 109 (f. 144v). A 6 line initial quartered as above begins the canticles on f. 187r. Flourished type initials (2–3 square indent) alternate in blue and red ink with contrasting penwork in combinations of red, blue, yellow, and purple and begin hymns and some neumed sections throughout the manuscript.

b. Plain initials (1–2 line square inset) alternate in red and blue ink (ff. 220r–223r, in red ink only); initials 2 lines in height begin sections of the text (e.g., Litany, f. 202r); 1 line versals run throughout the manuscript.

c. Cadels (3 line square inset) in black ink heightened in red occur within staves; cadels contain no illustrations.

III. Borders & Frames: Yellow and purple outer flourishing of initials with sprays and marginal extensions form partial borders (e.g., ff. 8r, 32r, 37v, 68v, 86v, 127r).

Calendar: One month per page; dominical letter **a** in red ink; Roman time marked in red ink.

Music & Staves: Four-line staves in red ink; 10 mm; square neumes in black ink.

Contents:

1. Calendar (Dominican)—ff. 1r–6v.

Liturgical calendar in black and red ink. Several feasts indicate Dominican use and permit a localization to a Dominican house in the diocese of Bamberg, likely in the Katharinenkloster Nuremberg: Erhard (Jan. 8), translation of Thomas Aquinas (Jan. 28; red; totum duplex), *anniuersarium patrum et matrum* (Feb. 4), Kunigunde (Mar. 3; red; simplex), Thomas Aquinas (Mar. 7; red; totum duplex), octave of Thomas Aquinas (Mar. 14; memorie), Adalbert (Apr. 24; 3 lectiones), Peter Martyr (Apr. 29; red; totum duplex), translation of Peter Martyr (May 7; red; totum duplex), Apparition of St. Michael the Archangel (May 8; totum duplex), translation of Dominic (May 24; red; totum duplex), Ulric (Jul. 4), Translation of Martin (Jul. 4; subsequent addition), *anniuersarium in cymiteriis nostris sepultorum* (Jul. 12), Henry (Jul. 13; red; simplex), Margaret (Jul. 14; red; simplex), Dominic (Aug. 5; red; totum duplex), octave of Dominic (Aug. 12; simplex), Sebald (Aug. 19; red; simplex), *anniuersarium familiarum et benefactorum ordinis nostri* (Sept. 5), translation of Kunigunde (Sept. 9; red; simplex), Wenceslas (Sept. 28), Michael (Sept. 29; red; totum duplex), Otto (Sept. 30; red), octave of Michael (Oct. 6; memorie), *anniuersarium omnium fratrum et sororum ordinis nostri* (Oct. 10), Elizabeth (Nov. 19; red; semiduplex), Katherine (Nov. 25; red; totum duplex), Conrad (Nov. 26); cf. calendars in cod. Lat. b. 1, and San Marino, Huntington Library, HM 25771. German text about the Golden Numbers added in the lower margin for January (f. 1r) and March (f. 2r).

2. Psalter, neumed—ff. 7r–187r.

Invitatory *Venite exultemus* and hymn *Nocte surgentes* on f. 7r; neumed. Pss 1 (f. 8r), 21 (f. 32r), 26 (f. 37v), 38 (f. 54v), 51 (f. 68v), 52 (f. 70v), 68 (f. 86v), 80 (f. 106v), 97 (f. 125r), 101 (127r), 109 (f. 144v), 119 (f. 164v), and 142 (f. 180r) are emphasized with varying types of flourished initials [see Decoration].

3. Canticles—ff. 187r–202r.

Six ferial canticles; *Benedicite omnia* (f. 196v), *Te deum* (f. 197v), *Benedictus dominus deus* (f. 198v), *Magnificat* (f. 199r), *Nunc dimittis* (f. 199v), *Quicumque uult* (f. 199v).

4. Litany and Collects—ff. 202r–207r.

4.1. Litany (Dominican)—ff. 202r–206r.

The Litany prominently features Dominican saints and others pointing toward Nuremberg; notable saints include: Peter Martyr, Dominic (doubled), Thomas Aquinas, Katherine (doubled), Margaret, Ursula, Kunigunde.

4.2. Collects—ff. 206r–207r.

Identical to those in cod. Lat. b. 1 and Claremont, Claremont Colleges, Honnold/Mudd Library, Crispin 8 and Crispin 9 (see Dutschke et al. 1986, 24–36). Dominican saints named in four of the prayers: Dominic (4.2.2), Peter Martyr (4.2.3), and Thomas Aquinas (4.2.4). Due to the earlier date, Vincent of Ferrer is lacking.

4.2.1. f. 206r. rub.: oratio; inc.: protege domine famulos tuos subsidiis pacis . . . a cunctis hostibus redde securos [*CO* 4756b].

4.2.2. f. 206r. rub.: oratio; inc.: concede quesumus omnipotens deus ut qui peccatorum . . . beati dominici confessoris tui patrocinio subleuemur [*CO* 766].

4.2.3. f. 206r. rub.: oratio; inc.: preces quas tibi domine offerimus intercedente beato petro martyre . . . sub tua protectione custodi [*CO* 4625].

4.2.4. f. 206r–v. rub.: oratio; inc.: deus qui ecclesiam tuam mira beati thome confessoris tui erudicione . . . et que egit imitacione complere [cf. *CO* 1566].

4.2.5. f. 206v. rub.: oratio; inc.: ineffabilem misericordiam tuam domine nobis clementer . . . pro hiis meremur eripias [*CO* 3129].

4.2.6. f. 206v. rub.: oratio; inc.: pretende domine famulis et famulabus tuis dexteram celestis . . . que digne postulant assequantur [*CO* 4587a].

4.2.7. f. 206v. rub.: oratio; inc.: ecclesie tue domine preces placatus admitte ut destructis aduersitatibus . . . ac dirige in uiam salutis eterne [*CO* 2404b].

4.2.8. ff. 206v–207r. rub.: oratio; inc.: deus a quo sancta desideria recta consilia et iusta sunt opera . . . sint tua protectione tranquilla per [*CO* 1088a].

5. Seasonal Variations—ff. 207r–219v.

5.1. Advent—ff. 207r–209v.

Includes antiphons, chapter, hymns (*Verbum supernum; Vox clara*), etc.

5.2. Septuagesima and Quadragesima—f. 209v–211v.

Verses and hymns (*Summi largitor; Iam Christe sol*); antiphons.

5.3. Passion Sunday—ff. 211v–213r.

Antiphons and verses.

5.4 Easter—ff. 213r–219v.

Antiphons, invitatory; verses; hymns (*Pange lingua gloriosi*; *Lustra sex*; *Aurora lucis*; *Sermone blando*).

6. Additions (*post* 1456)—ff. 220r–223v.

Additional material written by M2 [see SCRIPT]; all initials are plain, in red ink [see DECORATION]; rubrics in Latin with some German. A date after 1456 is evidenced by mention of Vincent of Ferrer in a commemoration [see 6.2.4].

6.1. Capitula—f. 220r.

6.1.1. Ioel 2.12–13. RUB. [f. 219v]: capitulum in quadragesima in die fera; INC.: conuertimini ad me in toto corde . . . et non uestimenta uestra ait dominus omnipotens.

6.1.2. 2 Cor 6.1–2. RUB.: in dominca; INC.: hortamur uos ne in uacuum gratiam dei . . . in die salutis adiuui te. deo.

6.1.3. Ier 11.20. RUB.: capitulum; INC.: tu autem domine sabaoth . . . reuelaui causam meam domine deus meus.

6.2. Commemorations—ff. 220r–221v.

Vincent of Ferrer is included in the commemoration of Dominican saints (6.2.4), placing the date of the addition after 1456. The Katherine mentioned after Vincent in 6.2.4 is likely the patroness of the convent, not Catherine of Siena.

6.2.1. Daily Commemoration—f. 220r–v. RUB.: die teglichen memorie; INC.: sub tuum praesidium . . .; OR.: protege domine famulos tuos subsidiis . . . a cunctis hostibus redde securos per [*CO* 4756b].

6.2.2. Holy Cross—f. 220v. RUB.: memorie de sancte crucis mat.; INC.: saluator mundi salua nos . . .; OR.: adesto nobis domine deus noster et quos sancte crucis . . . defende subsidiis per christum [*CO* 158].

6.2.3. Dominic—ff. 220v–221r. ANT.: benedictus redemptor omnium . . . dedit sanctum dominicum; OR.: deus qui ecclesiam tuam beati dominici . . . semper proficiat incrementis per christum [*CO* 1559].

6.2.4. Dominican Saints—ff. 221r–222v. ANT.: o quam felix gloria semper sanctorum . . . predicatorum . . .; OR.: concede quesumus omnipotens deus ut ad meliorem uitam sanctorum petri thome uincecii [*sic*] et katherine . . . actus imitemur per christum [cf. *CO* 739].

6.3. Chapter Office—ff. 221v–223v. INC.: preciosa est in conspectu domini . . .; EXPL.: . . . fidelium deus omnium conditor et redemptor . . . piis supplicacionibus consequantur qui uiuis et regnas per omnia secula seculorum. amen [*CO* 2684b].

Includes Latin and German rubrics; some forms specifically in the feminine (e.g., *famule tue* on f. 222r).

Binding: s. xv; brown leather over boards; blind tooled; metal catches on upper board; remnants of leather straps on lower board; metal finger tabs throughout; sewing on four double cords; binding is broken (front cover through f. 7 detached).

Owners & Provenance: General Rush C. Hawkins (1831–1920), on whom see Stillwell 1923; D. G. Francis Bookseller (label on pastedown); acquired by the university sometime after the 1887 Hawkins sale, but prior to 1935 as evidenced by entry in De Ricci.

Sales & Catalogues: George A. Leavitt & Co., March 21–25, 1887, lot 1568.

Former Shelfmarks: MS 2 (Notre Dame).

Bibliography: De Ricci 1:714, no. 2; Corbett 1951 (misidentified as De Ricci 1:714, no. 1); Corbett no. 2; D'Alverny 1981, 106; Emery, Jr. and L. Jordan 1998, 499–500.

cod. Lat. b. 3

Origin: France, s. xiv^{2}–xv^{1}.
Content Overview: Magister Iohannes, *Facetus* (*cum nihil utilius*); John 1.1–15.

In Latin, on parchment; i +11 ff. +i; 153 x 120 mm (page) [see Layout for ruling]; foliated in modern pencil with Arabic numerals; flyleaves modern acid-free paper.

Collation: i +1$^{12-1}$ +i

Quires: The manuscript is comprised of a single sexternion, F/F, lacking the eleventh leaf; does not obey Gregory's Rule; ff. 1 and 11 were formerly a wrapper. The manuscript has been trimmed; evidence of fire damage.

Layout:

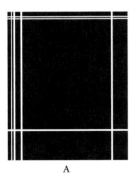

A

A ff. 2r–10r. Lead; 115 x 95 mm; 14 lines.

Pattern A is traced lightly in lead on ff. 2r–10r; single column; writing below the top line; no prickings are visible.

Decoration:
I. Rubrication: Rubric and paraph mark on f. 2r in brown ink.
II. Initials: One plain initial (2 line square inset) in brown ink begins the *Facetus* on f. 2r.

Script: The text of the *Facetus* is written by at least two discernable hands (M1–M2) at various levels of execution. M1 begins the text in Northern Textualis Formata with distinct hairlines and quadrangles in a brownish ink. M1 begins to write more rapidly and the quality of the script degrades toward Libraria: single compartment **a** begins to replace the two compartment form as quadrangles and hairlines disappear (e.g., f. 5r). On f. 6r, the script becomes a rapid Textualis Currens, however the ductus appears to be that of M1. M2 writes Northern Textualis under the influence of Cursiva on ff. 7v–10r. The use of two compartment **a** is consistent, but straight **s** often extends below the baseline (e.g., f. 9r) and some forms of **g** show a Cursiva influence (e.g., f. 7v). Ascenders are generally loopless, but some looped forms do appear (e.g., **l**, f. 8r; **h**, f. 8v; **d**, f. 10v). M3 writes Hybrida Currens under the influence of Bastarda on f. 11r–v and in the margins. A four-line addition [see Contents 2] is written on f. 10v by a fourth hand, M4, in Semihybrida.

Contents:

1. Magister Iohannes, *Facetus* (*cum nihil utilius*)—ff. 2r–10r.

rub.: facetus; inc.: [f. 2r] cum nichil utilius hu<m>ane credo saluti quam morum nouisse modos et moribus uti quod unus [*sic*] exequitur . . .; expl.: [f. 10r] . . . raro breues humiles uidi rufosque fideles albos audaces miror magnos sapientes. explicit facetus. deo gratias.

The final two lines do not appear in Morawski 1923.

Edition: Morawski 1923.

2. Addition [unidentified]—f. 10v.

inc.: post deum petro laudes et helueciis gratias unitas helueciorum heroum errorum propulsatrix.

Text added by M4 [see Script]; Switzerland was inferred as the origin by B. Rosenthal from this text.

3. John 1.1–15—f. 11r–v.

inc.: in principio erat uerbum et uerbum erat . . .; expl.: [f. 11v] . . . plenum gratie et ueritatis.

Text of John added by M3 [see Script].

Binding: s. xx (June 1999); bound at Notre Dame in a conservation pamphlet; gray. The previous non-contemporary binding of brown velvet is housed with the manuscript.

Owners & Provenance: J. Rosenthal (1926), B. Rosenthal (1954); acquired by the university during the 1956–1957 fiscal year.

Sales & Catalogues: J. Rosenthal, Cat. 83, no. 66; B. Rosenthal, Cat. 1, no. 59.

Former Shelfmarks: no. 5 (unknown); MS 6 (Notre Dame).

Bibliography: Faye and Bond, 186, no. 6; Corbett no. 6; Fuderer 1994, 177; Mann 2006, 43, 45–47, 68 n. 13; Nolan 2006, 3.

cod. Lat. b. 4

Origin: France, s. xiii^2 (Paris?, *post* 1282).
Content Overview: Carthusian Psalter, Diurnal and hymns, neumed; numerous additions (s. xiii–xvi).

In Latin with some French, on parchment; iii +350 ff. +vi; generally 175 x 123 mm (page) [see Layout for ruling]; flyleaves i, ii, viii, ix modern paper; flyleaves iii, iv, v medieval parchment [see Contents 1, 29–32]; flyleaves vi and vii modern parchment.

Collation: iii + 1–2^8 +3^{8+1} +4–16^8 +17^{2+1} +18–21^8 +22^{12} +23^8 +24^4 +25–30^8 +31^{12+4} +32–41^8 +42^{12} +43$^{8-2}$ +vi

Quires: Parchment quaternions, F/F, are the normal quire forms. Quire 3 is a quaternion with a singleton with stub added (f. 21); text uninterrupted. Quire 17 is a bifolium with a singleton with stub added (f. 132); text uninterrupted. The parchment is of variable quality with numerous imperfections (e.g., ff. 30, 52, 118, 120) and some damage (e.g., ff. 79, 107, 117). Quire 31 has been modified: a binion (ff. 241r–244v) has been inserted asymmetrically into the sexternion between ff. 240v and 245r. Quire 43 is a quaternion with the last two leaves canceled (stubs pasted to f. 350v). Multiple sets of quire marks, catchwords, and signatures remain in the manuscript, corresponding to the division of contents and stages of production.

Quire Marks: Quires 1–2 do not have quire marks; varying quire marks occur in the psalter (ff. 17r–132v). Quire 4 has the abbreviated *secundus* mark centered in the lower margin. Quires 3–17 also have later quire marks in Arabic numerals written in the inner margin of the versos; that for quire 16 has faded and is barely visible. The diurnal (quires 18–43; ff. 133r–350v) was created separately and quire marks begin anew. Quires 18–22, 25, 26 have Roman numerals in the lower margins; quires 23 and 24 have no quire marks. Quires 27–30, 32–36, 38, and 39 use Roman numerals as ordinals in the same position; quires 31, 37, 42, and 43 have no quire marks. All are written in the same brown and black ink as text (red ink on ff. 228v and 236v).

Catchwords: Quires 1–2 do not have catchwords; horizontal catchwords are written by the text hand in brown ink for quires 3–16 in the lower right margin; red ink used for quire 3 on f. 25v (not a rubric); catchword for quire 13 on f. 105v is in a different script. In the diurnal, horizontal catchwords appear in the lower right margins for quires 18–30, 32–36, and 38–42; all written by the text hand in brown and black ink; red ink used for quire 29 on f. 228v (not a rubric); all catchwords correspond.

Signatures: Quires 1–2 do not have signatures; *ad hoc* signatures are visible in the lower right corners of quires 3–9 (a–g) and 14–16 (n–o); those for quires 10–13 trimmed away; signatures use letters only (e.g., quire 3: a, aa, aaa, aaaa.); all signatures written in faded brown ink with a greenish tint. A different system of *ad hoc* signatures using letters and symbols is employed for quires 18–42 (e.g., quire 19: a⁺, b⁺, c⁺, d⁺); the opening of each quire is marked with an *x* in addition to those in the inner margin added by J. S. Kebabian [see Foliation]; all signatures and markings written in faded ink with an almost greenish tint similar to those in quires 3–16.

Foliation: Multiple sets of modern and medieval foliation occur. The entire manuscript was foliated in modern pencil with Arabic numerals in the lower inner margin by J. S. Kebabian in 1978 for H. P. Kraus (collation statement on flyleaf IX; quires also numbered and openings marked with an *x*). Psalter portion contains Arabic numerals (s. xv) in red ink: 22 (f. 1r), 30 (f. 9r), 31 (f. 10r), 37 (f. 16r), 38 (f. 17r); ff. 1r–133v foliated in modern pencil with Arabic numerals in the upper right corner (ff. 122r–131v have Kraus foliation only). Roman numerals in red (occasionally brown) ink are written in the upper margin throughout ff. 133r–318v (those on ff. 317r and 318r by A1; see Script); some folios skipped and others erased (e.g., ff. 235r, 236). Numerals are not properly a foliation, but reference specific openings (r/v) as well as sections.

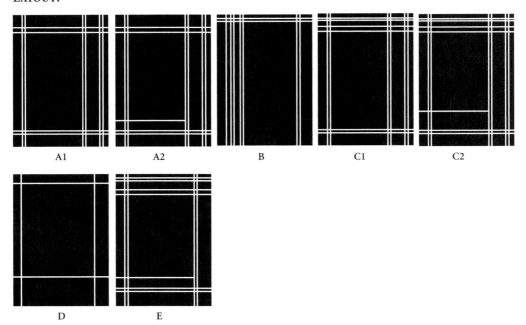

Layout:

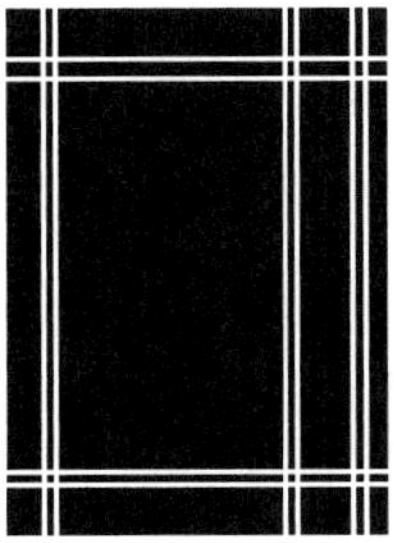
A1

A2

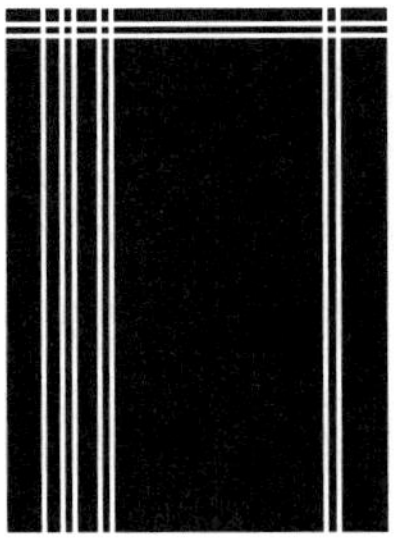
B

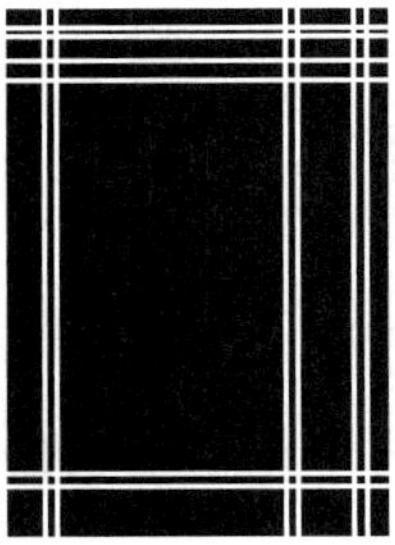
C1

C2

D

E

A ff. 1r–9v, 16r–132r. Combined technique; 122 x 76 mm; 20 lines.
B ff. 10r–15v. Lead; 150 x 96 mm; cols. 7/4/8/4/73/4 mm; 33 lines.
C ff. 133r–240v, 245r–344v. Combined technique; 116 x 74 mm; 20 lines.
D ff. 241r–244v. Ink; 123–133 x 90 mm; approx. 30–36 lines.
E ff. 345r–350r. Combined technique; 117 x 75 mm; approx. 30 lines.

Pattern **A** is traced on ff. 1r–9v and 16r–132r; using a combined technique of lead with the occasional use of brownish crayon (e.g., ff. 39r, 103r); single column; writing below top line; prickings visible in the upper and lower margins for vertical bounding lines; prickings for horizontal through lines (double only) in the outer (upper lines) and inner (lower); outermost vertical bounding lines often lost due to trimming. The variant, **A2**, occurs on some folios (e.g., f. 33r). Pattern **B** is traced on ff. 10r–15v in lead with later additional lines added in brown ink (e.g., f. 10r); six calendric columns (7/4/8/4/73/4 mm); writing below top line; prickings for verticals in the left area of the third line. Pattern **C** is traced on ff. 133r–240v and 345r–344v in lead with occasional use of brownish crayon (e.g., ff. 148r, 251r, 269r); single column (two columns used but not ruled for the Litany on ff. 321v–323r); writing below top line; prickings for vertical bounding lines, and upper and lower horizontal through lines visible; outer vertical bounding lines often lost to trimming. A pricking pattern distinctly different from that of **A** is most visible at the intersection of the outer bounding lines and upper and lower horizontals, which results in a double pricking aligned with a single pricking. The variant, **C2**, occurs on some folios (e.g., ff. 224r, 250r). Pattern **D** is traced in brown ink for a fourteenth-century addition on ff. 241r–244v; single column; writing below top line; height depending on the number of staves; number of lines is approximate. Pattern **E** is traced in lead and crayon on ff. 345r–350r [see Contents 27]; single column; writing below top line; prickings visible for vertical bounding lines in the upper and lower margins, and near the inner margin for the horizontal through lines; number of lines varies depending on music.

Script: The calendar, psalter, diurnal, and major texts are written in Northern Textualis of the late thirteenth century. Corrections abound in different techniques: erasure (e.g., ff. 35v, 41v), cross-outs (e.g., ff. 64r, 72r; black ink), and interlinear insertions (e.g., f. 325r). Several hands (s. xiii^{2}–xv) have made additions, annotations, and corrections in different scripts. Eight identifiable hands have made substantial additions (A1–A8). A1 writes Cursiva Antiquior (s. xiv) on ff. 9v and 16r–v [see Contents 4.4, 6, 7], and in the margins (e.g., ff. 246v, 247v, 248r). A2 writes Hybrida Libraria (s. xv) on ff. 132r–v, 258v, 259r, 260r, 300v, 328r, 335r, and 344r [see Contents 9, 11, 12.1, 12.6, 21, 23, 26]. A3 and A4 write Northern Textualis (s. xiv) on ff. 241r–244v [see Contents 10]. A5 writes Cursiva Formata (Bastarda) (s. xv) on f. 283r, flyleaf v (recto) [see Contents 12.2, 31.2]; A5 also adds prayers in Semihybrida on the final flyleaf [see Contents 31.1, 31.3, 31.4]. A6 writes Northern Textualis (s. xiii^{ex} with documentary intrusions) on f. 288r [see Contents 12.4]. A7 writes Northern Textualis (s. xv) on ff. 300r, 328r [see Contents 12.5, 20.2.4], and a correction on f. 71v. A8 writes Semihybrida on flyleaf IVr [see Contents 29]. Cursiva as a documentary script is used in flyleaves IVv and Vv [see Contents 1, 30, 32].

Decoration:

I. Rubrication: Rubrics in red ink; letter heightening of majuscules and cadels in red ink. Many cadels are stylized with grotesques and other designs.

II. Initials: Littera duplex, flourished, and plain initials occur in hierarchy.

a. Littera duplex initials (4 line square inset) occur in the psalter for the twelve-part division of the psalms on ff. 17r, 34r (taken up 1 line), 38v, 44v, 53v, 57v, 67v, 75r, 86v, 88r (taken up 1 line), 98v; initial on f. 62v is standing (4 line). For the diurnal, littera duplex initials (4 line square inset) occur in the Temporale, on ff. 133r, 149v, 161v, 219r, 220v, 230v, 235v (5 line square inset), and 236v; in the Sanctorale on ff. 259v, 262v, 266r, 286r, 298v; church dedication, on f. 301v; common of saints, on f. 303r; Office of the Dead, on f. 323v (4+4 line stepped); canticles, f. 335v.

b. Flourished initials in red and blue ink with contrasting penwork alternate throughout manuscript: initials, 3 line standing, are used for settings of the invitatory (ff. 1r–7r); initials, 2 line square inset, for *benedictiones mensae* (f. 9r–v) and in the calendar (ff. 10r–15v); subsequent initials (2 line square inset; hanging **is**) begin all psalms not part of the major division. Corrections to initials occur (e.g., ff. 107r, 108r, 119v); guide letters often are visible in the inner and outer margins. Identical flourished initials (2 line square inset; hanging **is**) run throughout the entire diurnal and section of hymns.

c. Plain initials (1 line versals) alternate in red and blue throughout the psalter; some initials corrected in black ink (e.g., ff. 81v, 100r); guide letters visible in the inner and outer margins. In the diurnal, plain initials (1 line versals) alternating in red and blue ink occur throughout the Litany (ff. 321v–323r), hymns (ff. 328v–335r), monastic canticles and hymns (ff. 335v–344r); two versals occur in the Office of the Dead on f. 323v.

III. Line Fillers: Line fillers occur occasionally in black and red ink (e.g., ff. 25v, 161r); and red ink (e.g., ff. 130r and 321v–323r).

IV. Borders & Frames: Partial borders of red and blue flourishes occur with littera duplex initials; upper and inner margins on ff. 17r, 133r, and 259v; inner margin only on ff. 34r, 38v, 44v, 53v, 57v, 62v, 67v, 75r, 86v, 88r, 98v, 149v, 161v, 219r, 220v, 230v, 235v, 236v, 262v, 266r, 286r, 298v, 301v, 303r, 335v; upper margin only on f. 323v.

Calendar: One month per page; dominical letter **a** in red ink; Roman time marked in red ink.

Music & Staves: Four-line staves ruled in red ink with square neumes in black ink (s. xiii^2; ff. 241r–244v, s. xiv); 7 mm; additional staves and neumes drawn in brown and black ink (e.g., f. 287v, flyleaf IVr).

Contents:

1. Fragmentary Document—flyleaf IIIr.

Fragment of a document in French written in Cursiva as a documentary script [see Script]; the fifth line is dated 8 March 1456.

2. Instructions for Cantor—flyleaf IIIv.

INC.: cantor hebdomarius caputium remouet antequam inuitatorium incipiat . . .

Added by a later hand of the sixteenth century [see SCRIPT].

3. Invitatory, neumed—ff. 1r–8v.

Three settings of *Venite exultemus* with multiple settings of *Gloria* and *Sicut erat*.

4. *Benedictiones Mensae*—f. 9r–v.

4.1. RUB.: benedictio prandii tempore ieiunii; INC.: edent pauperes et saturabuntur . . .

4.2. RUB.: quando bis comeditur in mane benedictio; INC.: oculi omnium in te sperant domine . . .

4.3. RUB.: in sero benedictio cene; INC.: edent pauperes et cetera ut supra . . .

4.4. RUB.: in cena domini post mandatum in refectorio . . .; INC.: potum seruorum suorum filius dei benedicat. amen.

4.4 written in brownish ink by A1 in the lower margin [see SCRIPT].

5. Calendar—ff. 10r–15v.

Liturgical calendar in black and red ink with later additions (s. xiii[2]–xv). Carthusian characteristics are conveyed in feasts and grading; examples in the unmodified calendar include: Hugh of Grenoble (Apr. 1; 12 lectiones), Bernard (Aug. 20; 12 lectiones; capitulum), Regimius (Oct. 1), *dedicatio ecclesie* (Oct. 3; 12 lectiones), Holy Relics (Nov. 8; 12 lectiones; capitulum; sollempnitas), Hugh of Lincoln (Nov. 17; 12 lectiones; regraded as a solemnity ca. 1339), Silas (Nov. 28). Notable additions include: Genevieve (Jan. 2; 12 lectiones), *obitus* [*ut uid.*] *mater mea* (Jan. 13), Maurus (Jan. 15), *obitus comitissa de de blois* [*sic*] (Jan. 29; Jeanne de Blois-Châtillon, 1253–1291), Thomas (Mar. 7), Benedict (Mar. 21; 12 lectiones; capitulum), Peter Martyr (Apr. 29), *dedicatio ecclesie* (Jun. 26). Visitation (Jul. 2; sollempnitas), Anne (Jul. 26), Louis (Aug. 25; 12 lectiones; capitulum), 11,000 Virgins (Oct. 21; capitulum; ca. 1352), Presentation of the Virgin (Nov. 21; sollempnitas), Barbara (Dec. 3), Conception (Dec. 8; sollempnitas; corrected from 'Sanctification' ca. 1341), *obiit dominus karolus* (Dec. 16).

6. Computistic fragment—f. 16r.

INC.: sciendum est quod annus incarnationis dominice qui data communiter nuncupatur semper in romana curia in circumcisione domini renouatur . . .; EXPL.: . . . regule uerissime ad inueniendum diem pasche. apres la sainte agathe prime lune querons le samedi apres la ueille des brandons item . . .

Latin text and two lines in French are written by A1 [see SCRIPT] and followed by a list to calculate Easter (*quando luna currit* . . .).

7. Benedictions for Matins—f. 16v.

RUB. [*in sup. marg.*]: benedictiones in matutinis super lectiones et euangelia.

Benedictions for three nocturns, Sundays, and other feast days; seasonal variations added by A1 in brown ink [see SCRIPT] and rubrics underlined in red.

8. Psalter and Canticles—ff. 17r–132v.

Twelve-part division: Pss 1 (f. 17r), 26 (f. 34r), 32 (f. 38v), 38 (f. 44v), 52 (f. 53v), 59 (f. 57v), 68 (f. 62v), 73 (f. 67v), 80 (f. 75r), 97 (f. 86v), 101 (f. 88r), 109 (f. 98v). Antiphons are written in the text with rubrics and also added in the margins throughout the psalter. Ferial canticles (ff. 122r–128v); *Te deum* (f. 128v), *Benedicite omnia opera* (f. 129r), *Benedictus dominus deus* (f. 129v), *Magnificat* (f. 130r), *Nunc dimittis* (f. 130v), *Quicumque uult* (f. 130v).

9. Additions—f. 132r–v.

9.1. Iacobus de Voragine, *Legenda aurea,* cap. xliv (de Cathedra Sancti Petri)—f. 132r. ubi [-petri] deprecatoria beati petri apostoli in carcere apud anthiochiam ihesu criste miserorum adiutor adiuua me in his tribulationibus deficientem. cum dominus respondit. petre credis tu [*sic*] derelictum a me mee bonitati derogas si contra me talia dicere non formidas presto est qui tue subueniat miserie [cf. MAGGIONI 1998, 1:271].

9.2. Suffrage—f. 132v. INC.: mon createur redempteur et vrai pere verite vie et la voie dadresse . . .; EXPL.: . . . tu espandis en croix et en torture par mon meffait et desobeissance. amen [SONET/SINCLAIR/RÉZEAU 1163].

9.3. Prayer—f. 132v. RUB.: nota orationem sequentem; INC.: deus caritatis et pacis qui pro salute mundi . . .; EXPL.: . . . ubi lux permanet et uita regnat perpetua amen ita fiat [*CO* 1117].

Later additions by A2 in Latin and French [see SCRIPT].

Diurnal

The major sections of the neumed diurnal include the Temporale, Sanctorale, church dedication, common of saints; the Office of the Virgin, Office of the Dead, hymns, monastic canticles, and Mass chants follow. The entire portion of the manuscript contains numerous additions.

10. Temporale, neumed—ff. 133r–259r.

From Saturday before the first Sunday of Advent to the twenty-fifth Sunday after the octave of Pentecost; feast of Corpus Christi added (ff. 241r–244v) by A3 and A4 [see SCRIPT].

11. Added Prayer—ff. 259r, 258v.

RUB. [f. 259r]: nota bene orationem sequentem; INC.: mater summe ueritatis templum trine deitatis . . . ueris donis exornare et per filium saluare in celis spes unica . . .; EXPL.: [f. 258v] . . .

ergo decus feminarum ac sanctissima sanctarum conseruatirx puellarum . . . quem lactasti properarum sacro lacte mamillarum summi patris filia amen.

Text begins on f. 259r then continues on f. 258v via a *signe-de-renvoi*; the entry includes the beginning and end of each section due to the nonlinear presentation in the manuscript. The text is written by A2 [see SCRIPT].

12. Sanctorale, neumed—ff. 259v–300v.

Contains: Andrew (f. 259v), Nicholas (f. 260r), Conception of the Virgin Mary (f. 260r), Eulalia (f. 260r), Lucia (f. 260r), Thomas (f. 260r), Silvester (f. 260r), Paul (f. 260r), Hilary (f. 260r), Felix of Nola (f. 260r), Marcellus (f. 260r), Prisca (f. 260v), Fabian and Sebastian (f. 260v), Agnes (f. 260v), Vincent (f. 261r), Conversion of St. Paul (ff. 261r–262r), Polycarp (f. 262r), Agnes (f. 262r), Purification (ff. 262v–264v), Blaise (f. 264v), Agatha (f. 264v), Valentine (f. 264v), Chair of St. Peter (ff. 264v–265v), Gregory (f. 265v), Benedict (ff. 265v–266r), Annunciation (f. 266r–268r), Hugh of Grenoble and Ambrose with common for a martyr and martyrs (ff. 268r–270r), Tiburtius, Valerian, and Maximus (f. 270r), George (f. 270r), Mark (f. 270r–v), Vitalis (f. 270v), Philip and James (ff. 270v–272r), Alexander, Eventius, and Theodolus (f. 272r–v), Invention of the Holy Cross (f. 272r–v), John (f. 272v; stricken in red ink), Gordian and Epimachus (f. 272v), Nereus, Achilles, and Pancratius (f. 272v), Urban (f. 272v), Marcellinus and Peter (f. 272v), Barnabas (f. 273r), Marcus and Marcellianus (f. 273r), Gervasius and Protasius (f. 273r), John the Baptist (ff. 273r–276v), John and Paul (f. 276v), Leo (f. 276v), Peter and Paul (ff. 276v–279r), Commemoration of St. Paul (ff. 279r–280r), Processus and Martinianus (f. 280r), Seven Brothers (f. 280r–v), Margaret (f. 280v), Praxedis (f. 280v), Mary Magdalane (ff. 280v–282v), Apollinaris (f. 282v), Christina (f. 282v), James (ff. 282v–283r), Christopher (f. 283r), Nazarius et Celus (f. 283r), Felix, Simplicius, Faustinus, and Beatrice (f. 283r), Abdon and Sennen (f. 283r–v), Germain (f. 283v), St. Peter in Chains (f. 283v), Stephen (ff. 283v–284r), Invention of St. Stephen (f. 284r), Dominic (f. 284r), Sixtus (f. 284r), Felicissimus and Agapitis (f. 284r), Cyriacus and companions (f. 284r), Laurence (vigil and feast; ff. 284r–285r), Tiburtius (f. 285r), Hippolytus (f. 285r), Eusebius (f. 285r), Assumption (vigil and feast; ff. 285r–288r), Agapitus (f. 288r), Timothy and Symphorianus (f. 288r), Bartholomew (f. 288r), Augustine (f. 288v), Hermes (f. 288v), Julian (stricken in brown ink; f. 288v), Decollation of John the Baptist (ff. 288v–289v), Sabina (f. 288v), Felix and Audactus (f. 289v), Nativity of the Virgin Mary (ff. 289v–290v), Gorgonius (f. 290v), Protus and Hyacinthus (f. 290v), Exaltation of the Holy Cross (ff. 290v–291r, and 291v–293v), Cornelius and Cyprianus (f. 291v), Octave of the Nativity (f. 293v) Nicomedes (f. 293v), Lucia and Geminianus (f. 293v), Eufemia (f. 293v), Matthew (vigil and feast; ff. 293v–294r), Maurice and companions (f. 294r), Tecla (f. 294r), Cosmas and Damian (f. 294r), Michael (ff. 294v–296r), Jerome (f. 296v), Remigius (f. 296v), Faith (f. 296v), Mark (f. 296v), Denis and companions (f. 296v), Callixtus (f. 296v), Luke (ff. 296v–297r), Crispin and Crispinianus (f. 297r), Simon and Jude (vigil and feast; f. 297r), All Saints (vigil and feast; ff. 297r–299v), Eustace and companions (f. 299v), Relics (f. 299v), Four Crowned Martyrs (ff. 299v–300r), Theodore (f. 300r), Martin (f. 300r), Menas (f. 300r), Brictius (f. 300r), Hugh (f. 300r), Columbanus (f. 300r), Cecilia

(f. 300v), Clement (f. 300v), Felicity (f. 300v), Chrysogonus (f. 300v), Katherine (f. 300v), Linus (f. 300v), Agricola and Vitalis (f. 300v), Silas (f. 300v), and Saturnin (f. 300v).

Correction [s. xiv] of *sanctificatione* to *conceptione* (f. 260r); later additions (s. xiv–xv) for Genevieve, Anne, Louis, Hugh of Lincoln, and Katherine (see below).

12.1. Genevieve—f. 260r. RUB.: de sancta genouefa uirgine; INC.: beate genouefe uirginis domine deus gloriosis meritis . . . sanitate gaudentes gratia cooperante saluemur per dominum.

Text and date (Jan. 3) are written in brown ink by A2 in the lower margin [see SCRIPT]; cf. Paris, Bibliothèque Sainte-Geneviève, MS 1131, f. 139v, and *Missale Cart[h]usiense*, Thielman Kerver, Paris, 1541.

12.2. Anne—f. 283r. RUB.: beate anne matris beate marie oratio [*in dex. marg.*]; INC.: deus qui beate anne tantam gratiam conferre dignatus es . . . ad celestem iherusalem peruenire mereamur qui uiuis [*CO* 1366a].

Text is written in brownish ink by A5 in Cursiva Formata (Bastarda) in the lower margin and rubric in right margin [see SCRIPT]; A5 has also corrected part of the prayer to St. Christopher on the same folio via erasure.

12.3. Common for a confessor (neumed)—f. 287v. INC.: in fide et lenitate ipsius sanctum fecit illum dominus et ostendit illi gloriam suam . . .; R.: sint lumbi uestri precincti et lucerne . . .

Text and notation added in brownish ink in the lower margin by A6 [*ut uid.*]; both are worn heavily and faded [see SCRIPT].

12.4. Louis—f. 288r. INC.: deus qui beatum ludouicum confessorem tuum de terreno . . . et eiusdem regni tribuas esse consortes per eundem [*CO* 1457]; V.: uigilate ergo quia nescitis . . .

Text written in the lower margin by A6 in a rapid Northern Textualis with strong documentary influences [see SCRIPT]; cues and directive rubrics for response and music added above the prayer.

12.5. Hugh of Lincoln—f. 300r. RUB.: de sancto hugone; ANT.: ecce sacerdos; R.: magnum s. [*ut uid.*] beatus seruus; INC.: deus qui beatum hugonem confessorem tuum atque pontificem et cetera quere in fine libri.

Text is written in the lower margin by A7 [see SCRIPT]; antiphon, response, etc. given in cue form and underlined; the prayer is found on f. 344r using the directive text [see CONTENTS 26].

12.6. Katherine—f. 300v. RUB.: ad uesperas et tertiam oratio de beata katherina; INC.: deus qui dedisti legem moysi . . . ut eius meritis et intercessione ad montem qui cristus est ualeamus peruenire. per eundem dominum nostrum et cetera [*CO* 1521].

Text is written in the lower margin by A2 [see SCRIPT].

13. Dedication of a Church, neumed—ff. 300v–303r.

Rubric begins on f. 300v, text on 301r.

14. Common of saints, neumed—ff. 303r–312v.

Apostle and apostles (ff. 303r–305r), martyrs (ff. 305r–306v), martyr (ff. 306v–308r), confessor and bishop (ff. 308r–309v), confessor not a bishop, and abbots (ff. 309v–310r), abbot (f. 310r–v), virgin and martyr, and not a martyr (ff. 310v–312v).

15. Office of the Virgin, use of the Carthusians—ff. 312v–318r.

16. Propers for St. Louis—f. 318r–v.

RUB.: de sancto ludouico.

16.1. f. 318r–v. RUB.: oratio; INC.: deus qui beatum ludouicum confessorem tuum . . . et eiusdem regni tribuas esse consortes per eundum.
16.2. f. 318v. RUB.: secreta; INC.: presta quesumus omnipotens deus ut sicut beatus ludouicus confessor tuus . . . ita eius oratio nos tibi reddat acceptos per eundem.
16.3. f. 318v. RUB.: postcommunio; INC.: deus qui almum confessorem tuum ludouicum mirificasti . . . ab omni aduersitate liberare digneris per dominum.

17. Commemorations—ff. 318v–320v.

Commemorations for the Holy Cross, Virgin Mary, John the Baptist, and All Saints (ff. 318v–319v); variants for Advent on ff. 319v–320v; all antiphons are neumed when written fully.

17.1. Holy Cross—ff. 318v–319r. RUB.: de sancta cruce ad uesperas commemoratio; ANT.: nos autem gloriari oportet . . .; OR.: perpetua quesumus domine pace custodi . . . redimere dignatus es saluator mundi qui cum patre et spiritu sancto uiuis et regnas deus [*CO* 4221b].
17.2. Virgin Mary—f. 319r–v. RUB.: de beata semper uirgine maria ad uesperas; ANT.: salue regina misericordie uite . . .; OR.: famulorum tuorum domine delictis ignosce . . . genitricis filii tui domini dei nostri intercessione saluemur per eundem [*CO* 2649].
17.3. John the Baptist—f. 319v. RUB.: de sancto iohanne baptista ad uesperas commemoratio; ANT.: inter natos mulierum non surrexit . . .; OR.: perpetuis nos domine sancti iohannis baptiste tuere . . . tanto magis necessariis attolle suffragiis per [*CO* 4222b].

17.4. All Saints—f. 319v. RUB.: de omnibus sanctis ad uesperas commemoratio; ANT.: fulgebunt iusti sicut sol . . .; OR.: ut tuam domine misericordiam consequamur . . . toto corde tibi esse deuotos per dominum nostrum.

17.5. All Saints—ff. 319v–320r. RUB.: per totum aduentum domini. de omnibus sanctis ad uesperas antiphona et uersus ut supra; OR.: consciencias nostras quesumus domine uisitando purifica ut ueniens ihesus christus filius tuus . . . in nobis inueniat mansionem qui tecum uiuit et regnat in unitate [*CO* 800f].

17.6. Holy Cross—f. 320r. RUB.: de sancta cruce ad laudes antiphona et uersus ut supra; OR. respice quesumus domine super hanc familiam tuam . . . et crucis subire tormentum qui tecum uiuit et regnat in unitate spiritus sancti deus per [*CO* 5104].

17.7. Virgin Mary—f. 320r. RUB.: de beata semper uirgine de genitrice maria; ANT.: tota pulcra es amica mea . . .; OR.: deus qui de beate marie uirginis utero uerbum tuum . . . dei genitricem credimus eius apud te intercessionibus adiuuemur per eundem [*CO* 1518].

17.8. John the Baptist—f. 320r. RUB.: de sancto iohanne baptista ad laudes antiphona et uersus ut supra; OR.: omnipotens sempiterne deus da cordibus nostris . . . quam beatus iohannes baptista in deserto uox clamantis edocuit per [*CO* 3817].

17.9. All Saints—f. 320r–v. RUB.: de omnibus sanctis ad laudes antiphona et uersus ut supra; OR.: deus qui nos concedis omnium sanctorum merita uenerari da nobis in eterna beatitudine de eorum societate gaudere per [cf. *CO* 1874c].

18. Rubrics—ff. 320v–321r.

18.1. ff. 320v–321r. RUB.: quid sit agendum festis duodecim lectionum et qualiter et primo de apostolis; INC.: in festis apostolorum duodecim lectionum . . .; EXPL.: . . . ad ultimas uesperas sollempnitatis primo fit conmemoratio de festo et de dominica fit ultimo.

18.2. f. 321r. RUB.: quid sit agendum et qualiter de festis trium lectionum; INC.: in festis trium lectionum . . .; EXPL.: . . . non tamen in ea dicitur uirgo sed beata [-illa] martyr inploret.

18.3. Vespers, response and verse for martyrs (neumed)—f. 321r–v. RUB.: ad uesperas plurimorum martyrum; R.: iustorum anime in manu . . .; V.: deus temptauit illos et inuenit . . .

19. Litany and Collects—ff. 321v–323r.

19.1. Litany—ff. 321v–323r.

Litany is general and contains no Carthusian saints. Among the confessors, Jerome has been added between Gregory and Martin in the margin, and Hugo between Augustine and Paul (s. xv). *Martyrs*: Stephen, Linus, Cletus, Clement, Sixtus, Cornelius, Cyprian, Laurence, Vincent, Ignatius, Fabian, Sebastian, Denis (*cum soc.*), Maurice (*cum soc.*); *Confessors*: Silvester, Gregory, Martin, Jerome (added), Nicholaus, Hilary, Remigius, Ambrose, Augustine, Hugo (added), Paul, Anthony,

Hilarion, Benedict; *Virgins*: Felicitas, Perpetua, Agatha, Agnes, Lucia, Cecilia, Anastasia, Blandina, Scholastica, Euphemia, Petronilla, Mary Magdalene.

19.2. Collects—f. 323r.

19.2.1. INC.: deus cui proprium est misereri semper parcere . . . miseratio tue pietatis absoluat per [*CO* 1142].

19.2.2. INC.: pretende domine famulis et famulabus tuis . . . et que digne postulant assequantur per [*CO* 4587a].

19.2.3. INC. [cue form]: fidelium deus omnium conditor et cetera [*CO* 2684b].

20. Office of the Dead, use of the Carthusians—ff. 323v–328r.

OTTOSEN nos. 14-36-46, 67-51-33, 60-95-53.

20.1. Votive Prayers—ff. 323v–324v.

20.1.1. f. 323v. RUB.: pro benefactoribus [-decti] defunctis oratio ; INC.: inclina domine aurem tuam ad preces nostras . . . et sanctorum tuorum iubeas esse consortem per [*CO* 3116b].

20.1.2. f. 323v. RUB.: item pro clerico siue laico uel laicis recenter mortuus oratio; INC.: deus cui proprium est misereri semper et parcere propiciare anime famuli tui . . . transire mereatur ad uitam per [*CO* 1141].

20.1.3. ff. 323v–324r. RUB.: pro femina defuncta oratio; INC.: quesumus domine pro tua pietate anime famule tue . . . in eterne saluationis parcem restitute per [*CO* 4843].

20.1.4. f. 324r. RUB.: pro sacerdote siue pro sacerdotibus recenter mortuis oratio; INC.: da nobis domine ut animam famuli et sacerdotis tui . . . sanctorum cetui tribuas esse consortem per [*CO* 913].

20.1.5. f. 324r. RUB.: pro omni anniuersario oratio; INC.: deus indulgenciarum domine da anime famuli tui . . . quietis beatitudinem et luminis claritatem per [*CO* 1251].

20.1.6. f. 324r. RUB.: pro sacerdotibus uel episcopis oratio; INC.: deus qui inter apostolicos sacerdotes famulos tuos pontificali . . . eorum perpetuo consortio letentur in celis per [*CO* 1757c].

20.1.7. f. 324r. RUB.: pro congregatione oratio; INC.: deus uenie largitor et humane salutis auctor . . . ad perpetue beatitudinis consortium peruenire concedas per [*CO* 2205].

20.1.8. f. 324r–v. RUB.: pro fratribus et benefactoribus oratio; INC.: omnipotens sempiterne deus cui nonquam [*sic*] sine spe . . . sanctorum tuorum numero facias aggregari per [*CO* 3809].

20.1.9. f. 324v. RUB.: pro cunctis fidelibus defunctis oratio; INC.: fidelium deus omnium conditor . . . piis supplicationibus consequantur qui uiuis et regnas cum domino patre et cetera requiescant in pace amen [*CO* 2684b].

20.2. Prayers—ff. 327v–328r.

20.2.1. f. 327v. RUB.: pro patre et matre oratio; INC.: deus qui nos patrem et matrem honorare precepisti . . . meque cum illis in eterne claritatis gaudio construe per [cf. *HE* p. 111].

20.2.2. f. 328r. RUB.: de magnis laboribus in cymiterio oratio; INC.: deus in cuius miseratione anime fidelium requiescunt . . . ut a cunctis reatibus absoluti tecum sine fine letentur per eundem [*CO* 1170].

20.2.3. f. 328r. RUB.: primo die antequam operari incipiamus in cymiterium conuenimus et ibi psalmos dicimus; [cues follow].

20.2.4. f. 328r. INC.: actiones nostras quesumus domine et aspirando . . . et a te semper incipiat et per te cepta finiatur per dominum nostrum ihesum christum filium tuum qui tecum uiuit et cetera [*CO* 74].

20.2.4 is written by A7 in brownish ink [see SCRIPT].

21. Prayer for the 11,000 Virgins—f. 328r.

RUB.: de undecim milia uirginum oratio ad uesperas tertiam et missam; INC.: deus qui digne sacratis uirginibus . . .; EXPL.: . . . in celestibus fecisti triumphare per dominum [*CO* 1527]. ad sextam et nonam quere orationem post himnos.

Text and rubric are written in brownish ink in the lower margin by A2 [see SCRIPT]; note following the prayer directs the reader to f. 335r [see CONTENTS 23].

22. Hymns—ff. 328v–335r.

Hymns for the Office: *Eterne rerum conditor* (f. 328v; neumed); *Splendor paterne glorie de luce* (ff. 328v–329r); *Iam lucis orto* (f. 329r; staves only); *Iam lucis orto* (f. 329r–v; neumed); *Nunc sancte nobis spiritus* (f. 329v; neumed); *Rector potens uerax* (f. 329v; neumed); two settings of *Rerum deus tenax* (f. 330r; neumed); *Deus creator* (f. 330r–v; neumed); *Venit redemptor gentium* (ff. 330v–331r; neumed; *cum diuisione*); *Audi benigne conditor* (f. 331r; neumed); *Christe qui lux es* (f. 331r–v; staves only); *Vexilla regis prodeunt* (ff. 331v–332r; neumed; *cum diuisione*); two settings of *Hic est dies uerus* (f. 332r–v; neumed; *cum diuisione*); *Optatus uotis omnium sacratus* (ff. 332v–333r; neumed; *cum diuisione*); *Veni creator spiritus* (f. 333r; neumed); *Iam Christus astra* (f. 333r–v; neumed); *Inpleta gaudent uiscera* (f. 333v); two settings of *Aue maris stella* (ff. 333v–334r; neumed); *Mysterium ecclesia hymnum* (f. 334r; neumed); *Vere gratia plena es* (f. 334v); *Christe redemptor omnium* (ff. 334v–335r; neumed); *Ihesu saluator seculi* (f. 335r). Following the hymn on f. 335r, a rubric to find *Vt queant laxis* directs the reader to ff. 343v–344r: hymnum sancti iohannis batiste quere in decimo folio post statim post cantica qui sic uocatur ut queant laxis et cetera.

23. Prayer for the 11,000 Virgins—f. 335r.

RUB.: ad sextam et nonam oratio undecim milia uirginum; INC.: deus qui nos in tantis periculis constitutos pro humana scis . . .; EXPL.: . . . que pro peccatis nostris patimur te adiuuante uincamus per dominum nostrum ihesum cristum filium tuum qui [*CO* 1898].

Text and rubric are written in brownish ink in the lower margin by A2 [see SCRIPT and CONTENTS 21].

24. Monastic Canticles—ff. 335v–343v.

Monastic canticles for Sundays (Mearns, set 1), Advent (Mearns, set 2), Christmas, Lent, Easter (Mearns, set 1), common of apostles and martyrs (Mearns, set 9 reordered), of a martyr or confessor (Mearns, set 1), of virgins (Mearns, set 2).

25. Hymn for the Nativity of John the Baptist—ff. 343v–344r.

rub.: de sancto iohanne baptista ad uesperas hymnus; inc.: [f. 343v] ut queant laxis resonare . . .; rub.: ad matutinas hymnus; inc.: antra deserti teneris . . .; rub.: [f. 344r] ad laudes hymnus; inc.: o nimis felix meritique . . .

Hymn for John the Baptist divided for Vespers, Matins, and Lauds; for the hymn, see *AH* 50: no. 96.

26. Prayer for Hugh of Lincoln—f. 344r.

rub.: oratio de beato hugone [-linli] lincolniensi episcopo ordinis cartusi<ensis>; inc.: deus qui beatum hugonem confessorem tuum atque pontificem . . .; expl.: . . . et uirtutes illustrant per dominum nostrum ihesum christum filium tuum qui tecum et cetera [*CO* 1446].

Text and rubric are written in brownish ink in the lower margin by A2 [see Script].

27. Hymns, Antiphons, Mass Chants, etc., neumed—ff. 344v–350r.

Iube donne [*sic*] *benedicere*, *Te deum*, different settings for Mass chants (*Kyrie*, *Gloria*, *Sanctus*, *Agnus dei*, *Ite missa est*, *Benedicamus domino*, etc.). The hymn *Crux fidelis inter omnes* on f. 350r is not neumed.

28. John 1.1–14 and Prayer—f. 350v.

rub.: initium sancti ewangelii secundum iohannem; inc.: in principio erat uerbum . . . premum gratie et ueritatis [Io 1.1–14]; rub.: sequitur oratio; inc.: protector in te sperancium deus et cetera [cf. *CO* 4738–4745]; rub.: quarta dominica post trinitatem; [blank].

29. Added Responsory, partially neumed—flyleaf IVr.

inc.: <c>redo quod redemptor meus uiuit et nouissimo . . .; expl.: . . . <n>e intres in iudicium.

30. Fragmentary document—flyleaf IVv.

Fragmentary document in French written in Cursiva as a documentary script [see Script]; the date survives partially, with the year 1451; with notarial mark.

31. Additions—flyleaf Vr.

Four additions in two script types written by A5 [see Script]: 31.1, 31.3, 31.4 in Semihybrida, and 31.2 in Cursiva Formata (Bastarda).

31.1. INC.: concede quesumus omnipotens deus ut unigeniti tui noua per carnem natiuitas liberet quos sub peccati iugo uetusta seruitus tenet [*CO* 778a].
31.2. INC.: tu quoque uigilla [*sic*] in omnibus labora opus fac euangeliste sobrius esto [cf. 2 Tim 4.5].
31.3. INC.: deus illuminator omnium gencium da populis tuis . . . quod trium manroum mentibus aspirasti dominum nostrum ihesum christum filium tuum [*CO* 1228].
31.4. INC.: pro[-c]tector in te et cetera.

32. Fragmentary Document—flyleaf Vv.

Fragmentary document in French written in Cursiva as a documentary script [see SCRIPT]; the datum survives partially: May 1451; same notarial mark as that previous fragment [see CONTENTS 30].

BINDING: s. xix; green morocco over pasteboard; diced; gilt borders; Phillipps number on paper pasted to spine; gilt tooled turn-ins; marbled pastedowns and endpapers; Middle Hill stencil with Phillipps number on flyleaf IIIr.

OWNERS & PROVENANCE: Amans-Alexis Monteil (1769–1850), on whom see LEMAITRE 2006; Jean François Royez (1757?–1823); Sir Thomas Phillipps (1792–1872), Middle Hill stencil with Phillipps number on flyleaf IIIr; H. P. Kraus (1979); Maggs Bros. (1990, 1992); Antiquariaat Forum (1994); Les Enluminures (1995). Acquired from Les Enluminures (Chicago, IL) by the university in 2010. The manuscript may have been at the Chartreuse de Vauvert-lès-Paris beginning in the late thirteenth century.

SALES & CATALOGUES: H. P. Kraus, Cat. 153, no. 38; Christie's, 21 June 1989, lot 15; Maggs Bros., Cat. 1110, no. 2; ibid., European Bulletin 15, no. 1; ibid., B17, no. 78; Antiquariaat Forum (Utrecht), Cat. 102, no. 1; Les Enluminures, Cat. 4, no. 24.

FORMER SHELFMARK: Phillipps MS 1312.

BIBLIOGRAPHY: PHILLIPPS no. 1312; MUNBY 3:21, 148; HOGG 2009.

cod. Lat. b. 5

Origin: Southern France, s. xiii^{ex}/xiv^{in}.
Content Overview: Nicholas de Byard, *Tractatus de uitiis et uirtutibus*; Humbert of Romans, *De dono timoris*; Ps.-Bernard of Clairvaux, *Meditations.*

In Latin, on parchment; i +241 ff. +i; generally 168 x 116 mm (page) [see Layout for ruling]; foliated in modern pencil with Arabic numerals; flyleaves paper folded in quarto; ff. 164r–165v blank; ff. 240r–241r blank but ruled.

Collation: i +1–3^{12} +4^{12+1} +5–13^{12} +14^{8} +15–20^{12} +21^{4} +i

Quires: Parchment sexternions, F/F, are the normal quire forms; quire 14 is a quaternion, H/H; all quires obey Gregory's Rule except quires 4 and 21. Quire 4 has a leaf added (f. 48); text is uninterrupted. Quire 21 is a constructed binion comprised of four singletons with parchment reinforcement strips which originally were two bifolia: the first, F/F (ff. 238r–239v); the second, H/H (ff. 240r–241v). The manuscript has been trimmed.

Catchwords: Horizontal catchwords are written in the lower right margins for quires 1–13; stylized in black and red ink; all correspond (those for quires 2–4, 8, 13 very trimmed). A different hand writes horizontal catchwords within the lower superfluous horizontal through lines near the inner margin for quires 15–20 (no stylization); all correspond.

Layout:

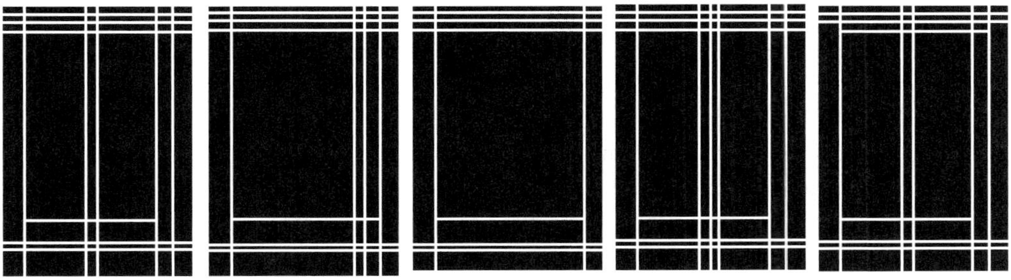

A1 A2 A3 A4 B

A ff. 1r–158v. Lead. 118 x 81 mm; intercol. 7 mm; 34 lines
B ff. 166r–239r. Lead. 118 x 81 mm; intercol. 7 mm; 34 lines

Pattern **A1** is traced in lead on ff. 1r–158v; two columns (intercol. 7 mm); writing below top line; prickings visible in all margins for all vertical bounding lines and horizontal through lines. The lists of *adaptationes* and chapters (ff. 159r–163v) use variations of **A1** (**A2–A4**) with modified pricking patterns: **A2** is used for the list of sermon *adaptationes* (ff. 159r–160r), adding an additional vertical bounding line and pricking to create a column for biblical citations (intercolumnium not traced); **A3** continues the *adaptationes* (ff. 160v–162v) with a pricking pattern identical to **A2** (only outermost vertical bounding lines traced); **A4** (f. 163r–v) augments the pricking pattern of **A2** to add another vertical to the right of the intercolumnium; when traced, **A4** is identical to **A1** with the additional vertical. Dimensions of **A2**, **A3**, and **A4** are identical to **A1**, but the ruling is used differently; ff. 164r–165v have the pricking pattern of **A1**, but are blank and unruled. Pattern **B** is traced in lead on ff. 166r–238r; two columns (intercol. 7 mm); writing below top line; prickings visible for vertical bounding lines and horizontal through lines; dimensions of the ruling are identical to **A**, but the pricking pattern and tracing differ. A ruling pattern for two columns is traced lightly in brown ink on ff. 240r–241v.

Script: There is a clear division of labor between two scribal bookhands (M1–M2). M1 writes a Semitextualis Libraria in black ink on ff. 1r[a]–163v[b]; M1 uses two compartment **a** occasionally, and frequently uses trailing **s** at word end. M2 writes a more rapid Semitextualis Libraria on ff. 166r[a]–239r[b], admitting two compartment **a** more regularly than M1. M2 favors straight **s** at word end and is averse to the trailing form; the Southern influence on the script is weaker than on M1. A third hand, M3, corrects the text and writes additions in a thin script clearly of Italian origin in a light brownish ink. M3 employs both Semitextualis and Hybrida forms (s. xiv) using the abbreviations of Rotunda. Other contemporaneous hands write marginal glosses; the autograph of a Giovanni Battista del Poggiardo (fl. 1597) supplies provenance information on f. 239v; that of an Andreas apostolus praedicator (s. xvi) writes on f. 241v[a] [see Owners & Provenance].

Decoration:

I. Rubrication: Rubrics and running titles in red ink; paraph marks alternate in red and blue ink; letter heightening of majuscules in red ink; numerous guide letters for initials and instructions for the rubricator are visible; rubrics for quires 16–21 (ff. 178r–241v) were never added.

II. Initials: Littera duplex and flourished initials occur in hierarchy within each text, but not in the manuscript as a whole.

a. Littera duplex initials with partial border begin the text on ff. 1r[a] (4 line square inset) and 164r[a] (2 line square inset).

b. Flourished initials (2 line square inset) in red and blue ink with contrasting penwork alternate throughout the manuscript.

III. Line Fillers: Simple line fillers in red ink on ff. 158r–163v.

CONTENTS:

1. Nicholas de Byard, *Tractatus de uitiis et uirtutibus*—ff. 1r^{a}–163v^{b}.

RUB.: sunt hec [*sic*] collecta libro uulgalia multa ex alphabeto distincte scripta teneto et positum titulo quodlibet est proprio; INC.: [f. 1r^{a}] duplex est abstinentia detestabilis et laudabilis detestabilis ut in ypocritis auaris et gulosis . . .; EXPL.: [f. 158r^{b}] . . . que preparauit dominus electis suis ad que nos perducere dignetur qui uiuit et regnat peri [i *del. M1*] omnia secula seculorum i [i *del. M1*] amen explicit.

Lists of sermon *adaptationes* (ff. 158v–162v) and chapters (ff. 162v–163v) follow. The work is also known as the *Summa de abstinentia* and *Dictionarius pauperum*.

EDITION: Incunabular editions include BASEL 1481, DEVENTER 1484, PARIS 1498, and PARIS 1500.
BIBLIOGRAPHY: STEGMULLER no. 5695; KAEPPELI no. 3046; BLOOMFIELD no. 1841.

2. Humbert of Romans, *De dono timoris*—ff. 166r^{a}–227r^{a}.

RUB.: incipit tractatus de habundancia exemplorum in sermonibus ad omnem materiam incipit prologus; INC.: [f. 164r^{a}] quoniam plus exempla quam uerba mouent secundum gregorium et facilius intellectu capiuntur . . .; EXPL.: [f. 227r^{a}] . . . mirum est nisi ualde timeat eos omnis homo; SCRIBAL COLOPHON: [f. 227r^{a}] explicit expliceat ludere scriptor eat. benedictus deus et pater domini nostri ihesu christi qui cum deo patre uiuit et regnat deus per omnia secula seculorum amen.

EDITION: BOYER 2008.
BIBLIOGRAPHY: KAEPPELI no. 2012.

3. Ps.-Bernard of Clairvaux, *Meditationes*—ff. 227r^{a}–239r^{b}.

RUB.: [*in det. marg. M3*] incipit liber meditationum beati bernardi abbatis et post de interiori homine; INC.: [f. 227r^{a}] multi multa sciunt et semet ipsos nesciunt et semet [met *add. M3*] ipsos deserunt . . .; EXPL.: [f. 239r^{b}] . . . uideas et meridiem solem iusticie in quo sponsum cum sponsa uideas perspiciensque unum eundemque dominum glorie qui uiuit et regnat in secula seculorum amen. expliciunt meditationes beati bernardi.

The text is also known as *De interiori homine*, or *Meditationes piissimae de cognitione humanae conditionis* (and other various forms).

EDITION: *PL* 184.485–508.
BIBLIOGRAPHY: BLOOMFIELD no. 3126.

BINDING: s. xvii; stiff vellum over pasteboards.

Owners & Provenance: Ownership marks on f. 239v identify a Giovanni Battista Marsu del Poggiardo (fl. 1597), the procurator of the convent of San Paolo in Brindisi (Apulia); on f. 240r Marsu names a Marinello de Marinelli; another ownership mark (s. xvi) on f. 241v[a] records an Andreas apostolus praedicator. Acquired from Herbert Reichner (New York, NY/Stockbridge, MA) by the university in January 1966.

Sales & Catalogues: Reichner, Cat. 31, no. 2096.

Former Shelfmark: MS 15 (Notre Dame).

Bibliography: Corbett no. 15; Emery, Jr. and L. Jordan 1998, 498–499; Delmas 2014, 314.

cod. Lat. b. 6

Origin: Northern France, s. xv^{2}
Content Overview: Ascetic and devotional treatises including works of Jean Gerson, Pierre d'Ailly, Gerard van Vliederhoven, Anselm, Richard of Wetheringsett, Eckbert of Schönau, Ps.-Augustine, Arnulfus de Boeriis, Bonaventure, Ludolph of Saxony, and a verse anthology.

In Latin, on parchment; i +100 ff.; generally 169 x 120 mm (page) [see Layout for ruling]; flyleaf is medieval parchment with s. xv^{2} writing 'papillon' repeatedly; foliated twice in brown ink (s. xv^{ex}) and modern pencil with Arabic numerals [see Foliation].

Collation: i +1–5^{8} +6$^{8-6}$ +7$^{8-2}$ +8$^{8-6}$ +9–11^{8} +12$^{8-6}$ +12–15^{8}

Quires: Parchment quaternions, F/F, are the normal quire forms. Quire 6 lacks three bifolia; quire 7 lacks one bifolium; quire 12 lacks its three inner bifolia. Beginning with quire 11, the quaternions are H/H.

Catchwords: Horizontal catchwords are written in the lower margins for quires 1, 3–5, 7–13; catchwords for quires 5 and 12 do not correspond; those for quires 3 and 13 are mutilated due to trimming.

Signatures: Roman numerals as *ad hoc* signatures (iii, iiii) appear in quire 13 on ff. 79r and 80r.

Foliation: Arabic numerals in modern pencil; a previous foliation (s. xv^{ex}) in brownish ink with Arabic numerals is visible in the upper right margin beneath the current folio number; many have been erased but some remain. The previous foliation in brownish ink accounts for the now missing sections and another seven leaves.

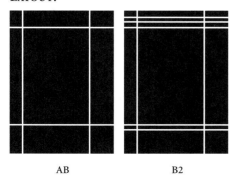

Layout:

AB

B2

A ff. 1r–16v. Ink; 120 x 76 mm; 29 lines.
B ff. 17r–110v. Ink; approx. 116 x 76 mm; 29 lines.

Pattern **A** is lightly traced in ink on ff. 1r–16v, though mostly indistinguishable; single column; writing above top line. Pattern **B** is traced throughout the rest of the manuscript in variable dimensions in darker ink; single column; writing mostly above top line; prickings visible for bounding lines. Pattern **B** is augmented into the deviant pattern, **B2**, in various configurations and dimensions on ff. 85v, 86v, 87v–92r. Writing often extends beyond the ruling horizontally near the end of the codex.

Script: Two main scribal bookhands (M1–M2) can be distinguished. M1 writes Semihybrida (Bastarda) in quires 1–2 (ff. 1r–16v) with a strong preference for loopless forms. Looped forms are so few that the script in most instances appears as Hybrida (Bastarda). M2 writes the remaining texts in a script where the tension between Hybrida (Bastarda) and Cursiva (Bastarda) is apparent, resulting in a more consistent display of Semihybrida (Bastarda) forms than M1; looped ascenders, however, occur on ff. 90v–93r with great consistency. Overall, the level of formality and execution of M2 degrades quickly (especially after f. 77r). Additional hands correct the text throughout the manuscript with erasures and cancellations and add text in the margins.

Decoration:

I. Rubrication: Rubrics, paraph marks, and letter heightening in red ink; lemmata underlined in red; guide letters for many initials still visible.

II. Initials: Flourished, plain, and cadel initials occur in an incongruous hierarchy.

a. One flourished initial (3 line square inset) in red ink with brown penwork begins the *Cordiale* on f. 19r.

b. Plain initials (2 line square inset) in red ink are drawn throughout the manuscript.

c. A single cadel (standing, approx. 4 lines) is drawn above the top line on f. 17r, flourished in brownish ink with red inner augmentation.

III. Line Fillers: Simplistic line fillers in red ink occur often at the end of texts.

Contents:

1. Jean Gerson, *Lamentatio anime agonizantis*—ff. 1r–9r.

rub.: incipit tractatus de meditacione mortis a magistro iohanne iarson parisiensi cancellario editus; inc.: [f. 1r] quacumque impugnacione seu temptacione impugnaris . . .; expl.: [f. 9r] . . . cum quibus est unus deus benedictus et gloriosus in secula amen et oremus pro inuicem ut saluemur. explicit tractatus de meditacione mortis a magistro iohanne iarson parisiensi cancellario editus.

The work is alternatively titled *De meditatione mortis* [see Ouy 1998]. In Ouy's edition this manuscript is siglum *N*.

Edition: Ouy 1998, 94–124.
Bibliography: Ouy 1998, li–lx.

2. Pierre d'Ailly, *Epilogus de quadruplici exercitio spirituali*—ff. 9r–16v.

rub.: incipit tractatus de excercitacione mentali abbreuiatus ex dyalogo domini bonauenture extractus; inc.: [f. 9r] anima deuota cupiens ad diuinam contemplationem spiritualiter excerceri tria debet . . .; expl.: [f. 16v] . . . perducantur gaudia sempiterna quia est benedictus in seculorum secula amen; scribal colophon: [f. 16v] explicit et frequenter legatur.

Edition: Strasbourg 1490.
Bibliography: Mohan 26*; Schneider 1989; *DSAM* 1:256–260; Salembier 1886, 333–334.

3. Florilegium—ff. 17r–18v

inc.: [f. 17r] quicumque primatum desiderauerit in terra confusionem inueniet in celo nec inter suos christi computabitur qui de primatu tractauerit . . .; expl.: [f. 18v] . . . nemo audeat resistere uiribus quoniam nisi fugeat cito sucumbet hoc idem ieronimus.

Extracts of John Chrysostom, Jerome, Gregory, Isidore, Bernard, Cyprian, Ambrose, and Augustine; names underlined in red; red line fillers separate each author's quotations.

4. Gerard van Vliederhoven, *Cordiale* [incomplete]—ff. 19r–64v.

rub.: incipit liber quattuor nouissimorum qui dicitur cordiale; inc.: [f. 19r] memorare nouissima tua et in eternum non peccabis ecc. [Sir 7.40] sicut dicit in libro suarum meditacionum beatus augustinus plus uitanda est sola peccati feditas quam . . .; expl.: [f. 64v] . . . utinam saperent et intelligerent at nouissima prouiderent. explicit tractatus de quatuor nouissimis qui dicitur cordiale. incertum est quo loco mors te expectat ideo tu illam in omni loco expecta seneca stultum est in tali statu uiuere in quo quis non audeat mori augustinus.

Lemmata underlined in red ink.

Bibliography: Bloomfield no. 3057; Dusch 1975, 1–69; Rudolf 1957, 87.

5. Anselm, *Second Meditation*—ff. 64r–67r.

rub.: [f. 64v] meditacio beati anselmi ad concitandum timorem domini in se et de ultimo iudicio et de penis inferni; inc.: [f. 65r] terret me uita mea namque [*corr.*] diligenter discussa apparet michi aut sterilitas fere tota uita mea . . .; expl.: [f. 67r] . . . qui cum patre et spiritu sancto gloriaris per interminata seculorum secula amen. explicit.

Edition: *PL* 158.721–725.

6. Richard of Wetheringsett, verse extract of *Summa 'Qui bene presunt'*—f. 67v.

INC.: [f. 67v] sanc[ti](ficatur) timet est pauper regnat perit inde superbit . . .; EXPL.: [f. 67v] . . . li(bera) sapit est pacis et filius et uenus exit. hiis uersibus continentur septem petitiones dominice orationis septem dona spiritus sancti septem beatitudines septem felicitates et septem peccata mortalia.

GOERING 1995, 149 n. 25 contains the verses transcribed from London, British Library, Royal MS 9 A XIV, f. 30r[a].

7. Eckbert of Schönau, *Stimulus amoris*; or Ps.-Bernard of Clairvaux, *Sermo de uita et passione Domini*—ff. 67v–74v.

RUB.: tractatus de passione domini nostri ihesu christi a beato augustino editus uel a beato anselmo; INC.: [f. 67v] ihesum nazarenum a iudeis innocenter condempnatum a gentibus crucifixum nos . . .; EXPL.: [f. 74v] . . . ut auerteret indignacionem tuam a nobis et consedere sibi nos faceret in celestibus amen. explicit tractatus de passione domini a beato anselmo editus.

EDITION: *PL* 184.953–966; *PL* 158.748–761.
BIBLIOGRAPHY: BESTUL 1996, 188.

8. Ps.-Augustine, *Manuale* [incomplete]—ff. 74v–76v.

RUB.: incipit manuale beati augustini studiose et deuote editum; INC.: [f. 74v] quoniam in medio laqueorum positi sumus facile a celesti desiderio refrigestimus [*sic*] . . .; EXPL.: [f. 76v] . . . ut christo in gloria et sanctis eius possemus sotiari [*sic*] nonne.

The text contains *praefatio*, chapters 1, 2 (imperfect), 13 (imperfect), 14, and 15 (imperfect). The work has also been attributed to Alcher of Clairvaux and Hugh of St. Victor.

EDITION: *PL* 40.951–958.
BIBLIOGRAPHY: BLOOMFIELD no. 4957.

9. Ps.-Augustine, *Speculum peccatoris* [incomplete]—ff. 77r–81v.

INC.: [f. 77r] finem miserum tendant miseri non actendunt [*sic*] o utinam saperent [cap. 6] . . .; EXPL.: [f. 81v] . . . ut per hoc eternam dampnacionem euadas et cum domino nostro ihesu christo uitam eternam possideas quod tibi concedat qui est benedictus in secula amen.

The text begins imperfectly in chapter 6.

EDITION: *PL* 40.988–992.

10. Ps.-Jerome, *Regula monachorum* [excerpts]—ff. 81v–82r.

RUB.: [fol. 81v] ieronimus ad eustochium uirginem; INC.: [cap. 22] inter uos numquam de uita disputetur alterius maneat diuino examini iudicium omne . . .; EXPL.: [fol. 82r] . . . [cap. 30] omnes simul nobilitatem et dignitatem unam habeatis ex sponso breuiter [*ut uid.*] idem ieronimus.

Text contains excerpts of chapters 22 and 30 only (according to the divisions in Migne's *PL*).

EDITION: *PL* 30.410, 417.

11. Ps.-Cyril of Jerusalem, *Epistola de miraculis Hieronymi* [excerpt]—ff. 82r–87v.

RUB.: [fol. 82r] extracta de epistola ciuili de morte sancti eusebii; INC.: adueniente autem die quo uenerabilis eusebius a beato ieronimo in uisione . . .; EXPL.: [f. 87v] . . . beato eusebio qui tunc erat ex hoc seculo migraturus gloriam finis adipisci nesciam quam nobis probare dignetur omnipotens et misericors deus qui uiuat et cetera. explicit.

The text includes most of chapter 3.

EDITION: *PL* 22.292–297; cf. *PL* 33.1128–1132.
BIBLIOGRAPHY: *BHL* 3868.

12. (Ps.-) Bernard of Clairvaux (attr.), verses—f. 87v.

INC.: [f. 87v] ad quid uenisti rogo te meditare frequenter . . .; EXPL.: [f. 87v] . . . et locus iste dei saluabit sufficienter.

EDITION: HAURÉAU 1890, 48.
BIBLIOGRAPHY: WALTHER, *Initia* 429.

13. Arnulfus de Boeriis, or Ps.-Bernard of Clairvaux, *Speculum monachorum*—ff. 87v–90r.

RUB.: [f. 87v] incipit speculum [-pt] monachorum a beato bernardo editum; INC.: [f. 88r] si quis emendatioris uite desiderio tactus cogitacionum locucionum operumque suorum sollicitus explorator uniuersos excessus suos corrigere nititur . . .; EXPL.: [f. 90r] . . . ab interiori tamen rigore et excercicio id est bonis operibus et oratione se inuictus animus non relaxet. explicit breuiarium seu speculum monachorum a beato bernardo editum. COLOPHON: nunc lege nunc ora nunc cum feruore labora sic erit hora breuis et labor ipse leuis.

EDITION: *PL* 184.1176–1178.
BIBLIOGRAPHY: BLOOMFIELD no. 5582.

14. Bonaventure, *De perfectione uitae ad sorores* (cap. 1.1–6)—ff. 90v–93r.

RUB.: [f. 90r] bonauentura de perfecta sui ipsius cognitione; INC.: [f. 90v] ad perfectioris uite fastigium famulo dei cupienti conscendere [*del.* consederare] primum necesse est ut a se incipiat ita ut omnium exteriorum oblitus ingrediatur in secretum conscientie sue . . .; EXPL.: [f. 93r] . . . hoc et beatus bernardus orabat dicens deus non det michi aliud scire quam ut me ipsum cognoscam quicquid agant alii sis memor ipse tui. explicit tractatus de perfecta cognitione sui ipsius.

The text contains chapter 1.1–6.

EDITION: QUARACCHI 8:108–109.
BIBLIOGRAPHY: MOHAN 42*; BESTUL 1996, 189.

15. Verse Florilegium—ff. 93r–100v.

INC.: [f. 93r] articuli fidei quod sit deus trinus et unus christus homo factus natus passusque sepultus descendens surgens scandens iudexque futurus debita dat surgant omnes quod sacra sacrum dant . . .; EXPL.: [f. 100r] pax est in cella foris instant iurgia bella . . . semper obedito te discute qualibet hora.

There are over a hundred selections indicated with red paraph marks; the anthology begins with an excerpt of Richard of Wetheringsett's verse summary on twelve articles from his *Summa 'Qui bene presunt'* [see GOERING 1995, 148].

16. Ludolph of Saxony, *Vita Christi* [excerpt]—f. 100v.

INC.: [f. 100v] qui dicit se in christo manere debet sicut ipse ambulauit et ipse ambulare quod non est ambire . . .; EXPL.: [f. 100v] . . . numquam suam sed conditorem [*sic*] gloriam semper querere et quos ualet secum ad superna erigere hec beda.

The excerpt is drawn from the proem, section 9.

EDITION: RIGOLLOT 1870, 1:7.
BIBLIOGRAPHY: BESTUL 1996, 191.

17. Added Verses—f. 100v.

INC.: [f. 100v] inconstans animus occulus [*sic*] uagus instabilis pes sunt homini [*sic*] signa de quo michi nulla boni spes.

The verse is copied twice in two different hands; see WALTHER, *Initia* 12215.

Binding: s. xv^{ex}/xvi; dark brown leather over pasteboards; blind tooled; sewn on three double thongs; perforations for ribbon or vellum ties on both boards.

Owners & Provenance: Ownership mark erased in the lower margin of fol. 1r; J. Rosenthal (1926); B. Rosenthal (1954, 1959). Acquired from B. Rosenthal (New York, NY) by the university in June 1959.

Sales & Catalogues: J. Rosenthal, Cat. 83, no. 45; B. Rosenthal, Cat. 1, no. 41; ibid., Cat. 9, no. 28.

Former Shelfmark: MS 11 (Notre Dame).

Bibliography: Corbett no. 11; Mohan 16*; Ouy 1998, liv.

cod. Lat. b. 7

Origin: Bohemia, s. xv^{1} (dated Blatná, 30 October 1417).
Content Overview: Bible.

In Latin, on parchment; i +714 ff. +i; generally 181 x 132 mm (page) see [Layout for ruling]; foliated in modern pencil with Arabic numerals; f. 1r post-medieval calligraphic title page (medieval parchment); ff. 9v–10v blank.

Collation: i $+1^{10-1+1}$ $+2\text{–}11^{10}$ $+12^{8}$ $+13\text{–}19^{10}$ $+ 20^{12}$ $+21\text{–}71^{10}$ $+72^{4}$ +i

Quires: Parchment quinions, F/F, are the normal quire forms. The tenth leaf of quire 1 has been canceled; a leaf (f. 1) has been added before the first; f. 1 is inserted asymmetrically and was likely the canceled leaf (ff. 1 and 2 are singletons with stubs). Quire 12 is a quaternion, quire 20 is a sexternion, and quire 72 is a binion. All quires are generally F/F, though the parchment is very thin and well scraped; the manuscript has been trimmed significantly.

Catchwords: Horizontal catchwords are visible in the lower right margins for quires 23–28; all correspond; other quires lack catchwords.

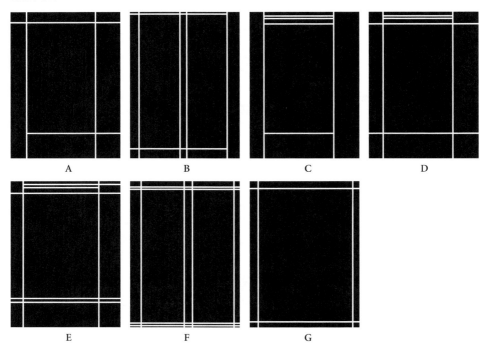

Layout:

A

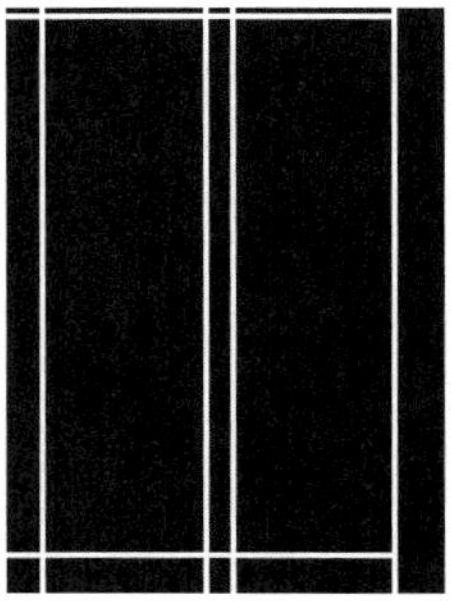
B

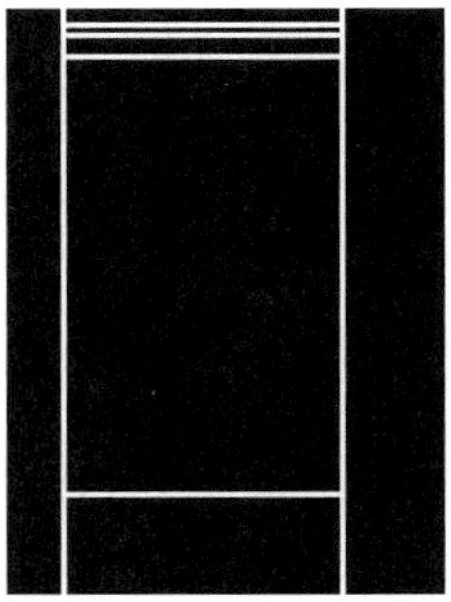
C

D

E

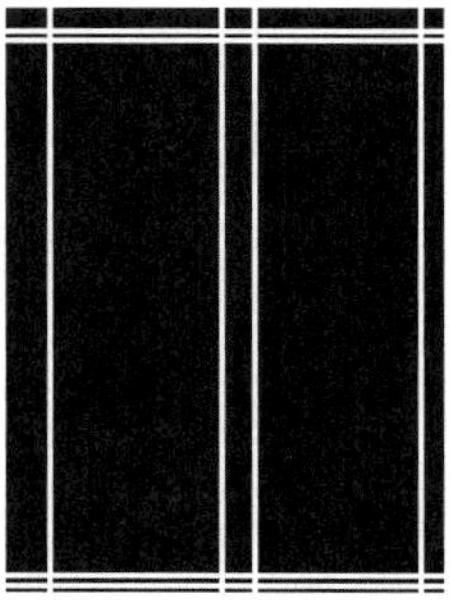
F

G

A ff. 2r–4r. Ink; 137 x 38 mm; 43–47 lines.
B ff. 4v–10v. Lead; 167 x 107 mm; intercol. 8 mm; 59–64 lines.
C ff. 11r–220v. Ink; 135 x 84 mm; 44 lines.
D ff. 221r–600v; 605r–606v; 611r–690v. Ink; 133 x87 mm; 44–46 lines.
E ff. 601r–604v; 607r–610v. Ink; 135 x 91 mm; 46 lines.
F ff. 691r–700v. Ink; 166 x 112 mm; intercol. 10 mm; 52 lines.
G ff. 701r–710v. Ink; 165 x 114 mm; 49–52 lines.
H ff. 710v–714v. Ink; variable dimensions and configurations.

Pattern **A** is frame-ruled in brown ink (ff. 2r–4r); single column; writing below top line; no prickings visible. Pattern **B** is traced lightly in lead on ff. 4v–10v; ruled for two columns (intercol. 8 mm); writing below top line; no prickings visible; use of ruling on ff. 5r–9r is a single column using Pattern **B** as frame-ruling. Pattern **C** is traced in brown ink on ff. 11r–220v; single column; writing below top line; prickings for single vertical bounding lines and all horizontals visible in the lower and outer margins when not trimmed; horizontals for running titles in upper margin. Pattern **D** is traced in brown ink on ff. 221r–600v, 605r–606v, and 611r–690v; single column; writing below top line; prickings as **C**; horizontal through lines extend the width of the page. Pattern **E** is traced in brown ink and interrupts **D** on ff. 601r–604v and 607r–610v; single column; writing below top line; prickings as **D**; **E** adds double horizontal through lines in the upper (by extension) and lower margins. Pattern **F** is traced in brown ink on ff. 691r–700v; ruled for two columns (intercol. 10 mm); writing below the top line; no prickings visible; use of ruling is single column using Pattern **F** as frame-ruling. Pattern **G** is frame-ruled in brown ink on ff. 701r–710v; single column; writing below top line; no prickings visible. Pattern **H** is not a true ruling pattern, but adds three to six columns per page (up to nine for doubles on ff. 711v–712r) to arrange Epistle and Gospel readings for the liturgical year [see CONTENTS 5]; occasional double verticals in red and black ink; *ad hoc* verticals in red ink; no horizontals or prickings.

SCRIPT: Cursiva Libraria and Cursiva Formata are written in black and brown (faded) ink; letter forms are clearly Eastern European/Germanic; strokes often very thick and dark; frequent use of **w**; multiple hands add marginal glosses and annotations in Cursiva using black and red ink.

DECORATION:

I. RUBRICATION: Rubrics, chapter numbers, and running titles in red ink; letter heightening of majuscules and paraph marks in red ink; guide letters for initials and guide numerals (Arabic) for chapters present.

II. INITIALS: Decorated, flourished, and plain initials occur inconsistently in hierarchy.

A. Decorated initials (4–8 lines square inset) in combinations of pink, red, silver, blue, gold, green, and white with marginal acanthus sprays occur on ff. 11r, 40r, 59v, 92v, 110v, 122v, 137v, 138v, 409v, 412r, and 416r (general prol., Ex, Lv, Dt, Ios, Idc, Prol. Rg, 1 Rg, Lam, Bar, Ez).

B. Flourished initials (4–8 lines square inset; hanging **is**; stepped **p**, 6+3 lines) mainly in blue ink with red penwork and white stylization, occasionally red with blue penwork, and one occurrence of gold with green penwork (f. 415v, Prol. Ez) begin all other books and some prologues; flourished initials do not alternate in color regularly; some plain initials were to be flourished, but have only white stylization or no penwork (e.g., ff. 378r, 459r, 524v).

C. Plain initials (2–8 lines square inset; hanging **is**; stepped **ps**) alternate in blue and red ink on ff. 11r–653v; most (2 line square indent) begin chapters; some have red penwork added later, but not of the flourished type (e.g., ff. 443r, 506v); ff. 2r–10r have plain initials in red only (2–3 lines square inset); the psalter (ff. 653v–688r) uses red only (2–5 lines square inset; stylization on f. 653v); Langton's *Interpretation of Hebrew Names* (f. 688r) also uses red initials only (2–5 line square inset; white stylization on f. 653v) and red paraph marks; decoration stops on ff. 694v and 695v.

CONTENTS:

1. Survey of the Bible's subdivisions—ff. 2r–4r.

INC.: [f. 2r] secundum augustinum in primo libro super genesin ad litteram capitulo primo sacra scriptura cannonis biblie habet duas partes principales . . .; **EXPL.**: [f. 4r] . . . per quos manu ducimur fideles ad eterne beatitudinis participationem ad [*deest*] [STEGMÜLLER 8846].

2. 4–5 Ezra—ff. 4v–9r.

5 Esr begins on f. 4v in two columns then switches to a single column on f. 5r [see LAYOUT]; 4 Esr ends imperfectly at the beginning of 11.24; ff. 9v–10v are blank.

2.1. 5 Esr—ff. 4v–5r. **INC.**: liber esdre prophete tercius filii zarie filii azarie filii elchie filii salanie filii sadoch . . .; **EXPL.**: . . . uade annunctia [*sic*] populo meo qualia et quanta mirabilia domini tu uidisti [STEGMÜLLER 96].

2.2. 4 Esr—ff. 5r–9r. **RUB.**: explicit liber tertius ezdre incipit quartus; **INC.**: anno tricesimo ruine ciuitatis eram in babillone . . .; **EXPL.**: . . . nisi tria capita in corpore quiescentia et sex pennacula [*sic*] et uidi et ecce de sex pennaculis [*sic*] [4 Esr 11.24] [STEGMÜLLER 95].

3. Bible—ff. 11r–688r.

Old Testament (ff. 11r–506v); New Testament (ff. 506v–653v); the psalter (ff. 653v–688r) follows Apc and contains *argumenta* written in the margins; *tituli* and marginal glosses occur sporadically throughout the entire Bible.

Order of books: Gn; Ex; Lv; Nm; Dt; Ios; Idc; Rt; 1–4 Rg; 1–2 Par with prayer of Manasses [STEGMÜLLER 93,2]; 1 Esr; Neh; 2 Esr (=3 Esr) [STEGMÜLLER 94,1]; Tb; Idt; Est; Prv; Ecl; Ct; Sap; Sir; Iob; Is; Ier; Lam; Bar; Ez; Dn; Os; Ioel; Am; Abd; Ion; Mi; Na; Hab; So; Agg; Za; Mal; 1–2 Mcc; Mt; Mc; Lc; Io; Rm; 1–2 Cor; Gal; Eph; Phil; Col; 1–2 Th; 1–2 Tim; Tit; Phlm; Hbr; Act; Iac; 1–2 Pt; 1–3 Io; Iud; Apc; Ps.

Prologues (56 in total, including the introduction to Sir and Lc 1.1–4; see above for Ps) are as follows:

				Stegmüller nos.
1.	f. 11r	Prol.	frater ambrosius . . .	284
2.	f. 13v	Pent.	desiderii mei desideratas . . .	285
3.	f. 110r	Ios	tandem finito pentatheuco . . .	311
4.	f. 110v	Ios	ihesus filius naue . . .	307
5.	f. 137v	1 Rg	uiginti duas esse litteras . . .	323
6.	f. 204v	1 Par	si septuaginta interpretum pura . . .	328
7.	f. 239r	1 Esr	utrum [esdrum *post corr.*] difficilius sit . . .	330
8.	f. 260v	Tb	chromatio et heliodoro episcopis . . .	332
9.	f. 265v	Idt	aput hebreos liber iudith . . .	335
10 +11.	f. 272v	Est	librum hester uariis . . .; rursum in libro . . . [f. 273r]	341+343
11.	f. 279v	Prv	iungat epistola quos iungit . . .	457
12.	f. 307r	Sir	multorum nobis et magnorum . . .	[Sir 1]
13.	f. 332v	Iob	cogor per singulos diuine scripture . . .	344
14.	f. 349r	Is	nemo cum prophetas uiderit uersibus . . .	482
15.	f. 378r	Ier	ieremias propheta cui hic prologus scribitur . . .	487
16.	f. 409v	Lam	et factum est postquam in captiuitatem . . .	29
17.	f. 415v	Ez	ezechiel propheta cum ioachim . . .	492
18.	f. 443r	Dn	danielem prophetam iuxta septuaginta . . .	494
19.	f. 455v	Proph. Min.	non idem ordo est . . .	500
20.	f. 459r	Ioel	iohel filius fatuel descripsit terram . . .	510
21.	f. 461r	Am	amos pastor et rusticus . . . audiendi uerbum domini.	512
22.	f. 464r	Abd	abdias qui interpretatur . . .	516
23.	f. 464v	Ion	ionas interpretatur columba naufragio suo . . .	522
24.	f. 465v	Mi	micheas de morastini coheres . . .	525
25.	f. 468r	Na	naum consolator orbis . . .	527
26.	f. 469r	Hab	abacus luctator fortis . . .	529
27.	f. 470r	So	sophonias speculator et archanorum . . .	532
28.	f. 471r	Agg	aggeus festiuus et letus . . .	535
29.	f. 472r	Za	zacharias memor domini sui . . .	540
30.	f. 476v	Mal	malachias latine interpretatur . . .	545
31.	f. 506v	Mt	matheus ex iudea sicut in ordine . . .	590
32.	f. 507r	Mt	matheus cum primo predicasset . . .	589
33.	f. 524r	Mc	marcus ewangelista dei electus . . .	607
34.	f. 535v	Lc	lucas syrus nacione anthiocensis . . .	620
35.	f. 536r	Lc	quoniam quidem multi . . .	[Lc 1.1–4]
36.	f. 555r	Io	hic est iohannes ewangelista . . .	624
37.	f. 571r	Rm	romani sunt partes italie hii preuenti . . .	cf. 677
38.	f. 579r	1 Cor	corinthii sunt achaici et hii similiter . . .	685
39.	f. 586v	2 Cor	post actam ab eis penitenciam . . .	699
40.	f. 591r	Gal	galathe sunt greci hii uerbum primum . . .	707
41.	f. 593v	Eph	ephesii sunt asyani hii accepto uerbo ueritatis . . .	715
42.	f. 596r	Phil	filippenses sunt macedones hii accepto uerbo . . .	728

				Stegmüller nos.
43.	f. 598r	Col	colosenses et hii sicut et laodicenses sunt asiani . . .	736
44.	f. 599v	1 Th	thessalonicenses sunt macedones qui . . .	747
45.	f. 601r	2 Th	ad thessalonicenses secundam scribit . . .	752
46.	f. 602r	1 Tim	timotheum instruit et docet de ordinacione . . .	765
47.	f. 604r	2 Tim	item timotheo scribit . . .	772
48.	f. 605v	Tit	thitum commonefacit . . .	780
49.	f. 606v	Phlm	filemoni familiares litteras facit . . .	783
50.	f. 607r	Hbr	in primis dicendum est cur apostolus paulus . . .	793
51.	f. 613r	Act	lucas anthiocensis nacione syrus . . .	cf. 637, 640
52.	f. 634r	Iac	non ita est ordo aput grecos . . .	809
53.	f. 636v	1 Pt	simon petrus iohannis filius prouincie galilee . . .	816
54.	f. 642r	2 Io	apostolos a deo ad sanctam feminam . . .	823
55.	f. 642v	3 Io	gayum pietatis causa . . .	824
56.	f. 643v	Apc	omnes qui pie uolunt . . .	839

4. Stephen Langton, *Interpretation of Hebrew Names*—ff. 688r–710v.

inc.: [f. 688r] aaz apprehendens uel apprehensio . . .; expl.: [f. 710v] . . . zuzim consiliantes eos uel consiliatores eorum [Stegmüller 7709]; scribal colophon: finis interpretacionum a(nno) d(omini) .m.cccc.xvij. die sabbati proxima ante uictorini in blathna.

The feast of St. Victorinus of Pettau is usually celebrated on Nov. 3.

5. Lectionary—ff. 710v–714v.

List of Epistle and Gospel readings for the liturgical year; titles in red ink and incipits and explicits in black ink are arranged in various columns [see Layout].

Binding: s. xvii/xviii?; stiff vellum over pasteboards; blind tooled; ink titles on spine.

Owners & Provenance: William Davignon (1867–1924); Gilhofer and Ranschburg, Vienna (ca. 1935); Very Rev. Urban de Hasque of Oklahoma City, OK (1875–1954); donated to the university by de Hasque according to Faye and Bond, 186, no. 7 and Corbett no. 7; no other documentation exists to confirm the donation or de Hasque's ownership.

Sales & Catalogues: Gilhofer & Ranschburg, Cat. 218, no. 240; ibid., Cat. 233, no. 1.

Former Shelfmark: MS 7 (Notre Dame)

Bibliography: Faye and Bond, 186, no. 7; Corbett no. 7; D'Alverny 1981, 107.

cod. Lat. b. 8

Origin: Low Countries, s. xv^{2}
Content Overview: Alan of Lille, *Liber parabolarum.*

In Latin, on paper; i +16 ff. +i; 205 x 144 mm (page) [see Layout for ruling]; pen trials and opening of *Liber parabolarum* written on second flyleaf recto; foliated in modern pencil with Arabic numerals; ff. 1v, 15r–16v blank.

Collation: i +1^{12} +2^{4} +i

Quires: A single sexternion and one binion folded in quarto comprise the manuscript.

Bibliographical Format: 4°.

Watermarks: Four occurrences of one watermark: Letter P (**A**) occurs on flyleaf II/f. 11, ff. 1/10, ff. 3/8, and ff. 6/7; cf. Piccard 111933 (Geldern, 1462–1463).

Layout:

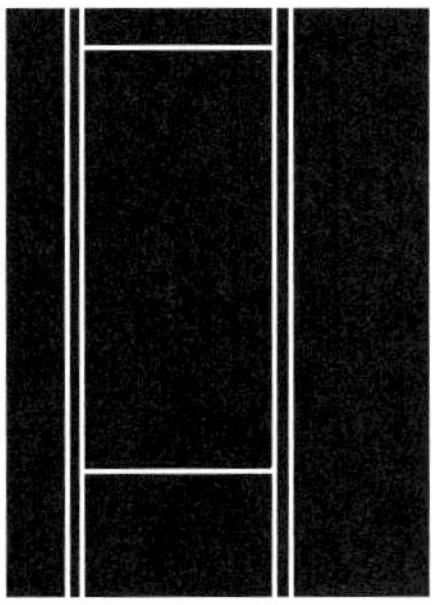

A

A ff. 1–16. Hard-point; 140 x 85 mm; 22–23 lines.

Pattern **A** is ruled using hard-point technique; single column; writing below top line; indentations on the verso. Interruptions at the intersection of verticals and horizontals cannot be seen clearly, though board-ruling is a possibility.

Script: A single hand (M1) writes the text in Semihybrida Libraria. Most ascenders are loopless, but some looped forms occur. Interlinear corrections appear on f. 1r.

Decoration:
I. Rubrication: Letter heightening of majuscules in red ink.
II. Initials: Plain initials (2–5 line square inset) in red ink occur in varying sizes on ff. 2r (5 line), 4v and 6v (2 line), 9r (4 line), 11r and 13r (3 line).

Contents:

1. Alan of Lille, *Liber parabolarum*—ff. 2r–14v.

inc.: [f. 2r] a phebo phebe lumen capit [rapit *add. sup. uersum*] a sapiente . . .; **expl.:** [f. 14v] . . . primitus in siluas doctus ut ire queat.

The text ends after VI.6.

Edition: Limone 1993; Hunt 2005, 158–178 and Hunt 2007, 115–133 provide the Latin text as appendices, though neither is a critical edition.
Bibliography: See also Raynaud de Lage 1951, 15–17; D'Alverny 1965, 51–52.

Binding: s. xix/xx; binder's board; green paper cover (diced print).

Owners & Provenance: Acquired from H. P. Kraus (New York, NY) by the university in September 1968.

Sales & Catalogues: H. P. Kraus, Cat. 117, no. 39.

Former Shelfmark: MS 55 (Notre Dame).

Bibliography: Corbett no. 55; D'Alverny 1981, 106; Mann 2006, 52; Nolan 2006, 3.

cod. Lat. b. 9

Origin: Italy, s. xiv[1].
Content Overview: William Peraldus, *Summa de uitiis.*

In Latin, on parchment; 408 ff.; generally 180 x 128 mm (page) [see Layout for ruling]; foliated in black ink (medieval) with Arabic and Roman numerals; twice foliated in modern pencil with Arabic numerals [see Foliation].

Collation: $1–28^{12} + 29^{10} + 30^{12} + 31^{10} + 32–34^{12} + 35^{1+1+1+1}$

Quires: Parchment sexternions, F/F, are the predominant quire forms; quires 29 and 31 are quinions, F/F; quire 35 is constructed from four singletons with stubs folded together, F/F; all quires obey Gregory's Rule; wormed; the manuscript has been trimmed.

Catchwords: Horizontal catchwords in the lower right margins for all quires (except quires 30, 32–35); stylized in brown ink (except quires 29 and 31); all correspond (quires 5, 6, 31 are trimmed).

Foliation: Medieval foliation in Arabic numerals 1–320 (ff. 9–339) with errors. Foliator combines Roman numerals for 100 with Arabic (e.g., CC9 for 209); modern foliation throughout with errors (corrected beginning on f. 339 with transformations, erasures, and strikes).

Layout:

A

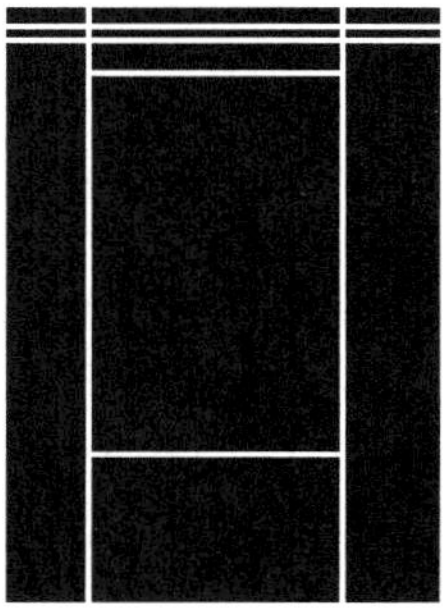
B

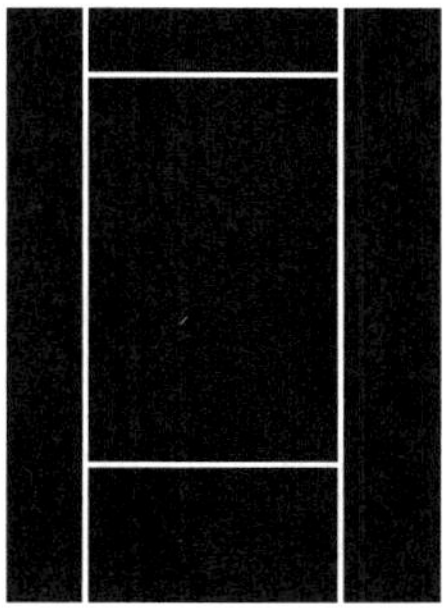
C

A ff. 1r–8v. Lead; 115 x 77 mm; cols. 3/6/4/8/56 mm; 27 lines.
B ff. 9r–336v. Lead; 115 x 75 mm; 27 lines.
C ff. 337r–408v. Lead; 115 x 75mm; 27 lines.

Pattern **A** is traced in lead on ff. 1r–8v in five columns (3/6/4/8/56 mm) to form the index and list of chapters; writing below top line; prickings for verticals visible in upper and lower margins. Pattern **B** is traced in lead on ff. 9r–336v; single column; writing below top line. The pricking pattern of **A** is visible on ff. 9–12, which complete quire 1, but **B** is traced. Pattern **C** is traced in lead on ff. 337r–408v; single column; writing below top line; prickings visible for verticals; dimensions of the ruling are identical with **B**; **C** lacks the upper horizontals and displays its own pricking pattern.

SCRIPT: A single hand (M1) copies the text in Southern Textualis (Rotunda); abbreviations are Italian. Glosses are written sparsely in the margins by another hand (M2) under the influence of Italian Semihybrida.

DECORATION:
I. RUBRICATION: Rubrics, chapters, and sections in red ink; paraph marks alternate in red and blue ink; instructions to rubricator and guide letters visible throughout the manuscript; Arabic numerals in red ink indicate chapter numbers in the margins.
II. INITIALS: Littera duplex and flourished initials occur in hierarchy.
A. Littera duplex (4–5 line square inset) occur on ff. 9r, 51v, 153r, 199r, 334v, 340r, and 361v.
B. Flourished initials (hanging) in red and blue ink with contrasting penwork (including major paraph marks) alternate throughout the manuscript; zoomorphic flourishes on f. 81v; a second painter is responsible for initials for quires 29–34. Small flourished initials in red and blue ink with contrasting penwork alternate by the letter in the upper margin (vices in abbreviated form); these switch to plain initials and write the vices fully for quires 29–34 (ff. 337–408) coinciding with the shift in decoration.

CONTENTS:

1. William Peraldus, *Summa de uitiis*—ff. 9r–408v.

RUB.: [f. 9r] de uitio in communi; INC.: dicturi de singulis uitiis cum oportunitas se offeret incipiemus a uitio gule . . .; EXPL.: [f. 408v] . . . ultimo ad commendationem silentii potuit ualere idem sapientis locutum esse aliquando penituit tacere uero numquam; SCRIBAL COLOPHON: explicit hic liber sit scriptor crimine liber. christi solam [*lac.*] qui dixerit amen.

Includes table of contents for the prologue and chapters on ff. 1r–8v with rubrics.

EDITION: ANTWERP 1588.
BIBLIOGRAPHY: BLOOMFIELD no. 1628; KAEPPELI no. 1622 (A).

Binding: s. xix/xx; paper pulp boards; sewn on three cords; brown marbled cover.

Owners & Provenance: Harras (1 December 1896); J. Rosenthal (1926); B. Rosenthal (1954, 1959). Acquired from B. Rosenthal (New York, NY) by the university in June 1959.

Sales & Catalogues: Sotheby's, 1–4 December 1896, lot 595; J. Rosenthal, Cat. 83, no. 50; B. Rosenthal, Cat. 1, no. 48; ibid., Cat. 9, no. 30.

Former Shelfmark: MS 12 (Notre Dame).

Bibliography: Corbett no. 12; D'Alverny 1981, 106; Kaeppeli 4:106; Emery, Jr. and L. Jordan 1998, 499.

cod. Lat. b. 10

Origin: Italy, s. xv^2 (Rome).
Content Overview: Two humanist miscellanies of classical, patristic, and scientific texts, recipe collections, and commentaries bound together.

In Latin and Italian, on paper with a few Greek annotations; two manuscripts have been bound together; iv +182 ff. +132 ff. +i; Part I, ff. 52v–53v, 72v–73v, 88v–89v, 151r–v, 179r–181v blank; Part II, ff. 114r–116v, 152v blank.

Collation: iii $+1^{18}$ $+2–7^{12}$ $+8–9^{20}$ $+10^{10}$ $+11^{12}$ $+12^{10}$ $+13^{20}$ $+14–21^{12}$ $+22^{24+1}$ $+23^{2}$ $+24^{9}$ +i

Bibliographical Format: 4°.

Quires: Paper sexternions and quinions folded in quarto are the predominant quire forms; quire 1 is comprised of nine bifolia; quires 8–10 and 13 are comprised of ten bifolia; quire 22 of twelve bifolia with a leaf pasted in during rebinding (f. 141). Quire 23 is a bifolium; quire 24 is comprised of three bifolia added asymmetrically (pasted in various configurations in rebinding).

Catchwords: Horizontal catchwords written in the lower right margins for quires 1–3, 8–9, 12, 14–20, 22; all correspond except for quire 22 where the manuscript ends imperfectly.

Foliation: Part I is foliated in early modern ink (ff. 1–179) and modern pencil (ff. 180–182) with Arabic numerals. Part II, quires 14–15 are paginated in ink with Arabic numerals (pp. 1–42); foliation begins in quire 15 (p. 43 = f. 42r); ff. 42–112 foliated in ink with Arabic numerals by the same hand as Part I; ff. 113–152 in modern pencil with Arabic numerals which adjust ink foliation (f. 117 = 113 in ink).

Watermarks: There are seventy-seven occurrences of seventeen different watermarks (**A–Q**) in Parts I and II of the manuscript.

Forty-five occurrences of seven different watermarks (**A–G**) are found in Part I (quires 1–13): (**A**) partial circle on flyleaf IV; unidentifiable. (**B**) Bird; occurs in quire 1 (ff. 1/16) and quire 12; cf. Piccard 42381 (Rome, 1563). (**C**) Stag, full body horizontal, antlers consisting of two lines; occurs in quires 1–4 and 13 (ff. 168/175, 171/172); distance between chainlines 44 mm; approx. 36 x 38 mm. (**D**) Bird; occurs in quires 5–6; cf. Briquet 12152 (Naples, 1495). (**E**) Crown; occurs in quires 7 and 10; cf. Piccard 51694 (Ravenna, 1500).

(F) Bird; occurs in quires 8–9; cf. Piccard 52388 (Ellwangen, 1495). (G) Bird; occurs in quire 13 (ff. 162/181, 165/178, 167/176); cf. Briquet 12205 (Florence, 1497).

Thirty-two occurrences of ten different watermarks (H–Q) are found in Part II (quires 14–24): (H) Crown; occurs in quires 14 (pp. 1/23), 16 (ff. 47/54), 17 (ff. 62/63), and 18 (ff. 70/79, 73/76); cf. Piccard 51068 (Florence, 1486). (I) Crown; occurs in quires 14 (pp. 7/17, 9/15), 15, 16 (ff. 58/67, 59/66), 18 (ff. 71/78); cf. Piccard 51004 (Rome, 1486). (J) Scissors with star; occurs in quire 16 (ff. 45/56); cf. Piccard 122549 (Genova, 1485). (K) Letter P; occurs in quire 19 and 20 (ff. 94/103); cf. Briquet 8492 (Rome, 1484). (L) Anchor; occurs in quire 20 (ff. 95/102, 98/99); cf. Briquet 429 (Udine, 1489). (M) Crown; occurs in quire 21 (ff. 107/114); cf. Piccard 51049 (Quinzano, 1483). (N) Bull's Head; partial watermark; occurs in quire 21 (f. 116). (O) Bird; occurs in quire 22; cf. Piccard 42386 (Rome, 1490). (P) Sun/star; occurs in quire 23 (ff. 142/143); cf. Piccard 41202 (Rome, 1530). (Q) Tower; occurs in quire 24 (ff. 150/151); distance between chainlines 49 mm; approx. 40 x 25 mm.

Layout: No distinctive ruling pattern is used; text is often aligned with chainlines, or folds along chainlines; single column (3 cols. on ff. 64v–65r; 2 cols. f. 65v); generally 147 x 87 mm with great variability; number of lines variable; text often slanted, especially near the bottom of the page.

Script: A single hand (M1) of the late fifteenth century writes all texts in Humanistic cursive at different levels of execution and rapidity. The Pomponian **g** occurs frequently at the beginning of words and as a majuscule; the graph points toward Rome and Pomponio Leto's circle. A later hand adds cursive on ff. 141r–152r.

Decoration:

I. Rubrication: Rubrics in red and brown ink.

II. Initials: Plain initials occur loosely in hierarchy.

a. Plain initials (hanging; 1 line versals) with Romanesque stylization are painted in red and brown ink throughout the manuscript.

Diagrams: Diagram of an apparatus is drawn within the text on f. 137v.

Contents, Part I:

1. Ps.-Messalla Coruinus, *De Augusti progenie* [incomplete]—ff. 1r–15v.

inc.: [f. 1r] regnante de creta cum manu electissimorum iuuenum forte noui regni fama concitum teucrum ad phrygiam patriis sedibus expulsum . . .; expl.: [f. 15v] . . . aeternum uale saeculi perenne ac immortale decus caesar auguste. finis.

The text begins in section III.

Edition: Bipontine 1789, 335–354.

Bibliography: H. Jordan 1869.

2. Ps.-Sextus Rufus, *Curiosum Vrbis Romae*—ff. 15v–20v.

RUB.: sexti ruffi de urbe opusculum; INC.: [f. 15v] regio prima porta capena continet aedem honoris et uirtutis camoenas lacum promothei [*sic*] balneanum [*sic*] torquati thermas seuerinus et comodianas aream apollinis et spelnis [*sic*] uicum uitrarium aream pannarium mutatorium caesaris balneum abascantis et mamertini aream carrucae . . .; EXPL.: [f. 20v] . . . tabellariorum uictimariorum mensae olearine per totam urbem duo .m.cccc. finis.

Falsely attributed to Sextus Rufus by Flavio Biondo.

EDITION: VALENTINI and ZUCCHETTI 1940–1953, 89–164; NORDH 1949.

3. Latin excerpts of Pausanias, *Description of Greece*—ff. 20v–43v.

3.1. ff. 20v–33v. RUB.: ex libro primo pausaniae qui inscribitur ἀτθίσ [*sic*]; INC.: atheniensium portus sub munychia et inibi munichiae dianae templum . . .; EXPL.: . . . graeciae pluuiam impetrauit eurystheus a menelao megaris peremptus.

3.2. ff. 33v–43v. RUB.: ex secundo pausaniae libro qui inscribitur κορινθιακα; INC.: corinthii dicunt uenisse neptunnum [*sic*] cum sole . . .; EXPL.: . . . polemotines filius mahaonis frater alexamonis. τελοσ.

Marginal scholia in Latin and Greek in both columns; text begins at 1.1.4 and ends around 2.23.4. The text is a partial translation and summary of Pausanias.

4. Latin excerpts of Philostratus, *Vita Apollonii*—ff. 44r–51v.

4.1. Book 1—ff. 44r–45r. RUB.: ex libro primo philostrati de uita apollonii thyanei; INC.: uestitum ex morticina materia renuisse pycthagorum [*sic*] dicunt linthea usurpantem . . .; EXPL.: . . . si respondit apollonius honoraueris multos credideris autem paucis.

4.2. Book 2—ff. 45r–46v. RUB.: ex libro philostrati secundo; INC.: bacchus nyseus a nysa que in india est dicitur . . .; EXPL.: . . . a cibo a uino autem triduum.

4.3. Book 3—ff. 46v–48v. RUB.: ex libro tertio; INC.: in hyphaside fluuio indiae belua est albo uermiculo persimilis . . .; EXPL.: . . . et hoc est unum genus indicae margaritae.

4.4. Book 4—ff. 48v–49r. RUB.: ex libro quarto; INC.: in lesbo orphei aditum est ubi reddebantur olim responsa cum ex thracia caput eius aduertum esset . . .; EXPL.: . . . nunc ad aethiopas nunc ad olympum proficiscuntur.

4.5. Book 5—ff. 49r–50v. RUB.: ex quinto libro; INC.: apud gades quo . . .; EXPL.: . . . sin autem nunc dum licet abire.

4.6. Book 6—ff. 50v–51r. RUB.: ex sexto libro; INC.: memnonem damas refert occubuisse non apud troiam . . .; EXPL.: . . . si eam actingere [att- *corr.*] rabiosus audeat.

4.7. Book 7—f. 51r. RUB.: ex septimo libro; INC.: python reginus cum ad dionysium siciliae tyrannum profugisset . . .; EXPL.: . . . signum libertatis esse propositum.

4.8. Book 8—f. 51r–v. RUB.: ex octauo libro; INC.: leges nisi rex regni sui damnatas esse putauerit non ipse damnabitur . . .; EXPL.: . . . solis diis datum nec senescere nec unquam [*sic*] mori. τελοσ.

5. Marcantonio Coccio Sabellico, *Annotations to Livy*—ff. 51v–52r.

RUB.: m. antonii sabellici in liuium annotationes ex primo libro; INC.: [f. 51r] facturusne sim operae pretium legendum auctore quintiliano facturusne operae pretium sim . . . [*Praef.* 1]; EXPL.: [f. 52r] . . . lauinii hostiam lanuuii hastam lege [21.62.].

Textual annotations for Books 1–3, 5–6, 8, 10, 21 of Livy, *Ab urbe condita.*

EDITION: OGILVIE 1974 (see *Sabellicus* in the *app. crit.*).

6. Definitions—ff. 54r–65v.

RUB.: graphionis [grapluonis *ut uid.*] deffinitiones [*sic*]; INC.: [f. 54r] deffinitio [*sic*] est uniuscuiusque rei aperte ac breuiter explicatae notio . . .; EXPL.: [f. 64r] . . . contentio est oratio acris ad confirmandum et infirmandum idonea.

An index for this section follows on ff. 64v–65v; ff. 51r–64r are numbered in the upper right corner on each recto as 1–10 (ff. 63r and 64r are both 10); the numbers correspond to an alphabetical list on ff. 64v–65v. A brief excerpt of Origen in Latin occurs near the bottom of f. 64r [see CONTENTS 7].

7. Origen, *Commentary on Romans* [Rufinus (tr.)]—f. 64r.

RUB.: origenes super epistolam pauli ad romanos; INC.: [f. 64r] iniquitas sane a peccato hanc habet differentiam quod iniquitas in his dicitur quae contra legem committuntur . . .; EXPL.: [f. 64r] . . . si contra quam natura docet et conscientia arguit delinquatur.

In Rom. IV.1.19 is written at the bottom of f. 64r between the definitions and their alphabetical index [see CONTENTS 6].

EDITION: HAMMOND BAMMEL 2010, 200.

8. Cassiodorus, *Expositio psalmorum* [selections]—ff. 66r–72r, 74r–75r.

RUB.: casiodorus in prologo psalmorum; INC.: [f. 66r] prophetia est aspiratio diuina quae euentus rerum aut per facta aut per dicta quorundam immobili ueritate pronuntiat . . .; EXPL.: [f. 75r] . . . hymnus est laus diuinitatis metri alicuius lege composita.

Psalms are numbered in left margin with Arabic numerals; ff. 72v–73v are blank; text resumes on f. 74r.

EDITION: STOPPACCI 2012; ADRIAEN 1958.

9. Medical recipe collection—ff. 75v–88r.

INC.: [f. 75v] ad incarnare denti recipe sangue de dracone . . .; EXPL.: [f. 88r] . . . et uidebis mirabilia.

Eighty-nine recipes in Italian and Latin, including a few prayers.

10. Alexius Africanus, *Compendium aureum*—ff. 90r–95r.

RUB.: incipit tractatus alaxii [*sic*] africani de uirtutibus septem herbarum secundum cursum planetarum; INC.: [f. 90r] alaxius [*sic*] africanus discipulus belbenis coladeo [*sic*] atheniensi eplogiticis studium continuare cum laude dei . . .; EXPL.: [f. 95r] . . . est quod serues id nec doctas quemquam nec reueles. finis.

EDITION: DELATTE 1942, 213–233.
BIBLIOGRAPHY: CARMODY 1956, 57; SINGER 1931, 766–773.

11. (Ps.-)Thessalus of Tralles, *De uirtutibus herbarum* (Latin)—ff. 95r–104v.

RUB.: incipit tractatus thessali philosophi de duodecim herbis duodecim signorum attributis necnon de aliis septem herbis secundum cursum septem planetarum; INC.: [f. 95r] thessalus philosophus germanico claudio regi et deo aeterno salutem et amorem o caesar uenerabilis multis intromittentibus . . .; EXPL.: [f. 104v] . . . humidus ut utere et cetera.

EDITION: cf. FRIEDRICH 1968 (multiple versions).
BIBLIOGRAPHY: PINGREE 1976; PINGREE 1992.

12. Arnau de Villanova, *Liber de uinis*—ff. 104v–123v.

RUB.: tractatus de conpositione uinorum****[*rasura*] ad carolum francorum.

12.1. Dedication—ff. 104v–105r. INC.: sacrae et semper uirtuosae regiae maiestati ***[*rasura*] seruitor uester humilis . . .; EXPL.: . . . et de grato efficiat gratiorem.

12.2. *De uinis*—ff. 105r–123v. INC.: cum igitur instat tempus in quo medicinalia . . .; EXPL.: . . . ualet ad uictoriam conperandam. finis.

Parts of the rubric and text on f. 104v have been erased.

EDITION: SIMÓ SANTONJA 2007; PARIS 1500.
BIBLIOGRAPHY: MCVAUGH 2005; PEREIRA 2004.

13. Ps.-Ramon Llull, *Ars operatiua medica*—ff. 124r–132v.

RUB.: tractatus de morbis incurabilibus per raimundum lulli de insula maiorica; INC.: [f. 124r] cum ego raimundus dudum bride [*sic*] existens rogatus affectuose a quibusdam carris amicis meis . . .; EXPL.: [f. 132v] . . . hoc bibitum ieiuno stomaco sanat arenam in uesica et dissoluit omnem lapidem in uesica [*ut uid.*].

EDITION: BASEL 1597, 150–178; see PEREIRA 1989, 66 no. I.6 for others.
BIBLIOGRAPHY: PEREIRA 1989, 66 no. I.6; PEREIRA 2004.

14. Medical recipe collection—ff. 132v–139v.

INC.: [f. 132v] hec sunt remedia singularia per ipocratonem [*ut uid.*]; impleatur amphora uini floribus rose marine . . .; EXPL.: [f. 139v] . . . capiat partiens onzas .8. bis in ebdomada.

Twelve recipes in Latin and Italian; diagram of an apparatus embedded in the text on f. 137v.

15. Ps.-Seneca, *De uerborum copia*—ff. 140r–150v.

RUB.: lucii annei senecae de copia uerborum opusculum incipit; INC.: [f. 140r] quisquis prudentiam sequi desideras tunc per rationem ratione [*sic*] uiues . . .; EXPL.: [f. 150v] . . . naufragium raro pertulit qui uentorum rationem bene inspexit. finis.

Text contains additional proverbs ending with Vegetius, *Mil.* 4.38.17.

EDITION: FOHLEN 1980.

16. Ambrose, *De bono mortis*—ff. 152r–178v.

RUB.: diui ambrosii de bono mortis opusculum aureum; INC.: [f. 152r] quoniam de anima superiori libro sermonem aliquem conteximus . . .; EXPL.: [f. 178v] . . . perpetuitas a saeculis et nunc et semper et in omnia saecula saeculorum. Amen.

EDITION: WIESNER 1970.

CONTENTS, PART II:

17. Petronius, *Satyricon*—pp. 1–42, ff. 42r–61v.

RUB.: petronius arbiter; INC.: [p. 1] cum alio genere furiarum declamatores inquietantur qui clamant . . .; EXPL.: [f. 61v] . . . multa loquor quod uis nummis praesentibus opta et ueniet clausum possidet arca iouem. petronius arbiter finit.

This section is partially paginated [see FOLIATION]; text ends at *Sat.* 137.9.

EDITION: MÜLLER 1995.
BIBLIOGRAPHY: T. RICHARDSON 1984.

18. Vibius Sequester, *De fluminibus*—ff. 62r–77v.

RUB.: uibius sequester de fluminibus fontibus lacubus nemoribus paludibus montibus gentibus ad uirgilianum filium; INC.: [f. 62r] quanto ingenio et studio fili carissime apud plerosque poetas fluminum mentio habita sit tanto labore sum secutus eorum et regiones et uocabula et qualitates . . .; EXPL.: [f. 77v] . . . thessali macedones europae uolsci italici europae. finis.

EDITION: GELSOMINO 1967; PARRONI 1965.

19. Suetonius, *De grammaticis et rhetoribus*—ff. 77v–100v.

RUB.: suetonii tranquilli de grammaticis et rhetoribus clarrissimis [*sic*] libellus incipit; INC.: [f. 77v] grammatica romae ne in usu quidem olim nedum in honore ullo erat rudi scilicet ac bellicosa etiam tum ciuitate necdum magnopere liberalibus disciplinis uacante . . .; EXPL.: [f. 100v] . . . conuocataque plebe causis propter quas mori destinasset diu ac more contionantis redditis abstinuit cibo. finis.

EDITION: KASTER 1995; VACHER 1993.
BIBLIOGRAPHY: COLKER 1983; KASTER 1992.

20. Symmachus, *Epistolae*, Book I [excerpts]—ff. 101r–113r.

RUB.: quinti aurelii simmachi consulis et praefecti urbis epistolarum liber; INC.: [f. 101r] ne mihi uitio uertatur intermissio litterarum malo esse promptus officii . . .; EXPL.: [f. 113r] . . . libet ut rideas plura desino ne qui strictim meliora detexui in minoribus uidear immorari uale.

Selected letters from Book I: 1, 5, 6, 14, 23, 25, 28, 31, 32, 34, 36–38, 43, 45, 46; initial s on f. 113v with no text [s<ilentii> *fort. rect.*; cf. *Ep.* I.47].

EDITION: CALLU 1972.

21. Commentary on Cicero, *Paradoxa Stoicorum*—ff. 117r–137v.

INC.: [f. 117r] animaduerti brute titulus huius operis talis est marci tulii ciceronis paradoxa ad marcum brutum et ideo hoc nomen acceperunt paradoxa . . .; EXPL.: [f. 137v] . . . quanto magis aestimanda uirtus quae nullum patitur detrimentum. finis.

22. Commentary on Statius, *Siluae* I—ff. 138r–140v [incomplete].

RUB.: [*mutil.*]; INC.: [f. 138r] cessent mendaces obliqui carminis astus non ulterius stella scribet et poetarum more quasdam elegias quibus mentiatur . . .; EXPL.: [f. 140v] . . . extra aut<em> intelligit laconicum nam ibi erant aquae frigidae et pellucide.

Begins at *Sil.* 1.2.27 and ends at 1.5.51; catchword trimmed in lower margin.

BIBLIOGRAPHY: H. ANDERSON 2009, 1:267–268; T. RICHARDSON 1984, 91.

23. Later Additions, unidentified—ff. 141r–152v.

Later additions in rapid cursive.

BINDING: s. xix/xx; brown leather over pasteboards; paper cover; gilt spine; broken.

Owners & Provenance: Acquired by a Henry Stoy Rigden of Chicago, IL, on 22 December 1918 in Italy according to a typewritten note pasted to flyleaf I; donated to the university by Rigden in June 1922; see also Henry Stoy Rigden to Library (Donated Books), June 1922, UPWL 12/60, Archives of the University of Notre Dame.

Former Shelfmark: 162558, Z6605 L349 M681 (Treasure Room, Notre Dame); MS 58 (Notre Dame).

Bibliography: Corbett no. 58; D'Alverny 1981, 108; Colker 1983; T. Richardson 1984; Iter 5:361–362; Kaster 1992, ix, 4–5 n. 8; Vacher 1993, lxxviii–lxxx; Kaster 1995, lx; Müller 1995, x, xlvii; H. Anderson 2009, 1:267–268; Vannini 2010, 42–43, 64; Stoppacci 2012, 136.

cod. Lat. b. 11

Origin: France, s. xiii.
Content Overview: Philip the Chancellor, sermons with index.

In Latin, on parchment; 65 ff.; generally 205 x 145 mm (page) [see Layout for ruling]; disbound, but gathered.

Collation: $1–7^{8} + 8^{8-4} + 9^{1+1+1+1+1}$

Quires: Parchment quaternions, H/H, are the normal quire forms; quire 8 lacks the inner bifolium and last two leaves; quire 9 is comprised of five singletons with stubs, F/H. Gregory's Rule is observed for all quires except quire 9. The manuscript has been trimmed; dimensions of the page vary; some prickings and marginal annotations are lost.

Quire Marks: Quire marks appear in the lower left margin for quires 1–4 and 7; that of quire 5 has been completely trimmed away.

Catchwords: Horizontal corresponding catchwords are visible in the lower right margin for quires 1 and 3.

Foliation: Medieval foliation in Roman numerals centered in the upper margin in black and brownish ink; foliated with Arabic numerals in modern pencil in the lower right margin.

Layout:

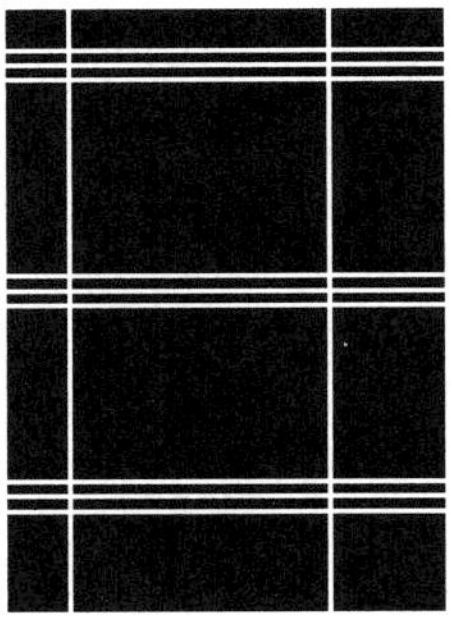

A1

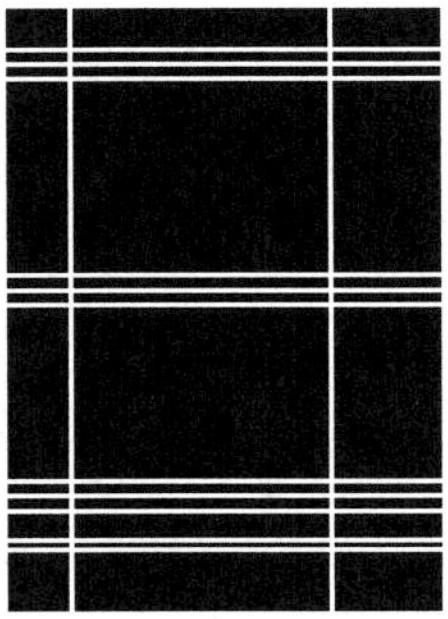

A2

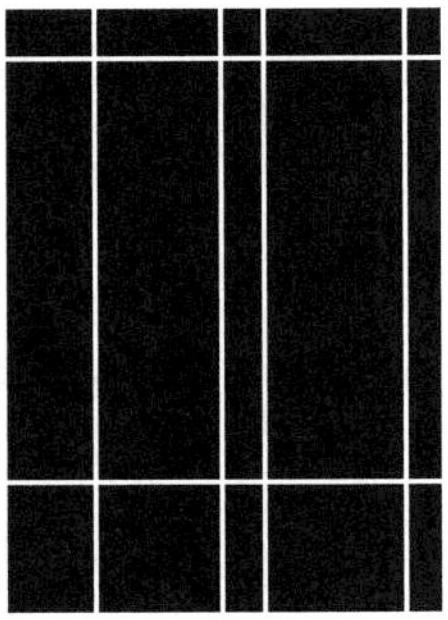

B

A ff. 1r–60v. Lead; 160 x 98 mm; 33 lines.
B ff. 61r–65v. Crayon; 144 x 107 mm; intercol. 14 mm; 34 lines.

Pattern **A** is traced in lead on ff. 1r–60v; single column; writing below top line. **A1** is used consistently with three sets of three horizontal through lines at the top, middle, and bottom extending beyond the vertical bounding lines; prickings visible in upper and lower margins for verticals, in the outer margin for horizontals; double pricking for first of the bottom horizontals. The variant pattern, **A2**, adds superfluous double through lines in the lower margin variously throughout the manuscript (e.g., ff. 9r–10v, 16r–v, 17v–18r, etc.). Pattern **B** is traced in brown crayon on ff. 61r–65v for the index; two columns (intercol. 14 mm); writing below top line. Combined technique for ruling is possible (hard-point traced in crayon); prickings are visible in the upper margin for verticals.

Script: A single hand (M1) writes a Northern Textualis of the thirteenth century in black and brown ink; heavily abbreviated.

Decoration:
I. Rubrication: Lemmata underlined occasionally in red or black ink; paraph marks in black and brown ink.
II. Initials: A single littera duplex initial occurs.
a. One littera duplex initial (9 line hanging) without flourishing begins the sermons on f. 1r.

Contents:

1. Philip the Chancellor, sermons—ff. 1r–60v.

inc.: [f. 1r] iocundum psalterium et cithara et cetera [Ps 56.9] prouerbia .xi. bene consurgit diluculo qui inquirit bona [Prv 11.27] que sunt hec bona intelligere quid sit . . . [Schneyer 4:848, no. 392]; expl.: [f. 60v] . . . ingressus ecclesie quia non intrant nisi [Schneyer 4:854, no. 496].

Ninety-two sermons; alphabetical index to the work occupies ff. 61r–65v. Most lemmata are underlined in red or black, but several are not underlined. Sermons listed below in order of occurrence in the manuscript; this list also corrects the errors found in Corbett [1978], 66–74.

Edition: Paris 1523.
Bibliography: Schneyer 4:848–868.

1. f. 1r–v. inc.: iocundum psalterium et cithara et cetera [Ps 56.9] prouerbia .xi. bene consurgit diluculo qui inquirit bona [Prv 11.27] que sunt hec bona intelligere quid sit . . .; expl.: . . . nominari uel a digniori nominatur [Schneyer 4:848, no. 392].

2. ff. 1v–2r. INC.: <b>eatus uir et cetera [Ps 1.1] iohannis in fine hec scripta sunt ut credatis et credentes . . .; EXPL.: . . . sic confirma precedentia per auctores.
3. f. 2r–v. INC.: et erit tamquam lignum et cetera [Ps 1.3] hoc lignum quod sic plantatur potest dici uir spiritualis . . .; EXPL.: . . . maledixit in qua fructum non inuenit .luc. iij. [Schneyer 4:848, no. 393].
4. ff. 2v–3v. INC.: nouit dominus uiam iustorum et cetera [Ps 1.6] uia hec uia est uiri iusti . . .; EXPL.: . . . lassati sumus in uia perditionis et iniquitatis [Schneyer 4:848, no. 394].
5. f. 3v. INC.: quare fremuerunt gentes et cetera [Ps 2.1] quattuor hic increpantur a propheta que nos infestant . . .; EXPL.: . . . destruimus in redemptorem delinquimus [Schneyer 4:848, no. 395].
6. ff. 3v–4v. INC.: disrumpamus uincula eorum et cetera [Ps 2.3] uideamus primo que sint uincula . . .; EXPL.: . . . proiecto uestimento exiliens uenit ad eum [Schneyer 4:848, no. 396].
7. ff. 4v–5v. INC.: apprehendite disciplinam et cetera [Ps 2.12] flagellum domini quia disciplina aduersitas siue infirmitas . . .; EXPL.: . . . pena eterna in temporalem conmutatur [Schneyer 4:848, no. 398].
8. ff. 5v–6r. INC.: seruite domino in timore et cetera [Ps 2.11] timor domini bonus est seruus . . .; EXPL.: . . . nisi te tenueris in timore domini cito corruet domus tua [Schneyer 4:848, no. 397].
9. f. 6r–v. INC.: ego dormiui et soporatus sum et cetera [Ps 3.6] nota quod duplex est sompnus culpe et gratie . . .; EXPL.: . . . exurgit per mentis excessum suscipitur per raptum [Schneyer 4:848, no. 399].
10. ff. 6v–7v. INC.: <f>ilii hominum usquequo graui corde et cetera [Ps 4.3] duplex est grauitas bona et mala . . .; EXPL.: . . . in infernum locum habebunt inferiorem [Schneyer 4:848, no. 400].
11. ff. 7v–8r. INC.: mane astabo tibi et cetera [Ps 5.5] notandum quod hic bis ponatur mane . . .; EXPL.: . . . per bonum exemplum illuminare [Schneyer 4:848, no. 402].
12. f. 8r–v. INC.: sepulcrum patens est guttur eorum [Ps 5.11] est sepulcrum clausum occultus peccator et simulator . . .; EXPL.: . . . beati quorum remisse iniquitates et cetera [Ps 31.1] [Schneyer 4:848, no. 403].
13. ff. 8v–9r. INC.: domine ne in furore tuo arguas et cetera [Ps 6.2] quattuor hic notantur furor ira argutio correctio . . .; EXPL.: . . . hoc nota contra sodomitas [Schneyer 4:849, no. 404].
14. ff. 9r–10r. INC.: laboraui in gemitu meo et cetera [Ps 6.7] loquitur de penitente ad modum parturientis . . .; EXPL.: . . . cur exceptus genibus cur lactatus uberibus [Schneyer 4:849, no. 405].
15. f. 10r–v. INC.: si reddidi retribuentibus mihi mala et cetera [Ps 7.5] tria sunt que nos obligant beneficia . . .; EXPL.: . . . per impatientiam factus sim sterilis et inanis [Schneyer 4:849, no. 406].

16. ff. 10v–11r. INC.: exurge domine in precepto quod mandasti et cetera [Ps 7.7] licet iste uersus in glosa exponatur de precepto humilitatis . . .; EXPL.: . . . de quibus magis curant quam de spiritualibus et ideo uolare non possunt [SCHNEYER 4:849, no. 407].
17. f. 11r–v. INC.: conuertetur dolor eius in caput eius . . . [Ps 7.17] potest istud conuenienter legi de cupido et auaro . . .; EXPL.: . . . per uerticem signatur ad caritatem amplius inflammatur [SCHNEYER 4:849, no. 408].
18. ff. 11v–12r. INC.: quoniam uidebo celos tuos et cetera [Ps 8.4] astrologorum est contemplari celum et lunam et stellas . . .; EXPL.: . . . hii sunt qui a se uerum gaudium peccando excluserunt [SCHNEYER 4:849, no. 409].
19. ff. 12r–13r. INC.: quid est homo quod memor es eius [Ps 8.5] quantum deus fecerit hominem preciosum manifestum est . . .; EXPL.: . . . contumeliam fraudem circa depositum natale passio [SCHNEYER 4:849, no. 410].
20. f. 13r–v. INC.: quoniam fecisti iudicium meum et causam meam et cetera [Ps 9.5] plerumque contingit quod aliquis in causa sit iusta . . .; EXPL.: . . . iudicant et uincam contra diabolum [SCHNEYER 4:849, no. 411].
21. f. 14r–v. INC.: annuntiate inter gentes studia eius [Ps 9.12] tria domini studia possumus mirari . . .; EXPL.: . . . constitui custos et cetera [SCHNEYER 4:849, no. 412].
22. ff. 14v–15r. INC.: cuius maledictione os plenum est et amaritudine et dolo et cetera [Ps 9.28] hic notantur tria uicia lingue primum quod est maledica . . .; EXPL.: . . . hic est a detractore ex adulatore [SCHNEYER 4:849, no. 413].
23. f. 15r–v. INC.: tibi derelictus est pauper orphano tu eris adiutor . . [Ps 9.35] pauper dicitur dupliciter pauper spiritu . . .; EXPL.: . . . et uarietatem uirtutum de perseuerantia [SCHNEYER 4:849, no. 414].
24. ff. 15v–16v. INC.: in domino confido quomodo dicitis anime mee transmigra in montes sicut passer [Ps 10.2] duo conmendabilia in uiro sancto confidentia in deo . . .; EXPL.: . . . cadent omnes qui descendunt in terram [Ps 21.30] [SCHNEYER 4:849, no. 416].
25. ff. 16v–17v. INC.: dominus in templo sancto suo et cetera [Ps 10.5] anima templo comparatur quia que solent fieri . . .; EXPL.: . . . incenderunt igni sanctuarium tuum [Ps 73.7] [SCHNEYER 4:849, no. 417].
26. ff. 17v–18r. INC.: illumina oculos meos et cetera [Ps 12.4] per hoc innuit dauid se habere oculos . . .; EXPL.: . . . uero sampson et sedechie de quibus supradictum est [SCHNEYER 4:849, no. 419].
27. f. 18r. INC.: eloquia domini eloquia casta argentum igne examinatum [Ps 11.7] castitas proprie est uirtus coniugatorum . . .; EXPL.: . . . unde prouerbia .xix. doctrina uiri per patenciam noscitur [Prv 19.11] [SCHNEYER 4:849, no. 418].
28. ff. 18r–19r. INC.: domine quis habitabit in tabernacula tuo aut quis requiescet in monte sancto tuo [Ps 14.1] per montem intelligimus templum quod factum fuit in monte . . .; EXPL.: . . . ne malitia peruerteret sensum illius et cetera [Sap 4.11] [SCHNEYER 4:850, no. 421].

29. f. 19r–v. inc.: domine pars hereditatis mee et cetera [Ps 15.5] duplex est hereditas spiritualium et mundanorum . . .; expl.: . . . in carcere fui et cetera [Mt 25.36] [Schneyer 4:850, no. 422].
30. ff. 19v–21r. inc.: igne me examinasti et cetera [Ps 16.3] quedam in igne consumuntur ut palee et stupa et stipula . . .; expl.: . . . ut in luca .xv. de filio prodigo [Schneyer 4:850, no. 423].
31. f. 21r–v. inc.: preocupauerunt me laquei mortis [Ps 17.6] laqueus mortis dicitur quicquid nos trahit aut ligat . . .; expl.: . . . ante uero poterat que sunt septem dona spiritus sancti [Schneyer 4:850, no. 425].
32. ff. 21v–22r. inc.: ascendit fumus in ira eius et cetera [Ps 17.9] dupliciter est fumus in uiro iusto . . .; expl.: . . . qui per solitudinem contemplationis ad eternorum surgit speculationem [Schneyer 4:850, no. 426].
33. ff. 22r–23r. inc.: eduxit me in latitudinem et cetera [Ps 17.20] nouus homo et uetus homo spiritus . . .; expl.: . . . extirpatis igitur uitiis sentiens se spiritus dilatari dicit eduxit me in latitudinem et cetera [Ps 17.20] [Schneyer 4:850, no. 427].
34. f. 23r–v. inc.: quoniam in te eripiar a temptatione et in deo meo transgrediar murum [Ps 17.30] per murum intelligitur congeries peccatorum . . .; expl.: . . . inmittit totum consumit [Schneyer 4:850, no. 428].
35. ff. 23v–24r. inc.: et precinxisti me uirtute ad bellum [Ps 17.40] solet ita distingui succingimur ituri . . .; expl.: . . . et eligite lapides et eleuate signum ad populos [Is 62.10] [Schneyer 4:850, no. 429].
36. f. 24r–v. inc.: filii alieni mentiti sunt . . . [Ps 17.46] hic reprobat tria genera filiorum quod mendaces sunt . . .; expl.: . . . mitti in gehennam ignis [Mt 18.9] [Schneyer 4:850, no. 430].
37. ff. 24v–25r. inc.: lex domini immacula conuertens animas [Ps 18.8] lex ista dupliciter est ita est serui ista non est immaculata . . .; expl.: . . . sed ubi non sperant deprehenduntur in miseriis scilicet augustiis infirmitatibus [cf. Schneyer 4:850, no. 431].
38. f. 25r–v. inc.: memor sit omnis sacrificii tui et cetera [Ps 19.4] dominus christus obtulit se sacrifitium in sartagine . . .; expl.: . . . uocauit aduersum me tempus. in natali [Schneyer 4:850, no. 433].
39. ff. 25v–26r. inc.: domine p<re>uenisti eum in benedictionibus dulcedinis et cetera [Ps 20.4] hic primo attendum est unde principium maledictionis . . .; expl.: . . . benedictio illius quasi fluuius inundabit [Sir 39.27] [Schneyer 4:850, no. 434].
40. f. 26r–v. inc.: quoniam pones eos dorsum [Ps 20.13] dominus ponit aliquos dorsum diuersis modis quantum ad semet ipsos . . .; expl.: . . . quasi dicat qui domino terga uertunt sit deus fatiet eis [Schneyer 4:850, no. 435].
41. ff. 26v–27r. inc.: ego sum uermis et non homo [Ps 21.7] tria sunt genera uermium quibus deus se ipsum comparat . . .; expl.: . . . nescio utrum dicatur bomber uel bombex uermis ille [Schneyer 4:851, no. 436].

42. f. 27r–v. INC.: edent pauperes et saturabuntur et cetera [Ps 21.27] quatuor consideranda sunt circa mensam domini . . .; EXPL.: . . . qui statuam suam ab aliis adorari uolebat [SCHNEYER 4:851, no. 438].
43. ff. 27v–28r. INC.: parasti in conspectu meo mensam et cetera [Ps 22.5] mensa est uita eterna circa quam tria sunt consideranda . . .; EXPL.: . . . unde quod oculus non uidit et cetera [Is 64.4] [SCHNEYER 4:851, no. 441].
44. f. 28r–v. INC.: hec est generatio querentium . . . [Ps 23.6] quatuor sunt attendenda circa generationem querentium . . .; EXPL.: . . . et iohannis .xi. eamus in iudeam iterum [Io 11.7] [SCHNEYER 4:851, no. 442].
45. f. 28v. INC.: tollite portas principes uestras [Ps 23.7] hoc quidam intelligunt de portis concupiscentie que a nobis tollende sunt . . .; EXPL.: . . . defixe sunt in terra porte eius id est sensus ad terrena [cf. SCHNEYER 4:851, no. 443].
46. ff. 28v–29v. INC.: firmamentum est deus omnibus timentibus eum [Ps 24.14] timor domini securitatem prestat et mentis iocunditatem . . .; EXPL.: . . . quia qui timet dominum nihil negligit [SCHNEYER 4:851, no. 445].
47. f. 29v. INC.: odiui ecclesiam malignantium et cetera [Ps 25.5] ecclesia ista fundamentum habet malum . . .; EXPL.: . . . quando enim uolunt dicunt esse consuetudinem contra quos iacobi decimo ue qui dicunt leges iniquas et cetera [Is 10.1] [SCHNEYER 4:851, no. 446].
48. f. 30r–v. INC.: hec dominus illuminatio mea et salus mea quem timebo [Ps 26.1] dominus illuminat cecum sanat infirmum protegit . . .; EXPL.: . . . luca decimo domine non est tibi cure et cetera [Lc 10.40] [SCHNEYER 4:851, no. 447].
49. ff. 30v–31r. INC.: unam petii a domino et cetera [Ps 26.4] unam id est beatitudinem eternam . . .; EXPL.: . . . unam petii et luca .x. porro unum est necessarium [Lc 10.42] [SCHNEYER 4:851, no. 448].
50. f. 31r–v. INC.: ad te domine clamabo et cetera [Ps 27.1] legitur in exodo .xxv. faties propitatorium auro mundissimo . . . [Ex 25.17]; EXPL.: . . . sed per se redire non potest [SCHNEYER 4:851, no. 450].
51. f. 31v. INC.: uox domini concutientis desertum et cetera [Ps 28.8] desertum est malum desideria carnalia et sceleraria . . .; EXPL.: . . . hoc est irriguum superius et inferius ut habetur iudic. duo [SCHNEYER 4:852, no. 452].
52. ff. 31v–32r. INC.: uox domini preparantis ceruos [Ps 28.9] ceruus est animal uelox pauidum . . .; EXPL.: . . . ceruus emissus dans eloquia pulcritudinis [Gn 49.21] id est intelligentie purioris [SCHNEYER 4:852, no. 453].
53. f. 32r. INC.: exaltabo te domine quem suscepisti me [Ps 29.2] tria sunt que nos reuocare dicunt a peccato . . .; EXPL.: . . . luca .xv. gaudium est in celo et cetera [Lc 15.7] [SCHNEYER 4:852, no. 454].
54. f. 32r–v. INC.: ego dixi in habundantia mea non mouebor et cetera . . . [Ps 29.7] duo sunt que maxime subministrant occasiones ad peccandum . . .; EXPL.: . . . nisi ab alio et miserum est aliene incumbere fame [SCHNEYER 4:852, no. 455].

55. ff. 32v–33r. INC.: in manus tuas conmendo spiritum meum et cetera [Ps 30.6] dicitur sapientie .iij. iustorum anime in manu domini sunt et cetera . . . [Sap 3.1]; EXPL.: . . . dicitur iob .xl. sub umbra dormit in secreto calami in locis humentibus [Iob 40.16] [SCHNEYER 4:852, no. 456].
56. f. 33r–v. INC.: odisti omnes obseruantes uanitates et cetera [Ps 30.7] uanitas dicuntur omnia temporalia et mutabilia . . .; EXPL.: . . . timeant ergo diuites [SCHNEYER 4:852, no. 457].
57. ff. 33v–34r. INC.: qui uiderunt me foras fugerunt a me et cetera [Ps 30.12] tria sunt que maxime interiori aspectione intuenda sunt . . .; EXPL.: . . . dicitur in naum tertio omnis qui uiderit te resiliet a te [Na 3.7] [SCHNEYER 4:852, no. 458].
58. f. 34r–v. INC.: quam magna multitudo dulcedinis tue domine quam abscondisti timentibus te [Ps 30.20] dulcedo ista duplex est gratie et glorie . . .; EXPL.: . . . parasti in dulcedine tua pauperi deus [Ps 67.11] [SCHNEYER 4:852, no. 459].
59. ff. 34v–35r. INC.: retribuet dominus habundanter facientibus superbiam [Ps 30.24] superbia singularis est in culpa . . .; EXPL.: . . . unde osee quinto respondebit israel arrogantia sua [Os 5.5] [SCHNEYER 4:852, no. 460].
60. f. 35r–v. INC.: dixi confitebor et cetera [Ps 31.5] differentia est inter forum ciuile et penitentiale . . .; EXPL.: . . . qui nudat archana amici fidem perdit [Sir 27.17] [SCHNEYER 4:852, no. 461].
61. ff. 35v–36r. INC.: nolite fieri sicut equus et multus et cetera [Ps 31.9] est equus fortitudinis de quo iob . . .; EXPL.: . . . id est ad insolitum opus et nefandum abusum [SCHNEYER 4:852, no. 462].
62. f. 36r. INC.: congregans sicut in utre aquas maris [Ps 32.7] aque maris sunt tribulationes quas dominus in hoc mundo . . .; EXPL.: . . . et conuentus uirtutum confessionem comitatur [SCHNEYER 4:852, no. 463].
63. ff. 36r–37r. INC.: beata gens cuius est dominus deus eius [Ps 32.12] et alibi beatus populus cuius est dominus deus eius [Ps 143.15] hic populus triplex est seculares ut laici . . .; EXPL.: . . . claustrales ergo quando peccant ortum domini excirpant [SCHNEYER 4:852, no. 464].
64. f. 37r. INC.: custodit dominus omnia ossa eorum [Ps 33.21] habet homo interior sicut exterior pellem carnem neruos et ossa . . .; EXPL.: . . . plaga autem lingue conminuit ossa [Sir 28.21] [SCHNEYER 4:852, no. 467].
65. ff. 37r–38r. INC.: in domino laudabitur anima mea et cetera [Ps 33.3] ad contemptum laudis humane consideranda sunt aut enim laudatur de bonis . . .; EXPL.: . . . pulcrum est monstrari digito dicior hic est [SCHNEYER 4:852, no. 465].
66. f. 38r–v. INC.: gustate et uidete quem suauis est dominus et cetera [Ps 33.9] est cibus cibo melior spiritualis scilicet quam carnalis . . .; EXPL.: . . . unde psalmus saciabor cum apparuerit gloria tua [Ps 16.15] [SCHNEYER 4:852, no. 466].
67. ff. 38v–39v. INC.: fiant tamquam puluis ante faciem uenti et cetera [Ps 34.5] quatuor hic notantur hic circa malos . . .; EXPL.: . . . lubricauerunt uestigia mea et cetera [Lam 4.18] [SCHNEYER 4:853, no. 468].

68. ff. 39v–40r. INC.: ego autem cum mihi molesti essent induebar cilicio humiliabam in ieiunio animam et oratio mea in sinu meo conuertetur [Ps 34.13] in hoc instruimur quid facere debeamus cum temptationibus quasi quibusdam hostibus molestamur . . .; EXPL.: . . . ut sic aptius uolet ideoque ieiunium et eleemosyna orationi sociantur [SCHNEYER 4:853, no. 469].
69. ff. 40r–41r. INC.: apud te est fons uite et cetera [Ps 35.10] scriptum est uersa haurietis aquas in gaudio . . .; EXPL.: . . . fulgor pertinet ad intellectum [SCHNEYER 4:853, no. 470].
70. ff. 41r–42r. INC.: custodi innocentiam et uide equitatem et cetera [Ps 36.37] duplex est mensa consolationis . . .; EXPL.: . . . reliquie homini pacifico [SCHNEYER 4:853, no. 473].
71. ff. 42r–43v. INC.: quoniam iniquitates mee supergresse sunt capud meum [Ps 37.5] supergresse dicit quasi aquarum inundationes . . .; EXPL.: . . . stigmata domini et cetera [Gal 6.17] [SCHNEYER 4:853, no. 474].
72. ff. 43v–44v. INC.: quod mutuabitur peccator et non soluet et cetera [Ps 36.21] duo sunt creditores a quibus peccator mutuatur . . .; EXPL.: . . . ingratus sensu delinquit liberantem se [Sir 29.22] [SCHNEYER 4:853, no. 472].
73. f. 45r–v. INC.: cor meum conturbatum est dereliquit me uirtus mea et lumen oculorum meorum et cetera [Ps 37.11] tria genera temptationis denotat . . .; EXPL.: . . . hoc est quod dicit dereliquit me uirtus mea et lumen oculorum meorum et ipsum non est mecum [Ps 37.11] [SCHNEYER 4:853, no. 475].
74. ff. 45v–46r. INC.: dixi custodiam uias meas et cetera [Ps 38.2] omni custodia custodi cor tuum . . .; EXPL.: . . . et claude hostia tua super uias tuas id est sensus [SCHNEYER 4:853, no. 476].
75. ff. 46r–47r. INC.: thesaurizat et ignorat cui congregabit ea et cetera [Ps 38.7] considandum [*sic*] de quibus faciendus est thesaurus . . .; EXPL.: . . . quam speciosa est ueteranis sapientia [Sir 25.7] [SCHNEYER 4:853, no. 477].
76. f. 47r–v. INC.: inmisit in os meum canticum nouum et cetera [Ps 39.4] quatuor hic consideranda sunt quid sit canticum nouum . . .; EXPL.: . . . de ierusalem percusso philisteo [SCHNEYER 4:853, no. 478].
77. ff. 47v–48r. INC.: ego autem mendicus sum et pauper dominus sollicitus est mei [Ps 39.18] multe cause sunt pro quibus necesse habemus . . .; EXPL.: . . . nolite timere pusillus grex [Lc 12.32] [SCHNEYER 4:853, no. 479].
78. ff. 48r–49v. INC.: homo pacis mee in quo speraui et cetera [Ps 40.10] uidetur dominus conqueri de quocumque penitente . . .; EXPL.: . . . manus tradentis me mecum est in mensa [Lc 22.21] [SCHNEYER 4:853, no. 480].
79. ff. 49v–50r. INC.: fuerunt mihi lacrime mee panes et cetera [Ps 41.4] ad hoc quod animis laute et splendide . . .; EXPL.: . . . in uoce exultationis et confessionis sonus epulantis [Ps 41.5] [SCHNEYER 481].
80. f. 50r–v. INC.: effudi in me animam meam et cetera [Ps 41.5] quidam effunduntur in malum extra se per luxuriam . . .; EXPL.: . . . de uase contumelie in uas honoris et glorie [SCHNEYER 4:853, no. 482].

81. ff. 50v–51v. INC.: introibo ad altare domini et cetera [Ps 42.4] considerandum est qui [*sic*] significantur per altare . . .; EXPL.: . . . ergo ad hec spiritualia semper iuuenes sumus [SCHNEYER 4:853, no. 483].
82. ff. 51v–53r. INC.: quoniam propter te mortificamur tota die et cetera [Ps 43.22] dupliciter est mortificatio hominis propter diabolum . . .; EXPL.: . . . et tales mortue anime suscitationem non impetrant [SCHNEYER 4:854, no. 485].
83. ff. 53r–54r. INC.: lingua mea calamus scribe uelociter scribentis et cetera [Ps 44.2] dominus habet scribas suos et calamum . . .; EXPL.: . . . omnes isti sunt scribe et notarii et de cancellaria diaboli [SCHNEYER 4:854, no. 486].
84. ff. 54r–55r. INC.: sedes tua deus in seculum seculi et cetera [Ps 44.7] primo considerandum que sit diuersitas sedium . . .; EXPL.: . . . non enim bene sedem suam regebat [SCHNEYER 4:854, no. 487].
85. f. 55r–v. INC.: astetit regina a dextris tuis et cetera [Ps 44.10] regina uirtutum est caritas regina . . .; EXPL.: . . . et sic nota aliis uirtutibus [SCHNEYER 4:854, no. 488].
86. ff. 55v–56v. INC.: omnis gloria eius filie regis ab intus et cetera [Ps 44.14] primo ostenditur quod non est glorificandum de exterioribus . . .; EXPL.: . . . magnificant fimbrias suas et dilatant philacteria sua [Mt 23.5] [SCHNEYER 4:854, no. 489].
87. ff. 56v–57v. INC.: elegit nobis hereditatem suam speciem iacob quam dilexit [Ps 46.5] ad speciem iacob pertinet prudentia spiritualis negociationis . . .; EXPL.: . . . fortiter aget id est religio que semper prosperatur [SCHNEYER 4:854, no. 491].
88. ff. 57v–58r. INC.: ibi dolores ut parturientis et cetera [Ps 47.7] ibi id est in penitente primo uidendum est qualis dolor sit in penitente . . .; EXPL.: . . . et occasiones aliorum bursas emungunt [SCHNEYER 4:854, no. 492].
89. f. 58r–v. INC.: ponite corda uestra in uirtute eius et cetera [Ps 47.14] ponendum est cor nostrum in uirtute domini per conatum . . .; EXPL.: . . . palliant sue uite enormitatem [SCHNEYER 4:854, no. 493].
90. ff. 58v–59v. INC.: tabernacula eorum in proienie [*sic*] et proienie [*sic*] uocauerunt nomina sua in terris suis [Ps 48.12] mundus uult suos nominari in mundo . . .; EXPL.: . . . cum eo gloria do. eius [Ps 48.18] [SCHNEYER 4:854, no. 494].
91. ff. 59v–60r. INC.: diues cum interierit non sumet omnia et cetera [Ps 48.18] carnalis et mundanus duplici morte moritur . . .; EXPL.: . . . ita sepe contingit de diuitiis clericorum [SCHNEYER 4:854, no. 495].
92. f. 60r–v [incomplete]. INC.: congregate illi sanctos eius qui ordinat testamentum eius super sacrificia [Ps 49.5] dominus christus suum fecit testamentum . . .; EXPL.: . . . quia non intrant nisi [SCHNEYER 4:854, no. 496].

BINDING: The manuscript is disbound.

OWNERS & PROVENANCE: G. F. Laruelle; acquired from B. Rosenthal (New York, NY) by the university in May 1961.

Sales & Catalogues: Delvaux-Liege, *Livres de la bibliotheque de feu G.F. Laruelle*, no. 47MSVF; B. Rosenthal, Cat. 12, no. 36.

Former Shelfmark: MS 9 (Notre Dame).

Bibliography: Corbett no. 9; D'Alverny 1981, 106.

cod. Lat. b. 12

Origin: Bohemia, s. xv^2.
Content Overview: Florilegium; *Miracula et indulgentiae urbis Romae*

In Latin, on paper; i +8 ff. +i; generally 196 x 140 mm (page) [see Layout for ruling]; foliated in modern pencil with Arabic numerals; modern paper flyleaves.

Collation: i +1^8 +i

Bibliographical Format: 4°.

Quires: A paper quaternion folded in quarto is used. No quire mark, catchword, or signature is visible; the manuscript has been trimmed.

Watermarks: A single watermark occurs: (A) Mill wheel with crank; cf. Piccard 122906 (1463).

Layout:

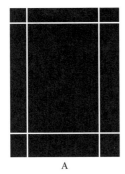

A

A ff. 1r–8v. Ink; 151 x 92 mm; 33 lines.

Pattern A is traced in brownish ink; single column; writing below top line. The vertical bounding lines and horizontals are often slanted, creating an asymmetrical text frame.

Script: A single hand (M1) writes the text in black ink and rubrics in red ink. M1 writes Cursiva Libraria of the fifteenth century.

Decoration: Rubrics in red ink; reserved space for an initial (2 line square inset) on f. 1r; no guide letter.

Contents:

1. Florilegium—ff. 1r–2r.

Extracts of Bernard of Clairvaux, Augustine, Ps.-Chrysostom, Gregory the Great, Caesarius of Arles, etc.; the compiler may be drawing on Thomas of Ireland's *Manipulus florum* for some of the quotations.

1.1. Bernard of Clairvaux, *De contemptu mundi*—f. 1r. rub.: sequitur breuiloquium bernhardi de contemptu mundi et de terrore inferni et amore dei; inc.: <si> quis aures habeat audiendi audiat excors in se reddeat . . .; expl.: . . . rex celi dator gratie uirtutum doctor optime et uite fons uberrime et cetera [*AH* 33: no. 245].

1.2. Various extracts—f. 1r–v.

1.2.1. f. 1r. rub.: nota; inc.: et beatissimus augustinus dicit uincula inquit mundi asperitatem habent ueram iocunditatem falsam . . .; expl.: . . . pax est in cella sunt foris non nisi bella [Walther, *Proverbia* 21035].

1.2.2. f. 1r–v. rub.: nota; inc.: uerum dicit idem doctor augustinus in effectu sic numquam uidi meliores quam qui in religione profecerunt . . .; expl.: . . . benedictus deus qui recepit et perfecit.

Quotations mainly from the corpus of Augustine; rubrics identify the two continuous blocks of text as *notae*. Cf. Manipulus florum, Mundus e (2); Augustine, *Ep.* 26.2.1–5; Augustine in *Io. Ev. Tract.* 38 (*PL* 35.1677); Manipulus florum, Religio e; and Augustine, *Ep.* 78.9.15–17, among others.

1.3. Bernard of Clairvaux, *dictum*—f. 1v. rub.: auctoritas sancti bernhardi; inc.: quoniam ut ait sanctus bernhardus non est nisi turpis amor in hoc seculo . . .; expl.: . . . et a potentibus huius seculi quasi peregrinus ignoratur.

1.4. Gregory the Great, *dictum*—ff. 1v–2r. rub.: auctoritas sancti gregorii; inc.: sunt quidam qui de omni re male iudicant homines . . .; expl.: . . . boni faciunt totum mali uertunt in uenenum.

1.5. Ps.-Chrysostom, *dictum*—f. 2r. rub.: auctoritas sancti iohannis crisostomi; inc.: arbor iuxta uiam posita sit . . .; expl.: . . . tecum habeat neque tu cum eo et cetera.

Excerpt of Ps.-Chrysostom, *Opus imperfectum in Matthaeum;* cf. *PG* 56.845–846.

1.6. Bernard of Clairvaux, *Sermo in Ressurectione*, 1.3—f. 2r. RUB.: de cruce christi bernhardus dicit; INC.: cristus in cruce pacientiam exhibet humilitatem commendat obedienciam implet tacitatem . . .; EXPL.: . . . radix omnium uirtutum humilitas in profundo.

Cf. *Manipulus florum*, Crux i.

Edition: *SBO* 5:76.

1.7. Bernard of Clairvaux, *Sermo in natali Sancti Andreae*, 1.5—f. 2r. RUB.: idem; INC.: qui iniciatur a timore christi crucem sustinet pacienter . . .; EXPL.: . . . qui consumitur in caritate amplectitur eam ardenter [*PL* 183.506].

Edition: *SBO* 5:430.

1.8. Caesarius of Arles, sermon 41.2—f. 2r. RUB.: gregorius; INC.: de castitate inter cuncta christianorum certamina maiora sunt castitatis prelia ubi frequens est pungna [*sic*] et rara uictoria.

Cf. *Manipulus florum*, Castitas et continencia i; Auct. Incert. (Ps.-Aug.?) *Serm.* 293.2 (*PL* 39.2302); here attributed to Gregory the Great.

1.9. Bernard of Clairvaux, *Epistola* 42.9—f. 2r. RUB.: bernhardus; INC.: castitas sine caritate lampas est sine oleo subtrahe oleum lampas non lucet tolle caritatem castitas non placet.

Manipulus florum, Castitas et continencia n.

Edition: *SBO* 7:108.

2. Ps.-Bernard of Clairvaux—ff. 2v–3r.

RUB.: incipit erudicio beati augustini de facto hominis quomodo quelibet potest temporalia et eterna pericula euitare et gaudia celestia eternaliter possidere et cum sanctis omnibus feliciter permanere; INC.: [f. 2v] si uis perfectus esse hec regulariter teneas semper habeas pre oculis tuis . . .; EXPL.: [f. 3r] . . . et reseruata opere facito et omnia tibi uenient cum habundancia et cetera [Bloomfield no. 5677].

In addition to the manuscripts listed in Bloomfield, the text is also found in Praha, Knihovna Národního muzea v Praze, XV. D.7, f. 1r[a], and Olomouc, Vědecká knihovna v Olomouci, M. I.349, f. 52r; cf. Praha, Národní knihovna Česke republiky, V. F.22, f. 59v.

3. *Miracula et indulgentiae urbis Romae*—ff. 3r–8v.

3.1. *Miracula*—ff. 3r–5v. RUB.: incipiunt miracula urbis romane et primo considera; INC.: quod a creatione mundi usque ad constructionem urbis romane . . .; EXPL.: . . . debite et honorifice terminaret uitam eorum in secula seculorum amen.

3.2. List of churches and indulgences—ff. 5v–8v. RUB.: nota indulgencie ecclesiarum in urbe romana; INC.: fuerunt enim mille quingente quinque ecclesie . . .; EXPL.: . . . et omnibus aliis peccatis ueraciter est absolutus. expliciunt indulgencie.

Rubrics subdivide the text into different architectural and topographical features, such as gates, hills, bridges, palaces, columns, etc.; some sections lack rubrics, but have space reserved. A list of churches in Rome follows the *Miracula urbis Romane* with notes on indulgences. Tournai, Bibliothèque de la Ville, Cod. 3 A (no. 26), ff. 4r–9v contains the same list of churches and indulgences without the *Miracula*.

Binding: Modern conservation pamphlet; white.

Owners & Provenance: Acquired from H. P. Kraus (New York, NY) by the university in September 1968.

Sales & Catalogues: H. P. Kraus, Cat. 117, no. 38.

Former Shelfmark: MS 56 (Notre Dame).

Bibliography: Corbett no. 56; D'Alverny 1981, 106.

cod. Lat. b. 13

Origin: France, s. xiii^2 (additions s. xiii^2–xv^2).
Content Overview: Missal, neumed (use of Coutances).

In Latin, on parchment; i +261 ff. +i; generally 212 x 149 mm (page) [see Layout for ruling); medieval and modern foliation [see Foliation].

Collation: i +1$^{6-2}$ +2^2 +3$^{12-1}$ +4–12^{12} +13$^{12-1}$ +14–17^{12} +18^{10} +19–20^{12} +21–24^8 +25^4

Quires: Parchment sexternions, F/F, are the predominant quire forms. Quire 1 is a ternion lacking the first and second leaves; ff. 3 and 4 are inserted asymmetrically by their stubs; flyleaf I is attached by its stub to f. 4v. Quire 2 is a bifolium, F/F. Quire 3 is a sexternion, H/F, lacking the first leaf. Quire 13 is a sexternion, F/H, lacking the last leaf. Quire 18 is a quinion, F/F. Quires 21–23 are quaternions, F/F. Quire 25 is a binion, F/F, which does not obey Gregory's Rule; final folio is flyleaf II.

Quire Marks: Roman numerals and Roman numerals as ordinals function as quire marks for quires 3–12 (one through ten); black ink; centered in lower margin.

Catchwords: Horizontal catchwords in black ink are written in the lower right margins for quires 3–12 and 13–20; all correspond.

Signatures: Signatures of the *ad hoc* type written in red ink are visible for quires 4–13 and 17–23; quires also numbered with small Roman numerals in the lower right margin of the first verso; the numerals are visible for most quires and agree with the quire marks. Quire 24 contains signatures in Roman numerals in red ink (i–v), despite currently being a quaternion.

Foliation: Medieval foliation with Roman numerals in black ink of ff. 7r–299r (ii–ccxliiii); foliation is aligned with the vertical bounding line in the upper right margin; folio references are given throughout the manuscript with cue forms. Modern foliation appears in the upper right margin with Arabic numerals in pencil.

Layout:

A

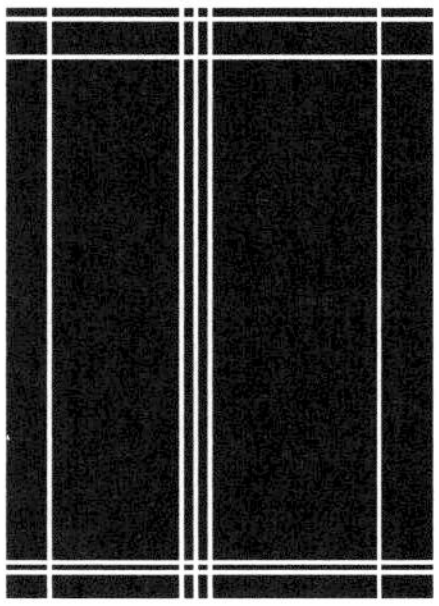

B

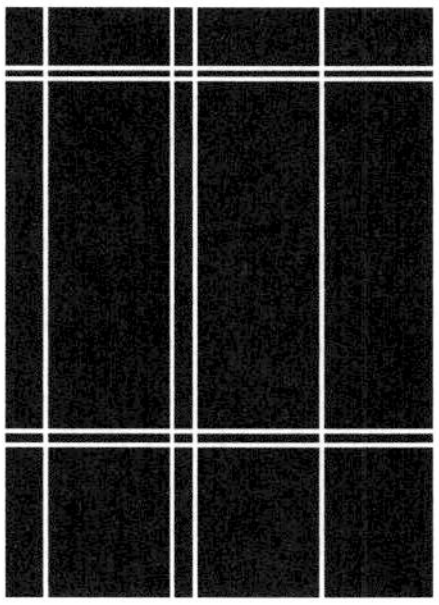

C

D

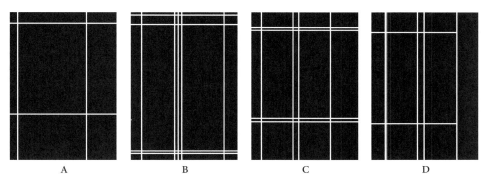

A ff. 1r–4v. Lead; 130 x 96 mm; 34 lines.
B f. 6r–v. Lead; 182 x 117 mm; intercol. 10 mm; 37 lines.
C ff. 7r–250v. Lead; 130 x 96 mm; intercol. 8 mm; 32 lines.
D ff. 251r–258v. Lead; 131 x 100 mm; intercol. 9 mm; 32 lines.

Pattern **A** is traced lightly in lead on ff. 1r–4v; calendric columns are present, but ruling for additional verticals is not visible; writing above and below top line depending on folio; prickings in the upper and lower margin for vertical bounding lines and horizontal through lines. Pattern **B** is traced in lead on f. 6r (variant on f. 6v); two columns (total intercol. 10 mm); writing below top line; prickings visible only in the upper margin for the intercolumnium, though it does not align. Pattern **C** is traced throughout the thirteenth-century portion of the manuscript in lead (ff. 7r–250v); two columns (intercol. 8 mm); writing below top line; prickings visible in the upper and lower margins for vertical bounding lines, intercolumnium, and horizontal through lines. Pattern **D** is traced in lead on ff. 251r–258v; two columns (intercol. 9 mm); writing below top line; prickings visible in upper and lower margins for vertical bounding lines, intercolumnium, and horizontal through lines.

Script: Several hands (s. xiii^{2}–xv^{2}) write and modify the text. The majority of the text is written in Northern Textualis Formata (s. xiii^{2}) in black ink; marginal additions throughout in Textualis, Anglicana, and Cursiva. Substantial additions (s. xiv) are written in Semitextualis Libraria (ff. 251r–256v), though two-compartment **a** has a strong presence along with a deliberate single-compartment form. Substantial additions (s. xiv–xv) by at least three hands are written in Anglicana Libraria (ff. 226v, 259r–260v, 261v); Anglicana letter forms of **e**, **g**, **r**, **s**, are used alongside exclusive use of two-compartment **a** (except f. 261v). Prayers to St. Etheldreda are added in an attempt at Northern Textualis Formata, but with minimal integration of Anglicana forms; Anglicana **s** and **g** appear; loops present on some ascenders; **f** and straight **s** on the line.

Decoration:

I. Rubrication: Rubrics in red ink; added rubrics in black and brownish ink underlined in red or black or brown; letter heightening in red and yellow; paraph marks alternate in red and blue.

II. Initials: Littera duplex, flourished, and plain initials occur in complex hierarchy; cadels used mainly in neumed sections.

a. Littera duplex initials (3–9 square inset; hanging **i**s) mark the major divisions of the manuscript and emphatic feast days.

b. Flourished initials (2 line square inset; hanging **i**s) in red and blue ink with contrasting penwork alternate throughout the manuscript.

c. Plain initials (1 line versals) in red and blue ink alternate within hierarchy.

d. Cadels are written in black ink and heightened in red ink; occur mostly in neumed passages; grotesques rare.

Calendar: Fragmentary liturgical calendar with later additions; one month per page; dominical letter **a** alternates in red ink and blue ink with yellow heightening; Roman time marked in red and black ink with yellow and red heightening.

Music & Staves: Four-line staves in red ink; 5 mm; square neumes in black ink.

Contents:

1. Prayers to Etheldreda—flyleaf Iv.

1.1. rub.: [*ut uid.*] ad consequenciam; inc.: aue gemma pretiosa uirgo desens [*sic*] et formosa etheldreda deo digna pia mater . . .; expl.: . . . beata etheldreda uirgo dei electa intercede pro nobis et cetera.

1.2. inc.: deus qui eximie castitatis priuilegeo [*sic*] sanctissimam uirginem tuam etheldredam multipliciter decorasti . . .; expl.: . . . per eius interuentum nostri memoria apud te semper habeatur in celis per [cf. *CO* 1612].

2. Calendar (incomplete)—ff. 1r–4v.

Liturgical calendar with feast days in red and black ink with various grades (see below); only May through December remains; additions in several hands throughout, including many obituaries of the thirteenth, fourteenth, and fifteenth centuries. The calendar contains many Parisian features, but many Norman and English saints are also present; almost identical to the calendar in København, Kongelige Bibliothek, NKS 36 8°.

Notable feast days include: Marculf (May 1; *semiduplum in crastino*), Brendan (May 16; *semiduplum*), Augustine of Canterbury (May 26; *tres lectiones sine regimine*), Germain (May 28; *tres lectiones sine regimine*), Petroc (Jun. 4; *more octaue)*, Alban (Jun. 22; *nouem lectiones*), Gallican (Jun. 25; *memoria*), translation of Eligius (Jun 25; *memoria*), ordination and translation of Martin (Jul. 4; in red; *nouem lectiones tres medie de apostolis*), translation of Thomas Becket (Jul. 7; *more octaue*), Wandregisil (Jul 22; *memoria*), translation of Crown of Thorns (Aug. 10), Taurin (Aug. 11; *nouem lectiones*), Helena (Aug. 18), Magnus (Aug. 19; *memoria*), Philebert (Aug. 20; *memoria*), Ouen (Aug. 24; *memoria et tres*), Bernard (Aug. 25 *sic*; *nouem lectiones*), Genesius (Aug. 25; in red; *memoria et tres medie lectiones*), Euverte (Sept. 7; *tres lectiones sine regimine*), Floscellus (Sept. 17; *nouem lectiones*), Laudus (Sept. 21; in red; *duplum*), Firmin (Sept. 25; in red; *memoria si dominica fuerit tres medie lectiones*), octave of Laudus (Sept. 28; *nouem lectiones*), relics of Coutances (Sept. 30; in red; *duplum*), Piatus (Sept. 30 *sic*; *memoria*), octave of the Relics (Oct. 7; in red; *nouem lectiones*), Denis (Oct. 9; in red; *nouem lectiones*), Nigasius [*sic*] (Oct. 11; *more octaue*), Michael in Tumba (Oct. 16; *nouem lectiones*), Justus (Oct. 18; *memoria*), Mellon (Oct. 22; in red; *semiduplum*), Romain (Oct. 23; *more octaue*), Magloire (Oct. 24; *more octaue*), Quintin (Oct. 31; *tres lectiones sine regimine*), Malo (Nov. 15; *memoria*), Anian (Nov. 17; *memoria*); Rumpharius (Nov. 18; *semiduplum in crastino oct.*), Sapientia (Dec. 16; in red).

Several later feasts have been added by two hands. Notable additions include: Erasmus (Jun. 3), Etheldreda (Jun. 23), translation of Vigor (Jul. 14; *nouem lectiones*), translation of Clair (Jul. 18; *nouem lectiones*), Arnulf (Jul. 18; *memoria et tres medie lectiones*), Germain (Jul. 31; *nouem lectiones*), Dominic (Aug. 5 *sic*; *more octaue*), translation of Etheldreda (Oct. 17), Vigor (Nov. 1; *semiduplum*), octave of Vigor (Nov. 8; *nouem lectiones*).

Obituaries (s. xiii^2–s. xiv^1) are added throughout the calendar by contemporary hands; surnames known in Lower Normandy during the respective periods: Bartholomeus de Alnetis (May 5, 1286), Nicholaa [*sic*] domina de Brehallo (May 5?, 1289), Maria soror mea (May 7, 1317), Basilis ux(or) G. Lemaignen (May 19, 1320), G. p(er)ag. de Briqueuilla (May 20, 1298), Geruasius de Alnetis (May 21, 1286), Guillelmus de Alnetis rector ecclesie de Briqueuilla (Aug. 10, 1299), Geruasius Lemaygnen clericus (Aug. 21, 1308), Iohannes de Purleio [*dub.*] (Sept. 20, 1312), The. Lemaignen, (Sept. 25, 1*26), Iohannes de Fontibus presbiter de Tribehou (Oct. 9, 1274), Nich(olas) Lemaignen rector de Lingreuilla (Nov. 13, 1326), Michaelis de Alnetis (Nov. 28, 1263).

3. Prayers—f. 5r.

3.1. INC.: a cunctis nos domine quesumus mentis et corporis deffende periculis . . .; EXPL.: . . . ecclesia tua tibi secura seruiat libertate per [*CO* 4].

3.2. INC.: exaudi nos domine deus noster ex intercedente pro nobis beata et gloriosa dei genetrice maria et beatis apostolis tuis petro et paulo cum omnibus sanctis a cunctis nos mentis et corporis hostibus tuearis gratiam tribuas in presenti et gloriam in futuro per [cf. *CO* 2506].

3.3. INC.: mundet et muniat nos quesumus domine munus oblatum et intercedente . . .; EXPL.: . . . peruersitatibus expiatos et aduersitatibus expeditos per [*CO* 3408].

3.1. is marked as *secreta* and 3.2. as *postcommunio* following the closing formula.

4. Note—f. 5v.

INC.: anno domini millesimo ducentesimo octogesimo quinto die mercurii post quasimodo in sancta synodo iussum fuit omnibus quod cotidie [-mi] in missa post pater noster dicerent psalmum et orationes in folio primo huius libri notatas pro uictoria obtinenda in regnum aragonie et ualencie et dominus guillelmus pag^v. miles mouit de briqueuilla supra mare die sabbati post inuocauit me ultimo preterita et nobilis phylipus [-rex] rex francorum mouit de sancto dyonisio in francia ad mediam quadragesimam proximo sequentem cum exercitu suo pro eundo in regnis supradictis.

A thin paper sheet containing modern transcription (with errors and omissions) and translation is pasted below the text; [see CONTENTS 5] for the psalms and prayers mentioned.

5. War prayers and masses—f. 6r^{a-b}.

5.1. f. 6r^{a}. RUB.: oratio facienda singulis diebus; INC.: deus in adiutorium meum intende . . .; OR.: deus qui conteris bella . . . actione laudemus. per christum dominum nostrum amen [*CO* 1501].

5.2. Masses—f. 6r^{b}.

RUB.: [*in sup. marg.*] in missa pro domino rege francorum coadiutoribus immediate post pater noster flexis genibus dicatur hic presens psalmus cum uersu et oratione sequentibus; RUB.: item singulis edomadis celebretur una missa in qualibet ecclesia pro iam dicto rege et pro bellatoribus nostris siue per mare siue per terram. hoc modo .xxvj.

5.2.1. RUB.: oratio pro rege; INC.: quesumus omnipotens deus ut famulus tuus philipus rex noster . . .; EXPL.: . . . ueritas et uita es graciosus ualeat peruenire. per [*CO* 4880a].

5.2.2. RUB.: secreta pro rege; INC.: munera domine quesumus oblata sanctifica ut et nobis . . . et regi nostro philippo . . .; EXPL.: . . . te largiente usquequaque proficiant. per [*CO* 3413b].

5.2.3. RUB.: postcommunio pro rege; INC.: hec domine salutaris oratio famulum tuum philippum regem . . .; EXPL.: . . . post istius temporis decursum ad eternam perueniat herditatem [*CO* 2793].

Prayers *pro rege* written fully [CONTENTS 5.2.1–5.2.3]; additional prayers *pro bellatoribus* and *pro pace* given in cue form with folio numbers; postcommunio *pro bellatoribus* is written in-full: INC.: sumpta quesumus domine misterii celestis sacramenta . . . et eos ad salutaria cuncta perducant. per.

6. Rules of date of Easter—f. 6v^{a}.

INC.: [f. 6v^{a}] quando luna currit per .i. proxima dominica post nonas aprilis erit pascha . . .; EXPL.: [f. 6v^{a}] . . . tercia dominica tercie lunationis post epiphaniam domini erit dies pasche.

7. "Lusus calami"—f. 6v^{a}.

INC.: [f. 6v^{a}] in grauibus kausis hostis graue iustior heres laudatur ius gracia karis hoste grauandis krudeles homines furor incitat hoste latentes.

BIBLIOGRAPHY: WALTHER, *Proverbia* cf. 3807, cf. 11790.

8. 2 Th 1.3.10—f. 6v^{b}.

RUB.: ad thessalonicenes; INC.: [f. 6v^{b}] fratres gratias agere debemus deo semper pro nobis . . .; EXPL.: [f. 6v^{b}] . . . qui crediderunt dominum ihesum christum; R.: protector noster. xl. et cetera pro ut retro.

9. Distich for "cursed days"—f. 6v^{b}.

INC.: augurior decies audito lumine clangor linquit olens abies coluit colus excute gallum.

10. Temporale [incomplete]—ff. 7r^{a}–136r^{b}, 137r^{a}–168v^{a}.

Begins imperfectly due to missing leaf [see QUIRES]; INC.: <lucu>stas et mel siluestre edebat et predicabat dicens . . .

11. Ordo Misse [incomplete]—f. 136v^{a-b}.

Confiteor, *Mieseratur*, *Absolutionem* through the *Credo* ending imperfectly (EXPL.: . . . et resurrexit tercia die secundum . . .); *preces* are as follows:

11.1. f. 136v^{a}. RUB.: oratio; INC.: aufer a nobis domine iniquitates . . .; EXPL.: . . . mentibus introire ad sancta sanctorum. qui uiuis [*CO* 352b].

11.2. f. 136v^{a}. RUB.: alia oratio; INC.: deus qui tribus pueris . . .; EXPL.: . . . non exurat flamma uitiorum. per [*CO* 2136].

11.3. f. 136v^{a-b}. RUB.: alia oratio; INC.: actiones nostras quesumus domine . . .; EXPL.: . . . per te cepta finiatur. per christum [*CO* 74].

11.4. f. 136v^{b}. RUB.: alia oratio; INC.: ure igne sancti spiritus renes . . .; EXPL.: . . . mundo corde placeamus. per eiusdem [*sic*] [cf. *CO* 6025].

12. Church dedication—ff. 168v^{a}–169v^{a}.

13. Sanctorale—ff. 169v^{b}–226r^{b}.

Notable saints include: Genevieve, Maurus, Sulpicius Severus, Proiectus, Aubsert, Peter Martyr, Augustine of Canterbury, Alban, translation of Martin, Wandregisil, Cucuphas, Dominic, translation of the Crown of Thorns, Taurin, Magnus, Philebert, Ouen, Floscellus, Laudus, Nigasius [*sic*], Justus, Magloire, Quentin, Anian.

Later additions in the margins for the translation of Thomas Becket (f. 194r), Clair (f. 194v), Arnulf (f. 194v), Anne (f. 197r), Martha (f. 197v), Francis (f. 215r), Vigor (f. 220v), Elizabeth (f. 222r), Katherine (f. 223r), and Barbara (f. 225r).

Contains: Silvester (f. 169v^{b}) Genevieve (ff. 169v^{b}–170r^{a}), Hilary and Remigius (f. 170r^{a}), Felix (f. 170r^{a-b}), Maurus (f. 170r^{b}–v^{a}), Sulpicius (f. 170v^{a-b}), Anthony (f. 170v^{b}), Prisca (ff. 170v^{b}–171r^{a}), Fabian and Sebastian (f. 171r^{a-b}), Agnes (f. 171v^{a}), Vincent (f. 171v^{a-b}), Emerentia (ff. 171v^{b}–173r^{a}), Conversion of Paul (ff. 172r^{a}–173r^{a}), Proiectus (f. 173r^{b}), Julian (f. 173r^{b}–v^{a}), Agnes (f. 173v^{a}), Purification (ff. 173v^{b}–175v^{a}), Blaise (f. 175v^{a-b}), Agatha (ff. 175v^{b}–176r^{b}), Vedast and Amand (f. 176r^{b}), Aubsert (f. 176r^{b}–v^{a}), Scholastica (f. 176v^{a-b}), Valentine (f. 176v^{b}), Juliana (ff. 176v^{b}–177r^{a}), Chair of

St. Peter (ff. 177r^{a}–178v^{b}), Albinus (f. 178v^{b}), Perpetua and Felicity (ff. 178v^{b}–179r^{a}), Gregory (f. 179r^{a}–v^{a}), Benedict (f. 179v^{a-b}), Annunciation (ff. 179v^{b}–181r^{a}), Ambrose (f. 181r^{a}), Leo (f. 181r^{b}), Eufemia (f. 181r^{b}–v^{a}), Tiburtius and Valerian (f. 181v^{a-b}), George (ff. 181v^{b}–182v^{a}), Mark (ff. 182v^{a}–183r^{a}), Vitalis (f. 183r^{a}), Peter Martyr (f. 183r^{a-b}), Philip and James (ff. 183r^{b}–184r^{a}), Invention of the Holy Cross (ff. 184r^{a}–185r^{a}), Alexander, Eventius, and Theodolus (f. 185r^{a-b}), John (f. 185r^{a}), Gordian and Epimachus (f. 185r^{a}–v^{a}), Nereus, Achilles, and Pancratius (f. 185v^{a-b}), Urban (ff. 185v^{b}–186r^{a}), Augustine of Canterbury (f. 186r^{a}), Petronilla (f. 186r^{b}), Marcellinus and Peter (f. 186r^{b}–v^{a}), Medard and Gildard (f. 186v^{a-b}), Primus and Felician (ff. 186v^{b}–187r^{a}), Barnabas (f. 187r^{a}), Basilides, Quirinus, Nabor, and Nazarius (f. 187r^{a-b}), Vitus, Modestus, and Crescentia (f. 187r^{b}–v^{a}), Marcus and Marcellianus (f. 187v^{a-b}), Gervasius and Protasius (ff. 187v^{b}–188r^{a}), Alban (f. 188r^{a-b}), John the Baptist (vigil and feast; ff. 188r^{b}–190r^{b}), John and Paul (f. 190r^{b}–v^{b}), Leo (f. 190v^{b}), Peter and Paul (vigil and feast; ff. 190v^{b}–192r^{b}), Commemoration of St. Paul (ff. 192r^{b}–193r^{a}), Martial (f. 193r^{a-b}), Processus and Martinianus (f. 193r^{b}), translation of Martin (f. 193r^{b}–v^{a}), Octave of Peter and Paul (ff. 193v^{a}–194r^{b}), Seven Brothers (f. 194r^{b}–v^{a}), translation of Benedict (f. 194v^{a-b}), Margaret (ff. 194v^{b}–195r^{a}), Praxedis (f. 195r^{a}), Mary Magdalene (ff. 195r^{a}–196r^{a}), Wandregisil (f. 196r^{a}), Apollinaris (f. 196r^{a-b}), James (vigil and feast; f. 196r^{b}–v^{b}), Christopher and Cucuphas (ff. 196v^{b}–197r^{a}), Seven Sleepers (f. 197r^{a}), Pantaleon (f. 197r^{a-b}), Samson (f. 197r^{a}–v^{a}), Nazarius and Celsus (f. 197v^{a}), Felix, Simplicius, Faustinus, and Beatrice (f. 197v^{a-b}), Abdon and Sennen (ff. 197r^{b}–198r^{a}), Germain (f. 198r^{a-b}), St. Peter in Chains (f. 198r^{b}–v^{a}), Maccabees (f. 198v^{a-b}), Stephen (f. 198v^{b}), Invention of Stephen, Nicodemus, Gamaleil, and Abidon (ff. 198v^{b}–199r^{a}), Dominic (f. 199r^{a-b}), Sixtus, Felicissimus, and Agapitus (f. 199r^{b}–v^{a}), Donatus (f. 199v^{a}), Cyriacus and companions (f. 199v^{a-b}), Romain (ff. 199v^{b}–200r^{a}), Laurence (vigil and feast; ff. 200r^{a}–201r^{a}), translation of the Crown of Thorns (ff. 201r^{a}–202r^{a}), Taurin (f. 202r^{a}), Tiburtius (f. 202r^{a-b}), Hippolytus and companions (f. 202r^{b}–v^{a}), Eusebius (f. 202v^{a}), Assumption (vigil and feast; ff. 202v^{a}–205r^{a}), Octave of St. Laurence (f. 205r^{b}–v^{a}), Agapitus (f. 205v^{a}), Magnus (f. 205v^{a-b}), Philebert (ff. 205v^{b}–206r^{a}), Octave of the Assumption (f. 206r^{a-b}), Timothy and Symphorianus (f. 206r^{b}), Timothy and Apollinaris (f. 206r^{b}–v^{a}), Bartholomew (vigil and feast; ff. 206v^{a}–207r^{a}), Ouen (f. 207r^{a-b}), Rufus (f. 207r^{b}), Augustine (f. 207r^{b}–v^{a}), Hermes (f. 207v^{a-b}), Decollation of John the Baptist (ff. 207v^{b}–208v^{a}), Sabina (f. 208v^{a}), Felix and Adauctus (f. 208v^{a-b}), Giles (ff. 208v^{b}–209r^{a}), Priscus (f. 209r^{a}), Nativity of the Virgin Mary (ff. 209r^{a}–210r^{a}), Adrian (f. 210r^{a-b}), Gorgonius (f. 210r^{a}), Protus and Hyacinthus (f. 210r^{a}–v^{b}), Exaltation of the Holy Cross (ff. 210v^{b}–211r^{b}), Cornelius and Cyprianus (f. 211r^{b}), Octave of the Nativity (f. 211r^{b}), Nicomedes (f. 211v^{a}), Eufemia (f. 211v^{a-b}), Floscellus (ff. 211v^{b}–212r^{a}), Lambert (f. 212r^{a}), Matthew (vigil and feast; f. 212r^{a}–v^{b}), Laudus (ff. 212v^{b}–213r^{a}), Maurice and companions (f. 213r^{a-b}), Cosmas and Damian (f. 213r^{b}–v^{a}), Michael (ff. 213v^{a}–214v^{b}), Jerome (f. 214v^{b}), Germain, Remigius, and Vedast (ff. 214v^{b}–215r^{a}), Leodegar (f. 215r^{a-b}), Faith (f. 215r^{b}–v^{b}), Marcus (f. 215v^{b}), Marcus and Marcellinus (ff. 215v^{b}–216r^{a}), Demetrius (f. 216r^{a}), Denis and companions (f. 216r^{b}), Paulinus (f. 216r^{b}–v^{a}), Augustine (f. 216v^{a}), Nigasius [*sic*] and companions (f. 216v^{a-b}), Callixtus (ff. 216v^{b}–217r^{a}), Michael at Monte Tumba (f. 217r^{a-b}), Justus (f. 217r^{b}–v^{a}), Romain (f. 217v^{a-b}), Magloire (ff. 217v^{b}–218r^{a}), Crispin and Crispinianus (f. 218r^{a-b}), Simon and Jude (vigil and feast; f. 218r^{b}–v^{b}), Quentin (ff. 218v^{b}–219r^{a}), All Saints (vigil and feast; ff. 219r^{a}–220v^{a}), Eustace (f. 220v^{a-b}), Leonard (f. 220v^{b}), Claudius, Nicostratus, Symphorianus, Castorius, and Simplicius (ff.

220v^{b}–221r^{a}), Theodore (f. 221r^{a-b}), Martin (f. 221r^{a}–v^{a}), Menas (f. 221v^{a}), Brictius (f. 221v^{a-b}), Anian (ff. 221v^{b}–222r^{a}), Octave of St. Martin (f. 222r^{a}), Cecilia (f. 222r^{a-b}), Clement (f. 222r^{b}–v^{a}), Felicity (f. 222v^{a-b}), Chrysogonus (f. 222v^{b}), Katherine (f. 223r^{a-b}), Saturnin (f. 222r^{b}), Andrew (vigil and feast; ff. 222r^{b}–225r^{a}), Chrysanthus, Maurus, and Daria (f. 225r^{a}), Nicholas (f. 225r^{a}–v^{a}), Octave of St. Andrew (f. 225v^{a-b}), Conception of the Virgin Mary (f. 225v^{b}), Eligius (ff. 225v^{b}–226r^{a}), Lucia (f. 226r^{a}), Thomas (vigil and feast; f. 226r^{a-b}).

14. Trental of St. Gregory—f. 226v.

14.1. INC.: ordo trigintalis quod quidam apostolicus pro liberacione anime matris sue a penis purgatorii . . .; EXPL.: . . . sub ordine proximiores prime orationes.

14.2. RUB.: oratio; INC.: deus summa spes nostre redemptionis qui in terra promissionis . . .; EXPL.: . . . per tuam magnam succurre pietatem per dominum nostrum.

14.3. RUB.: secreta; INC.: omnipotens et misericors deus redemptor animarum saluandarum . . .; EXPL.: . . . in uiam salutis eterne misericorditer dirigendo per dominum.

14.4. RUB.: postcommunio; INC.: deus cuius misericordie non est numerus cui soli competit . . .; EXPL.: . . . auxilii tui piissime largiendo per dominum.

EDITION: PFAFF 1974, 82–83.
BIBLIOGRAPHY: PFAFF 1974.

15. Common of saints, neumed—ff. 227r^{a}–243v^{a}.

An apostle (vigil and feast; ff. 227r^{a}–229v^{a}), a martyr (ff. 229v^{a}–230v^{b}), a confessor as well as a martyr (ff. 230v^{b}–231v^{b}), a martyr and bishop (ff. 231v^{b}–232v^{a}), martyrs (ff. 232v^{a}–237r^{a}), a confessor (ff. 237r^{a}–239v^{a}), an abbot (ff. 239v^{b}–240v^{a}), confessors (ff. 240v^{a}–241r^{a}), a virgin (ff. 241r^{a}–243r^{b}), virgins (f. 243r^{b}–v^{a}).

16. Votive and Requiem masses—ff. 243v^{a}–250r^{a}.

Votive masses: de trinitate (f. 243v^{a}); in suffragium angelorum (f. 243v^{a-b}); de sancta cruce domini (ff. 243v^{b}–244r^{a}); officium beate marie uirginis in sabbatis (f. 244r^{b}–v^{a}); in memoria saluatoris (f. 244v^{a}); missa pro seipso (f. 244v *in marg.*); de omnibus sanctis missa (f. 244v^{b}); de reliquiis ecclesie (ff. 244v^{b}–245r^{a}); pro congregatione (f. 245r^{a}); pro seipso missa (f. 245r^{a-b}); pro familiaribus missa (f. 245r^{b}); pro iter agentibus missa (ff. 245r^{b}–v^{a}); missa contra hostes (f. 245v^{a}); pro infirmo missa (f. 245v^{a-b}); missa pro pace (f. 245v^{b}); missa generalis (f. 246r^{a-b}); missa communis (f. 246r^{b}).

Requiem masses and prayers: missa pro fidelibus defunctis (f. 246v^{a}); pro presenti defuncto (f. 246v^{a}); pro femina oratio (f. 246v^{a}); pro quolibet defuncto (f. 246v^{a}); pro laicis et mulieribus (f. 246v^{a}); pro quibusuis defunctis in tempore paschali, pro principibus et militibus, in minoribus et maioribus anniuersariis (ff. 246v^{b}–247v^{a}); pro mulieribus (f. 247v^{a}); pro laicis (f. 247v^{a-b}); pro regibus et principibus et militibus (ff. 247v^{b}–248r^{a}); pro femina (f. 248r^{b}); pro quoblibet (f. 248r^{b}); pro presenti (f. 248v^{a}); pro defuncta (f. 248v^{a}); pro quolibet (f. 248v^{a}); missa pro patre et matre (f. 248v^{a}); missa pro quibuslibet defunctis (f. 248v^{a}); missa pro benefactoribus (f. 248v^{b}); missa pro fratribus congregationis (ff. 248v^{b}–249r^{a}); missa pro quiescentibus in cimiterio (f. 249r^{a-b}); in aniuersario (f. 249r^{b}); missa pro episcopo uel sacerdote (f. 249r^{b}–v^{a}); pro sacerdote missa (f. 249v^{a}); pro cunctis fidelibus missa (f. 249v^{a-b}).

Votive masses: missa contra temptationem carnis (f. 249v^{b}); ad poscendam sancti spiritus gratiam (ff. 249v^{b}–250r^{a}).

17. Litany—ff. 250r^{a}–250v^{b}.

RUB.: letania ad fontes.

Martyrs: Stephen, Cletus, Clement, Sixtus, Cornelius, Cyprian, Laurence, Leodegar, Denis (*cum soc.*), Julian, Nichostratus, Saturnin; *Confessors*: Silvester, Gregory, Augustine, Julian, Ambrose, Samson, Martin, Benedict; *Virgins*: Mary Magdalene, Maria of Egypt, Scholastica, Agatha, Agnes, Petronilla, Cecilia, Katherine, Lucia, Juliana, Columba, Fides, Spes, Caritas.

18. *Benedictio fontis* [incomplete]—ff. 251r^{a}–253v^{a}.

The first litany is general; the second litany contains Laudus, Taurin, Germain, and Genevieve; the third litany contains Romain, Ouen, and Columba.

19. Ordinary chants—ff. 253v^{a}–255v^{b}.

20. Feast of Relics of Coutances—f. 256r^{a}.

RUB.: in festo reliquarum ecclesie const(antie); INC.: [f. 256r^{a}] <s>apientiam sanctorum. oratio. <p>ropitiare quesumus domine nobis famulis tuis . . . semper protegamur aduersis [*CO* 4703a]; EXPL.: [f. 256r^{a}] . . . postcommunio. <s>umpta nos quesumus domine sacramenta uiuificent et uite nobis conferent remedia et per sanctorum merita quorum reliquie in nostra continentur ecclesia ad superna nos subleuent gaudia. per.

21. Mass for Corpus Christi—f. 256r^{b}–v^{b}.

INC.: [f. 256r^{b}] cibauit eos ex adipe. deus qui nobis sub sacramento mirabili . . . fructum percipere mereamur qui uiuis et regis [cf. *CO* 1828]; EXPL.: [f. 256v^{b}] . . . fac nos quesumus domine . . . perceptio prefigurat qui uiuis et [*CO* 2597].

22. Additions, neumed—ff. 257r^{a}–258v^{b}.

23. Added Prayers—f. 259r–v.

23.1. f. 259r. RUB.: orationes dicendi in ferris [*sic*] quadregesima [-feria -tercia]; [-offertorium]; INC.: sanctissime dei genitricis semperque uirginis marie et beatarum omnium celestinum uirtutum sanctorum . . .; EXPL.: . . . peccatorum et requiem sempiternam. per eundum [*CO* 5309].

23.2. f. 259r. RUB.: secreta; INC.: in conspectu domine maiestatis tue quesumus omnipotens deus . . .; EXPL.: . . . concede et omnibus fidelibus tuis uitam sempiternam largire. per eundem [*CO* 3081].

23.3. f. 259r. RUB.: postcommunio; INC.: per huius sacramenti misterium atque uirtutem quesumus domine . . .; EXPL.: . . . et omnes fideles tui uitam eternam adipisci mereantur [-mereantur]. per eundem [*CO* 4183].

23.4. f. 259v. RUB.: oracio; INC.: omnium sanctorum tuorum intercessionibus quesumus domine gratia tua nos semper . . .; EXPL.: . . . defuncti remissionem mereantur suorum omnium accipere peccatorum. per dominum [*CO* 4103].

23.5. f. 259v. RUB.: secreta; INC.: oblationes nostras quesumus domine propiciatus intende et ob tuorum . . .; EXPL.: . . . et presentis uite subsidia et future premia eterna acquirat. per dominum [*CO* 3630].

23.6. f. 259v. RUB.: postcommunio; INC.: hec sacrificia que sumpsimus domine meritis et intercessionibus . . .; EXPL.: . . . eterna ac temporalia premia benigne adquirant. per dominum [*CO* 2876a].

24. Mass for Feast of the Relics—f. 259v.

24.1. f. 259v. RUB.: in die reliquiarum; INC.: ad processionem. concede nobis . . . communio. gaudet.

24.2. f. 259v. RUB.: oracio de reliquiis; INC.: presta quesumus omnipotens deus ut sanctorum tuorum quorum reliquie . . .; EXPL.: . . . tranquilla pace in tua iugiter laude letemur. per christum [*CO* 4556].

24.3. f. 259v. RUB.: secreta; INC.: munera tua misericors deus maiestatis oblata benigne . . .; EXPL.: . . . sacratissime in basilica hac reliquie sunt recondite. per.

24.4. f. 259v. RUB.: postcommunio; INC.: diuina libantes misteria quesumus domine ut . . .; EXPL.: . . . quorum hic sacra gaudemus habere patrociniam. per dominum.

25. Mass for St. Anne—f. 260r.

RUB.: in festo sancte anne ad missam; INC.: officium. gaudeamus. oratio. deus qui beatam annam dilectissime genetricis tue matrem egregiam hodierna . . . dignatus es carnem qui uiuis et cetera [*CO* 1381] . . .; EXPL.: . . . offertorium. filie regnum. communio. diffusa est.

26. Mass for Thomas Becket—f. 260v.

RUB.: missa in conmemoratione sancti thome martiris; INC.: officium. letabitur iustus; .ccxxv. oratio. deus pro cuius ecclesia . . . consequantur effectum per [*CO* 1315] . . .; EXPL.: . . . postcommunio. adiuuet nos omnipotens et misericors deus . . . pro tui nominis honore glorioso meruit coronari /cum meo\ martirio. per [*CO* 202].

27. Mass for St. Dunstan—f. 260v.

RUB.: in festo sancti dunstani ad missam; INC.: officium. sacerdotes tui .ccxxxij. oratio. deus qui beatum dunstanum pontificem tuum ad regnum . . . ad gaudia transire perhennia. per [*CO* 1438] . . .; EXPL.: postcommunio. beati dunstani confessoris tui . . . in cuius ueneracione tua contingimus sacramenta. per [*CO* 410].

28. Mass for the Church—f. 261v.

28.1. f. 261v. RUB.: pro uniuersali ecclesia. oratio; INC.: ecclesie tue quesumus domine preces placatus . . .; EXPL.: . . . secura tibi seruiat libertate [*CO* 2404b].

28.2. f. 261v. RUB.: secreta; INC.: protege nos quesumus domine misteriis . . .; EXPL.: . . . famulemur et mente per christum [*CO* 4766a].

28.3. f. 261v. RUB.: postcommunio; INC.: quesumus domine deus noster . . .; EXPL.: . . . non sinas subiacere periculis. per. [*CO* 4828a].

Binding: s. xix; brown leather over boards; blind tooled; gilt spine; very tight; seven raised bands; modern conservation work.

Owners & Provenance: Medieval provenance points to Lower Normandy in the diocese of Coutances [see Contents 2 for place names and individuals]; acquired from Les Enluminures (Chicago, IL) by the university in August 2012.

cod. Lat. b. 14

Origin: Germany, s. xvi^{in}.
Content Overview: Sermon collection.

In Latin and German, on paper; i + 50 ff. +i; generally 200 x 136 mm (page) [see Layout for ruling]; flyleaves modern paper; foliated in modern pencil with Arabic numerals; f. 50v blank.

Collation: i + 1–5^{10} +i

Bibliographical Format: 4°.

Quires: Paper quinions folded in quarto are used for all quires; conservation treatment visible on f. 1; paper in good condition otherwise; trimmed.

Signatures: Contemporary Arabic numerals in black ink are written on the first recto of each quire in the lower right margin; signature for quire 3 missing (trimmed).

Watermarks: Eleven occurrences of seven different watermarks: (A) Letter P; occurs in quires 1 and 2 (ff. 3/8, 11/20); cf. Piccard 109359 (Arnhem, 1499). (B) Letter P; occurs in quires 1 and 2 (ff. 11/20, 14/17); corresponds closely to Piccard 110465 (Strasbourg, 1505). (C) Letter P; occurs in quire 2 (ff. 12/19); cf. Piccard 110122 (Mecheln, 1505). (D) Hand; occurs in quire 3 (ff. 21/30, 24/27); corresponds closely to Piccard 154597 (Düsseldorf, 1506). (E) Letter P; occurs in quires 4 and 5 (ff. 31/40, 42/49); cf. Piccard 110365 (1513). (F) Letter P; occurs in quire 4 (ff. 34/37); generally cf. Piccard 109713 (Löwen, 1486). (G) Letter P; occurs in quire 5 (ff. 43/48); cf. Piccard 111394 (Middelburg, Zeeland, 1494).

Layout:

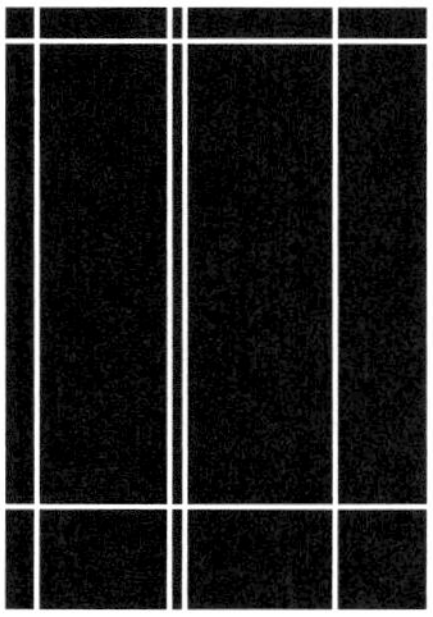

A

A ff. 1r–50v. Hard-point; 147 x 104 mm; intercol. 5 mm; 31–45 lines.

Pattern **A** is incised throughout the manuscript using hard-point technique (not board); two uneven columns (intercol. 5 mm); writing below top line; number of lines varies with size of script from 31 to 45 lines per page; single vertical bounding lines and horizontal through lines.

Script: A single hand (M1) writes the text on ff. 1r^{a}–48v^{a}. M1 begins writing Hybrida Libraria (ff. 1r^{a}–9v^{a}) with occasional bifurcation of ascenders and attempted hairlines, then switches to Semitextualis Libraria (ff. 9v^{a}–48v^{a}) using the same letter forms with the exception of **f** and straight **s**. The final sermon (ff. 48v^{a}–50r^{b}) written in Semitextualis Libraria is likely a later addition by M1 with an attempt at a more formal presentation with quadrangles frequently at the base of minims. The size of the script varies throughout the manuscript, accounting for the great flux in the number of lines; incipits often in larger, more formal Semitextualis in an attempt to create hierarchy.

Decoration:
I. Rubrication: Rubrics and letter heightening of majuscules in red ink.
II. Initials: Flourished and plain initials occur.
A. One flourished initial (5 line square inset) with floral spray drawn completely in red ink on f. 1r.
B. Plain initials (2 line square inset) in red ink begin sermons on ff. 9v–48v [see Contents 3–13].

Contents:

1. Sermons—ff. 1r^{a}–50r^{b}.

Thirteen sermons for Easter, Pentecost, Corpus Christi, Assumption, Nativity, Purification; nos. 1 and 2 present alternating text in Latin and German.

1. ff. 1r^{a}–2r^{b}. **inc.**: surrexit ioab et abiit in gessur et adduxit absolon in iherusalem ita scribitur secundo regum .14. [2 Rg 14.23] originaliter atque ad nostram exhortacionem hodierne festiuitatis uerba sunt pre [*sic*] assumpta thematizaliter . . .; **expl.**: . . . sicud enim sidus celeste calorique solaris terram sub se iacentem fructificat sic dei gratia cor humile sibi substratum uariis donis fructificat et fecundat et cetera.

2. ff. 2r^{b}–9v^{a}. **inc.**: surrexit ioab loco et capitulo preallegatis [2 Rg 14.23] pro introductione thematis occurrit michi uenerabilis doctor dominus hugo cardinalis libro sexto didascolicon dicens in doctrina fieri oportet ut prius historiam discas et rerum gestarum ueritatem [*DS* 6.3] . . .; **expl.**: . . . debeamus bonis uirtutibus si uolumus cum christo spiritualiter et surgere ut amigdalus ut rosa ut lilium ut palma thronis salomonis et hec fuit secunda causa necessaria christum resurgere.

3. ff. 9v^{a}–15v^{a}. **rub.**: sermo de resurrectione; **inc.**: ihesum queritis naza<renum> crucifixum surrexit non est hic sic scribitur marci .xiij. et ultimo [Mc 16.6] pro aliquali presencium uerborum explanacione . . .; **expl.**: . . . ad quam societatem simulque beatificatam uisionem nos perducat qui sine fine uiuit et regnat amen.

4. ff. 15v[a]–20v[b]. INC.: ihesum queritis nazarenum crucifixum surrexit marci ultimo [Mc 16.6] et in ewangelio hodierno festiuitatis hec verba angelus domini dixit sanctis mulieribus que uenerant mane hodierno ad ungendum corpus christi in sepulcro . . .; EXPL.: . . . accedamus itaque o charissimi et mente uideamus christum ac si presentem et osculemur eius uulnera rogemus quoque et cetera.

5. ff. 20v[b]–25v[a]. INC.: surrexit scilicet ihesus non est hic ecce locus ubi posuerunt eum marci ultimo [Mc 16.6] et in ewangelio hodierno ccharissimi [*sic*] hodie tam angeli iocun<de> de resurrectionibus annunciantes quam ecclesia hortantur ut laudemus deum pro letabunda resurrectione christi . . .; EXPL.: . . . nos ergo peccatores rogemus christum ut dimittat peccata et benedicat nos dando graciam et gloriam amen.

Attributed to Pelbartus de Themesvar in HAGENAU 1498.

6. ff. 25v[a]–30v[b]. INC.: sol egressus est super terram genesis .xix. [Gn 19.23] uidemus multociens quod tempore ueris flos qui delicate oritur interdum a transeuntibus tam hominibus quam animalibus conculcatur et ex hoc languet et marcescit et quasi mortuus apparet . . .; EXPL.: . . . corpus et anima de miseria et penalitate ad eternam gloriam et felicitatem sicut hoc testatur leo papa dicens post passionem domini ruptis uinculis mortalitatis infirmitas in uirtutem mortalitas in eternitatem et contumelia transit ad gloriam.

Identical to sermon 49 attributed to Meffret(h) in the *Hortulus reginae*.

7. ff. 30v[b]–32v[b]. INC.: hec est dies quam fecit dominus exultemus et letemur in ea psalmus [Ps 117.24] post auram pluuialem sequitur serenitas post tempestatem tranquillitas magna pluuia fuit in die parasceues non solum lacrimarum que fluxerunt de oculis christi et martiris eius . . .; EXPL.: . . . apocalipsis .xxj. absterget deus omnem lacrimam ab oculis sanctorum et mors ultra non erit neque luctus neque clamor neque dolor erit ultra que prima abierit [Apc 21.4] ad hec gaudia nos perducat ihesus christus amen [SCHNEYER 43:212, no. 77].

Attributed to Graeculus (T28) (SCHNEYER 43:212, no. 77); also found in Berlin, Preußische Staatsbibliothek, theol. qu. 47, f. 1, and attributed to Gerlacus de Monte (ROSE 1901, 2:433, no. 533); and among the sermons in Trier, Stadtbibliothek, Cod. 274, ff. 2r–221r, ascribed to Tilmannus (Dilmannus) Sengelberge de Eschwege in the colophon on f. 221r (ZUMKELLER 1966, 391, no. 833).

8. ff. 32v[b]–37r[b]. RUB.: in die sancto penthecostes sermo; INC.: emitte spiritum tuum et creabuntur et renouabis faciem terre ps. .ciij. [Ps 103.30] pro introductione thematis dicit beatus augustinus maxima insania est hominem erumpnosam uitam . . .; EXPL.: . . . et ideo significatur periit psalmus spiritu principali confirma cor meum deus et alibi emitte spiritum tuum et creabuntur.

9. ff. 37r[b]–40v[a]. RUB.: de corpore christi sermo; INC.: caro mea uere est cibus et sanguis meus uere est potus ioh. .vj. [Io 6.56] et habetur de conse. dis. .ij. ca. quia corpus dicit beatus thomas contra gentiles libro .iiij. ca. sexagesimo sicut corporalis uita alimento

materiali [*SCG* 4.61] . . .; EXPL.: . . . et dator gratie continetur dominus noster ihesus christus qui es super omnia benedictus et cetera.

10. ff. 40v[a]–42v[a]. RUB.: de assumptione beate marie uirginis; INC.: assumpsit me spiritus ezechielis .iij. [Ez 3.13] quasi diceret propheta pater et filius et spiritus sanctus assumpserunt me et singulariter exaltauerunt me super omnes choros angelorum . . .; EXPL.: . . . iusti fulgebunt sicut sol in regno patris eorum [Mt 13.43] o quis erit splendor quando solis fulgorem habebit lux cor- [f. 42v[a]] porum dotes animarum sunt tres scilicet uisio fruicio comprehensio amen.

11. ff. 42v[a]–45v[b]. RUB.: de natiuitate christi sermo; INC.: natus est uobis saluator mundi luc. .ij. [Lc 2.11] secundum naturales uer premittit uarios nuncios aliqui sunt uiole . . .; EXPL.: . . . et cum peccatoribus manducare mat. .ix. [Mt 9.11] et sic christus in orto suo tamquam saluator omnia pacificauit.

12. ff. 46r[a]–48v[a]. RUB.: de purificatione beate uirginis sermo; INC.: postquam impleti sunt dies purgacionis marie secundum legem moysi tulerunt illum in iherusalem ut sisterent eum domino id est offerrent eum domino luc. .ij. [Lc 2.21] racionabile est ut ponens aliquam legem eam seruet et adimpleat propter quod dicitur actus primo capitulo cepit ihesus facere et docere [Act 1.1] et hoc ideo ut nos suam legem et doctrinam implemus [*sic*] . . .; EXPL.: . . . tercio consolatus est symeon a [f. 48v[a]] patre per finem pacificum unde ad patrem ait nunc dimittis seruum tuum domine secundum uerbum et cetera [Lc 2.29] quia uiderunt oculi mei salutare tuum [Lc 2.30] quod nobis concedat ihesus christus amen.

Also found in Trier, Bistumarchiv, Abt. 95, Nr. 38, ff. 301v–302v [see FRECKMANN 2006, 134–146].

13. ff. 48v[a]–50r[b]. INC.: angelus domini secundum tempus descendebat in piscinam mouebatur aqua et qui prior descendebat saniis [*sic*] fiebat ioh. .v. [Io 5.4] charissimi fratres secundum historialem intellectum horum uerborum nichil aliud in istis uerbis intelligendum . . .; EXPL.: . . . dignatus est suo patri cum quo post hanc uitam regnare debemus sine fine quod nobis praestare—.

BINDING: s. xxi; brown leather over binder's board; blind tooled; five raised bands.

OWNERS & PROVENANCE: Acquired from King Alfred's Notebook (Cayce, SC) by the university in April 2013. The manuscript formed part of a larger codex, which was split into five pieces that were bound individually. The five codices are:

Ann Arbor, Univ. Michigan, Hatcher Graduate Library, Mich. MS 290
Cambridge, Harvard Univ., Houghton Library, MS Lat 447
Cambridge, Harvard Univ., Houghton Library, MS Lat 448
Cambridge, Harvard Univ., Houghton Library, MS Lat 449
Notre Dame, Univ. Notre Dame, Hesburgh Library, cod. Lat. b. 14

cod. Lat. b. 15

ORIGIN: Switzerland or Germany, s. xvi^{1}.
CONTENT OVERVIEW: Antiphonary.

In Latin with some German, on paper; 188 ff. +i; generally 213 x 158 mm (page) [see LAYOUT for ruling]; foliated in modern pencil with Arabic numerals; ff. 184r–188v blank but ruled.

COLLATION: 1^{14+2} $+2^{14+1}$ $+3–11^{16}$ $+12^{12+1}$ +i

BIBLIOGRAPHICAL FORMAT: 4°.

QUIRES: Various forms of paper quires folded in quarto are used; the predominant forms are gatherings of eight bifolia. Quire 1 is a gathering of seven bifolia with two leaves added (ff. 1 and 16). Quire 2 is a gathering of seven bifolia with one leaf added (f. 17). Quire 12 is a sexternion with one leaf added (f. 182). Paper is in good condition; minimal frying.

WATERMARKS: Forty-five occurrences of two distinct watermarks: (**A**) Bear; occurs in quires 1–11; cf. PICCARD 84070 (Basel, 1514). (**B**) Grapes; occurs in quires 11 (ff. 164/171, 166/169) and 12; cf. PICCARD 129375 (Schwyz, 1517).

LAYOUT:

A

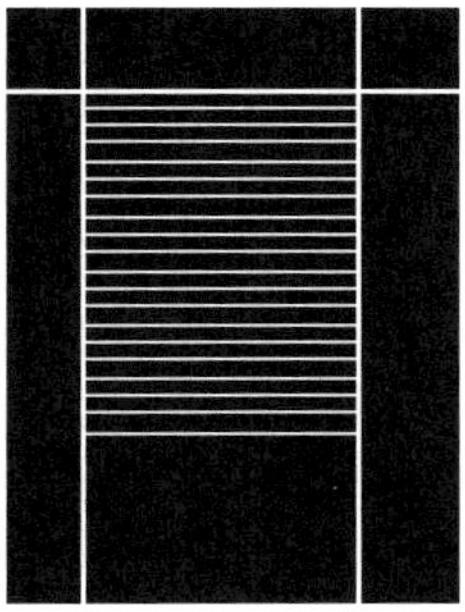

B

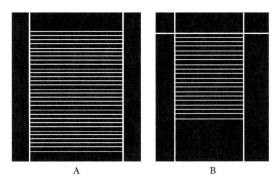

A f. 1r–v. Combined technique; 136 x 110 mm; 6 four-line staves.
B ff. 2r–188v. Red ink; 121 x 96 mm; 6 four-line staves.

Pattern **A** is traced on f. 1r–v using a combined technique of lead (verticals) and red ink (staves); single column. Pattern **B** is traced on ff. 2r–188v in red ink; single column; top line part of first staff.

Script: Four hands (M1–M4) write throughout the manuscript. M1 writes the text on f. 1r–v in a late script (s. xvi[1]) imitative of Northern Textualis and influenced by Hybrida using single compartment **a**, straight **s** on the line, and loopless ascenders. M2 writes the text on ff. 2r–182r in Northern Textualis Libraria (s. xvi[1]); size of script decreases on f. 135v, but the hand remains the same. M3 adds text (1.5 lines) on f. 182r in Hybrida Libraria. M4 writes text on ff. 182r–183v in a calligraphic sixteenth-century Textualis.

Decoration:
I. Rubrication: Rubrics and letter heightening in red ink.
II. Initials: Plain initials with occasional ornamentation occur in hierarchy.
a. Plain initials (1 line versals; hanging forms) are painted in red ink throughout the manuscript.

Music & Staves: Four-line staves in red ink; 13 mm; black neumes.

Contents:

1. *Cum rex gloriae Christus*—f. 1r–v.

rub.: das singt man andem hailgen ostertag so balt die herren zu der cor diir in gand so facht man an; **inc.**: [f. 1r] cum rex glorie cristus infernum debellaturus intraret . . .; **expl.**: [f. 1v] . . . spes desperatis magna consolacio in tormentis alleluya.

2. Sanctorale [incomplete]—ff. 2r–172v.

Rubrics in Latin and German; the text begins imperfectly. Contains: Visitation (ff. 2r–6r; incomplete), Anne (ff. 6r–15r), Transfiguration (ff. 15r–29v), Trinity (ff. 29v–38v), John the Baptist (ff. 39r–49r), John and Paul (ff. 39r–51r), Peter and Paul (ff. 51v–52r), Peter (ff. 52r–64v), Paul (ff. 64v–76r), dedication of a church (ff. 76r–86r), Mary Magdalene (ff. 86r–99v), Dominic (ff. 99v–110r), Laurence (ff. 110v–122v), Tiburtius (ff. 122v–123r), Assumption (ff. 123r–135v), Augustine (ff. 135v–138v), Decollation of John the Baptist (ff. 138v–140r), Nativity of the Virgin Mary (ff. 140r–142v), Exaltation of the Holy Cross (ff. 142v–144r), Michael (ff. 144r–146r), All Saints (ff. 146r–149r), Ursula (ff. 149r–155v), Martin (ff. 156r–159r), Elizabeth (ff. 159r–161v), Cecilia (ff. 162r–163v), Clement (ff. 163v–164v), Katherine (ff. 165r–169v), Catherine of Siena (ff. 169v–172v).

3. Common of the saints—ff. 173r–182r.

Rubrics in Latin and German; apostles (ff. 173r–174v), Evangelists (ff. 174v–176r), martyr (f. 176r–v), martyrs (ff. 176v–177v), confessors (ff. 177v–178v), virgins (ff. 178v–180v), Virgin (*von unser frowen*; ff. 180v–182r), all saints (added; f. 182r).

4. *Nisi manducaueritis carnem* (Io 6.54–55)—f. 182r–v.

INC.: [f. 182r] nisi manducaueritis carnem filii hominis et biberitis eius sanguinem non habebitis uitam in uobis . . .; EXPL.: [f. 182v] . . . sanguinem habet eternam et ego rescuscitabo eum in nouissimo die.

5. Corpus Christi—f. 183r–v.

RUB.: offertorium de sacramento; INC.: [f. 183r] sacerdotes incensum domini et panes offerunt deo . . .; EXPL.: [f. 183v] . . . uel biberit calicem domini indigne reus erit corporis et sanguinis domini alleluia.

BINDING: s. xvi; stiff vellum over pasteboard; modern rebacking.

OWNERS & PROVENANCE: Acquired from Les Enluminures (Chicago, IL) by the university in September 2014.

SALES & CATALOGUES: Les Enluminures, TextManuscripts Cat. 4, no. 4.

cod. Lat. c. 1

Origin: Bohemia, s. xv. (dated 15 July 1435).
Content Overview: Nicholas Biskupec of Pelhřimov (Mikuláš of Pelhřimov), *Scriptum super quattuor euangelia in unum concordata* (part I, *redactio prima*).

In Latin, on paper; 240 ff.; generally 210 x 148 mm (page) [see Layout for ruling]; ff. 215r–239v blank; no flyleaves.

Collation: $1–20^{12}$

Bibliographical Format: 4°.

Quires: Paper sexternions folded in quarto are the normal forms; paper in good condition; little damage.

Quire Marks: Arabic numerals in the lower right margins for quires 1–17.

Watermarks: Sixty-one occurrences of two different watermarks: (**A**) unidentifiable; occurs in quires 1–17; distance between chainlines 38/39 mm; approx. 87 mm in height; above rod consisting of one line with three-leaf clover/flower. (**B**) Bell; occurs in quires 18–20; cf. Piccard 40433 (Toru, 1426).

Layout:

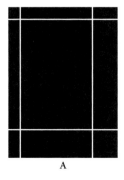

A

A ff. 1r–240v. Ink; 154 x 98 mm; approx. 38 lines.

Pattern A is frame-ruled in brown ink; single column; writing below top line; prickings visible for verticals in the upper and lower margins, and for horizontals in the outer margin; number of lines variable.

Script: A single scribal bookhand (M1) writes the text in Cursiva Libraria of the fifteenth century; pericopes are copied in a larger script. Other hands in addition to M1 write various marginalia in Cursiva.

Decoration:

I. Rubrication: Paraph marks, letter heightening, and chapter numbers in red ink; sources and lemmata often underlined in red.

II. Initials: Plain initials occur sparsely.

a. Plain initials (2–4 line square inset) in red ink occur on ff. 1r, 2r, 18r, 31v; initial on f. 41v (2 line square inset) contains minimal flourishing in black ink.

Contents:

1. Nicholas Biskupec of Pelhřimov, *Scriptum super quattuor euangelia (pars I, redactio prima)*—ff. 1r–203r.

1.1. Prologue—ff. 1r–2r. inc.: lex seu doctrina ewangelica perfectissima est per se sufficiens ad regimen ecclesie militantis cui non licet quidquam addere uel subtrahere christus enim eius dator est summus anime humane medicus ut ex fide supponitur sed non perfecte . . .; expl.: . . . sed sicut unicuique inspiratum est non superflua [*sic*] cooperacionem sui laboris adiunxit [Augustine, *cons. ev.* I.2.4; *CPL* 273].

1.2. Text—ff. 2r–203r. inc.: [f. 2r] in principio erat uerbum . . . [f. 2v] plenum gratie et ueritatis [Io 1–14] postquam premissa est excellentia et legis ewangeliorum commendacio . . .; expl.: [f. 203r] . . . per quorum medium ire cum christo debemus ne eis in operibus malis consenciamus; scribal colophon: [f. 203r] finis huius prime partis anno domini .1435. in diuisionis apostolorum commemoratione.

Contains 1–152; folio numbers, range of contents, and date from the colophon are exactly those of the "Wien, Nat. cod. s.n. (acquired 1964)" listed in Stegmüller 6007,8. Missing sections added on ff. 203v–214v; cue found on f. 8r; folio numbers and marginal comments for missing sections (*sermo post quintum* and *sermo post uicesimum tertium*) are exactly those of the above manuscript [see Stegmüller 6007,10 and 6007,11].

Bibliography: Stegmüller 6007,8; Bartoš 1919; Molnár 1970, 154; Spunar 1995, 76–77 contains the full bibliography.

Binding: s. xv; brown leather over wooden boards; four raised bands; two metal clasps (broken); catches on upper board; black ink on front cover "prima pars" and possible former shelf number.

Owners & Provenance: B. Rosenthal (ca. 1967); Aleksander Janta-Połczyński (Alexander Janta; 1908–1974); acquired from Janta (Elmhurst, NY) by the university in November 1967.

Sales & Catalogues: B. Rosenthal, Cat. 19, no. 155.

Former Shelfmark: MS 27 (Notre Dame).

Bibliography: Corbett no. 27; Spunar 1995, 76.

cod. Lat. c. 2

Origin: Italy, s. xvi^{1}.
Content Overview: Gradual, use of the Franciscans [part 1].

In Latin, on parchment; ii +229 ff. +ii; generally 235 x 165 mm (page) [see Layout for ruling]; f. 224v blank but ruled; modern parchment flyleaves; medieval foliation in red ink with Roman numerals; modern foliation in modern pencil with Arabic numerals [see Foliation].

Collation: ii +1–18^{8} +19^{4+1} +20–29^{8} +ii

Quires: Quaternions, F/F, are the normal quire forms; quires 1–18, 20–29 obey Gregory's Rule. Quire 19 is a binion, F/F, with a singleton with stub added (f. 149); does not obey Gregory's Rule; quire 19 has been inserted into the manuscript after original foliation; script and decoration are consistent with the other quires.

Catchwords: Horizontal catchwords centered in the lower margins for quires 1–8 and 20–28; all correspond. The catchwords are stylized minimally with flourishes.

Foliation: Roman numerals in red ink on ff. 1–144 (ff. i–cxxxxiiii); ff. 145–149 in quire 19 lack Roman numerals; Roman numerals resume in red on ff. 150–229 (ff. cxxxxv–ccxxiiii). Arabic numerals are traced in the upper right corner in modern pencil throughout the manuscript. When folio references appear in rubrics, a different system of Roman numerals is used which does not always match the numeral of the folio (e.g., xc refers to f. lxxxx).

Layout:

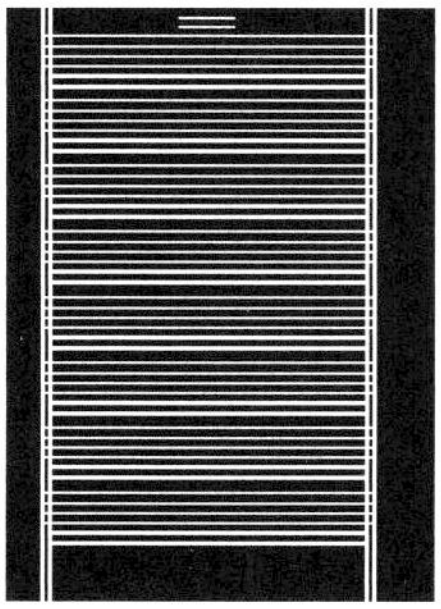

A

A ff. 1r–229v. Ink; 190 x 129 mm; 8 staves; 8 text lines.

Pattern A is traced on ff. 1r–229v; single column/full-music layout; eight four-line staves traced in red ink; each unit has one line of script beneath it ruled in light brown ink (upper and lower); ruling for folio number in light brown ink within the upper margin; double vertical bounding lines in red ink. Additional lines for rubrics and cues in smaller script are traced in light brown ink when necessary (e.g., ff. 9r, 101r, etc.).

Script: A single hand (M1) writes Southern Textualis Formata (Rotunda) of the sixteenth century in black and red ink. A contemporary hand (M2) has made a few corrections to the text, but not rubrics, in black ink.

Decoration:

I. Rubrication: Rubrics in red ink; most rubrication completed after the initials and decoration, yet some are the reverse; letter heightening of majuscules, cadels, and some rubrics in yellow and green ink.

II. Initials: Littera duplex style and flourished initials occur in hierarchy, but do not conform strictly to the normal types.

a. Littera duplex style initials (4 line square inset) on gold grounds with bianchi girari interiors are painted on ff. 1r, 19v, 30v, 150r, 169v, 182v, 184v; occasionally augmented with green; some marginal sprays and extensions form partial borders [see Borders & Frames].

b. Flourished initials (2 line square inset) in red and blue ink on gold grounds with bianchi girari interiors and contrasting penwork occur in correct color alternation; occasional floral sprays and extensions into the margins. Flourished initials (1 line versals) alternate in red and blue ink with contrasting penwork throughout the manuscript.

III. Borders & Frames: Floral and penwork borders in red, blue, gold, and green accompany the initials of 4 line size; borders are drawn in the outer, lower, or upper margin.

Music & Staves: Four-line staves in red ink; 12 mm; square neumes in black ink.

Contents:

1. Temporale—ff. 1r–113r; ff. 150r–229v.

First Sunday of Advent through Holy Saturday (ff. 1r–107v); Easter through the twenty-third Sunday after Pentecost (ff. 145r–224r). Litany (ff. 108r–111r) includes Bonaventure, Francis, Anthony, Bernadine, Catherine, Clare, Elizabeth. Francis begins with a majuscule heightened in yellow and green.

2. Ordinary Chants—ff. 113r–134v.

Settings for *Kyrie, Gloria, Sanctus, Benedictus, Agnus dei*, etc.; three settings of the *Credo* (ff. 129v–134v).

3. Sequences—ff. 134v–145v.

3.1. Christmas—ff. 134v–135v. RUB.: in natiuitate domini sequentia; INC.: letabundus exultet fidelis . . . [*AH* 54: no. 2].

3.2. Easter—ff. 135v–138r. RUB.: de resurrectione domini sequencia; INC.: surgit christus cum tropheo . . . dic maria quid uidisti . . . [*AH* 54: no. 230 *var.* p. 366].

3.3. Easter and Mary Magdalene—ff. 138r–139v. RUB.: de resurrectione domini et de maria magdalena; INC.: mane prima sabbati surgens dei filius nostra spes et gloria . . . [*AH* 54: no. 143].

3.4. Sundays in Easter—ff. 139v–140r. RUB.: tempore pascali in diebus dominicis sequentia; INC.: uictime pascali laudes immolent christiani . . . [*AH* 54: no. 7].

3.5. Holy Spirit—ff. 140v–142r. RUB.: [f. 140r] sequentia de spiritu sancto in die penthecostes et per octauam; INC.: sancti spiritus adsit nobis gratia . . . [*AH* 53: no. 70].

3.6. Holy Spirit—ff. 142r–143r. RUB.: alia sequentia de spiritu sancto; INC.: ueni sancte spiritus et emitte . . . [*AH* 39: no. 24].

3.7. Corpus Christi—ff. 143r–145v. RUB.: in festo corporis christi sequentia; INC.: lauda syon saluatorem lauda ducem . . . [*AH* 50: no. 385].

4. *Credo*—ff. 145v–147r.

5. Palm Sunday—ff. 147r–149v.

ANT.: cum appropinquaret dominus . . .; HYM.: gloria laus et honor tibi sit . . .; R.: ingrediente domino in sanctam ciuitatem . . .

BINDING: s. xix; bound in London by Ramage (John Ramage, 1836–1891); light brown leather; five bands; gilt spine and gilt border on turn-ins; gilt pages; gilt binder's stamp on front turn-in; identical binding to cod. Lat. c. 3.

OWNERS & PROVENANCE: Convent of the Annunciata in Ventimiglia (see cod. Lat. c. 3 for ownership marks); G. H. Tolson. The convent became an observant house, which was founded in 1509 (MOORMAN 1983, 504), but the years 1503 and 1509 are also attested (see G. ROSSI 1886, 189). Additionally, there was an earlier Franciscan foundation in Ventimiglia ca. 1230 and relocated ca. 1313 to another site (MOORMAN 1983, 504). Acquired from Les Enluminures (Chicago, IL) by the university in 2010.

SALES & CATALOGUES: Sotheby's, 11 July 1960, lot 122; ibid., 12 December 1966, lot 213; Christie's, 16 July 1969, lot 145.

cod. Lat. c. 3

Origin: Italy, s. xvi[1].
Content Overview: Gradual, use of the Franciscans [part 2].

In Latin, on parchment; ii +136 ff. +ii; generally 237 x 170 mm (page) [see Layout for ruling]; modern parchment flyleaves; medieval foliation in red ink with Roman numerals, and modern foliation in pencil with Arabic numerals.

Collation: ii +1–17^{8} +ii

Quires: Parchment quaternions, F/F, are the normal quire forms; all quires obey Gregory's Rule. The manuscript has been trimmed.

Catchwords: Horizontal catchwords written in black ink (f. 24v in red ink) are centered in the lower margins for quires 1, 3–16; all correspond. The catchwords are stylized minimally with flourishes; lines for catchwords ruled in light brown ink [see Layout].

Signatures: Signatures are also visible on the lower right corner of the rectos. Many have been trimmed.

Layout:

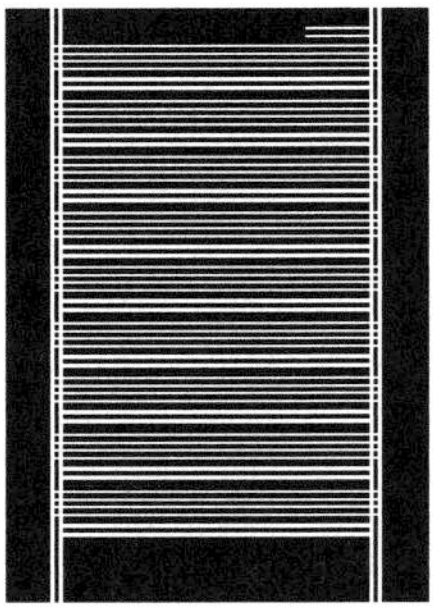

A

A ff. 1r–136v. Ink; 190 x 126 mm; 9 staves; 9 text lines.

Pattern A is traced on ff. 1r–136v; single column/full-music layout; nine four-line staves in red ink; each unit has one line of script beneath it ruled in light brown ink (upper and lower); ruling for folio number in light brown ink in upper right margin; lines for catchwords also ruled; double vertical bounding lines in red ink. Additional lines for rubrics and cues in smaller script are traced in light brown ink when necessary (e.g., ff. 42v, 43r, etc.).

Script: All text is written by a single hand M1 in Southern Textualis Formata (Rotunda) of the sixteenth century in black and red ink.

Decoration:

I. Rubrication: Rubrics in red ink; heightening of majuscules and cadels in yellow with green wash.

II. Initials: Littera duplex and flourished initials occur in hierarchy, but do not conform strictly to the normal types.

a. Littera duplex style initials (4 line square inset) on gold grounds with bianchi girari interiors occur on ff. 22v, 35r, 41r, 43r, 49v, 52v, 112v; occasionally augmented with green; some marginal sprays and extensions form partial borders [see Borders & Frames]. Littera duplex initials (2 line square insets) styled identically with marginal sprays occur throughout the manuscript (e.g., ff. 1r–18r).

b. One flourished initial (4 line square inset) in red with blue contrast is painted on gold ground with bianchi girari interior on f. 126v (*Mandatum*). Flourished initials (1 line versals) alternate in red and blue ink with contrasting penwork throughout the manuscript; occasional floral sprays into the margins.

III. Borders & Frames: Floral and penwork borders in red, blue, gold, and green accompany the initials of 4 line size; borders are drawn in the outer, lower, or upper margin. Piece borders are often formed by marginal sprays and extensions on all sizes of initials (e.g., f. 90v).

Music & Staves: Four-line staves in red ink; 10 mm; square neumes in black.

Contents:

1. Ordinary Chants—ff. 1r–18r.

Asperges (f. 1r); settings of the *Kyrie, Gloria, Sanctus, Benedictus, Agnus dei* (ff. 1r–14r); three settings of the *Credo* (f. 14r–18r).

2. Sanctorale—ff. 18r–52r.

Notable feasts include: Bernadine, Anthony, Transfiguration, Clare, Stigmata, and Francis.

Contains: Andrew (vigil and feast; ff. 18r–19r), Conception of the Virgin Mary (ff. 19r–20v), Lucia (f. 20v), Thomas (ff. 20v–21r), Silvester (f. 21r), Fabian and Sebastian (f. 21r), Agnes (f. 21r), Conversion of St. Paul (ff. 21r–22r), Agnes (f. 22r), Purification (ff. 22r–24r), Agatha (f. 24r–v),

Valentine (f. 25r–v), Chair of St. Peter (ff. 25v–27r), Gregory (f. 27r–v), Annunciation (ff. 27v–29r), Tiburtius and Maximus (f. 29r), George (f. 29r), Mark (f. 29r), Vitalis (f. 29r), Philip and James (ff. 29r–30r), Invention of the Holy Cross (ff. 30r–31r), Gordian and Epimachus (f. 31r), Bernardine (f. 31r–v), Anthony (ff. 31v–32v), John the Baptist (vigil and feast; ff. 32v–34v), John and Paul (f. 34v), Peter and Paul (vigil and feast; ff. 34v–35v), Commemoration of St. Paul (ff. 35v–36v), Octave of Peter and Paul (f. 36v), Mary Magdalene (f. 36v), St. Peter in Chains (ff. 36v–37r), Transfiguration (ff. 37r–38r), Laurence (vigil and feast; ff. 38v–40v), Clare (ff. 40v–41r), Hippolytus and companions (f. 41r), Assumption (ff. 41r–42r), Octave of Laurence (f. 42r–v), Agapitus (f. 42v), Louis (f. 42v), Timothy, Hippolytus and Simphorianus (f. 42v), Bartholomew (f. 42v), Augustine (f. 42v), Decollation of John the Baptist (ff. 42v–43r), Felix and Adauctus (f. 43r), Nativity of the Virgin Mary (ff. 43r–46r), Gorgonius (f. 46r), Protus and Hyacinthus (f. 46r), Exaltation of the Holy Cross (ff. 46r–47r), Stigmata (f. 47r–v), Nicomedes (f. 47v), Matthew (vigil and feast; f. 47v), Cosmas and Damian (f. 47v), Michael (ff. 47v–49v), Francis (ff. 49v–51r), Callistus (f. 51r), Luke (f. 51r), Simon and Jude (vigil and feast; f. 51r), All Saints (vigil and feast; f. 51r–v), Four Crowned Martyrs (f. 51v), Martin (f. 51v), Cecilia (f. 51v), and Clement (ff. 51v–52r).

3. Common of saints—ff. 52r–99r.

Rubrics divide the common as follows: an apostle (vigil; f. 52r–v), apostles (vigil; f. 52v), an apostle (ff. 52v–56v), a martyr and bishop (ff. 56v–57r), a martyr not a bishop (ff. 57r–62v), a martyr from Easter to Pentecost (f. 63r–v), martyrs from Easter to Pentecost (ff. 63v–64v), martyrs (ff. 64v–80r), a confessor and bishop (ff. 81r–88v), a confessor not a bishop (ff. 88v–90r), virgins (ff. 90r–99r).

4. Church dedication and other masses—ff. 99r–107v.

Church dedication (ff. 99r–110v), commemoration of the Virgin Mary from Advent to Christmas (ff. 100v–101v), Trinity (ff. 101v–103r), Holy Spirit/Pentecost (ff. 103r–105r), variant introit from Septuagesima to Easter (f. 105r–v), missa in agenda pro mortuis (ff. 105v–107v).

5. Sequences—ff. 108r–122r.

Sequences for the dead, the Purification, Annunciation, Anthony, John the Baptist, Clare, the Assumption, and Francis. The sequence for the dead (5.1) is followed by *Patrem omnipotentem factorem* (ff. 110r–111v), *Sanctus*, *Benedictus*, *Agnus dei*, and *Ite missa est* (ff. 111v–112r).

5.1. Dead—ff. 108r–110r. RUB.: [f. 107v] sequentia defunctorum; INC.: dies ire dies illa soluet . . . [*AH* 54: no. 178].

5.2. Purification—ff. 112v–114r. RUB.: [f. 112r] de domina; INC.: aue gratia plena dei genitrix uirgo . . .

5.3. Annunciation—ff. 114r–115v. RUB.: in annunciatione beate marie uirginis. sequentia; INC.: ab arce siderea lux descendit . . . [*AH* 8: no. 5].

5.4. Anthony—ff. 115v–117r. RUB.: in sancti antonii de padua ordinis minoris [*sic*]. sequentia; INC.: hodierne lux diei celebris . . . [*AH* 55: no. 72].

5.5. John the Baptist—ff. 117r–119r. RUB.: in sancti iohannis baptiste [*sic*]. sequentia; INC.: helisabeth zacharie magnum uirum . . . [*AH* 9: no. 240; *AH* 55: no. 185].
5.6. Clare—ff. 119r–120r. RUB.: in sancte clare uirginis [*sic*]. sequentia; INC.: letabundus clare cleri psallat chorus alleluya . . .
5.7. Assumption—ff. 120r–122r. RUB.: in assumptione beate marie uirginis. sequentia; INC.: aurea uirga prime matris . . . [*AH* 7: no. 107].
5.8. Sequences for Francis—ff. 122r–125v.
5.8.1. ff. 122r–124v. INC.: surgit uictor uirtualis hic franciscus . . . [*AH* 55: no. 133].
5.8.2. ff. 124v–125v. INC.: letabundus francisco decantet . . . [*AH* 55: no. 131].
5.8.3. ff. 125v–126v. INC.: corda pia inflammantur dum francisci celebrantur . . . [*AH* 34: no. 233].

6. *Ad Mandatum*—ff. 126v–132v.

INC.: [f. 126v] mandatum nouum do nobis ut diligatis . . .; EXPL.: . . . secula per infinita seculorum. amen.

7. Antiphons—ff. 132v–136v.

7.1. ff. 132v–133r. INC.: alma redemptoris mater . . . [*RH* 861].
7.2. f. 133r–v. INC.: aue regina celorum . . . [*RH* 2070].
7.3. f. 133v. INC.: regina celi letare . . . [*RH* 17170].
7.4. f. 134r. INC.: uirgo mater resurgentis . . . [*RH* 21829].
7.5. ff. 134r–135v. INC.: salue regina misericordie . . . [*RH* 18147].
7.6. ff. 135v–136. INC.: quam pulchra es . . . [*RH* 32196].
7.7. f. 136r–v. INC.: celorum candor splenduit . . . [*RH* 3589].
7.8. f. 136v. INC.: plange turba paupercula . . . [*AH* 52: no. 195, p. 179].

BINDING: s. xix; bound in London by Ramage (John Ramage, 1836–1891); light brown leather; five bands; gilt spine and border on turn-ins; gilt pages; gilt binder's stamp on front turn-in; identical binding to cod. Lat. c. 2.

OWNERS & PROVENANCE: Ownership marks of the convent of the Annunciata in Ventimiglia are written on ff. 1r and 55r; G. H. Tolson. The convent became an observant house, which was founded in 1509 (MOORMAN 1983, 504), but the years 1503 and 1509 are also attested (see G. ROSSI 1886, 189). Additionally, there was an earlier Franciscan foundation in Ventimiglia ca. 1230 and relocated ca. 1313 to another site (MOORMAN 1983, 504). Acquired from Les Enluminures (Chicago, IL) by the university in 2010.

SALES & CATALOGUES: Sotheby's, 11 July 1960, lot 122; ibid., 12 December 1966, lot 213; Christie's, 16 July 1969, lot 145.

cod. Lat. c. 4

Origin: France, s. xiii^{1}.
Content Overview: Peter Comestor, *Historia scholastica* [incomplete]; additional texts.

In Latin, on parchment; 116 ff.; generally 230 x 157 mm (page) [see Layout for ruling]; no flyleaves; pastedowns lifted; foliated in modern pencil with Arabic numerals.

Collation: 1–5^{8} +6–14^{8} +15^{4}

Quires: Parchment quaternions, H/H, are the normal quire forms. Quires 6 and 7 are quaternions which each contain a bifolium constructed of two singletons with stubs: the third bifolium of quire 6 (ff. 43/46), and the fourth bifolium of quire 7 (ff. 52/53). Quire 15 is a binion, H/H. The manuscript has been trimmed, resulting in the loss of some marginal glosses, prickings, and instructions to the rubricator.

Quire Marks: Quires 1, 3, and 8 have quire marks. Both quires 1 and 8 bear the *primus* mark.

Catchwords: Horizontal catchwords are visible in the lower right margins of quires 1–3, 5, 8, and 9; all catchwords correspond.

Layout:

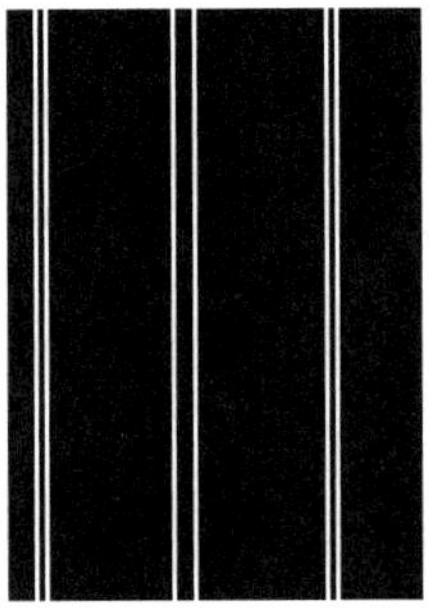
A1

A2

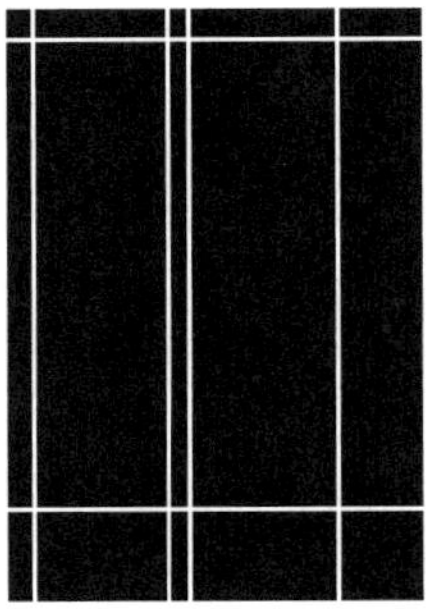
B

A ff. 1r–37v. Lead; 174–188 x 106 mm; intercol. 7–8 mm; 43–47 lines.
B ff. 38r–116v. Lead; 190 x 117 mm; intercol. 7–8 mm; 49 lines.

Pattern **A** is traced in lead with variable dimensions and number of lines on ff. 1r–37v; two columns (with insets); writing above top line (except ff. 4v and 5r; below top pricking on ff. 5v and 6r); prickings in upper and lower margins for vertical bounding lines; prickings for horizontals in the outer margin. **A** is a scholastic presentation often ruled for marginal glosses (**A2**), without clearly defined upper and lower through lines. The *Additiones* are written in inset columns of varying lengths traced in lead and red ink (e.g., ff. 1r, 2v, 3r, 4r, 5v, 6r, etc.). Pattern **B** is traced in lead on ff. 38r–116v; two columns; writing above top line. **B** uses single vertical bounding lines and horizontal through lines; the marginal rulings used in **A1** are not traced. Prickings in **B** are visible as in **A**; single prickings for vertical bounding lines begin on f. 41r.

SCRIPT: Several hands have written text and glosses. Three scribal bookhands (M1–M3) can be discerned conservatively based on letter forms and idiosyncrasies in tachygraphic abbreviations. All write Northern Textualis of the thirteenth century (s. xiii[1]) in black and brown ink. M1 writes the text of the *Historia* on ff. 1r^{a}–35v^{a}; M2 on ff. 35v^{b}–54r^{b} and 57r^{a}–116r^{a}; M3 on ff. 54r^{b}–56v^{b} and f. 116r^{a}–v^{b} (*ut uid.*). Both the front and rear paste-downs have been lifted, but the transfer left on the boards is the work of an earlier hand in a late Caroline minuscule.

DECORATION:

I. RUBRICATION: Rubrics in reddish orange and red ink throughout the manuscript; numerous instructions to the rubricator in black ink remain in all margins. Glosses in the margins often outlined in red ink; inset column partitions for the *Additiones* marked in red ink [see LAYOUT].

II. INITIALS: Plain initials (1–2 line square inset) in reddish orange and red ink begin the major divisions of texts. The initials retain vestiges of "Romanesque" design, and are not fully Gothic in appearance.

CONTENTS:

1. Peter Comestor, *Historia scholastica* [incomplete]—ff. 1r^{a}–54v^{b}, 57r^{a}–116v^{a}.

The text ends imperfectly in 2 Mcc at *PL* 198.1522. Many of the individual sections contain most of the *Additiones* as in the *PL*; when present, each *Additio* is incorporated into an inset column parallel to the text [see LAYOUT]. Additional texts are written between Dt and Ios [see CONTENTS 2]. Multiple sets of marginal (and some interlinear) glosses occur throughout the text.

EDITION: *PL* 198.1053–1522C; SYLWAN 2005 (Gn).
BIBLIOGRAPHY: SYLWAN 2005; STEGMÜLLER 6543–6565.

1.1. Prol.—f. 1r^{a}. INC.: imperatorie maiestatis est tres in palacio habere mansiones . . .; EXPL.: . . . prima planior secunda acutior tercia suauior [*Additio* 2] a fundamento loquendi sumemus principium . . . qui omnium princeps est et principium [*PL* 198.1053–1056; Sylwan 2005, 4–5].

1.2. Gn—ff. 1r[a]–27v[b]. rub.: de creatione empirei celi et quattuor elementorum; inc.: in principio erat uerbum et uerbum erat principium in quo et per quod pater creauit mundum . . .; expl.: . . . in hebron post translati sunt in sichem [*PL* 198.1055–1142; Sylwan 2005, 6–184].

1.3. Ex—ff. 27v[b]–41r[a]. rub.: hic terminata [*corr.*] istoria genesis explanatio exodi; inc.: hystoria exodi non alia quidem est a predicta sed eadem continuata . . .; expl.: . . . et dum stabat super tabernaculum et ipsi stabant eratque ignis in nocte [*PL* 198.1141–1104].

1.4. Lv—ff. 41r[a]–45v[a]. rub.: liber leuiticus; inc.: tercia distinctio historie quam scripsit moises . . .; expl.: . . . ne etiam digniorem aliis se putant [*sic*] in emptione eius rei quia eam dederat [*PL* 198.1193–1216].

1.5. Nm—ff. 45v[a]–51v[b]. rub.: liber numeri; inc.: quarta huius historie distinctio hebraice dicitur uaiedaber quod sonat et locutus est . . .; expl.: . . . set maneant ut a domino separate sunt [*PL* 198.1215–1248].

1.6. Dt—ff. 51v[b]–54v[b]. rub.: exposicio libri deuteronomii; inc.: quinta et ultima huius historie distinccio [*sic*] hebraice dicitur elledebarin . . .; expl.: . . . sicut ab illo loco ascendit moises usque ad hunc ferunt iosue apposuisse [*PL* 198.1247–1260].

1.7. Ios—ff. 57r[a]–59v[b]. rub.: incipit liber iosue; inc.: liber iosue a nomine auctoris censetur qui et ihesus dictus est . . .; expl.: . . . uno tantum superstite qui regnauit post eum [*PL* 198.1259–1272].

1.8. Idc—ff. 59v[b]–65r[b]. rub.: istoria iudicum; inc.: liber iudicum hebraice sophthim dicitur qui iudices describit usque ad heli sacerdotem . . .; expl.: . . . ideo /forte\ uidetur quod circa idem tempus utrumque factum fuerat [fuerit *ante corr.*] [*PL* 198.1271–1292].

1.9. Rt—f. 65r[b]–v[b]. rub.: de ruth; inc.: post samsonem iudicauit israel heli sacerdos . . .; expl.: . . . hic est pater ysai patris dauid [*PL* 198.1293–1296].

1.10. 1 Rg—ff. 65v[b]–73r[b]. rub.: de parentibus samuhelis; inc.: liber regum in quattuor uoluminibus distinguitur apud nos . . .; expl.: . . . alio modico tempore antequam olimpiades inciperent [*PL* 198.1295–1324].

1.11. 2 Rg—ff. 73r[b]–79r[b]. rub.: de planctu dauid super saul et ionatan; inc.: factum est post mortem saul adolescens fugiens de prelio uenit ad dauid in sicelec . . .; expl.: . . . decreuit dauid ut locus ille uocaretur area populi [*PL* 198.1323–1348].

1.12. 3 Rg—ff. 79r[b]–88v[b]. rub.: de unctione salomonis in regem; inc.: incipit secundum hebreos malachim quod sonat . . .; expl.: . . . qui prius albula dicebatur undecimus siluius agrippa [*PL* 198.1347–1386].

1.13. 4 Rg—ff. 88v[b]–98v[b]. rub.: de occhosia rege israel; inc.: porro ochozias filius aca[b>p] regnare cepit in samaria . . .; expl.: . . . uel quia regna quandoque sine rege fuerant [*PL* 198.1385–1432].

1.14. Tb—ff. 98v^{b}–101r^{a}. RUB.: istoria tobie; INC.: historia tobie exordium habuit in captiuitate decem tribuum . . .; EXPL.: . . . prosequentes altius ordiemur [*PL* 198.1431–1442].

1.15. Ez—f. 101r^{a}–v^{b}. RUB.: de ezechiele; INC.: ezechiel propheta de terra cisare fuit filius buzi de genere sacerdotum . . .; EXPL.: . . . ad uescendum sic quoque multis deficientibus uitam restituit [*PL* 198.1441–1446].

1.16. Dn—ff. 102r^{a}–107v^{a}. RUB.: de danyele; INC.: prophetauit et in caldea daniel qui secundum iosephum et epiphanium de semine regio fuit . . .; EXPL.: . . . porro sub cambise factum est quod in historia iudith legitur [*PL* 198.1447–1476].

1.17. Idt—ff. 107v^{a}–110r^{b}. RUB.: de iudith; INC.: hanc historiam transtulit ieronimus ad petitionem paule et eustochii de calde<o> in latinum . . .; EXPL.: . . . hic ab hebreis dicitur assuetus [*sic*] sub hoc isteria [*sic*] hester conscripta est [*PL* 198.1475–1490].

1.18. Est—ff. 110r^{b}–113r^{a}. RUB.: de hester; INC.: librum hester transtulit ieronimus ad petitionem paule et eustochii de hebreo in latinum . . .; EXPL.: . . . et adiudicauit antiocus facere peticionem eorum [*PL* 198.1489–1506].

1.19. 1 Mcc—ff. 113r^{a}–116r^{b}. RUB.: de macabeis; INC.: tunc multi iudeorum sponte quidam [*sic*] timore regis iussa secuti sunt; EXPL.: . . . et factus est princeps sacerdotum post patrem suum [-expliciunt historie regum] [*PL* 198.1505–1520].

1.20. 2 Mcc [incomplete]—f. 116r^{b}–v^{a}. INC.: secundus liber machabeorum non est historie profecto [*sic*] sed prosecute recapitulatio . . .; EXPL.: . . . due mulieres delate sunt natas [*sic*] suos circum<cidisse> [*PL* 198.1521–1522].

2. Additional Texts—ff. 54r^{b}–56v^{b}.

Texts not part of the *Historia scholastica* are written between Dt and Ics; each text begins with a plain initial (2 line square inset), except 2.7, an incomplete text on virginity, which follows the Passion of St. James (2.6) and is set off with a paraph mark like the other sections.

2.1. f. 54r^{b}–v^{b}. INC.: archa in qua continebantur federa domini scilicet tabula testamenti et urna aurea in qua erat manna . . .; EXPL.: . . . de sacramentis prosperat ad allegoriam inuenitur tractasse.

2.2. ff. 54v^{b}–55r^{a}. INC.: sciendum est ierusalem tribus uicibus fuisse destructam . . .; EXPL.: . . . et pro destructione illa dauid composuit ut quid deus repulisti in finem.

2.3. f. 55r^{a}. INC.: sciendum est quod tria sunt genera peccati peccatum uoluntatis peccatum operis peccatum consuetudinis . . .; EXPL.: . . . quia non habuisti tantam delectacionem in faciendo quantam amaritudinem in confitendo.

2.4. f. 55r^{a}–v^{a}. INC.: locutus est dominus ad moisen et aaron mensis iste sit principium omnium mensium . . . sciendum est fratres karissimi quod dum filii israel essent in egipto . . .; EXPL.: . . . determinare et comedere festinanter id est sine dubitatione.

2.5. ff. 55v^{a}–56v^{a}. INC.: nota est istoria a beato gregorio octo antiphonas conpositas . . .; EXPL.: . . . hoc peracto assummit de corpore sancto et ponit in calice silendo [cf. *PL* 77.896].

2.6. Passion of St. James—f. 56v^{a-b}. INC.: iacobus apostolus christi frater iohannis euangeliste predicauit omnem iudeam et samariam . . .; EXPL.: . . . hora cum apostolo martir effectus est [*BHL* 4057].

2.7. f. 56v^{b}. INC.: uirginitas quasi dicat [*ut. uid. post corr.*] partita est <pro>pria uiolentie . . .; EXPL.: . . . qua prouenit ex dei munere.

Binding: s. xiii (with some s. xx componants); tan leather over wooden boards; pastedowns lifted, but reverse transfer is visible on front and rear boards; remnants of strap on upper board; rebound and rebacked in 1988.

Owners & Provenance: The manuscript was likely acquired from Laurence Witten (New Haven, CT) by the university in 1962 (does not appear in Faye and Bond). Three lines of erased text in brown ink on f. 116v may have been a later ownership mark; "1449" is barely visible at the end of line three.

Sales & Catalogues: Laurence Witten, Cat. 5, no. 37.

Former Shelfmark: MS 13 (Notre Dame).

Bibliography: Corbett no. 13; D'Alverny 1981, 107.

cod. Lat. c. 5

Origin: Italy, s. xv^{2}.
Content Overview: Nicholas of Osimo [Nicolaus de Ausmo/Ausimo], *Supplementum summae pisanellae.*

In Latin, on parchment; i + 286 ff. +i; generally 229 x 159 mm (page) [see Layout for ruling]; foliated in modern pencil with Arabic numerals with errors [see Foliation]; flyleaves medieval parchment.

Collation: i +1$^{10-1}$ +2–28^{10} +29$^{8-1}$ +i

Quires: Parchment quinions, F/F, are the normal quire forms. Quire 1 lacks the first leaf (H/F). Quire 29 is a quaternion with the last leaf canceled (F/H). Parchment is well scraped but hairy in sections; likely sheepskin; all quires obey Gregory's Rule.

Catchwords: Vertical catchwords in the lower inner margins for quires 1–27; all correspond.

Foliation: Arabic numerals in modern pencil are misnumbered: 4 *bis* (= ff. 4, 4a); f. 202 is skipped (i.e., ff. 201, 203); flyleaf II foliated as f. 287; actual folio count is 286.

Layout:

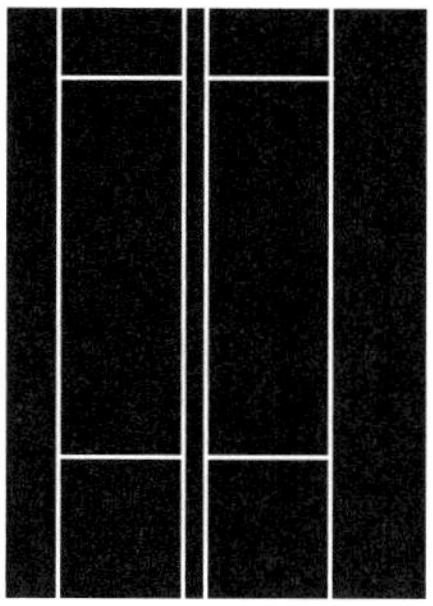

A

A ff. 1r–286v. Combined technique; 147 x 104 mm; intercol. 8.5 mm; 45 lines.

Pattern **A** is traced on ff. 1r–286v using a combined technique of lead and light black ink; lead often used for vertical bounding lines and ink for all horizontals; some instances have faded and appear as hard-point technique; two columns of text (intercol. 8.5 mm); writing below top line; prickings visible occasionally in upper and lower margins for the vertical bounding lines.

Script: A single hand (M1) writes the text and marginal additions in Southern Textualis Libraria (Rotunda); the rapidity at times admits a seemingly single compartment **a**. M1 uses Southern Textualis Formata (Rotunda) as a display script. Occasionally, M1 writes Hybrida Libraria (e.g., f. 118v) using the abbreviations of Rotunda in the margins.

Decoration:

I. Rubrication: Some marginal *tituli* in red ink (e.g., f. 267v); rubric and book references to *Digesta* also in red ink (ff. 285v–286v); paraph marks alternate in red and blue ink.

II. Initials: Flourished initials occur in hierarchy.

a. Flourished initials (1–8 lines square inset) in red and blue ink with contrasting penwork occur throughout the manuscript. Larger (4–8 lines) and better executed initials begin each section of the alphabet (one zoomorphic initial; f. 146v); medium-sized initials (3 lines) for each alphabetical item; 1 line versals in red ink with blue penwork, and red ink with brownish penwork alternate (A and B for each section, respectively).

Contents:

1. Nicholas of Osimo, *Supplementum summae pisanellae* [incomplete]—ff. 1r[a]–282r[b].

inc.: [f. 1r[a]] absoluere numquam tenetur homo reiterare nisi uelit immo etiam dicit thomas in quadam questione de quolibet quod non potest . . .; **expl.**: [f. 282r[b]] . . . . A. zelus etiam capitur pro feruore seu commotione diuine caritatis psalmo .lxuiij. zelus domus tue comedit me; **auth. colophon**: [f. 282r[b]] et hic zelus me fratrem nicolaum de ausmo ordinis minorum indignum pro aliquali simpliciorum subsidio ad huius supplementi compilationem excitauit quod fauente domino nostro yhsu christo excepta tabula capitulorum et abreuiaturarum et rubricarum expletum est apud locum nostrum sancte marie de angelis uulgariter sancti angeli nuncupatum millesimo quadrigentesimo uicesimo secundo nouembris uicesimo septimo die sabbati proxime ante aduentum hora quasi sexta et omnia que in eo [-acceperis] ac ceteris opusculis per me compilatis compilandisue incaute seu minus bene posita continentur peritorum et presertim sancte ecclesie submitto correctioni. finis.

Edition: Venice 1474.

Alphabetical index without folio numbers on ff. 282v[a]–285v[a]; alphabetical index of rubrics and book numbers of the *CIC*, and *Digesta* on ff. 285v[a]–286v[b]. A marginal gloss on f. 267v is attributed to Antoninus of Florence (Antonio Pierozzi, 1389–1459): RUB.: frater antoninus archiepiscopus florentinus; INC.: [f. 267v *in lae. marg.*] forte posset sic dici quod similiter potest retrahere dotem eius non curat . . .; EXPL.: . . . uel exponere licite lucris et multo magis si non habet alia unde uiuat.

Binding: s. xviii?; green morocco over pasteboards; gilt tooled; gilt edges; parchment endpapers; blind tooled turn-ins; present binding differs from earlier descriptions of a broken binding of brown leather over oak boards with gilt edges.

Owners & Provenance: Allegedly owned by Pope Leo X (Giovanni di Lorenzo de' Medici, 1475–1521) based on bookseller descriptions, though no evidence to support this provenance can be found in current state of the manuscript; Sir Edward Dering of Surrenden, Kent (1598–1644); Sir Robert Leicester Harmsworth (1870–1937); acquired from J. Rubinstein (Tucson, AZ) by the university in 1967.

Sales & Catalogues: Puttick and Simpson, 13 July 1865, lot 661; Puttick and Simpson, 6 December 1866, lot 106; Sotheby's, 22 July 1918, lot 531; Sotheby's, 15 October 1945, lot 2111; Gutekunst & Klipstein, 13 November 1947, lot 347; Sotheby's, 29 January 1951, lot 8; J. Rubinstein, Cat. 3, no. 56.

Former Shelfmark: MS 29 (Notre Dame).

Bibliography: Corbett no. 29; Emery, Jr. and L. Jordan 1998, 500–501.

cod. Lat. c. 6

Origin: Iberian Peninsula, s. xiii^{1} (ca. 1220 *ut uid.*).
Content Overview: Peter Riga, *Aurora.*

In Latin, on parchment; i +225 ff. +i; 238 x 143 mm generally (page) [see Layout for ruling]; foliated in modern ink and pencil multiple times [see Foliation]; flyleaves medieval parchment fragments of Justinian [see Contents 1].

Collation: i $+1–23^{8}$ $+24^{8+1}$ $+25^{14}$ $+26^{10}$ $+27^{12-4}$ +i

Quires: Parchment quaternions, H/H, are the normal quire forms, but irregular forms abound. Quires 4, 7, 8, 10, 16, and 19 are constructed quaternions in which the third bifolium is comprised of two singletons joined with their stubs. Quire 13 is a quaternion which does not obey Gregory's Rule; first two bifolia are constructed of singletons joined to singletons with stubs; f. 98 is added and disrupts Gregory's Rule. Quire 24 is a quaternion, F/F, with an added singleton with stub (f. 186). Quire 25 is comprised of seven bifolia, F/F, obeying Gregory's Rule. Quire 26 is a quinion, F/F, and does not obey Gregory's Rule. Quire 27 is a sexternion with the last four leaves canceled.

Catchwords: Quires 1–23 have horizontal catchwords in the far right margins; stylized in red ink; all correspond. Quires 23–24 have horizontal catchwords; not stylized; all correspond. Quires 25–26 have vertical catchwords; all correspond.

Foliation: Arabic numerals in brownish ink are occasionally visible (e.g., ff. 1–12; folio count on f. 225r); Arabic numerals in modern pencil subsequently corrected by transformation, strikethroughs, and erasures (three sets in total).

Layout:

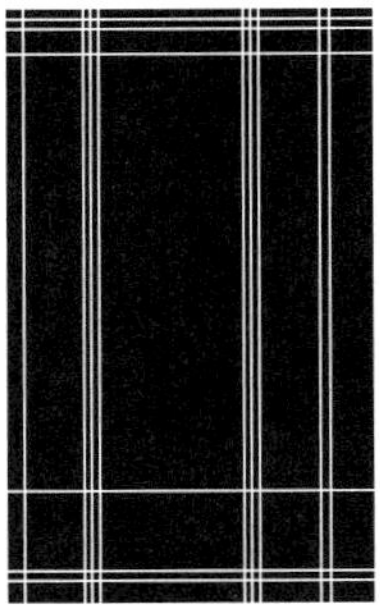

A

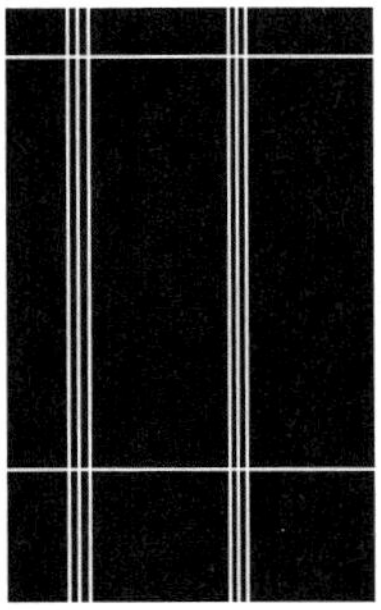

B

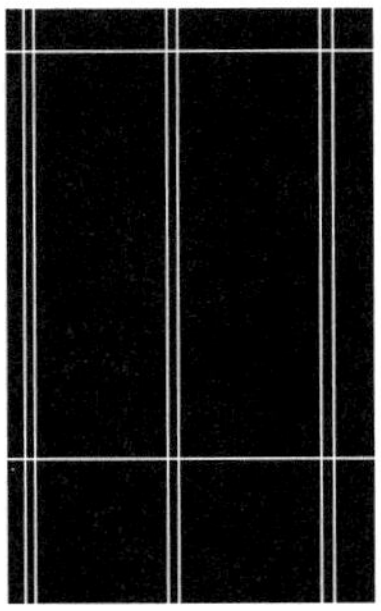

CD

A ff. 1r–96v, 99r–177r. Crayon; 172 x 70 mm; 39 lines.
B ff. 97r–98v. Lead; 165 x 70 mm; 39 lines.
C ff. 177v–184v. Lead; 159 x 116 mm; intercol. 4mm; 34 lines.
D ff. 185r–225r. Lead and crayon. 155–159 x 116 mm; 34–36 lines.

Pattern **A** is traced in brown crayon and occasionally lead on ff. 1r–96v and 99r–177r; single column of text; writing above top line; triple vertical bounding lines at left and right for initial and final letter of each line; additional verticals in the outer left (single) and right (double) margins; double horizontals for running titles in upper margin; superfluous double horizontals in lower margin; horizontals often ruled across entire page, typical of glossing formats. The pricking pattern for **A** presents clear prickings for all verticals and horizontals (unless trimmed). Pattern **B** is traced in lead on ff. 97r–98v for the inserted leaves [see Quires]; single column of text; writing below top line; triple vertical bounding lines similar to **A** and single horizontals; prickings visible for all verticals and horizontals. Pattern **C** is traced in lead on ff. 177v–184v; two columns of text (intercol. 4 mm); writing below top line; double vertical bounding lines and single horizontal through lines. Pattern **C** has the pricking pattern of **A** with additional prickings for the intercolumnium and outer verticals; intercolumnium holds initials for column two. Pattern **D** is traced in lead and brown crayon on ff. 185r–225r; two columns of text; writing below top line. **D** is traced identically to **C** but has its own pricking pattern; prickings visible for double vertical bounding lines and intercolumnium.

Script: Two scribal bookhands (M1–M2) copy the text of the *Aurora*. M1 writes a very bold Iberian Southern Textualis Libraria (early phase) using pregothic **a**, **i** longa in all positions, characteristic **t**, and uncial **d** exclusively; M1 may be Portuguese. M2 begins on the final line of f. 177r and writes all text in the two column configuration. M2 writes an Iberian Semitextualis Libraria admitting two compartment **a** occasionally, using trailing **s** at word end, and **9** (-**us** abbreviation) on the line.

Decoration:

I. Rubrication: Rubrics and book titles (in upper margin) in red ink; guide letters and instructions for the rubricator are often visible.

II. Initials: Littera duplex, flourished, and plain initials do not occur in hierarchy.

a. Flourished initials (and paraph marks) of various sizes and configurations (mostly 1–9 lines square insets; initials with descenders often stepped) in red and blue ink with contrasting penwork mostly alternate through ff. 1r–176v.

b. Various initials are drawn on ff. 177v–198r and 207v by a different painter: most are plain initials (2 line square inset) in red and black ink; some are transformed into littera duplex initials (e.g., ff. 185r, 188v) and some executed as such (e.g., f. 191v); others two colors only, lacking the blue for true littera duplex style (e.g., ff. 180r, 186v); others transformed into flourished types (e.g., f. 194r); faces drawn on ff. 177v, 182v, 185v, 187v; guide letter visible throughout the section.

Contents:

1. Justinian, *Digesta* with glosses [binding fragment]—flyleaves I–II.

Both flyleaves are cut from the same folio, of which the flesh side was the recto.

1.1. "Recto"—flyleaves IIv, Ir: inc.: . . . [IIv^{a}] [*Dig.* 34.1.16.pr.] moderati heredes eius respondit et heredibus eius teneri . . .; expl.: [Ir^{b}] [*Dig.* 34.1.18.1] . . . si conditio extitisset nichil proponitur [*sic*] /cur\ non possent [*Dig.* 34.1.18.2] ab.

1.2. "Verso"—flyleaves IIr, Iv: inc.: . . . [IIr^{a}] [*Dig.* 34.1.18.2] heredibus sticum manumitti uoluit eique si cum seio moraretur cibaria et uestiaria prestari uoluit a seio . . .; expl.: [Iv^{b}] [*Dig.* 34.20.pr.] . . . et libros legauit his quoque uiuis pre<st>abat dari.

2. Peter Riga, *Aurora*—ff. 1r–225v.

The manuscript contains the third medieval edition of the *Aurora*, with some of the accretions from the first redaction of Aegidius of Paris, *Lamentationes Ieremie*, *De agno paschali* (following Iob). Most of Aegidius's verses are copied sparsely in the margins by M3 and positioned in the text via *signes-de-renvoi* (e.g., ff. 2r, 4r, 89r).

Order of books: "Peter Riga's Preface" [Beichner 1965, 1:7–8]; Gn; Ex; Lv; Nm; Dt; Ios; Idc; Rt; 1–4 Rg (rubrics only for 1–2); Tb (without Misterium Tobie); Dn (no allegoria); Idt (no allegoria); Est (no allegoria); 1–2 Mcc (no prol.); "Interea salomon sapientie peritior omni" of Aegidius [Beichner 1965, 1:298–299]; Ct with the first preface of Aegidius; Iob; Mysterium de agno paschali; Recapitulationes; prol. to Gospels; Euangelium; Act (expl.: . . . hic finit liber et consumat linea metrum); "Peter, What is the World?" [Beichner 1965, 1:18].

Edition: Beichner 1965.

Bibliography: Beichner 1965; Stegmüller 6823–6825; Dinkova-Bruun 2007; Dinkova-Bruun 2011; Dinkova-Bruun 2012, esp. 185–189.

Binding: s. xvi; limp vellum (broken and detached).

Owners & Provenance: William Bragge (1823–1884); Francois-Jean Olivier (ca. 1886); William Morris (1834–1896). Date of acquisition by the university is unknown (prior to 1962).

Sales & Catalogues: Sotheby's, 7 June 1876, lot 38; F-J. Olivier, 30 March 1886, no. 672; Sotheby's, 5 December 1898, lot 862.

Former Shelfmarks: MS 8 (Notre Dame); Beichner cites the manuscript as MS 3, which corresponds neither to Corbett nor to De Ricci numbers.

Bibliography: Beichner 1956, 143 n. 29; Beichner 1965, 1:liv; Faye and Bond, 186, no. 8; Corbett no. 8; D'Alverny 1981, 107; Lapidge 2006, 32–33, 40 n. 72; Nolan 2006, 2.

cod. Lat. c. 7

Origin: England, s. xv^{2}.
Content Overview: Augustine, *Rectractationes* [II.4]; Augustine, *De doctrina christiana.*

In Latin, on parchment; iii +72 ff. +iii; generally 240 x 160 mm (page) [see Layout for ruling]; foliated in modern pencil with Arabic numerals; flyleaves blank.

Collation: iii $+1–9^{8}$ +iii

Quires: Parchment quaternions, F/F, comprise the manuscript. The parchment is stiff, extremely coarse, and well scraped; flesh sides and hair sides often indistinguishable in sections. All quires appear to obey Gregory's Rule. Quire 5 has sustained damage forming singletons and stubs; glued during subsequent binding, which has disturbed the original quire form.

Catchwords: Contemporary horizontal catchwords in the lower right margins for quires 1–8; most outlined in ink; all correspond.

Signatures: Signatures (a–i) are visible on rectos of the first four leaves of all quires; some have been trimmed partially or completely.

Layout:

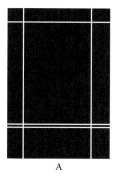

A

A ff. 1r–78v. Ink; 165 x 107 mm; 30 lines.

Pattern **A** is traced in black ink on ff. 1r–78v; single column; writing below top line; prickings visible in the upper and lower margins for single vertical bounding lines, and in the right margin for all horizontals.

SCRIPT: A single hand (M1) writes all the text in English Cursiva Formata of the fifteenth century which displays clearly the influence of European Cursiva on Anglicana, notably in the consistent use of single compartment **a** and in the forms of **d**, **g**, and the continental form of **r**. Shafts of ascenders do not have the marked bold bifurcation; Anglicana letter forms of **e**, **r**, and round **s** are used frequently. A mild influence of documentary script manifests itself in the exaggerated elongation of ascenders (e.g., f. 42v) and descenders (e.g., f. 42r), first and last line respectively (*litterae elongatae*). Anglicana Formata with two compartment **a** occurs occasionally as a display script (e.g., f. 49r).

DECORATION:

I. RUBRICATION: Rubrics, book numbers, and chapter numbers have been added in the margins and text in red ink; paraph marks and letter heightening of cadels and majuscules in red ink.

II. INITIALS: Initials of the dentelle and flourished types occur in hierarchy.

A. Dentelle initials (3 lines square inset) begin each of the four books on ff. 3r, 14r, 32v, 49r. The dentelles have red and blue backgrounds in contrast, rather than red and blue alternations; white penwork; marginal sprays in green and gold with vegetal and botanical elements.

B. Flourished initials (2 lines square inset) in blue ink with red penwork only occur throughout the manuscript, typical of English decoration.

III. LINE FILLERS: Rudimentary line fillers in black (e.g., f. 49r) and red ink (e.g., f. 3r).

CONTENTS:.

1. Augustine, *Rectractationes* [II.4]—f. 1r.

RUB.: augustinus [*in sup. marg.*]; INC.: [f. 1r] libros de doctrina christiana cum inperfectos comperissem perficere malui quam eis sic relictis ad alia retractanda transire . . .; EXPL.: [f. 1r] . . . in libro eius legitur quem de sacramentis siue de philosophia scripsit. hoc opus sic incipit.

EDITION: MUTZENBECHER 1984, 92–93.

2. Augustine, *De doctrina christiana*—ff. 1r–72r.

INC.: [f. 1r] sunt precepta quedam tractandarum scripturarum que studiosis . . .; EXPL.: [f. 72r] . . . aliis etiam laborare studenti quantulacumque potui facultate disserui. expliciunt quattuor libri de doctrina christiana secundum saunctum [*sic*] augustinum.

Prologue (ff. 1r–3r), Book 1 (ff. 3r–13v), Book 2 (ff. 14r–32v), Book 3 (ff. 32v–49r), Book 4 (ff. 49r–72r); four lines of text have been written on f. 72v, but are worn [see CONTENTS 3].

EDITION: MARTIN 1962, 1–167.

3. Erased text—f. 72v.

3.1. INC.: forma fauor populi feruor iuuenilis opesque surripuere tibi noscere quid sit homo [WALTHER, *Proverbia* 9745]
3.2. INC.: domine qui natus es de uirgine gloria tibi.
3.3. INC.: o mater quod fili peto te dulcissima baba [WALTHER, *Initia* 12762].
3.4. INC.: ihesus est amor meus.

All items have been erased, but are visible under ultraviolet light; a line between 3.2 and 3.3 is too obliterated to react under the ultraviolet light.

BINDING: s. xvii; English black velvet over wooden boards; sewn on four cords; metal furniture, clasp, and armorial; covers now detached; silk doublures with floral patterns.

OWNERS & PROVENANCE: Grosvenor (Westminster); acquired from Charles W. Traylen (Guildford, Surrey) by the university in March 1967.

SALES & CATALOGUES: Sotheby's, 11 July 1966, lot 231; C.W. Traylen, Cat. 66, no. 22.

FORMER SHELFMARK: MS 31 (Notre Dame).

BIBLIOGRAPHY: CORBETT no. 31.

cod. Lat. c. 8

Origin: Italy, s. xv^{ex}–xvi (Milan).
Content Overview: Rule of the Compagnia Ambrosiana (Ambrosian Society of Milan).

In Latin and Italian, on parchment; ii +63 ff. +i; generally 251 x183 mm (page) [see Layout for ruling]; parchment and paper flyleaves with one engraving [see Contents 14]; contemporary foliation and two sets of modern foliation [see Foliation].

Collation: ii +1–5^{8} +6$^{8-4+8+4}$ +7^{2} +8$^{8-3}$ +i

Quires: Parchment quaternions, F/F, are the normal quire forms. Quire 6 is irregularly structured: ff. 41–44 were gathered as a quaternion with the last four leaves canceled and then added to another quaternion (ff. 45–52); internal catchword on f. 44v corresponds to f. 45r; subsequently two bifolia, ff. 53/54 and 55/56, were inserted asymmetrically between the stubs of ff. 43/44 and 41/42; outer sides of quire 6 are F/H with insertions. Quire 7 is a bifolium, F/F. Quire 8 is a quaternion, F/H, with the last three leaves canceled; all quires obey Gregory's Rule except quire 6 where asymmetrical insertions cause disruptions.

Catchwords: Horizontal catchwords are written in the lower margins for quires 1–5; stylized; all correspond. A corresponding catchword in a different hand appears within quire 6 (f. 44v) to join the irregularly structured quire [see Quires].

Foliation: Original foliation with Roman numerals in red ink (running i–xlix) is centered in the upper margin of the rectos on ff. 3r–50r; foliation erased on ff. 59r, 60r, 61r, 62r. Two sets of modern foliation with Arabic numerals in pencil are present; the first set continues where the Roman numerals stop and includes rear flyleaves; the second set foliates all folios in the manuscript consecutively (ff. 1–63) and the flyleaves separately; the second set is referred to in this description.

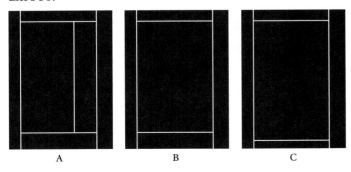

Layout:

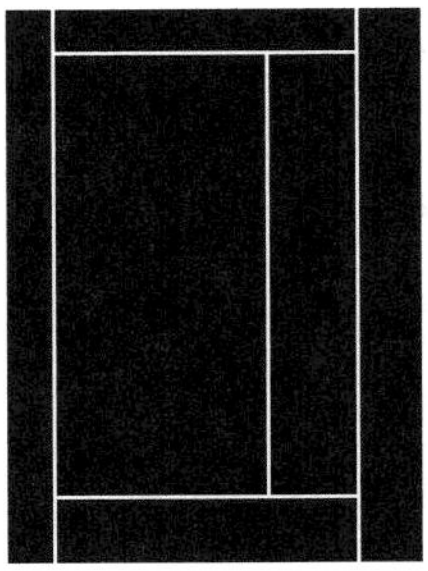
A

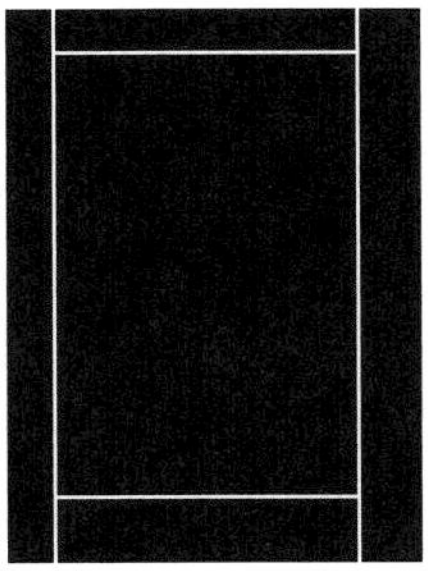
B

C

A f. 1r–v. Lead; 201 x 137 mm; cols. 100/35 mm; 31 lines.
B ff. 2r–55r, 59r–62v. Combined technique; 201–204 x 132–137 mm; 31 lines.
C ff. 55v–58v. Combined technique; 216 x 133 mm; 33 lines.

Pattern **B** is traced lightly in lead (verticals) and diluted brown ink (horizontals) on ff. 2r–55r and 59r–62v; single column; writing below top line; prickings occasionally visible for verticals. Pattern **A** modifies **B** with an additional vertical to create the table contents for the chapters [see Contents 1]; **A** is traced entirely in lead on f. 1r and partially on f. 1v. Pattern **C** is similarly traced in lead and ink on ff. 55v–58v; single column; writing below top line; prickings visible for verticals; f. 63r–v is not ruled.

Script: Three scribal book hands (M1–M3) of the end of the fifteenth and beginning of the sixteenth century write Southern Textualis (Rotunda). M1 writes ff. 1r–50r and 59r–62v and M2 writes ff. 50v–52v in Rotunda Formata. M3 writes ff. 53r–59r in a slender and more elongated Rotunda (M2 and M3 may be identical). Later additions in the upper margins on ff. 59r, 60r, and 62v by M4 in a clear sixteenth-century script in black ink; M5 adds the obit for Gio. Marco de Capponi in the lower margin of f. 62v in a minuscule (s. xvi) in brownish ink [see Contents 12]; M6 (s. xvi) adds Office section on f. 63r–v [see Contents 13]; autograph of Carlo Trivùlzio (1715–1789) on flyleaf IIIv.

Decoration:
I. Rubrication: Rubrics, paraph marks, and contemporary foliation in red ink.
II. Initials: Decorated, flourished, plain, and cadels initials occur loosely in hierarchy.
a. Decorated initial (2 line square inset); gold on blue grounds with white penwork and red marginal spray begins the first chapter on f. 2r; other decorated types (3–4 line square inset) in red with white and brown penwork and vegetal motifs on ff. 50v, 55v; a later initial (4 line square inset) in red on greenish grounds is painted on f. 53r.
b. Flourished initials (2–3 line square inset) are painted throughout the manuscript exclusively in red with brown penwork.
c. Plain initials (2 lines square inset) occur in red on ff. 45v–50r.
d. Cadels occasionally in red ink; a standing cadel with a face in red and brownish ink is drawn on f. 52v.
III. Borders & Frames: Miniatures on ff. 1v and 2r are enclosed in red frames with golden faceted motifs; frames outlined in blue (f. 1v) and green (f. 2r).

Miniatures: Nativity (f. 1v), 117 x 140 mm; the rule of the Compagnia is presented before St. Ambrose (f. 2r), 90 x 140 mm.

Contents:

1. Chapter List—f. 1r–v.

rub.: iesus de aue maria. infrascripte sono le ordinatione de le compagnie nostre ambrosiane. intitulate a le solemnitade de la madona; inc.: capitulo primo de la ordinatione de la regula nostra in folie .i. capitulo secundo . . .; expl. [f. 1v] . . . capitulo decimo octauo de commemoratione commemoranda fratribus siue sociis congregationis nostre huius ambrosiane in folie .xlviiij.

2. Gio. Marco de Capponi (compiler), rule for the Ambrosian Society—ff. 2r–50r.

rub.: capitulo primo de la ordinatione de la regula nostra ambrosiana; inc.: [f. 2r] nec arrogans uideri existimo si inter socios meos suscipiam affectum huius regule docendi . . .; expl. [f. 50r] . . . ut constat in predicta regula capituli rogationum instituit et confirmauit.

3. Ambrosian Litany—ff. 50v–52r.

rub.: letanie deuotissime domini nostri yhesu christi secundum morem ambrosianum; or.: [f. 52r] deus qui uoluisti pro redemptione mundi a iudeis filium tuum reprobari . . . confitemur peruenisse yhesum christum dominum nostrum. amen.

4. Indulgences—f. 52r.

4.1. rub.: [-papa iohanne a concesso atuti quilli che dirano la infrascripta oratione cum uno pater et una aue maria deuotamente su li cimiterrii che abiano tanti anni de plenaria induglentia quanti corpi morti sono et giaseno in quello cimiterio et atuti quili che la insegnarano ad altri o uero darano in scripto [-i] harano tri anni de indulgentia per ogni uolta chi li in signarano o uero darano in scripto]; inc.: auete anime chirsti fideles quorum [*sic*] corpora hic et ubique requiescit det . . .; expl.: . . . ut uobiscum associemur et in celis uobiscum coronemur. amen.

Rubric stricken in brown ink; the prayer is often attributed to John XII; cf. Leroquais 2:341.

4.2. rub.: [-oratio ista habet duodecim milia annorum per papam sixtum quartum]; inc.: aue sanctissima maria mater dei regina celi porta paradisi . . .; expl.: . . . libera me ab omni malo et ora pro peccato meo. amen.

Rubric stricken in brown ink as in 4.1; the prayer is attributed to Sixtus IV, and was to be recited before an image of *Maria in Sole*; also in Leroquais 1:299, 336; 2:29, 190; Luttikhuizen 2011, 209 n. 21 provides the full prayer, but gives no citation for the source of the text therein printed.

5. Various—f. 52v.

5.1. Meditational compilation—f. 52v. RUB.: in quid [*sic diuid.*] diuus bernardus; INC.: agnosce homo aspice et diligenter considera quid fuisti quid es et quid eris . . .; EXPL.: . . . cuius conceptus culpa nasci miseria mori angustia ergo deo serui.

5.2. Anonymous verses—f. 52v. RUB.: de miseria mundi; INC.: quid mundus ualet iste miser nihil utile cerno omne fugit spe pereunte perit . . .; EXPL.: . . . ergo animis mansura piis celumque petamus mentibus ex nostris stet procul omne fugax.

5.3. Epitaph of Frederick II—f. 52v. RUB.: fiderici imperatoris epitaphium super eius sepulcrum; INC.: tu qui transis ut mundum spernere possis hic lege et disce quam falax sit mundus iste . . .; EXPL.: namque in tali domo clauditur omnis homo ergo nouissima tua recordare uelis et in eternum non peccabis nec timorem mortis timebis.

See Deér 1959, 20–21; Corbett [1978], 184–185 provides a full transcription with errors: *guidve* (for *quidue* at line 14) and *extinctus* (for *extintus* at line 19).

5.4. f. 52v. RUB.: tabula ordinata per presbiterum iohannem marcum canonicum de caponibus.

Rubric only.

6. Iacobus de Voragine, *Legenda aurea* [cap. 55]—f. 53r.

INC.: [f. 53r] ambrosius dicitur ab ambra que est species ualde redolens et preciosa . . .; EXPL.: . . . esca [-i] angelorum per gloriosam fruitionem eius uitam scripsit paulinus nolanus episcopus ad augustinum ipponensem episcopum doctorem eminentissimum. explicit. hec de ethimologia nominis gloriosissimi [-i] patris nostri ambrosii.

De nomine section preceding chapter 55, *De Sancto Ambrosio*, in the *Legenda aurea.*

Edition: Maggioni 1998, 1:378.

7. Ps.-Ambrose, *Epistola* IV—ff. 53r–54v.

RUB.: epistola beatissimi doctoris ambrosii [-o] mediolanensis archiepiscopi de moribus et honesta uita; INC.: [f. 53r] dilecte fili dilige lacrimas et noli differre eas tanto esto prumptus [*sic*] ad [-i] lamenta . . . si non potest [*sic*] iram uitare saltem tempera . . .; EXPL.: [f. 54v] . . . uide quisquis hec legis ut [*sic*] [-i] quod legendo respicis uiuendo contemnas. deo gratias amen.

The text is also attributed to Isidore of Seville and Valerius Bergidensis.

Edition: *PL* 17.749–752.
Bibliography: Bloomfield no. 1655. *CPPM* 2: nos. 28b, 3006, 3431, 3482, 3541.

8. Commemoration of Ambrose—f. 54v.

RUB.: antiphona in commemoratione sanctissimi doctoris ambrosii; INC.: o clara lux fidelium ambrosi doctor inclite . . .; V.: ora pro nobis beatissime pater ambrosi; R.: ut digni efficiamur . . .; OR.: deus qui beatum ambrosium pontificem tuum . . . ut eius pia intercessione eterne felicitatis gloriam consequi mereamur. per christum dominum nostrum amen. RUB.: alia antiphona; INC.: o ambrosi doctor optime pastor et dux mediolanensium . . . et intercede pro salute omnium populorum.

9. Selections from Ambrose, *De officiis*—ff. 54v–55r.

RUB.: de ratione tacendi in primo de officiis; INC.: [f. 54v] rarum est tacere quemquam cum sibi loqui [-i] nihil prosit . . .; EXPL.: [f. 55r] . . . ita in adolescentibus uerecundia uelut [-i] quadam dote commendatur nature.

Selections mainly from Book 1 of Ambrose's *De officiis* are compiled and divided under the rubrics *de ratione tacendi*, *de elemosina*, and *de uerecundia adolescente*.

EDITION: cf. DAVIDSON 2002.

10. Disputation between Death and a Sinner—ff. 55v–59r.

RUB.: questa si e una disputatione che fa la morte con lo peccatore imprima parla la morte et dice; INC.: [f. 55v] io son per nome chiamata more ferischo ognuno achi tocha la sorte non ne homo cossi forte che da mi possa scampare . . .; EXPL. [f. 58v] . . . che si degna a uoy perdonare [f. 59r] ognia offesa a luy facta e la morte sempre contemplare a laude de iesu christo crucifixo. deo gratias amen.

EDITION: FINZI 1893, 171–177.

11. Commemorations—ff. 59r–62v.

Nativity, Stephen, John the apostle, Circumcision, Epiphany, Anthony abb., Purification, Matthias, Annunciation, Easter, Mark, Philip and James, Ascension, Pentecost, Corpus Christi, John the Baptist, Peter and Paul, Visitation, James, Christopher and Christine, Laurence, Assumption, Bernard, Bartholomew, Virgin Mary, Matthew, Michael, Jerome, Simon and Jude, All Saints, Martin, Catherine, ordination of Ambrose, and Thomas. Holy Innocents (f. 59r) and invention of the Holy Cross (f. 60r), and Andrew (f. 62v) added by M4 [see SCRIPT].

12. Obit for Giovanni Marco de Capponi—f. 62v.

INC.: die decimo septimo martii anno .1550. hora uigesima secunda qui fuit die lune obiit reuerendus dominus presbiter iohannes marcus de caponibus primus fundator huius societatis aetatis uero sue annorum nono***.

Text added by M5 [see SCRIPT]; according to the obituary, Giovanni Marco de Capponi, the founder of the Compagnia, died on March 17, 1550.

13. Office of St. Ambrose—f. 63r–v.

RUB.: orationes et responsus sancti ambrosii.

13.1. Matins—f. 63r. OR.: sancti ambrosii nos quesumus domine iugiter . . . pro nobis interuentione prestetur per dominum [*CO* 5324].

13.2. Prime—f. 63r. OR.: dominus mundi auctor et conditor qui hodierne . . . tue pietatis consequatur auxilium per dominun nostrum et cetera [*CO* 1270a].

13.3. Terce—f. 63r. OR.: creator et conditor omnium deus qui per sumum [*sic*] sacerdotem . . . intercedente sanctifica et congregationem istam benedicere dignari de celesti glorie tue regno per dominum nostrum [*CO* 853].

13.4. Sext—f. 63r–v. OR.: repleti sumus domine muneribus tuis . . . ut eorum emun*** effectu et muniamur auxilio per dominum nostrum et cetera [*CO* 5072].

13.5. None—f. 63v. OR.: exaudi domine preces nostras . . . ambrosii nos tuere ubique presidiis per dominum nostrum et cetera [*CO* 2473b].

13.6. Vespers—f. 63v. OR.: deus qui beatum ambrosium pontificem . . . quoque imitemur exempla per dominum nostrum et cetera [cf. *CO* 1444].

13.7. Compline—f. 63v. OR.: per huius domine operationem misterii . . . tuo ambrosio iusta desideria compleantur per dominum nostrum et cetera [cf. *CO* 5708].

The text is added by M6 [see SCRIPT]; all material is given in cue form except the *orationes* for each hour.

14. Engraving by Gerolomo Cattanio—flyleaf IIIr.

According to the provenance notes supplied by Carlo Trivulzio on the verso, the engraving was done by a "Gerolomo Cattanio" in 1753 based on a painting by Ambrogio Borgognone (1470s–1523/24).

15. *Documento santissimo con quello . . .* (fragmentary)—rear pastedown.

A fragmentary copy of a prayerbook, *Documento santissimo con quello che acquisitano quei figliuoli che osservano i Precetti d'ubbidire ai loro Padri e Madri*, printed by Giuseppe Magnaza, Milan, 1740 is affixed to the rear pastedown.

BINDING: s. xvi; calf over wooden boards; blind tooled; wormed; front and rear boards detached; previously rebacked using gilt spine.

OWNERS & PROVENANCE: Ownership mark of Santa Liberata on front pastedown; Trivùlzio-Trotti family; U. Hoepli(?) of Milan; G. A. Leavitt (sold 6 February 1888); bookplate of Alphonse Labitte (1853–?); William S. Semple (sold by Anderson Galleries Inc.); bookplate of Lenore (1899–1971) and James Marshall (1896–1986). According to CORBETT [1978], 189, the manuscript passed to B. Quaritch (1972), then to E. Pozzi of 'Libreria

Antiqua' (Milan), before it was acquired by the university from Pozzi in 1974. A similar manuscript is described as an autograph of Giovanni Marco de Capponi in the Biblioteca Silva in Cinisello Balsamo (see SILVA 1811, *Nota VI*, no. 57).

SALES & CATALOGUES: G. A. Leavitt & Co., 6 February 1888, lot 143; Anderson Galleries, 21 October 1926, Cat. 2087, lot 186.

FORMER SHELFMARK: N. 44 bis (Trivùlzio-Trotti); MS 42 (Notre Dame).

BIBLIOGRAPHY: NOVATI 1887, 177–178; CORBETT no. 42; D'ALVERNY 1981, 107.

cod. Lat. c. 9

Origin: Italy, s. xvi¹.
Content Overview: Francesco da Fiesso (Fiessi), *De uisitatione* with two prefaces by Giovanni Agostino Folperti.

In Latin, on paper; i +51 ff. +i; generally 274 x 198 mm (page) [see Layout for ruling]; flyleaves modern paper; ff. 50r–51v blank.

Collation: i +1^{10+1} +2–5^{10} +i

Bibliographical Format: 4°.

Quires: Paper quinions folded in quarto comprise the manuscript; f. 1 is a singleton pasted to f. 2; paper in good condition but water-damaged in the upper margin; occasionally wormed and trimmed.

Catchwords: Horizontal catchwords are written in the lower right margins for quires 1–4; all correspond [see Signatures].

Signatures: Signatures as catchwords occur in the lower right margins of the versos for the first half of quires 2–5 (ff. 3v, 4v, 5v, 6v only for quire 1); all correspond.

Watermarks: Thirteen occurrences of two different watermarks: (**A**) Bull's head; occurs in quires 1, 2, 3, and 5 (ff. 2/11, 4/9, 6/7, 15/18, 26/27, 42/51, 44/49, 45/47); no likeness remotely close can be found; approx. 56 x 21 mm; distance between chainlines 25 mm; bull's head, eyes only, above rod consisting of one line with above flower (5 petals). (**B**) Bull's head; occurs in quires 2–5 (ff. 14/19, 23/30, 24/29, 34/39, 36/37); no likeness remotely close can be found; approx. 54 x 23 mm; distance between chainlines 26 mm; same general parameters as **A** but a very different mark.

Layout:

A

A ff. 1r–51v. Hard-point; 190 x 125 mm; 23 lines.

Pattern **A** is frame-ruled using hard-point technique (not board); single column; writing above top line; indentations on rectos (f. 1 indentations on verso); likely ruled by the quire.

Script: A single hand (M1) writes all text in brownish ink using a cursive script of the sixteenth century informed by Humanistic cursive.

Decoration:
I. Rubrication: Rubrics with paraph marks are written in brownish ink.
II. Initials: Hanging capitals and cadels in brownish ink throughout the text; no insets.

Contents:

1. Giovanni Agostino Folperti, *Praefationes*—ff. 1v–5r.

Both prefaces contain dedications to Filippo Arrivabene, archbishop of Monemvasia (Malvasia, Μονεμβασία); the first preface is dated Cremona, 10 May 1529; second preface precedes that which usually circulates with the *De uisitatione* [see Contents 2.1].

1.1. First Preface—ff. 1v–2v. rub.: ad reuerendissimum d. d. ac patronum philipum ariuabenem archiepiscopum monouasiensem iohannis augustinus folpertus iuris utriusque doctor in tractatu uisitationis prefatio. inc.: que me potissimum ratio duxerit ut tibi hoc nostri qualiscumque operis dicarem reuerendissime domine ob illud precipue exponam . . .; expl.: . . . castigationem nullam omnino refugiamus eo magis appetamus tuam atque sedulo efflegitemus quo illam ex iuditio candidiore ex doctrina uberiore ex maiore tandem in nos beniuolentia procesuram existimamus. uale cremone sexto idus may millesimo quingentesimo uicesimo nono.

1.2. Second Preface—f. 3r–v. rub.: iohannis augustini folperti papiensis iuris consulti ad reuerendissimum d(ominum) philipum ariuabenem archiepiscopum monouasiensem super nouo uisitationis tractatu prefatio; INC.: intellectum tibi dabo et instruam te in uia hac qua gradieris ait dominus omnipotens per os prophete in libro psalmorum [Ps 31.8] intellectus igitur est munus diuinum seu benefitium ab illa summa luce perfluens . . .; EXPL.: . . . subditos uestros illuminatis et purgatis duxi humiliter destinandum ut lima correctionis uestre politum prodeat in publicum quod sine illa prodire non audet.

2. Francesco da Fiesso (Fiessi), *De uisitatione*—ff. 5r–49v.

The *De uisitatione* with this preface is found in two mid-fifteenth-century manuscripts: Paris, Bibliothèque nationale de France, MS lat. 738, and Modena, Biblioteca Estense Universitaria, alfa.v.10.14.

2.1. Preface—ff. 3v–5r. INC.: quam uero fuerit utilis quemque [*sic*] necessaria reuerendissime domine ad bene beateque uiuendum uisitationum institutio . . .; EXPL.: . . . que cum his libellus persenserit audax fiat quocumque proficisci tue reuerendissime dominationi [*sic*] numine tutus cui me comendo.

2.2. *De uisitatione*—ff. 5r–49v. INC.: antequam latiorem uisitationis materiam de uariis locis ac diuersis doctorum sententiis magno labore et studio collectam agrediar pauca de ipsius rei diuisione ac huius uoluminis ordine mihi uidentur esse tractanda . . .; EXPL.: . . . nam uelut in principio dixi huius libelli te censorem facio ut si quid in eo prefecitum [*sic*] fuerit addas si quid superfluum aut male compositum minuas uel emendas quod ut facias oro ne si quid erroris aut uitii remanserit tue possim ascribere culpe ualeat semper tua reuerendissima d(ominatio) cui meque plurimum comendo. finis deo gratias.

Binding: s. xx; white paper over modern binder's board.

Owners & Provenance: Giovanni Angelo Altemps (d. 1620); acquired by the university from Joseph Rubinstein (Tucson, AZ) in March 1967.

Sales & Catalogues: J. Rubinstein, Cat. 3, no. 27.

Former Shelfmark: MS 33 (Notre Dame).

Bibliography: Corbett no. 33; D'Alverny 1981, 107.

cod. Lat. c. 10

Origin: Italy, s. xvi[1].
Content Overview: Zanobi Acciaiuoli (tr.), *Olympiodorus, In Ecclesiasten* with *praefatio.*

In Latin, on paper with Greek and Latin marginalia; ii +64 ff. +ii; 282 x 202 mm (page) [see Layout for ruling]; f. 64 blank; foliated in modern pencil with Arabic numerals.

Collation: ii +1–6^{10} +7^{4} +ii

Bibliographical Format: 2°.

Quires: Six paper quinions and one binion folded in folio comprise the manuscript.

Quire Marks: Arabic numerals (1–6) used as quire marks are also written below the catchwords.

Catchwords: Vertical catchwords are written in the lower right margins of quires 1–6; all correspond.

Watermarks: Thirty-four occurrences of two different watermarks: (**A**) Fruit; occurs on flyleaves I and III; cf. Briquet 7386 (Florence, 1507); (**B**) eagle with crown; occurs in quires 1–7; cf. Piccard 42599 (Ravenna, 1500).

Layout:

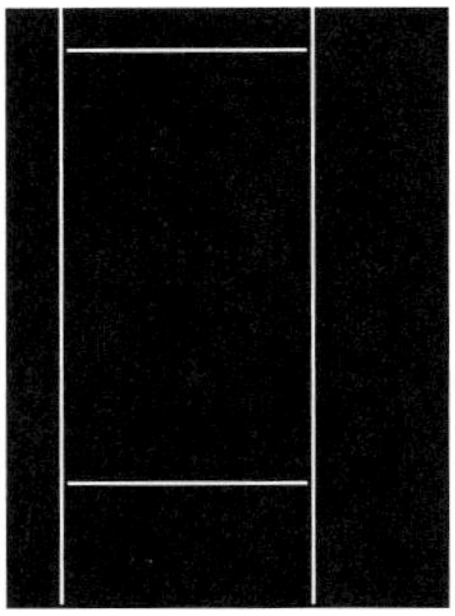

A

A ff. 1–64. Board-ruled; 204 x 115 mm; 30 lines.

Pattern A is ruled in hard-point throughout the entire manuscript; single column; writing below top line; indentations on recto. The intersections of verticals and horizontals appear to have very slight interruptions, suggesting the use of a ruling board.

Script: A single hand (M1) writes text and rubrics in Humanistic cursive in black and red ink. M1 also uses capitalis as a display script (e.g., f. 2r).

Decoration: No decoration is present other than rubrication in red ink. Spaces remain for square inset initials never drawn (2–4 lines).

Contents:

1. Zanobi Acciaiuoli, *Praefatio*—ff. 1r–2r.

rub.: fratris zenobii acciaioli ordinis praedicatorum praefatio in tralationem olympiodori super ecclesiasten salomonis ad reuerendum in christo presbiterem d. guglelmum brisonettum episcopum lodonensem [*sic*]; **inc.**: [f. 1r] <e>x litteris tuorum certior factus rem tibi non ingratam esse facturum siquis olympiodori graeca scholia in solomonis ecclesiasten latinitate donaret . . .; **expl.**: [f. 2r] . . . ut deum creatorem suum toto ex corde mente et anima diligendum suscipiat. uale.

Dedicated to Guillaume Briçonnet (ca. 1472–1534); Briçonnet became bishop of Lodève on 24 April 1489.

Edition: Rice 1972, 285–287.
Bibliography: Rice 1972, 283–287; Stegmüller 6164.

2. Zanobi Acciaiuoli (tr.), *Olympiodorus, Commentary on Ecclesiastes*—ff. 2r–63r.

rub.: olympiodori expositio in ecclesiasten salomonis argumentum primi capitis; **inc.**: [f. 2r] <r>erum certam cognitionem cum a deo salomon accepisset qui fuit filius . . .; **expl.**: [f. 63r] . . . cum quo et per quem deo patri est gloria sanctoque spiritui et nunc et in saecula saeculorum. amen. finis.

Edition: Paris 1512.
Bibliography: Stegmüller 6164.

Binding: s. xvi; tan sheepskin over wooden boards; blind tooled; scallop catches on lower board; two metal clasps on upper boards (one remaining); sewn on three double cords; binding is severely worn and partially detached.

Owners & Provenance: Hoepli (1931); acquired from J. Rubinstein (Tucson, AZ) by the university in March 1967.

Sales & Catalogues: Hoepli, 21 May 1931, no. 72; J. Rubinstein, Cat. 3, no. 58.

Former Shelfmarks: H. [*uix potest legi*] (on spine); MS 28 (Notre Dame).

Bibliography: Rice 1972, 283, 285–287; Corbett no. 28; D'Alverny 1981, 107; Iter 5:362.

cod. Lat. c. 11

Origin: Italy, s. xv^{2} (*post* 1463).
Content Overview: Pietro Perleone, *Vita Homeri*; Plutarch, *Vita Camilli* (tr. Ognibene da Lonigo); Angelo Decembrio, *Vergiliana Panegyris* on Carlos de Viana; Ps.-Plutarch, *Parallela minora* (tr. Guarino Veronese); William Heytesbury, *Termini naturales*; Albert of Saxony, *Tractatus proportionum*.

In Latin, on paper with a few marginal comments in Greek; i +39 ff. +i; generally 295 x 228 mm (page) [see Layout for ruling]; modern paper flyleaves; ff. 1, 13, 18v–20v, 35v–39r blank.

Collation: i +1^{12-1} +2^{6-2} +3^{6-1} +4^{2} +5^{12-1} +6^{6} +i

Bibliographical Format: 2°.

Quires: Quires do not have a uniform structure, but sexternions and ternions folded in folio are the predominant quire forms. Quires 1 and 5 are sexternions lacking a leaf; quires 2 and 3 are ternions lacking leaves; quire 4 is a bifolium glued to the outer reinforcement strip of quire 3; quire 6 is a ternion. Stubs are present where leaves are missing, but the manuscript has been rebound since it was broken [see Owners & Provenance]; heavy water damage throughout; wormed; no quire marks, catchwords, or signatures.

Foliation: Foliated in modern pencil with Arabic numerals in the upper right margin and lower inner margin. Foliation and numbering of quires in the gutter was done by J. S. Kebabian for H. P. Kraus in December 1966 (collation statement on rear pastedown); only f. 39v is paginated in black ink (p. 40).

Watermarks: Twenty-one occurrences of a single watermark: (A) Hat; occurs on ff. 2, 3, 5, 7, 8, 11, 13, 14, 17–18, 22–25, 29–30, and 34–35; cf. Briquet 3369 (Pesaro, 1455) and 3370 (Florence, 1465).

Layout:

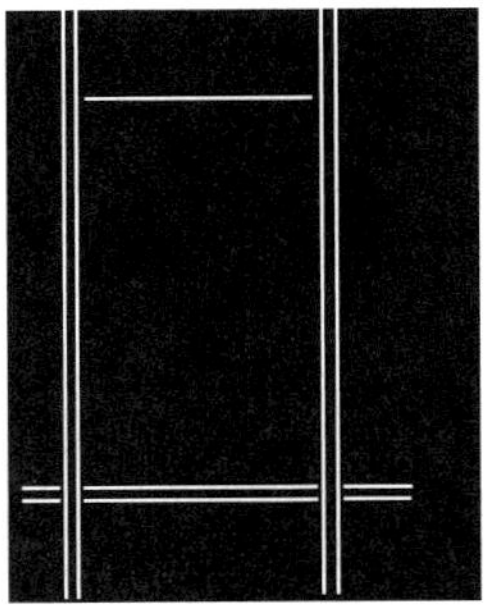

A

A ff. 1–37. Board-ruled; 160 x 115 mm; 30 lines.

Pattern **A** is board-ruled with indentations on the verso; single column; writing below top line. Interruptions at intersections of verticals and horizontals from the ruling board are visible; **A** is an inversion of Derolez no. 34 (though used in a paper manuscript here).

Script: A single hand (M1) of the fifteenth century writes all texts in Humanistic cursive in black ink and adds rubrics in red. M1 is also responsible for the minimal marginal scholia (both Latin and Greek) in black and red inks.

Decoration:

I. Rubrication: Rubrics and marginal *tituli* in red ink; two geometric shapes on f. 35r.

II. Initials: A plain initial (2 line square inset left, but initial is hanging) is drawn in red ink on f. 35r; spaces left for other 2 line square insets that are unfilled (e.g., f. 2r), and some filled using only one line (e.g., f. 29v). Smaller majuscule forms in red ink (1 line hanging) occur throughout the manuscript (e.g., ff. 21r–28v).

Diagrams: Two geometric diagrams are traced in lead then red and brown ink in the margins of f. 35r [see Contents 6].

Contents:

1. Pietro Perleone (Petrus Parleo), *Vita Homeri*—ff. 2r–10v.

rub.: uita homeri.

1.1. Dedication—ff. 2r–3r. inc.: <r>em profecto pulchram sed laboriosam inprimis atque difficilem a me petiisti ioannes uir praestantissime ut de uita homeri omnium maximi excelentissimique poete certi aliquid ad te perscriberem . . .; expl.: . . . sed iam ad rem nostram redeamus et eorum uideamus opiniones qui de homero quicquam scripserunt qua in re cum alios multos quos potui tum per plutrarchum in eo libro quem in primis nobis inmitandum proposuimus.

1.2. *Vita Homeri*—ff. 3r–10v. INC.: igitur ephorus cumaeus in eo [-eo] libro quem de patriis rebus inscripsit ostendit homerum fuisse cumaeum . . .; EXPL.: . . . si te ut de uita et genere ita et de doctrina quoque eius dubitare intellexissem quam summi excellentissimique uiri et graeci et latini omnes ut diuinam coluerunt semper ac uehementer sunt admirati. τέλος.

This life of Homer has been falsely ascribed to Pier Candido Decembrio. The false ascription seems to originate from Bandini's description of Firenze, Biblioteca Medicea Laurenziana, Plut. 63.30 (BANDINI 1774–1777, 2:702, col. 2); see HANKINS 1990, 2:415–417, esp. n. 4 and n. 5, which also include a list of other manuscripts of Perleone's *Life of Homer.*

BIBLIOGRAPHY: MOREL-FATIO 1896, 122–123; KRISTELLER 1985, 562 (appendix III to chap. 17); SUÁREZ-SOMONTE 1988; HANKINS 1990, 2:415–417.

2. Ognibene da Lonigo (tr.), *Plutarch, Vita Camilli*—ff. 11r–12v.

RUB.: fabii [*sic*] camilli uita; INC.: [f. 11r] nondum satis constitueram clarissime princeps hanc lucubratiunculam tibi tuoque uouendam nomini suspicere cum mihi subuereri uenit in mentem ne cui forte impudens ac temerarius esse uiderer . . .; EXPL.: [f. 12v] . . . causa et ratione carens que quidem naturale haberet initium terrorem incussit. nouus enim autumnus erat.

Dedicated to Gianfrancesco Gonzaga (ca. 1433).

EDITION: PADE 2007, 2:53–54
BIBLIOGRAPHY: CORTESI 1995, 151–156; CORTESI 1997, 441–444; PADE 2007, 1:229–230, 2:230.

3. Angelo Decembrio, *Vergiliana Panegyris* on Carlos of Viana—ff. 14r–18r.

RUB.: uirgiliana panaegyris angeli poetae mediolanensis ad diuum carolum aragonesium principem ex celicolarum ordine de eius natali felicissimo uita moribus morte exequiis mirabilis deificatione; INC.: [f. 14r] stirpis aragoniae regum pulcherrime princeps carole prima tui soboles genitoris honesta . . .; EXPL.: [f. 18r] . . . sic facias regnique tui quod nuper adeptus consortes maneatque tuum per secula nomen. τέλος. acta panaegeris; COLOPHON:[f. 18r] acta panaegeris hec caesarauguste primo assentientibus eiusdem ciuitatis citerioris hispaniae consulibus idibus maiis anni dominici .1463. iterum acta barcellonae senatus decreto et anno sequenti tibicine poetam comitante et iuniorum ordine feliciter.

EDITION: REEVE 1991a, 148–157.

4. Guarino Veronese (tr.), *Ps.-Plutarch, Parallela minora*—ff. 21r–29r.

RUB.: mutuae graecorum ac romanorum barbarorumque comparationes a plutarcho succintae descriptae et per guarinum ueronensem latine factae incipiunt; INC.: [f. 21r] complurimi sunt qui uetustissimas historias ob rerum gestarum admirationem fictiones et fabulamenta esse existiment . . .; EXPL.: [f. 29r] . . . ab quo declinatum preneste romani uocitant ut aristocles tertio rerum italicarum scriptum reliquit. expliciunt plutarchi comparationes. τέλος.

EDITION: BONANNO 2008, 75–92.
BIBLIOGRAPHY: CACCIATORE 2006; PACE 2006, 205–230.

5. William Heytesbury, *Termini naturales*—ff. 29v–34v.

RUB.: termini naturales burlei; INC.: [f. 29v] na [*sic*] natura est principium alicuius et causa motus et quietis eius in quo est . . .; EXPL.: [f. 34v] . . . corpus planum est tale cuius ultima superficies est plana non gerens ad sp(a/e)rcitatem [*sic*] ut tabula et de aliis. finiunt termini naturales burlei.

The text is attributed to Walter Burley in the rubric on f. 29v.

BIBLIOGRAPHY: WEISHEIPL 1968, esp. 198; WEISHEIPL 1969, esp. 212 and 216–217; TABARRONI 1984.

6. Albert of Saxony, *Tractatus proportionum*—f. 35r.

RUB.: albertutii sansoniani dialectici ac philosophi doctissimi de proportionbus libellus; INC.: [f. 35r] proportio communiter accepta est duorum comparatorum in aliquo uniuoco ad inuicem habitudo et dico uniuoco quia licet stilus sit actus et etiam uox dicatum acuta tamen quia acuties non dicitur . . .; EXPL.: [f. 35r] . . . proportio autem inrationalis non reperitur nisi in continuis et propter hoc arimetrica [*sic*] quem [*sic*] de numeris.

The text is incomplete, ending around section 36 (BUSARD 1971, 59); the end of the fragment is corrupt textually compared to Busard's edition; two geometric drawings in the margins [see DIAGRAMS].

EDITION: BUSARD 1971, 57–72; PARKER 1959; PATAR 2001, 1:97–98 for manuscripts and printed editions.

7. Spurious Ovidian quotation—f. 39v (p. 40).

INC.: omnia diuino cantauit carmine uates.

The line occurs in Benvenuto da Imola's commentary on Dante, and has been spuriously attributed to Ovid speaking of Vergil; cf. "omnia diuino monstrauit carmine uates," which occurs in Argum. VII (XIII).16 to *Georgics* III, also a spurius Ovidian attribution.

Bibliography: Rossi-Casè 1889; cf. Heyne 1819, 4617.

Binding: s. xx; green paper over cardboard; water-damaged.

Owners & Provenance: Acquired by Sir Thomas Phillipps (1792–1872) from Longman. The manuscript was separated sometime before auction at Sotheby's sale; H. P. Kraus (New York, NY) sold the current manuscript to the university in September 1967, and the first portion to the University of Kansas in 1968; now Lawrence, Univ. Kansas, Kenneth Spencer Research Library, Pryce MS P4 (see Iter 5:268).

Sales & Catalogues: Sotheby's, 29 November 1966, lot 67.

Former Shelfmarks: Phillipps MS 3542; MS 43 (Notre Dame).

Bibliography: Phillipps no. 3542; Munby 1:15, 4:189, 191, 205; Corbett no. 43; D'Alverny 1981, 107; Iter 4:230; 5:362; Pade 2007, 2:230; Bonanno 2008, 52–53.

cod. Lat. c. 12

Origin: Southern France, s. xiv^{2}.
Content Overview: Pontifical, neumed (incomplete).

In Latin, on parchment; ii +152 ff; generally 241 x 167 mm (page) [see Layout for ruling]; flyleaves i–ii are the medieval chapter list on parchment [see Contents 1].

Collation: ii +1–19^{8}

Quires: Parchment quaternions, F/F, comprise the manuscript; parchment is well scraped with few imperfections (e.g., ff. 35, 45, 52); an indeterminate number of folios are missing after quire 19; flyleaves are medieval parchment singletons.

Catchwords: Horizontal catchwords are centered in the lower margins for quires 1–9; stylized with grotesques and bestial figures in ink [see Decoration]; all correspond. Vertical catchwords in the inner margin are written for quires 10–19; vertical catchwords are stylized, but lack pen-and-ink drawings present in quires 1–9; all correspond, except that of quire 19 (f. 151v) since the manuscript ends imperfectly [see Quires]. The vertical catchwords suggest an Italian influence on the production of quires 10–19 [see Script].

Foliation: Medieval foliation in Roman numerals is centered in the upper margins; later foliated with Arabic numerals in modern pencil in the upper right margins; f. 142 numbered twice in medieval (cxlii) and modern foliation (f. 142 *bis*), now f. 142a; beginning of each quire numbered (1–19) in the lower inner margin with Arabic numerals in modern pencil.

Layout:

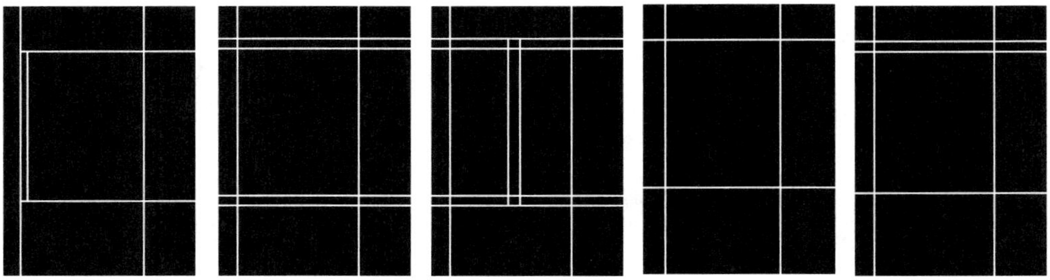

A B C D E

A flyleaves I–II. Purple and brown ink; 142 x 105 mm; 16 lines.
B ff. 1r–15v, 18v–74v, 79r–80r. Rose and purple ink; 143 x 103–105 mm; 16 lines.
C ff. 16r–18r. Rose and brown ink; 143 x 103–105 mm; intercol. 10 mm; 16 lines.
D ff. 75r–78v. Purple ink; 137–138 x 102 mm; 16 lines.
E ff. 81r–151v. Rose and brown ink; 142 x 105 mm; 16 lines.

Pattern **A** is traced in purple ink on flyleaves Ir–IIr (flyleaf IIv in brown ink); single column; writing below top line; prickings for vertical bounding and horizontal through lines visible in the upper, lower, and outer margin; an additional vertical is drawn to align the initial of each chapter. As a result of rapid execution in **A**, horizontals do not always extend to the far right edge of the page. Pattern **B** is traced in rose and purple ink on ff. 1r–80v (except ff. 16v–18r and 74r–78v); single column; writing below top line; prickings in the upper, lower, and outer margins, with double prickings for the first lower horizontal through line. Pattern **C** is traced in rose and brown ink on ff. 16r–18r (Litany), beginning partially on f. 16r (full pattern begins on f. 16v); two columns (intercol. 10 mm); writing below top line. Two verticals are traced in brown ink through the middle of **B** to form **C**; the added verticals are contained by the outermost horizontals. Pattern **D** is traced in purple ink on ff. 75r–76v; single column; writing below top line; single prickings visible in upper, lower, and outer margins. Pattern **E** is traced in rose and brown ink for quires 10–19 (ff. 81r–151v); single column; writing below top line; prickings as **D**.

Script: Two distinguishable scribal bookhands of the fourteenth century (M1–M2) write the text of the pontifical in Northern Textualis Formata. M1 and M2 can be distinguished by differences in letter forms (particularly **g**), but most notably by their graphs for Tironian **et** and abbreviations for **per**. M1 writes the text on ff. 1r–74v, and M2 on ff. 75r–151v. M1 and M2 write scripts under the influence of Southern Textualis (Rotunda), though M1 exhibits more Northern features, particularly a fuller usage of superfluous hairlines than M2. M2 exhibits more features of Rotunda including use of the characteristic a form alongside both Northern forms, and the use of figure-2 **r** in initial position. The shift in hands corresponds to the change in ruling [see Layout]; the shift to vertical catchwords, suggestive of Italian influence, can be associated with M2 [see Catchwords]. A third hand, M3, adds corrections and marginalia in Southern Textualis of the fourteenth century (e.g., ff. 14r, 19r).

Decoration: The manuscript features pen-and-ink illustrations around the horizontal catchwords used in quires 1–9 on ff. 8v, 16v, 24v, 32v, 40v, 48v, 56v, 64v, 72v; most are grotesques and bestial motifs. Cadels are similarly decorated with faces and grotesques [see Decoration II.d.]. Various forms of *maniculae* and faces used as *maniculae* often accompany the marginal rubrics *sine mitra* and *cum mitra*.

I. Rubrication: Rubrics in red ink; inflections for plural forms also written in red ink above the line; many cadels and majuscules heightened in red; paraph marks in red and blue ink mark chapter headings.

II. Initials: Littera duplex, flourished, and plain initials occur.

A. Littera duplex initials (3–6 line square inset) occur throughout quires 1–10: ff. 14r (6 lines), 16r, 30r (3 lines), 73r (4 lines).

B. Flourished initials (2–4 line square inset) in red and blue ink with contrasting penwork (red or brown) alternate through the manuscript. Chapters begin with the larger sizes; subsections begin with initials 2 lines in size.

C. Plain initials (1 line versals) alternate in red and blue ink mainly in the Litany (ff. 16r–18r), and occur sparsely in the rest of the manuscript.

D. Cadels (1–3 line square inset) in black ink occur within staves; most are decorated with pen-and-ink faces and grotesques and heightened in red ink.

III. Line Fillers: Line fillers in red ink occur in the table of contents (flyleaves I–II), and alternate in red and blue ink in the Litany (ff. 16r–18r).

Music & Staves: Four-line staves ruled in red ink; 14 mm; square neumes in black ink.

Contents:

1. Chapter List—flyleaves Ir–IIv.

RUB.: secuntur rubrice istius pontificatus [*sic*].

The list contains fifty-five chapters and at least 205 folios. The list functions similarly to Durand's prologue, which is lacking in this manuscript; the list of chapters does not match Durand's identically, but there is no additional material [see Contents 2].

2. Pontifical, neumed [incomplete]—ff. 1r–151v.

The pontifical is incomplete, ending imperfectly at II.iv.9 (f. 151v). The text included is that of William Durand's *Pontificale*, but significant sections have been omitted; reference to the *Speculum iudicale* on f. 44r. The *partes* used in Durand's division of the text are not indicated, nor is the prologue included. A list of chapters similar to those of the prologue appear on flyleaves Ir–IIv [see Contents 1]. Chapters omitted: I.iv (*de barba tondenda*), I.xvi (*missa in anniuersiario die consecratione episcopi*; listed in the contents on flyleaf Ir), I.xvii (*ordo romanus ad romanum pontificem ordinatum*), I.xx (*de confirmatione et benedictione regularis abbatis*), I.xxi (*de benedictione abbatisse*), I.xxii (*de ordinatione diaconisse*), I.xxiii (*de benedictione et consecratione uirginum*), I.xxiv (*de benedictione uidue*), I.xxv (*ordo romanus ad benedicendum regem uel reginam imperatorem uel imperatricem coronandos*), I.xxvi (*de benedictione et corronatione aliorum regum et reginarum*), I.xxvii (*de benedictione principis siue comitis palatini*), and I.xxviii (*de benedictione noui militis*). Localizable variants do not appear; Durand's text specifying Bourges is transmitted on ff. 47v and 68r. Greek and Latin alphabets written fully on f. 95r–v; the Greek alphabet contains the letters themselves, but omits the pronunciations. The saints appearing in the Litany (ff. 16r–18r) are virtually identical to those in Andrieu 1940, except Yleri and Lucia are omitted and Enimia is replaced with Eugenia.

Edition: Andrieu 1940.

2.1. I.i—ff. 1r–3v. INC.: pontifex pueros in fronte crismare uolens . . . in nostris constitutionibus synodalibus plenius continet [*sic*].

2.2. I.ii—f. 3v. RUB.: de psalmista faciendo; INC.: psalmista id est cantor . . . tondeat bene facit.

2.3 I.iii—ff. 3v–6r. RUB.: de clerico faciendo; INC.: primo notandum est quod quando fiunt ordines [*sic*] generales . . . deo placere studeant.

2.4. I.v—ff. 6r–7r. RUB.: de septem ordinibus clericorum; INC.: de septem ordinibus ecclesiasticis dicturi premictimus . . . prout sequitur seriatim.

2.5. I.vi—ff. 7v–9r. RUB.: [f. 7r] de ordin<ation>e hostiarii; INC.: factis tonsuris que fiunt . . . reddeunt [*sic*] ad sedes suas.

2.6. I.vii—ff. 9r–10v. RUB.: de ordinatione lectoris; INC.: hostiariis ordinatis pontifex accedit ad sedem suam . . . reddeant sedes suas.

2.7. I.viii—ff. 10v–12v. RUB.: de ordinatione exorciste; INC.: lectoribus ordinatis presul accedit ad sedem suam . . . reddeant sedes suas.

2.8. I.ix—ff. 12v–15r. RUB.: de ordinatione acoliti; INC.: exorcistis ordinatis presul accedit ad sedem suam . . . reddeant ad sedes suas.

2.9. I.x—f. 15r–v. RUB.: de sacris ordinibus; INC.: sacri et maiores ordines sunt sed subdyaconatus dyaconatus . . . et precedenti ieiunare.

2.10. I.xi—ff. 15v–21v. RUB.: de ordinatione subdiaconi; INC.: acholitis ordinatis pontifex ad sedem accedit . . . ministrauit dicat epistolam.

2.11. I.xii—ff. 21v–30r. RUB.: de ordinatione dyachoni; INC.: subdiachonibus ordinatis accedit pontifex ad sedendum . . . reddeant ad loca sua.

2.12. I.xiii—ff. 30r–42r. RUB.: de ordinatione presbiteri et cetera; INC.: dyachonibus ordinatis ponthifex ad sedendum accedit . . . uel piscina fundatur.

2.13. I.xiv—ff. 42r–69r. RUB.: de examinatione et ordinatione et consecatione [*sic*] epischopi; INC.: ad consecratione [*sic*] et ordinationem electi in episcopum . . . et consecrandi episcopos.

2.14. I.xv—ff. 69r–73r. RUB.: edictum quod metropolitanus tradit scriptum consecrato; INC.: dilecto nobis fratri coepiscopo ill. quoniam ut credimus . . . in gaudium domini tui.

2.15. I.xviii—ff. 73r–76r. RUB.: de manacho [*sic*] uel alio religioso faciendo; INC.: quando monachus uel alius religiosus sit . . . supra de clerico faciendo.

2.16. I.xix—ff. 76r–78v. RUB.: de professione nouitiorum; INC.: nouicius professionem facere uolens . . . in choro ultimus.

2.17. II.i—ff. 78v–83r. RUB.: sequitur de benedictione et impositione primarii lapidis in ecclesie fundatione; INC.: nemo hedificet ecclesiam priusquam episcopi . . . mentibus exequamur per dominum nostrum ihesum christum.

2.18. II.ii—ff. 83r–124v. RUB.: de ecclesie dedicatione; INC.: ecclesiarum consecrationes quamuis omni die fieri de iure . . . necessariam non esse.

2.19. II.iii—ff. 124v–150r. RUB.: de altaris consecratione que fit sine ecclesie dedicatione; INC.: quando altare solum et non ecclesia consecratur . . . meritis imploratur per dominum nostrum ihesum christum.

2.20. II.iv.1–9.2 [incomplete]—ff. 150r–151v. RUB.: de altaris portatilis consecratione; INC.: ad consecrandum tabulam siue altare . . . de oleo sancto cathecuminorum in eisdem <locis>.

Binding: s. xv; brown leather over boards (rebacked); four raised bands; blind tooled; brass bosses (later addition); two metal catches on upper board; metal clasps with leathers on lower board.

Owners & Provenance: Ownership mark of "Nostre Dame de Grace" (?) on f. 1r; Phillip J. Pirages (McMinnville, OR); John Windle (San Francisco, CA); acquired from Les Enluminures (Chicago, IL) by the university in September 2011.

Sales & Catalogues: Pirages, Cat. 53, no. 1; John Windle, Cat. 48, no. 3.

cod. Lat. c. 13

Origin: Spain, s. xiv.
Content Overview: Missal, neumed (incomplete).

In Latin, on parchment; 235 ff.; generally 271 x 192 mm (page) [see Layout for ruling]; three sets of foliation from different periods [see Foliation]; pastedowns lifted.

Collation: $1–8^{8} +9^{8-4} +10–12^{8} +13^{8-5} +13–21^{8} +22^{8-1} +23^{8} +24^{8-1} +25^{8-2} +26–27^{8} +28^{8-1} +29^{8} +30^{2+1} +31^{8} +32^{8-1}$

Quires: Parchment quaternions, F/F, comprise the manuscript. Quire 9 lacks the last four leaves. Quire 13 lacks five leaves. Quire 22 lacks the sixth leaf. Quire 24 lacks the first leaf (H/F). Quire 25 lacks the inner bifolium. Quire 28 lacks the third leaf. Quire 30, F/H, is a binion (ff. 218–219) with an added singleton (f. 220); the quaternion preceding quire 30 is missing (catchword on f. 217v does not correspond). Quire 32 lacks the eighth leaf (F/H). All complete quires obey Gregory's Rule. Parchment is torn and stained; modern conservation treatment and repairs are evident.

Catchwords: Horizontal catchwords appear in the lower margins for most quires; quires 13, 19, 30, and 32 are fragmentary and lack catchwords; all correspond except those at the end of quires 23 and 29; many catchwords are stylized with various motifs, grotesques, beasts, and faces.

Signatures: Signatures of the *ad hoc* type using Roman numerals remain in blue and red ink for most quires in the lower margins; some lost from trimming.

Foliation: Modern foliation is written with Arabic numerals in pencil in the upper right margin (ff. 2r–235r); early modern foliation with Roman numerals in the upper right corner in faded black ink on ff. 2r–226r (xlix–cclxxxvii); gaps accordingly with missing sections. A previous modern foliation with Arabic numerals in pencil appears on ff. 227r–235r (288–297).

LAYOUT:

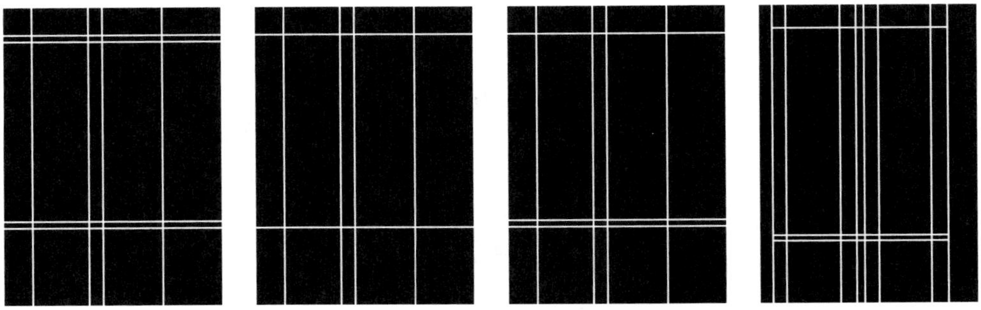

A1 A2 A3 B

A ff. 1r–218r, 221r–235v. Crayon; 176 x 114.5 mm; intercol. 11.5 mm; 30 lines.
B ff. 218r–219v. Crayon; 183 x 142 mm; intercol. 21 mm; 38 lines.

Pattern **A** is traced in brown crayon in various configurations with identical dimensions (**A1–A3**) throughout the manuscript; very faded in parts; two columns (intercol. 11.5 mm); writing below top line; prickings visible in the upper and lower margins for vertical bounding lines, intercolumnium, and occasionally in the outer margin for horizontal through lines. Pattern **B** is traced in brown crayon on ff. 218r–219v to create a multi-column (seven ruled, four used) lectionary index; writing below top line; prickings for verticals and intercolumnia visible in the upper and lower margins; f. 220r–v, which contains added material, displays the pricking pattern for **B**, but is used and ruled lightly for a two-column layout.

SCRIPT: The text of the missal is written in Southern Textualis Formata by two hands (M1–M2). M1 (ff. $1r^{a}$–$79v^{b}$, $96r^{a}$–$142v^{b}$, $221r^{a}$–$230r^{b}$) and M2 (ff. $79v^{b}$–$95v^{b}$, $143r^{a}$–$219v^{b}$, $230v^{a}$–$235v^{b}$) both display an Iberian treatment of letter forms, particularly **a** which does not have the distinctive form of Italian Rotunda. M2 exhibits a tendency for ligature, minims terminating *sine pedibus*, and overall displays a more Iberian presentation than M1. Additions for Corpus Christi [see CONTENTS 5] on f. $220r^{a}$–v^{b} are made by M3 in Southern Textualis; other additions [see CONTENTS 6] on f. $220v^{a-b}$ are written by M4 in Northern Textualis Formata.

DECORATION:

I. RUBRICATION: Rubrics in red ink; letter heightening of majuscules and cadels in yellow ink.

II. INITIALS: Littera duplex, flourished, and plain initials occur in hierarchy.

A. Littera duplex initials (3–5 lines square inset) mark major divisions and emphatic portions of the manuscript (e.g., ff. 93r, 96r, 102r, 143r).

B. Flourished initials (2 lines square inset) alternate in red and blue ink with contrasting penwork throughout the manuscript.

C. Plain initials (1 line versals) in red and blue ink alternate in hierarchy; plain initials (2 line square inset) in red ink only on f. 220r–v.

Music & Staves: Four-line staves traced in red ink (occasionally black); 11.5 mm; many staves are blank; neumes (post-medieval) added later in black ink to some staves.

Contents:

1. Temporale [incomplete]—ff. 1r^{a}–142v^{b}.

Begins imperfectly with Gospel reading for the fourth ferial day of Lent (inc.: . . . terre audite sapientiam salominis . . . [Mt 12.42–50]).

2. Sanctorale [incomplete]—ff. 143r^{a}–196v^{a}.

Contains: Andrew (ff. 143r^{a}–145r^{a}; vigil and feast), Nicholas (f. 145r^{a}), Damasus (f. 145r^{a-b}), Lucia (f. 145r^{b}–v^{a}), Thomas (ff. 145v^{a}–146r^{a}), Felix of Nola (f. 146r^{b}–v^{a}), Marcellus (ff. 146v^{b}–147r^{a}), Marius, Martha, Audifax, and Abachum (f. 147va), Fabian and Sebastian (ff. 147v^{a}–148v^{a}), Agnes (ff. 148v^{a}–149v^{a}), Vincent and Anastasius (f. 149v^{a-b}), Emerentiana (f. 149v^{b}), Conversion of St. Paul (ff. 149v^{a}–151r^{b}), Agnes (ff. 151r^{a}–152r^{a}), Purification (ff. 152r^{a}–154r^{b}), Agatha (f. 154r^{b}–v^{b}), Apollonia (f. 154v^{b}), Valentine (ff. 154v^{b}–155r^{b}), Chair of St. Peter (ff. 155r^{b}–156r^{a}), Matthew (f. 156r^{a}–v^{b}), Perpetua and Felicity (ff. 156v^{b}–157r^{a}), Forty Martyrs (f. 157r^{a}), Gregory (f. 157r^{a}–v^{b}), Benedict (ff. 157v^{b}–158r^{b}), Annunciation (ff. 158r^{b}–159r^{b}), Tiburtius, Valerian, and Maximus (f. 159v^{a-b}), George (ff. 159v^{b}–160r^{a}), Mark (f. 160r^{a}–v^{b}), Vitalis (ff. 160v^{b}–161r^{a}), Phillip and James (ff. 161r^{a}–162r^{a}), Invention of the Holy Cross (ff. 162r^{a}–163r^{b}), John (f. 163r^{b}), Apparition of St. Michael (f. 163r^{b}), Gordian and Epimachus (f. 163r^{b}–v^{b}), Nereus, Achilles, and Pancratius (ff. 163v^{b}–164r^{a}), Primus and Felician (f. 164r^{a-b}), Barnabas (f. 164r^{b}–v^{a}), Basilides, Quirinus, Nabor, and Nazarius (ff. 164v^{a}–165r^{a}), Anthony (f. 165r^{a}–v^{b}), Vitus and Modestus and Crescentia (f. 166r^{a}), Marcus and Marcellianus (f. 166r^{a-b}), Gervasius and Protasius (f. 166v^{a-b}), John the Baptist (vigil and nativity; ff. 166v^{b}–168v^{b}), John and Paul (ff. 168v^{b}–169r^{b}), Leo (f. 169v^{a}), Peter and Paul (vigil and feast; ff. 169v^{a}–171r^{b}), Commemoration of St. Paul (ff. 171r^{b}–172r^{b}), Processus and Martinianus (f. 172r^{b}–v^{a}), Octave of Peter and Paul (ff. 172v^{a}–173r^{a}), Seven Brothers, Rufina, and Secunda (f. 173r^{b}–v^{b}; incomplete), Mary Magdalene (f. 174r^{a-b}; incomplete), Apollinaris (f. 174r^{b}–v^{b}), James (ff. 174v^{b}–175r^{a}), Nazarius, Celsus, Victor, and Innocent (f. 175r^{b}–v^{a}), Felix, Simplicius, Faustinus, and Beatrice (f. 175v^{a-b}), Martha (f. 175v^{b}), Abdon and Sennen (ff. 175v^{b}–176r^{a}), St. Peter in Chains (ff. 176r^{b}–177r^{a}), Stephen (f. 177r^{a}–v^{b}), Invention of St. Stephen (f. 177v^{b}), Dominic (f. 177v^{b}), Sixtus, Felicissimus, and Agapitus (f. 178r^{a-b}), Donatus (f. 178r^{b}–v^{a}), Cyriacus, Largus, and Smaragdus (ff. 178v^{a}–179r^{a}), Laurence (vigil and feast; ff. 179r^{a}–180v^{a}), Tiburtius and Susanna (f. 180v^{a}), Hippolytus and companions (ff. 180v^{a}–181r^{a}), Assumption (vigil and feast; ff. 181r^{a}–182v^{a}), Octave of St. Laurence (f. 182v^{a-b}), Agapitus (ff. 182v^{b}–183r^{a}), Timothy, Hippolytus, and Symphorianus (f. 183r^{a-b}), Bartholomew (f. 183r^{b}–v^{b}), Augustine and prayer for Hermes (f. 183v^{b}; incomplete), Nativity of the Virgin Mary (f. 184r^{a}–v^{b}; incomplete), Gorgonius (ff. 184v^{b}–185r^{a}), Protus and Hyacinthus (f. 185r^{a-b}), Exaltation of the Holy Cross (ff. 185r^{b}–186r^{a}), Nicomedes (f. 186r^{a-b}), Lucia, Geminianus, and Eufemia (f. 186r^{b}–v^{a}), Matthew (vigil; ff. 186v^{a}–187r^{a}), Eustace and companions (f. 187r^{a-b}), Matthew (ff. 187r^{b}–188r^{a}), Maurice and companions (f. 188r^{a}), Cosmas and Damian (f. 188r^{a}–v^{a}), dedication of St. Michael's at Monte Gargano (ff. 188v^{a}–189r^{b}), Francis (ff. 189r^{b}–190r^{a}), Sergius and Bacchus (f. 190r^{a-b}), Denis, Rusticus, and Eleutherius (f. 190r^{a}–v^{a}), Callixtus (f. 190v^{a-b}), Luke (ff. 190v^{b}–191v^{b}), Chrysanthus and Daria

(f. 191v^{a-b}), Simon and Jude (vigil and feast; ff. 191v^{b}–192r^{b}), All Saints (vigil; ff. 192r^{b}–193r^{b}), All Saints and Caesarius of Africa (ff. 193r^{a}–194v^{a}), Four Crowned Martyrs (f. 194v^{a-b}), Theodore (ff. 194v^{b}–195r^{a}), Martin of Tours and Menas (f. 195r^{a-b}), Elizabeth (f. 195r^{b}–v^{a}), Cecilia (f. 195v^{a-b}), Clement and Felicity (ff. 195v^{a}–196r^{a}), Chrysogonus (f. 196r^{a}), and Katherine (f. 196r^{a}–v^{a}).

3. Common of saints [incomplete]—ff. 197r^{a}–217v^{b}.

Vigil for an apostle (f. 197r^{a}–v^{a}), vigil for apostles (f. 197v^{b}), apostle (f. 198v^{a-b}), apostles (ff. 198v^{b}–201r^{a}), martyr and bishop (ff. 201r^{a}–203v^{b}), martyr not a bishop (ff. 203v^{b}–204v^{a}), saint from Easter to Pentecost (ff. 204v^{a}–205r^{a}; incomplete), martyrs (ff. 205r^{a}–209v^{b}), confessor and bishop (ff. 209v^{b}–214r^{b}), confessor not a bishop with variants if abbot or doctor (ff. 214r^{b}–215v^{a}), virgins (ff. 215v^{a}–217v^{b}; incomplete).

4. Lectionary index—ff. 218r^{a}–219v^{b}.

5. Corpus Christi—f. 220r^{a}–v^{a}.

RUB.: incipit officium de sacrosancto corpore christi; INC.: [f. 230r^{a}] cibauit eos ex adipe frumenti . . .; EXPL. [f. 230v^{a}] . . . temporalis perceptio prefigurat qui uiuit.

6. Benedictions—f. 220v^{a-b}.

6.1. f. 220v^{a}. RUB.: ad sportam benedicendum; INC.: in nomine domini ihesu christi accipe sportam itineris tui . . .; EXPL.: . . . subfragiis eius merearis custodiam.

6.2. f. 220v^{a}. RUB.: benedictione baculi; INC.: in nomine domini ihesu christi accipe hunc baculum ad sustentationem tui itineris . . .; EXPL.: . . . et peracto cursu ad nos reuertaris cum gaudio per [Franz 1909, 2:280, no. 6].

6.3. f. 220v^{a-b}. RUB.: benedictio agni in festo pasche non in ecclesia sed in domo. benedictio agni; INC.: deus qui uniuerse carnis noe et filiis eius . . .; EXPL.: . . . et gratia tua repleantur in bonis per dominum nostrum ihesum christum.

6.4. f. 220v^{b}. RUB.: oratio; INC.: benedic domine creaturam istam panis sicut . . .; EXPL.: . . . quam anime recipiat sanitatem per christum dominum [Franz 1909, 1:248, no. 2].

7. Dedications—ff. 221r^{a}–222r^{b}.

Church dedication, anniversary of a church dedication, and dedication of an altar.

8. Votive and Requiem Masses [incomplete]—ff. 222r^{b}–235v^{b}.

Votive Masses: missa in honore sanctorum quorum corpora habentur (f. 222r^{b}); missa in honore sancte trinitatis (f. 222v^{a}); missa ad postulandam gratiam spiritus sancti (f. 222v^{a-b}); missa in honore sancte crucis (f. 222v^{b}); missa in honore beate marie uirginis (f. 223r^{a}); missa in honore angelorum (f. 223r^{a-b}); missa in honore apostolorum petri et pauli (f. 223r^{b}); missa ad poscenda suffragia sanctorum (f. 223v^{a}); alia missa ad poscenda suffragia sanctorum quam fecit dominus innocentius papa tercius (f. 223v^{a-b}); missa pro persecutoribus ecclesie (ff. 223v^{b}–224r^{a}); missa pro pace (f. 224r^{a}); missa pro papa (f. 224r^{a-b}); missa apostolica sede uacante (f. 224r^{b}–v^{a}); missa pro iter agentibus (f. 224v^{a-b}); missa pro infirmis (f. 224v^{a}); missa in anniuersario pontificis (ff. 224v^{b}–225r^{a}); missa pro seipso sacerdote (f. 225r^{a-b}); alia missa pro seipso sacerdote (f. 225r^{b}–v^{a}); alia missa pro seipso sacerdote (f. 225v^{a-b}); missa pro congregatione (ff. 225v^{b}–226r^{a}); missa pro omni gradu ecclesie (f. 226r^{a-b}); alia missa pro congregatione (f. 226r^{b}); alia missa pro congregatione (f. 226r^{b}–v^{b}); missa pro concordia fratrum (f. 226v^{b}); missa pro temptatione carnis (ff. 226v^{b}–227r^{a}); missa pro peccatis (f. 227r^{a-b}); alia missa pro peccatis (f. 227r^{a-b}), alia missa pro peccatis (f. 227r^{b}); missa pro remissione peccati (f. 227r^{b}–v^{a}); missa ad repellendas malas cogitationes (f. 227v^{a}); missa pro petitione lacrimarum (f. 227v^{b}); missa pro amico (ff. 227v^{b}–228r^{a}); alia missa pro amico (f. 228r^{a-b}); missa pro salute uiuorum (f. 228r^{b}); missa pro deuotis amicis (f. 228r^{b}–v^{a}); missa ad pluuiam postulandam (f. 228v^{a-b}); missa ad serenitatem poscendam (f. 228v^{b}); missa ad repellendas tempestates (ff. 228v^{b}–229r^{a}); missa generalis sancti augustini pro uiuis et defunctis (f. 229r^{a-b}); missa generalis (f. 229r^{b}–v^{b}); missa contra paganos (f. 229v^{b}); pro quacumque tribulatione (ff. 229v^{b}–230r^{a}); alia missa pro quacumque tribulatione (f. 230r^{a}); missa pro imperatore (f. 230r^{a-b}); missa pro rege (f. 230r^{b}–v^{a}); missa contra persecutores et male agentes (f. 230v^{a}); missa pro nimiis pressuris (ff. 230v^{b}–231r^{a}); missa in tempore belli (f. 231r^{a}); missa pro quacumque nessessitate (f. 231r^{b}); missa ad postulandam sanctam sapientiam (f. 231r^{b}–v^{a}); missa ad postulandam fidem et caritatem (f. 231v^{a}); missa ad postulandam humilitatem (f. 231v^{a-b}); missa ad postulandam caritatem (ff. 231v^{b}–232r^{a}); missa ad postulandam pacientiam (f. 232r^{a-b}); missa pro stabilitate loci (f. 232r^{a}); missa pro confitente peccata sua (f. 232r^{b}–v^{a}); missa pro inimicis (f. 232v^{a}); pro elemosinis [*sic*] nobis facientibus (f. 232v^{b}); missa pro amico in captione posito (f. 233r^{a}); missa pro nauigantibus (f. 233r^{a-b}); missa pro sterilitate terre (f. 233r^{b}); missa pro peste animalium (f. 233v^{a}); missa pro mortalitate hominum (f. 233v^{a-b}); missa pro infirmo qui proximus est morti (ff. 233v^{b}–234r^{a}).

Requiem Masses: in agenda defunctorum (f. 234r^{a}); in die depositionis defuncti (ff. 234r^{a}–235v^{b}); missa in die tercio septimo uel tricessimo depositionis defuncti (f. 235v^{b}; incomplete).

Binding: s. xiv–xv; calf over wooden boards; blind tooled; sewing on five double thongs; metal catches on lower board.

Owners & Provenance: Acquired from King Alfred's Notebook (Cayce, SC) by the university in November 2011.

cod. Lat. c. 14

Origin: Southern Germany or Austria, s. xiv^{1}.
Content Overview: Gradual.

In Latin, on parchment; 214 ff.; generally 220 x 163 mm (page) [see Layout for ruling]; multiple sets of medieval and modern foliation [see Foliation].

Collation: 1^{10} $+2^{10-2}$ $+3\text{–}14^{10}$ $+15^{8}$ $+16^{10}$ $+17^{8}$ $+18\text{–}21^{10}$ $+22^{4}$ $+23^{6}$

Quires: Parchment quinions are the predominant quire forms; all obey Gregory's Rule, however H/H and F/F quires occur. Quire 2 is irregular and lacks two leaves according to early foliation, though not a bifolium. Quires 15 and 17 are quaternions, F/F. Quire 22 is a binion. Quire 23 is a ternion. The manuscript has been disturbed by conservation efforts; parchment treatments and repairs apparent; parchment is thick and dirty.

Quire Marks: Roman numerals as ordinals are used for quires 17–22; a quire may be lacking between quires 17 and 18 (quire 18 signed as the nineteenth).

Catchwords: Horizontal catchwords occur for quires 1–16; often stylized; all correspond.

Foliation: Arabic numerals in modern pencil are written in the upper right margin of the entire manuscript, including the paper leaf (f. 120). Earlier foliation with Roman numerals in brownish ink is centered in the upper margin on ff. 1r–147r (i–cxlviiii); two missing folios between ff. 13 and 14 (xiii and xvi); Roman numerals in the upper margin on ff. 148r–156r (i–viiii); Arabic numerals in the upper right margin in black ink on ff. 165r–189r (1–125).

Layout

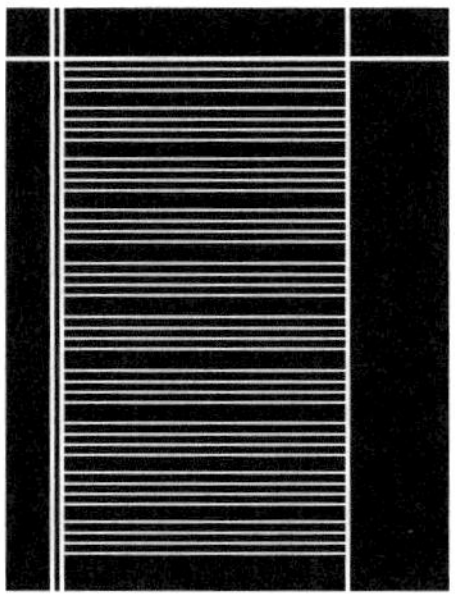

A

A ff. 1r–214v. Red ink and lead; 169 x 110 mm; 10 staves units.

Pattern **A** is traced on ff. 1r–214v in red ink, and lead is visible occasionally for the text line; single column/full-music layout; top line used as first staff; prickings visible in upper and lower margins for vertical bounding lines; ten groups of two prickings in the outer margin correspond to text lines; final set of prickings is doubled for endline.

Script: The majority of text is written by a single hand (M1) in Northern Textualis Libraria with Germanic features, particularly in the **a** form and avoidance of box-**a** on ff. 1r–164v, 205v–207v; execution becomes less rapid on ff. 165r–205v, and frequent use of box-**a** likely indicates a second hand (M2). A third hand (M3) adds sequences in a larger Northern Textualis with more pronounced quadrangles. A fourth hand (M4) adds ff. 210v–214v in a rapid Northern Textualis Libraria often admitting single compartment **a** in the manner of Semitextualis. A fifth hand (M5) adds the final *Alleluia* melody on f. 214v in Cursiva Libraria. Another hand (M6) writes Semitextualis Libraria on f. 156r in dark black ink. Additional hands (s. xv–xvi²) make additions, modifications, and corrections throughout the entire manuscript; front pastedown written in Northern Textualis Formata (s. xv) with Germanic features.

Decoration:

I. Rubrication: Rubrics and staves in red ink; rubrics often copied in backward configurations.

II. Initials: Littera duplex, flourished, and plain initials occur in hierarchy.

a. Littera duplex initials (2–5 stave units square inset) mark major liturgical divisions in the manuscript; the largest mark the first Sunday of Advent on f. 1r (5 stave units square inset) and Christmas on f. 12v (3 stave units square inset +2 units stepped); others (2–3 stave units square insets) occur on ff. 17v (with flourished border), 26v, 73v, 89v, 104r, 105v, 109r, 128v, 131r.

b. Flourished initials (1–2 stave units square inset) in red with red, blue, or brown penwork occur on ff. 15r, 31r, 38v (hanging i), 125v, 147r.

c. Plain initials (1–2 stave units square inset) in red are painted throughout the entire manuscript; plain initials in black ink (no inset) are drawn on top of the staves on ff. 207v–214v.

d. Cadel initials in black, red, and brown throughout the manuscript; most incorporate grotesques and other faces.

Music & Staves: Four-line staves traced in red ink; 10 mm; Hufnagel neumes in black ink throughout the manuscript; a typical stave unit incorporates four red lines and one line of text with approx. 7 mm between each unit. Added music on ff. 162v–163r uses five-line staves with Hufnagel neumes in brownish or black ink.

CONTENTS:

1. Temporale—ff. 1r–125v.

First Sunday of Advent through the twenty-third Sunday after Pentecost.

2. Sanctorale—ff. 125v–147r.

Primus and Felician (ff. 125v–126r), Marcellinus and Peter (f. 126r–v), Quirinus, Nazarius, and Nabor (ff. 126v–127r), Vitus and Modestus (f. 127r), Marcus and Marcellianus (f. 127r–v), Gervasius and Protasius (f. 127v), John the Baptist (vigil and feast; ff. 127v–129r), John and Paul (ff. 129r–130r), Peter (vigil and feast; ff. 130r–132r), Conversion of St. Paul (ff. 132r–133r), Processus and Martinianus (f. 133r–v), Seven Brothers (f. 134r), translation of Nicholas (f. 134r), translation of Benedict (f. 134r), Margaret (f. 134r), Mary Magdalene (f. 134v), Apollinaris (f. 134v), Felix, Simplicius, and Faustinius (ff. 134v–135r), Stephen (f. 135v), Sixtus (f. 135v), Affra (f. 136r), Cyriacus and companions (f. 136r–v), Laurence (vigil and feast; ff. 136v–138r), Tiburtius (f. 138r–v), Hippolytus and companions (f. 138v), Eusebius (f. 139r), Assumption (f. 139r–v), Octave of Laurence (ff. 139v–140r), Timothy and Symphorianus (f. 140r), Agapitus (f. 140r), Bartholomew (f. 140r), Hermes (f. 140r–v), Augustine (f. 140v), Sabina (ff. 140v–141r), Decollation of John the Baptist (f. 141r), Giles (f. 141r), Felix and Adauctus (f. 141r–v), Nativity of the Virgin Mary (f. 141v), Gorgonius (ff. 141v–142r), Protus and Hyacinthus (f. 142r), Exaltation of the Holy Cross (f. 142r), Cornelius and Cyprianus (f. 142r), Nicomedes (f. 142r), Eufemia (f. 142r), Matthew (vigil and feast; f. 142r), Maurice and companions (f. 142v), Cosmas and Damian (f. 142v), Michael (ff. 142v–143v), Jerome (f. 143v), Remigius (f. 143v), Marcus (f. 143v), Denis and companions (f. 143v), 11,000 Virgins (ff. 143v–144r), Simon and Jude (vigil and feast; f. 144r), All Saints (vigil and feast; f. 144r), Four Crowned Martyrs (f. 144r), Theodore (f. 144v), Menas (f. 144v), Martin (f. 144v), Cecilia (f. 144v), Clement (ff. 144v–145r), Chrysogonus (f. 145r), Andrew (vigil and feast; ff. 145r–146r), Trinity Sunday (ff. 146r–147r).

3. Church dedication—ff. 147r–148r.

4. Office of the Virgin—ff. 148r–150r.

5. Common of saints (Alleluia melodies and verses)—ff. 150r–154r.

Alleluia melodies: apostles (f. 150r), martyrs (f. 151r), a martyr (f. 152r), confessors (f. 152v), virgins (f. 153r), and evangelists (f. 154r).

6. Alleluia melodies and verses—ff. 154r–156r.

6.1. f. 154r. INC.: aeuia. sancta dei genitrix uirgo semper . . .

6.2. f. 154v. INC.: alleluia [natiuitas /concepcio\ gloriose uirginis marie ex semine abrahe orta de tri<bu>. *add.*] aeuia. felix es sacra uirgo maria et omni laude . . .

6.3. f. 155r. RUB.: katherine uirginis; INC.: aeuia. beata uirgo katherina tu a prece uos . . .

6.4. f. 155r. RUB.: elizabeht; INC.: aeuia. o pia regum filia felix alumpna pauperima . . .

6.5. f. 155r–v. INC.: aeuia. gaudete syon filie pastor reduxit hodie . . . [*RH* 7161].
6.6. f. 155v. INC.: aeuia. imperatrix egregia ihesu mater . . .
6.7. ff. 155v–156r. INC.: aeuia. o maria rubens rosa delicatum . . . [*RH* 13217].
6.8. ff. 156r. INC.: aeuia. filii syon letamini et exultate . . .

7. Ordinary chants—ff. 156v–164v.

Later additions of five-line staves in black ink with Hufnagel neumes on ff. 162v–163r.

8. Sequences—ff. 165r–207v.

8.1. Christmas—f. 165r. INC.: grates nunc omnes reddamus domino deo qui sua natiuitate nos liberauit de dyabolica potestate . . . [*AH* 53: no. 10].
8.2. ff. 165r–166v. INC.: eya recolamus laudibus piis digna . . . [*AH* 53: no. 16].
8.3. f. 166r–v. RUB.: ad publicam missam; INC.: natus ante secula dei filius inuisibilis interminus . . . [*AH* 53: no. 15].
8.4. Stephen—ff. 166v–167r. RUB.: stephano de sancto [*sic*]; INC.: hanc concordi famulatu colamus sollempnitatem . . . [*AH* 53: no. 215].
8.5. John—ff. 167r–168r. RUB.: iohanne de sancto [*sic*]; INC.: iohannes ihesu christo multum dilecte uirgo . . . [*AH* 53: no. 168].
8.6. Holy Innocents—f. 168r–v. RUB.: de innocentibus; INC.: laus tibi criste patris optimi nate deus omnipotencie . . . [*AH* 53: no. 157].
8.7. Epiphany—ff. 168v–169v. RUB.: nie domini in epipha [*sic*]; INC.: festa christi omnis cristianitas celebret . . . [*AH* 53: no. 29].
8.8. Octave—ff. 169v–170r. RUB.: domini taua in oc [*sic*]; INC.: letabundus exultet fidelis chorus alleluia . . . [*AH* 54: no. 2].
8.9. Conversion of St. Paul—ff. 170r–171r. RUB.: in conuersione sancti pauli; INC.: dixit dominus ex basan conuertam conuertam in profundum maris quod dixit . . . [*AH* 50: no. 269].
8.10. Purification—ff. 171r–172v. RUB.: sancte marie in purificatione [*sic*]; INC.: concentu parili hic te maria ueneratur populus . . . [*AH* 53: no. 99].
8.11. Easter—ff. 172v–174r. RUB.: in die sancto; INC.: laudes saluatori uoce modulemur supplici . . . [*AH* 53: no. 36].
8.12. Easter—ff. 174r–175r. RUB.: feria secunda; INC.: pangamus creatori atque redemptori gloriam . . . [*AH* 53: no. 46].
8.13. Easter—f. 175r–v. INC.: agni pascalis esu potuque dignas . . . [*AH* 53: no. 50].
8.14. Easter—ff. 175v–176r. RUB.: in octaua pasce; INC.: uictime paschali laudes ymmolent christiani . . . [*AH* 54: no. 7].
8.15. Ascension—ff. 176r–177r. RUB.: in asscensione domini; INC.: summi [*sic*] triumphum regis prosequamur laude . . . [*AH* 53: no. 67].
8.16. Pentecost—ff. 177r–178r. RUB.: sancto in die [*sic*]; INC.: sancti spiritus assit nobis gracia que corda . . . [*AH* 53: no. 70].

8.17. Pentecost—f. 178r–v. RUB.: de sancto spiritu; INC.: ueni sancte spiritus et emitte celitus lucis tue radium . . . [*AH* 54: no. 153].

8.18. Trinity—f. 179r–v. RUB.: [f. 178v] de sancta trinitate; INC.: benedicta semper sancta sit trinitas deitas scilicet unitas coequalis gloria . . . [*AH* 53: no. 81].

8.19. Corpus Christi—ff. 180r–181v. RUB.: [f. 179v] christi de corpore [*sic*]; INC.: lauda syon saluatorem lauda ducem et pastorem in ympnis et canticis . . . [*AH* 50: no. 385].

8.20. John the Baptist—ff. 181v–182r. RUB.: de sancto iohanne; INC.: sancti baptiste christi preconis . . . [*AH* 53: no. 163].

8.21. Peter—ff. 182v–183r. RUB.: [f. 182r] de sancto petro; INC.: petre summe christi pastor et paule gencium doctor . . . [*AH* 53: no. 210].

8.22. Dedication—f. 183r–v. RUB.: dedicacione templi [*in dex. marg.*]; INC.: psallat ecclesia mater illibata et uirgo sine ruga honorem huius ecclesie . . . [*AH* 53: no. 247].

8.23. Division of the Apostles—ff. 183v–185v. RUB.: in diuisione apostolorum; INC.: celi enarrant gloriam dei filii uerbi incarnati facti de terra celi . . . [*AH* 50: no. 267].

8.24. Mary Magdalene—ff. 185v–187r. RUB.: madale maria [*sic*]; INC.: laus tibi christe qui es creator et redemptor . . . [*AH* 50: no. 268].

8.25. James—ff. 187r–188r. RUB.: de sancto iacobo; INC.: pangat chorus in hac die nouum genus melodye clara dans preconia . . . [*AH* 55: no. 172].

8.26. Laurence—ff. 188r–189r. RUB.: de sancto laurencio; INC.: laurenti dauid magni martir milesque fortis . . . [*AH* 53: no. 173].

8.27. Assumption—ff. 189r–190r. RUB.: in assumpcione sancte marie; INC.: congaudent angelorum chori gloriose uirgini . . . [*AH* 53: no. 104].

8.28. Augustine—ff. 190r–191r. RUB.: de sancto augustino; INC.: de profundis tenebrarum mundo lumen exit clarum et scintillat hodie . . . [*AH* 55: no. 75].

8.29. Decollation of John the Baptist—ff. 191r–192v. RUB.: in decollatione sancti iohannis; INC.: psallite regi nostro psallite psallice psallite prudenter . . . [*AH* 50: no. 270].

8.30. Nativity *BMV*—ff. 192v–193r. RUB.: in natiuitate beate marie; INC.: stirpe maria regia procreata regem generans ihesum . . . [*AH* 53: no. 95].

8.31. Evangelists—ff. 193r–194r. RUB.: gelistis de ewange [*sic*]; INC.: plausu chorus letabundo hos attollat per quos mundo sonat . . . [*AH* 55: no. 6].

8.32. Michael—f. 194r–v. RUB.: de sancto michahelo; INC.: magnum te michahelem habentem pignus . . . [*AH* 53: no. 191].

8.33. All Saints—ff. 194v–195v. RUB.: [-de sanct***]; INC.: omnes sancti seraphin cherubin throni quoque dominacionesque . . . [*AH* 53: no. 112].

8.34. Martin—ff. 195v–196v. RUB.: de sancto martino; INC.: sacerdotem christi martinum cuncta per orbem canat ecclesia pacis katholice . . . [*AH* 53: no. 181].

8.35. Elizabeth—ff. 196v–197v. RUB.: elizabet de sancta [*sic*]; INC.: laude [*sic*] syon quod egressus a te decor et depressus tui fulgor speculi . . . [*AH* 55: no. 120].

8.36. Katherine—ff. 197v–198r. RUB.: de sancta katherina; INC.: sanctissime uirginis uotiua festa recolamus . . . [*AH* 55: no. 203].

8.37. Andrew—ff. 198r–v. inc.: deus in tua uirtute sanctus andreas gaudet et letatur eadem comitatus . . . [*AH* 53: no. 122].

8.38. Nicholas—ff. 199r–200v. rub.: [f. 198v] nycolay de sancto [*sic*]; inc.: laude christo debita celebremus inclita nycolay merita . . . [*AH* 55: no. 265].

8.39. Apostles—ff. 200v–201r. rub.: de apostolis; inc.: clare sanctorum senatus apostolorum princeps orbis terrarum rectorque regnorum . . . [*AH* 53: no. 228].

8.40. Martyrs—f. 201r–v. rub.: tiribus de mar [*sic*]; iohannis et pauli [*in dex. marg.*]; inc.: agone triumphali militum regis summi dies iste celebris est populis christo regi credulis . . . [*AH* 53: no. 229].

8.41. Confessors—ff. 201v–202v. rub.: de confessoribus; inc.: rex regum deus noster colende . . . [*AH* 53: no. 243].

8.42. Virgins—ff. 202v–203v. rub.: de uirginibus; inc.: exultent filie syon in rege suo nescientes thorum delicti crimine sordidatum . . . [*AH* 50: no. 271].

8.43. Virgin Mary—ff. 203v–205r. rub.: de beate [*sic*] uirgine; inc.: aue preclara maris stella in lucem gencium maria diuinitus orta . . . [*AH* 50: no. 241].

8.44. Virgin Mary—f. 205r–v. rub.: item alia sequentia; inc.: uerbum bonum et suaue personemus illud aue per quod christi fit conclaue uirgo mater filia . . . [*AH* 54: no. 218].

8.45 Virgin Mary—ff. 205v–206r. inc.: hodierne lux diei celebris in matris dei agitur memoria . . . [*AH* 54: no. 219].

8.46. Virgin Mary—ff. 206r–207r. inc.: imperatrix gloriosa potens et imperiosa ihesu christi generosa mater atque filia . . . [*AH* 54: no. 221].

8.47. Virgin Mary—f. 207r–v. inc.: marie preconio seruiat cum gaudio feruens desiderio uerus amor . . . [*AH* 54: no. 249].

9. Additions—ff. 207v–214v.

Sequences and Alleluia melodies added subsequently.

9.1. ff. 207v–208v. inc.: aue cella noue legis aue parens noui regis sine uiri semine . . . [*AH* 54: no. 227].

9.2. ff. 208v–210v. inc.: salue mater saluatoris uas electum uas honoris uas celestis gracie . . . [*AH* 54: no. 245].

9.3. ff. 210v–211v. inc.: <a>d celebres rex celice laudes cuncta . . . [*AH* 53: no. 190].

9.4. f. 212r. inc.: aeuia a[-u]ue benedicta maria iesu christi mater et filia flos dulcoris dos amoris . . .

9.5. ff. 212v–213r. inc.: mundi renouacio noua parit gaudia resurgenti domino conresurgunt omnia . . . [*AH* 54: no. 148].

9.6. ff. 213r–214v. inc.: <u>irginalis turma sexus iesu christi qui connexus dono sentis gracie . . . [*AH* 55: no. 333].

9.7. f. 214v. inc.: alleluya. prophete sancti predicauerunt nasci saluatorem de uirgine matre sancta maria.

Binding: Brown leather over boards; restored, but incorporates some leather from an earlier binding; blind stamped; modern bosses, straps, and clasps.

Owners & Provenance: Early ownership marks, *sententiae*, and names with titles on rear pastedown: Leonardus Hainer de Peillstain; Steffel Choll. fr. Spitall.; Hennsel fr. von Perger; Hanns Swab; Ulreich Ledere [*ut uid.*]; Räppel Schuester; Her Steffan Kreuzer, unser pharrer. Acquired from Les Enluminures (Chicago, IL) by the university in February 2014.

Sales & Catalogues: Reiss & Sohn, ca. May 2012; Les Enluminures, TextManuscripts Cat. 4, no. 11.

cod. Lat. c. 15

Origin: France, s. xiii².
Content Overview: Gradual.

In Latin, on parchment; i +106 ff. +iv; generally 276 x 195 mm (page) [see Layout for ruling]; foliated in modern pencil with Arabic numerals; some contemporary foliation remains in sections [see Foliation].

Collation: i $+1^{12}$ $+2^{12-1}$ $+3^{12}$ $+4^{12-1}$ $+5^{12-2}$ $+6-7^{12}$ $+8^{12-1}$ $+9^{12-1}$ $+10^{4}$ +iv

Quires: Parchment sexternions, F/F, are the normal quire forms (quires 1–9). Quire 2 lacks the first leaf, H/F; obeys Gregory's Rule within the quire. Quire 4 lacks the fifth leaf; does not obey Gregory's Rule. Quire 5 lacks the fourth and eighth leaves; does not obey Gregory's Rule. Quire 8 lacks the sixth leaf; does not obey Gregory's Rule. Quire 9 lacks the tenth leaf; does not obey Gregory's Rule. Quire 10 is a constructed binion, F/F, of singletons with stubs; text ends imperfectly; original form likely a sexternion. Parchment is damaged throughout with rips, tears, and heavy frying (e.g., ff. 69–74, 76, 81–84).

Foliation: Contemporary foliation marks each opening with Roman numerals in the outer margin of each verso, and 'A' and 'B' in the lower margins of each verso and recto; method continues through f. 82r. The modern foliation in pencil with Arabic numerals is referred to in this description.

Layout:

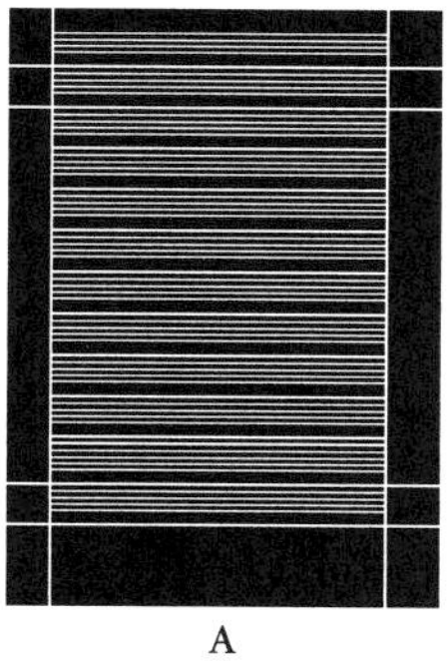

A

A ff. 1r–106v. Ink; 214 x 151 mm; 12 four-line staves, 12 text lines.

Pattern A is traced in brown, yellow, and red ink [see Music & Staves]; single column/full-music layout; first four-line staff above top line; most prickings lost due to trimming, but some occasionally visible in the lower margin for verticals.

Script: A single hand (M1) writes all text in Northern Textualis Formata of the thirteenth century. Sparse marginal additions (e.g., ff. 19r, 31r) and folio numbers in Roman numerals (e.g., f. 36r), and by a later hand (s. xvi).

Decoration:
I. Rubrication: Rubrics in red ink; letter heightening of majuscules and cadels in red ink.
II. Initials: Littera duplex, flourished, plain, and cadel initials occur in hierarchy.
a. Littera duplex initials (1 four-line staff and text line; 5 four-line staves and text lines) occur on ff. 1r, 7r, 43r, 49r, 51r (unfinished), 58v, 59v, 66v, 77v. Initials mark the major divisions of the manuscript and emphatic feasts: First Sunday of Advent (f. 1r), Christmas (f. 7r), Easter (f. 43r), Ascension (f. 49r), Trinity (f. 51r; unfinished), church dedication (f. 58v), Sanctorale (f. 59v), common of saints (f. 66v), and common of saints for a virgin (f. 77v; breaks hierarchy).
b. Flourished initials (1 four-line staff and text line square inset) in red and blue ink with contrasting penwork alternate and begin the initial chant for each feast (except those with littera duplex initials).
c. Plain initials (1 line versals) in red and blue ink alternate and begin all chants except the verses.
d. Cadels in black ink with heightening in red begin verses within the staves.
III. Line Fillers: Line fillers in blue and red ink occur within staves.
IV. Borders & Frames: Partial borders of red and blue flourishes in the outer and upper margins occur with littera duplex initials on ff. 1r, 7r, 43r, 49r, 59v, 66v, and 77v.

Music & Staves: Four-line staves traced in brown ink; C in yellow ink; F in red ink; 10 mm; 12 staves per page; square neumes in black ink.

Contents:

1. Temporale—ff. 1r–58v.

First Sunday of Advent through the twenty-third Sunday after the Octave of Pentecost.

2. Church dedication—ff. 58v–59r.

3. Sanctorale [incomplete]—ff. 59v–66v.

Contains Andrew (vigil and feast; f. 59v), Conversion of Paul (ff. 59v–60r), Purification (f. 60r–v), Agatha (f. 60v), Valentine (f. 61r), Chair of St. Peter (f. 61r–v), Gregory (f. 61v), Annunciation (ff. 61v–62r), Phillip and James (f. 62r), Holy Cross (f. 62r–v), Corpus Christi (f. 62v), John (vigil and feast; ff. 62v–63r), Peter and Paul (vigil and feast; f. 63r–v), Commemoration of Paul (ff. 63v–64r), Thomas Becket (f. 64r), Mary Magdalene (f. 64r), Chains of St. Peter (f. 64r), Laurence (ff. 64r–65r; vigil and feast), Octave of Laurence (f. 65r–v), Giles (f. 65v), Nativity (f. 65v), Michael (ff. 65v–66r), Martin (f. 66r), Clement (f. 66r–v).

4. Common of saints—ff. 66v–80v.

Apostle (vigil and feast; ff. 66v–68r), martyr (ff. 68v–70r), martyr in Easter and Pentecost (f. 70v), saints in Easter and Pentecost (f. 70v), saints throughout the year (ff. 70v–74v), confessor and bishop (ff. 74v–77r), confessor not a bishop (f. 77r–v), virgin (ff. 77v–80v).

5. Votive Masses—ff. 80v–83r.

Virgin Mary (ff. 80v–81v), dead in Easter and Pentecost (f. 81v), dead (ff. 81v–83r).

6. Ordinary Chants—ff. 83r–85v.

Settings of *Kyrie* and *Gloria*.

7. Sequences—ff. 86r–106v.

7.1. Christmas [incomplete]—f. 86r. INC.: prestrinxit claritas militum dei . . . [*AH* 53: no. 15].

7.2. Christmas—f. 86r. RUB.: ad publicam missam; INC.: grates nunc omnes reddamus domino deo qui sua natiuitate nos liberauit de dyabolica potestate . . . [*AH* 53: no. 10].

7.3. Christmas—f. 86r–v. RUB.: item; INC.: iubilemus saluatori quem celestes laudant chori concordi leticia . . . [*AH* 40: no. 378].

7.4. Christmas—ff. 86v–87r. RUB.: ad summam missam; INC.: eya recolamus laudibus piis digna . . . [*AH* 53: no. 16].

7.5. Stephen—f. 87r–v. RUB.: de sancto stephano; INC.: hanc concordi famulatu colamus sollempnitatem . . . [*AH* 53: no. 215].

7.6. John—ff. 87v–88r. RUB.: iohannis; INC.: iohannes ihesu christo multum dilecte uirgo . . . [*AH* 53: no. 168].

7.7. John—f. 88r–v. RUB.: item; INC.: speciale dedit munus uiuens regnans trinus unus qui est pater luminum . . .

7.8. Holy Innocents—ff. 88v–89r. RUB.: innocentium; INC.: laus tibi christe cui sapit quod uidetur ceteris esse surdastrum . . . [*AH* 53: no. 156].

7.9. Virgin Mary—f. 89r–v. RUB.: de beata uirgine; INC.: letabundus exultet fidelis chorus aeuia . . . [*AH* 54: no. 2].

7.10. Epiphany—ff. 89v–90r. RUB.: in epyphania; INC.: festa christi omnis cristianitas celebret . . . [*AH* 53: no. 29].

7.11. Epiphany—f. 90r–v. RUB.: item; INC.: maiestati sacrosancte militans cum triumphante iubilet ecclesia . . . [*AH* 55: no. 331].

7.12. Agnes—ff. 90v–91v. RUB.: agnetis uirginis; INC.: laus sit regi glorie cuius formam gracie solis splendor obstupescit . . . [*AH* 55: no. 51].

7.13. Conversion of Paul—ff. 91v–92r. RUB.: in conuersione pauli; INC.: dixit dominus ex basan conuertam conuertam in profundum maris quod dixit . . . [*AH* 50: no. 269].

7.14. Purification—f. 92r–v. RUB.: in purificatione; INC.: concentu parili hic te maria ueneratur populus . . . [*AH* 53: no. 99].

7.15. Easter—ff. 92v–93v. RUB.: in die sancto pasche; INC.: laudes saluatori uoce modulemur supplici . . . [*AH* 53: no. 36].

7.16. Easter—ff. 93v–94r. RUB.: feria secunda; INC.: mane prima sabbati surgens dei filius nostra spes et gloria . . . [*AH* 54: no. 143].

7.17. Easter—f. 94r–v. RUB.: feria tertia; INC.: agni paschalis esu potuque dignas . . . [*AH* 53: no. 50].

7.18. Easter—f. 94v. INC.: uictime paschali laudes immolent christiani . . . [*AH* 54: no. 7].

7.19. Holy Cross—ff. 94v–95r. RUB.: in inuentione sancte crucis; INC.: salue crux sancta arbor digna . . . [*AH* 53: no. 82].

7.20. Holy Cross—f. 95r–v. RUB.: item; INC.: salue lignum sancte crucis salue signum summi ducis . . . [*AH* 54: no. 122].

7.21. Ascension—ff. 95v–96r. RUB.: in ascensione domini; INC.: summi triumphum regis prosequamur laude . . . [*AH* 53: no. 67].

7.22. Pentecost—f. 96r–v. RUB.: in die pentecostes; INC.: sancti spiritus assit nobis gracia que corda . . . [*AH* 53: no. 70].

7.23. Pentecost—f. 97r. RUB.: item; INC.: ueni sancte spiritus et emitte celitus lucis tue radium . . . [*AH* 54: no. 153].

7.24. Trinity—ff. 97r–98r. RUB.: de trinitate sequentia; INC.: profitentes trinitatem ueneremur trinitatem pari reuerentia . . . [*AH* 54: no. 161].

7.25. Trinity—f. 98r–v. RUB.: item; INC.: benedicta semper sancta sit trinitas deitas scilicet unitas coequalis gloria . . . [*AH* 53: no. 81].

7.26. Trinity—ff. 98v–99r. RUB.: item; INC.: benedictio trine unitati simplici deitati semper omnifaria . . . [*AH* 50: no. 248].

7.27. Corpus Christi—ff. 99r–100r. RUB.: de corpore domini; INC.: laureata plebs fidelis sacramenta christi carnis iherusalem superna . . . [*AH* 8: no. 37].

7.28. Ten Thousand Martyrs [incomplete]—f. 100r–v. RUB.: de decem milibus martirum; INC.: hic est dies celebrandus laudibusque presentandus dies decem milium . . . [*AH* 55: no. 42].

7.29. Division of the Apostles [incomplete]—ff. 101r–102r. INC.: angelus istud consilium lapso homini auxilium est . . . [*AH* 50: no. 267].

7.30. Thomas Becket—f. 102r. RUB.: thome martiris; INC.: spe mercedis et corone stetit thomas in agone ad mortem obediens . . . [*AH* 55: no. 9].

7.31. Mary Magdalene—ff. 102r–103r. RUB.: marie magdalene; INC.: laus tibi christe qui es creator et redemptor . . . [*AH* 50: no. 268].

7.32. Laurence—f. 103r–v. RUB.: de sancto laurentio; INC.: laurenti dauid magni martyr milesque fortis . . . [*AH* 53: no. 173].

7.33. Assumption—ff. 103v–104r. RUB.: in assumptione beate uirginis; INC.: congaudent angelorum chori gloriose uirgini . . . [*AH* 53: no. 104].

7.34. Assumption—f. 104r–v. RUB.: item; INC.: in celesti ierarchia iubius cum symphonia festi dat iudicia . . .

7.35. Virgin Mary—ff. 104–105r. RUB.: de beate uirgine; INC.: aue maria gratia plena ominus [*sic*] tecum uirgo serena . . . [*AH* 54: no. 216].

7.36. Decollation of John the Baptist—ff. 105r–106r. RUB.: in decollatione iohannis baptiste; INC.: psallite regi nostro psallite psallice psallite prudenter . . . [*AH* 50: no. 270].

7.37. Giles—f. 106r–v. RUB.: de sancto egidio; INC.: laudem dei ueneretur supplicum deuotio . . . [*AH* 34: no. 184].

7.38. Nativity *BMV*—f. 106r. RUB.: in natiuitate beate marie uirginis; INC.: stirpe maria regia procreata regem generans ihesum . . . [*AH* 53: no. 95].

7.39. Nativity *BMV* [incomplete]—f. 106v. RUB.: item; INC.: est ex iacob sydus ortum ducens ad salutis portum mundi . . .

BINDING: s. xvii; calf over wooden boards; blind tooled; sewing with four double cords (mostly detached); metal catches on the upper board; remnants of leather straps on lower board; edges dyed red; paper flyleaves.

OWNERS & PROVENANCE: Acquired from J & J Lubrano (Syosset, NY) by the university in April 2015.

cod. Lat. d. 1

Origin: Southern Germany or Austria, s. xv.
Content Overview: Peregrinus of Opole, sermons *De tempore* and *De sanctis*; sermons of Antonius de Parma; sermon collections and material; various texts attributable to Narcissus Herzburg, Nicolaus von Dinkelsbühl, Peter Reicher of Pirchenwart, Thomas Ebendorfer de Haselbach.

In Latin with some German, on paper; 282 ff.; generally 285 x 205 mm (page) [see Layout for ruling]; f. 113v blank; select medieval foliation in ink with Arabic numerals; modern foliation in pencil with Arabic numerals [see Foliation].

Collation: $1–2^{12} + 3^{12+3} + 4–8^{12} + 9–10^{12+1} + 11–15^{12} + 16^{12+1} + 17–18^{12} + 19^{12+2} + 20^{12} + 21^{12+2} + 22^{12} + 23^{12-4}$

Bibliographical Format: 2° (ff. 30 and 33 in 4°).

Quires: Paper sexternions folded in folio are the normal quire forms. Quire 3 contains an additional singleton with stub (f. 37), and an inserted bifolium (ff. 30 and 33) folded in quarto. Quires 9 adds one leaf (f. 11). Quire 10 adds one leaf (f. 113). Quire 16 adds one leaf (f. 198). Quire 19 adds two leaves (ff. 235 and 236). Quire 21 adds two leaves (ff. 249 and 261). Quire 23 is a sexternion with the last four leaves canceled. Parchment strips cut from a document in German reinforce the opening of each quire.

Catchwords: Horizontal catchwords appear in the lower right margins; all correspond; quires 1, 9, 14, 16, 20, 21–23 lack catchwords.

Signatures: Arabic numerals (1–9) as ordinals are written on the first recto for quires 10–18.

Foliation: Contemporary foliation in Arabic numerals (1–62) in the upper margins on ff. 114r–175r corresponds to the register on f. 113r; the entire manuscript is foliated in modern pencil with Arabic numerals in the upper right margin.

Watermarks: One hundred thirty-six occurrences of six different watermarks: (A) Scales in quarterfoil with straight scale; occurs in quires 1, 16, 21–22; corresponds closely to Piccard 117475 (Bavaria, 1461). (B) Scales in circle with straight scale; occurs in quires 2–9; cf. Piccard 116697 (Triest, 1498). (C) Bull's head with above flower; occurs in quire 3 (ff. 30/33) folded in quarto; cf. Piccard 65246 (Nuremberg, 1430) and 65255 (Haselbach, 1436). (D) Anvil in circle; occurs in quires 10–11 and 23; corresponds closely to Piccard 122666 (Grätz, 1457). (E) Scale in circle with straight scales; occurs in quires 15, 17–19; cf. Piccard 116755 (Wiener Neustadt, 1450). (F) Anvil in circle; occurs in quire 20; cf. Piccard 122662 (Vienna, 1455).

Layout:

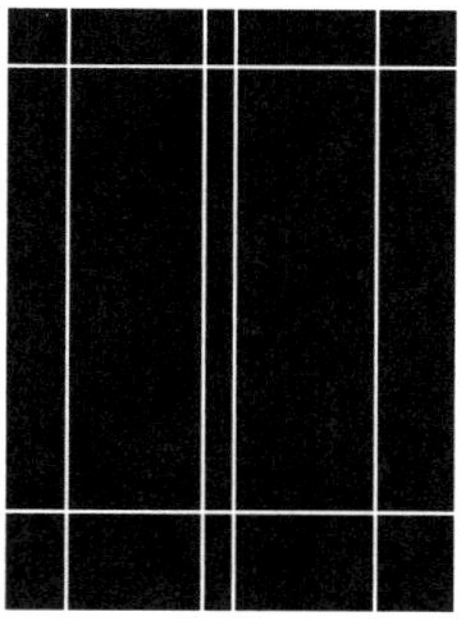
A

B

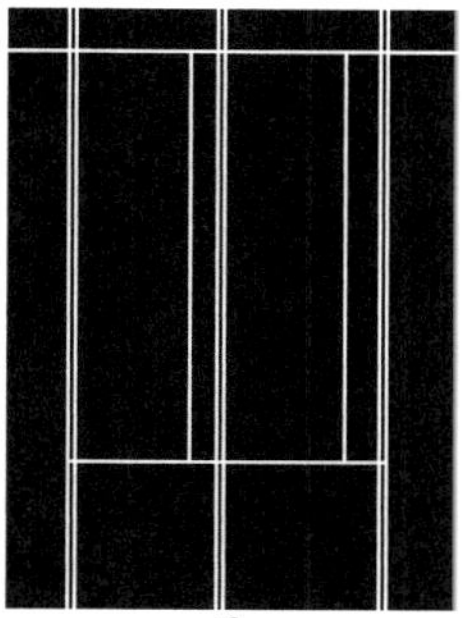
C

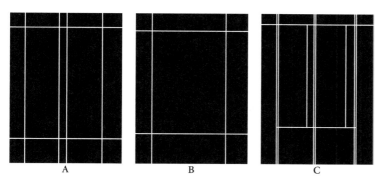

A ff. 1r–12v. Lead; 210 x 146 mm; intercol. 14 mm; 35 lines.
B ff. 13r–112v, 114r–281v. Ink; 193–203 x 135–145 mm; 35 lines.
C f. 113r. Ink; 196 x 147 mm; 40 lines.

Pattern A is frame-ruled in lead on ff. 1r–12v; two columns (intercol. 14 mm); writing below top line; prickings occasionally visible for verticals. Pattern B is frame-ruled in black and brownish ink throughout the manuscript in varying dimensions; single column; writing below top line; prickings seldom visible. Pattern C is traced on f. 113r in ink to form the register for the sermons *De sanctis* [see Contents 6]; two columns converted to four with additional verticals; no true intercolumnium.

Script: Several fifteenth-century hands write, correct, and annotate the manuscript. A conservative grouping of the scribal bookhands based on script type and levels of execution reveals five bookhands (M1–M5), of which two write the majority of the manuscript. M1 writes Hybrida Formata on ff. 1r–12v (loops extremely rare); M2 writes Cursiva Formata (loopless forms rare) on ff. 13r–29v, 31–32v, 34r–170v, 237–245r, 275r–280r, but briefly slipping into Semihybrida without consistency; M3 writes Cursiva Libraria on ff. 30r–v and

33r (inserted leaves); M4 writes Hybrida at varying levels of execution: Hybrida Libraria on ff. 171r–175v, 199r–235v, 245r–260v (occasional looped forms in initial position), Hybrida Libraria and Currens on ff. 176r–198r, Hybrida and Semihybrida under the influence of Bastarda on ff. 260v–274r; M5 writes a Semihybrida Formata (Bastarda) on f. 236r–v.

DECORATION:

I. RUBRICATION: Rubrics in red and black ink; lemmata underlined in red ink; guide letters often visible.

II. INITIALS: Initials of the flourished, plain, and cadel types occur loosely in hierarchy.

A. Flourished initials (3–7 lines square inset) in red ink with brown penwork on f. 1r.

B. Plain initials (2–4 lines square inset) in red ink occur throughout the manuscript.

C. Cadels drawn in black ink begin texts on ff. 113r, 236v, and 272r.

CONTENTS:

1. Narcissus Hertz de Berching, *De passione*—ff. $1r^{a}$–$12v^{b}$.

INC.: [f. $1r^{a}$] en morior cum nichil horum fecerim que isti false aduersum me testificantur danielis tertio decimo [Dn 13.43] licet originaliter hec uerba dixerit sancta susanna falso testimonio in mortem dampnata . . .; EXPL.: [f. $12v^{b}$] . . . et sic post hanc uitam eterne uite uidebimur esse ascripti quod nobis concedat dominus noster ihesus christus maria amen et cetera.

Authorship attributed to Narcissus Hertz de Berching or possibly (Ps.-)Nicolaus von Dinkelsbühl. The text is also found in Klosterneuburg, Bibliothek des Augustiner-Chorherrenstifts, Cod. 417, ff. 133r–144v, München, Bayerische Staatsbibliothek, Clm 26693, ff. 301v–311v, Graz, Universitätsbibliothek, Cod. 137 (LVI), ff. 231v–239v, and Melk, Stiftsbibliothek, Cod. 1926. TKACZ 2004, 288 contains a partial transcription from Klosterneuburg, Bibliothek des Augustiner-Chorherrenstifts, Cod. 417, but is unaware of the other manuscripts of the text and attributed authors, and lacks bibliography.

BIBLIOGRAPHY: MADRE 1965, 308–309; STEGMÜLLER 5658,2.

2. Peregrinus of Opole, *Sermones de tempore*—ff. 13r–105r.

RUB.: dominica prima in aduentum; INC.: [f. 13r] ecce rex tuus ueni tibi [Za 9.9; Mt 21.25] in hys uerbis consolatur prophetia sanctos patres qui diuersis tribulationibus afflicti fuerunt ante aduentum christi [no.1/T1] . . .; EXPL.: [f. 105r] . . . nec auris audiuit nec in cor hominis ascendit et cetera [1 Cor 2.9] rogemus ergo. explicit peregrinus. COLOPHON: [f. 105r] .a. age .b. bene cole deum egenti fac graciam humilitatem iustitiam karitatem legem meditare nobilis olaue pacem quere rege sapienter tene ueritatem christum yhesum zela.

Order of sermons according to TATARZYŃSKI 1997: nos. 1–22, 24, 26, 31–33, 34–64, 23, 25, 27–30 [T1–T8, T10–T23, T25, T28/2, T32–T34, T36–T37, T39–T65, T24, T28, T28/3–T31]. Quarto inserts in Latin and German on ff. 30 and 33; notes in Latin on f. 37r; adaptation of John of Freiburg on ff. 50r–51v [see CONTENTS 3] between T34 and T36; pericopes preceding those of T35, T37, and T39 written in larger-sized Cursiva Formata on ff. 52r (Mc 16.14–20), 53v (Io 15.26–27;

16.1), and 55r (Io 15.7). Four additional sermons not in the corpus of Peregrinus are interspersed on ff. 97v–99r between T24 and T28 [see CONTENTS 4].

EDITION: TATARZYŃSKI 1997, 3–304.
BIBLIOGRAPHY: KAEPPELI no. 3194.

3. Adaptation of John of Freiburg, *Summa confessorum*—ff. 50r–51v.

INC.: [f. 50r] nota si musca uel aranea ante consecracionem in calicem ceciderit uel etiam uenenum in calicem missum; EXPL.: [f. 51v] . . . nec propter hoc efficitur transgressor constitucionis ecclesie quia ab ea que frequentius accidunt leges aptantur [*Sup. Sent.* 4. d. 10. q. 1. a. 4. qc. 3 ad 1 (15277)].

BIBLIOGRAPHY: CORBETT [1978], 13.

4. Sermons—ff. 97v–99r.

Four sermons not found in TATARZYŃSKI 1997 are included among those of Peregrinus's *Sermones de tempore.*

4.1. f. 97r–v. RUB.: de passione [f. 96v]; INC.: o uos omnes et cetera [Lam 1.12] uerbum istud conpetit singulariter passioni christi et significat passionem . . .; EXPL.: . . . quod est contra naturam cum ipse sit uita iudit si bene egistis cum ieroboal et cetera. [Idc 7.16] [Schneyer 9:431, no. 37].

Also found in Koblenz, Landeshauptarchiv, Best. 701, no. 247, f. 65r, and, according to SCHNEYER 9:431, no. 37, Roma, Biblioteca Angelica MS 1057.

4.2. ff. 97v–98r. RUB.: de passione domini; INC.: o uos omnes qui transitis per uiam et cetera ieren. primo [Lam 1.12] multa sunt que ad dolorem deo grauissima fuerunt . . .; EXPL.: . . . nam quia mortem suam paucis prodere uidebatur. ys. .xlix. in uacuum laboraui sine causa et uane fortitudinem meam consumpsi et cetera [Is 49.4].

4.3. f. 98r. RUB.: sermo in paraszauen [*sic*]; INC.: stabat iuxta crucem iesu et cetera. io. .xix. [Io 19.3] nota quod beata uirgo stetit in cruce et iuxta crucem . . .; EXPL.: . . . quia per eam in celum ascendimus genesis .xxviij. [Gn 28.12] uidit iacob scalam.

Also found in Paris, Bibliothèque nationale de France, MS lat. 3737, f. 20r^{a-b} (rub. on 19v^{b}), and, according to SCHNEYER 8:489, no. 68, London, British Library, Add. MS 16590, and München, Bayerische Staatsbibliothek, Clm 2638.

4.4. ff. 98r–99r. RUB.: ad idem; INC.: inclinatio capite emisit spiritum ioh. [Io 19.30] nota quod christus quattuor fecit in cruce primum quod locutus est secundum fleuit . . .; EXPL.: . . . unde ante passionem dixit uide fac quod facis cicius.

Also found in Innsbruck, Universitäts- und Landesbibliothek Tirol, Cod. 712, f. 70v.

5. Antonius Azaro de Parma, *Sermones de tempore*—ff. 105r–112v.

The six sermons [T32, T33, T37, T39–T41] are attributed to Antonius Azaro de Parma.

5.1. [T32]—ff. 105r–106r. RUB.: dominica quarta; INC.: uado ad eum qui misit me et cetera ioh. [Io 16.5] consweuit [*sic*] dominus quando facturus ad opus grande predicare . . .; EXPL.: . . . laudabo eum coram patre meo hec laudacio est diuine gratie collacio siue argumentacio rogemus ergo [SCHNEYER 1:305, no. 200].

5.2. [T33]—ff. 106r–107r. RUB.: dominica quinta; INC.: amen amen dico uobis si quid petieritis patrem in nomine meo et cetera [Io 16.23] reges solent in die coronationis sue magna munera largiri . . .; EXPL.: . . . quia est omni laude dignissimus rogemus [SCHNEYER 1:305, no. 201].

5.3. [T37]—ff. 107r–108v. RUB.: dominica infra ascensionem; INC.: cum uenerit paraclitus quod mittam uobis apoc. [Io 15.26] iohannes in sequenti dominica retolit ecclesia aduentum spiritus sancti in apostolos . . .; EXPL.: . . . eis huius et in futuro nisi peniteant et a peccato custodiant [SCHNEYER 1:305, no. 202].

5.4. [T39]—ff. 108v–110r. RUB.: in die sancto; INC.: si quis diligit me sermonem meum seruabit et cetera iohannis nono [Io 14.23] hodie mater ecclesia celebrat aduentum spiritus sancti in discipulos . . .; EXPL.: . . . ut pro deo prelatis nostris exhibeamus deuotam obedientiam per quam perueniet ad graciam rogemus [SCHNEYER 1:305, no. 203].

5.5. [T40]—ff. 110r–111v. RUB.: in octaua pentecosten [*sic*]; INC.: erat homo ex pharizeis nycodemus nomine et cetera ioh. tertio [Io 3.1] hodie facimus festum sancte trinitatis hoc est cum solempnitate laudamus dominum deum . . .; EXPL.: . . . quia quidquid agimus nichil esse uidetur si acerbitas dominice passionis cogitetur [SCHNEYER 1:305, no. 204].

5.6. [T41]—ff. 111v–112v. RUB.: dominica prima post trinitatis [*sic*]; INC.: homo quidem erat diues et induebatur purpura et bysso [Lc 16.19] cum dominus quadam uice predicabat uidit in populo quosdam phariseos . . .; EXPL.: . . . quos numquam uiderat in hac uita sequitur et clamans dixit pater abraham [Lc 16.24] patrem eum uocauit [SCHNEYER 1:305, no. 205].

EDITION: PARIS 1515.
BIBLIOGRAPHY: KAEPPELI no. 264; SCHNEYER 1:305, nos. 200–205.

6. Peregrinus of Opole, *Sermones de sanctis*—ff. 114r–169r.

RUB.: incipit peregrinus de sanctis; INC.: [f. 114r] uestigia illius secutus est pes meus uiam illius custodiui et non declinaui ab ea iob uicesimo tertio [Iob 23.11] dominus uocans petrum et andream dixit uenite post me [Mt 4.19; Mc 1.17] uolens autem ut uenirent non solum gressu corporis . . .; EXPL.: [f. 169r] . . . ut cononicis [*sic*] legitur terra deglutiuit nunc autem infernus omnes absorbuit rogamus ergo dominum.

List of saints with folio numbers in Arabic numerals for the sermons (RUB.: registrum super peregrinum de sanctis) on f. 113r; a sermon attributed to Antonius Azaro de Parma (SCHNEYER 1:312, no. 305) on ff. 135v–138r occurs among those of Peregrinus. Order of sermons according to TATARZYŃSKI 1997: nos. 1–13, 15–18, 21, 19, 22 [Antonius Azaro de Parma; SCHNEYER 1:312, no. 305], 23–27, 29–39, 42–54 [cf. SCHNEYER 4:563, no. 186], 40–41. [S1, S3, S7–S8, T6, S9–S13, S17–S19, S21–S24, S28, S25, S4, T26 (Antonius Azaro de Parma; SCHNEYER 1:312, no. 305), S29–S30, S32–S33, S35, S42, S44, S46–S46/2, S47, S49–S50, S52, S56, S59, S61, S65–S67, S70, S75, S77–S84, S85 (cf. SCHNEYER 4:563, no. 186), S63–S64].

EDITION: TATARZYŃSKI 1997, 304–570.
BIBLIOGRAPHY: KAEPPELI nos. 3194 and 264.

7. Sermons—ff. 169r–175v.

Eleven sermons follow those of Peregrinus without attribution. Topics include the Circumcision (7.1–2), Epiphany (7.3–4), and saints Blaise (7.5; also found in München, Bayerische Staatsbibliothek, Cgm 660, f. 251v[b], and Clm 14899), Ulrich (7.6–7), Stephen (7.8–9), Afra (7.10), and Giles (7.11).

7.1. ff. 169r–170r. RUB.: in circumcisione domini sermo; INC.: in carne eius fecit stare testamentum ecclesiastici .xliiij. [Sir 44.21] conuenit enim hec auctoritas puero ihesu in cuius carne deus pater stare fecit preceptum circumci[-o]sionis huius . . .; EXPL.: . . . que tunc fiet circumcisio quando reuelata facie gloriam domini speculabimur ad quam nos perducat qui sine fine uiuit et regit.

7.2. f. 170r–v. RUB.: de eodem; INC.: uocatum est nomen eius ihesus et cetera luc. secundo [Lc 2.21] nomina ponuntur ad notifficationem [*sic*] et secundum morem antiquorum inponabantur . . .; EXPL.: . . . qui confugerit saluabitur et cetera igitur rogamus deum et cetera.

7.3. f. 171r–v. RUB.: de epiphania; INC.: ubi est qui natus est rex iudeorum math. .ij. [Mt 2.2] uox ista uox magorum est et potest esse uox inquirencium conpacientium . . .; EXPL.: . . . per me reges regnant et legum conditores iusta decernunt.

7.4. ff. 171v–172v. INC.: duce [*sic*] splendida fulgebis naciones uenient ex longinquo ad te et munera deferentes adorabunt te dominum th. .xiij. [Tb 13.13–14] in uerbis istis quatuor occurrunt notabilia . . .; EXPL.: . . . si procidens adoraueris me sed sathan ipse debuit procidere sicut magi procidentes adorauerunt eum.

7.5. ff. 172v–173r. RUB.: de sancto blasio; INC.: beatus seruus quem cum uenerit dominus inuenerit uigilans luc. .xij. [Lc 12.37/43] consolatur autem dominus seruos suos in promissione . . .; EXPL.: . . . qui enim tollerauerunt mala propter christum debuit habere gloriam cum christo ro. .ix. si fuimus et cetera [SCHNEYER 8:703, no. 8].

7.6. f. 173r–v. RUB.: de sancto walrico [*sic*]; INC.: benediccio domini super caput iusti sap. .x. [Prv 10.6] uerba ista dici ponunt de beato udalrico qui benediccionem domini promeruit . . .; EXPL.: . . . benedicta incipit filia a domino et hec ideo quia nuru sua uenerat de longinqua terra in bethleem.

7.7. f. 173v. RUB.: de eodem; INC.: uenite ascendamus ad montem domini et ad dominum dei iacob et docebit nos uias suas ysa. secundo [Is 2.3] duo tanguntur in uerbis istis primum quid facere [-habeant] debeant qui hodie huc conueniunt . . .; EXPL.: . . . rogemus ergo beatum udalricum ut nobis impetret ab istis sanctis doctoribus ut sic uias suas nos doceant ut ad ipsos peruenire mereamur.

7.8. ff. 173v–174r. RUB.: de sancto stephano; INC.: gloria et honore coronasti eum domine [Ps 8.6] dominus beatum stephanum dupliciter coronauit gloria in celo quo ad animam honore in terra quo ad corpus . . .; EXPL.: . . . delatum est enim corpus eum [*sic*] a iersualem romam et ibi sepultum in sepulchro beati laurencii recipe legendam.

7.9. f. 174r–v. INC.: quasi effodientes thesaurum uehementer cum inuenerunt sepulchrum gaudent iob tertio [Iob 3.21] in familia principum plus ceteri honorantur milites et precipue primus militum . . .; EXPL.: . . . namque et tres tunc a uariis lang<uoribus> et cetera rogemus.

7.10. ff. 174v–175r. RUB.: de sancta affra; INC.: raab meretricem fecit iosue uiuere cum omni domo sua et habitat in medio israhel usque ad presentem diem iosue sexto [Io 6.25] hodie karissimi agimus festum et diem que unicuique peccatori et peccatrici dat spem et fiduciam . . .; EXPL.: . . . quia lacrimas in oratione pro ea domino fuderit ut in legenda eius habetur unde iac. .v. multum ualet oratio iusti assidua [Iac 5.16].

7.11. f. 175r–v. RUB.: de sancto egidio; INC.: uidi angelum dei ascendentem ab ortu solis habentem signum dei uiui et cetera uerba proposita legunt in apok. septimo [Apc 7.2] sed possunt adtribui beato egidio cuius festum hodie colimus qui propter uite sanctitatem angelus dicitur . . .; EXPL.: . . . ut quam diu uiueret ipsum wlnus [*sic*] numquam sanaretur quod a domino impetrauit rogemus igitur et cetera.

8. Sermon material—ff. 176r–198v.

INC.: [f. 176r] cum appropinquaret ihesus mt. uicesimo primo [Mt 21.1] mons olиueti est prope iherusalem decorus et plenus arboribus oliuarum . . .; EXPL.: [f. 198v] . . . et potest resuscitari per penitentiam [*ut uid.*] et cetera sunt plana. et sic est finis huius materie.

9. Sermon material—ff. 199r–216v.

INC.: [f. 199r] cum appropinquasset ihesus iherosolimis et uenisset betphage mt. uicesimo primo [Mt 21.1] auicenna philosophus dicit quod lapis cadens in aquam quatuor efficit in ea et relinquit primo spummam gingnit strepitum facit aquam sursum salire facit et cogit circulum describit . . .; EXPL.: [f. 216v] . . . et talem humilitatem habuit iste princeps de quo ewangelium hodiernum dicit in illo tempore et cetera. et sic est finis huius materie.

10. Peter Reicher of Pirchenwart, *De poenitentia*—ff. 217r–235v.

INC.: [f. 217r] circa illam particulam ut temptaretur a dyabalo illius ewangely ductus est ihesus in desertum [Mt 4.1] et notandum secundum magistrum sententiarum di. 21.9.ii. temptacio est motus mentis operacio cum qua anima spiritus . . .; EXPL.: [f. 235v] . . . contra proximum quia inhumanum est facere deteriorem et cetera. et sic sufficit amen. et sic est finis huius tractatuli.

Also attributed to Nicolaus von Dinkelsbühl.

Bibliography: Madre 1965, 285–288.

11. Iacobus de Voragine, *Legenda aurea* [chapter 35]—f. 236r

RUB.: rationes de quatuor temporibus per doctores etiam [*sic*]; INC.: [f. 236r] ieiunia quatuor temporum a calixto papa institutas legimus fiunt autem hec ieiunia quatuor in anno secundum quattuor tempora anni . . .; EXPL.: [f. 236r] . . . quia in sepulchro iacuit et quia tristes erant apostoli de nece sui domini et cetera. amen.

Edition: Maggioni 1998, 230–232.

12. *De decem uirtutibus misse*—f. 236v.

RUB.: sic notantur uirtutes misse; INC.: [f. 236v] unde bernhardus prima uirtus est audire missam quantum spacium terre quod si homo interim transiret . . .; EXPL. [f. 236v] . . . quicumque libenter audit missam per quam homo tam salubriter saluatur.

Edition: Franz 1902, 43–44; excerpted in W. Simon 2003, 101 n. 271.
Bibliography: Franz 1902, 43–44; W. Simon 2003, 100–102.

13. Sermons—ff. 237r–249v.

13.1. ff. 237r–245r. INC.: probet autem seipsum homo et sic de pane illo edat et de calice bibat qui enim indigne manducat et cetera primo ad corinth. undecimo [1 Cor 11.28–29] in hac epistola beatus paulus ostendit formam institutionis huius sacramenti scilicet corporis . . .; EXPL.: . . . si in umbra mortis iacentem quere reconcilacionem sub figura agni pascalis.

Also found in Herzogenburg, Stiftsbibliothek, Cod. 9, Graz, Universitätsbibliothek, Cod. 1264, f. 10r, and Zwettl, Zisterzienserstift, Cod. 356, f. 48r[b].

13.2. ff. 245r–249v [incomplete]. INC.: <a>ccipite et comedite hoc est corpus meum et iterum bibite ex hoc omnes hic est enim sagwis [*sic*] meus math. .xxvj. [Mt 26.26–27] karissimi hodierna dies que nobis de bonitate et gratia dei illuxit et ostendit nobis precipuam et maximam caritatem ipsius dei . . .; EXPL.: . . . circa sextum scilicet quare deus dederit nobis corpus suum uelatum et non in forma manifesta de hoc requere in precedenti sermone et in sermone angelorum esca nutristi populum [Sap 16.20] in ultimo membro.

Incomplete, but also occurs in Graz, Universitätsbibliothek, Cod. 128 (CCXV), 56v; according to Corbett [1978], 29, the complete version is found München, Bayerische Staatsbibliothek, Clm 16164.

14. *Tractatus artis bene moriendi* (*Speculum artis bene moriendi*)—ff. 250r–260r.

inc.: [f. 250r] cum de presentis exilii miseria mortis transitus propter moriendi inpericiam multis non solum laiicis uerum etiam religiosis atque deuotis . . .; expl.: [f. 260r] . . . cum uideritis abraham ysaac et iacob et omnes prophetas in regno dei uos autem expelli foras de quo nos custodiat qui sine fine uiuit et regnat ihesus christus filius dei et marie et uirginis filius qui est benedictus in secula seculorum amen; colophon: deo gratias. et sic est finis huius tractatuli de arte moriendi conpositi egrery uiri magistri nicolay de dinkchelspuechel.

The work has been attributed to Jean Gerson, Nicolaus von Dinkelsbühl, Matthew of Krakow, Domenico Capranica, and Eberhard Mardach among others.

Bibliography: Rudolf 1957, 75–82; Madre 1965, 292–295; Palmer 1993, 318; Akerboom 2003, 210 n. 5; Kaeppeli no. 965; Bloomfield no. 1076.

15. Verse—f. 260r[a]–v.

inc.: [f. 260r[a]] ne sis dampnatus mori sis semper paratus . . .; expl.: [f. 260v] . . . tali namque domo clauditur omnis homo. deo gracias.

Cf. similar verses found in Graz, Universitätsbibliothek, Cod. 538, 233r.

16. *Speculum naturale* (excerpt)—f. 260r[b].

inc.: [f. 260r[b]] plinius in speculo naturali naturali [*sic*] igitur balsamum . . .; expl.: [f. 260r[b]] . . . uirtutibus ingerit brutales autem petulantia fuit semper.

17. Iacobus de Voragine, *Legenda aurea* [chapters 31–34]—ff. 260v–262v.

inc.: [f. 260v] septuagesima signat tempus deuiacionis sexagesima tempus uiduacionis quadragesima tempus remissionis . . .; expl.: [f. 262v] . . . ut digni ualeamus conmedere agnum uite que nobis concedere dignetur qui sine fine uiuit et regnat amen.

Edition: Maggioni 1998, 219–229.

18. Jacques de Nouvion, *Disputatio cum Hussitis*—ff. 263r–271v.

inc.: [f. 263r] utrum uiris ecclesiasticis sew [*sic*] clericis liceat aliquid possidere in hac questione respondit iacobi de nouiano . . .; expl.: [f. 271v] . . . post hanc uitam me benignissime saluator agregare queso dignare amen. explicit tractatum iacobi de monano [*sic*] factus contra obiectiones et questiones fautorum et disciplorum damnati heresiarche wicleff.

Updated list of manuscripts from SEDLÁK 1914 is available at Pavel Soukup, *Repertorium operum antihussiticorum*, on-line database, www.antihus.eu.

EDITION: SEDLÁK 1914.
BIBLIOGRAPHY: SEDLÁK 1914; CORBETT [1978], 30.

19. Nicolaus von Dinkelsbühl and Peter von Pulkau(?), *De uiginti quattuor senioribus*—ff. 272r–274v.

RUB.: copia de .xxiiij. senioribus qui dicuntur sancti ficti nichil in rerum natura existentes; INC.: [f. 272r] uenerabili prouido ac sollicito uiro domino .n. in superiori styria archedyacono [*sic*] decanus et magistri sacre theologie uniuersitatis study wiennensis iugem karitatis affectum . . .; EXPL.: [f. 274v] . . . ad cultum demonum pertinens aut aliud illicitum latere; COLOPHON: datum wienne iudicali [*sic*] collegio in nostra generali congregacione super hoc sollemniter celebrata anno domini millesimo quadringentesimo uicesimo primo .xvij. die mensis octobris sub nostri sigilli appensione ad maiorem certitudinem prescriptorum.

EDITION: SCHMIDT 1938, 354–362.
BIBLIOGRAPHY: MADRE 1965, 260–263; GIRGENSOHN 1964, 179–180.

20. Thomas Ebendorfer de Haselbach, Sermon—ff. 275r–280r.

INC.: [f. 275r] egressus ihesus perambulat iericho et cetera luce .19. [Lc 19.1] legimus in tertio libro de gaudio et solempnitate populi iudaici in dedicatione templi salomonis . . .; EXPL.: [f. 280r] . . . mox ipse cum populo egrediente statim cum grandi strepitu et ullulatu ecclesiam istam subueritit et cetera. sermo magistri thome de haselbach et cetera.

The sermon is also found in Klosterneuburg, Bibliothek des Augustiner-Chorherrenstifts, Cod. 327, ff. 61r[a]–66r[a], and Leipzig, Universitätsbibliothek, MS 597, f. 399r[a].

BIBLIOGRAPHY: LHOTSKY 1957, 78, no. 56.

BINDING: s. xvi?; calf over wooden boards; stamped; two metal catches on upper board; metal clasps on lower board; metal bosses and furniture.

OWNERS & PROVENANCE: Mgr. Andrew Arnold Lambing of Pittsburgh, PA (1842–1918) acquired the manuscript on 7 April 1874 according to his note; donated to the university by Lambing at an unknown time.

FORMER SHELFMARK: no. 438 (Lambing); MS 3 (Notre Dame).

BIBLIOGRAPHY: DE RICCI 1:714, no. 3; O'CONNOR 1942, 112; KAEPPELI no. 3194 (lists the manuscript as having *De tempore* only); CORBETT no. 3; D'ALVERNY 1981, 106; EMERY, JR. and L. JORDAN 1998, 500.

cod. Lat. d. 2

Origin: Southern France, s. xv^{2}.
Content Overview: Cyprian and Ps.-Cyprian, works with glosses.

In Latin, on parchment and paper; i +229 ff. +i; generally 287 x 210 mm [see Layout for ruling]; parchment flyleaves (medieval).

Collation: i +1–18^{12} +19$^{12-1}$ +20^{1+1} +i

Bibliographical Format: 2°.

Quires: Mixed sexternions are the normal forms for quires 2–18; the outer and inner bifolia are parchment with four paper bifolia folded in folio between them; both H/H and F/F arrangements occur. Quire 1 uses a paper singleton for f. 1, and f. 12 is a parchment singleton attached by its stub; quire 19 lacks the last parchment leaf; quire 20 is comprised of two singletons with stubs folded over each other (ff. 228–229); transfer of green paint is visible on flyleaf Iv.

Catchwords: Vertical catchwords written in the inner margins for quires 1–18; all correspond.

Foliation: Foliation in Roman numerals in ink is written in the upper right margin by M1 [see Script]; Roman numerals correspond to folios in the index [see Contents 25]; later foliated in modern pencil with Arabic numerals; collation statement for H. P. Kraus written in pencil on the rear pastedown (December 1964).

Watermarks: Seventy-eight occurrences of various Bull's Head watermarks (eyes, nose, and other facial features without additional motifs); arrangement of text obscures too many of the separative features of the motifs to classify individually; cf. Piccard 79681 (1446), 79699 (1452), 79679 (Chambéry, 1466), and 79700 (1452); distances between chainlines 38–40 mm; approx. dimensions are 55–62 x 26–35 mm.

Layout:

A

B

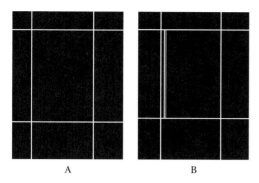

A ff. 1r–227r. Combined technique; 179 x 115 mm; 33 lines.
B ff. 228r–229v. Rose ink; 172 x 110 mm; 24 lines.

Pattern **A** is traced on ff. 1r–227r using a combined technique of lead and hard-point; single column; writing above top line; prickings often visible in outer right margins. Deviant patterns within **A** are rare, but do occur (e.g., two upper through lines on f. 36r). Pattern **B** is traced in rose ink for the index on ff. 228r–229v; single column appropriated into three; writing below top line; additional verticals added to align flourished initials.

Script: A single hand (M1) writes the text in Hybrida Libraria of the fifteenth century, though Cursiva characteristics begin to lapse and straight **s** and **f** may sit on the line (e.g., f. 98r). A second hand (M2) adds marginal glosses blending Cursiva letter forms and features of the sixteenth century (e.g., forms of straight **s**, **f**, and **d**).

Decoration:

I. Rubrication: Rubrics in red ink; letter heightening of majuscules in yellow.

II. Initials: Foliate and flourished initials occur in hierarchy.

a. Foliate initials (5–6 line square inset) begin each text; the interiors of the initials contain faces occasionally in lieu of the normal tendril motifs (e.g., ff. 96r, 116r, 192v), animals (e.g., f. 108r), other plant matter (e.g., ff. 108v, 174r, 193r), and zoomorphic foliates (e.g., f. 69v).

b. Flourished initials (1 line versals) in blue ink with red penwork and gold with blue penwork alternate throughout the index on ff. 228r–229v.

III. Line Fillers: Line fillers in blue ink and gold are painted throughout the index on ff. 228r–229v.

IV. Borders & Frames: Piece borders of black and gold rinceaux, acanthus, and vegetal motifs in blue, gold, green, and red accompany all foliate initials.

CONTENTS:

1. Cyprian, *Ad Donatum*—ff. 1r–5v.

RUB.: d. cecilii cipriani ad donatum liber de gratia dei; INC.: [f. 1r] bene admones donate carissime nam et promisisse me memini . . .; EXPL.: [f. 5v] . . . si sit nobis spiritualis auditio prolectet aures religiosa mulcedo. explicit ad donatum [SIMONETTI 1976, 3–13].

2. Cyprian, *De habitu uirginum*—ff. 6r–12r.

RUB.: incipit de disciplina et de habitu uirginum; INC.: [f. 6r] disciplina custos spei retinaculum fidei . . .; EXPL.: [f. 12r] . . . cum incipiet in uobis uirginitas honorari. [f. 12v] de habitu uirginum explicit [VON HARTEL 1868-1871, 1:187–205].

3. Cyprian, *De lapsis*—ff. 12v–22r.

3.1. ff. 12v–18v. RUB.: incipit de lapsis; INC.: pax ecce dilectissimi fratres ecclesie reddita est . . .; EXPL.: . . . quamuis nec dum dies uenerit pene. de lapsis explicit.

3.2. ff. 18v–22r. RUB.: incipit de [-catholice ecclesie unitate] ultione lapsorum; INC.: plectuntur interim quidam quo ceteri dirigimur exempla sunt omnium tormenta paucorum . . .; EXPL.: . . . nec iam solam die ueniam merebitur sed coronam. explicit de [-catholice] ultione [-ecclesie unitate] lapsorum.

Text is divided between chapters 22 and 23, each beginning with an initial and piece border; see BÉVENOT 1972, 221–242.

4. Cyprian, *De ecclesiae catholicae unitate*—ff. 22r–30v.

RUB.: incipit de [-oratione] ecclesie unitate [-dominica]; INC.: [f. 22r] cum moneat dominus et dicat uos estis . . .; EXPL.: [f. 30v] . . . serui uigiles christo dominante regnabimus. de catholice ecclesie unitate explicit [BÉVENOT 1972, 250–268].

5. Cyprian, *De dominica oratione*—ff. 30v–40v.

RUB.: incipit de oratione dominica; INC.: [f. 30v] euangelica precepta fratres dilectissimi nihil aliud sunt quam magisteria diuina . . .; EXPL.: [f. 40v] . . . hic quoque orare et deo gratias agere non desinamus. de oratione dominica explicit [MORESCHINI 1976, 90–113].

6. Cyprian, *De opere et eleemosynis*—ff. 40v–48v.

RUB.: incipit de ope et elemosinis; INC.: [f. 40v] multa et magna sunt fratres carissimi beneficia diuina . . .; EXPL.: [f. 48v] . . . in persecutione purpuream pro passione geminabit. de ope et elemosinis explicit [SIMONETTI 1976, 155–172].

7. Cyprian, *De mortalitate*—ff. 48v–55r.

7.1. RUB.: incipit de mortalitate; INC.: etsi apud plurimos uestrum fratres dilectissimi mens solida est et fides firma . . .; EXPL.: . . . ad quorum conuiuium congregatur quisque fidelis et iustus et laudabilis inuenitur. de mortalitate explicit [SIMONETTI 1976, 17–26].

7.2. Cap. 18—ff. 53r–55r. RUB.: incipit de contempnenda morte; INC.: meminisse debeamus uoluntatem nos non nostram sed dei facere . . .; EXPL.: . . . quorum circa se fuerunt desideria maiora. de contempnenda morte explicit [SIMONETTI 1976, 26–32].

Text is divided between chapters 17 and 18, each beginning with an initial and piece border; see SIMONETTI 1976, 17–32.

8. Cyprian, *Ad Demetrianum*—ff. 55r–62v.

RUB.: incipit ad demetrianum; INC.: [f. 55r] oblatrantem te et aduersus deum qui unus est et uerus est . . .; EXPL.: [f. 62v] . . . qui cum morti fuisset obnoxius factus in mortalitate securus. cecilii cipriani ad demetrianum explicit [SIMONETTI 1976, 35–51].

9. Cyprian, *De bono patientiae*—ff. 62v–69v.

RUB.: incipit de bono pacientie; INC.: [f. 62v] de paciencia locuturus fratres carisimi et utilitates et eius comoda predicaturus unde pocius incipiam . . .; EXPL.: [f. 69v] . . . sed cum iustis et deum timentibus honoremur. de [-zelo et liuoi] bono pacientie explicit [MORESCHINI 1976, 118–133].

10. Cyprian, *De zelo et liuore*—ff. 69v–74v.

RUB.: incipit de zelo et liuore; INC.: [f. 69v] zelare quod bonum uideas et inuidere melioribus . . .; EXPL.: [f. 74v] . . . si placituri semper in regno in hoc mundo ante placeamus. cecilii cipriani de zelo et liuore explicit [SIMONETTI 1976, 75–86].

11. Cyprian, *Epistolae*—ff. 74v–108v.

Letters 6, 10, 28, 37, 11, 38, 39, 60, 57, 59, 52, 47, 45, 44, 51, 49, 50, 61, 46, 78, 13, 43, 76, 77; see DIERCKS 1994 and 1996.

12. Cyprian (dub.), *Quod idola dii non sint*—ff. 108v–111v.

RUB.: incipit quod ydola dii non sint et quod unus deus sit et quod christum credentibus salus data sit; INC.: [f. 108v] quod ydola dii non sunt et quod unus deus sit et quod intercedentibus datum sit . . .; EXPL.: [f. 111v] . . . quod est christus erimus christiani si christum fuerimus secuti. quod ydola dii non sint explicit [VON HARTEL 1868–1871, 1:19–31].

13. Cyprian, *Epistolae*—ff. 111v–118v.

Letters 66, 54, 32, 20, 30; see DIERCKS 1994 and 1996.

14. Cyprian, *Ad Fortunatum*—ff. 118v–128v.

RUB.: incipit ad fortunatum de exortatione martirii; INC.: [f. 118v] desiderasti fortunate carissime ut quoniam persecutionum et pressurarum pondus incunbit . . .; EXPL.: [f. 128v] . . . in persecutione milicia in pace consciencia coronatur. de exortatione martirii explicit [WEBER 1972, 183–206].

15. Cyprian, *Epistolae*—ff. 128v–140v.

Letters 63 and 55; see Diercks 1996.

16. Ps.-Cyprian, *De laude martirii*—ff. 141r–148v.

rub.: incipit de laude martirii; inc.: [f. 141r] etsi incongruens est fratres karissimi in hoc fauore dicendi aliquid trepidationis afferre ac minime deceat . . .; expl.: [f. 148v] . . . sed hoc dominus poterit efficere quod uobis petentibus creditur non negare. de laude martirii explicit [von Hartel 1868–1871, 3:26–52].

17. Cyprian, *Epistolae*—ff. 148v–196r.

Letters 58, 73, 70, 74, 40, 65, 1, 69, 67, 64, 2, 31, 70, 7, 14, 4, 56, 3, 72, 12, 16, 15, 17, 18, 19, 26, 24, 25, 9, 29, 27, 23, 36, 33, 34, 80; see Diercks 1994 and 1996.

18. Ps.-Cyprian, *Aduersus Iudaeos*—ff. 196r–199r.

inc.: [f. 196r] attendite sensum et intelligenciam uestram in spiritu sancto . . .; expl.: [f. 199r] . . . sic dominus florere uoluit gentes uidetis quemadmodum uos christus dilexit [Diercks 1972, 265–278].

19. Ps.-Cyprian, *De aleatoribus*—ff. 199r–202r.

inc.: [f. 199r] magna nobis ob uniuersam fraternitatem curo fidelis maxime et rea perditorum omnium audacia id est aleatorum . . .; expl.: [f. 202r] . . . puras manus ad christum extende ut promereri deum possis aleam noli respicere [von Hartel 1868–1871, 3:92–104].

20. Ps.-Cyprian, *De montibus Sina et Sion*—ff.. 202r–206v.

rub.: probatio capitulorum ueteris testamenti; inc.: [f. 202r] probacio capitulorum que in scripturis deificis continentur . . .; expl.: [f. 206v] . . . in contentione iudicium et in nomine eius gentes credant [von Hartel 1868–1871, 3:104–119].

21. Ps.-Cyprian, *Ad Vigilium episcopum de iudaica incredulitate*—ff. 206v–210r.

inc.: [f. 206v] etsi plurimos gentilium scio uigili sanctissime ab ordine atque ratione ueritatis aduersos . . .; expl.: [f. 210r] . . . in domini misericordia in mente habe puerum tuum celsum sanctissime [von Hartel 1868–1871, 3:119–132].

22. Cyprian, *Epistolae* 75—ff. 210v–217r.

Letter 75; see Diercks 1996.

23. Ps.-Cyprian, *Exhortatio ad poenitentiam*—ff. 217r–219v.

rub.: incipit de penitencia; inc.: [f. 217r] per penitenciam posse omnia peccata dimitti ei qui ad deum toto corde conuersus sit . . .; expl.: [f. 219v] . . . sin autem ueniam tibi cito et candelabrum de loco suo mouebo [Ciccolini 2011, 132–138].

24. Ps.-Cyprian, *De duodecim abusiuis saeculi*—ff. 219v–227r.

INC.: [f. 219v] sequitur duodecim abusiones sancti cipriani episcopi et martiris gloriosissimi . . .; EXPL.: [f. 227r] . . . ne sine nobis christus esse incipiat in futuro amen. explicit deo gratias [HELLMANN 1909, 1–62].

An edition is in progress by Aidan Breen; see CLAYTON 2012, esp. p. 141 n. 1.

BIBLIOGRAPHY: BREEN 2002.

25. Index—ff. 228r–229v.

BINDING: s. xv/xvi; brown leather (mostly lifted) over pasteboards; blue and tan endbands; sewing on five double cords.

OWNERS & PROVENANCE: George John Warren Vernon (1803–1866), 5th Baron of Vernon (Sudbury Hall, Derbyshire); acquired from H. P. Kraus (New York, NY) by the university in March 1967.

SALES & CATALOGUES: Sotheby's, 10 June 1918, lot 167; Maggs Bros., Cat. 369, no. 216; ibid., Cat. 380, no. 1665; ibid., Cat. 395, no. 30; H. P. Kraus, Cat. 115, no. 3.

FORMER SHELFMARK: MS 44 (Notre Dame).

BIBLIOGRAPHY: CORBETT no. 44; D'ALVERNY 1981, 107.

cod. Lat. d. 3

Origin: England (Wales?), s. xv[1].
Content Overview: Martin of Troppau, *Chronicon pontificum et imperatorum* (excerpt) with continuation of popes; Geoffrey of Monmouth, *Historia regum Britanniae* (with associated contents); Ps.-Methodius, *Apokalypsis*; Bede, *Historia ecclesiastica gentis Anglorum* [excerpt]; unidentified chronicle, from Noah to Henry V.

In Latin, on parchment; iii +57 ff.; generally 345 x 245 mm (page) [see Layout for ruling]; flyleaves i–iii and ff. 1v–2v, 11r–12v, 36r–37v, 48r–57v blank; foliated in modern pencil with Arabic numerals.

Collation: iii $+1^{2}$ $+2^{10-2}$ $+3^{2}$ $+4^{12}$ $+5^{10+1}$ $+6^{2}$ $+7^{8+2}$ $+8^{6}$ $+9^{1+1}$ $+10^{2}$

Bibliographical Format: 2° (paper quires).

Quires: The manuscript has been rebound and quire structures have been disturbed. Quire 1 is a parchment bifolium (s. xvii). Quire 2 is a quinion, H/F, lacking the fourth and tenth leaves; does not obey Gregory's Rule. Quires 3, 6, 9, and 10 are paper bifolia folded in folio and inserted between and within the other quires to divide the texts. Quire 4 is a parchment sexternion, F/F; obeys Gregory's Rule. Quire 5 is a parchment quinion, F/H, with a leaf inserted asymmetrically (f. 35); obeys Gregory's Rule. Quire 7 is a parchment quaternion, F/F, with a paper bifolium (ff. 40–41) inserted asymmetrically; parchment sections obey Gregory's rule. Quire 8 is a paper ternion. Quire 9 is comprised of two singletons. Quire 10 is a paper bifolium. Conservation treatment has disturbed the original quire forms with the addition of Japanese paper, paste, and new stitching. In quire 1, f. 8 was inserted asymmetrically (new stitching visible), where the stub was previously between ff. 5v–6r [see Contents 1].

Watermarks: Nine occurrences of a single watermark: (**A**) Pot with handle, three-pronged crown with quarter flower above, letters **po**; occurs in paper quires 3, 6, 8, 9, 10 (ff. 12, 36, 40, 49, 51, 53, 54, 55, 56); approx. 25 x 15 mm; distance between chainlines 24 mm; general similarity to Heawood 3556 (no place, no date).

Catchwords: A single horizontal catchword in lower right margin of f. 24v; corresponds.

LAYOUT:

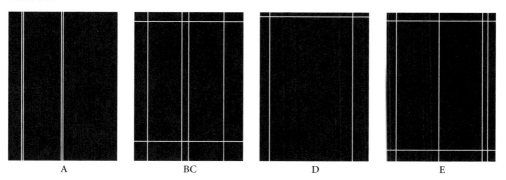

A BC D E

A ff. 3r–10v. Combined technique; variable dimensions (see below).
B ff. 13r–38v. Lead; 278 x 170 mm; intercol. 14 mm; 70–74 lines.
C f. 39r–v. Lead; 285 x 174 mm; intercol. 15 mm; 71 lines.
D ff. 42r–46v. Red ink; 329 x 186 mm; variable use of frame.
E f. 47r–v. Red ink; 300 x 193 mm; no true intercol.; 76 lines.

Pattern **A** is traced on ff. 3r–10v for Martin of Troppau's *Chronicon* [see CONTENTS 1]; two double lines (3 mm) are traced in brown ink over brown crayon and filled with yellow and green; double roundels are positioned along the lines (18 mm in diameter) [see DIAGRAMS]; text area is frame-ruled in brown crayon (see f. 4r), generally 289 x 195 mm; two columns; writing below top line. Pattern **B** is traced in lead on ff. 13r–38v; two columns (intercol. 14mm); writing below top line; prickings visible for verticals in the upper and lower margins. Pattern **C** is a modified version of **B** traced on f. 39r–v to accommodate added text [see CONTENTS 4]; two columns (intercol. 15 mm); writing below top line. Pattern **D** is traced on ff. 42r–46v in red ink consistently with an upper horizontal, and vertical bounding lines only (no lower); additional verticals in red ink are added to create frames for text and various line configurations for roundels (13 mm in diameter) [see DIAGRAMS]; writing below top line; prickings visible occasionally in upper margin for verticals; text written in various arrangements. Pattern E is frame-ruled in red ink on f. 47r–v, which continues the chronicle without diagrams; two columns (no intercol., but approx. 15 mm gaps); writing below top line; no prickings visible.

SCRIPT: Four scribal bookhands (M1–M4) write all texts in Anglicana and English Cursiva at various levels of execution. Additional hands correct the text or make additions in Anglicana (e.g., 3r^{b}). M1 writes Cursiva Libraria on ff. 3r–10v, 39r–46v, 47r^{a}–v^{a} using Anglicana forms for **d**, **e**, **g**, **r**, **s** with great regularity, though normal Cursiva forms are also used; single compartment **a** is consistently used, though two compartment **a** occurs as a deviant form occasionally in initial position; there is an obvious continental influence on the script despite its definitively English character and use of Anglicana forms; Textualis used in roundels. M2 writes Anglicana Formata (Cursiva Antiquior) against the influence of Cursiva on ff. 13r–35v; M2 admits single compartment **a** alongside the normal two compartment form as an alternative form, which begins to become regular; M2 also uses Cursiva **g**. M3 writes Anglicana Currens on ff. 38r–47v with two compartment **a**, and the characteristic forms of **e**, **g**, **r**, and **s**, though the influence of Bastarda is apparent. M4 writes Anglicana Libraria beginning in the lower margin on f. 46v through the middle of f. 47v[a]; M4 consistently uses all Anglicana letter forms without exception. Description of contents in English and ownership marks in the autograph of Valentine Leigh (1560) are found on f. 1r; ownership mark of James Sotheby (1687) in upper margin of f. 1r, and a John Conwell (s. xv) on f. 9v. [See OWNERS & PROVENANCE].

DECORATION: In addition to medieval decoration there is sixteenth-century decoration (dragons) on f. 1r with the ownership mark of Valentine Leigh [see OWNERS & PROVENANCE].

I. RUBRICATION: Rubrics in red ink; letter heightening of majuscules in yellow and red ink.

II. INITIALS: Littera duplex, flourished, and plain initials occur loosely in hierarchy.

A. Littera duplex initials (4 line square inset) occur on ff. 13r[a] and 38r[a] (hanging **i**) with red flourished marginal sprays.

B. Flourished initials (3 line square inset) are painted exclusively in blue with red penwork, as is typical of the English practice.

C. Plain initials (1 line versals) alternate in red and blue ink on ff. 39r–39v and 42r–47v.

DIAGRAMS: Succession diagrams are drawn in two columns on ff. 3r–10v; double roundels 18 mm in diameter traced in black (outer) and red (inner) ink, and *lineae* filled with yellow and green; larger roundels in green, red, yellow, and black on f. 4r for Augustus (22 mm in diameter) and Christ (25 mm in diameter) [see LAYOUT, Pattern **A**]. Genealogical diagrams drawn in red ink in various configurations on ff. 42r–45v; roundels 13 mm in diameter; larger triple roundels 19 mm in diameter for Lucius (f. 43v), Woden (f. 44r), Arthur with crown (f. 44r); 23 mm in diameter for Egbert (f. 44v); 25 mm for St. Edward with crown (f. 45v) [see LAYOUT, Pattern **D**].

CONTENTS:

1. Martin of Troppau, *Chronicon pontificum et imperatorum* (excerpt with additions)—ff. 3r[b]–10v[b].

Due to the missing leaf between ff. 5v and 6r, the *Chronicon* lacks the entries for John III through Gregory II. The rubricator has added years with red Arabic numerals next to encircled names in diagrams.

1.1. *Chronicon pontificum et imperatorum*—ff. 3r^{b}–9v^{a}. INC.: <s>ecundum orosium ad augustinum a creatione mundi ad urbem . . .; EXPL.: . . . et fuit iste fredericus .95. imperator ab augusto primo cesare.

Edition: Weiland 1872.
Bibliography: Ikas 2002, 195–198.

1.2. *Notitiae breues de pontificibus maximis*—ff. 9v^{b}–10v^{b}. INC.: <g>regorius .9. campanus annis .14. elizabet filiam . . .; EXPL.: . . . iohannes .23. anno domini .1414. celebrant consilium in constancia ciuitate alemannie ubi et ipse depositus est.

Edition: Ikas 2004, 280–289.
Bibliography: Ikas 2004, 53–56; Ikas 2002, esp. 18–19, 21, 195–198, 203; Crick 1991, 57–58.

2. Geoffrey of Monmouth, *Historia regum Britanniae* [*De gestis Britonum*] (with associated contents)—ff. 13r^{a}–35v^{b}.

2.1. *Ab origine mundi circa annos tria milia*—f. 13r^{a-b}. RUB.: de prima inhabitacione regni anglie et cetera; INC.: ab origine mundi circa annos tria millia . . .; EXPL.: [f. 13r^{b}] . . . ex eorum nomine britanniam uocauerunt sicut patet in sequenti.

Bibliography: Crick 1991, 22; Carley and Crick 1995, 50.

2.2. Genealogy: *Trojans*—f. 13r^{b}–v^{a}. RUB.: genelogia [*sic*] priami regis troie et enee usque ad brutum; INC.: ciprus quidam filius cetini in cypro insula primus regnauit . . .; EXPL.: . . . filius iaphet filius noe.

Bibliography: Crick 1991, 43–44.

2.3. Dares Phrygius, *De excidio Troiae historia* (XII)—f. 13v^{a-b}. RUB.: de forma quorundam ducum grecorum et troianorum; INC.: dares frigius qui historiam troianorum scripsit ait se militasse . . .; EXPL.: . . . que sua formositate omnes superauit animo simplici largam dapsilem.

Edition: Meister 1991, 14–16.
Bibliography: Crick 1991, 35–39.

2.4. Geoffrey of Monmouth, *Historia regum Britanniae* [*De gestis Britonum*] ('vulgate' text)—ff. 13v^{b}–35v^{b}.

2.4.1. Prologue [§§1–3]—f. 13v^{b}. RUB.: translacio gaufridi arciri [*sic*] monemutensis de gestis britonum; INC.: cum mecum multa et de multis sepius animo reuoluens in historiam regum britannie inciderem . . .; EXPL.: . . . unde britannia tibi nunc temporibus nostris ac si alterum henricum adepta interno gratulatur affectu.

2.4.2. Description of the Island [§5]—ff. 13v^{b}–14r^{a}. RUB.: prologus; INC.: britannia insularum optima in occidentali occeano inter galliam et hiberniam sita . . .; EXPL.: . . . applicuerunt restat nunc parare ut in subsequentibus explicabitur.

2.4.3. Book 1 [§§6–53]—ff. 14r^{a}–19v^{a}. RUB.: liber primus; INC.: eneas post troianum bellum excidium urbis cum astanio filio diffugiens in italiam . . .; EXPL.: . . . ipse eciam diademate priscanus illis et tocius insule imperabat principibus.

2.4.4. Book 2 [§§54–72]—ff. 19v^{a}–21v^{a}. RUB.: liber secundus; INC.: interea contigit ut in romanis reperitur historiis iulium cesarem . . .; EXPL.: . . . nullatenus opus fuit ut inferiori stilo renouaretur.

2.4.5. Book 3 [§§73–88]—ff. 21v^{a}–23v^{a}. RUB.: liber tertius; INC.: interea gloriosus rex lucius cum infra regnum suum cultum . . .; EXPL.: . . . ad conciues suos in armoricam que iam altera britannia uocabatur.

2.4.6. Book 4 [§§89–208]—ff. 23v^{a}–35v^{b}. RUB.: liber quartus; INC.: gracianus municeps cum de nece maximiani audiuisset . . .; EXPL.: . . . in honore predicatorum principum hoc modo in latinum sermonem transferre curaui. explicit historia britonum.

The contents are listed according to the book division of the rubrics in the manuscript; the *Prophetiae Merlini* [§§109–117] begins on f. 26r^{a} (prologue) and f. 26r^{b} (text). For rubrics and book divisions in the manuscript tradition, see CRICK 1991, 121–157, and REEVE and WRIGHT 2007, lx–lxi.

EDITION: REEVE and WRIGHT 2007.
BIBLIOGRAPHY: CRICK 1989, 212–214; CRICK 1991, 129; REEVE 1991b; REEVE and WRIGHT 2007, xliii.

3. Ps.-Methodius, *Apokalypsis* (Latin)—ff. 38r^{a}–39r^{a}

3.1. RUB.: incipit liber methodii de millenariis seculi; INC.: [f. 38r^{a}] in nomine ihesu christi incipit liber methodii episcopi ecclessie paterenys . . .; EXPL.: [f. 38r^{a}] . . . in opusculis suis collaudauit.

3.2. RUB.: de primo millenio seculi; INC.: [f. 38r^{a}] sciendum namque est nobis fratres . . .; EXPL.: [f. 39r^{a}] . . . uiuit et regnat deus per infinita secula seculorum amen.

Rubrics in red ink are also present on f. 38r: *de primo millenio seculi; de secundo millenio seculi; de tertio millenio seculi; de quarto millenio seculi; de quinto millenio seculi*; and on f. 38v: *de sexto millenio seculi; quid continget in fine seculorum.*

EDITION: AERTS AND KORTEKAAS 1998 (edition of Rec. I, which differs from this version).
BIBLIOGRAPHY: CRICK 1991, 58–59.

4. Bede, *Historia ecclesiastica gentis Anglorum* [5.24]—f. 39r[a]–v[a].

INC.: [f. 39r[a]] uerum ea que temporum distinctione latius digesta sunt . . . [5.24]; EXPL.: [f. 39v[a]] . . . ad lucem propria est reuersa. hec de historia ecclesiastica secundum bedam de britannia et maxime gentis anglorum.

EDITION: COLGRAVE and MYNORS 1969.
BIBLIOGRAPHY: CRICK 1991, 33–35.

5. Chronicle, from Noah to Henry V (unidentified)—ff. 42r[a]–47v[a].

INC.: [f. 42r[a]] ab hiis tribus filiis noe texuntur generaciones .lxxij. post diuisionem in edificacione babel in agro . . .; EXPL.: [f. 47v[a]] . . . quod multi magistri suspecti dicebantur de lollardria.

Close textual parallels and verbatim sections are also found in Aberystwyth, National Library of Wales, Roll 55.

BINDING: s. xvi/xvii; calf over pasteboards; rebacked (modern); gilt tooled; boards detached.

OWNERS & PROVENANCE: John Conwell (s. xv; see f. 9v); ownership inscription of 1560 Valentine Leigh (d. 1563) on f. 1r; William Cecil, Lord Burghley (1521–1598); inherited by Robert Bruce, First Earl of Ailesbury (1626–1685); acquired by James Sotheby (1655–1720) in 1687, thus passing into Ecton Hall presumably by descent to Charles William Hamilton Sotheby (1820–1887), Frederick Edward Sotheby (1837–1909), and Herbert George Sotheby (1871–1954) until the "Sotheby Heirlooms" sale of 1955; James G. Commin (bookseller; unverified); E. Hauswedell (1961); H. P. Kraus (ca. 1962); acquired from H. P. Kraus (New York, NY) by the university in April 1964.

SALES & CATALOGUES: Bentley & Walford, 21 November 1687, p. 80, lot 12; Sotheby's, 21 November 1955, lot 156; Hauswedell, 3 June 1961, lot 1; H. P. Kraus, Cat. 100, no. 19.

FORMER SHELFMARK: MS 40 (Notre Dame).

BIBLIOGRAPHY: CORBETT no. 40; D'ALVERNY 1981, 107; CRICK 1989, 212–214; CRICK 1986, 159; CRICK 1991, 22, 34, 43–44, 57–58, 59, 129, 161–162, 173–175, 190, 201; IKAS 2002, 18, 21, 195–198, 203; IKAS 2004, 53, 117–118; REEVE and WRIGHT 2007, xliii.

cod. Lat. d. 4

Origin: Italy, s. xv.
Content Overview: Walter Burley, *Expositio super artem ueterem Porphyrii et Aristotelis* (incomplete) with scholia.

In Latin, on paper; 107 ff.; generally 343 x 228 mm [see Layout for ruling]; foliated in modern pencil with Arabic numerals.

Collation: 1^{10-1} $+2$–10^{10} $+11^{8-1}$

Bibliographical Format: 2°.

Quires: Paper quinions folded in folio are the normal quire forms. Quire 1 is lacking most of the final leaf (f. 10), though a small fragment of marginal commentary remains. Quire 11 is a paper quaternion folded in folio lacking the final leaf. The manuscript is water-damaged severely and stained; paper conservation treatments are present.

Catchwords: Vertical catchwords are written in the inner right margins for quires 1–6 and 8–9; all correspond. Quire 7 contains a horizontal catchword in the lower right margin; corresponds.

Watermarks: Fifty-three occurrences of six different watermarks: (**A**) Hat; occurs in quire 1 (ff. 2, 4, 6, 8); corresponds closely to Briquet 3387 (Florence, 1465). (**B**) Griffon; occurs in quires 2–4 (ff. 12, 16–18, 20, 21, 26, 27–29, 33, 34, 36, 39) and quires 10, 11 (ff. 96, 97, 99–102; damaged on ff. 105, 106); cf. Piccard 123882 (Padua, 1461) and 123881 (Central Italy, 1464–1465). (**C**) Semi-Griffon; occurs in quires 4 and 7 (ff. 40, 63, 66, 67, 69, 70); cf. Piccard 123874 (Florence, 1385). (**D**) Horn; occurs in quires 5, 6, 9, 10 (ff. 42, 46–48, 50–52, 56–58, 83, 93); cf. Briquet 7684 (Padua, 1416) and Piccard 119603 (Udine, 1423). (**E**) Bird with eye, two-line legs, tail feathers; occurs in quires 8 and 9 (ff. 72, 73, 76, 77, 80, 87, 89, 90); cf. Piccard 42178 (Naples, 1476). (**F**) Crown with three prongs in a circle; occurs in quire 9 (f. 85); cf. Briquet 4689 (Venice, 1482).

Layout:

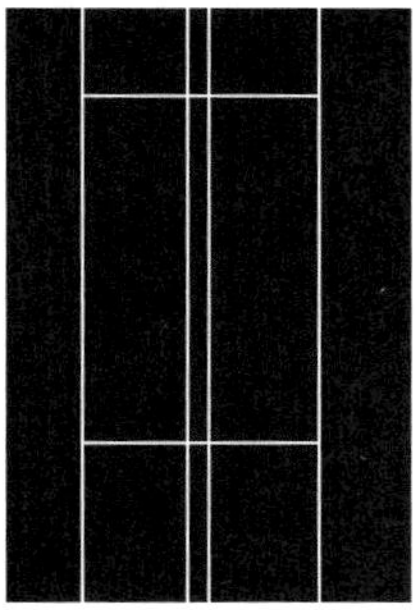

A

A ff. 1r–107v. Combined technique; 200 x 133 mm; intercol. 12 mm; 29–36 lines.

Pattern **A** is traced on ff. 1r–107v using a combined technique of hard-point and lead; lead is visible on most folios; frame-ruled only; two columns (intercol. irregular, but approx. 12 mm); writing above top line; number of lines variable; no prickings visible.

Script: A single hand (M1) writes all text in a rapid Humanistic script, combining minuscule and cursive elements; execution is erratic as is the script. Lemmata are written in a larger script mixing Textualis forms with Humanistic ones. Another hand (M2) has added text in a fully developed Humanistic cursive in the right and lower right margins on f. 6v.

Decoration:

I. Rubrication: Rubrics usually in brownish and blackish ink; a single rubric in red ink; paraph marks in red ink throughout the manuscript.

II. Initials: Plain initials occur in various sizes; many insets blank with guide letters; some insets also have lead tracings for initials.

a. Plain initials (3–8 line square inset) are painted in red ink with a few in blue and black; some have been transformed subsequently into flourished types with brownish ink (e.g., ff. 1r, 74v).

Contents:

1. Walter Burley, *Expositio super artem ueterem Porphyrii et Aristotelis*—ff. $1r^{a}$–$107v^{b}$.

1.1. Prologue—ff. $1r^{a}$–$5r^{a}$. inc.: quia de dictis in loica intendo quoddam conpendium compilare uidenda sunt primo tria circa loicam in communy deinde descendendum est ad scientiam traditam in libro porfiriy [*sic*] . . .; expl.: . . . prohemium.

1.2. *Porphyry*—ff. 5r^{b}–24v^{a}; INC.: cum sit necessarium grisorori [*sic*] iste liber qui est primus in ordine doctrine inter libros loice continet prohemium et duos tractatus in primo tractatu auctor determinat de unoquoque uniuersali . . .; EXPL.: . . . ab illis quibus accidit sed secundum magis et minus igitur [*ut uid.*] et cetera. finis huius capituli. expliciunt universalia burley. incipiunt predicamenta.
1.3. *Praedicamenta*—ff. 24v^{b}–28r^{a}. INC.: <c>irca librum predicamentorum est sciendum quod subiectum contentiuum totius scientie tradite in libro predicamentorum est ens dicibile inconplexum inordinabile in genere . . .; EXPL.: . . . ad coppulandum extrema id inuicem uel diuidendum extrema ad inuicem. explicit prologus burley incipit tractatus predicamentorum.
1.4. *Praed.* [text; incomplete]—ff. 28r^{b}–107v^{b}. INC.: equiuoca dicuntur iste liber qui est de predicamentis ut eis insunt intentiones secunde continet tres tractatus . . .; EXPL.: . . . sicut enim albedo et nigredo sunt contraria sic motus ad nigredinem.

The text of the *Praedicamenta* ends imperfectly; lemmata written in larger script.

EDITION: VENICE 1497.
BIBLIOGRAPHY: LOHR 1968, 174–176; WEISHEIPL 1969, 189; SHARPE 710–712; VON PERGER 2001, 237–238.

2. Anonymous commentary on Burley's *Expositio sup. ars. uet.*—ff. 1r–69r.

2.1. *Porph.*—ff. 1r–18r. INC.: [*in lae. marg.*] ipse burleus prius incipit traditque regulam communem circa loicam . . .; EXPL.: [*in dex. marg.*] . . . sed propriis quod est inseparabile repugnat separabile.
2.2. *Praed.*—ff. 27v–69r. INC.: [*in dex. marg.*] qualiter duplex sit conpositio scilicet realis et intellectualis modo non est inconueniens . . .; EXPL.: [*in dex. marg.*] . . . [*mutilo*] ut hic preter [*ut uid.; fort.* pater] et cetera.

The commentary is written in the margins by M1; the comments on Burley's *Porph.* are fuller and more frequent than those on the *Praed.*, which are extremely sparse after the first few sections.

BINDING: Limp vellum; arms on front cover; sewn on three split thongs; ownership mark of a Gerardinus de Buschitis.

OWNERS & PROVENANCE: Gerardinus de Buschitis (s. xv?); a Jacomus Jacomini is named on inner rear cover; donated to the university by William F. Mulrenan (1915–1974; class of 1937).

FORMER SHELFMARK: MS 19 (Notre Dame).

BIBLIOGRAPHY: CORBETT no. 19.

cod. Lat. d. 5

Origin: Italy, s. xv^{2} (Venice).
Content Overview: Boethius, *De consolatione philosophiae*; works of Filippo da Strada [Philippus Ligurensis].

In Latin and Italian, on parchment; ii + 84 ff. +ii; generally 351 x 234 mm (page) [see Layout for ruling]; foliated in modern pencil with Arabic numerals; flyleaves modern parchment (s. xix); ff. 1r and 84v blank.

Collation: ii +1^{2} +2–9^{10} +10^{2} +ii

Quires: Parchment quinions, F/F, are the normal quire forms (quire 2, H/H). Quires 1 and 10 are bifolia, F/F, which were pastedowns formerly (ff. 1r and 84v).

Catchwords: Horizontal catchwords in lower center margins of quires 3–8; stylized; all correspond.

Signatures: Signatures of the *ad hoc* type occur in quires 2–9 (using letters **a** and **b** with Roman numerals).

Layout:

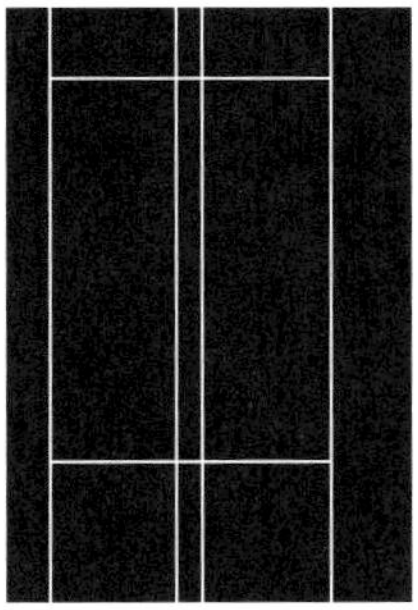

A

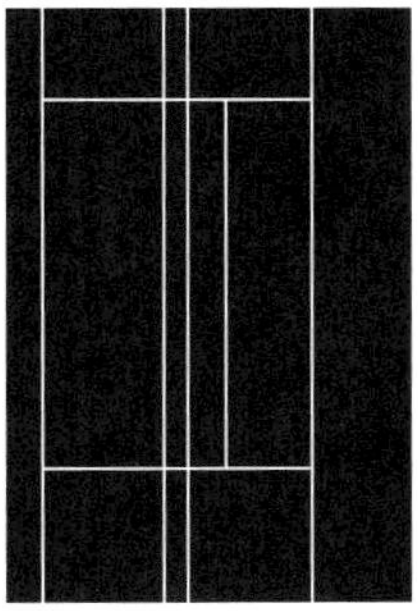

A1

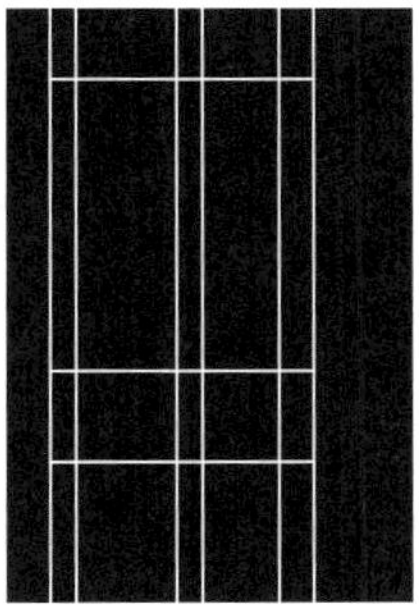

B1

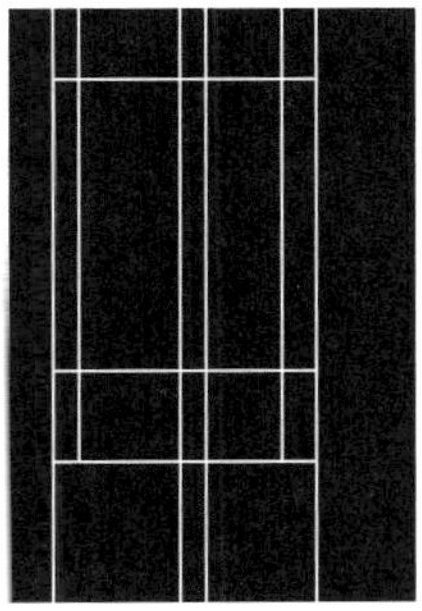

B2

A ff. 2r–12v, 83r–v. Combined technique; variable dimensions.
B ff. 13r–82v. Combined technique; variable dimensions.

The ruling patterns are variable and often idiosyncratic per folio; patterns are not always homogenous with the use of the ruling; dimensions of the ruling vary. Pattern **A** is ruled on ff. 2r–83v using hard-point technique (New Style); prickings for verticals visible in the upper margins; in various sections the hard-point ruling is retraced in brown ink, lead, crayon, or combinations of each. **A** is used as a single column on ff. 2r–3v; writing above top line (inverted additions in lower margin); ff. 10r–12v and 83r–v use **A** as two columns (approx. 226 x 142 mm; intercol. 15 mm; 33 lines; 70 lines on f. 83r–v). **A1** adds an additional vertical on ff. 4r–9v to contain writings of Filippo da Strada in a marginal column to the right of the calendar; dimensions of **A1** differ per folio (approx. 218–226 x 155–175 mm); no additional calendric columns are ruled; writing above top line (inverted additions in lower margin). Pattern **A** is modified with additional verticals to create pattern **B** for the text of Boethius and the works of Filippo da Strada. **B** is traced inconsistently, resulting in variants **B1** and **B2**. The text of Boethius is written in a single column (approx. 172 x 112 mm; 23–24 lines); writing below top line (additional line blank if rubric does not begin the folio); prickings for additional verticals in the upper and lower margins for the text of Boethius (inner vertical bounding lines). Prickings in the inner and outer margin mark the final line of Boethius per folio; six ruled lines follow last line marked by pricking. The works of Filippo da Strada are written below the text of Boethius; single column (approx. 92 x 147 mm; outer vertical bounding lines; 16–18 lines); two lines of Humanistic minuscule are written in one ruled line; text often exceeds bounding lines in the outer margin. Former flyleaves, now ff. 1v and 84r, contain text written in a single column with a variable number of lines, but are not ruled.

Script: Humanistic minuscule and cursive throughout the manuscript are written by a single hand (M1), which has been identified as the autograph of Filippo da Strada (see Dell'Oso 2013, 44–49); the manuscripts used by Dell'Oso for comparison were Firenze, Biblioteca Riccardiana, Ricc. 1213, and Milano, Biblioteca Braidense, AC. IX. 34 (see Dell'Oso 2014, 81–82 for plates). A second hand (M2) writes Southern Textualis (Rotunda) of the late fifteenth century on ff. 3r–v and 10r–12v; the script displays great angularity, is prone to heavy forking of ascenders, and the Rotunda **a** is often closed with a hairline; M2 is also likely the hand of Filippo da Strada. A third hand (M3) writes the liturgical calendar on ff. 4r–9v in Southern Textualis Formata (Rotunda). A fourth hand (M4) writes the text of Boethius (ff. 13r–82v) in Southern Textualis Formata (Rotunda) of the late fifteenth century; the script is heavily compressed, very round, and ascenders and descenders are short.

Decoration:

I. Rubrication: Rubrics in red and brown ink; paraph marks alternate in red and blue ink; letter heightening of majuscules and cadels in red ink.

II. Initials: Plain initials and capitals occur loosely in hierarchy.

a. Plain initials (2–6 line square inset; 1 line versals) in red and blue; some outlined only in black ink; versals in red ink only (f. 10r); influence of capitalis present in many examples which begin text written in the Humanistic scripts.

CALENDAR: One month per page; dominical letters **a** in red ink; Roman time marked in red ink.

CONTENTS:

1. Filippo da Strada, *In laude Boetii*—f. 1v.

RUB.: in laude boetii innocenter expulsi ab urbe romana carmina digressum facientia ut postea melius concludant; INC.: [f. 1v] o miles molis dicam te degenerasse ab prisca ex uenetis nobilitate tui . . .; EXPL.: [f. 1v] . . . eris illo ex numero facio te qui decus urbis romanae pepulit philosophia leuet.

2. Filippo da Strada, prologue to verse commentary on Boethius, *De consolatione*—f. 2r.

RUB.: prologus super commentum nouum boetii per carmina subiuncta singulis prosis eiusdem autoris per ordinem; INC.: [f. 2r] quoniam superbiae nubilo turpiter execati [*sic*] plures hominum latinorum imperiti pertinacitatem exprimentis palatinam . . .; EXPL.: [f. 2r] . . . eorum qui quottidie subintrant componentum nugacitatem indoctam sapienter perdocentis. finis prologi in commentantia boetium carmina senis interpretis leniora. RUB.: sequere post hanc praefatione [*sic*] uersus adiectos.

EDITION: MCDONALD 2013, 45–49.

3. Filippo da Strada, verses—f. 2v.

INC.: [f. 2v] supplicat o proles faustissima proficientis officio in gentes lectas comitis ueterani oppressus frater senior defende clientem qui uocat ausilium de quo lux diua refulget . . .; EXPL.: [f. 2v] . . . dicta georgica sit comitis patris intimus heres heres uirtutum uenetis ueneratus amicis.

4. Filippo da Strada, *Obiectio fratrum praedicatorum*—f. 2v.

RUB.: obiectio fratrum praedicatorum in minoristas de uirgine maria concepta; INC.: [f. 2v] cum sanctissima uirgo dei genitrix in humanis dignata fuerit ad templum progredi purificationis sue causa pretensa . . .; EXPL.: [f. 2v] . . . ut dicunt omnes doctores sanctificatus erat.

5. Filippo da Strada, poem on eight virtues—f. 3r.

RUB.: paret hic est humilis pauper patiensque pudicus diliget est iustus pax puer iste deus. in natiuitate yhesu christi sermo; INC.: [f. 3r] octo deus uenit uirtutes figere nostris pectoribus nisi sint pectora nostra lapis paruit is primum patris regnantis olimpo consilio subiens quod monuisset opus . . .; EXPL.: [f. 3r] . . . angelus e supero delapsus cardine mandat regibus ite lares uisere calle rudi sic fecere citi delusus tuncque futurus improbus occisor uhe gregis ense uago.

6. Filippo da Strada, petition to the Council of Ten—f. 3r.

INC.: [f. 3r] uobis insignibus decem dominis iustitie uenetiarum executioni mandande nullo maiore consilio contra statuta uestra refragante . . .; EXPL.: [f. 3r] . . . supplicat bone fidei relligiosus praedicator quatenus qui fefellit innocentem perficiat quod tenetur libram uidelicet unam paruorum quae periit sui culpa.

7. Filippo da Strada, *Supplicatio magistri cuiusdam*—f. 3v.

RUB.: supplicatio magistri cuiusdam thesaurizandae theologiae ad integerrimam iustitiam uenetiarum; INC.: [f. 3v] esse decem dominos plectentes crimina uulgi . . .; EXPL.: [f. 3v] . . . crimina cum studeant qui peccant ludere iustos.

8. Calendar (Venice)—ff. 4r–9v.

Liturgical calendar in black ink with graded feasts in red ink, and few entries specify particular grades (e.g., *duplex maius*). The calendar points toward Venetian use and contains many Italian saints and several feasts particular to Venice; feasts of note include: Hyginus (Jan. 11), John Chrysostom (Jan. 27), Geminiano (Jan. 30), translation of Mark (Jan. 31), Faustinus and Jovita (Feb. 15), Ercolano of Perugia (Mar. 1), Anselm (Mar. 18), Vincent Ferrer (Apr. 5), translation of Monica (Apr. 9), procession of Isidore of Chios (Apr. 16), George (Apr. 23; red), Isidore of Chios (May 15), translation of Bernardine (May 17), Bernardine (May 20), translation of Francis (May 25), Secundus of Asti (Jun. 1), Anthony of Padua (Jun. 13), apparition of Mark (Jun. 25), Transfiguration (Aug. 6; red), Clare (Aug. 12), Moses (Sept. 4), dedication of St. Michael (Sept. 28; red), Francis (Oct. 4), Magnus of Oderzo (Oct. 6), dedication of the basilica St. John Lateran I (Nov. 9; red; here, *dedicatio basilice saluatoris et theodori*), dedication of the basilica of Peter and Paul (Nov. 18; red), Lucia (Dec. 13; red).

BIBLIOGRAPHY: MCDONALD 2013, 32–44 (detailed examination).

9. Filippo da Strada, *Accipe sub modicis certamina*—f. 4r.

INC.: [f. 4r] accipe sub modicis certamina uasta scientum est pudor in populo . . .; EXPL.: [f. 4r] . . . sollicitare ducem non est equitum sed honeste exeruisse bonum que possint laedere turmas.

10. Filippo da Strada, *Est prior hic noster*—f. 4v.

INC.: [f. 4v] est prior hic noster senior dignus ueneratu addictus uestris grauitatibus o generati sanguine magnifico . . .; EXPL.: [f. 4v] . . . pro re martirii quod pertulit integer heros.

11. Filippo da Strada, *Nunc placeat domini Mathiae*—ff. 4v–5r.

INC.: [f. 4v] nunc placeat domini mathiae laudibus ora laxemus dulci carmine . . .; EXPL.: [f. 5r] . . . instar ouis quem fugiamus adest nobis cautela duobus istis discussis quemque sequemur humi.

12. Filippo da Strada, *Notabile prohemium*—f. 5v.

RUB.: notabile prohemium; INC.: [f. 5v] non deerunt monaci qui tecum stent pater orent si pueros prohibes dormire thoro proprie fratres et monachos fractos . . .; EXPL.: [f. 5v] . . . probra hominum nisi sit uerax sententia scripti non tibi do legens potius discedo tumultu.

13. Filippo da Strada, Text against print—f. 5v.

INC.: [f. 5v] chi legera la presente compillatione sopra le prose de boetio . . .; EXPL.: [f. 5v] . . . cossi trouo in altre dictione senza fine.

EDITION: DELL'OSO 2013, 41.

14. Filippo da Strada, *Auribus accepi quae sunt*—f. 5v.

INC.: [f. 5v] auribus accepi quae sunt praemissa dolendo murmura de fetido nexu . . .; EXPL.: [f. 5v] . . . ut non credantur muliebria gaudia in illis uultibus extersis puerorum nocte seccuti.

15. Filippo da Strada, *Tollete amici le versi veraci*—f. 6r.

RUB.: tollete amici li uersi ueraci qual canta philippo predicatuore al buon poeta niun stia auaro; INC.: [f. 6r] carta et scrittura in optimo decore ben constan piu cha il libro fedo ingrato ma fante hauer perpetuale honore . . .; EXPL.: [f. 6r] non mai sera fatto opinione de homeni amanti compresse buggie libri di man te fan gran barone.

EDITION: DELL'OSO 2013, 126–127; DELL'OSO 2014, 88–89; DELL'OSO 2015, 29.

16. Filippo da Strada, Text against print—f. 6r.

INC.: [f. 6r] questa la tauola sopra uno confessionario che compuosi el dottissimo padre messer frate michel milanese del orden de san francesco . . .; EXPL.: [f. 6r] . . . trouati nel discorso da capo ad piedi comme uedera chi scontrara questo scritto a mano col uiciato ad torculo.

EDITION: DELL'OSO 2013, 43.

17. Filippo da Strada, *Viuacem puerum lecto locatum*—f. 6v.

INC.: [f. 6v] uiuacem puerum lecto locatum amicus quidam rubicundo colore possidebat . . .; EXPL.: [f. 6v] . . . amiciciamque deturbat seram foetu ac faenore praestituto lego diuum mortaliumue rectorum.

18. Filippo da Strada, *Consilium posco de te*—ff. 6v–7v.

INC.: [f. 6v] consilium posco de te pater o uenerande o decus ingentis grauitatis qui pia cernas . . .; EXPL.: [f. 7v] . . . hortamenta scies colubros extrudere ab antris ad sua quisque me et facies tibi deinde triumphus.

19. Filippo da Strada, *Te uolo scire breui*—f. 8r.

INC.: [f. 8r] te uolo scire breui pater o lepidissime quod sit res horrenda uiro propius retinere cloacas . . .; EXPL.: [f. 8r] . . . dignus uterque odiis turbabitur accubus infans.

20. Filippo da Strada, *Non prestat paucas in festis dicere missas*—f. 8v.

INC.: [f. 8v] non praestat paucas in festis dicere missas quam quod quis celebret nocte abeunte rutus . . .; EXPL.: [f. 8v] . . . dum desit mulier pro muliere mares femina tunc parui fiunt feruent uiduati coniuge sicque petunt coniugis inde uicem.

21. Filippo da Strada, *Vidimus infausti feruoris decus atrum*—f. 9r.

INC.: [f. 9r] uidimus infausti feruoris dedecus atrum nunc et auariciae morbus in ora uenit . . .; EXPL.: [f. 9r] . . . ut tu prouideas gemmis istic [*sic*] memoratis culpis ex uicio carnis opumque fame.

22. Filippo da Strada, *Est bonus ille putas uir dignus*—f. 9v.

INC.: [f. 9v] est bonus ille putas uir dignus amoreque gentis qui petit ut dentur . . .; EXPL.: [f. 9v] . . . posco ne fraude uelit mea damna rectori uestroque meo fac nota tot ausa.

23. Liturgical texts and prayers—ff. 10r–12v.

Mass prayers, readings, nuptial blessings in Latin (ff. 10r^{a}–11v^{a}); rubrics in Italian and text in Latin (ff. 11v^{b}–12v^{a}).

24. Filippo da Strada, verses to the Council of Ten—f. 12v.

RUB.: ad sapientissimi segniori sopra lo ariento conseglio de legge; INC.: se non credete de poter tirare ad la iustitia i damnificatuori . . .; EXPL.: . . . ben lo sa sopra chi e de illustro lampo prego o segniori ad uui sia qua grato.

EDITION: DELL'OSO 2013, 128–130.

25. Boethius, *De consolatione philosophiae*—ff. 13r–82v.

RUB.: <i>ncipit liber boecii malii [*sic*] torquati anitii seurini [*sic*] de consolatione ad instruendum pacienciam in aduersis et humilitatem in prosperis et ad diuine cognitionis apetitum et amorem eterne felicitatis et summi boni; INC.: [f. 13r] carmina /qui quon\dam studio florente peregi flebilis heu mestes cogor inire modos . . .; EXPL.: [f. 82v] . . . uultis neccesitas indicta probitatis cum ante oculos agitis iudicis cunca [*sic*] cernentis. explicit liber quintus boecii. deo gratias. amen.

EDITION: MORESCHINI 2000.

26. Fillipo da Strada, verse commentary to Boethius—ff. 13r–82r.

26.1. Introduction—f. 13r. INC.: nil tangens carmen quod tu canis alme boeti in prosas tendam flamina sana lirae . . .; EXPL.: . . . his finem faciens ambitebus ad mea pergo pensa cano in primam plana minuta prosam.

26.2. Book 1—ff. 13v–22r. RUB.: incipit expositio elegans per uersus elegos super prosas boetii per ordinem ad informationem iuuenum qui gaudent suauitate carminis lepidi; INC.: dum tacitus mecum curis agitarer ineptis musarum lugens carmina uana notans . . .; EXPL.: . . . tunc tibi succurret solatrix lux animarum eiectis umbris quae uia praepediens.

26.3. Book 2—ff. 22r–37r. RUB.: finis primi et principium secundi libri qui incipit post haec paulisper et cetera; INC.: haec modulata piis de labris philosophia obticuit pausans oraque mesta tuens . . .; EXPL.: . . . diuitiae marcere queunt non marcet amicans dum uiuit uiuit corde retentus amor.

26.4. Book 3—ff. 37v–52v. RUB.: [f. 37r] explicit liber secundus boetii incipit tertius iam cantum illa finierat sequitur expositio primae prosae; INC.: finierat iam uerba modos et carmina mater dulcis et inspiciens auribus esse citis . . .; EXPL.: . . . hec bonitas deus est felicia regna uidere atque frui tali simplice luce bona. finis libri tertii.

26.5. Book 4—ff. 55r–61v, 62v–63v, 64v, 65v–68r, 69v–70r. RUB.: prosa prima quarti libri; INC.: talia dum dulci dignoque tenore locuta esset amans mater philosophia mihi . . .; EXPL.: . . . aspera non sternat gnaros quia praeparat ornat exercet punit pace ferenda quidem.

26.6. Book 5—ff. 70v–82r. INC.: hactenus immensum spaciis confecimus aequor exacta est uersu scibilis ampla uia . . .; EXPL.: . . . magnorumque uirum si sit modo dente molenda nec mola nec lapis est laptus ad acre meus.

EDITION: McDONALD 2013, 50–54 (introduction and excerpts from Book 1).

27. Filippo da Strada, sermon on St. Cyprian and virginity—ff. 45v–46v.

INC.: [f. 45v] tra quelle duote che receue el feruente martiro cipriano dal summo dio fi detta esser la uirginita . . .; EXPL.: [f. 46v] . . . da questi lazzi mondani transferitta la sua orante anima in la diuina gloria infinita amen.

EDITION: DELL'OSO 2013, 132–135.

28. Filippo da Strada, nuptial sermon—ff. 53r–54v.

INC.: [f. 53r] uuole ogni legge descritta che la concupiscentia libidinosa che e radicata in la nostra carne humana . . .; EXPL.: [f. 54v] . . . non glie mancharebbe altro se non adiuttarsi col peccato de la sua persona nuda.

EDITION: DELL'OSO 2013, 136–139.

29. Filippo da Strada, nuptial sermon—ff. 62r, 64r, 65r.

INC.: [f. 62r] el glie ad sapere che nel mondo non se troua la piu laudabel forma de uiuere allegramente cha questa forma . . .; EXPL.: [f. 65r] . . . credendo lui chel stia sconsolato se uuol conformare al suo infortunio et essergli liale si in male comme in bene e stato.

EDITION: DELL'OSO 2013, 140–143.

30. Filippo da Strada, on the marriage of Sebastiano Erizzi and Cipriana Trevisan—ff. 68v–69r, 73r.

INC.: [f. 68v] io piccolo studiante in le sante scritture uorrebbe metterine ad commendare due cose honeste cio e . . .; EXPL.: [f. 73r] . . . cossi per lo simele posso dir de uui che sete uir et uxor inuicem bene consentientes paulo apostolo confermante.

EDITION: DELL'OSO 2013, 144–146.

31. Filippo da Strada, sermon on marriage—f. 70r.

INC.: [f. 70r] ut matrimonium commendaret dominus yhesus christus dixit sic ad discipulos luce undecimo nisi quis oderit pa. et cetera. odium in parentes et in uitam suam carnalem propter amplectendam crucem christi . . .; EXPL.: [f. 70r] . . . et belli non ineundi contra fortiorem quod tutius est stare in foedere communi hymeneo quam carpere ardua monachatus proposita.

32. Filippo da Strada, verses—f. 82v^{a-b}.

INC.: [f. 82v^{a}] sum tibi tam carus quamuis ego nullius ad te sim precii o cesar seu genitore comes . . .; EXPL.: [f. 82v^{b}] . . . si mala non sumet decus a se magna tonanti sed sua facta dabunt ridendum ceu leue latrans.

33. Filippo da Strada, verses—f. 82v [*in det. marg.*].

INC.: [f. 82v^{a} *in det. marg.*] uult cicero nihil esse magis dignum /in\ quot habentur . . .; EXPL.: [f. 82v^{b} *det. marg.*] . . . sed laudaret eam uocem quae docta fuisset.

34. Filippo da Strada, verses—f. 83r [*in sup. marg.*].

INC.: [f. 83r *in sup. marg.*] christofore aspalatine tibi ieronimiana nomina distribuam quia sis ieronimus haustu . . .; EXPL.: [f. 83r *in sup. marg.*] . . . ne mirere igitur uolo sis ieronimus ut nunc tanquam *icaris [*sic*] nautis tu portus et aura.

Nearly identical with CONTENTS 38.

35. Filippo da Strada, verses—f. 83r^{a}–v^{b}.

INC.: [f. 83r^{a}] consulis o plebis rector me quae bona factu in re nummorum qui gignant pacis honorem . . .; EXPL.: [f. 83v^{b}] . . . concentu rostri sulce modulantis ad annos continuisse cibis tali modulamine fotum.

36. Filippo da Strada, *In laudem Boetii*—f. 84r.

RUB.: in laudem boetii non digne oppressi a romanis elegi uersus. applicabiles auaritiae aduocatorum adulantium iudicibus in fauorem perfidiae ratione nummi; INC.: [f. 84r] omnis honestatis ratio tutanda uidetur res inhonesta pio proicienda sinu . . .; EXPL.: [f. 84r] . . . istius autoris non digna oppressio cautos efficiat reges nolle fauere lupis.

37. Filippo da Strada, Sonnet—f. 84r [*in dex. marg.*].

RUB.: sonetto di grande iniquita di uno; INC.: [f. 84r *in dex. marg.*] un buono amico qual terro coperto hammi furatto ad simulatione . . .; EXPL.: [f. 84r *in dex. marg.*] . . . non me uuol dir la scielta ueritatte perche el se crede che dormi ben uechia.

EDITION: DELL'OSO 2013, 131.

38. Filippo da Strada, verses—f. 84r [*in dex. marg.*].

INC.: [f. 84r *in dex. marg.*] ingenio celeber bene uir ieronimiana nomina fausta capis quia sis ieronimus alter . . .; EXPL.: [f. 84r *in dex. marg.*] . . . nam uelut is quondam sic tu nunc portus et umbra aduenis afflictis estu pelagique furore.

39. Filippo da Strada, verses—f. 84r [*in det. marg.*].

INC.: [f. 84r *in det. marg.*] attulit unus amans gratissima scripta miloni quae ciceronis erant /bene\ condita mente manuque . . .; EXPL.: [f. 84r *in det. marg.*] . . . premia uocis agunt pessum quaecunque proterua.

INVERTED CONTENTS

Inverted texts are written in the lower margins of ff. 1v–13r; when the manuscript is rotated, texts can be read in order on ff. 13r–1v.

40. Filippo da Strada, *Libro de la conception de la madre vergene*—ff. 13r–10v.

RUB.: libro de la conception de la madre uergene; INC.: [f. 13r] perche son puochi chi entendino bene che cosa sia la originale . . .; EXPL.: [f. 10v] . . . debiti da adam ma poi sanctificata con gratia excelsa et duoni accumulati.

EDITION: DELL'OSO 2013, 108–115.

41. Filippo da Strada, sermon to Guido de Gonzaga—ff. 10r–8v.

RUB.: ad reuerendissimum d. d. guidonem de gonzaga commendatarium monasterii sancti benedicti diocesis mantuane. sermo; INC.: [f. 10r] guido magne regens reuerende tuae grauitati congruit ut monachum teneas qui relligiose . . .; EXPL.: [f. 8v] . . . o decus ecce hominis superarier omni animante noster inops mentis corradus [*sic*] sic bona praefert.

42. Filippo da Strada, verses—ff. 8r–7v.

42.1. f. 8r. INC.: si sale conditus si sanae mentis habendus intradi [*sic*] meditans diceret egre fero . . .; EXPL.: . . . proponam uersus uulgares fando facete ultima uerba mei sicque ferendus ero.

42.2. ff. 8r–7v. INC.: un zentilhomo haueua una mugliere bella del corpo quanto se poteua . . .; EXPL.: . . . ad dio ad dio marito hora uechieto questo amo in sposo in dolce mio delecto.

42.3. f. 7v. INC.: se apprecii persuona tua respondente non glie accostare alcun molto apparente . . .; EXPL.: . . . ad homeni bassi accostite securo quegli non sconfiano et tu restarai azuro.

EDITION: DELL'OSO 2013, 116–118 (vernacular only).

43. Filippo da Strada, *Liber de nouis medicis*—ff. 7r–6v.

RUB.: liber de nouis medicis liberaliter egra corpora curantibus absque mortis periculo; INC.: [f. 7r] o gonzaga manus cui cura est sub benedicto cogere confector monachos in carceris antra . . .; EXPL.: [f. 6v] . . . utilitate frui contemptis legibus almis ad quid non cogis mortalia pectora crassa auri sacra fames tundantur fuste proterui.

44. Filippo da Strada, *De medico cenobita gratioso exempla*—ff. 6r–3r.

RUB.: de medico cenobita gratioso exempla notanda; INC.: [f. 6r] credo equidem nec uana fides si femina quaeuis languorem fingens cum sit tentata flagranti . . .; EXPL.: [f. 3r] . . . dedere se lubricis mulcentibus actibus in rem carnis set augendi census per fasque rapinam.

45. Filippo da Strada, *Un Dio eterno se debbe adorare*—ff. 2v, 1v.

INC.: [f. 2v] un dio eterno se debbe adorare . . .; EXPL.: [f. 1v] . . . e gran peccato la affectione auara del frutto al qual non hai carta primara.

EDITION: DELL'OSO 2013, 119–121.

46. Filippo da Strada, *Ho io mirato che peccati mortali*—f. 2r.

INC.: [f. 2r] ho /io\ mirato che peccati mortali fanno odioso ad santi homini reali . . .; EXPL.: [f. 2r] . . . nulla se acquista la doglia del profecto in li compagni ma danno in lui infecto.

EDITION: DELL'OSO 2013, 122–124.

47. Filippo da Strada, *Per dilection de le alme electe*—f. 2r.

INC.: [f. 2r] per dilection de la alme electe fin proponute le colpe ad fi recte . . .; EXPL.: [f. 2r] . . . dal ben saputo sorge lo operare chi nol connosce mal pol meritare.

EDITION: DELL'OSO 2013, 125.

BINDING: s. xix; armorial binding; calf over stiff pasteboards; gilt tooled covers, spine, and turn-ins; gilt stamp of Henry Pelham Fiennes Pelham-Clinton, 4th Duke of Newcastle-under-Lyme (1785–1851). The manuscript was bound by Charles Lewis (1786–1836) according to the description in Kraus, Cat. 100, no. 17.

Owners & Provenance: Henry Joseph Thomas Drury (1778–1841); Henry Pelham Fiennes-Pelham-Clinton, 4th Duke of Newcastle-under-Lyme (1785–1851); sold in Sotheby's 1937 sale upon the death of Henry Pelham Archibald Douglas Pelham-Clinton, 7th Duke of Newcastle-under-Lyme (1864–1928); H. P. Kraus (1951, 1962); acquired from H. P. Kraus (New York, NY) by the university in October 1968.

Sales & Catalogues: Evans, 19 February 1827, lot 804; Sotheby's, 12 June 1937, lot 935; Kraus, Cat. 56, no. 32; ibid., Cat. 100, no. 17.

Former Shelfmark: MS 53 (Notre Dame).

Bibliography: Ives 1943 (for H. P. Kraus); Corbett no. 53; Emery, Jr. and L. Jordan 1998, 499; McDonald 2013; Dell'Oso 2013; Dell'Oso 2014; Dell'Oso 2015.

cod. Lat. d. 6

ORIGIN: Austria or Bohemia, s. xv^{2}.
CONTENT OVERVIEW: Works of Aeneas Siluius Piccolomini (Pius II); epistolary extracts from Gregory the Great, Leonardo Bruni, Cyprian, and others.

In Latin, on paper; 201 ff. +i; generally 300 x 213 mm (page) [see LAYOUT for ruling]; flyleaf medieval parchment; medieval and modern foliations present [see FOLIATION]; ff. 71r–72r, 100r–v, 119v–124v, 140r, 151r–152r, 155v, 166r–v, 174r–175v, 180v–184v, 189v, 194v–196v, 200v blank.

COLLATION: 1–6^{12} +7^{4} +8–11^{12} +12$^{4-2}$ +13^{14} +14^{12} +15^{14-3+2} +16^{10} +17$^{12-2}$ +18^{12} +19^{4+1} +i

BIBLIOGRAPHICAL FORMAT: 2°.

QUIRES: Paper sexternions folded in folio are the predominant quire forms, but other forms occur. Quire 7 is a binion. Quire 12 is a binion lacking the last two leaves. Quires 13 and 15 are comprised of seven bifolia. Quire 15 lacks the last three leaves and contains a bifolium (ff. 164 and 165) inserted asymmetrically. Quire 16 is a quinion. Quire 17 is a sexternion lacking the seventh and twelfth leaves. Quire 19 is a binion with one leaf added. The manuscript has been trimmed.

CATCHWORDS: Horizontal catchwords appear in the lower margins for quires 8 and 10.

SIGNATURES: Graphic leaf signatures are used to order the errant text on ff. 168v–173v [see CONTENTS 33].

FOLIATION: Arabic numerals are written in black ink in the upper margins on ff. 167r–201r (1–36). Modern foliation with Arabic numerals in pencil is written throughout the manuscript.

WATERMARKS: One hundred two occurrences of seven distinct watermarks: (**A**) Bull's head; occurs in quires 1–6; corresponds closely to PICCARD 65964 (Schwabach, 1466). (**B**) Bull's Head; occurs in quire 7; cf. PICCARD 65181 (Różan, 1475) and 64813 (Brescia, 1434). (**C**) Triple Mount in circle with cross; occurs in quires 8–11, 13–14; cf. PICCARD 153457 (Vicenza, 1452). (**D**) Scales at angle with straight scales; occurs in quires 12 and 15 (f. 164);

cf. Piccard 116205 (1457). (E) Bull's Head; occurs in quires 15–18; cf. Piccard 65641 (Könitz, 1459). (F) Head with diadem; occurs in quire 19 (ff. 197 and 199); cf. Piccard 20368 (Innsbruck, 1436) and 20346 (Innsbruck, 1436). (G) Bull's Head; occurs in quire 19 (f. 200r); cf. Piccard 70359 (Königsberg, 1440).

Layout:

A

B

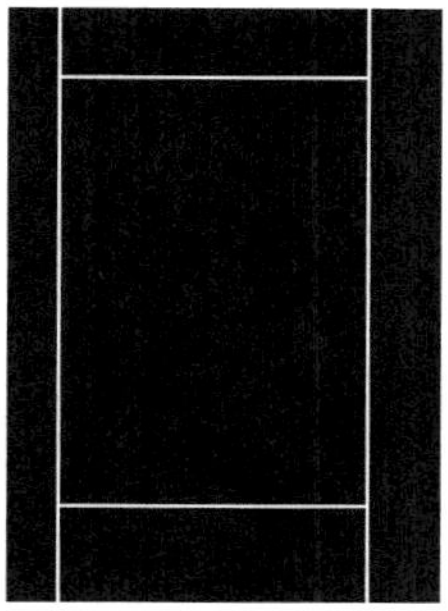
C

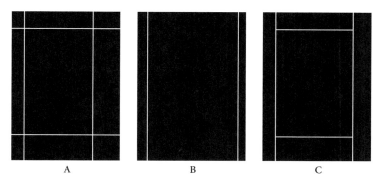

A ff. 1r–72v. Ink; 213–219 x 135–140 mm; 32 lines.
B ff. 73r–76v. Hard-point; 255 x 180 mm; 50 lines.
C ff. 77r–200r. Hard-point; 216 x 152 mm (text frame; variable use); 46–52 lines.

Pattern **A** is frame-ruled in brown ink on ff. 1r–72v with variable dimensions; single column; writing below top line. Pattern **B** is executed in hard-point technique to rule verticals only, creating the frame; single column; top line approximated. Pattern **C** also uses hard-point technique to rule the verticals (multiple leaves ruled at a time; often each half of the quire separately similar to Old Style); top line and bottom line of frame not ruled, but indicated with a single prick in the outer right margin; the use of frame (height) and number of lines vary.

Script: Three distinct scribal bookhands (M1–M3) write all texts. M1 writes Cursiva Formata on ff. 1r–72v; script of M1 is large compared to those of M2 and M3. M2 writes Semihybrida Libraria on ff. 73r–76v in brownish ink. M3 writes Semihybrida Libraria on ff. 77r–201r in dark black ink, displaying great similarities to M2. Ownership marks on the front pastedown are written in a dark black Hybrida Formata followed by Hybrida Libraria (autograph of a Martin Leheure, 1484).

Decoration:
I. Rubrication: Rubrics in red and black ink.
II. Initials: Flourished initials, cadels, and other majuscules occur closely in hierarchy.
a. Flourished initials (3–4 line square inset) in blue ink with red penwork and red ink with brown penwork occur on ff. 1r, 2v,17r, 30r, 44r, and 60v.
b. Cadels are drawn in initial position for most texts and excerpts.

Contents:

1. Aeneas Siluius Piccolomini (Pius II), *Historia bohemica*—ff. 1r–70v.

RUB.: [ad alfonsum sicilie et arragonum regem *in sup. marg.*] cronica bohemorum compilata per dominum eneam siluium poetam laureatum et postea episcopum senensem demumque in summum pontificem sub nomine pii secundi in ecclesia militante sublimatum; INC.: [f. 1r] interitura esse queque nascuntur atque homines in primis quos ea de causa mortales appellant omnes norunt plurimi damnant . . .; EXPL.: [f. 70v] . . . quod metus extorserit nobis persuasum est armis acquiri regna non legibus.

Edition: Hejnic and Rothe 2005.

2. Aeneas Siluius Piccolomini (Pius II), *Bulla de profectione in Turcos*—ff. 73r–76v.

INC.: [f. 73r] pius episcopus seruus seruorum dei uniuersis et singulis christi fidelibus salutem et apostolicam benedictionem ezechielis prophete magni sententia est . . .; EXPL.: [f. 76v] . . . datum rome aput sanctum petrum anno incarnationis dominice .m°.cccc°.lviij. .xj. kalends nouembris pontificatus nostri anno sexto.

Edition: Basel 1551, 914–923.
Bibliography: Bertalot, *Initia* 2: no. 7342.

3. Nicolaus de Tudeschis, *Quoniam ueritas uerborum*—ff. 77r–97v.

RUB.: casus summarius habitorum in sacro(sancto) basiliensis concilio per reuerendissimum dominum nicolaum archiepiscopum panormitanum recollectus ihesus christus; INC.: [f. 77r] quoniam ueritas uerborum lenocinio non indiget ideo quanto uerbis simplicionibus proponitur tanto maiori claritate relucet . . .; EXPL. [f. 97v] . . . non aliter in hoc negocio presentis dissidii futuris speramus quod ut cito fiat christus concedat amen.

Edition: Herre and Quidde 1928, 440–538.
Bibliography: Bertalot, *Initia* 2: no. 19371.

4. Gerhardus Landrianus, *Oratio prima ad regem Enricum VI*—ff. 97v–99v.

RUB.: oracio ad imitandum principem ut suos ad concilium dirigat; INC.: [f. 97v] facite quod dei est et ipse faciet quod uestrum est . . .; EXPL.: [f. 99v] . . . et diffinitum in celo locum obtinebitis ad laudem et gloriam omnipotentis dei eterni et tocius triumphantis amen.

Edition: Mansi 29:463–468.
Bibliography: Bertalot, *Initia* 2: no. 7426.

5. Giuliano Cesarini, *Oratio* [20 December 1437]—f. 101r.

RUB.: responsio domini iuliani ad requisicionem promotorum sacri concilii basiliensis ut interesset congregacioni et sessioni citatorium; INC.: [f. 101r] uobis dominis promotoribus requirentibus me legatum et presidentem apostolicum ut intersim congregacioni generali faciende . . .; EXPL.: [f. 101r] . . . hoc eciam dixi cum correctione cuiuscumque me melius sencientis salua potestate premissa corrigendi.

EDITION: MANSI 31a:234–237.

6. Lodovico Pontano, *Presens citatio*—ff. 101r–106r.

RUB.: responsio domini ludouici de roma prothonotarii sedis apostolice ad predicta modo sequitur per optima; INC.: [f. 101r] presens citacio qua per sacram basiliensis sinodum interpellatur sanctissimus dominus noster papa primo fortificatur ex assistencia plene caritatis . . .; EXPL.: [f. 106r] . . . quid est in usu homini bono ac licito unde non posset pernicies irrogari dicit tex [*sic*] relatus .xxiij. .q. .v. de occidendis.

EDITION: WOELKI 2011, 548–576.

7. Lodovico Pontano, *Primum diligenter*—ff. 106v–115v.

RUB.: alia responsio eiusdem domini prothonotarii facta nomine concilii ad ultimas peticiones domini iuliani legati; INC.: [f. 106] primum diligenter mente reuoluens metuendissimi patres uerbum illud elegans . . .; EXPL.: [f. 115v] . . . ut deinde ad uestras aures hinc uenientes non facilius admittatis nec a uobis excommunicatos ultra in communionem uelitis recipere et cetera.

EDITION: WOELKI 2011, 577–635.

8. *Oratio Ambasiatoris regis Portugalliae*—ff. 115v–117v.

RUB.: proposicio ambasiatorum [*sic*] regis portugallie; INC.: [f. 115v] plato grauissimus stoice discipline imitator in eo sermone in quo socratem de immortalitate animorum diuinitus disputantem facit . . .; EXPL.: [f. 117v] . . . uniuersali sanitate redacta tota pulchra sit et decora. amen.

BIBLIOGRAPHY: BERTALOT, *Initia* 2: no. 15666.

9. Augustinus Iauriensis, *Oratio ad Nicolaum V papam*—ff. 117v–119r.

RUB.: proposicio pro parte electorum imperii coram papa; INC.: [f. 117v] mandatum susceperam laborem quem hodierna iubet explere dies sanctitati tue pater beatissime . . .; EXPL.: [f. 119r] . . . ultra conspicium in terris immortale testimonium te exutum corpore suscipient in gloria domini nostri ihesu christi qui uiuit in secula benedicens. amen.

BIBLIOGRAPHY: BERTALOT, *Initia* 2: no. 11592.

10. Epistolary excerpts—ff. 125r–129v.

Extracts varying in length mostly from Piccolomini's *Epistole*; epistle numbers in the description refer to those used in Van Heck 2007 unless indicated; page numbers refer to entire letter. Letters from other authors are also indicated.

10.1. f. 125r–v. rub.: de remedio amoris; inc.: eneas siluius ipolito mediolanensi salutem plurimam dicit querebaris mecum nocte preterita quod amori operam dares . . .; expl.: . . . uirumque alium te prestabis deo gratum et celo dignum uale et quod tibi dampno est auertere stude ex wyennensi. [*Ep.* 7, Wolkan 1912, 33–39].

10.2. *Ep.* 193—f. 125v. rub.: ad idem ad quendam iohannem secretarium colonie qui tristabatur ob recessum amasie; inc.: si amicus mortuus est moriturum hunc scire debebas . . .; expl.: . . . non te lesit sed alium lesura recessit gaude quia fugit et cetera. [Van Heck 2007, 495–496]. iacula que preuidentur minus feriunt.

10.3. *Ep.* 152 (*De duobus amantibus historia*)—f. 125v. rub.: eneas mario ad idem; inc.: rem petis haud conuenientem etati mee tue uero et aduersam et repungnantem [*sic*] . . .; expl.: . . . tu uale et historie que me scribere cogis attentus esto [Van Heck 2007, 311–347].

10.4. *Ep.* 94—f. 125v. rub.: historiam scriptor omisit quia sacerdos cui non competebat. notat tamen aliqua; inc.: huc non reueniens nisi uxoris prius aut licentia aut sacietas intercesserit . . .; expl.: . . . ego ex his sum qui melius scio predicare quam facere [Van Heck 2007, 196–198].

10.5. f. 126r. rub.: ad idem; inc.: uiro prestanti ac singulari iohanni frunt [*sic*] insignis ciuitatis agrippe secretario et amico suo precaro . . . pauci dies sunt quibus . . .; expl.: . . . sensi aliquando quod nunc sentis sed et tu aliquando sencies quod ego sencio et cetera [*Ep.* 6, Wolkan 1912, 30–33].

10.6. *Ep.* 152 (*De duobus amantibus historia*)—f. 126r–v. rub.: procacionis materia pro mania [*sic*]; inc.: nec suauis illi quicquam illustrium aspectu feminarum ego dubius si facies ille humane sint . . .; expl.: . . . humiles tantum gazas habitat castitas solaque pauperies effectu sano tenetur et cetera [Van Heck 2007, 311–347].

10.7. *Ep.* 104—f. 126v. rub.: ex cuiusdam philocapti principis epistola pro mania protandi; inc.: se ipsum singulari domine sue insigni et formosissime uirgini lucreae [*sic*] regis epyrotharum filie . . .; expl.: . . . uale animula mea corculum meum et mee delicie [Van Heck 2007, 225–226].

10.8. Francesco dei Conti di Acquaviva—f. 127r. rub.: epistola domini francisci de comitibus ad regem polonie; inc.: consilium michi fuit fortasse non improbum illustrissime ac inuictissime princeps . . .; expl.: . . . sed maximarum rerum procuracionibus suffragari et cetera. obmisi [also found in Praha, Národní knihovna Česke republiky, VI. A.7, ff. 233v–237; Prochaska 1882, 879–885].

10.9. Francesco da Fiano, *Contra ridiculos oblocutores et fellitos detractores poetarum*—f. 127v. rub.: in epistola contra detractores poetarum franciscus de comitibus; inc.: christus in euangelio sepius usus est specie allegorici sermonis que theologi parabolam uocant . . .; expl.: . . . nonne scriptum est in lege uestra ego dixi dii estis et cetera.

10.10. Michael von Pfullendorf—f. 127v. RUB.: anthonius duobus fratribus monachis scribit; INC.: numquam adeo putaui uos ueros monachos sicut iam experior monachus enim mortuus esse debet mundo . . .; EXPL.: . . . quam uestra taciturnitas que inhumanior est hircanis tigridibus et cetera. ideo scribite [*Ep.* 118 (Wolkan, CXVIII), WOLKAN 1909, 188–189].

10.11. Francesco dei Conti di Acquaviva—ff. 128r–129v. INC.: cunctos dies cunctas noctes piissime patrum in tui memoria ac ueneracione consumo utinam ueluti animo sic et tecum corpore inseparabiliter copularer . . .; EXPL.: . . . nonne risu et ludibrio digni sunt et cetera. tu excede omnes et cetera [also found in Praha, Národní knihovna Česke republiky, VI. A.7, ff. 219v–233r].

10.12. *Ep.* 151 (*Somnium de fortuna*)—f. 129v. RUB.: describit amenitatem cuiusdam loci eneas siluius poete laureatus; INC.: intraui illic florea prata riui cum lacte uinoque currentes frigidi fontes lacus piscibus pleni . . .; EXPL.: . . . ibi dispensationes bachus uenus et cheres silua mirtea concubitus admittebat et cetera [VAN HECK 2007, 301–310].

11. Gregory the Great, *Registrum Epistolarum* (excerpts)—ff. 130r–132v.

RUB.: ex registro beati gregorii pape.

11.1. *Ep.* 8.1—f. 130r. INC.: beatus gregorius epistola prima ibidem mittit anastasio episcopo anthiochie scilicet solidos ad comparanda . . .; EXPL.: . . . qui baptisandi fuerunt et cetera. uideamus si hodie simile faciat romana curia.

11.2. *Ep.* 8.2—f. 130r. RUB.: epistola secunda eidem; INC.: suscepi epistolas suauissime beatitudinis uestre . . .; EXPL.: . . . post longa adhuc tempora uos ad celestis patrie gaudia perducat.

11.3. *Ep.* 8.3—f. 130r. RUB.: tertia epistola; INC.: nostis enim antiquam nostram consuetudinem . . .; EXPL.: . . . fidelitatem corporibus pensam facere debemus et cetera.

11.4. *Ep.* 8.22—f. 130r. RUB.: promissa elemosina. .xxij. epistola; INC.: peto ut gratia que uobis concessit eas . . .; EXPL.: . . . ne unde uos peccata tergitis nos inde maculemur et cetera.

11.5. *Ep.* 8.25—f. 130r. RUB.: uictori episcopo panormitano .25.; INC.: sicut iudeis non debet esse licentia . . .; EXPL.: . . . preiudicium sustinere et cetera. nec debent in eorum ceremoniis inpediri [*ut uid.*]

11.6. *Ep.* 8.28—f. 130r. RUB.: eulogio episcopo allexandrino. 28.; INC.: utilis est semper docti uiri allocucio . . .; EXPL.: . . . cum uestra beatitudo scribere studuit hoc uel hoc et cetera.

11.7. *Ep.* 8.31—f. 130r–v. RUB.: uinencio episcopo carthaginensi .30.; INC.: magna uirtus caritatis est que sinceritatis . . .; EXPL.: . . . gratia operibus nos exhibere concedat.

11.8. *Ep.* 8.34—f. 130v. RUB.: adeodate illustri epistola .34.; INC.: magnam nobis [-letitie gloriam] leticiam glorie uestre ingessit epistola . . .; EXPL.: . . . et in sanctarum matronarum sorte recipiat et cetera.

11.9. *Ep.* 9.1—f. 130v. RUB.: ianuario episcopo caralithano .37.; INC.: predicator omnipotentis [-dei] domini paulus dicit seniorem . . .; EXPL.: . . . dictum quippe mihi est quod et cetera.

11.10. *Ep.* 9.9—f. 130v. RUB.: ianuario episcopo sardinie .38.; INC.: non terrenarum rerum curam sed animarum te ducatum suscepisse cognosce . . .; EXPL.: . . . sicut in culpa tua dilaceror ita in bona accione letificor et cetera.

11.11. *Ep.* 9.135—ff. 130v–131r. RUB.: anastasio anthioco .75.; INC.: certe beatum iacob qui pro uxoribus diu seruierat . . .; EXPL.: . . . ac mensuram superaffluentem ad eterna gaudia reportare concedat.

11.12. *Ep.* 9.147—f. 131r. RUB.: secundo incluso alias [*ut uid.*] inclauso .82. INC.: dilectionis tue scripta suscepi . . .; EXPL.: . . . patrie amore flabant et cetera.

11.13. *Ep.* 9.219—f. 131r. RUB.: aragio episcopo francie .119.; INC.: indecens est de illis tedium afflictionis adici . . .; EXPL.: . . . ut non contristemini sicut et ceteri qui spem non habent.

11.14. *Ep.* 9.222—f. 131r. RUB.: siragrio episcopo. 121.; INC.: magistra bonorum omnium caritas que nil sapit extraneum . . .; EXPL.: . . . eadem caritate te preditum multorum testificacione comperio et cetera.

11.15. *Ep.* 9.227—f. 131r–v. RUB.: leandro episcopo epistola .127.; INC.: sanctitatis tue suscepi epistolam solius caritate calamo scriptam . . .; EXPL.: . . . et ei quem multum diligo parum loquor.

11.16. *Ep.* 9.228—f. 131v. RUB.: rocaredo regi gothorum .126.; INC.: uigilanti studio cauende sunt antiqui hostis insidie . . .; EXPL.: . . . quanto maiora sunt dona que portat et cetera.

11.17. *Ep.* 9.232—f. 131v. RUB.: ytalie patricio [*sic*] .cxxvij.; INC.: quosdam de silicia [*sic*] uenientes affectu quo debui . . .; EXPL.: . . . et mortis remedium expectando suspiro et cetera.

11.18. *Ep.* 10.12—f. 131v. RUB.: libertino expretori .cxlj.; INC.: quanta uos seculi huius premat angustia . . .; EXPL.: . . . et super hec gaudia eterna prestantur et cetera.

11.19. *Ep.* 10.14—ff. 131v–132r. RUB.: eulogio patriarche allexandrino gregorius .cxlij. epistola; INC.: transacto anno suauissima sanctitatis uestre scripta suscepi . . .; EXPL.: . . . scripsit autem mihi dulcissima et semper honoranda beatitudo et cetera.

11.20. *Ep.* 10.15—f. 132r. RUB.: .cxliiij.; INC.: nolite de talibus omnino contristari . . .; EXPL.: . . . felices nos extiment dies habuisse.

11.21. *Ep.* 11.1—f. 132r. RUB.: palladio presbytero de monte syna .151.; INC.: epistolis dilectionis tue susceptis filium meum simplicium requirere curaui . . .; EXPL.: . . . esto mihi in deum protectorem et in locum mu(nitum) ut sal(uum) me facis.

11.22. *Ep.* 11.42—f. 132r. RUB.: aregio episcopo galliarum .180.; INC.: cum in fraterna dilectione unum cor et unus sit animus . . .; EXPL.: . . . et animum ad consolacionem rediisse cognouimus.

11.23. *Ep.* 12.1—f. 132r. RUB.: dominico episcopo carthaginensi .207.; INC.: quam copiosa cordis uestri sit caritas lingua interprete demonstratis . . .; EXPL.: . . . postmodum paratus ad iudicium ueniat et cetera.

11.24. *Ep.* 13.2—f. 132r–v. RUB.: denuncciacio [*sic*] pro septiformi letania; INC.: oportet fratres karissimi ut flagella dei que metuere uentura debuimus . . .; EXPL.: . . . uiduarum uitalis martiris pauperum et infantium letania ab ecclesia beate cecilie.

Excerpts from books 8–13; book numbers and epistle numbers correspond to the critical edition of Ewald and Hartmann 1992.

12. Letter to John of Capistrano—f. 133r–v.

rub.: reuerendo patri ac religioso homini fratri iohanni de capi(strano) uerissime ihesu christi preconi domino et patri nostro colendissimo; inc.: [f. 133r] nemo nostrum dubitat reuerende pater quin uirtus dei omnipotentis operetur in uobis . . .; expl.: [f. 133v] . . . animo uobiscum aut moriamur aut certe uiuamus. superiorum partium uniuersi nobiles ac proceres regni hungarie ad uestre reuerende paternitatis noticiam hec peruenire uoluerunt.

13. Guarino Veronese (tr.), Comparison of Philopoemen and Flamininus (Plutarch, *Lives*)—f. 134r.

rub.: iudicium et comparacio philopoemenis et t. q. flaminii [*sic*]; inc.: [f. 134r] mutuam ipsorum comparacionem intueri iam tempus postulat . . .; expl.: [f. 134] . . . romano autem iusticie ac bonitatis palmam reddentes arbitri minime contendendi fore uideamus. ex plutarcho de greco in latinum uerso per guarinum ueronensem.

Bibliography: Pade 2007, 2:75–77.

14. Leonardo Bruni, Latin translation of Ps.-Plato, *Epistolae* (preface)—f. 134v.

rub.: platonis epistole per leonardum aretinum e greco in latinum tradite; inc.: [f. 134v] inter clamosos strepitus negociorum procellas quibus florentina pallacia . . .; expl.: [f. 134v] . . . non tam uerbis quam lectione operibusque tibi non frustra collatum ostendas.

Edition: Baron 1928, 135–136.

15. Leonardo Bruni, Latin translation of Xenophon, *Tyrannus* [*Hiero*] (preface)—f. 135r.

rub.: epistola leonardi aretini ad nicolaum florentinum in xenofontem; inc.: [f. 135r] xenofontis philosophi quendam libellum quem ego ingenii exercendi gratia e greco sermone in latinum conuerti . . .; expl.: [f. 135r] . . . nullo modo ausi sumus attingere. uale .n. suauissime et in tuis ut cepisti perseuera moribus.

Edition: Baron 1928, 100–101.

16. Aeneas Siluius Piccolomini (Pius II), *Epistola* 99 (excerpt)—ff. 135v–137r.

rub.: ex epistola enee siluii ad sigis(mundum) ducem austrie missa; inc.: [f. 135v] in cesaris curiam quam primum migraui magna me cupido incessit tibi . . .; expl.: [f. 137r] . . . digna uox que tuo progredientur ex ore et quam omnis laudatura sit etas et cetera. cetera huius epistole ad finem adhuc multa sunt obmissa.

Edition: Van Heck 2007, 204–217.

17. Aeneas Siluius Piccolomini (Pius II), *Epistole* (excerpts)—f. 137v.

17.1. *Ep.* 150—f. 137v. RUB.: eneas siluius campisio iohannis insigni philosopho et amico singulari. salutem plurimam dicit; INC.: uellem tibi per singulos dies aliquid scribere . . .; EXPL.: . . . tum necessarios tum utiles exponet et cetera [VAN HECK 2007, 297–300.

17.2. *Ep.* 106—f. 137v. RUB.: eneas ad siluestrum episcopum chiemenem; INC.: non miror quod ad me nihil scribis quia nil me indiges . . .; EXPL.: . . . uidi nuper litterarum copias et cetera [VAN HECK 2007, 228–229].

17.3. *Ep.* 195—f. 137v. RUB.: eneas domino iohanni schindel astronomio uiroque probatissimo. salutem plurimam dicit; INC.: reuersus nunc ad cesarem insignis miles procopius . . .; EXPL.: . . . totisque uiribus amo uale [VAN HECK 2007, 497–498].

17.4. *Ep.* 121—f. 137v. INC.: cum tanto principi seruio . . .; EXPL.: . . . aliquod officium apud aquilas [VAN HECK 2007, 258–259].

18. Bernard of Clairvaux, *Epistola* 174—ff. 138r–139r.

RUB.: epistola beati bernardi missa ad canonicos lugdunenses de concepcione beate marie; INC.: [f. 138r] reuerendo conuentui lugdunensium canonicorum frater bernardus clareuallensis uocatus abbas salutem in christo inter ecclesias gallie constat profecto . . .; EXPL.: [f. 139r] . . . ipsius si quid aliter sapio paratus iudico emendare ualete.

EDITION: *SBO* 7:388–392.

19. Aeneas Siluius Piccolomini (Pius II), *Epistola* 37—f. 139r.

RUB.: eneas siluius ad anthonium suum nepotem; INC.: [f. 139r] retulit michi nannes pater tuus te dum puer adhuc fores . . .; EXPL.: [f. 139r] . . . possis bene uiuere cras dicas incipiam uale.

EDITION: VAN HECK 2007, 112–113.

20. Aeneas Siluius Piccolomini (Pius II), *Epistole* (excerpts)—f. 139v.

20.1. *Ep.* 70—f. 139v. RUB.: enee siluii epistola amicalis ad socium; INC.: mirabar dudum quid rei esset quod me nichil scriberes . . .; EXPL.: . . . et duplum recipies et cetera tuarum litterarum unas [*sic*] suscepi [VAN HECK 2007, 163–164].

20.2. *Ep.* 2—f. 139v. INC.: nichil est quod magis affectem quam te sanum hilaremque esse . . .; EXPL.: . . . quam rem scribendo sepius efficies uale [VAN HECK 2007, 14].

20.3. *Ep.* 7—f. 139v. INC.: litteris tuis quas hic suscepi utor iocundissime . . .; EXPL.: . . . tunc enim quod aculei corculum meum tetigisse et cetera [VAN HECK 2007, 21–22].

20.4. *Ep.* 55—f. 139v. INC.: expecto te itaque mi iohanni magna cum animi alacritate et gaudio . . .; EXPL.: . . . sed philosophorum legibus immutabilem et cetera [VAN HECK 2007, 147–148].

21. Aeneas Siluius Piccolomini (Pius II), *Epistola* 38—f. 140v.

RUB.: eneas siluius laudat agriculturam; INC.: [f. 140v] elegisti ut audio senectuti tue uitam conuenientissimam . . .; EXPL.: [f. 140v] . . . quibus nec pluuia nocet nec estus uale.

EDITION: VAN HECK 2007, 113–114.

22. Aeneas Siluius Piccolomini (Pius II), *Epistola* [402]—ff. 141r–147r.

INC.: [f. 141r] reuerendissimo in christo patri domino sbigneo sacrosancte romane ecclesie tituli sancte prisce presbytero cardinali ac pontifici cracouiensi domino suo colendissimo . . .; EXPL.: [f. 147r] . . . uale et iam non epistolam sed librum cum uacauerit legito ex noua ciuitate austrie.

EDITION: BASEL 1551, 934–946.

23. Bernard of Clairvaux, *Sermo super Canticum Canticorum* 26 (incomplete)—ff. 147v–150r.

RUB.: epistola beati bernardi de morte fratris sui gerardi super canticum; subtracto fratre meo per quem mea in domino studia utcumque libera esse solebant simul et cor meum dereliquit me quousque enim disimulatio. sunt alibi principium [*ut. uid.*]; INC.: [f. 147v] quamquam et meror finem imperat et calamitas quam pacior . . .; EXPL.: [f. 150r] . . . repetisti commendatum recepisti tuum finem uerborum indicunt lacrime tu illis domine finem modumque indixeris.

EDITION: *SBO* 1:171–181.

24. Bernard of Clairvaux, *Sermo super Canticum Canticorum* 27 (excerpt)—f. 150r.

RUB.: bernardus; INC.: [f. 150r] debitis humanis officiis amicum reuertentem in patriam . . .; EXPL.: [f. 150r] . . . et tolerabilius fiat nobis quod nobiscum non est quia cum deo est.

EDITION: *SBO* 1:181.

25. Aeneas Siluius Piccolomini (Pius II), *Epistole* (excerpts)—f. 150v.

RUB.: ex epistolis enee siluii.

25.1. *Ep.* 166 (de curialium miseriis)—f. 150v. INC.: quidam sapiens ait apud priuatos uiros optimam uitam . . .; EXPL.: . . . non apud magnates nec curienses et cetera [VAN HECK 2007, 393–421].

25.2. *Ep.* 166 (de curialium miseriis)—f. 150v. INC.: moneo uos ut agrum hunc histriones . . .; EXPL.: . . . qui nigrum in candida uertunt [VAN HECK 2007, 393–421].

25.3. *Ep.* 166 (de curialium miseriis)—f. 150v. INC.: giges lidorum rex qui se pre ceteris fortunatissimum reputabat . . .; EXPL.: . . . numquam excesserat felicem esse respondit [VAN HECK 2007, 393–421].

25.4. *Ep.* 190—f. 150v. INC.: apud italos anthonius massetanus ex ordine minorum magnus . . .; EXPL.: . . . quia per episcopatum his liberatus sum et cetera [VAN HECK 2007, 481–484]. nota dignum et tu fac similiter.

25.5. f. 150v. INC.: iohanni compisio quare senes magis curant diuicias quam iuuenes et cetera.

25.6. *Ep.* 117—f. 150v. INC.: aliorum litteras que ad me scribuntur semel dumtaxat lego . . .; EXPL.: . . . iuuenalis inquit haud facile emergunt quorum uirtutibus obstat res angusta et cetera [VAN HECK 2007, 250–253].

25.7. *Ep.* 117—f. 150v. INC.: michi curandum est ut uiuam utque auro non caream quo nocte dieque corpus eget [VAN HECK 2007, 250–253].

25.8. *Ep.* 117—f. 150v. INC.: da ueniam si emptor quam nimium [*sic*] dare cupio nam et qui uendit quam maxime optat uendere et cetera. [VAN HECK 2007, 250–253].

25.9. *Ep.* 117—f. 150v. INC.: quod mihi scribis bona te uerba ex summo pontifice audisse . . .; EXPL.: . . . presertim si tibi adiutores sint tales et cetera [VAN HECK 2007, 250–253].

25.10. *Ep.* 155—f. 150v. INC.: fortunet deus hunc hominem uitamque sibi cornicis prebeat et annos nestoris [VAN HECK 2007, 368–375].

25.11. f. 150v. INC.: irundo recessisti et tardius boue reuerteris. [*Ep.* 5, WOLKAN 1912, 28–30].

25.12. f. 150v. INC.: uale et me tuum tuissimum facito.

26. Aeneas Siluius Piccolomini (Pius II), *Epistola* 78 (excerpt)—f. 152v.

RUB.: anthonius senensis in nuptialibus iocis; INC.: [f. 152v] leteris an doleas quod mihi sobolem dominus dederit et cetera . . .; EXPL.: [f. 152v] . . . nec scio quis eo careat late patet pestis si pestis est et cetera.

EDITION: VAN HECK 2007, 176–179.

27. Hilduin, *Life of St. Denis*—ff. 153r–155r.

RUB.: dyonisii; INC.: [f. 153r] atheniensium ciuitas munitissimis meniis mare florido mellitis ut sic dictum sit riuulis et fluminibus satis pinguissimis . . .; EXPL.: [f. 155r] . . . ex hoc male habens uespere enim erat et cetera. transeo hanc uisionem. tunc sequitur historia passionis beati dyonisii que habetur alibi.

Text begins with chapter 4 and ends imperfectly in chapter 15.

EDITION: *PL* 106.26–33.

28. Bernard of Clairvaux, *Epistole* (excerpts)—ff. 156r–160r.

28.1. *Ep.* 2—ff. 156r–157v. RUB.: ihesus christus. epistola beati bernardi ad fulconem puerum qui postea fuit lingonensium archydyaconus; INC.: bone indolis adolescenti f(ulconi). frater bernardus peccator inde letari in adolescentia unde in senectute non peniteat . . .; EXPL.: . . . non quibus mulierculis uel similari uel placere studeamus et cetera.

28.2. *Ep.* 8—f. 157v. RUB.: ad brunonem coloniensem archiepiscopum; INC.: queris a me consilium uir illustris an uolentibus promouere te . . .; EXPL.: . . . uel si cui forte reuelauerit ipse. sed uide tuam uitam.

28.3. *Ep.* 13—f. 158r. RUB.: ad honorum papam bernardus; INC.: aiunt apud uos ualere pauperis precem . . .; EXPL.: . . . quod caritas suggerit. et sequitur narracio.

28.4. *Ep.* 14—f. 158r. RUB.: ad eundem; INC.: quanto ad uos timore scribam nouit ipse . . .; EXPL.: . . . que imperat et uobis pro. narracio.

28.5. *Ep.* 15—f. 158r. RUB.: ad aimericum cancellarium; INC.: uiro illustri domino a(imerico) apostolice sedis cancellario . . .; EXPL.: . . . contra quam ne amicum quidem respicere fas est uale.

28.6. *Ep.* 16—f. 158r. RUB.: ad petrum cancellarium; INC.: ego causam non habeo causam tamen .n. qui uir religiosus . . .; EXPL.: . . . eam sic tamen ut et iuste et cetera.

28.7. *Ep.* 266—f. 158r. RUB.: ad suggerium; INC.: amico karissimo et intimo b(ernardus) gloriam que intus est . . .; EXPL.: . . . hac fiducia mittimus uobis panem benedictionis. uale.

28.8. *Ep.* 379—f. 158r. INC.: amicum pauperem amico diuiti mittimus . . .; EXPL.: . . . inopia aliquatenus releuetur.

28.9. *Ep.* 31—f. 158r. RUB.: ad hugonem comitem; INC.: si causa dei factus es ex comite miles . . .; EXPL.: . . . scientes quia hec est mutacio dextere excelse.

28.10. *Ep.* 40—f. 158v. INC.: dilectissimo suo et olim et modo .n. duo uobis commendamus in homine isto . . .; EXPL.: . . . cum tanto labore de longe requirere curauit.

28.11. *Ep.* 41—f. 158v. INC.: timeo uos grauari in tam crebris nostris scriptitacionibus . . .; EXPL.: . . . hunc itaque senem et cetera.

28.12. *Ep.* 43—f. 158v. INC.: primis [*sic*] precis nostre benigna suscepcio prebet ampliora . . .; EXPL.: . . . me faciat debitorem quatenus uidelicet hoc et cetera.

28.13. *Ep.* 44—f. 158v. INC.: uidetis certe quantum presumam de uestra beniuolentia . . .; EXPL.: . . . quoniam de caritate non de temeritate descendit.

28.14. *Ep.* 117—f. 158v. RUB.: ad ermendgardem comitissam britanie; INC.: recepi delicias cordis mei pacem tui . . .; EXPL.: . . . in te alacritatis natum est de spiritu sancto est et cetera.

28.15. *Ep.* 125—f. 158v. INC.: odor in flore in fructu sapor requiritur . . .; EXPL.: . . . ex fructu operis cangnoscere [*sic*] te.

28.16. *Ep.* 133—f. 158v. RUB.: ad mediolanenses ciues; INC.: ut ex uestris percipio scriptis . . .; EXPL.: . . . divinitus credo datum et cetera.

28.17. *Ep.* 136—f. 158v. RUB.: ad innocencium papam; INC.: si tristia semper acciderent quis sustineret . . .; EXPL.: . . . raptores et predones compuncti humiliantur et cetera.

28.18. *Ep.* 152—ff. 158v–159r. RUB.: ad innocencium papam pro cretensi episcopo; INC.: insolentia clericorum cuius mater est neglegentia episcoporum . . .; EXPL.: . . . semper uitam alienam rodere negligere suam et cetera.

28.19. *Ep.* 169—f. 159r. RUB.: ad innocencium papam; INC.: dignacio uestra fecit me familiare . . .; EXPL.: . . . uel aliquatenus excusare et cetera. narracio.

28.20. Ep. 170—f. 159r. INC.: si totus orbis aduersum me coniuraret . . .; EXPL.: . . . quod pietati resistit dei ordinacioni resistit et cetera.

28.21. *Ep.* 171—f. 159r. INC.: qui in aliorum negociis tociens exauditus sum . . .; EXPL.: . . . a se dicat alienum quod capitis sit et cetera.

28.22. *Ep.* 177—f. 159r. INC.: dico tamen ius phas honestas religio in nostris partibus perierunt et cetera.

28.23. *Ep.* 178—f. 159r. INC.: confidenter loquor et scribo quia fidem amo.

28.24. *Ep.* 183—f. 159r. INC.: scripta uestra et salutaciones tam deuotus . . .; EXPL.: . . . dignitate sed non deuocione. narracio.

28.25. *Ep.* 185—f. 159r. INC.: salutem tibi uir illustrissime etsi non scribo tamen opto . . .; EXPL.: . . . nec inuitatus sed quid si caritas iubet et cetera.

28.26. *Ep.* 191—f. 159r. INC.: sermonem facio abbreuiatum prolixo negocio.

28.27. *Ep.* 196—f. 159r. INC.: a(rnaldus) de b(rixia) cuius conuersacio mel et doctrina uenenum . . .; EXPL.: . . . supra modum ut uereor nociturus et cetera.

28.28. *Ep.* 193—f. 159r. INC.: magister p(etrus) de s. sine regula monachus sine sollicitudine prelatus . . .; EXPL.: . . . nichil scit que in celo et que in terra sunt preter se ipsum et cetera.

28.29. *Epp.* 198, 199—f. 159v. RUB.: in aliqua causa calumpniosa; INC.: puto satis apparet et lacescentis iniuria . . .; EXPL.: confugere ad uestram presentiam et cetera. [*Ep.* 199] usquequo superabit impius et incenditur pauper.

28.30. *Ep.* 200—f. 159v. INC.: lacrimas magis dare quam litteras libet . . .; EXPL.: . . . qui ex tali re scandalizantur et cetera.

28.31. *Ep.* 201—f. 159v. INC.: epistola quam misisti affectum tuum redolet . . .; EXPL.: . . . non possum rescribere et cetera.

28.32. *Ep.* 111—f. 159v. RUB.: ex persona helye monachi ad suos parentes; INC.: sola causa qua non licet obedire . . .; EXPL.: . . . ad lutum ad seculum reducere moliuntur.

28.33. *Ep.* 112—ff. 159v–160r. RUB.: ad ganfredum lexouiensem; INC.: doleo super te fili mi ganfrede doleo super te et merito . . .; EXPL.: . . . quia hic filius noster mortuus fuerat et reuixit perierat et inuentus est.

28.34. *Ep.* 206—f. 160r. INC.: audiunt homines quod locum gratie habeam apud uos . . .; EXPL.: . . . strenuus in armis suauis in moribus et cetera.

28.35. *Ep.* 214—f. 160r. INC.: si cura si memoria quantulacumque mei extat . . .; EXPL.: . . . et omnium que pro illo facere ualeo debitorem et cetera.

28.36. *Ep.* 216—f. 160r. INC.: scriptum est quos [*sic*] deus coniunxit non homo separet . . .; EXPL.: . . . contra deum disiungere et cetera.

28.37. *Ep.* 217—f. 160r. INC.: tribulacio et angustia inueniunt nos . . .; EXPL.: . . . diuitum quoque uinculis et carceribus et cetera.

EDITION: *SBO* 7–8.

29. Cyprian and Ps.-Cyprian, excerpts—ff. 160v–162r.

RUB.: ex epistolis beati cipriani.

29.1. *Ep.* 77—f. 160v. INC.: karissime litteris tuis laborantia pectora recreasti . . .; EXPL.: . . . et tetrum odorem fumi discussisti et cetera.

29.2. *Ep.* 31—f. 160v. INC.: illuxerunt enim nobis littere tue ut in tempestate quadam serenitas . . .; EXPL.: . . . sicut quam qui et docuit et cetera.

29.3. *Ep.* 78—f. 160v. INC.: quibus perlectis cepimus in uinculis laxamentum . . .; EXPL.: . . . et excitati sumus et robustius animati et cetera.

29.4. Ps.-Cyprian, *De laude martirii*—f. 160v. INC.: quod si te dignitas ambiciosa deterret . . .; EXPL.: . . . et in futuro uitam eternam possidebit et cetera [VON HARTEL 1868–1871, 3:26–52].

29.5. *Ep.* 63—f. 160v. INC.: quod auida et esurienti cupiditate suscipitur plenius et uberius hauritur.

29.6. *Ep.* 59—f. 160v. INC.: non qui audit sed qui facit conuicium . . .; EXPL.: . . . sed qui fratrem cedit in lege peccator est.

29.7. *Ad Donatum*—f. 161r. RUB.: ciprianus ad donatum epistola prima; INC.: bene ammones donate karissime nam et promisisse me memini . . .; EXPL.: . . . animam simul et auditus instruit et pascit obtutus et cetera [SIMONETTI 1976, 3–13].

29.8. *Ad Demetrianum*—f. 161v. RUB.: ciprianus ad demetrianum; INC.: scire debes senuisse iam mundum . . .; EXPL.: . . . hominem morbida ualitudo consumat hec omnia peccatis prouocantibus eueniunt [SIMONETTI 1976, 35–51].

29.9. Ps.-Cyprian, *De laude martirii*—f. 162r. RUB.: cyprianus in epistola de laude martirii; INC.: seuiens locus cui nomen gehenna est . . .; EXPL.: . . . quibus maiora his repromissa sunt quibus auctiora sunt premia et cetera [VON HARTEL 1868–1871, 3:26–52].

For the *Epistolae* see DIERCKS 1994 and 1996; editions for other works are listed in relevant entries.

30. Epistolary extracts of Abelard and Heloise—ff. 162v–163r.

RUB.: ex epistolis abaelardi parisiensis rapulata [*sic*] et heloyssa sua [*sic*]; INC.: [f. 162v] sepe humanos affectus aut prouocant aut mitigant amplius exempla quam uerba . . .; EXPL.: [f. 163r] . . . nunc proch dolor patuit quod latebat et colubri soporati tandem aculeos suscitasti. recitacio facti.

The extracts are transcribed fully and sourced in LUSCOMBE 1983, 539–544.

31. Aeneas Siluius Piccolomini (Pius II), *Epistole* (excerpts)—f. 163v.

RUB.: ex epistolis enee in cardinalatu.

31.1. *Ep.* [189]. INC.: intelligo quantum debeo tue [*sic*] at unde persoluere possim debitum non intelligo [BASEL 1551, 763].

31.2. *Ep.* [228]. INC.: suauissime littere ab amantissimo pectore prodeuntes et cetera [BASEL 1551, 775].

31.3. *Ep.* [228]. INC.: quis tam euiscerate caritate satisfacere aut unde deus potest [BASEL 1551, 775].

31.4. *Ep.* [228]. INC.: scio quid debeo facio quod ualeo [BASEL 1551, 775].

31.5. *Ep.* [228]. INC.: non omnia prodit senex que facturus est [BASEL 1551, 775].

31.6. *Ep.* [251]. INC.: natura comparatum est ut nulli laus onerosa uideatur [BASEL 1551, 784].

32. Iohannes, *Epistola ad patrem*—ff. 164r–165v.

RUB.: filii ad patrem epistola [*in marg.*]; INC.: [f. 164r] etsi pater mi amantissime non modice uerebar quotiescumque lapsis retro temporibus me scribere contingebat . . .; EXPL.: [f. 165v] . . . etati ignoscite postea quam anni succrescent sanius scribam iohannes filius uestre magnifice dominacionis bononie rector ad omnia semper pronus.

33. Aeneas Siluius Piccolomini (Pius II), *Oratio*—ff. 168r–171v, 167r, 172r–173v.

RUB.: [f. 168r] responsio pii pape secundi oratoribus regis francie facta mantue .1459. mensis decembris; INC.: [f. 168r] responsuri uerbis uestris insignes oratores que superioribus diebus adhibita longe . . .; EXPL.: [f. 167r] . . . potissimum iure merito et erit uocabitur christianissimus.

EDITION: MANSI 32:230–251.
BIBLIOGRAPHY: BERTALOT, *Initia* 2: no. 20100.

34. Aeneas Siluius Piccolomini (Pius II), *Oratio*—ff. 176r–180r.

RUB.: oracio pii pape secundi ad principes contra thurcum facta; INC.: [f. 176r] cum bellum hodie aduersus impiam thurcorum gentem pro dei honore ac salute rei publice christiane . . .; EXPL.: [f. 180r] . . . quam ut mentibus nostris inserat ille rogamus qui cum patre et spiritu sancto sine fine regnat christus yhesus amen.

EDITION: MANSI 32:207–221.
BIBLIOGRAPHY: BERTALOT, *Initia* 2: no. 3021.

35. Aeneas Siluius Piccolomini (Pius II), *Epistola* 166 (*De curialium miseriis*)—ff. 185r–189r (excerpts).

RUB.: ex epistola enee siluii de statu curiensium excerpta; INC.: [f. 185r] eneas siluius salutem plurimam dicit domino iohanni ayth perspicaci et claro iurisconsulto stultos esse qui regibus seruiunt uitamque tum infelicem tumque miserrimam ducere curiales et cetera. obmisi quasi dimidiam. iam de tactu peragamus in quo uenus potissime dominatur . . .; EXPL.: [f. 189r] . . . ex pruk supra murum salzburgis dyocesis pridie kalendas decembris anno domini .m°.cccc°.xliiij. indictione septima.

EDITION: VAN HECK 2007, 393–421.

36. Aeneas Siluius Piccolomini (Pius II), *Epistola* 166 (*De curialium miseriis*)—ff. 190r–193r (excerpts).

RUB.: eneas siluius poeta laureatus salutem plurimam dicit domino iohanni de ayth perspicaci et claro iurisconsulto stultos esse qui regibus seruiunt uitamque tum infelicem; INC.: [f. 190r] uereor ne qui me arguant michique maledicant . . .; EXPL.: [f. 193r] . . . hec si quis sapiat mutus pocius esse uelit quam audire.

EDITION: VAN HECK 2007, 393–421.

37. Gabriel Veronensis, *Epistola ad Georgium regem*—ff. 193v–194r.

RUB.: epistola fratris gabrielis de uerona missa ad g(eorgium) de pod(iebrad); INC.: [f. 193v] nuper delate sunt copie siue transsumpta quarundam litterarum apostolicarum . . .; EXPL.: [f. 194r] . . . eya clementissime domine et moras rescinde quam cicius mihi rescribas et cetera.

EDITION: PRIBRAM 1890, 172–174 [209–211].

38. Aeneas Siluius Piccolomini (Pius II), *Epistola* 47—ff. 197r–199v, 201r.

INC.: [f. 197r] uiro insigni et singulari uirtute predito domino artongo iuris utriusque doctori eneas poeta salutem dicit. in aula cesaris cum nuper otiosi essemus . . .; EXPL.: [f. 199r] . . . illud eciam uelim deesse ut aliorum monitiis non adquiescam uale.

Omitted text is written on ff. 199v and 201r.

EDITION: VAN HECK 2007, 129–140.

39. Council of Basel, Session 36 [17 September 1439]—f. 200r.

RUB.: decretum concilii basiliensis de concepcione sancte marie; INC.: [f. 200r] sacrosancta generalis sinodus basiliensis in spiritu sancto legitime congregata uniuersalem ecclesiam . . . elucidantibus diuine gratie misteria mercedem gloriosam . . .; EXPL.: [f. 200r] . . . datum basiliee in sessione nostra publica in maiori ecclesia basiliensi solempniter celebrata .xv. kalendas octobris anno a natiuitate .m°.cccc°.xxxix. apostolica sede uacante.

EDITION: *CCCOGD* 2.2:1074–1076.

40. Verses—flyleaf Iv.

40.1. cur dantur frustra pro psalmis carmina pulchra plus prodesset ei ter miserere mei.
40.2. hic pro defunctis studeas pia fundere uota temporibus certis assimulandus eis.

Binding: s. xv; brown leather over boards; blind tooled; two metal catches on upper board; sewing on four split thongs; rear board with hasp and chain; rear board is detached.

Owners & Provenance: The late-fifteenth-century provenance is recorded on the front pastedown: Iohannes Andrea of Neisse; Jos. Czeyskendorff of Krakow; given to a Martin Leheure in 1484 by a Nicholas Halbendorff and Martin Kwinesye; church in Reichenbach, 1493; see Luscombe 1983, 537–538. The source and date of the acquisition by the university are unknown.

Sales & Catalogues: Galerie Fischer, 28 June 1962, lot 384; B. Rosenthal, Cat. 15, no. 33.

Former Shelfmark: MS 30 (Notre Dame).

Bibliography: Corbett no. 30; D'Alverny 1981, 107; Iter 5:362; Luscombe 1983; Barrow et al. 1984–1985, nos. 91, 377; Hankins 1991, no. 107; Hankins 1997, no. 2372; Woelki 2011, 548, 809; Luscombe 2013, xliii, lv, lxxxviii, ciii.

cod. Lat. e. 1

Origin: Southern France or Italy, s. xiv.
Content Overview: Boniface VIII, *Liber sextus*; Iohannes Monachus, *Glossa aurea.*

In Latin, on parchment; iii +69 ff. +i; generally 436 x 280 mm (page) [see Layout for ruling]; foliated in ink with Roman numerals (medieval) and in modern pencil with Arabic numerals; flyleaves medieval parchment; flyleaf iv part of quire 8 [see Quires].

Collation: iii $+1–2^{8} +3^{2+2} +4–7^{10} +8^{8+2}$

Quires: Parchment quaternions, F/F, and quinions, F/F, are the normal quire forms. Quire 3 is a bifolium, F/F, with two singletons with stubs added (ff. 17 and 20). Quire 8 is a quaternion, F/F, (ff. 61–flyleaf iv) with a bifolium (ff. 68–69) inserted asymmetrically between ff. 64–65; all quires obey Gregory's Rule. Flesh sides of the parchment are bright; hair sides are thick, and visible hair often remains.

Catchwords: Horizontal catchwords are written in the lower right margins for quires 1–7; stylized; all correspond.

Foliation: Roman numerals in black ink are written in the upper margin by the same hand as the table of contents; modern foliation in Arabic numerals in the upper right margin. Due to the asymmetrical insertion of the bifolium in quire 8 [see Quires], ff. 68–69 are between ff. 64 and 65; both sets of foliation are accurate.

Layout:

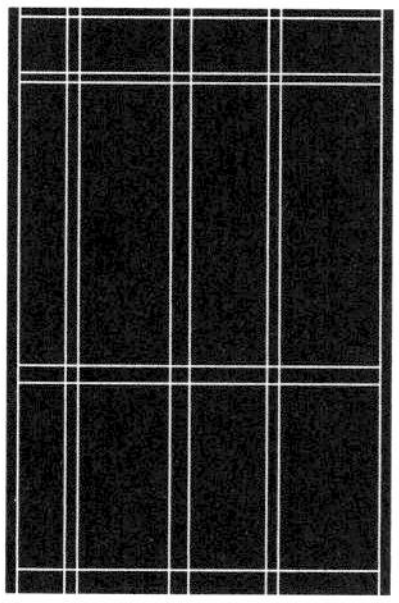

A1

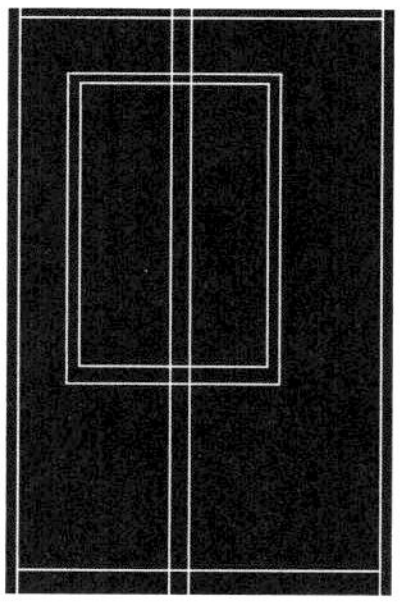

A2

A ff. 1r–69v. Combined technique; 410 x 256 mm (full frame); variable lines.

Pattern A is traced using brown crayon and hard-point technique on ff. 1r–69v; legal glossing layout of 4 columns (text inner, gloss outer); writing below top line; number of lines and size of frames are variable; A2 shows the typical use of the ruling.

SCRIPT: Several hands write text, glosses, corrections, and marginalia in Southern Textualis (Rotunda) at the Formata and Libraria levels; many Italian abbreviations are used, however the script also incorporates some Northern forms. Semitextualis Libraria is also used alongside Rotunda, especially in the *Glossa*; Northern features abound. A later hand has created a table of contents on flyleaf IIIr–v and foliated the manuscript [see FOLIATION].

DECORATION:
I. RUBRICATION: Rubrics in red ink; paraph marks alternate in red and blue ink.
II. INITIALS: Littera duplex, flourished, and plain initials occur in hierarchy.
A. Littera duplex initials are painted on f. 1r to begin the dedication (standing), prologue (5 line square inset), and gloss (hanging).
B. Flourished initials (2–3 line square inset; many 3–4 lines hanging) in red and blue ink with contrasting penwork alternate throughout the manuscript. Most resemble Italian types (cf. ff. 66v and 67v for a more Northern type).
C. Plain initials alternate in red and blue ink on ff. 68r–69v.

CONTENTS:

1. Boniface VIII, *Liber sextus*—ff. 1r[a]–69v[b].

1.1. Dedication. INC.: [f. 1r[b]] Bonifacius episcopus seruus seruorum [*in lae. marg. add.*] dei dilectis doctoribus et scolaribus uniuersis in romana /aliter bononie\ curia conmorantibus salutem et apostolicam benedictionem.

1.2. Prologue. INC.: [f. 1r[b]] sacrosancte romane ecclesie quam inperscrutabilis diuine prouidentie altitudo uniuersis dispositione incomutabili pretulit ecclesiis et totius . . .; EXPL.: [f. 1v[c]] . . . post editionem dicti uoluminnis [*sic*] promulgatas recepturi ulterius aud pro decretalibus habituri.

1.3. Text. RUB.: de summa trinitate et fide catholica; INC.: [f. 1v[c]] fideli ac deuota professione fatemur . . .; EXPL.: [f. 69v[b]] . . . certum est quod is committit in legem qui legis uerba conplectens contra legis nititur uoluntatem; COLOPHON: [f. 69v[a]] explicit sextus liber decretalium. datum rome apud sanctum petrum quinto nonas martii pontificatus domini bonifacii pape .viij. anno quarto.

Table of contents is arranged by book with folio numbers written on flyleaf IIIr–v.

EDITION: *CIC* 2:933–1124.

2. Iohannes Monachus (Jean Lemoine), *Glossa aurea* [incomplete]—ff. 1r[a]–67v[d].

INC.: [f. 1r[a]] in dei nomine amen. secundum philosophum scire est rem per causam cognoscere . . .; EXPL.: [f. 67v[d]] . . . sibi manducat et bibit.

EDITION: PARIS 1535 (repr. 1968).

3. Iohannes Andreae (Giovanni d'Andrea), *Declaratio arboris consanguinitatis* (fragmentary)—flyleaf IV.

INC.: [flyleaf IVv] p est in tertio frater patruellis est in quarto filius in quinto nepos in sexto et sic debet esse utraque puncta postea fac proauum . . .; EXPL.: [flyleaf IVr] . . . quid igitur inpediet des [*ut uid. sc.* istos] collaterales contrahere non uidet.

The text is inverted and begins on flyleaf IVv in section 13.

EDITION: *CIC* 1:1429–1430.

BINDING: s. xv; brown leather over wooden boards; blind tooled; sewn on six split thongs; metal catches on lower board.

OWNERS & PROVENANCE: Acquired from H. P. Kraus (New York, NY) by the university in November 1966.

SALES & CATALOGUES: H. P. Kraus, Cat. 115, no. 2.

FORMER SHELFMARK: MS 45 (Notre Dame).

BIBLIOGRAPHY: CORBETT no. 45.

cod. Lat. e. 2

Origin: Italy, s. xv.
Content Overview: Jean Buridan, *Quaestiones supra decem libros Ethicorum Aristotelis ad Nicomachum.*

In Latin, on paper; 246 ff.; 431 x 295 mm (page) [see Layout for ruling]; ff. 4v–6v blank.

Collation: $1^{6} + 2–20^{10} + 21^{10-1} + 22–24^{10} + 25^{10+1}$

Bibliographical Format: 2°.

Quires: Quires 2–25 are paper quinions folded in folio and reinforced with parchment strips on the outer and inner openings. Quire 1 is a ternion containing a table of contents to Buridan's *Quaestiones.* Quire 21 is a quinion lacking the sixth leaf. Quire 25 has an added singleton with stub (f. 246) which has been repaired with paper (see verso), yielding a paper reinforcement strip between the stub and the outer side of the quire. Additional repairs to the paper have been made (e.g., ff. 91, 110–115); wormed.

Catchwords: Horizontal catchwords are written in the lower margins (except quires 1, 2, and 25); all correspond.

Watermarks: One hundred twenty-three occurrences of a single watermark: (**A**) Dragon; occurs throughout quires 1–25; distance between chainlines 57 mm; generally cf. Briquet 2674 (Ferrara, 1505).

Foliation: Foliated in modern pencil with Arabic numerals in lower left margins by J. S. Kebabian for H. P. Kraus (collation statement on f. 245v; quires also numbered and openings foliated in inner margin); previous foliation visible in the upper right margins in ink, also Arabic numerals. All references in this description refer to the foliation in pencil.

Layout:

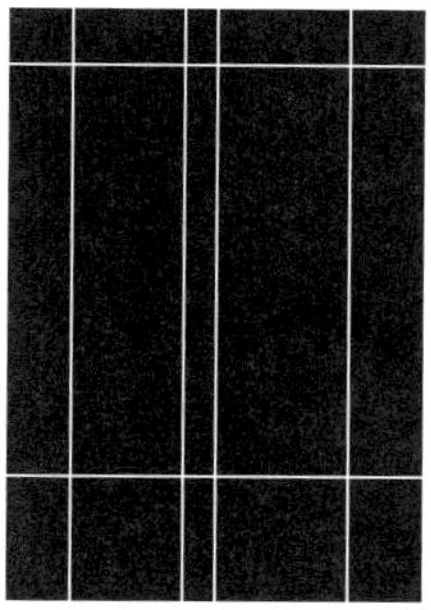

A

A ff. 1r–246v. Lead; 300 x 180 mm; intercol. 25 mm; 56 lines.

Pattern **A** is traced lightly in lead on ff. 1r–246v; two columns (intercol. 25 mm); writing mostly above top line; prickings visible in the upper and lower margins for vertical bounding lines.

Script: An Italian hand (M1) of the fifteenth century writes all text in Hybrida Libraria with a distinctive brownish ink; round **r** is used exclusively, including initial position. Textualis is used as a display script (e.g., f. 1r); colophon on f. 246r^{b} evidences M1 as a professional scribe [see Contents 1, scribal colophon]; a later hand (M2) corrects the text in black ink.

Decoration: In addition to the historiated initial on with marginal sprays, three conjoined heraldic lozenges appear at the bottom of f. 7r.

I. Rubrication: Paraph marks and rapid letter heightening alternating in red and blue ink throughout the index of *Quaestiones* (ff. 1r^{a}–4r^{b}); paraph marks in red (or alternating red and blue) occur sparsely throughout the text as well as a second underlining of lemmata in red ink (lemmata first underlined by M1 in brownish ink).

II. Initials: A single historiated initial is painted on f. 7r^{a}. Spaces for initials (4 line square inset) for *quaestiones* (6 line square inset for Books 2–10) are reserved at the beginning of each *quaestio* or book; guide letters remain.

a. One historiated initial 15 lines in height surrounded by display script occurs on f. 7r^{a}. The initial depicts either Buridan or Aristotle in medieval costume (or possibly the owner); pink ink with white penwork and blue interior on gold grounds; stylized with typical Italian motifs with vegetal tendrils spraying into the margins in blue, red, green, pink, orange, and gold with white penwork.

CONTENTS:

1. Jean Buridan, *Quaestiones supra decem libros Ethicorum Aristotelis ad Nicomachum*—ff. 7r[a]–246r[b].

INC.: [f. 7r[a]] diuinitatis et nobilitatis excellentiam philosophie moralis extollit aristoteles secundo ethicorum cum dicit eam esse non contemplationis gratia . . .; **EXPL.:** [f. 246r[b]] . . . coniunctum scilicet sensus uel appetitus sensitiui ex hiis sic est finis quoniam super decem libris ethicorum aristotelis secundum iohannem bridannum [*sic*]; **SCRIBAL COLOPHON:** [f. 246r[b]] finis adest mete mercedem quero diete quam nisi tu dederis cras minus actus [*sic*] eris amen amen amen amen.

Index for the *Quaestiones* written on ff. 1r[a]–4r[b], corresponding to the previous foliation in ink; see the colophon in Reims, Bibliothèque municipale, MS 1267 (J. 744), f. 91r; see also London, British Library, Harley MS 3220 [*COLOPHONS* 6: no. 21248]. Brugge, Stedelijke Openbare Bibliotheek, MS 488 [*COLOPHONS* 6: no. 21249], and Toledo, Biblioteca Capitular, MS 12.4 [GUTIÉRREZ CUADRADO 1992, 430], contain only the first line of the colophon.

EDITION: PARIS 1513 (repr. 1968).
BIBLIOGRAPHY: FARAL 1946; FARAL 1950, esp. 117–132; LOHR 1970; ZUPKO 2003, 227–242; generally, KLIMA 2009.

BINDING: s. xvi; half binding of brown leather over wooden boards; sewn on four split thongs; blind stamped; metal catches on lower board; leather thongs on upper board contain parchment fragments written in Italian in Hybrida; spine lined with legal fragments written in Italian Rotunda.

OWNERS & PROVENANCE: The three heraldic marks on f. 7r remain unidentified. The ownership mark of Ludovico Podocataro (ca. 1430–1504) appears in the upper right margin of f. 1r; acquired from H. P. Kraus (New York, NY) by the university in September 1967.

FORMER SHELFMARK: MS 22 (Notre Dame).

BIBLIOGRAPHY: CORBETT no. 22.

cod. Lat. e. 3

Origin: Italy, s. xiv^2 (Bologna).
Content Overview: Paulus de Liazariis, *Lectura super Clementinis*; added legal texts and verses.

In Latin, on parchment; i +50 ff. +i; 455 x 280 mm (page) [see Layout for ruling]; medieval parchment flyleaf; foliated in Roman (medieval) and Arabic (modern) numerals [see Foliation].

Collation: i +1^{10} +2^{4} +$3–5^{10}$ +6^{6} +i

Quires: Parchment quinions, F/F, are the normal quire forms. Quire 2 is a binion, F/F. Quire 6 is a ternion, F/F. All quires obey Gregory's Rule. Fire damage is visible throughout the manuscript; pecia marks occur in the margins of ff. $5v^b$, $11v^b$, $18r^a$, $20v^b$, $22r^a$, $29v^a$ [*ut uid.*], $36v^b$, and $39v^a$; the manuscript has been trimmed.

Catchwords: Horizontal catchwords appear in the lower right margins; all correspond; quires 3 and 6 lack catchwords.

Foliation: Medieval foliation with Roman numerals in ink is centered in the upper margins (i–xxiii, xxiiii–xliii, xlv–xlix); modern foliation with Arabic numerals in pencil in upper right corner (1–23, 23a, 24–49); description uses modern foliation.

Layout:

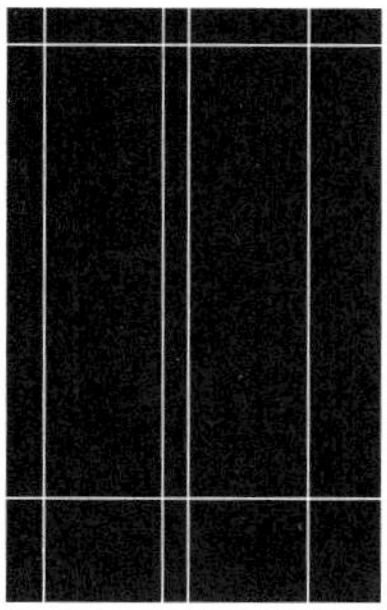

A

A ff. 1r–23r, 24r–48r. Lead; 347 x 198 mm; intercol. 19 mm; 94 lines.

Pattern A is traced in lead and occasionally brown crayon on ff. 1r–23r and 24r–48r; two columns; writing below top line; prickings visible in upper and lower margins for vertical bounding lines and horizontal through lines.

SCRIPT: Four discernable scribal bookhands (M1–M4) write all texts: M1 writes Southern Textualis Libraria (Rotunda) in rapid execution on ff. $1r^a$–$23r^b$ and $24r^a$–$48r^b$. M2 writes Cursiva Antiquior on ff. $23v^a$–$23vA^b$, $49v^a$–$49v^b$, varying between Libraria and Currens; consistent use of two compartment **a**; M3 writes Semitextualis at varying levels on f. $48r^b$ and transitions to Cursiva Libraria; M4 writes a Southern Textualis Libraria (Rotunda) on f. $48v^{(b)}$ which is similar to M1.

DECORATION:
I. RUBRICATION: Rubrics in red ink; paraph marks alternate in red and blue ink.
II. INITIALS: Historiated and flourished initials occur in hierarchy.
A. Historiated initials (8 lines square inset) of Bolognese canonists on gold grounds with vegetal sprays in green, red, and gray begin the two sections of the *Lectura* on ff. 1r and 24r.
B. Flourished initials (3 line square inset) alternate in red and blue with contrasting penwork throughout the manuscript.

CONTENTS:

1. Paulus de Liazariis, *Lectura super Clementinis* (I–II)—ff. $1r^a$–$22r^a$.

INC..: [f. $1r^a$] Bonus uir sine deo nemo est et non potest aliquis supra fortunam . . . iohannes obmissis questionibus que in principio decretalium et sexti libri super salutatione formantur . . .; EXPL.: [f. $22r^a$] . . . infinita possent de hoc exempla haberi. finis secundi libri.

BIBLIOGRAPHY: BERTRAM 2013, 91–101.

2. Paulus de Liazariis, *Repetitio de confessis*—ff. $22r^a$–$23r^b$.

RUB.: ista glosa super .c. ex parte extra de confessis; INC.: [f. $22r^a$] de confessis quod continuare sic sepe contingit quod libello oblato propter contumaciam rei suspenditur processus . . .; EXPL.: [$23r^b$] . . . et iuxta .v. sed numquid ecclesia paulus de iiaziariis [*sic*]. [*Decretal.* Gregor. IX. Lib. II.18].

3. Iohannes Calderinus, *Repetitio super spoliatione de ordine cognitionum* [*D.* II.10.4]—ff. $23v^a$–f. $23Av^b$.

INC.: rubrica de ordine cognitionum super spoliatione casus agens possessorio recuperande . . .; EXPL.: . . . ex certa causa obstet eidem postea super illa causa iterum uolenti agere notat [*ut uid.*] ipse innoc(ens) .i. t. .2. c. cum ecclesia iohannes cald(erin)us.

EDITION: VENICE 1496, ff. 17v–19v.

4. Ps.-Jerome, *Quindecim signa ante diem iudicii*—f. 23Av[b].

INC.: [f. 23Av[b]] antequam iudicii dies metuenda ueniat sunt mundi omnia conmouenda . . .; EXPL.: [f. 23Av[b]] . . . ut in die ualeat mala liberari. expliciunt carmina ieronimi.

EDITION: PELAEZ 1935, 67–68.
BIBLIOGRAPHY: WALTHER, *Initia* 1314; PELAEZ 1935, 61–63.

5. Verses—f. 23Av[b].

5.1. INC.: hanc in honore pie candelam porto marie . . .; EXPL.: . . . per lumen numen maiestatisque cacumen.

The verses are transmitted in the *Legenda aurea, De purificatione beatae Mariae uirginis.*

EDITION: MAGGIONI 1998, 1:248; cf. text of HERVIEUX 1884–1899, 4:350.

5.2. INC.: materia triplici [*ut uid.*]; EXPL.: . . . christi significatur.
5.3. *Versus de quatuor complexionibus.* INC.: largus amans ylaris ridens ruffique coloris cantans carnosos satis audax atque benignus. sanguineus . . .; EXPL.: . . . sollicitus tristis cupidus dextreque tenacis non expers fraudis timidus nigerque coloris. melancolicus.

EDITION: THORNDIKE 1958, 399 n. 3.
BIBLIOGRAPHY: THORNDIKE 1955, 177–180; THORNDIKE 1958, 399, esp. n. 3.

6. Paulus de Liazariis, *Lectura super Clementinis* (III–V)—ff. 24r[a]–48r[b].

RUB.: de uita et honestate clericorum; INC.: [f. 24r[a]] dyocesanis punit clericos coniugatos et alios si tercio moniti non desistunt . . .; EXPL.: [f. 48r[b]] . . . [*Clem.* 5.11.2] que summum bonum in rebus est .vij. .q. .ij. cum deuotissimam quam sic seruare in hoc seculo nobis concedat altissimus ut summum celeste bonum intercedente beatissima uirgine gloriosa cum omnibus sanctis eius in exitu mereamur amen. paulus de liaziis [*sic*] decretorum doctor egregius.

7. *Lectura* (?) *de exceptionibus* [incomplete]—f. 48r[b].

INC.: [f. 48r[b]] uiso de probatione in genere et in specie quia is qui excipit in se honus probacionis assumit . . .; EXPL.: [f. 48r[b]] . . . que opponitur contra exceptionem peccati de non.

Text begins with *Decretal.* Gregor. IX. Lib. II.25, *rubrica de exceptionibus* and cap. 2 (*a nobis*), but ends imperfectly.

8. Aegidius de Bellamera, *Praelectiones in decretalium libros* (*de exceptionibus c. a nobis*)—f. 48v[(b)].

INC.: [f. 48v[(b)]] <perempto>riam sibi competentem nisi ex quo fundata . . .; EXPL.: [f. 48v[(b)]] . . . sed non habebit necesse specialiter interloqui. iohannes an(dreae) decretorum doctor andreas de suchdol [*ut. uid.*].

The text corresponds to that of Aegidius de Bellamera (Gilles Bellèmere) printed in Lyon 1549, f. 4r^{a-b}.

Edition: Lyon 1549, f. 4r^{a-b}.

9. Unidentified—f. 49r^{a}–v^{b}.

inc.: [f. 49r^{a}] propositus est liber scriptus intus et foris intus diuinitate foris humanitate unus ergo liber semel est scriptus intus et foris bis primo per uisibilium condicionem [Hugh of St. Victor, *De sacramentis* I.5] . . .; **expl.**: [f. 49v^{b}] . . . non speremus ipse tamen uiuebat et uiuit in secula seculorum.

Binding: s. xv; brown leather over wooden boards; blind tooled; metal catches on lower board; remnants of leather thongs on upper board.

Owners & Provenance: Acquired from H. P. Kraus (New York, NY) by the university in November 1966.

Sales & Catalogues: H. P. Kraus, Cat. 100, no. 12; ibid., Cat. 115, no. 96.

Former Shelfmark: MS 46 (Notre Dame).

Bibliography: Corbett no. 46; Bertram 2013, 100.

cod. Lat. e. 4

Origin: England, s. xiv^2
Content Overview: Psalter.

In Latin, on parchment; iii +142 ff. +iii; generally 338 x 225 mm (page) [see Layout for ruling]; foliated in modern pencil with Arabic numerals; 81 *bis* (81, 81a); f. 102 foliated as 103 (i.e., 101, 103, 104, etc.); flyleaf iv foliated as f. 143; flyleaves i and vi modern parchment; flyleaves ii (blank, former pastedown) and iii (ruled) medieval parchment, which form part of quire 1 [see Quires]; flyleaves iv and v medieval parchment (ruled).

Collation: i +1–6^8 +7$^{8-1}$ +8–18^8 +iii

Quires: Quaternions, H/H are the normal quire forms. Flyleaves II and III form part of quire 1; though the binding is tight, ff. 2–3 and 1–4 are conjugate bifolia; quire 7 lacks the second leaf. The parchment is of high quality and well scraped; it is difficult to distinguish hair side from flesh side. The manuscript has been trimmed and undergone extensive conservation treatment (e.g., ff. 12, 42, 51, 57, 72, 74, 75); imperfections visible on ff. 27, 65, 81, 129.

Catchwords: Horizontal catchwords in the lower right margins for quires 2–15; all correspond; quires 16–18 lack catchwords; most catchwords are stylized with scroll borders or other penwork.

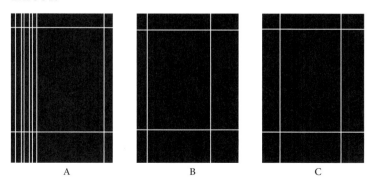

Layout:

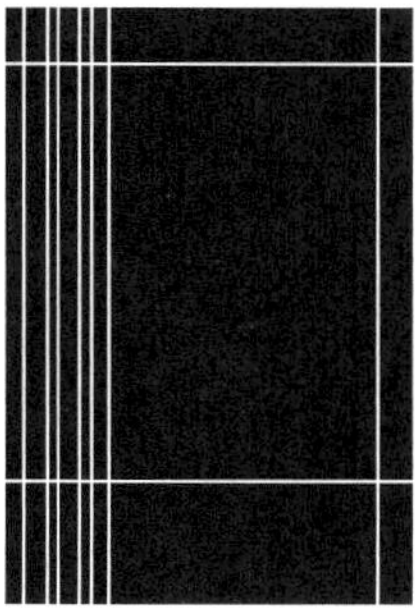

A

B

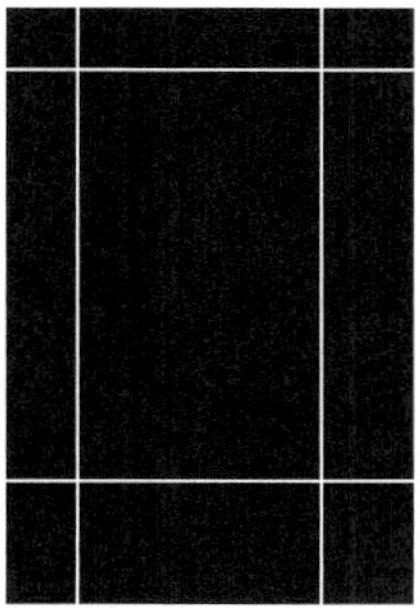

C

A ff. 1r–6v. Ink; approx. 237 x 153 mm; cols. 13/6/12/7/9/107 mm; 33 lines.
B ff. 7r–77v. Ink; 226 x 142–146 mm; 22 lines.
C ff. 78r–142v. Ink; 233 x 135–137 mm; 22 lines.

Pattern **A** is traced in ink on ff. 1r–6v; six calendric columns (approx. 13/6/12/7/9/107 mm); writing above top line; prickings visible in upper, lower, and outer margins; double prick for lower horizontal through line; right vertical bounding line (recto) rarely straight, sloping left from top down. Patterns **B** and **C** are identical in layout but differ in dimensions; writing below top line; prickings visible in upper, lower, and outer margins. The shift from **B** to **C** corresponds to the division of labor [see SCRIPT and DECORATION]; flyleaves III, IV, and V crudely ruled: III similar to **A**, IV and V similar to **B** and **C**.

SCRIPT: Two scribal bookhands (M1–M2) are discernable. M1 copies quires 2–10 (ff. 7r–77v) in Northern Textualis Formata of the fourteenth century. M2 copies the calendar (ff. 1r–6v) and quires 11–18 (ff. 78r–142v) in Northern Textualis Formata of the fourteenth century. Two hands (M3–M4) supply additional material. M3 writes *Gloria patri* in crayon in some margins (e.g., ff. 90r, 91v, 94r, 96r, 136v); M3 writes in Anglicana under the influence of European Cursiva of the fifteenth century. M4 (s. xvi^{2}/xvii) renumbers the psalms in the margins and adds instructions for ferial recitation.

DECORATION: The division of scribal labor between M1 and M2 [see SCRIPT] also marks a division in decoration. Two painters (P1–P2) can be distinguished in the initials, line fillers, and border decoration. P1 is responsible for quires 2–10 (ff. 7r–77v) and P2 for the calendar (ff. 1r–6v) and quires 11–18 (ff. 78r–142v). Stylized *litterae elongatae* have been added to some descenders (e.g., ff. 113r, 116r, 122r) but cannot be attributed reliably.

I. RUBRICATION: No rubrication or letter heightening; graded feasts in the calendar in red ink.

II. INITIALS: Historiated and dentelle initials occur in hierarchy.

A. Historiated initials (6 line square inset) begin Ps 1 (David with harp; f. 7r), Ps 26 (David in abstract pose; f. 25r), Ps 38 (David in abstract pose; f. 37r), Ps 68 (Jonah and the whale; f. 58r), Ps 80 (playing the bells; f. 72r), Ps 97 (choir singing; f. 85r), and Ps 109 (the Father and Son; f. 99r). Those on ff. 85r and 99r are likely the work of P2.

B. Dentelle initials (2–4 line square inset; 1 line versals; occasional hanging **i**s) occur throughout the manuscript. The 2 line initials begin the non-historiated psalms and mark the kalends abbreviation in the calendar; 1 line versals used in all psalms, initial position for calendar entries, and dominical letter **a**. P1 uses light pink and light blue grounds (ff. 7r–77v); P2 (ff. 1r–6v, 78r–142v) uses deep rose and darker, vivid blue grounds with more precise white penwork. The 2 line dentelles by P2 use a quartered contrast of rose and blue and incorporate sprays into the margins. A larger dentelle (4 line square inset) begins Ps 101 on f. 86v.

III. Line Fillers: Line fillers of the dentelle type in three styles are painted throughout by P1 and P2. P1 paints line fillers in the same palette as the dentelles; those on ff. 7r–47v are rectangular and notched; foliate-like interior filled with gold outlined in black. P1 switches style on ff. 48r–77v; line fillers are only rectangular; foliate interior designs are outlined in white and filled with darker pink or blue; bars separated by gold outlined in black. P2 paints line fillers on ff. 78r–142v using the same palette as the dentelles; rectangular in shape; foliate interior designs in crisp white penwork; bars separated by gold outlined in black.

IV. Borders & Frames: Full foliate borders and one partial border. Full foliate borders accompany the historiated initials. Borders by P2 on ff. 7r, 25r, 37r, 58r, and 72r are inhabited by grotesque birds and hybrids (knot work on ff. 7r and 72r); palette is the same light pinks and blues and gold as dentelles and line fillers. Borders by P2 on ff. 85r, 99r; uninhabited with more knot work; palette is the same deep rose and vivid dark blue as the dentelles and line fillers with crisp white penwork. A partial border via extension of initial in gold by P2 on f. 86v terminates in hairy foliate and floral sprays in deep rose and dark blue with white highlights.

Calendar: One month per page; dominical letter **a** in dentelle style; Roman time marked in red and black ink; forms of *papa* and Thomas Becket have been erased.

Contents:

1. Calendar—ff. 1r–6v.

Liturgical calendar in black and red ink with grades in far right column. The manuscript was in England after Henry VIII was declared supreme head of the Church of England, and all forms of *papa* have been erased as well as the name of Thomas Becket.

In red ink with nine *lectiones*: deposition of Wulfstan (Jan. 19), Gregory (Mar. 12), Edward (Mar. 18), Cuthbert (Mar. 20), Benedict (Mar. 21), Richard of Chichester (Apr. 3), Augustine of Canterbury (May 26), translation of Edmund (Jun. 9), translation of Richard of Chichester (Jun. 16), translation of Edward (Jun. 20), Alban (Jun. 22), translation of Thomas Becket (Jul. 7; erased), Edmund (Nov. 16), Thomas Becket (Dec. 29; erased). In black ink with nine *lectiones*: Dunstan (May 19), Aldhelm (May 25), Swithun (Jul. 3; *memoria*) translation of Swithun (Jul. 15), translation of Cuthbert (Sept. 4), Edith (Sept. 16), translation of Edward (Oct. 13), Malo (Nov. 15), Edmund (Nov. 20). In black ink with three *lectiones*: Bathild (Jan. 30), Alphege (Apr. 19), Kenelm (Jul. 17), Oswald (Aug. 5), Magnus (Aug. 19; *memoria*), Cuthberga (Aug. 31), translation of Oswald (Oct. 8), Bricius (Nov. 13).

2. Psalter—ff. 7r–130r.

Eight-part division of psalms marked by initials [see Decoration]: Ps 1 (f. 7r), Ps 26 (f. 25r), Ps 38 (f. 37r), Ps 68 (f. 58r), Ps 80 (f. 72r), Ps 97 (f. 85r), Ps 101v (f. 86v), and Ps 109 (f. 99r).

3. Canticles—ff. 130r–142v.

Six ferial canticles (ff. 130r–138r); *Te deum* (f. 138r); *Benedicite omnia* (f. 139r); *Benedictus dominus deus* (f. 140r); *Magnificat* (f. 140v); *Nunc dimittis* (f. 141r); *Quicumque uult* (f. 141v).

Binding: s. xix/xx; brown leather over boards; blind tooled; seven raised bands; two bosses on front cover, one on back; two brass clasps on upper board; catches on lower board; binding has been rebacked.

Owners & Provenance: Howel Wills (1854?–1901); Quaritch; William Morris (1834–1896); Richard Bennett (see De Ricci 1930, 171–173); Leighton; Charles Butler (1822–1910); Chas J. Sawyer (London); Marks and Co (London); John Edgar Park (1926–1944); Milton Anastos (1909–1997) and Rosemary Park Anastos (1907–2004) of Los Angeles, CA; gift of Milton and Rosemary Anastos to the university in 1977 or 1978.

Sales & Catalogues: Sotheby's, 11 July 1894, lot 1536 (Howel Wills Sale); Quaritch, Cat. 144, *a Rough List* no. 413 (August 1894); Sotheby's, 5 December 1898, lot 972 (Morris Sale); Sotheby's, 18 March 1912, lot 2630 (Butler Sale, Third Portion); Sotheby's, 18 July 1921, lot 499; Chas J. Sawyer, Cat. 100, no. 111; Sotheby's, 18 December 1933, lot. 363; Marks & Co, 1935, no. 1719.

Former Shelfmarks: A. II.26 (Howel Wills); MS 65 (Notre Dame).

Bibliography: Hilmo 2012, 182, 194–195, figs. 22, 35a.

MS Eng. d. 1

Origin: England, s. xv^{1}.
Content Overview: *A Mirror to Devout People* (*Speculum deuotorum*); *O intemerata*; *The Craft of Dying*.

In English and Latin, on parchment; ii +127 ff. +i; generally 300 x 209 mm (page) [see Layout for ruling]; flyleaves medieval parchment; f. 126v blank but ruled.

Collation: ii +1–15^{8} +16$^{8-1}$ +i

Quires: Parchment quaternions, H/H, are the predominant quire forms; quires 14–16 are F/F. The final folio of quire 16 has been canceled (F/H).

Catchwords: Horizontal catchwords with scroll decoration and examination marks are centered in the lower margins for quires 1–13; quire 14 has no catchword, but contains examination mark on f. 109r; quire 15 has a horizontal catchword in the inner right margin underlined in red ink on f. 126v; all correspond.

Signatures: Signatures (e.g., g1) are trimmed, but visible in the lower right margins of rectos for most quires.

Layout:

A

A ff. 1r–127v. Ink; 203–206 x 137 mm; 27 lines.

Pattern **A** is traced in brown ink throughout ff. 1r–127v; single column; writing below top line; prickings visible for all verticals and horizontals; double (occasionally triple) prick for lower penultimate horizontal.

Script: Two scribal bookhands (M1–M2) write all texts. M1 writes Cursiva of the fifteenth century under the influence of Bastarda on ff. 1r–108r; consistent use of single compartment **a**; M1 admits Anglicana **g**, **r**, **s** as alternative forms; Latin rubrics use two compartment **a**; M1 is identified with the initials W. H. in the colophon on f. 108r. M1 also writes a well-executed Northern Textualis Formata on ff. 108r–109r with distinctive hairlines and flourishes to tick forms of **i**. M2 writes Anglicana Libraria (Cursiva Antiquior) of the fifteenth century on ff. 108v–126r; M2 consistently uses two compartment **a** and Anglicana forms for **e**, **g**, **r**, **s** while admitting occasional continental alternative forms. Latin rubrics in Anglicana Formata written under the influence of Bastarda; use of continental **g**. M3 is identified with the initials W. M. in the colophon on f. 126r. Later additions on flyleaf Iv (s. xvii^{in}); copies of two legal documents in Cursiva on f. 127v and flyleaf IIIr; autograph of a Richard Savige (fl. 1686) on f. 127r.

Decoration:

I. Rubrication: Rubrics and some colophons in red ink; paraph marks and letter heightening in red.

II. Initials: Historiated (dentelles) and flourished initials occur in hierarchy.

a. Three historiated initials occur, of which all are of the dentelle type with miniatures: initial (4 line square inset) on f. 1r contains "the arms of the Scropes *azure*, a bend *or* with label *argent*, impaling those of Chaworth" (Edwards 2006, 110); St. John (*ut uid.*) holding chalice, Eucharist, and palm frond with Virgin crowned and child on f. 108r (5 line square inset with floral spray); figure asleep or dead in bed with red covers and bishop on f. 109v (5+4 line stepped with floral spray).

b. Flourished initials (4 line square inset) in blue ink with red penwork begin chapters on ff. 1r–108r; initials are 2 line square indents on ff. 109v–123r.

c. Plain initials (1 line versals) in blue ink occur on ff. 106r–107r in the cues for *O intemerata* [see Contents 2].

III. Line Fillers: Line fillers in black and red ink on ff. 108r and 109r.

IV. Borders & Frames: Acanthus border in blues, greens, pinks, and oranges with white penwork on f. 1r; floral sprays in black and green with gold; dentelle style frame.

Contents:

1. *A Mirror to Devout People* (*Speculum deuotorum*)—ff. 1r–108r.

inc.: [f. 1r] gostely sustre in ihesu criste i trowe it be nought 3it from yo mynde þat when we spake last togidre I behight yow a meditacioun of þe passioun of our lorde . . .; expl.: [f. 108r] . . . one everlastynge verrey and almyghty god to whome be all worship ioye and preysynge nowe and withoute ony edynge. amen; SCRIBAL COLOPHON: [f. 108r] finito libro sit laus et gloria christo soluite nunc mentem pro w.h. ad omnipotentem de uita christi libro finis datur isti paruos lactabit solidos quasi pane cibabit de bethlem pratum dedit hos ihesu tibi flores post hunc ergo statum reddas sibi semper honores.

The text is also known in Cambridge, University Library, MS Gg.1.6; PATTERSON 2006, 66–69 discusses the relationship of the two manuscripts very generally.

EDITION: PATTERSON 2016; PATTERSON 2006; HOGG 1973–1974; see also BANKS 1959 and WILSHER 1956.
BIBLIOGRAPHY: *IPMEP* 254; I. JOHNSON 1999.

2. *O intemerata* (masculine forms)—ff. 108r–109r.

RUB.: oracio bona et deuota ad beatam uirginem mariam matrem domini nostri ihesu christi et beatum iohannem euangelistam; INC.: [f. 108r] o intemerata et in eternum benedicta singularis atque incomparabilis uirgo . . . et esto michi peccatori . . . ego miser peccator . . .; EXPL.: [f. 108v] . . . qui patri et filio consubstancialis et coeternus cum eis et in eis uiuit et regnat omnipotens deus per omnia secula seculorum amen; COLOPHON: [f. 109r] nos tibi uirgo pia semper commendo maria nos rogo conserues christi dilecte iohannes uirgo maria dei genitrix quam scriptor honorat sis pia semper ei prout hic te sperat et orat ex aliaque uice iohannes christi dulcis amice da sibi solamen cum sanctis omnibus amen. in omni tribulacione temptacione necessitate et angustia succurre nobis piissima uirgo maria amen.

The last sentence of the colophon is also found in New Haven, Yale Univ., Beinecke Library, MS 535, fol. 90r.

EDITION: WILMART, 487–504.

3. *The Craft of Dying*—ff. 109v–126r.

INC.: [f. 109v] for als miche as þe passage of deth oute of the wrycchednesse of the exile of this world . . .; EXPL.: [f. 126r] . . . of our lord ihesu cryste þat is mediatour bytwix god and man. amen; COLOPHON 1: [f. 126r] esto memor mortis nam porta fit omnibus ortis sepe sibi iuuenes accipit ante senes [WALTHER, *Initia* 5892]; COLOPHON 2: [f. 126r] non homo leteris tibi copia si fluat eris hic non semper eris memor esto quod morieris es euanebit quod habes tunc alter habebit corpus putrebit quod agis tecum remanebit [WALTHER, *Initia* 12072]; COLOPHON 3: [f. 126r] finem siste pia mortis michi uirgo maria es quia regina manfeld defende ruina; [*in dex. marg.*]: w.m. amen.

EDITION: COMPER 1917, 1–47 (with modern spelling).
BIBLIOGRAPHY: *IPMEP* 234.

Binding: s. xv; tawed skin over wooden boards; sewn on seven split thongs; two clasps (missing); later red and gilt tooled title piece on spine.

Owners & Provenance: According to Edwards 2006, 122: John Scrope, 4th Baron of Masham (ca. 1388–1455) and Elizabeth Chaworth (1391–1466/67); Mrs. Bertram Bell; acquired by William Alfred Westropp Foyle (1885–1963) in 1946; purchased from Quaritch by the university in 2000. Bookplate of Marbury Library on front pastedown; price (s. xvii^{in}) "Cost .vi^{s}. .viii^{d}." written on flyleaf Iv.

Sales & Catalogues: Sotheby's, 3 June 1946, lot 112; Christie's, 11 July 2000, lot 73.

Former Shelfmarks: Case 8, no. 220 (Marbury); MS 67 (Notre Dame).

Bibliography: Salter 1964, 29 n. 16; Jolliffe 1974, 123 [L.4 (a)], 225; Sargent 1994, 66–67; I. Johnson 1999, 73; Selman 2000, 75 n. 4; Brantley 2006, 173–174, 194, 198, 200–201, 204–205, 215 (plates 1–3, on 8–10); Edwards 2006 (description on 120–122); Gillespie 2006, 129, 132, 138, 142–143, 146, 160 n. 2, 165 nn. 20 and 22, 166 n. 24, 167 n. 36, 168 n. 37, 170 n. 58; Nolan 2006, 4–6; Patterson 2006 (brief description on 4–7); Brantley 2007, 53, 347; Gillespie 2008, 136–137, 141, 144–147, 157 n. 3, 160 n. 21, 161 nn. 23 and 24, 163 nn. 36 and 37, 165 n. 63; Cole and Turville-Petre 2010, 27 (index, 138); Gillespie 2011, 190 n. 12; Patterson 2011, 134–135, 149; I. Johnson 2013, 155 n. 9; Patterson 2016.

MS Fr. c. 1

Origin: France, s. xvi^{1}.
Content Overview: *Le Sacre Couronnement et Entrée de Madame Claude Royne de France fille du Roy Loys XII et de Madame Anne de Bretaigne.*

In French with Latin rubrics, on parchment; i +36 ff. +i; generally 223 x 155 mm (page) [see Layout for ruling]; flyleaves modern marbled paper (versos); foliated in modern pencil with Arabic numerals.

Collation: i $+1^{6} +2^{2-1} + 3^{8-1} +4^{2-1} +5^{6} +6^{2} +7^{4-1} +8^{6-2} +9^{6}$ +i

Quires: Parchment ternions and quaternions are the predominant quire forms. Quire 2 is a bifolium with the first leaf canceled. Quire 3 is a quaternion with the sixth leaf canceled. Quire 4 is a bifolium with the last leaf canceled. Quire 7 is a binion with the second leaf canceled. Quire 8 is a ternion with the fourth and fifth leaves canceled. Cancellations create stubs for inserted illustrations, which are typical of this work, though none are found in this manuscript. Gregory's Rule is not observed due to cancellations; both outward H/H and F/F arrangements are found among the quires; occasional water damage; quire marks, catchwords, and signatures are absent.

Layout:

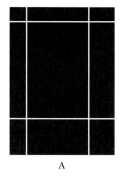

A

A ff. 1r–36v. Rose ink; 146 x 92 mm; 18 lines.

Pattern **A** is traced on ff. 1r–36v in rose ink; single column; writing below top line; prickings for bounding lines are seldom visible. **A** is often faded or traced very lightly.

Script: A single hand (M1) writes Cursiva Formata (Bastarda) of the sixteenth century using **g** forms drawn from Southern Textualis and Humanistic minuscule. Corrections are made via erasures by a contemporaneous hand (M2); M2 writes Hybrida Formata (Bastarda) using deviant forms of **g** similar to M1; later addition on f. 24v.

Decoration: In addition to initials, arms are painted in the margins on f. 1v.

I. Rubrication: Latin rubrics written in red ink by M1.

II. Initials: Decorated initials (3–4 line square indent) occur throughout the text; gold initials on blue, pink, or reddish grounds; blue initials with white penwork on pink or gold grounds (some with floral motifs); a hierarchy is not entrenched firmly.

Contents:

1. *Le Sacre Couronnement et Entrée de Madame Claude Royne de France fille du Roy Loys XII et de Madame Anne de Bretaigne.* [incomplete]—ff. 1r–36v.

inc.: [f. 1r] la noble dame arriua a saict [*sic*] denis le sabmedi au soir neusiesme jour de may bien acompaignee de princes et princesses et aultres grans seigneurs . . .; expl.: [f. 36v] . . . portoient le nom ainisi finit celle noble assemblee. nous prirous dieu et la uierge marie qui lur doiuet fruict bonne longue uie.

All miniatures have been excised. Other known manuscripts of the text are: Cambridge, Magdalen College, Pepys MS 1491; London, British Library Cotton MS Titus A. XVII and Stowe MS 582; Paris, Bibliothèque nationale, MSS Fr. 5750 and Fr. 14116; and Paris, École nationale supérieure des Beaux-Arts, MS 491.

Edition: C. Brown 2005, 273–313; Godefroy 1649, 472–486.

Bibliography: C. Brown 2005, 273–278; Kipling 1998, 69 n. 45; Booton 2010, 275–276.

Binding: s. xviii; stiff vellum over pasteboards; inked panels; with marbled end papers; gilt spine (rebacked).

Owners & Provenance: A Thomas Williams is mentioned on f. 28r (see also f. 35r); later given by Evan Evans (1731–1788) [Ieuan Fardd or Ieuan Brydydd Hir] to Evan Lloyd Vaughan (ca. 1709–1791) in 1771 (f. 1r: *donum Rev. Ev. Evans to Ev. Lloyd Vaughn, 1771*; *ex libris Ev. Ll. Vaughan*); front pastedown bears the bookplate of the Corsygedol Library [Cors-y-Gedol]; passed to the Mostyn estate after Vaughn's death and is recorded among the Mostyn manuscripts in the *Fourth Report of the Royal Commission on Historical Manu-*

scripts (London, 1874); bookplate of Wilfred Merton (1887–1957); B. Breslauer (1958); H. P. Kraus (1958; 1967); acquired from H. P. Kraus (New York, NY) by the university in November 1968.

Sales & Catalogues: Sotheby's, 13 July 1920, lot 53; H. P. Kraus, Cat. 88, no. 38; Breslauer, Cat. 90, no. 35; H. P. Kraus, Cat. 117, no. 19.

Former Shelfmark: MS 74 (Mostyn); MS 37 (Notre Dame).

Bibliography: Corbett no. 37; Great Britain, Royal Commission on Historical Manuscripts 1874, 1:350, no. 74.

MS Fr. c. 2

Origin: France, s. xv^{2} (dated 28 May 1464).
Content Overview: Cuvelier, *Chanson de Bertrand du Guesclin.*

In French, on paper; iii +298 ff. +iii; generally 276 x 201 mm (page) [see Layout for ruling]; 58v blank; paper flyleaves.

Collation: iii $+1^{16-1}$ $+2^{18}$ $+3^{16+1}$ $+4–5^{16}$ $+6^{18}$ $+7–9^{16}$ $+10^{16+2}$ $+11–14^{16}$ $+15–19^{12}$ $+20^{12-4}$ +iii

Bibliographical Format: 2°.

Quires: The manuscript is irregularly structured using various quire forms. The predominant forms are gatherings of eight bifolia folded in folio; gatherings of nine bifolia are used for quires 2 and 6; sexternions are used for quires 15–19. Rebinding and conservation treatments have disturbed many of the quire forms and relocated folios out of sequence. Quire 1 lacks the last leaf, which has been inserted (f. 35) into quire 3, and the second bifolium of quire 1 has been reversed (ff. 2 = 15 and 15 = 2). Quire 10 contains a constructed bifolium (ff. 152–153) which is inserted asymmetrically between ff. 151v and 154r; ff. 152–153 belong to the manuscript's final quire, quire 20 (quire mark on f. 153). Quire 20 is comprised of four bifolia, though ff. 153 and 152 would have formed its opening leaves; the quire was originally a sexternion with the last two leaves canceled, though its current state lacks four leaves.

Quire Marks: Quire marks in French using Roman numerals as ordinals appear on the beginning rectos for quires 2–19; quire mark for quire 20 on f. 153r [see Quires].

Foliation: Two sets of modern foliation with Arabic numerals appear. Set 1 was written in the upper right hand corner by J. S. Kebabian for H. P. Kraus in December 1966 (collation statement on rear pastedown). Set 1 does not foliate the manuscript in numerical order, but rather in order of content (i.e., f. 2 is marked as f. 15, and f. 152 is marked as f. 290v, etc.). Portions of set 1 were transformed at an unknown point between 2006 and 2010. As a result, the manuscript no longer corresponds fully to previous descriptions. Set 2 was added in 2014 for accuracy and consistency, in which all folios are numbered in the lower right corner in numerical order (i.e., f. 2 is marked as f. 2, and f. 152r is marked as f. 152, etc.). All references in the description refer to set 2.

Watermarks: One hundred fifty-two occurrences of five distinct watermarks: (A) Posts/Pillars with CC; occurs on flyleaves II and IV; Heawood 3514 (Paris, 1667). (B) Unicorn, vertical with mane; occurs in quires 1–6, 14–20, and parts of quires 10 (f. 152) and 13 (ff. 202, 205, 207, 209, 210, 212); Piccard 124423 (Wesel, 1460). (C) Anchor with single line flukes, beneath single line cross; occurs in quires 7–9, part of quire 10 (f. 158); cf. Piccard 118220 (Düsseldorf, 1463). (D) Gothic Letter P, two lines, divided vertical, above rod with flower or leaf in quatrefoil; occurs in quires 11–12, and parts of quires 10 (ff. 150, 151, 154, 156, 160, 162, 166) and 13 (ff. 213, 214); cf. Piccard 112407 (reference lacks dots) (Baden-Baden, 1469). (E) Pot (s. xvii^{2}); occurs on flyleaf VI; Heawood 3679 (no place, no date).

Layout:

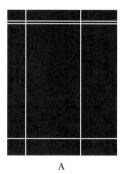

A

A ff. 1r–298v. Combined technique; 223 x 100 mm; 39 lines.

Pattern A is traced on ff. 1r–298v using hard-point technique and lead; single column; writing above top line; prickings visible in the right margins; double pricking for end of line; no visible prickings for verticals.

Script: A single hand (M1) writes all text (ff. 1r–298v) in Cursiva Formata (Bastarda). Additions, pen trials, and notarial marks (s. xv^{ex}) are written on f. 298v in the autograph (*ut uid.*) of an Anthoinette du Brouncq [see Owners & Provenance].

Decoration:

I. Rubrication: Rubrics and colophon in red ink; heightening of majuscules in yellow ink.

II. Initials: Flourished and plain initials occur outside of hierarchy.

a. Flourished initials (2–4 line square inset) in red and blue ink with contrasting penwork on f. 1r; red with brown penwork on f. 147r.

b. Plain initials (2 line square inset) in red ink are painted crudely throughout the manuscript; plain initials in blue ink occur on ff. 1v and 35r.

Contents:

1. Cuvelier, *Chanson de Bertrand du Guesclin*—ff. 1r–298v.

inc.: [f. 1r] seigneur or escoutez pour dieu le roy diuin que nostre sire dieux qui de leaue fist uin . . .; expl. [f. 298v] . . . dieux ait de luy pitie par son commandement et nous doinst joye et uie tout par amendement. amen.; **scribal colophon**: [f. 289v] explicit ce fut fait et par escript le lundy .xxviij^{e}. jour de may mil .iiij^{c}.lxiiij.

The manuscript is identified by the siglum *G* in Faucon 1990–1991.

Edition: Faucon 1990–1991, vol. 1, and 2:449–496.
Bibliography: Boulton 2006, 217–224, 232–233.

Binding: s. xvii; brown leather over pasteboards; blue and tan endbands; gilt tooled; gilt spine; edges dyed red; five raised bands; Phillipps paper shelfmark on spine.

Owners & Provenance: The name of an Anthoinette du Brouncq (s. xv^{ex}) is written twice on f. 298v with notarial marks; Alexandre Albert François Barthélémy de Bournonville (1662–1705); Richard Heber (1773–1833); Sir Thomas Phillipps (1792–1872); acquired from H. P. Kraus (New York, NY) by the university in September 1968; Comte Justin MacCarthy-Reagh (1744–1811) may have also owned the manuscript, but it does not appear in the 1815 catalogue by De Bure. Rear pastedown records the provenance: "Biblioth(èque) Bournon(ville), 5 Jan. 1707, no. 50."

Sales & Catalogues: Giffart, Bournonville sale, 1706, lot 239; Evans, 27 May 1825, lot 897 [unverified]; Evans, 10 February 1836, lot 820 (sold on 15 February 1836); Sotheby's, 29 November 1966, lot 70; H. P. Kraus, Cat. 117, no. 34.

Former Shelfmarks: Heber MS 824; Phillipps MS 8194; MS 51 (Notre Dame).

Bibliography: Phillipps no. 8194; Omont 1889, 8; Munby 1:1, 3:78, 163; Corbett no. 51; D'Alverny 1981, 107; Faucon 1990–1991, 2:445–496, 3:312, 327–328, 339–348; Boulton 2006, 217–224, 230, 232–233; Nolan 2006, 6–7.

MS Fr. d. 1

Origin: France, s. xv^2 (Normandy?).
Content Overview: Guillaume de Lorris and Jean de Meun, *Roman de la Rose.*

In French, on parchment; iii +140 ff. +i; generally 298 x 221 mm (page) [see Layout for ruling]; flyleaves post-medieval parchment; modern foliation with Arabic numerals in brown ink.

Collation: iii +1–8^8 +9^4 +10–12^8 +13^4 +14–18^8 +19^4 +i

Quires: Parchment quaternions, F/F, are the normal quire form. Quires 9, 13, and 19 are binions, F/F. The parchment has been treated and is extremely well scraped and rough in parts; hair sides and flesh sides often indistinguishable; collation statement by J. S. Kebabian for H. P. Kraus on rear pastedown.

Catchwords: Vertical catchwords are written in brown ink in the inner margins for quires 1–18; all correspond.

Signatures: Remnants of signatures are visible on the rectos for most quires; many have been trimmed.

Layout:

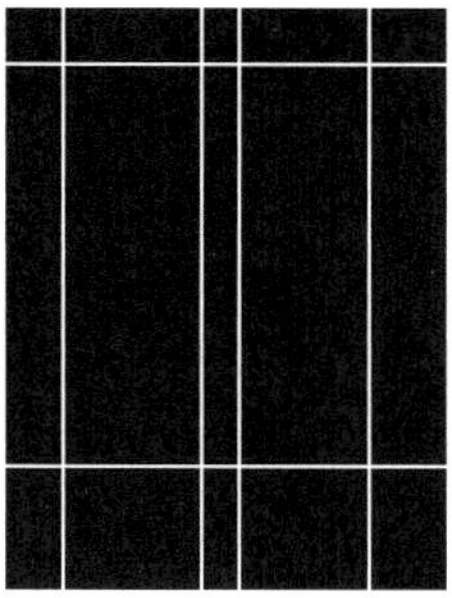

A

A ff. 1r–140r. Red ink; 206 x 153 mm; intercol. 19 mm; 39 lines.

Pattern **A** is traced in red ink on ff. 1r–140r; two columns (intercol. 19 mm); writing below top line; prickings visible for vertical bounding lines and intercolumnium in the upper and lower margins.

SCRIPT: A French hand (M1) writes all text in a Southern Textualis Libraria; M1 incorporates many Rotunda forms, but lacks precision and displays occasional Northern influences, particularly in the letter form for **a**; nearly exclusive use of upright **d** and ampersand. Marginal annotations are written in a similar script, but favor uncial **d**. Flyleaves contain stenciled (modern) and later descriptive text on the authors' identities (modern).

DECORATION:

I. RUBRICATION: Rubrics in red ink; letter heightening of majuscules in yellow ink; guide letters visible.

II. INITIALS: Historiated and decorated initials occur in hierarchy.

A. One historiated initial (9+ lines standing) is painted on f. 1r containing a presentation miniature.

B. Decorated initials (2 lines square inset) in gold on blue and red grounds in late French style alternate throughout the manuscript.

III. BORDERS & FRAMES: One border configuration occurs. An ownership mark (gules three escallops argent) is painted to the lower right of the border [see OWNERS & PROVENANCE].

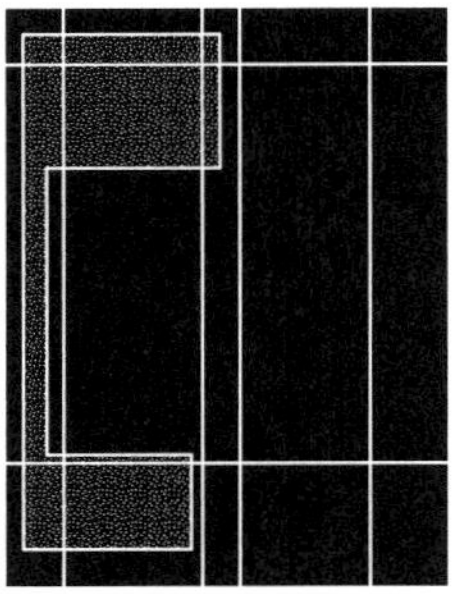

B

One functional bracket-left border (**B**) is painted on f. 1r with acanthus and vegetal motifs in blues, yellows, and green, red and orange strawberries, and black rinceaux. The area to be decorated is framed in red ink after the ruling pattern was executed. The historiated initial is situated within the border.

Contents:

1. Guillaume de Lorris and Jean de Meun, *Roman de la Rose*—
ff. 1r[a]–140r[a].

INC.: [f. 1r[a]] maintes gens dient que en songez na sinon fables et mensongez . . .; EXPL.: [f. 140r[a]] . . . ainxi eu la rose uermeille atant fut iour et ie mesueille.

Edition: Lecoy 1965–1970; Poirion 1974; Strubel 1992.
Bibliography: Boulton 2006.

Binding: s. xvii; brown leather over wooden boards; six raised bands; blind tooled; gilt spine.

Owners & Provenance: Charles-Paul Bourgevin de Vialart de Moligny (17??–1795); Ambroise Firmin-Didot (1790–1876); Charles Butler (1822–1910); Lt.-Col. William E. Moss (1875–1953); James Patrick Ronaldson Lyell (1871–1948). For the early provenance, see Boulton 2006, 226 and 234 n. 47, which indicates possible ownership by a descendant of a M. Robert de Fraidel from the identification of the arms painted on f. 1r. Acquired from H. P. Kraus (New York, NY) by the university in June 1968.

Sales & Catalogues: Hotel Drouot, 9 June 1881, lot 21; Sotheby's, 25 May 1906, lot 371; ibid., 18 March 1912, lot 2654; ibid., 2 March 1937, lot 944; Maggs Bros., Cat. 687, no. 190; Quaritch, Cat. 699, no. 95; ibid., Cat. 716, no. 315; ibid., Cat. 755, no. 14; ibid., Cat. 794, no. 14; H. P. Kraus, Cat. 100, no. 21; ibid., Cat. 115, no. 17.

Former Shelfmark: MS 34 (Notre Dame).

Bibliography: Corbett no. 34; D'Alverny 1981, 107; Boulton 2006, 217, 224–230, 234–236; Nolan 2006, 6–7.

MS Ger. a. 1

Origin: Germany, s. xv^{ex} (Niederrhein?).
Content Overview: Prayerbook.

In Middle Low German, on paper and parchment; iii +284 ff. +iii generally 135 x 96 mm (page) [see Layout for ruling]; foliated in modern pencil with Arabic numerals (ff. 200 and 211 *bis* = 200, 200a and 211, 211a); flyleaves paper and parchment.

Collation: iii $+1^{8+1}$ $+2^{10}$ $+3^{8}$ $+4^{10-2+1}$ $+5^{8}$ $+6^{10}$ $+7–12^{8}$ $+13^{10-1}$ $+14^{10}$ $+15–16^{8}$ $+17^{6+1}$ $+18–24^{8}$ $+25^{10}$ $+26–28^{8}$ $+29^{4}$ $+30^{10}$ $+31–34^{8}$ $+35^{4}$ +iii

Bibliographical Format: 8° (paper sections).

Quires: Mixed quires of parchment and paper; paper quaternions folded in octavo are the normal quire forms; quinions are used when parchment bifolia are added. Quire 1 is a quaternion with a leaf added (f. 5). Quire 4 is a quinion with the sixth and tenth leaves canceled and one leaf added (f. 36). Quire 17 is a ternion (ff. 139–140 inserted asymmetrically) with one leaf added (f. 138). Quires 29 and 35 are binions. Parchment bifolia are used only when border illustrations and gold painted initials occur [see Decoration]. The manuscript has been trimmed.

Quire Marks: Letters as quire marks are written in the lower left margin of the rectos for each quire; many trimmed.

Watermarks: Thirty-three occurrences of a single watermark: (**A**) Pot; visible in all quires except 25 and 29; cf. Piccard 31528 (Arnhem, 1532).

Layout:

A1

A2

A3

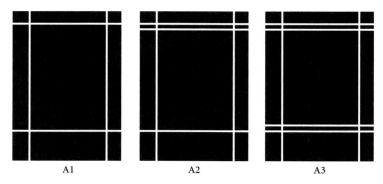

A ff. 1r–282v. Combined technique; 97 x 68 mm; 21 lines.

Pattern **A** is traced in brown ink (predominantly) and dark crayon throughout the manuscript in variant configurations (e.g., **A1**, **A2**, **A3**) in various stages of completion; single column; writing below top line; prickings visible in all margins for vertical bounding lines and horizontal through lines (double prick for second to last horizontal), and lines for text.

Script: A single hand (M1) writes all text in Hybrida Libraria of the end of the fifteenth century; occasional bifurcation of ascenders; nearly exclusive use of loopless forms. A later hand (s. xvi) writes additions on flyleaves IVr–Vv.

Decoration:

I. Rubrication: Rubrics in red ink; paraph marks alternate in red and blue ink; letter heightening of majuscules in red ink.

II. Initials: Foliate, dentelle style, flourished, and plain initials occur in hierarchy.

a. Foliate initials (5–7 line square inset) in blue ink with white penwork begin major sections of the text on ff. 1r, 45r, 67r, 112r, 172v, 200Ar, and 237r; vegetal motifs abound; initials are Northern in style.

b. Dentelle style initials (3–4 line square inset) are painted on ff. 58v and 181v; Northern in style.

c. Flourished initials (3–6 line square inset) in blue ink with red penwork occur throughout the manuscript; most have green ornamentation; larger sizes with borders on ff. 15r and 33v.

d. Plain initials (2 line square inset and 1 line versals) alternate in red and blue throughout the manuscript.

III. Borders & Frames:

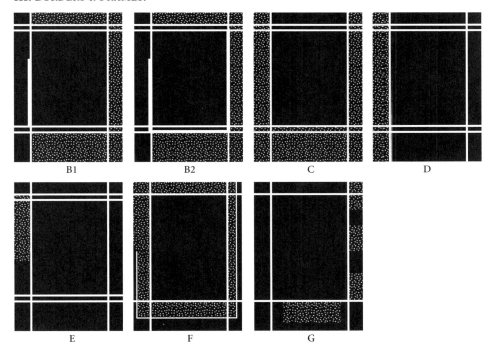

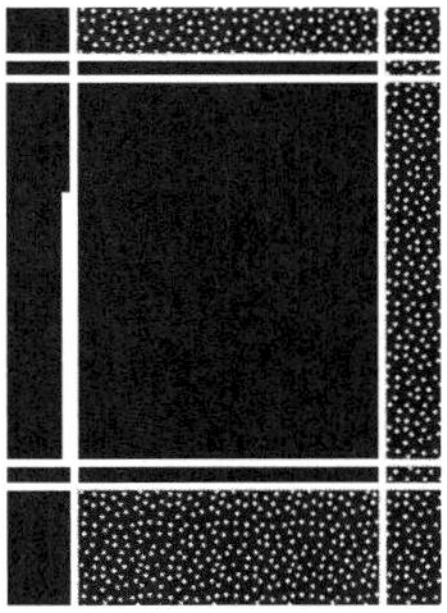
B1

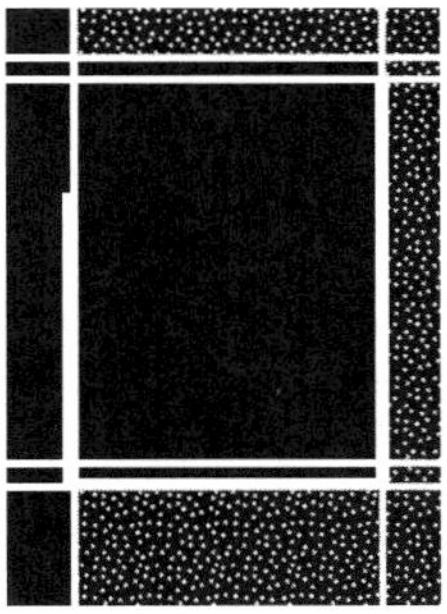
B2

C

D

E

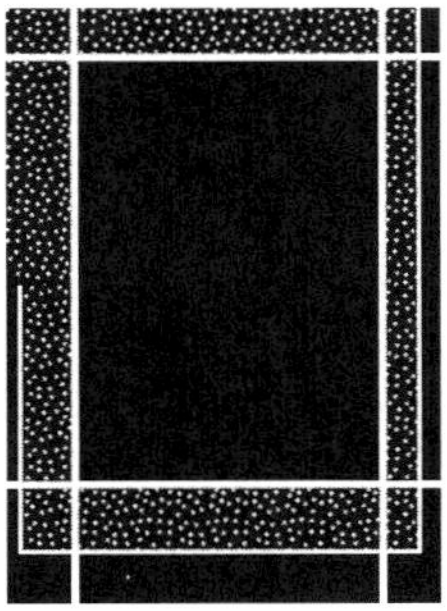
F

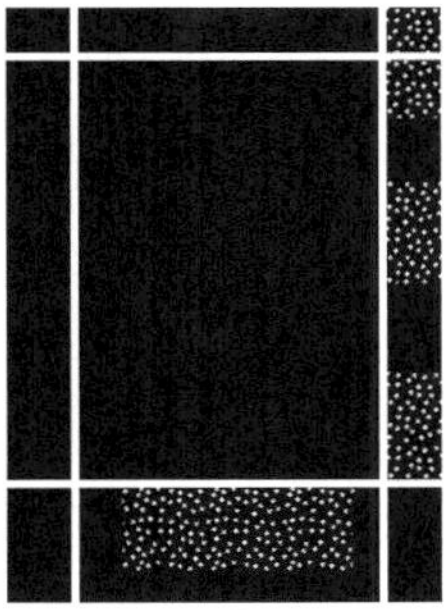
G

Three-margins-outer borders (**B**) are painted on ff. 1r and 45r; gold frames left (**B1**) and three-margins (**B2**) with black and gold rinceaux with blue, pink, and green; deep rose florals and orange added to **B1**. Three-margins border painted on f. 15r (**C**); no frames; black and gold rinceaux with blue, pink, and green; deep rose florals. Left border painted on ff. 33v and 172v (**D**); rinceaux and florals as **C**; no frames. Piece border sprays from initial on f. 58v (**E**); rinceaux as **C**; no florals; no frames. Four-margins border painted on f. 112r (**F**); black and gold rinceaux with blue and pink; florals in blue and deep rose; outer frame in rose ink. Other configurations comprised of four piece-borders on ff. 67r, 200Ar, and 237r of large florals in blue, rose, green, blue, gold, and black; no frames.

CONTENTS:

1. Gospel Harmony—ff. 1r–15r.

RUB.: her beghint dat auentmael ons lieuen heren ihesu christi alst sincte iohannes bescrijft; INC.: [f. 1r] dje feestdach der ioden nakede die pacschen giet was . . .; EXPL.: [f. 15r] . . . here sie twee sweerden sin hier ende hi segede hem het is genoech.

EDITION: cf. VAN DEN BERG ET AL. 2005, 67–81.
BIBLIOGRAPHY: See DESCHAMPS 1975, esp. 169–177.

2. Gospel Harmony—ff. 15r–33v.

RUB.: hier beghint die passie ons lieuen heren ihesus christi als sie die .iiij. ewangelisten bescrijft mandach; INC.: [f. 15r] alse ihesu dit ghespraken hadde ende die lauesanc ghesecht was ghinc hi wt ende genck nae ghewonten inden berch van oliueten . . .; EXPL.: [f. 33v] . . . ende bereyden gerruden ende salue m. op dat se quemen ende ihesum salueden.

EDITION: cf. VAN DEN BERG ET AL. 2005, 81–101.
BIBLIOGRAPHY: See DESCHAMPS 1975, esp. 169–177.

3. Gospel Harmony with prayer—ff. 33v–44v.

RUB.: hier beghint die verzisenisse ons lieuen heren ihesum christum als se die vier ewangelisten bescrijuen; INC.: [f. 33v] ende vroe op enen dach vander weken i doe noch diuister iussen waren . . .; EXPL.: [f. 44v] . . . ick meen dat die werlt niet begriepen en solde die boecken die te scriuen sijn. deo gracias. RUB.: ghebet; INC.: ghelouet ende ghecert ende ghebendijt . . . nict van di verscheiden en moet werden amen.

4. Jordan of Quedlinburg, *Sixty-five Articles of the Passion of Christ*—ff. 45r–58r.

RUB.: hier beghinnen .lxv. ghebede vander passien ons lieuen heren ihesu christi die mister jordanus gemaket heeft. die metten sondach dat ierste gebet; INC.: [f. 45r] o here ihesu christe des leuendighen godes sone die te metten tijt voer mi arme sundighemensche ende voer . . .; EXPL.: [f. 58r] . . . begrauen moet werden ende totter glorien der verzisenisse moet comen amen.

BIBLIOGRAPHY: WILLMEUMIER-SCHALIJ 1979.

5. Prayers attributed to Bernard of Clairvaux—ff. 58v–66v.

RUB.: [f. 58r–v] hier beghinnen simcte [*sic*] bernardus ghebeden uan betlaghinge der passien ons lieuen heren ihesu christi doer die weke ghedeiit gebet; INC.: [f. 58v] ghegruet sijstu mijn salicheit o du lieue here ihesu christe . . .; EXPL.: [f. 66v] . . . o versadinge alre reynce begereten comende blijf bi im inewicheit.

6. Henry Suso, *Hundred Articles of the Passion of Christ*—ff. 67r–86v.

RUB.: [f. 66v] hier beghinnen die .c. articulen der passien christi daer hen een yegelit deuoet iongher christi dagelix in oeffenen mach. des sondaghes die ierste artikel en op elch artikel; INC.: [f. 67r] eya ewighe wijsheit godes gheuadighe here ihesu christe . . .; EXPL.: [f. 86v] . . . ende hores goddienstigen mede doegens amen.

EDITION: cf. texts in VAN AELST 2005.

7. Prayers—ff. 87r–111v.

RUB.: hier beghint een ynnich gebet te offeren dat liden ons lieuen heren ihesu christi vette hemelsch vader onder nussen; INC.: [f. 87r] o hillighe vader ende guedertierene . . .; EXPL.: [f. 111v] . . . kint voer mi dat hi my alle mine sunden wil vergeuen amen.

8. Bernard of Clairvaux (attr.), Marian Psalter—ff. 112r–172v.

RUB.: desen psalter van onser lieuer vrouwen heeft sunte beren gemact; INC.: [f. 112r] o here doe op mine mont te lauen dijnen alre fueten ende onsprekelicsten name . . .; EXPL.: [f. 172v] . . . hillige eugelen mijn fielen moghen leyden totter vrouden des hemels amen.

9. Seven Psalms and Marian Litany—ff. 172v–181r.

RUB.: hier beghint onser lieuer vrouwen .vij. psalmen; INC.: [f. 172v] o vrouwe maria in der verbolghenheit godes . . .; EXPL.: [f. 181r] . . . alle gelouige fielen moeten rusten in vreden amen.

10. Prayers—ff. 181v–200v.

RUB.: [f. 181r–v] soe wie dijt gebet .xxx. dage lanc leest voer onser lieuer vrowenbeelde op sincknyen die verdient .v. dage aflates dici soe vaket leest ende men mach darene bede mede vertrighen gebet; INC.: [f. 181v] o edele coninginne der hemelen ende reyne maget maria moder alre barmherticheit ende myldicheit . . .; EXPL.: [f. 200v] . . . ende ghewerdiget mi te leiden in dat hemesche paradijs amen.

11. Marian Psalter and three rosaries—ff. 200Ar–236v.

RUB.: hier beghint een deuoet psalterken van drie roscukreuskens van onser lieuer vrouwen dat begauet is mit .lx. dusent iaer aflates pater noster aue maria gracia . . .; INC.: [f. 200Ar] weest gegruet maria reyne maget coninginne des hemels die vanden propheten voer gefiguert . . .; EXPL.: [f. 236v] . . . ende dat ic nummermeer van hem noch van di verscheiden en moet werden amen.

12. Marian Psalter and three rosaries—ff. 237r–286v.

RUB.: hier beghint onser lieuer vrouwen psalter van drie kreuskens die sie deuoeteliken leest die verdient daer mede .lx. m iaer aflats pater noster; INC.: [f. 237r] god gruete u weerde reyne maghet maria coninghinne des hemels die vanden propheeten voer ghefyguereert . . .; EXPL.: [f. 286v] . . . verghiffenisse al onser funden ouermides onsen heren ihesum christum amen.

13. Later additions—flyleaves IVr–Vv.

INC.: [flyleaf IVr] eijn schone gebet vnde vermaninge to cristum ijhesum van al sin hilligen . . .; EXPL.: [flyleaf Vv] . . . vaders in soete barmherticheit de do ges*.

BINDING: s. xix?; brown leather over pasteboards; blue and white marbled edges; gilt spine.

OWNERS & PROVENANCE: Acquired from a private collector by the university in 2008.

SALES & CATALOGUES: Reiss & Sohn, 28–31 October 2008, lot 865.

MS Ital. b. 1

Origin: Italy, s. xvi^{1}.
Content Overview: Italian poetry (Serafino Aquilano, Iacopo Sannazaro, Iacopo Corsi, Giovan Francesco Caracciolo).

In Italian, on parchment; ii +19 ff. +ii; generally 187 x 125 mm (page) [see Layout for ruling]; flyleaves modern paper; modern foliation in black ink with Arabic numerals.

Collation: ii +1$^{10-1}$ +2^{10} +ii

Quires: Parchment quinions, F/F, are the normal quire forms. Quire 1 is missing the first leaf (H/F). Both quires obey Gregory's Rule; the manuscript has been trimmed; fire damage to f. 1; no quire marks, catchwords, or signatures visible. A. Rossi 2005, 458 incorrectly identifies the manuscript as paper ("Cart.").

Layout:

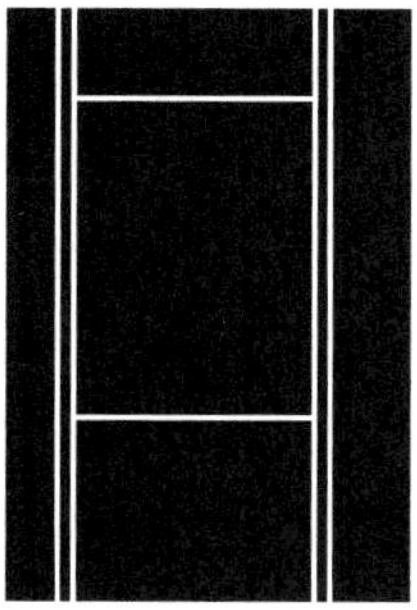

A

A ff. 1r–19v. Combined techinque; 100 x 85 mm; 15 lines.

Pattern A is traced on ff. 1r–19v using a combined technique of lead for the vertical bounding lines and red-brown ink for all horizontals; single columns; writing below top line; prickings for verticals visible in upper and lower margins of some folios; most vertical bounding lines very faded.

Script: A single hand (M1) writes all texts in Humanistic cursive of the sixteenth century; Humanistic monumental capitals used as display script.

Decoration:
I. Rubrication: Rubrics and initial letters of each line in red ink.
II. Initials: Red initials in monumental capitals (1 line in height).

Contents:

1. Serafino Aquilano, *Sonetti*—ff. 1r–7v.

Contains sonnets: 41 (f. 1r; A. Rossi 2005, 144–145); 32 (ff. 1v and 4v; A. Rossi 2005, 130); 34 (f. 2r; A. Rossi 2005, 133); 64 (f. 2v; A. Rossi 2005,181); 57 (f. 3r; A. Rossi 2005, 169–170); 58 (f. 3v; A. Rossi 2005, 171); 46 (f. 4r; A. Rossi 2005, 153); 75 (f. 5r; A. Rossi 2005, 199–200); 53 (f. 5v; A. Rossi 2005, 163–164); 69 (f. 6r; A. Rossi 2005, 181); 48 (f. 6v; A. Rossi 2005, 156); 67 (f. 7r; A. Rossi 2005, 186–187); 68 (f. 7v; A. Rossi 2005, 188). All sonnets prefaced with the rubric *seraphini*.

Edition: A. Rossi 2005.

2. Iacopo Sannazaro, *Sonetto* 100—ff. 8r–13r.

rub.: iacobi sanazarii ad laudem obitus marchionis piscariae; inc.: [f. 8r] <s>corto dal mio pensier fra i saxi e londe mera sospinto in la uezosa falda che pesilipo in mar bagna et ascende . . .; expl.: [f. 13r] . . . cosi dicendo al raggio di la luna chen gliocchi mi feriua riuolse el uiso por saluto le stelle ad una ad una et lieto se nando nel paradiso.

Edition: Mauro 1961, 212–216.

3. Iacopo Corsi—ff. 13v–14r.

3.1. rub.: iacobi corsi; inc.: [f. 13v] <o> suegliati pensier e spirti accesi o nocte eterne o feruido disio o ueloce memoria o tardo oblio o uoce o suspir mei mai non intesi . . .; expl.: [f. 13v] . . . o lachryme infinite a lungo affanno et tu uoglia noiosa et pertinace deh date ad altrui parte del mio danno.

3.2. rub.: iacobi corsi; inc.: [f. 14r] <d>al di chio nacqui prese ad balestrarme fortuna ne me ual fuga e diffesa ne renderme prigion cognhor piu accesa se monstra et obstinata ad lacerarme . . .; expl.: [f. 14r] . . . assai meglio e tacer choggi di raro un iusto lamentar gratia ritroua per proua el so che a mie mal spese imparo.

Edition: Cervigni 1979, 29.

4. Giovan Francesco Caracciolo, *Argo,* 11 (xxxv)—f. 14v.

RUB.: iacobi sanazarii; INC.: [f. 14v] <m>illi pungenti chiodi et milli dumi e 'l nocturo [*sic*] riposo del mio lecto . . .; EXPL.: [f. 14v] . . . tal che nha loco l'alma coue scampi.

Here attributed to Iacopo Sannazaro.

EDITION: GIOVANAZZI 2009, 477.
BIBLIOGRAPHY: SANTAGATA 1980.

5. Serafino Aquilano, *Capitolo* 5—ff. 15r–18r.

RUB.: seraphini ad somnum; INC.: [f. 15r] <p>lacido somno hor che dal cielo in terra descendi a tranquillar l'humane menti . . .; EXPL.: [f. 18r] . . . et al partir da me con lei presente ti prego i passi tuoi non sian si presti.

EDITION: A. ROSSI 2005, 372–375; see p. 569 for the variant lines 82–103.

6. Serafino Aquilano, *Sonetti*—ff. 18v–19v.

Sonnets 39 (f. 18v; A. ROSSI 2005, 141–142); 16 (f. 19r; A. ROSSI 2005, 103); 56 (f. 19v; A. ROSSI 2005, 168).

EDITION: A. ROSSI 2005.

BINDING: s. xix; stiff vellum; gilt spine; stamp of Bookbinders' Co-operative Society, Ltd., London on rear pastedown.

OWNERS & PROVENANCE: Giuseppe Martini (1870–1944) (signature on flyleaf IIv); H. P. Kraus (1948, 1956); various dealer marks in pencil on front pastedown. Date and source of acquisition by the university are unknown.

SALES & CATALOGUES: H. P. Kraus, Cat. 44, no. 176; ibid., List 189, no. 158.

FORMER SHELFMARK: MS 17 (Notre Dame).

BIBLIOGRAPHY: CORBETT no. 17; CERVIGNI 1979; SANTAGATA 1980; ITER 5:362; A. ROSSI 2005, 458; GIOVANAZZI 2009, 164.

MS Ital. b. 2

Origin: Italy, s. xv^{2}.
Content Overview: Catherine of Siena, *Letters*; Ugo Panziera, *Trattati spirituali* (selections); Feo Belcari, *Laude* (selections).

In Italian, on paper; i +108 ff. +i; generally 205 x 140 mm (page) [see Layout for ruling]; ff. 104r–108v blank but ruled; foliated in modern pencil with Arabic numerals (duplicate: ff. 70, 70a; numbering skips 102: 101, 103).

Collation: i $+1\text{–}3^{10} +4^{2} +5\text{–}9^{10} +10^{14} +11^{12}$ +i

Bibliographical Format: 4°.

Quires: Paper quinions folded in quarto are the normal quire forms; several quires contain constructed bifolia comprised of two different papers (e.g., ff. 31/32, 33/42). Quire 10 is a gathering of seven bifolia. No signatures or catchwords remain.

Watermarks: Thirty occurrences of six different watermarks: (**A**) Ladder; occurs in quires 1 (ff. 2/9, 5/6), 3, and 4 (partial); cf. Piccard 122760 (Milan, 1477). (**B**) Ladder; occurs in quires 1 (ff. 4/7), 2, and 5 (f. 33, partial; f. 34, partial); cf. Piccard 122751 (Venice, 1463). (**C**) Hat; occurs in quires 5 (f. 40, partial; f. 42, partial), 6–10; cf. Piccard 31981 (Como, 1483). (**D**) Eagle; occurs in quire 11; cf. Piccard 42605 (Ravenna 1500). (**E**) Triple Mount or top of Bell; occurs on flyleaf II (partial); distance between chainlines 60 mm. (**F**) circle; occurs on rear pastedown (partial).

Layout:

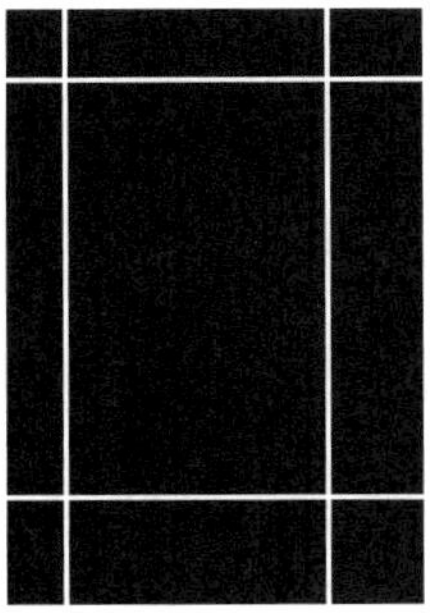
A

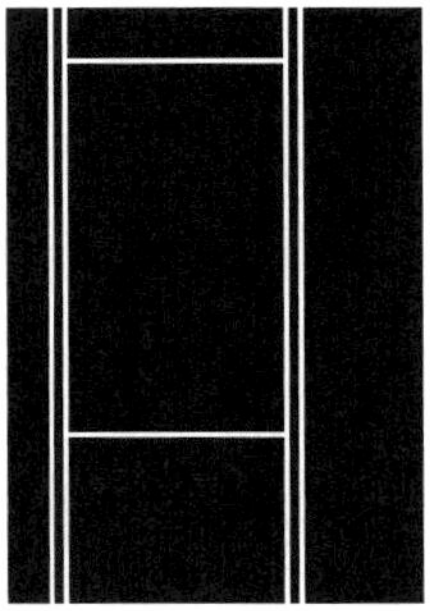
B

A ff. 1r–35v. Lead; 144 x 88 mm; 23–25 lines.
B ff. 36r–108v. Board-ruled; 129 x 74 mm; 25 lines.

Pattern **A** is traced in lead on ff. 1r–35r; single column; writing above top line; prickings visible for vertical bounding lines and horizontal through lines in the upper and lower margins. Pattern **B** is executed on ff. 36r–108v in hard-point technique using a ruling board; single column; writing above top line.

Script: A single hand (M1) writes all texts in Mercantesca (Semihybrida), but often employs Cursiva forms.

Decoration:
I. Rubrication: Rubrics in black ink.
II. Initials: Calligraphic hanging initials in black ink throughout the manuscript.

Contents:

1. Catherine of Siena, *Letters*—ff. 1r–35v.

Letters 188, 134, 148, 332, 156, 72, 361, 221, 20, 48, 155, 224, 247, 40, 9, 276, 202.

Edition: Volpato 2002; Di Ciaccia 1996–1999 (modern Italian).

2. Ugo Panziera, *Trattato spirituale IV*—ff. 36r–41r.

rub.: questa si e una spirituale epistola in uolghare la quale fu manda<ta> ad uenerabile religiose e sante donne in loro exercitatmento; **inc.**: [f. 36r] alle uenerabili spirituali religiose sante donne le quali anno tutta la loro presente uita . . .; **expl.**: [f. 41r] . . . di se gloriosamente dilettandoui per infinita a secula seculorum amenne. sempere sia laldato [*sic*] yhesu christo ella uergine maria.

Edition: Florence 1492.
Bibliography: Pacetti 1967.

3. Ugo Panziera, *Trattato spirituale XIII*—ff. 41r–43v.

inc.: [f. 41r] una epistola della amicitia al suo uenerabile in christo padre fratre [.n. *uix potest legi*] uno laico innutile creatura . . .; **expl.**: [f. 43v] . . . cruciato istato di cosi utile et delettabile e uirtuosa compagnia proueduti amenne yhesu amore.

Edition: Florence 1492.
Bibliography: Pacetti 1967.

4. Ugo Panziera, *Trattato spirituale XIV*—ff. 43v–49v.

rub.: [f. 43v] questa si e una diuota epistola la quale fue mandata alli ispirituali fratelli della compagnia del ceppo di prato; **inc.**: [f. 44r] a suoi in christo dilettissimi ispirituali fratelli equali nelle parti di ponente nella pro uinca di toscana et in prato dimorano . . .; **expl.**: [f. 49v] . . . nelle sue bracca amorose bracca istretti trionfalmente gloriosi ritenendo perr [*sic*] infinita secula seculorum amen; **authorial colophon**: data nelle parti di leuante doue sicongunge elmare maggiore doriente colmare che uiene dal ponente anni domini .m°.ccc°. xij°. titolo della soprascritta epistola saluato o lalberto o iacopo o mone procuratori de frati minori di prato sia data.

EDITION: FLORENCE 1492.
BIBLIOGRAPHY: PACETTI 1967.

5. Feo Belcari, *Venga ciascun devoto ed umil core*—f. 53r–v.

INC.: [f. 53r] uengha ciascuno deuoto et umil core a laldar [*sic*] chon feruore la nuoua santa di dio chaterina . . .; EXPL.: [f. 53v] . . . or chorri a pie di questa alta regina finita la lalda [*sic*] di santa chaterina da siena. yhesu amore amenne yhesu dolccie amore.

EDITION: GALLETTI 1863, 28–29; CREMONINI 2006.

6. Feo Belcari, *I' son l'Arcangel Rafael di dio*—ff. 54r–55r.

INC.: [f. 54r] i son larcangel raffel di dio dottore in medicina chetti uodare dottrina contral mondo la carne el demonio rio . . .; EXPL.: [f. 55r] . . . colla superna gratia allora iddio ringratia perche tua forze non uaglono un fio. yhesu amore yhesu amore maria dolccie.

EDITION: GALLETTI 1863, 30–31; CREMONINI 2006.

7. Catherine of Siena, *Letters*—ff. 55r–103v.

Letters 321, 184, 260, 26, 335, 240, 23, 25, 74, 151, Gardner II (addressed to *Samuelle da Rimine dottore di leggie* in rubric), Gardner III (also addressed to *Samuelle da Rimine dottore di leggie*), 294, 317, 10, 297.

EDITION: VOLPATO 2002; DI CIACCIA 1996–1999 (modern Italian).

BINDING: s. xvi?; limp vellum.

OWNERS & PROVENANCE: Giuseppe Martini (1870–1944) [Ioseph Martini. Luc.]; H. P. Kraus (1948, 1956); date and source of acquisition by the university are unknown (between 1966 and 1967).

SALES & CATALOGUES: Hoepli, 21 May 1935, lot 55; H. P. Kraus, Cat. 44, no. 54; ibid., List 189, no. 39.

FORMER SHELFMARK: MS 18 (Notre Dame).

BIBLIOGRAPHY: CORBETT no. 18; D'ALVERNY 1981, 107; EMERY, JR. and L. JORDAN 1998, 501; NOFFKE 2000-2008, 1:332–333.

MS Ital. d. 1

Origin: Italy, s. xv^{2}.
Content Overview: Henry Suso, *Horologium sapientiae* (Italian translation).

In Italian and Latin, on paper; i +180 ff.; generally 285 x 182 mm [see Layout for ruling]; foliated in modern pencil with Arabic numerals; paper flyleaf.

Collation: i+ 1–18^{10}

Bibliographical Format: 2°.

Quires: Paper quinions folded in folio form the manuscript; paper is dirty and stained; faint woodcuts stamped in black ink throughout containing the Virgin and Child (e.g., f. 137r).

Catchwords: Vertical catchwords are present for quires 1–17 in the lower right margin; often stylized; all catchwords correspond.

Watermarks: Ninety occurrences of three different watermarks: (**A**) Hat with divided brim; occurs through quires 1–18; cf. Piccard 31981 (Como, 1483). (**B**) Crown without arch, chainline as midline, two line midpoint; occurs in quires 16 (f. 158) and 18 (f. 173); distance between chainlines 53 mm, approx. 31 x 39 mm; cf. Piccard 51114 (Piacenza, 1480; slightly corresponds; **B** has an additional curved line in lower portion). (**C**) Horn; occurs in quire 17 (f. 166); cf. Piccard 119351 (Urbino, 1496).

Layout:

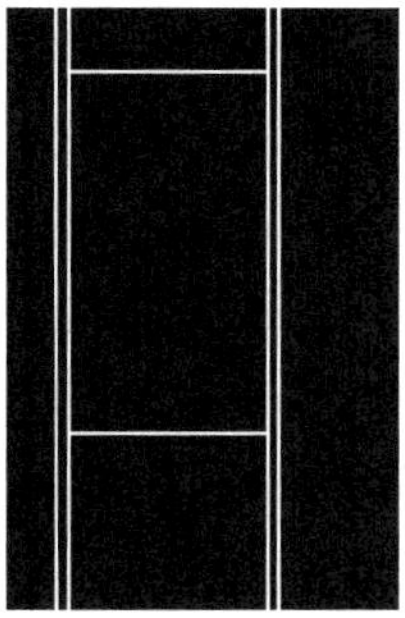

A

A ff. 2r–180v. Board-ruled; 171 x 92 mm; 27 lines.

Pattern A is ruled on ff. 2r–180v using a ruling board; single column; writing above top line.

SCRIPT: A single hand (M1) writes all text and rubrics in Humanistic cursive of the fifteenth century (s. xv^2).

DECORATION:
I. RUBRICATION: Rubrics and paraph marks in red ink.
II. INITIALS: A plain initial occurs in the manuscript.
A. One plain initial (3 lines square inset) in blue ink is painted on f. 1r; guide letters remain throughout the manuscript for initials never executed (1–2 line square inset).

CONTENTS:

1. Henry Suso, *Horologium sapientiae* [Italian trans.]—ff. 1r–169v.

1.1. Prologue—ff. 1r–5r. RUB.: incominciasi il prologo del libro il quale si chiama oriuolo della sapientia; INC.: sentite del signore in bonitade e con simplicita di chuore cerchate per lui . . .; EXPL.: . . . ad alchuna persona chomando che queste fussino chomunicate e participate con tutti coloro che amano iddio.

1.2. Chapters, Book 1—f. 5r–v. INC.: <l>a materia di questo primo libro e la pretiosissima paxione di christo . . .; EXPL.: . . . <l>od da singulare della uergine maria et del dolore chellebbe nella paxione di christo.

1.3. Book 1—ff. 6r–108r. RUB.: come alquanti electi preuenuti dalla diuina gratia sono tracti addio e come alchuno fu tracto; INC.: <l>a sapientia io amai et per lei cerchai infino da giouaneza e cerchai . . .; EXPL.: . . . menati chon allegrezza a quella celestiale gierusalem.

1.4. Chapters, Book 2—f. 108r. INC.: <d>ella diuersita marauigliosa delle doctrine e de discepoli . . .; EXPL.: . . . <f>ructo uario della diuina sapientia meritano.

1.5. Book 2—ff. 108v–169v. RUB.: [f. 108r] della diuersita della doctrine capitolo primo; INC.: <a>lchuno disideroso discepolo della sapientia cerchaua la sapientia di tutti gli antichi . . .; EXPL.: . . . di gloria et signore delle uirtudi nella tua bellezza gieso [*sic*] christo signor nostro il quale con padre e collo spirto sancto uiue et regna in secula seculorum. amen.

EDITION: VENICE 1511; KÜNZLE 1977 (Latin text); see BARTOLA 2010, 23 n. 12.
BIBLIOGRAPHY: KÜNZLE 1977, 263–267; KAEPPELI no. 1852; BARTOLA 2010 (not included in the list of manuscripts).

2. Henry Suso, Office of Eternal Wisdom—ff. 169v–174r.

RUB.: lufìcio della sapientia; INC.: [f. 169v] <c>hiumque [*sic*] desidera di farsi amicho e dimesticho della diuina sapientia dee queste ore continouamente leggere e dire . . .; EXPL.: [f. 174r] . . . eterna sapientia benedicat et custodiat corda et corpora nostra amen.

EDITION: KÜNZLE 1977, 606–618 (Latin text).

3. Henry Suso, Meditations on the passion of Christ—ff. 174v–179v.

RUB.: [f. 174r] queste sono cento meditationi con cento petitioni della paxione di christo le quali si uogliono dire ogni di con cento genue et tosto sentira il dolore di christo crucifisso; INC.: [f. 174v] <d>omine yhesu christe qui permisisti a maria madalena sanctos pedes tuos lacrimis deuotionis lauari et unguento ungi unge et compunge cor meum tua sanctissima paxione . . .; EXPL.: [f. 179v] . . . <d>omine yhesu christe qui tertia die a mortuis resucitasti resucita et uiuifica animam meam ut in ueritate te ualeam inuenire in nomine patris et filii et spiritus sancti. amen.

Excerpted from the *Little Book of Eternal Wisdom*; see EMERY, JR. and L. JORDAN 1998, 501.

EDITION: VENICE 1511.

BINDING: s. xv; brown leather over wooden boards; blind stamped; metal bosses; sewing on three split thongs; two metal catches on lower board; remnants of leather thongs on upper board.

OWNERS & PROVENANCE: George John Warren Vernon (1803–1866); sold in Sotheby's Vernon sale of 1918; Giuseppe Martini (1870–1944); H. P. Kraus (1948, 1956). This provenance is misattributed to another Italian translation of the *Horologium* (New Haven, Yale Univ., Beinecke Library, Marston MS 130) by SHAILOR 1992, 252. Acquired from H. P. Kraus (New York, NY) by the university in October 1968.

SALES & CATALOGUES: Sotheby's, 10–12 June 1918, lot 376; H. P. Kraus, Cat. 44, no. 185; ibid., Cat. 80, no. 24A; ibid., List 189, no. 173.

FORMER SHELFMARK: MS 50 (Notre Dame).

BIBLIOGRAPHY: CORBETT no. 50; EMERY, JR. and L. JORDAN 1998, 501.

Frag. I. 1

Origin: Low Countries, s. xv^2.
Content Overview: Prayerbook (leaf).

In Dutch, on parchment; 161 x 105 mm (page) [see Layout for ruling].

Layout:

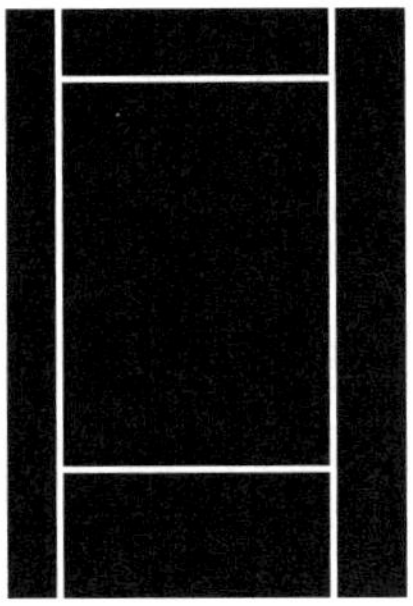

A

A Ink; 107 x 72 mm; 27 lines.

Pattern **A** is traced in brown ink; single column; writing below top line; prickings visible in the upper and lower margins for vertical bounding lines.

Script: A single hand (M1) writes all text in Northern Textualis Formata.

Decoration:
I. Rubrication: Rubrics in red ink; letter heightening of majuscules in red ink.
II. Initials: Flourished and plain initials occur in hierarchy.
a. Flourished initials (3–5 line square inset) in blue ink with purple penwork on green grounds with white vegetal motifs.
b. Plain initials (2 line square inset) in red ink begin the collects; plain initials (1 line versals) alternate in red and blue ink on the recto and verso.

CONTENTS:

1. Prayerbook [leaf].

INC.: [recto] doppende voer die hemelsche poerte ende in ghelaten vander conincliker hant ende di en wort . . .; EXPL.: [verso] . . . heuet hedaer in tesamen ghewreuen twe molen steuen der yoder scher ewen ende des euangelijs hie heuer te samen ghe-.

The fragment of a prayerbook (psalter, book of hours, or breviary) contains portions of suffrages from January: Agnes (Jan. 21), Vincent (Jan. 22), and the Conversion of Paul (*Pauwels bekeringe*; Jan. 25).

OWNERS & PROVENANCE: Date and source of acquisition by the university are unknown.

Frag. I. 2

Origin: Low Countries, s. xv^2 (Delft).
Content Overview: Book of Hours, Geert Groote, trans. (leaf).

In Dutch, on parchment; 177 x 122 mm (page) [see Layout for ruling].

Foliation: Foliated in modern pencil in the upper right corner (f. 90).

Layout:

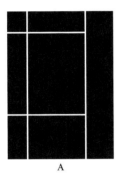

A

A Ink; 99 x 67 mm; 22 lines.

Pattern **A** is traced in brown ink; single column; writing below top line; no prickings are visible.

Script: A single hand (M1) writes all text in Northern Textualis Formata.

Decoration:
I. Rubrication: Rubrics in red ink; letter heightening of cadels and majuscules in red ink.
II. Initials: Flourished and plain initials occur in hierarchy.
a. Flourished initials (2 lines square inset) alternating in blue and red ink with contrasting penwork occur on the recto.
b. Plain initials (1 line versals) alternate in red and blue ink on the recto.
III. Borders & Frames: Flourished and feathered borders are drawn in blue and red ink in the style of Delft on the recto.

Contents:

1. Book of Hours, Geert Groote, trans. [leaf].

inc.: [f. 90r]: ofnemes die sonden der werelt ghif ons vrede criste hoor ons heer ontferm di onser criste ontferm . . . [van Wijk 1940, 153]; **expl.**: [f. 90v] . . . aen ende inropen dijns heilighen drie- [van Wijk, 1940, 154].

Fragment is from the Litany and contains the collects.

Edition: van Wijk 1940.

Owners & Provenance: Donated to the university by Ralph W. Dixon (1925–2013; class of 1950) in 1992; acquired by Dixon from Bruce P. Ferrini (Akron, OH) on 15 February 1992.

Leaves from the parent manuscript were included in Ferrini's portfolio of 15 leaves, which were mounted and issued in a box, known collectively as the "Liturgical Text Collection." The portfolios were sold ca. 1989, and two are known at Loyola Marymount University and the University of Delaware. Known leaves from the parent manuscript are:

Los Angeles, Loyola Marymount Univ., William H. Hannon Library, Coll. 25, 14
Newark, Univ. Delaware, Hugh M. Morris Library, Liturgical Text Collection, 14
Notre Dame, Univ. Notre Dame, Hesburgh Library, Frag. I. 2

Four other leaves from the Delft group also from manuscripts broken and sold by Ferrini are at Emory University, Pitts Theological Library. The present leaf shares the same ruling pattern and number of lines as Rudy 2012's 'Leaf A' and 'Leaf B', but decoration differs and no dimensions for comparison have been recorded; likely from a different parent manuscript. The shelfmarks of the Emory leaves are:

Atlanta, Emory Univ., Pitts Theological Library, RG 020-2, Box 1, Folder 2 (Rudy 2012, 'Leaf A')
Atlanta, Emory Univ., Pitts Theological Library, RG 020-2, Box 1, Folder 3 (Rudy 2012, 'Leaf B')
Atlanta, Emory Univ., Pitts Theological Library, RG 020-2, Box 1, Folder 5 (Rudy 2012, 'Leaf D')
Atlanta, Emory Univ., Pitts Theological Library, RG 020-2, Box 2, Folder 2 (Rudy 2012, 'Leaf C')

Sales & Catalogues: Ferrini #05-24.

Former Shelfmark: MSE/MR 9 (Notre Dame).

Frag. I. 4

Origin: Spain, s. xvi.
Content Overview: Psalter, neumed (6 leaves).

In Latin, on parchment; 6 ff.; generally 197 x 140 mm (page) [see Layout for ruling]; f. 6v blank; foliated in modern pencil with Arabic numerals.

Collation: 1^6

Quires: A single parchment ternion, H/H; obeys Gregory's rule; sewing remains.

Layout:

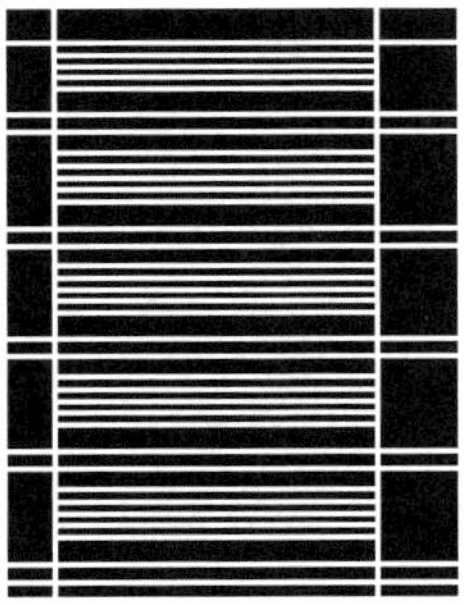

A

A Combined technique; 170 x 104 mm; 5 five-line staves, 5 text lines.

Pattern **A** is traced using a combined technique of lead (vertical bound lines, upper horizontal, text lines) and brown ink (staves); single column/full-music layout; prickings visible in the upper margin for the intersection of the verticals with the upper horizontal, and in the inner and outer margins for all text lines.

Script: A single hand (M1) writes all text in a thick sixteenth-century Southern Textualis with clear Iberian forms.

Decoration:

I. Initials: Cadels are used to begin verses and as majuscules; occasional stylization of descenders on final line of text.

Music & Staves: Five-line staves ruled in light brown ink; 17 mm; square neumes in dark brown ink.

Contents:

1. Psalter, neumed [6 leaves].

inc.: [f. 1r] uenite exultemus domino iubilemus deo salutari nostro . . . [Ps 94.1]; **expl.:** [f. 6r] . . . sicut erat in principio et nunc et semper et in secula seculorum amen.

The fragment is probably the invitatory from a psalter; contains *Venite exultemus* [Ps 94] (ff. 1r–5v) and *Gloria* (ff. 5v–6r).

Owners & Provenance: Date and source of acquisition by the university are unknown.

Former Shelfmark: MSE/MR 11 (Notre Dame).

Frag. I. 5

Origin: Low Countries, s. xv^{2}.
Content Overview: Book of Hours or Psalter (leaf).

In Latin, on parchment; 1 f.; 126 x 87 mm (page) [see Layout for ruling].

Layout:

A

A Rose ink; 81 x 56 mm; 19 lines.

Pattern **A** is traced in rose ink; single column; writing below top line; no prickings are visible.

Script: A single hand (M1) writes all text in Northern Textualis Formata.

Decoration:
I. Rubrication: Rubrics in red ink; letter heightening of majuscules and cadels in yellow ink.
II. Initials: Plain initials occur in hierarchy.
a. Plain initials (2 line square inset; 1 line versals) alternate in red and blue ink; initials 2 lines in height on the recto; 1 line versals used throughout the remainder of the Litany.

Contents:

1. Book of Hours or Psalter [leaf].

inc.: [recto] tantum exultat eternum bonum concupiscit qui cum laudatur extollitur . . .;
expl.: [verso] . . . sancte petre ora sancte paule ora sancte andrea ora sancte iohannes euuangelista ora.

Owners & Provenance: Donated to the university by Ralph W. Dixon (1925–2013; class of 1950) in 1992; acquired by Dixon from Bruce P. Ferrini (Akron, OH) on 15 February 1992.

Sales & Catalogues: Ferrini #VM 6780.

Former Shelfmark: MSE/MR 12 (Notre Dame).

Frag. I. 6

Origin: Southern France, s. xv^{2}.
Content Overview: Evangeliary (leaf).

In Latin, on parchment; 1 f.; 156 x 111 mm (page) [see Layout for ruling].

Foliation: Contemporary foliation in red ink with Roman numerals in the upper right corner (.cxxix.).

Layout:

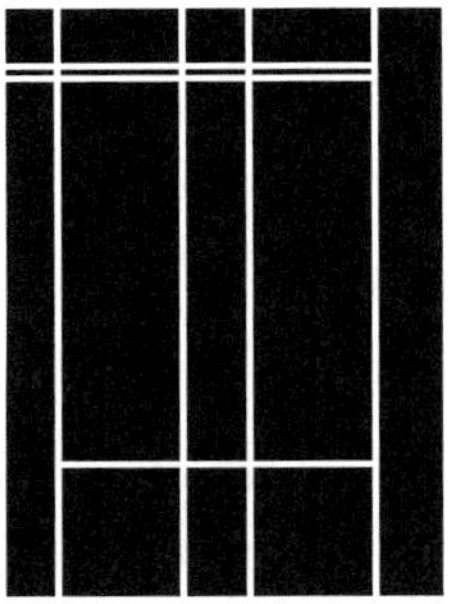

A

A Ink; 103 x 81 mm; intercol. 17 mm; 32 lines.

Pattern **A** is traced in brown ink; two columns (intercol. 17 mm); writing below top line; prickings in the upper and lower margins for vertical bounding lines and intercolumnium.

Script: A single hand (M1) writes all text in Southern Textualis Formata of the French variety with a strong Northern influence.

Decoration:
I. Rubrication: Rubrics in red ink; letter heightening of majuscules in yellow ink.
II. Initials: Plain initials occur in hierarchy.
a. Plain initials (2 line square inset) alternate in blue and red ink and begin Gospel readings; 1 line versals in red ink begin the prayers following the readings.

CONTENTS:

1. Evangeliary [leaf].

INC.: [recto[a]] sustinebit et alterum contempnet non potestis deo seruire et mamone . . . [Mt 6.23]; EXPL.: [verso[b]] . . . quod uobis uidetur de christo cuius filius [Mt 22.42].

Contains Mt 6.24–34, Lc 7.11–16, Lc 14.1–11, and Mt 16.1, 22.35–42 for the 15th–18th Sundays.

OWNERS & PROVENANCE: Date and source of acquisition by the university are unknown.

FORMER SHELFMARK: MSE/MR 13 (Notre Dame).

Frag. I. 7

Origin: France, s. xiii^{2} (Paris).
Content Overview: Pocket Bible (leaf).

In Latin, on parchment; 1 f.; 158 x 114 mm (page) [see Layout for ruling].

Layout:

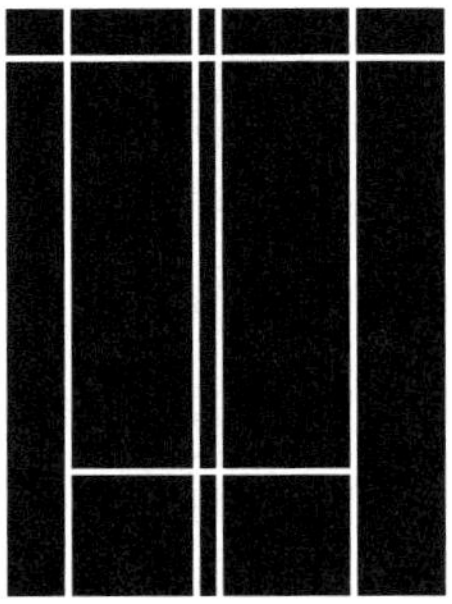

A

A Lead; 111 x 74 mm; intercol. 6 mm; 45 lines.

Pattern **A** is traced in lead; two columns (intercol. 6 mm); writing below top line; no prickings are visible.

Script: A single hand (M1) writes all text in a rapid Northern Textualis Libraria under the influence of Semitextualis, frequently admitting single compartment **a** (often in initial position). Documentary intrusions of **n** and **m** are seen in the curvature of the final limb below the line, similar to the uncial form of **m** in both forms.

Decoration:
I. Rubrication: Rubrics are not added but indents are reserved.
II. Initials: Flourished and plain initials occur outside of hierarchy.
a. Flourished initials (1 line square inset) alternate in red and blue ink with contrasting penwork and begin each chapter.
b. Plain initials are used for book titles in the upper margin with letters alternating in red and blue ink. Chapter numbers in plain style also alternate in blue and red ink contrasting with initials.

Contents:

1. Bible [leaf].

inc.: [recto[a]] uerba hec dixit azarias filius iosie et iohanna filius charee et omnis uiri superbi dicentes ad ieremiam . . . [Ier 43.1–2]; expl.: [verso[b]] . . . ethyopia et libiae tenentes scutum et lidii ar<rripientes> [Ier 46.9].

Contains Ier 43.1–46.9.

Owners & Provenance: Donated to the university by Ralph W. Dixon (1925–2013; class of 1950) in 1992; acquired by Dixon from Bruce P. Ferrini (Akron, OH) on 15 February 1992. Other leaves from the parent manuscript were also sold by Ferrini. Known leaves are:

Columbus, Ohio State Univ., Thompson Memorial Library, MS. MR. Frag.59.1
Columbus, Ohio State Univ., Thompson Memorial Library, MS. MR. Frag.59.2
Notre Dame, Univ. Notre Dame, Hesburgh Library, Frag. I. 7

Sales & Catalogues: Ferrini #45-03.

Former Shelfmark: MSE/MR 14 (Notre Dame).

Frag. I. 8

Origin: France, s. xv^{2}.
Content Overview: Book of Hours (leaf).

In Latin, on parchment; 1 f.; 210 x 149 mm (page) [see Layout for ruling].

Catchwords: One horizontal catchword centered in the lower margin of the verso; stylized.

Foliation: Foliated in modern pencil with Arabic numerals in the upper right corner (f. 129).

Layout:

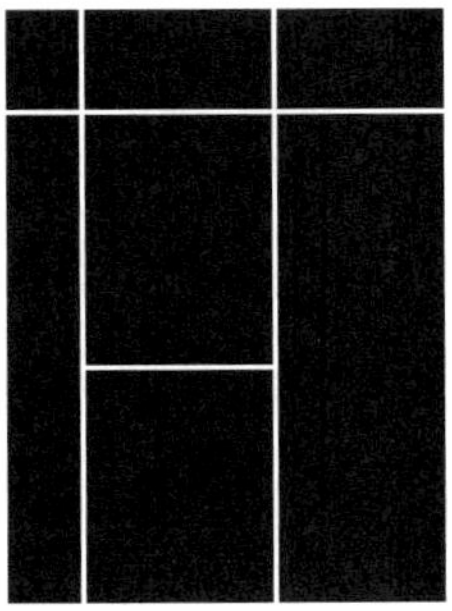

A

A Rose ink; 90 x 65 mm; 15 lines.

Pattern **A** is traced in rose ink; single column; writing below top line; prickings visible in the lower margin for vertical bounding lines, and in the outer margin for headline (double pricking) and text lines (single prickings); transfer from a black and gold rinceaux border is visible in the outer margin on the recto.

Script: A single hand (M1) writes all text in Cursiva Formata (Bastarda) of the fifteenth century.

Decoration:

I. Initials: Dentelle initials occur in hierarchy.

a. Dentelle initials (1 line versals) with alternating grounds begin each verse.

II. Line Fillers: Five line fillers are painted in dentelle style.

Contents:

1. Book of Hours [leaf].

inc.: [f. 129r] et exaudiuit preces meas et eduxit me de lacu miserie et de luto fecis . . . [Ps 39.3]; expl.: [f. 129v] . . . annunciaui iusticiam tuam in ecclesia magna ecce labia mea non prohibebo domine tu scisti [Ps 39.10].

Contains Ps 39.3–10 from matins of the Office of the Dead.

Owners & Provenance: Donated to the university by Ralph W. Dixon (1925–2013; class of 1950) in 1992; acquired by Dixon from Bruce P. Ferrini (Akron, OH) on 15 February 1992.

Sales & Catalogues: Ferrini #47-100.

Former Shelfmark: MSE/MR 15 (Notre Dame).

Frag. I. 9

Origin: France, s. xv^{2} (Rouen?).
Content Overview: Book of Hours (leaf).

In Latin, on parchment; 1 f.; 184 x 124 mm (page) [see Layout for ruling].

Layout:

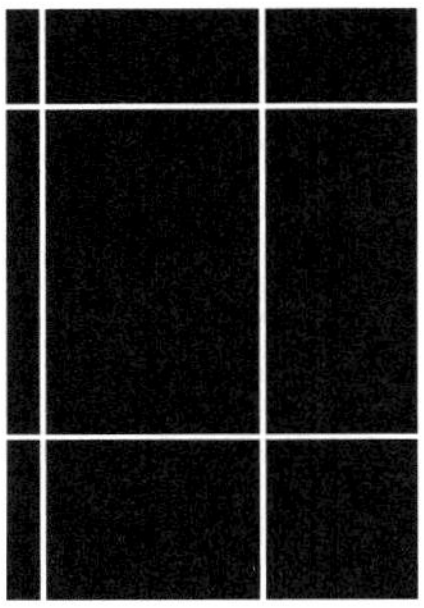

A

A Rose ink; 103 x 66 mm; 12 lines.

Pattern **A** is traced in rose ink; single column; writing below top line; no prickings are visible.

Script: A single hand (M1) writes all text in Northern Textualis Formata.

Decoration:
I. Rubrication: Rubrics in red ink; letter heightening of majuscules in yellow ink.
II. Initials: Decorated initials occur in hierarchy.
a. Decorated initials (2 line square inset; 1 line versals) in gold on light red grounds begin the psalm and verses.
III. Line Fillers: Line fillers are painted in the same style as initials.

IV. Borders & Frames:

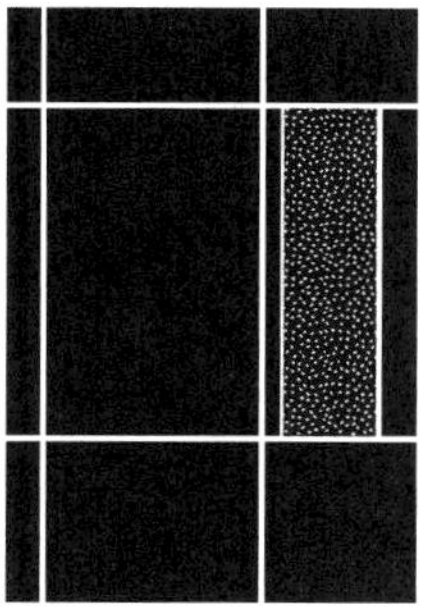

B

Outer border (**B**) with black and gold rinceaux, blue and gold acanthus, and purple and green floral section on gold grounds. Area to be decorated defined with red verticals; black ink is used to delineate section on gold grounds; patterns on recto mirrored on verso.

Contents:

1. Book of Hours [leaf].

inc.: [recto] est et propter legem tuam sustinui te domine . . . [Ps 129.4]; expl.: . . . super misericordia tua et ueritate tua quoniam magnificasti super [Ps 137.2].

Contains Ps 129.4–9 (recto) from vespers of the Office of the Dead; antiphons *Si iniquitates* and *Opera manuum* precede Ps 137.1–2 on the verso.

Owners & Provenance: Date and source of acquisition by the university are unknown.

Frag. I. 10

Origin: France, s. xv^{1}.
Content Overview: Book of Hours (leaf).

In Latin, on parchment; 1 f.; 164 x 129 mm (page) [see Layout for ruling].

Layout:

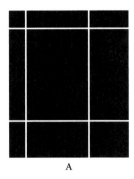

A

A Rose ink; 104 x 68 mm; 16 lines.

Pattern **A** is traced in rose ink; single column; writing below top line; prickings visible in the upper margin for outer vertical bounding line.

Script: A single hand (M1) writes all text in Northern Textualis Formata.

Decoration:
I. Initials: Dentelle initials occur in hierarchy.
a. Dentelle initials (1 line versals) begin verses of the psalm.
II. Line Fillers: Line fillers are painted in dentelle style.

III. Borders & Frames:

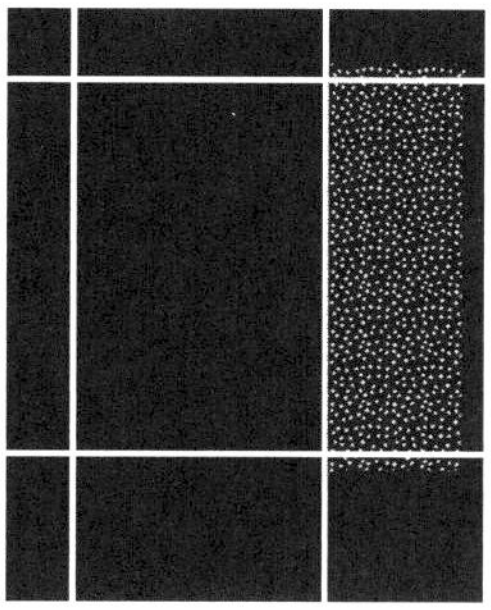

B

Black and gold rinceaux border (**B**); area to be decorated is not defined.

Contents:

1. Book of Hours [leaf].

inc.: [recto] annunciaui iusticiam tuam in ecclesia magna ecce labia mea non prohibebo domine tu scisti . . . [Ps 39.10]; expl.: [verso] . . . ferant confestim confusionem suam qui dicunt michi euge [Ps 39.16].

Contains Ps 39.10–16 from matins of the Office of the Dead.

Owners & Provenance: Date and source of acquisition by the university are unknown.

Frag. I. 11

ORIGIN: Germany, s. xv (dated Buxheim, 1434).
CONTENT OVERVIEW: Simon of Cremona, sermon (leaf).

In Latin, on paper; 1 f.; generally 298 x 211 mm (page) [see LAYOUT for ruling].

BIBLIOGRAPHICAL FORMAT: 2°

FOLIATION: Contemporary foliation in brown ink with Arabic numerals within the intercolumnium (f. 91).

LAYOUT: No ruling pattern is traced; text area approx. 213 x 140 mm; two columns (intercol. approx. 6 mm); 40 lines; chainlines and laid lines used as guides.

SCRIPT: A single hand (M1) writes all text in a bold Cursiva Libraria. The text was written by the Carthusian scribe Caspar Misnensis at Buxheim in 1434 according to the colophon in the parent manuscript [*COLOPHONS* 2: nos. 4841–4842]. München, Bayerische Staatsbibliothek, Clm 4402 and Augsburg, Universitätsbibliothek, Cod. II.1.2° 15 also contain texts in Caspar's hand.

DECORATION:
I. RUBRICATION: Letter heightening of majuscules in red ink; sources and some lemmata often underlined in red ink.

CONTENTS:
1. Simon of Cremona, sermon [leaf].
INC.: [recto[a]] pontifex dator futurorum bonorum que specie est assistens deo patri non per mediacionem aliam nisi per tabernaculum sue carnis . . .; EXPL.: [verso[b]] . . . que in conspectu omnium occisa sacerdos digitum suum sanguini eius intingens species aspergebat uersus.

EDITION: REUTLINGEN 1484.

OWNERS & PROVENANCE: Source and date of acquisition by the university are unknown. The parent manuscript contained 242 leaves and was produced at the Carthusian Charterhouse at Buxheim in 1434. The manuscript was broken ca. 1926 by Foliophiles, Inc. (New York, NY). Alfred W. Stites (Washington, DC) acquired Foliophiles, Inc. in 1963 and compiled portfolios of various leaves entitled "Pages from the Past" and "History of the Written Word." Many leaves of the manuscript were distributed by Stites between 1964 and 1967. Known leaves are:

Auburn, Auburn Univ., Ralph Brown Draughon Library, Z 105.5 . S56 S4 1434
Austin, Univ. of Texas, Harry Ransom Center, MS Leaf M3
Beaver Falls, Geneva College, McCartney Library, MS 1 [missing]
Chapel Hill, Univ. North Carolina, Wilson Library, MS 258
Columbia (MO), Univ. Missouri, Ellis Library, Rare Folio Z113 . P3, item 9
Columbia (SC), Univ. South Carolina, Thomas Cooper Library, Early MS 54
Evanston, Charles S. Jenson Collection, VL 93 (F6–18)
Kalamazoo, Western Michigan Univ., Waldo Library, Pages from the Past, Box 2, folder 3, item 3
Oberlin, Oberlin College, Harvey Mudd Center, MS P4
Orange, Chapman University, Leatherby Libraries, Z 105.5 . S56 S4 1434
Montréal, McGill Univ., McLennan Library, Rare Books and Special Collections, MS 122
New Haven, Yale Univ., Beinecke Library, MS 3.12 (two leaves)
Notre Dame, Univ. Notre Dame, Hesburgh Library, Frag. I. 11
Tampa, Tampa-Hillsborough County Public Library, MS 2 [possibly deaccessioned and sold]
Westerville, Otterbein Univ., Courtright Memorial Library, Archives, Clements Rare Manuscripts Collection, s.n.

Sales & Catalogues: Sale of Graf Hugo von Walbott-Bassenheim, Munich, 20 September 1883, lot 2756 (parent manuscript); Charles F. Gunter sale (New York, 11 November 1926, lot 268).

Former Shelfmark: MSE/MR 52 (Notre Dame).

Frag. I. 12

Origin: Low Countries, s. xiii (Flanders).
Content Overview: Psalter (leaf).

In Latin, on parchment; 1 f.; 246 x 169 mm (page) [see Layout for ruling].

Foliation: Paginated in modern ink with Arabic numerals in the upper right corner of the recto and verso (22, 23).

Layout:

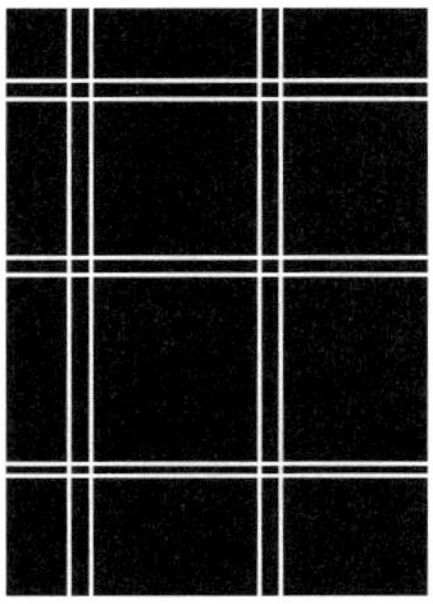

A

A Lead; 166 x 109 mm; 23 lines.

Pattern **A** is traced in lead; single column; writing above top line; prickings visible in the upper and lower margins for vertical bounding lines; superfluous middle through line.

Script: A single hand (M1) writes the psalter text in Northern Textualis Formata. A second hand (M2) writes Anglicana Libraria in the outer margin of the verso.

Decoration:
I. Initials: Dentelle and plain initials occur in hierarchy.
a. A dentelle initial (4 lines square inset) begins Ps 17 on the recto.
b. Plain initials (1 line versals) in gold with black outlines begin each verse.
II. Line Fillers: Line fillers are painted in red and blue ink on the recto and verso.

Contents:

1. Psalter [leaf].

inc.: [recto] exurge domine preueni eum et subplanta eum eripe animam meam ab impio . . . [Ps 16.13]; expl.: [verso] . . . et apparuerunt fontes aquarum et re<uelata> [Ps 17.16].

Contains Pss 16.13–15 and 17.1–16, skipping verse 14, which M2 adds in the left margin of the verso.

Owners & Provenance: The parent manuscript was in the collection of Otto F. Ege (1888–1951) by 1943 (Gwara 2013, 346); leaves were described by Ege as "English, ca. 1225." This leaf was acquired from King Alfred's Notebook (Cayce, SC) by the university in May 2015. Known leaves from the parent manuscript (including those in Gwara 2013, *Handlist* no. 125 with additions) are:

Cleveland, Cleveland Public Library, f 091.97 EG121M vol. 2
Houston, Univ. of Houston, M. D. Anderson Library, s.n. (framed)
Notre Dame, Univ. Notre Dame, Hesburgh Library, Frag. I. 12
Phoenix, Phoenix Public Library, MS Fragment 69
Phoenix, Phoenix Public Library, MS Fragment 79

Sales & Catalogues: King Alfred's Notebook, *Enchiridion* 18, no. 25; ibid., *Ench.* 19, no. 26; ibid., *Ench.* 21, no. 25.

Bibliography: Shailor 2009, 21; Gwara 2013, *Handlist* no. 125; Gwara 2013, 6, 37 n. 96, 58 nn. 152 and 154, 69, 74; Oliver 1985, no. 74 describes another leaf (*olim* Endowment Collection, MS Leaf 7); images of other leaves are Shailor 2009, color plates 2a–2b (Phoenix, PL, MS Fragments 69 and 79), and Gwara 2013, fig. 64 (Cleveland, PL, f 091.97 EG121M vol. 2).

Frag. I. 13

Origin: Austria, Germany, or Bohemia, s. xii[1].
Content Overview: Gradual, Temporale (binding fragment).

In Latin, on parchment; 1 piece; 255 x 118 mm (piece) [see Layout for ruling].

Foliation: A later hand has added Roman numerals in black ink in the upper margin and throughout the fragment for cues.

Layout: The fragment is badly damaged, and transfer from much glue remains; technique of ruling cannot be seen.

Script: A single hand (M1) writes all text in a late Caroline minuscule in brown ink displaying few transitional features; rubrics written using majuscule forms.

Decoration:
I. Rubrication: Rubrics in red ink.
II. Initials: Plain initials occur in hierarchy.
a. Plain initials (2–5 line half inset; 1 line versals) in red ink and brown ink occur; red initials of the larger size begin the introits for each Sunday; 1 line versals in brown ink begin the other chants.

Music & Staves: Adiastematic neumes written above text in brown ink.

Contents:

1. Gradual, Temporale [binding fragment].

inc.: [recto] <circuibo et immola>bo in tabernaculum colus hostiam eiius [*sic*] iu<bilationis cantabo et> psalmum dicam domino . . .; expl.: [verso] dum clamarem custodi me *** exul<tate>.

The manuscript was used as spine lining and is in a very fragmented state. Recto contains portions of: the *communio* for the Sixth Sunday after Pentecost (Dom. 6 p. Pent.); introit, invitatory, gradual, alleluia, offertory, verse for the offertory, and *communio* for the Seventh Sunday after Pentecost (Dom. 7 p. Pent.); introit and alleluia for the Eighth Sunday after Pentecost (Dom. 8 p. Pent). Verso contains portions of: alleluia verse, offertory, *communio* for the Eight Sunday after Pentecost; introit, gradual, verse for the gradual, alleluia, and *communio* for the Ninth Sunday after Pentecost (Dom. 9 p. Pent); introit, gradual, and alleluia for the Tenth Sunday after Pentecost (Dom. 10 p. Pent.).

Owners & Provenance: Acquired from King Alfred's Notebook (Cayce, SC) by the university in August 2012.

Frag. I. 14

Origin: France, s. xii^{ex}.
Content Overview: Isidore of Seville, *Origines* (2 leaves).

In Latin, on parchment; 2 ff.; generally 319 x 219 mm (page) [see Layout for ruling].

Collation: 1^2

Quires: One bifolium, F/F; the bifolium was likely the inner leaf of the quire.

Foliation: Foliated in modern pencil with Arabic numerals.

Layout: Ruled in lead; two columns (approx. 81 and 83 mm; intercol. 14 mm); the fragment has been trimmed significantly in the upper margin resulting in the loss of top line.

Script: A single hand (M1) writes all text in Praegothica of the late twelfth century in brown ink. A vestige of the hierarchy of scripts is visible on f. 2r^b where Uncial forms are used in the opening word. Multiple sets of corrections via rasura and expuncti are present throughout the fragment. A correcting hand (M2) writes in dark black ink on f. 2v^b.

Decoration:
I. Rubrication: Rubrics in red ink.
II. Initials: Plain initials occur in hierarchy.
a. Plain initials (2 line square inset) in red ink with Romanesque stylization begin chapters on f. 2r.

Contents:

1. Isidore of Seville, *Origines* [2 leaves].

inc.: [f. 1r^a] creata solui regnu(m) portendit alexandro ex muliere monstrum creatum . . . [*Orig.* 11.3]; **expl.:** [f. 2v^b] . . . sibique inuicem sucedentes nullum laborem pon<deris> [*Orig.* 12.19].

Contains *Orig.* 11.3.5–11.4.3 and 12.1–19.

1.1. *Orig.* 11.3.5–11.4.3. ff. 1r^{a}–2^{b}. INC.: creata solui regnu(m) portendit alexandro ex muliere monstrum creatum . . .; EXPL.: . . . scorpion exibit caudaque minabitur unca [*Met.* 15.369 in *Orig.* 11.4.3].

1.2. *Orig.* 12.1– f. 2r^{a}–2v^{b}. RUB.: capitula libri .xij. /.iii.\ .i. de pecoribus et iuuencis .ij. de bestiis .iij. de minutis animantibus .iiij. de serpentibus .v. de uermibus .vj. de piscibus .vij. de auibus .viij. de minutis uolatilibus. incipit liber .xij. capitulum .i. de pecoribus et iumentis; INC.: omnibus animantibus adam primum uocabula indidit . . .; EXPL.: . . . sibique inuicem sucedentes nullum laborem pon<deris>.

EDITION: LINDSAY 1911.

OWNERS & PROVENANCE: Thomas Malin Rodgers, Jr. (1943–2012); acquired from King Alfred's Notebook (Cayce, SC) by the university in December 2012.

SALES & CATALOGUES: Bonhams, 4 December 2012, lot 1010.

Frag. I. 15

Origin: Eastern Mediterranean (Crete), s. xii.
Content Overview: Evangeliary (leaf).

In Greek, on parchment; 211 x 142 mm (page) [see Layout for ruling].

Layout:

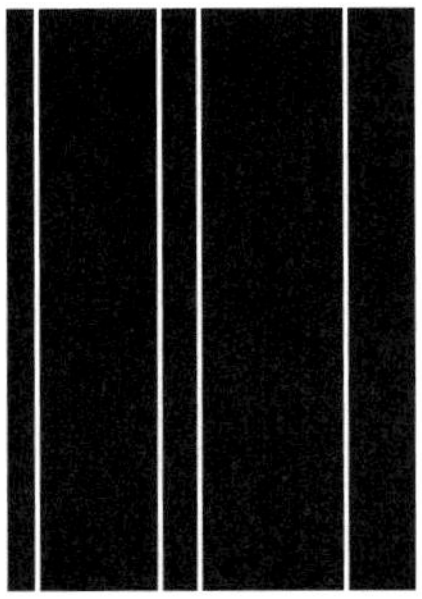

A

A Hard-point; approx. 171 x 108 mm; intercol. 14 mm; 32 lines.

Pattern **A** is traced using hard-point technique; two columns (intercol. 14 mm); only vertical bounding lines are traced; columns are very uneven (43 mm and 51 mm).

Script: All text is written in Greek minuscule of the twelfth century.

Decoration:
I. Initials: Ornamented initials (6 lines half inset; hanging) in red ink occur on the recto and verso of the fragment.

Contents:
1. Evangeliary [leaf].
inc.: [recto[a]] τῶι καιρῶι ἐκείνωι ἠρώτεσε τὸν πιλάτον ὁ ἰωσὴφ ὁ ἀπὸ ἀριμαθαίας . . . [Io 19.38]; **expl.:** [verso[b]] . . . τότε ἐπληρώθη τὸ ῥηθὲν διὰ [Mt 27.9].

Contains the Gospel readings: Io 19.38–42 [recto[a–b]], Mt 27.62–66 [recto[b]–verso[a]], and Mt 27.1–9 [verso[a–b]].

Owners & Provenance: Acquired from King Alfred's Notebook (Cayce, SC) by the university in March 2013.

Frag. I. 16

Origin: England, s. xiv^2.
Content Overview: Missal (binding fragments).

In Latin, on parchment; 2 pieces; generally 173 x 46 mm (piece) [see Layout for ruling].

Layout: The manuscript was ruled in black ink in two columns with single vertical bounding lines; double superfluous horizontal through lines in the lower margin are visible.

Script: A single hand (M1) writes all text in Northern Textualis Formata (Quadrata).

Decoration:
I. Rubrication: Rubrics in red ink; letter heightening of majuscules in yellow ink.
II. Initials: Flourished initials occur in hierarchy.
a. Flourished initials (2 line square inset) in blue with red penwork begin the Epistle readings; a hanging **i** is also visible on piece 1, recto.

Contents:

1. Missal [binding fragments].

Prayers and epistolary readings (*ad Romanos*) for the Seventh and Eight Sunday in the Octave of Pentecost. The two fragments align to form a larger textual unit.

1.1. Seventh Sunday in the Octave of Pentecost—Pieces 1 and 2, recto.
1.1.1. Piece 1, recto:
<sunt>t bona
<nutrias ac pieta>tis studio
<que sunt nutrita> custodias [*CO* 2210]
<per dominum ad ro>manos
<fratres> huma-
<anum dico pro>pter infir-
<mitatem carnis uest>re sicut
<enim exhibuistis m>embra ues-
<tre seruire immu>undicie et [Rm 6.19].

1.1.2. Piece 2, recto:
<nut>rias ac pi<et>a<tis studio>
<qu>e sunt nutr<i>ta <custodias> [*CO* 2210]
<per> dominum ad ro<manos>
fratres <huma->
num dico pro<pter infir->
<mi>tatem carnis u<estre sicut>
<enim> exhibuistis m<embra ues->
<tre> seruire immu<nditie et> [Rm 6.19].

1.2. Eighth Sunday in the Octave of Pentecost—Pieces 1 and 2, verso.
1.2.1. Piece 1, verso:
fallitur t<e supplices exora->
mus ut <noxia cuncta sub->
moueas <et omnia nobis profutura>
concedas [*CO* 1188] <per dominum ad romanos>
fr<atres debitores>
s<umus non carni ut>
secundum car<nem uiuamus si enim>
secundum car<nem uixeritis mo->
riemini <si> [Rm 8.12].

1.2.2. Piece 2, verso:
<mus ut nox>ia cuncta <sub->
<moueas> et omnia nobis pro<futura>
<concedas> [*CO* 1188] per dominum ad rom<anos>
<f>ratres debit<ores>
<s>umus non carni <ut>
<secundum car>nem uiuamus si <enim>
<secundum car>nem uixeritis <mo->
<riemini> si autem spiritu fa<cta> [Rm 8.12].

Owners & Provenance: The fragments were extracted from a book binding in the Hesburgh Library (unrecorded).

Frag. I. 17

Origin: England, s. xiii^{2}/xiv^{1}.
Content Overview: Breviary, Sanctorale (binding fragment).

In Latin, on parchment; 1 piece; 23 x 189 mm (piece) [see Layout for ruling].

Layout: Ruled in lead (mostly worn away); two columns (intercol. approx. 12 mm).

Script: A single hand (M1) writes all text in Northern Textualis Formata.

Decoration:
I. Rubrication: Rubrics in red ink; letter heightening of majuscules in red ink.
II. Initials: Flourished initials occur in hierarchy.
a. Flourished initials (2 lines square inset) alternate in red and blue ink with contrasting penwork.

Contents:

1. Breviary, Sanctorale [binding fragment].

inc.: [recto^{a}] <sexagin>ta annis duobus regnante imperatore christianissimo theodosio surrexit . . .; expl.: [verso^{b}] . . . pietas qui famulum suum in uia ueri<tatis>.

Contains part of the sanctorale for July; contents in very fragmentary form are: second reading, matins for the Seven Sleepers (Jul. 27) on recto^{a}; *oratio* and first reading, matins for Felix, Simplicius, Faustinus, and Beatrix (Jul. 29) on recto^{b}; first and second readings, matins for Abdon and Sennes (Jul. 30) on verso^{a}; second and third readings, matins for Germain of Auxerre (Jul. 31) on verso^{b}. Divisions of readings are different than those recorded in *SB* [cf. *SB* 556, 559, 561, 564].

Owners & Provenance: The fragments were removed from a book binding in the Hesburgh Library (unrecorded).

Frag. I. 18

ORIGIN: Germany, s. xiii^{in}.
CONTENT OVERVIEW: Missal, neumed (binding fragment).

In Latin, on parchment; 1 piece; 156 x 118 mm (piece) [see LAYOUT for ruling].

LAYOUT: Ruled using hard-point technique (indentation on flesh side); fragment formed the left column (recto) of a two-column layout.

SCRIPT: A single hand (M1) writes all text in a rapid Northern Textualis Libraria; a smaller script is used for the neumed sections on the recto.

DECORATION:
I. RUBRICATION: Rubrics in red ink; letter heightening of cadels and majuscules in red ink.
II. INITIALS: Flourished, plain, and cadel initials occur in broken hierarchy.
A. One flourished initial (2 lines square inset) in blue ink with red penwork begins the canon on the verso.
B. Plain initials (2 line square inset; hanging **i**) in red ink begin Mass prayers on the verso.
C. Cadels are used as versals throughout the fragment and are enlarged within staves on the recto.

MUSIC & STAVES: Four-line staves traced in red ink; 9 mm; square neumes in black ink.

CONTENTS:
1. Missal, neumed [binding fragment].
INC.: [recto] multi enim infirmi et imbecilles et dormiunt multi . . . [1 Cor 11.30]; EXPL.: [verso] . . . hanc igitur oblationem seruitutis nostre set.

Contains part of the mass of Holy Thursday; recto contains a fragment of the Epistle (1 Cor 11), the gradual and response (neumed); the verso contains the last word of the Gospel reading (Io 13), the offertory, secret, preface, and canon.

OWNERS & PROVENANCE: Found in a copy of Ovid's *Metamorphoses* printed by Sebastianus Gryphius (Lyon, 1541). The book was from the collection of José Durand (1925–1990), which was acquired by the university in 1995. The imprint is housed in the Hesburgh Library's Department of Rare Books and Special Collections as "Rare Books Small PA 6519 .M2 1541."

Frag. I. 19

Origin: England, s. xv[1].
Content Overview: John Chrysostom (sp.), *Homilia in sanctum Mattheum* (binding fragment).

In Latin, on parchment; 2 pieces; generally 42 x 172 mm (piece) [see Layout for ruling].

Layout: Ruled in ink; two columns (intercol. 13 mm); writing below top line; prickings visible on piece 1 in the upper margin for the intercolumnium and in the inner margin at the intersection of the inner vertical bounding line and top horizontal.

Script: A single hand (M1) writes all text in Anglicana Formata under the influence of European Cursiva.

Decoration:
I. Rubrication: Lemmata underlined in red ink; paraph marks in red and blue ink.

Contents:

1. John Chrysostom (sp.), *Homilia in sanctum Mattheum* [binding fragment].

inc.: [1 recto[a]] dilectio est cum nutrix dilectionis humilitas est et hodii mater superbia . . .; expl.: [1 verso[b]] . . . iusticia est secundum ergo quod eripuerit se quis a malis et fecerit bona . . . aut modice aut ***. inc.: [2 recto[a]] secundum fidem humiles sunt et <intelligentes dum nim>is de se adiutorium dei pulsare non . . .; [2 verso[b]] expl.: . . . diuerte a malo fac bonum non di<xit>.

Both fragments were cut from the same folio containing portions of *Hom.* 9.2–8. Textual order: 1 recto[a]–2 recto[b] (9.2), 1 recto[b] (9.3), 2 recto[b] (9.3–4), 1 verso[a] (9.4), 2 verso[a] (9.5–6), 1 verso[b] (9.7), 2 verso[b] (9.8).

Edition: *PG* 56.680–682.

1.1. Piece 1, recto–verso.

1.1.1. recto[a]. inc.: dilectio est cum nutrix dilectionis humilitas est et hodii mater superbia . . .; expl.: . . . et inicium salutis ab humiliate per christum ***.

1.1.2. recto[b]. inc.: consolabuntur in seculo illo qui aliena lugent quomodo consolabuntur numquid desinent . . .; expl.: . . . sunt in mundo nescientes dei prouidenciam nec intelli<gentes>***.

1.1.3. verso[a]. INC.: <trans>formatum et conforme factum corpori glorie christi erit terra uiuorum . . .; EXPL.: . . . et spiritualem et sanctam spirituales et sancti beat***.

1.1.4. verso[b]. INC.: iusticia est secundum ergo quod eripuerit se quis a malis et fecerit bona . . .; EXPL.: . . . aut turbulente aut munde aut modice aut ***.

1.2. Piece 2, recto–verso.

1.2.1. recto[a]. INC.: secundum fidem humiles sunt et <intelligentes dum nim>is de se adiutorium dei pulsare non . . .; EXPL.: . . . superbie est sine dubio et ra<dix>*****humilitas est et quia proprium est.

1.2.2. recto[b]. INC.: misertus est abraham ibi filio ardenti non quia fuerat [*sic*] epulator . . .; EXPL.: . . . iniuriam pati quam facere nam.

1.2.3. verso[a]. INC.: <pre>mia dei quam desideria auara sanctorum beati misericordes quoniam ipsis . . .; EXPL.: . . . scriptum est diligite inimicos uestros et benefacite hiis.

1.2.4. verso[b]. INC.: uere pacificus audi prophetam dicen<tem co>hibe linguam tuam a malo et l<abia tua> ne loquantur . . .; EXPL.: . . . diuerte a malo fac bonum non di<xit>.

OWNERS & PROVENANCE: Acquired from ElevenEleven Books (Clarkson, NY) by the university in April 2013. The book from which the fragments were extracted is unknown. Both pieces were cut from the same folio of the same parent manuscript by a binder (period unknown).

Frag. I. 20

Origin: Low Countries, s. xv^2 (Flanders).
Content Overview: Book of Hours (3 leaves).

In Latin and French (some rubrics), on parchment; 3 ff. generally 182 x 129 mm (page) [see Layout for ruling].

Layout:

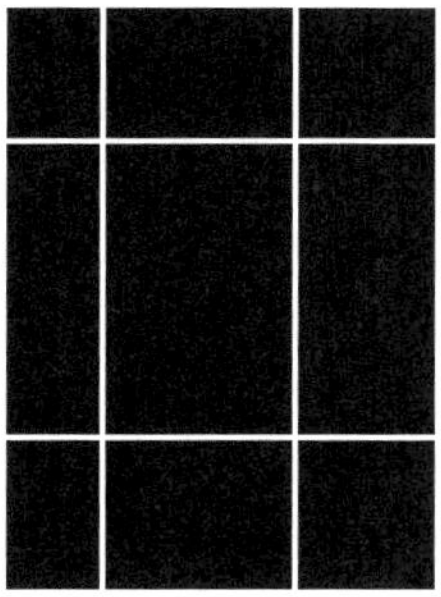

A

A Rose ink; 93 x 58 mm; 14 lines.

Pattern **A** is traced in rose ink; single column; writing below top line; no prickings are visible.

Script: A single hand (M1) writes all text in Northern Textualis Formata.

Decoration:
I. Rubrication: Rubrics in red ink; letter heightening of majuscules in yellow ink.
II. Initials: Foliate and dentelle initials occur in hierarchy.
a. Foliate initials (2 line square insets; **h** overflows 2 lines; hanging **i**) begin major sections of the text (e.g., prayers, readings, etc.).
b. One dentelle initial (1 line versal) begins the *Gloria* on leaf 2, recto.
III. Borders & Frames: Piece borders of acanthus leaves in blues, red, orange, white, and black and gold rinceaux spray from foliate initials; piece border on leaf 1, verso is inhabited by a figure wearing a red headpiece, blue hood, pink tunic, and red hose.

Contents:

1. Book of Hours [3 leaves].

1.1. Gospel Lessons—leaf 1. inc.: [recto] et duriciam cordis et qui uiderant eum resurrexisse a mortuis non crediderant . . . [Mc 16.14]; expl.: [verso] . . . quod factum est in ipso uita erat et uita [Io 1.3–4].

1.2. Hours of the Holy Spirit, compline and *recommendatio*—leaf 2. inc.: [recto] deus in adiutorium meum intende domine ad adiuuandum . . .; expl.: [verso] . . . benedicamus domino deo gratias pater noster passio domini nostri ihesu christi secundum iohannem.

1.3. Collects—leaf 3. inc.: [recto] <ab>soluat per christum oraison omnipotens sempiterne deus qui facis; expl.: [verso] . . . deus quo sancta desideria recta consilia et iusta.

The collects are likely those following the Litany.

1.3.1 recto [incomplete] <ab>soluat per christum [*CO* 1143].

1.3.2. recto. rub.: oraison; inc.: omnipotens sempiterne deus qui facis mirabilia magna solus pretende . . . super famulos tuos et super cunctas congregationis illis commissas . . . rorem tu benedictionis infunde per christum [cf. *CO* 3938c].

1.3.3. recto–verso. rub.: oraison; inc.: ure igne sancti spiritus renes nostros . . . et mundo corde placeamus per christum dominum [cf. *CO* 6025].

1.3.4. verso. rub.: orason [*sic*]; inc.: pretende domine famulis et famulabus tuis dexteram celestis . . . et que digne postulant assequantur [*CO* 4587a].

1.3.5. verso. rub.: oraison; inc.: acciones nostras quesumus domine aspirando preueni . . . et per te cepta finiatur per christum dominum [*CO* 74].

1.3.6. verso (incomplete). rub.: oraison; inc.: deus a quo sancta desideria recta consilia et iusta [*CO* 1088a].

Owners & Provenance: Acquired from King Alfred's Notebook (Cayce, SC) by the university in May 2014; the three leaves originate from the same parent manuscript.

Sales & Catalogues: King Alfred's Notebook, *Enchiridion* 25, nos. 26–28.

Frag. I. 21

Origin: France, s. xii^2 (Saint-Oyan de Joux/Abbey of Saint-Claude, ca. 1175).
Content Overview: Glossed Bible (Chronicles) (leaf).

In Latin, on parchment; 1 f.; 244 x 158 mm (page) [see Layout for ruling].

Layout:

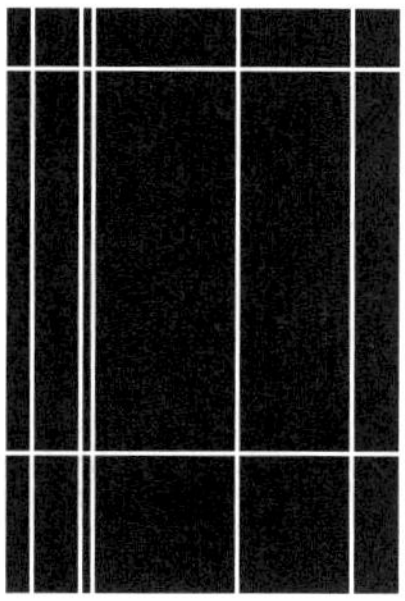

A

A Lead; 161 x 25/58/40 mm; 27 lines.

Pattern **A** is traced in lead; 3 columns (gloss/biblical text/gloss); writing above top line; no prickings are visible.

Script: A single hand (M1) writes all text and gloss in Praegothica of the late twelfth century.

Contents:

1. Bible (Chronicles with glosses) [leaf].

inc.: [recto] de curru in alterum currum qui sequebatur eum more regio et asportauerit in ierusalem . . . [2 Par 35.24]; expl.: [verso] . . . principes sacerdotum preuaricati sunt inique iuxta uniuersas abhominationes [2 Par 36.14].

Owners & Provenance: The parent manuscript was in the library of the Benedictine Abbey of Saint-Oyan de Joux (Saint-Claude) at least by 8 March 1492 (Castan 1889, 333, no. 56); then in collection of William L. Clements of Bay City, MI (1860–1934), who acquired it from Wilfrid Michael Voynich (1865–1930) according to De Ricci 2:1131, no. 1; in the possession of Otto F. Ege (1888–1951) by 1937 (Gwara 2013, 346); leaves for sale by Philip Duschnes (New York, NY) in 1943 and 1946 (Gwara 2013, 31); this leaf was acquired from King Alfred's Notebook (Cacye, SC) by the university in May 2013.

The remainder of the parent manuscript is hypothesized to be Cleveland, Cleveland Museum of Art, Ege dep., TR 12828/50 (see Gwara 2013, 71). Known leaves from the parent manuscript (including those from Gwara 2013, *Handlist* no. 77 with additions) are:

Austin, University of Texas, Harry Ransom Center, MS Leaf B2
Boston, Boston Univ., School of Theology Library, MS Leaf 18
Cayce, King Alfred's Notebook, *Enchiridion* 17, no. 3
Columbus, Ohio State Univ., Thompson Memorial Library, MS. MR. Frag.197
Dallas, Southern Methodist Univ., Bridwell Library, MS 56
Minneapolis, Univ. Minnesota, Elmer L. Andersen Library, MS 44
Notre Dame, Univ. Notre Dame, Hesburgh Library, Frag. I. 21
Oberlin, Oberlin College, Harvey Mudd Center, MS B2
Phoenix, Phoenix Public Library, 091 B471TC (two leaves)
Providence, RISD, Museum of Art, 1943.433

Sales & Catalogues: Unspecified leaves were listed in: Duschnes, Cat. 54, no. 15; ibid., Cat. 74, no. 30; other leaves King Alfred's Notebook, *Enchiridion* 17, no. 3 [1 Par 5.18–6.31]; ibid., *Enchiridion* 18, no. 3 [2 Par 21.4–34.9]; ibid., *Enchiridion* 19, no. 2 [ibid.]; ibid., *Enchiridion* 21, no. 2a.

Bibliography: Gwara 2013, *Handlist* no. 77; Castan 1889, 333, 354, no. 56 (parent manuscript); de Ricci 2:1131, no. 1 (parent manuscript); Gwara 2013, 31–32, 39, 41, 58 n. 152, 71–72 describes the complex provenance; Oliver 1985, nos. 23–24 describes two leaves from the parent manuscript.

Frag. I. 22

Origin: Germany, s. xi^{ex}.
Content Overview: Mass book (binding fragment).

In Latin, on parchment; 1 f.; 305 x 207 mm (page) [see Layout for ruling].

Layout:

A

A Hard-point; 255 x 150 mm; 29 lines.

Ruled using hard-point technique; single column; writing above top line; no prickings are visible.

Script: A single hand (M1) writes all text in a degraded Caroline minuscule in brown ink; artificial **ct** and **st** ligatures.

Decoration:
I. Rubrication: Rubrics in red ink; letter heightening of majuscules in red.
II. Initials: Plain initials occur in hierarchy.
a. Plain initials (hanging) in red and brown ink divide sections; rubrics written in capitalis.

Contents:

1. Mass book [binding fragment].

inc.: <dom>ibus eorum adduces enim super eos latronem repente quia foderunt foueam ut caperent me . . . [Ier 18.22]; expl.: . . . et hi cognouerunt quia tu me misisti et no<tum fe>ci eis nomen tuum et notum faciam ut dilectio [Io 17.25–26].

Contains the part of the readings, gradual, and gradual verse for Passion Sunday.

Owners & Provenance: Acquired from Philip Pirages (McMinnville, OR) by the university in May 2013. Another leaf from the parent manuscript, now sold, was McMinnville, Pirages, Cat. 65, no. 2.

Sales & Catalogues: Pirages #ST11913-1.

Frag. I. 23

Origin: France, s. xiv^{in}.
Content Overview: Unidentified binding fragment.

In Latin, on parchment; 1 piece; 29 x 10 mm (piece).

Script: The small amount of text is written by a single hand (M1) in Semitextualis; single compartment **a** is visible on the recto.

Decoration:
I. **Rubrication:** Underlining and letter heightening in red ink are visible.

Contents:
1. Unidentified binding fragment.

1.1. recto:
. . .]t per h(o)c [. . .
. . .]iuntur conp[. . .
. . .]artinus b[. . .
. . .]sus iste [. . .

1.2 verso:
. . .] ex illo [. . .
. . .] duas con[. . .
. . .](o/e)cessiue[. . .
. . .]t uidetur et i[. . .
. . .]**sat[. . .

Owners & Provenance: The fragment was removed from a book in the Hesburgh Library (unrecorded).

Frag. I. 24

Origin: Southern France (?), s. xv.
Content Overview: Breviary (binding fragment).

In Latin, on parchment; 1 piece; generally 55 x 56 mm (piece) [see Layout for ruling].

Layout: Ruled in brown ink; two columns (intercol. 4 mm); writing below top line.

Script: A single hand (M1) writes all text in Northern Textualis with a slight Southern influence.

Decoration:
I. Rubrication: Rubrics in red ink.
II. Initials: Flourished initials occur in hierarchy.
a. Flourished initials (2 line square inset; hanging **i**s) in blue ink with red penwork begin the readings; no alternation.

Contents:
1. Breviary [binding fragment].
inc.: [recto[a]] <summi>tas eius celos tangebat et descendentes angelos et dixit uere gloria uere . . .; expl.: [verso[b]] . . . populi tui et osten<de> eis uiam bonam per quam.

The fragment contains part of matins for a church dedication; recto contains in fragmentary form: the end of the first nocturn and second nocturn through the sixth reading; verso contains end of the second nocturn and third nocturn through the response before the eighth reading.

Owners & Provenance: The fragment was removed from a copy of Petrus de Palude (dub.), *Thesauri noui, vt vulgo vocatur, Sermones quadragesimales* printed by Iacobus Kerver (Paris, 1552). The book was from the collection of Rt. Rev. Astrik L. Gabriel, O. Praem. (1907–2005) who donated it to the library. The imprint is housed in the Hesburgh Library's Department of Rare Books and Special Collections as "Rare Books Small BV 4277 . T44," which contains two other fragments from the same parent manuscript used as spine lining.

Frag. I. 25

Origin: England, s. xii^2 (ca. 1175).
Content Overview: Breviary (binding fragment).

In Latin, on parchment; 1 piece; 210 x 77 mm (piece) [see Layout for ruling].

Layout: Ruled in lead; originally two columns.

Script: A single hand (M1) writes all text in an English Praegothica of the late twelfth century, incorporating most transitional features toward Northern Textualis.

Decoration:
I. Rubrication: Rubrics in red ink; letter heightening of ampersands and some majuscules in red ink.
II. Initials: Flourished and plain initials occur in hierarchy.
a. Flourished initials (hanging) in blue, green, and red ink with contrasting penwork in Romanesque style alternate on the verso.
b. Plain initials (1 line versals; hanging) in red ink occur.

Contents:
1. Breviary [binding fragment].
inc.: [recto] obmutesc<e et> exi ab eo et <statim liberatus est homo qui> per multos annos fuerat . . .; expl.: [verso] . . . adesto supplicantibus nostris o<mnipotens deus ut quibus fiduciam> sperand<e pie>tatis indulges *** [cf. *CO* 182].

Contains in fragmentary form the offices for Bartholomew (Aug. 24), Rufus (Aug. 27), and Augustine with *memoria* for Hermes (Aug. 28). The recto begins at the end of the second nocturn for Bartholomew; the verso ends with the collects for Hermes [cf. *CO* 1472a] and Augustine [*CO* 182].

Owners & Provenance: Acquired from King Alfred's Notebook (Cayce, SC) by the university in August 2013; dealer marks of Bruce P. Ferrini (Akron, OH) are visible in pencil on the recto.

Sales & Catalogues: Ferrini #VM 7067; King Alfred's Notebook, *Enchiridion* 16, no. 42.

Frag. I. 26

Origin: England, s. xii (ca. 1150).
Content Overview: Jerome, *Commentarii in Ezechielem* (binding fragments).

In Latin and one word in Greek, on parchment; 2 pieces; generally 195 x 61 mm (piece) [see Layout for ruling].

Layout: Ruled using hard-point technique; originally two columns (intercol. lost); writing above top line.

Script: A single hand (M1) writes all text in an English Praegothica; frequent use of the ampersand, **nt** and **st** ligatures, and **e** caudata.

Decoration:
I. Rubrication: Rubrics in red ink.
II. Initials: Plain initials occur in hierarchy.
a. Plain initials (1 line half inset) in red and green ink with Romanesque stylization occur.

Contents:

1. Jerome, *Commentarii in Ezechielem* [binding fragments].

inc.: [recto] theodotioque [*sic*] <στη>ρ<ι>γμα id est firmamentum interpretati quod autem opere . . . [1.4.1509]; expl.: [verso] . . . genitum posita est <ut quia e>rat notus in [2.5.73]

The fragments were cut from the same folio of the parent manuscript; pieces match to create a continuous flow of text; fragments in very mutilated condition from extraction; source unknown.

Edition: *CPL* 587.

Owners & Provenance: Acquired from King Alfred's Notebook (Cayce, SC) by the university in October 2013.

Frag. I. 27

Origin: Southern Italy, s. xii[ex] (Benevento).
Content Overview: Office book, neumed (binding fragment).

In Latin, on parchment; 1 piece; 141 x 261 mm (piece) [see Layout for ruling].

Layout: Ruled using hard-point technique; indentations on the flesh side; two columns.

Script: A single hand (M1) writes all text in Beneventan minuscule; later additions (s. xvi–xvii) are written on the recto and verso.

Decoration:
I. Rubrication: Rubrics in red ink; Beneventan-style letter heightening of majuscules in red and yellow.
II. Initials: Plain initials occur in hierarchy.
a. Plain initials in red ink occur within the staves (approx. 2 lines in height) and begin the antiphons.

Music & Staves: Three-line staves traced using hard-point technique with C traced in yellow ink and F in red ink; Beneventan neumes in black ink.

Contents:

1. Office book, neumed [binding fragment].

inc.: [recto[a]] mirra<m> offerimus si carnis uitia per abstinentiam mortificamus per mirram namque ut diximus agitur ne mortua caro putrefiat . . .; expl : [verso[b]] . . . uidimus stellam eius in oriente et uenimus cum muneribus ador<a>re dominum. ad magnificat. inter*.

The recto begins with Gregory the Great's *Homiliae in Euangelia* [*CPL* 1711, 1.10.6, p. 70]; the verso contains antiphons for the Epiphany.

Owners & Provenance: Mark Lansburgh (d. 2013); Ernst Boehlen Collection (Bern, Switzerland); acquired from King Alfred's Notebook (Cayce, SC) by the university in January 2014.

Sales & Catalogues: Sotheby's, 7 December 1999, lot 6; Christie's, 20 November 2013, lot 24 (Sale 1160); King Alfred's Notebook, *Enchiridion* 17, no. 28; ibid., *Enchiridion* 21, no. 25.

Former Shelfmark: MS. 1123 ES (Ernst Boehlen Collection; fragment cited as "s.n." by V. Brown 2008 when it was in the collection of Mark Lansburgh).

Bibliography: V. Brown 2008, 309, 327; V. Brown 2012, 251, 269.

Frag. I. 28

Origin: Italy, s. xi^{ex}.
Content Overview: Mass book, neumed (binding fragments).

In Latin, on parchment; 2 ff.; generally 323 x 217 mm (page) [see Layout for ruling].

Foliation: Each leaf is foliated in modern pencil with Arabic numerals in the upper right corners (1 and 1A); numbering may have been part of the shelfmark when the fragments were in the Ernst Boehlen Collection.

Layout:

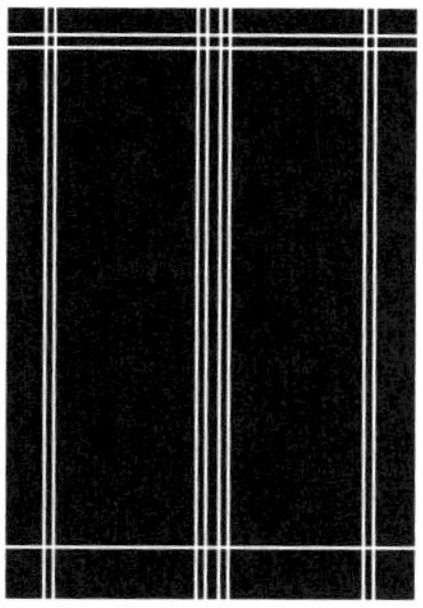

A

A Hard-point; 276 x 162 mm; intercol. 17 mm; 36 lines.

Pattern A is ruled using hard-point technique (New Style); two columns (intercol. 17 mm); writing above top line; prickings are visible in the outer margin for text lines (f. 1A).

Script: A single hand (M1) writes all text in a late Caroline minuscule; an ownership mark in (presumably) the autograph of Domenico Maria Manni is written in the upper margin of f. 1r: "di Domenico Maria Manni fortassis saeculi ix uel x."

Decoration:
I. Rubrication: Rubrics in red ink.
II. Initials: Plain initials occur in hierarchy.

A. Plain initials (2 lines half inset) drawn in red ink under the influence of capitalis begin each section of text; black initials mixing capitalis and uncial forms are used as versals (hanging) and begin some of the neumed sections.

Music & Staves: Adiastematic neumes are written in black ink above sung portions.

Contents:

1. Mass book, neumed [binding fragments].

INC.: [f. 1r[a]] mater eius et fratres stabant foris querentes loqui ei dixit autem ei quidam ecce mater tua . . .; **EXPL.:** [f. 1Av[b]] . . . et de excelso caelorum <habitaculo> et benedic populo*** [*mutil.*] [Dt 26.15].

Both leaves are sequential, containing in fragmentary form: Wednesday, first week of Lent (Fer. 4 Hebd. 1 Quad.), Thursday, First week of Lent (Fer. 5 Hebd. 1. Quad.), Friday, first week of Lent (Fer. 6 Hebd. 1 Quad.), and Saturday, first week of Lent (Sabb. Hebd. 1 Quad.). Much damage and mutilation remains from extraction; seven mutilated lines follow the recorded explicit from Dt. 26.

Owners & Provenance: Domenico Maria Manni (1690–1788); Mark Lansburgh (d. 2013) owned the leaves from 1978 to at least 1990 according to Sotheby's; Ernst Boehlen Collection (Bern, Switzerland); acquired from King Alfred's Notebook (Cayce, SC) by the university in January 2014.

Sales & Catalogues: Sotheby's, 6 July 2006, lot 8; Christie's, 20 November 2013, lot 32; King Alfred's Notebook, *Enchiridion* 17, no. 12.

Former Shelfmark: MS. 1108 ES (Ernst Boehlen Collection).

Frag. I. 29

Origin: Germany, s. xiii^{1}.
Content Overview: Gradual (binding fragment).

In Latin, on parchment; 1 piece; 263 x 51 mm (piece) [see Layout for ruling].

Layout: Ruled in brown ink.

Script: A single hand (M1) writes all text in Northern Textualis of the thirteenth century.

Decoration:
I. Initials: Plain initials occur in hierarchy.
a. Plain initials (1 line versals) in red ink begin the chants.

Music & Staves: Adiastematic neumes in black ink added above the text.

Contents:

1. Gradual [binding fragment].

inc.: [recto] <cre>do in unum deum patrem . . .; **expl.:** [verso] . . . <i>te pax uobis uite mis<ssa est>.

Fragment of a mass book used as spine lining; recto contains *Credo* and *Sanctus*; verso contains *Sanctus* trope (unidentified), *Agnus* trope (*Vulnere quorum*), *Ite missa est.*

Owners & Provenance: Acquired from King Alfred's Notebook (Cayce, SC) by the university in April 2014.

Frag. I. 30

Origin: Austria or Germany, s. xiii^{in}.
Content Overview: Breviary, neumed (binding fragment).

In Latin, on parchment; 1 piece; 165 x 290 mm (piece) [see Layout for ruling].

Layout: Ruled in brown ink in two columns; writing above top line; prickings visible in upper margin for double vertical bounding lines and intercolumnium (three prickings); prickings in the inner margin for all horizontals.

Script: A single hand (M1) writes all text in an early Northern Textualis which exhibits numerous transitional features. M1 employs a smaller script for the chanted portions [see Music & Staves].

Decoration:
I. Rubrication: Rubrics written in red ink; letter heightening of majuscules in red ink.
II. Initials: Flourished and plain initials occur in hierarchy.
a. Flourished initials (hanging) in blue and red ink with contrasting penwork occur on the recto.
b. Plain initials (1 line half inset) in red ink occur on the recto and verso.
III. Line Fillers: Lines in red ink connect divided syllables in neumed sections.

Music & Staves: Adiastematic neumes written above the smaller script for chanted portions.

Contents:
1. Breviary [binding fragment].
inc.: [recto[a]] litis uincula astringe pacis federa omni. lectio .vj. hoc ergo utrumque unus est christus . . .; expl.: [verso[b]] . . . dominum inuitantem et dicentem uenite ad me omnes qui labora<tis>.

Contains part of matins for Trinity Sunday.

Owners & Provenance: Acquired from King Alfred's Notebook (Cayce, SC) by the university in July 2014.

Sales & Catalogues: King Alfred's Notebook, *Enchiridion* 18, no. 66.

Frag. I. 31

Origin: Italy, s. xiv^{1}.
Content Overview: Giles of Rome, *Quaestiones.*

In Latin, on parchment; 7 ff.; generally 265 x 193 mm (page) [see Layout for ruling]; foliated in modern pencil with Arabic numerals.

Collation: $1^{2} + 2^{6-1}$

Quires: Quire 1 is an artificially constructed bifolium, H/H, with modern Japanese paper connecting ff. 1–2. Quire 2 is a ternion, H/F, with the last leaf canceled; the entire manuscript obeys Gregory's Rule; trimmed.

Layout:

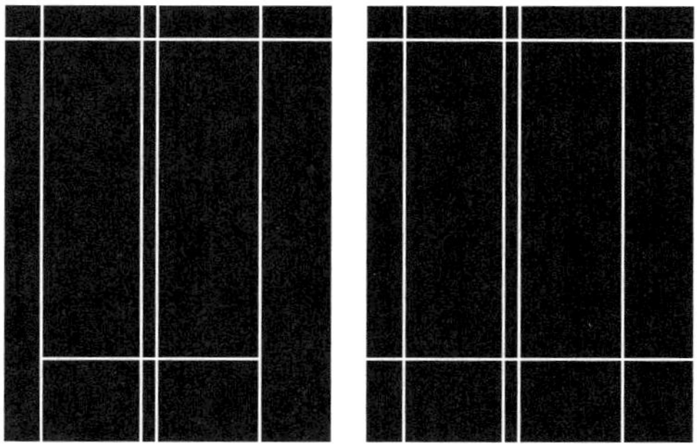

A A1

A ff. 2r–7v. Lead; 194 x 130 mm; intercol. 9 mm; 50–60 lines.

Pattern **A** is traced in lead on ff. 2r–7v; two columns (intercol. 9 mm); writing below top line; prickings visible for single vertical bounding lines and intercolumnium. The variant pattern **A1** is created on ff. 6v–7v by extending the lower horizontal the width of the pages; text lines of **A1** also traced through the vertical bounding lines more prominently than those of **A**; dimensions of **A1** identical to **A**.

Script: Two main scribal bookhands (M1–M2) can be discerned. M1 writes Semitextualis Libraria on ff. 2r–6r. M2 writes Semihybrida Currens on ff. 6v–7v with a strong preference for loopless forms, and admits deviant forms of **a** in initial position. M2 makes frequent corrections to the text of M1 using a variety of techniques: corrections within the text are inserted as additions over strikes, expuncted forms, and carets; other corrections use transformations, and those written in the margins are inserted with *signes-de-renvoi.* Corrections via rasura are those of M1. Elements of the script of M1 and M2 indicate clearly a university text. A third hand (M3) of the sixteenth century also corrects the text with expuncti and marginal text inserted with *signes-de-renvoi.* Various pen trials, Arabic numerals, and writing of the eighteenth century appear throughout the manuscript in dark black ink.

Decoration:

I. Initials: No initials are present, but 3 line square insets are reserved for the first three *quaestiones*, and one 2 line square inset for the fourth.

Contents:

1. Giles of Rome, *Quaestiones*—ff. 2r^{a}–7v^{a}.

RUB.: [*in sup. marg.*] questiones domini egidii.

1.1. *Quaestio*—f. 2r^{a}–v^{b}. INC.: <q>uestio est utrum substantia creata possit esse inmediatum principium alicuius operacionis ita quod posita anima non sit aliud superadditum substantie ipsius anime . . .; EXPL.: . . . simul cum substantia anime non incipiunt inmediate in substantia anime naturaliter fundari non possunt.

1.2. *Quaestio*—ff. 2v^{b}–4v^{b}. INC.: <q>uestio est utrum caritas siue aliquis habitus uel qualitas uel [-quia aut augetur] aliqua forma accidentalis possit augeri secundum essentiam et in quam /sic\ quia aut augetur secundum essentiam . . .; EXPL.: . . . ex alia et alia dispositione substantiali explicit ista questio.

1.3. *Quaestio*—ff. 4v^{b}–6r^{b}. INC.: <q>uestio est utrum idem sit augeri caritatem secundum substantiam et secundum uirtutem et uide[-a]tur quod non quia uirtus est mediatum inter substantiam et operacionem sed uirtus caritatis non est idem . . .; EXPL.: . . . augeri et perfici secundum agere et hec de quesito sufficiant.

1.4. *Quaestio*—ff. 6v^{a}–7r^{b}. INC.: <q>uestio est utrum scientia dei possit dici practica et utrum intellectus eius rationali aliorum a se possit dici practicus . . .; EXPL.: . . . facere disponeret siue uellet et hec de quesito sufficient explicit amen amen amen amen amen amen amen amen amen.

1.5. *Quaestio*—f. 7v^{a}. INC.: queritur utrum scientia que dicitur theologia que habitur hic . . . in uia sit eadem cum scientia beatorum; EXPL.: . . . perfecte hec erit in prima que est maior quam illa que est per fidem continetur.

The *quaestiones* in 1.1, 1.2, and 1.4. are also found in Nürnburg, Stadtbibliothek, Cent. I. 67 [see Schneider 1967, 78–81, nos. 9a, 9b, 9d].

Owners & Provenance: Acquired from Les Enluminures (Chicago, IL) by the university in 2014.

Sales & Catalogues: Libreria Alberto Govi di Fabrizio Govi Sas, Cat. 2013, no. 1.

Bibliography: Dumont, forthcoming.

Frag. I. 32

Origin: Italy, s. xiii^{2}.
Content Overview: Gregory the Great, *Homiliae in Ezechielem prophetam* (leaf).

In Latin, on parchment; 1 f.; 144 x 97 mm (page) [see Layout for ruling].

Layout:

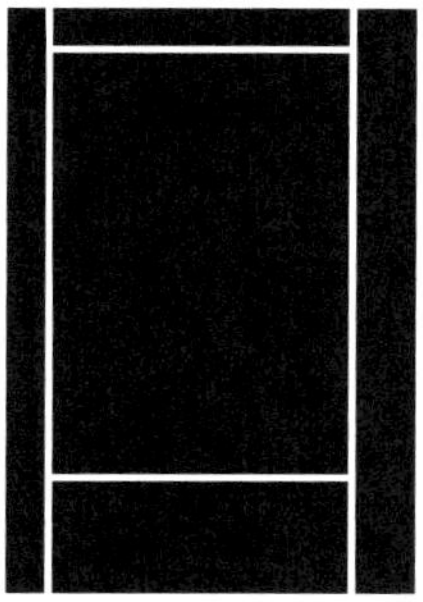

A

A Lead; 105 x 72 mm; 20 lines.

Pattern **A** is traced in lead; single column; writing below top line; no prickings are visible.

Script: A single hand (M1) writes all text in Semitextualis Libraria, admitting two compartment **a** occasionally; cursive forms of **d** intrude with some regularity on the recto; Tironian **et** crossed, which is unusual for Italian hands; a second hand (M2) adds missing text in the lower margin of the verso; a third hand (M3) adds marginal citations using Arabic numerals.

Decoration:
I. Rubrication: Letter heightening of majuscules in red ink.

Contents:

1. Gregory the Great, *Homiliae in Ezechielem prophetam* [leaf].

inc.: [recto] <suble>uare in altum et quibus subleuari ipse potuit in imis deponit . . . [1.4.101]; expl.: [verso] . . . quando ergo abdicamus mala que feci<mus> [1.4.154].

Contains Homily 4 from Book 1, 101–154.

edition: *CPL* 1710.

Owners & Provenance: Acquired from King Alfred's Notebook (Cayce, SC) by the university in May 2015. The parent manuscript was broken by Hartung & Hartung in 1993.

Sales & Catalogues: Swann, 22 March 1990, lot 131 (parent manuscript); Sotheby's, 17 December 1991, lot 49 (parent manuscript); King Alfred's Notebook, *Enchiridion* 21, no. 77.

Frag. I. 33

Origin: France, s. xv^2 (Rouen)
Content Overview: Calendar (leaf).

In French, on parchment; 1 f.; generally 171 x 128 mm (page) [see Layout for ruling]; edges of leaf dyed red.

Layout:

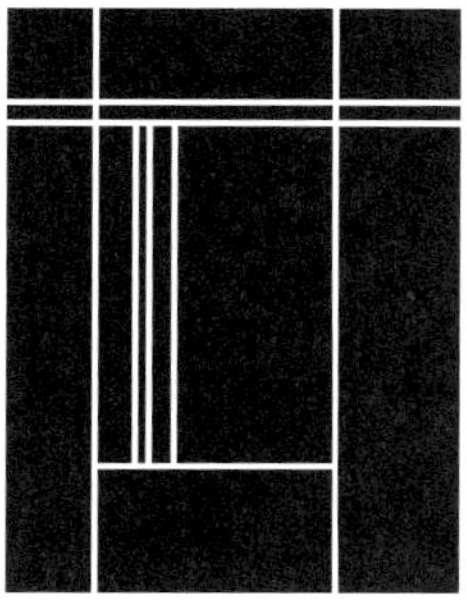

A

A Red ink; 100 x 68 mm; cols. 11.5/4/7/45 mm; 16 lines.

Pattern **A** is traced in red ink; four calendric columns (11.5/4/7/45 mm); writing below top line; no prickings visible.

Script: A single hand (M1) writes all text in Northern Textualis Formata.

Decoration:
I. Initials: Foliate initials occur in hierarchy.
a. One foliate initial (2 line half inset) occurs on the recto.

II. Borders & Frames:

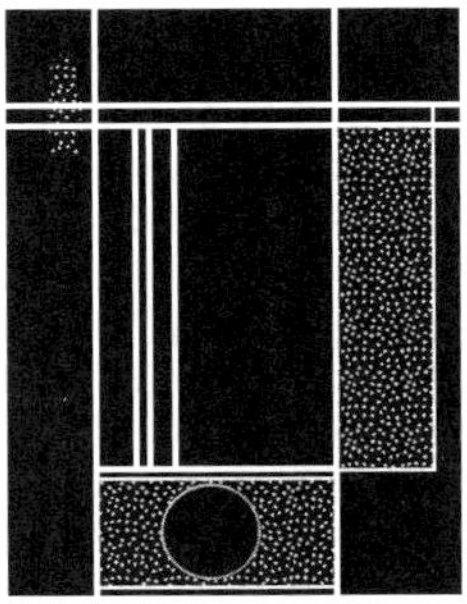

B

A functional outer border (**B**) comprised of blue and gold acanthus with blue, pink, red, and green florals incorporating gold grounds and black and gold rinceaux is painted on the recto (reverse on verso). A border of the same motifs in a rectangle frames the roundel containing the miniature in the lower margin. The area to be decorated for both borders is defined in red ink which is darker than the ruling. A functional piece border comprised of black and gold rinceaux and red and blue florals sprays from the initial in the inner margin.

Miniatures: A miniature in a roundel framed in black ink occurs in the lower margin. Miniature depicts the noble labors for May: two lovers on horseback with fronds courting; the man holds a hawk; white hunting dog.

Calendar: Two pages per month; recto/verso; non-composite calendar; historiated with monthly labors; all dominical letters in gold; Roman time with numerals alternates in red and blue ink.

Contents:

1. Calendar (Rouen) [leaf].

Calendar leaf for May in red and blue ink with graded feasts in gold; fifteen days filled; includes the translation of Ouen (May 5).

Owners & Provenance: Acquired from King Alfred's Notebook (Cayce, SC) by the university in July 2015.

Sales & Catalogues: King Alfred's Notebook, *Enchiridion* 21, no. 1.

Frag. I. 34

Origin: France, s. xiii^{2} (Paris).
Content Overview: Bible (leaf).

In Latin, on parchment; 1 f.; 230 x 160 mm (page) [see Layout for ruling].

Layout:

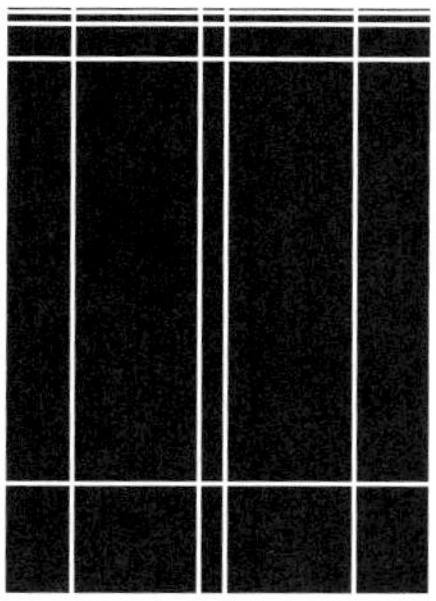

A

A Lead; 167 x 107 mm; intercol. 10 mm; 51 lines.

Pattern A is traced in lead; two columns (intercol.= 10 mm); writing below top line; no prickings remain.

Script: A single hand (M1) writes all text in Northern Textualis Formata.

Decoration:
I. Rubrication: Rubric in red ink.
II. Initials: Historiated and decorated initials occur in hierarchy.
a. One historiated initial P (9+22 lines taken up) is painted on the recto in Parisian style; depicts Moses leading a group. The historiated initial is attributed to the Dominican Painter (Branner 1977, 118–122).
b. Two decorated initials (3 lines square inset) begin the chapter on the verso; same style as above.

1. Bible [leaf].

INC.: [recto] <lit>tore maris habitat et in statione nauium pertingens usque ad sydonem . . . [Gn 49.13]; EXPL.: [verso] . . . de infantibus hebreorum est cum soror pu<eri> [Ex 2.7].

1.1. Gn 49.13–50.25—recto[a]–verso[a]. INC.: <lit>tore maris habitat et in statione nauium pertingens usque ad sydonem . . .; EXPL.: . . . et conditus aromatibus repositus est in loculo in egipto.

1.2. Ex 1.1–2.7—verso[a–b]. RUB.: incipit liber exodi; INC.: hec sunt nomina filiorum israel qui <i>ngressi sunt in egiptum cum iacob . . .; EXPL.: . . . de infantibus hebreorum est cum soror pu<eri>.

OWNERS & PROVENANCE: Acquired from De Brailes Medieval Art (Charleston, SC) by the university in August 2015. The parent manuscript, W.116, was one of the so-called Chester Beatty Bibles. W.116 was broken by Folio Fine Art (London) in 1969 after Sotheby's Beatty sale of December 1968. Known leaves are:

Gn 49.13–Ex 2.7	Notre Dame, Univ. Notre Dame, Hesburgh Library, Frag. I. 34
Ios 24.22–Idc 2.11	Notre Dame, Univ. Notre Dame, Snite Musuem of Art, Acc. 1989.20.2
2 Rg 24.21–3 Rg 1.53	Notre Dame, Univ. Notre Dame, Snite Musuem of Art, Acc. 1989.20.3
Ps 144.21–Prv 1	Boulder, Univ. Colorado, Norlin Library, MS 320
Prv 31.5–Ecc 2.17	Dublin, Chester Beatty Library, W 116 f. 54
12 leaves from Io	San Francisco, John Windle, March List 2014, no. 12

SALES & CATALOGUES: Sotheby's, 3 December 1968, lot 14 (parent manuscript).

Frag. I. 35

Origin: France, s. xiii.
Content Overview: Ovid, *Metamorphoses*, glossed (binding fragment).

In Latin, on parchment; generally 175 x 47 mm (piece) [see Layout for ruling].

Layout: Ruled in lead; single column of text in scholastic presentation for glossing.

Script: A single hand (M1) writes the text of the *Metamorphoses* in Northern Textualis Libraria under the influence of an early Semitextualis; the rapidity of writing also allows the scribe to admit single compartment **a**. Interlinear and marginal glosses display documentary intrusions in their letter forms.

Contents:

1. Ovid, *Metamorphoses* [binding fragment].

inc.: [recto] cognoscite uestrum <uerba animo desunt reson>at latratibus ether . . . [*Met.* 3.230–231]; expl.: . . . occuluere suis lact<isque alimenta dedere> [*Met.* 3.313].

In fragmentary form, the recto contains *Met.* 3.230–270; verso *Met.* 3.273–313. Instances of interlinear and marginal glosses from an unidentified commentary remain.

Owners & Provenance: Acquired from King Alfred's Notebook (Cayce, SC) by the university in October 2015.

Frag. I. 36

Origin: Low Countries, s. xiii^{2}.
Content Overview: Psalter-Hours (leaf).

In Latin, on parchment; generally 93 x 69 mm (page) [see Layout for ruling].

Layout:

A

A Lead; 68 x 45 mm; 12 lines.

Pattern A is traced in lead; single column; writing below top line; no prickings visible; trimmed.

Decoration:

I. Rubrication: Rubrics in red ink; letter heightening of majuscules in red ink.

II. Initials: Dentelle initials occur.

a. Dentelle initials (2 line square inset; 1 line versals) occur in hierarchy; initials of the 2 line size are inhabited with grotesques in blue, orange, and green.

III. Line Fillers: Line fillers in dentelle style are painted on the verso.

IV. Borders & Frames: Dentelle style borders spray from the 2 line initials on the recto and verso; border on the recto in three-margins style; border on verso sprays into inner and upper margin only. A dog chasing a hare is drawn in the lower margin of the verso.

Script: A single hand (M1) writes all text in Northern Textualis Formata of the thirteenth century.

Contents:

1. Psalter-Hours [leaf].

inc.: [recto] dolorem meum. [Iob 10.20] responsum. deus eterne in cuius humana conditio potestate consistit animas fidelium defunctorum . . .; **expl.:** [verso] . . . nam et si ambulauero in medio umbre mortis non timebo mala quoniam tu mecum est [*sic*] [Ps 22.2].

Contains a portion of the Office for the Dead; Ottosen nos. 18 (responsory) and 184 (versicle).

Owners & Provenance: Acquired from King Alfred's Notebook (Cayce, SC) by the university in November 2015.

Frag. II. 1

Origin: Italy, s. xii[1] (ca. 1140).
Content Overview: Atlantic Bible (leaf).

In Latin, on parchment; 1 f.; 404 x 261 mm (page) [see Layout for ruling].

Layout: Ruled using hard-point technique; two columns (intercol. 26 mm); writing above top line; indentations on flesh side; no prickings are visible.

Script: A single hand (M1) writes all text in an Italian Praegothica exhibiting many transitional features moving toward Southern Textualis (Rotunda).

Decoration:
I. Initials: Plain initials occur in hierarchy.
a. One plain initial (1 line half inset) in red ink begins Nm 15 on the verso[b]; the remnants of another beginning Nm 14 are visible on verso[a] (lost due to trimming).

Miniatures: Roundels on the recto depicting Jesus, Moses, and Aaron with vegetal motifs painted in pinks, reds, greens, grays, and yellow are modern forgeries (s. xx).

Contents:

1. Atlantic Bible [leaf].

inc.: [recto] contra moysen ait ascendamus et possideamus terram quoniam poterimus optinere eam . . . [Nm 13.31]; **expl.:** [verso] . . . et preceptum illius fecit irritum idcirco delebitur et portabit iniquitatem suam [Nm 15.30]

The leaf contains Nm 13.31–15.30; the outer portion of the leaf has been trimmed resulting in a small loss of text.

Owners & Provenance: Acquired from King Alfred's Notebook (Cayce, SC) by the university in May 2011.

Sales & Catalogues: King Alfred's Notebook, *Enchiridion* 4, no. 1.

Frag. II. 2

Origin: Italy, s. xv.
Content Overview: Antiphonary, Temporale (leaf).

In Latin, on parchment; 1 f.; generally 335 x 260 mm (page) [see Layout for ruling].

Layout:

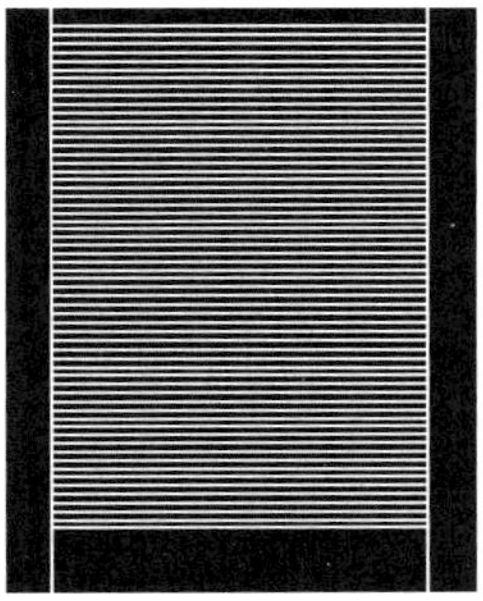

A

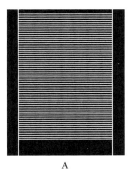

A Combined technique; 300 x 208 mm; 10 four-line staves, 10 text lines.

Pattern A is traced using a combined technique of red ink (staves) and lead (vertical bounding lines and text lines); single column/full-music layout; prickings are visible for text lines in the inner margin.

Script: A single hand (M1) writes all text in Southern Textualis Formata (Rotunda); corrections via rasura on the recto.

Decoration:
I. Rubrication: Rubrics in red ink.
II. Initials: Decorated and flourished initials occur in hierarchy.
a. Decorated initials (2 staves and two text lines square inset) executed in blue, green, orange, red, and white on gold grounds with floral motifs begin *Si oblitus fuero* on the verso.
b. Flourished initials (1 line versals) in blue ink with red penwork, and red ink with brown penwork alternate and begin antiphons and verses; many guide letters remain visible.

Music & Staves: Four-line staves traced in red ink with a rake; 15 mm; square neumes in black ink.

Contents:

1. Antiphonary, Temporale [leaf].

inc.: [recto] mundus autem gaudebit et uos gaudebitis et gaudium uestrum nemo tollet . . .; **expl.:** [verso] . . . super flumina babilonis illic sedimus et fleuimus dum recordaremur tui syon ad .lx. responsorum.

The recto contains portions of the Office for the Third Sunday after Easter (Dom. 3 p. Pascha); the verso contains portions of the Office for the Fourth Sunday after Easter (Dom 4 p. Pascha), but is rubricated as Dom. 3. p. Pascha.

Owners & Provenance: Date and source of acquisition by the university are unknown.

Frag. II. 3

Origin: Italy, s. xv.
Content Overview: Gradual, Common of the saints (binding fragment).

In Latin, on parchment; 1 piece; generally 432 x 284 mm (piece) [see Layout for ruling].

Foliation: Contemporary foliation in red and blue ink with Roman numerals is centered in the upper margin; partially visible (f. cx).

Layout: Ruled using combined technique of red ink (staves) and lead (vertical bounding lines and text lines); single column/full-music layout.

Script: A single hand (M1) writes all text in Southern Textualis Formata.

Decoration:
I. Rubrication: Rubrics in red ink.
II. Initials: Flourished and plain initials occur in hierarchy.
a. Flourished initials (1 text line, 2 staff lines versals) alternate in blue and red ink with contrasting penwork.
b. Plain initials alternating in red and blue ink mark the folio number on the recto.

Music & Staves: Four-line staves are traced in red ink; 23 mm; square neumes in black ink.

Contents:

1. Gradual, Common of the saints [binding fragment].

inc.: [recto] <defi>cient omni bono graduale pretiosa in conspectu domini mors sanctorum eius . . .; **expl.:** [verso] . . . laudate pueri dominum laudate nomen domini alleluya. uersus.

Common for the feasts of martyrs from Easter to Pentecost; contents identical to those of the *Missale Romanum Mediolani*, 1474; edited in Lippe 1899, 425, lines 32–37.

Owners & Provenance: Donated to the university by the Sisters of St. Francis of Perpetual Adoration (Mount Alverno in Mishawaka, IN).

Former Shelfmark: MSE/MR 16f (Notre Dame).

Frag. II. 4

Origin: Spain, s. xvi[1].
Content Overview: Calendar, Carthusian (6 leaves).

In Latin, on parchment; 6 ff.; generally 372 x 258 mm (page) [see Layout for ruling].

Collation: 1^6

Quires: A single ternion, F/F, comprises the calendar; obeys Gregory's Rule; sewing removed.

Layout:

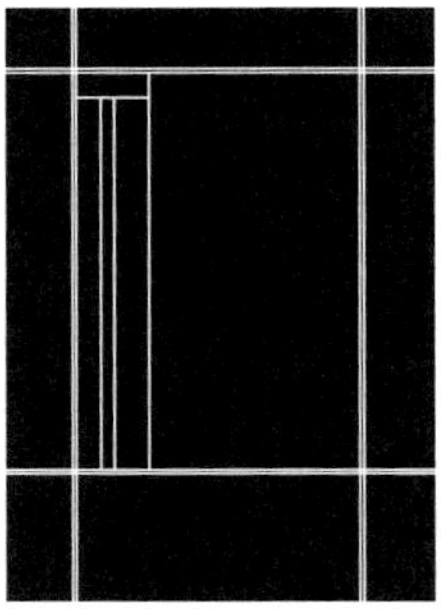

A

A Purple ink; 250 x 171 mm; cols. 15/18/21/127 mm; 33 lines.

Pattern **A** is traced in purple ink; four calendric columns (15/18/21/127 mm); writing below top line; thin double vertical bounding lines and horizontal through lines; no prickings are visible.

Script: A single hand (M1) writes all text in Southern Textualis Formata of the Spanish variety.

Decoration:
I. Rubrication: Rubrics and graded feasts in red ink.
II. Initials: Plain initials occur in hierarchy.
a. Plain initials (3 lines square inset) with white stylization mark **kl** alternating in red and blue ink per month.

Calendar: one page per month; dominical letter **a** in red ink; Roman time marked in red ink.

Contents:

1. Calendar (Carthusian)—ff. 1r–6v.

Liturgical calendar in black ink with graded feasts in red ink; one Spanish saint appears among several Carthusian saints; calendar is characteristically minimal. Significant feasts include: Illdefonso of Toledo (Jan. 23; *12 lectiones*); Hugo of Grenoble (Apr. 1; *12 lectiones*); Bruno (red; Oct. 6; *can. sermo*); Holy Relics (red; Nov. 8); *commemoratio defunctorum nostri ordinis* (red; Nov. 9; *memoria*); Hugo of Lincoln (red; Nov. 17; *can.*).

Owners & Provenance: Acquired from King Alfred's Notebook (Cayce, SC) by the university in July 2013; the parent manuscript is unknown.

Sales & Catalogues: King Alfred's Notebook, *Enchiridion* 16, no. 32.

Frag. II. 5

Origin: France or Low Countries, s. xv^2.
Content Overview: Missal (binding fragment).

In Latin, on parchment; 1 piece; 424 x 307 mm (piece) [see Layout for ruling].

Layout: Ruled in brown ink; 317 x 206 mm (ruling); two columns (intercol. 23 mm); 33 lines; no prickings are visible.

Script: A single hand (M1) writes all text in Northern Textualis Formata under English influence.

Decoration:
I. Rubrication: Rubrics in red ink; letter heightening of majuscules in yellow ink.
II. Initials: Flourished initials occur in hierarchy.
a. Flourished initials (2 lines square inset) in blue and red ink with contrasting penwork alternate on the recto and verso.

Contents:

1. Missal [binding fragment].

rub.: incipiunt officium uisitationis beate marie uirginis introitus misse; **inc.:** [recto] gaudeamus omnes in domino diem festum celebrantes in honore marie uirginis . . .; **expl.:** [verso] . . . per hoc sacrificium quod sumpsimus ut a tue uisitationis gracia nullatenus excidamus per.

Contains the feast of the Visitation BMV (Jul. 2).

Owners & Provenance: Anonymous donation to the university in December 2013; the book from which the fragment was extracted is unknown.

Frag. III. 1

Origin: France, s. xv (Brittany, ca. 1450).
Content Overview: Book of Hours, use of Vannes and Rennes.

In Latin, on parchment; 92 ff.; generally 173 x 135 mm (page) [see Layout for ruling]; ff. 89v and 111v blank but ruled.

Quires: The manuscript is now broken; a collation statement given in Pope 1999, no. 8 is conjectural and not forensically reliable.

Catchwords: Horizontal catchwords remain on ff. 28v and 121v; each correspond.

Foliation: Three sets of foliation in modern pencil with Arabic numerals appear; two sets in the upper right corner are those before the manuscript was broken and are used in this description; the third set is written in the lower right margin and differs in various increments as the manuscript was cut apart and disseminated.

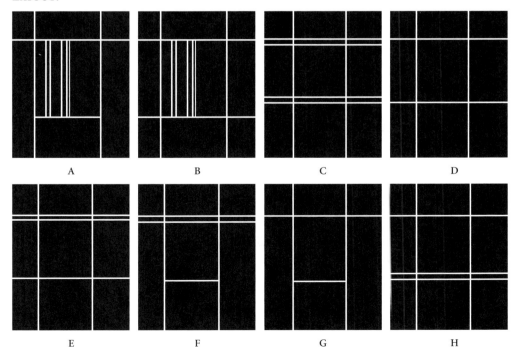

Layout:

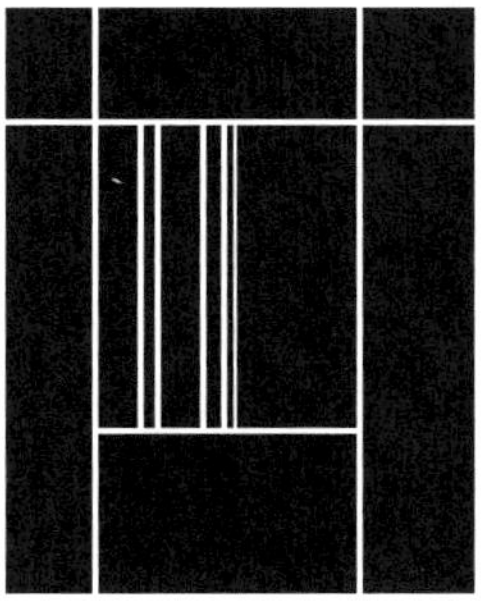
A

B

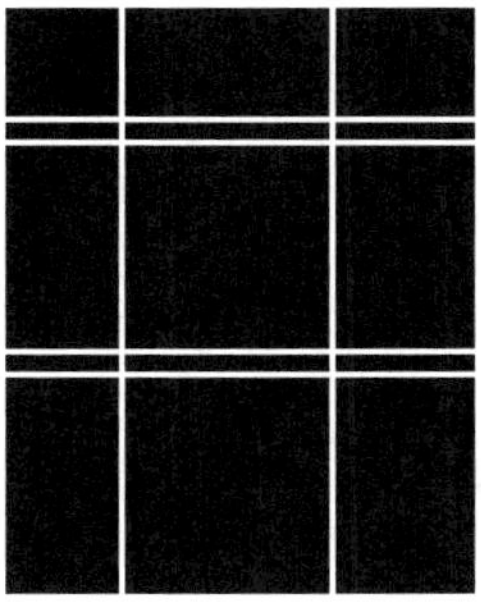
C

D

E

F

G

H

A ff. 1r–3v, 4v–5r, 6r–8v, 11r. Rose ink; 91–93 x 76 mm; cols. 13/5/13/6/2/40 mm; 17 lines.

B ff. 4r, 5v, 9r–10v, 11v–12v. Rose ink; 91–93 x 76 mm; cols. 13/5/13/6/2/40 mm; 17 lines.

C ff. 13r–v, 18v, 19r–21v, 24r–29v, 36r–v, 47r–58v, 64r–v, 66v, 69r–70v, 73r–v, 78r–v, 91v, 93v, 94r–v, 96r–v, 114r–v, 121r–v, 123r, 128r–v. Rose ink; 75 x 61 mm; 12 lines.

D ff. 14r–16v, 84r–v, 85v, 86r, 87r–v, 108r–v, 109r, 110v, 111v. Rose ink; 75 x 60 mm; 12 lines.

E ff. 18r, 31r–34v, 66r, 67r–v, 72r–v, 76v, 79r, 88r–v, 89v, 91r, 92r–93r, 95r–v, 98r–v, 101r–102v, 105r–v, 117v–118r, 122r–v, 125r–126v, 129r–v. Rose ink; 74 x 62 mm; 12 lines.

F ff. 68r–v, 71r–v, 74r–76r, 79v, 80r–v, 89r, 117r, 118v, 123v, 124r–v, 127r–v. Rose ink; 76 x 62.5 mm; 12 lines.

G ff. 85r, 86v, 106r–107v, 111r. Rose ink; 76 x 61 mm; 12 lines.

H ff. 109v, 110r. Rose ink; 76 x 62 mm; 12 lines.

Patterns **A** and **B** are traced in rose ink for the calendar; 6 calendric columns (13/5/13/6/2/40 mm; fifth col. is superfluous); writing below top line; prickings visible in the inner margins of ff. 9–12 only. Patterns **C**, **D**, **E**, **F**, **G**, **H** are traced in rose ink throughout the manuscript; single column; writing below top line; prickings only visible on ff. 15 and 16 in the inner margin. The manuscript was ruled by the opening which accounts for the variable patterns, especially between the recto and verso of the same folio.

Script: A single hand (M1) writes all texts in Northern Textualis Formata; a smaller script is used for many antiphons, verses, and responses.

Decoration:

I. Rubrication: Rubrics in red ink; letter heightening of majuscules and cadels in yellow ink.

II. Initials: Foliate and dentelle initials occur in hierarchy; plain initials in calendar only.

a. Foliate initials (3–4 line square inset) begin the hours *BMV* and some of the hours *SC* and *SS* on ff. 49r, 56r, 57r, 58r, 69r, 76r, 87r, 88r, 114r.

b. Dentelle initials (2 line square inset; 1 line versals) occur throughout the manuscript. Those of the 2 line size mark textual divisions (psalms, suffrages, prayers, etc.) as well as many of the canonical hours *SC* and *SS* on ff. 63r, 67v, 68v, 73v, 74v, 79v, and 80v.

c. Plain initials (1 line) in red and blue ink occur in the calendar only and mark the dominical letter **a**.

III. Line Fillers: Line fillers in dentelle style occur throughout the manuscript; unfinished example on. f. 102v.

IV. Borders & Frames:

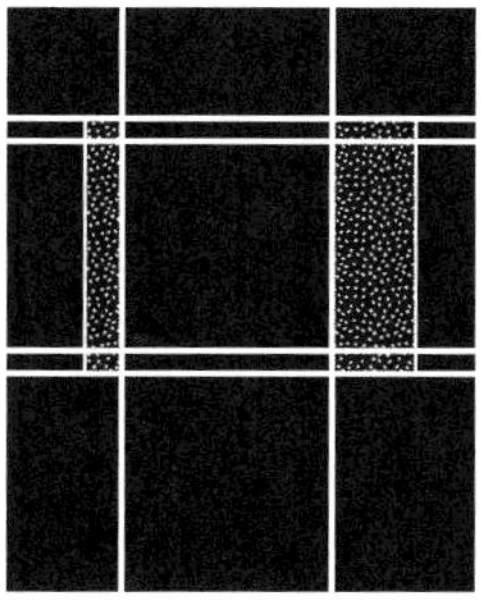

I

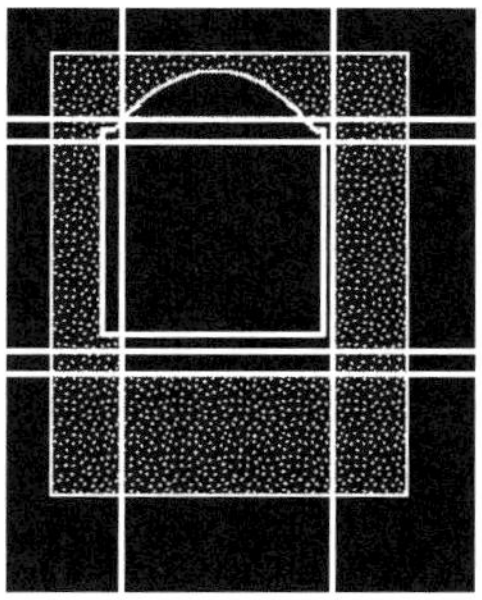

J

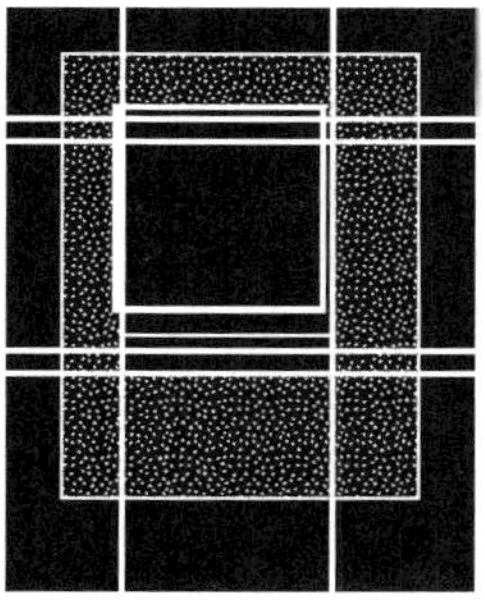

K

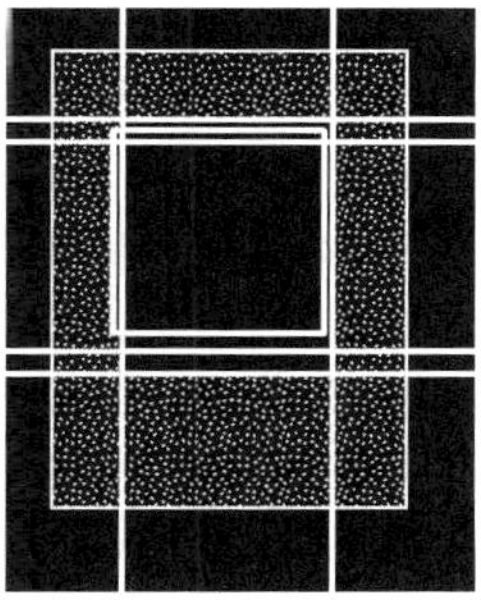

L

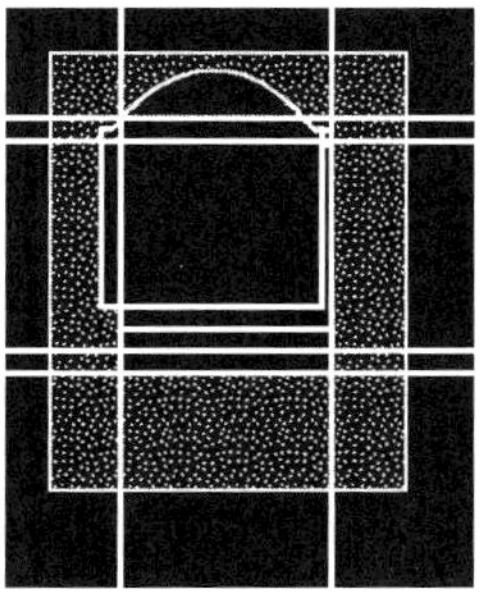

M

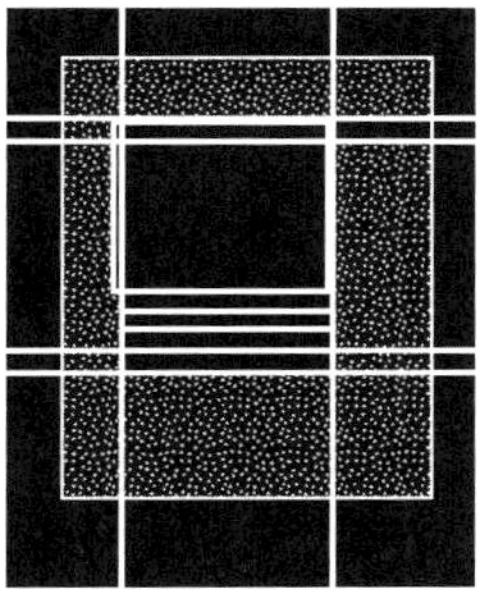

N

All text folios regardless of ruling pattern contain both left and outer borders (I) comprised of black and gold rinceaux and various floral, vegetal, and acanthus motifs in blues, greens, pinks, reds, oranges, and white; arrangement of the rectos mirrored on the versos; the area to be decorated often defined in the inner or outer side with lead. Four-margins borders comprised of black and gold rinceaux with the identical floral, vegetal, and acanthus motifs and palette are painted on all miniature folios; the area to be decorated is defined with lead; all frames are traced in black and gold, and vary in size and composition; the four-margins borders often incorporate dentelle style baguettes similar to line fillers to the left, right, or left and right of the miniature frames. Discernable types are: arch-topped frames with two text lines (J) on ff. 47r, 63r; square frames with three text lines (K) on ff. 48r, 58r, 87r, 88r; square frames with two text lines (L) on ff. 49r, 67v, 68v, 73v, 74v, 75v, 79v, 80v, 89r, 111r; arch-topped frames with three text lines (M) on ff. 50r, 56r, 57r; square frames with four text lines (N) on ff. 69v, 76r, 114r.

Miniatures: The calendar is historiated with twelve small miniatures depicting the monthly labors in both square and arch-topped frames. All miniatures except November (f. 11r) were originally in arch-topped frames; these were then converted to square frames except April (f. 4r) and May (f. 5r), which remain arch-topped. Miniatures are: man with hood and head-piece feasting (Jan.; f. 1r); man with hood warming feet by the fire (Feb.; f. 2r); man in tunic pruning vines with *falx* (Mar.; f. 3r); well-dressed man picking flowers (Apr.; f. 4r); well-dressed man with branch, courting (May; f. 5r); peasant mowing (Jun.; f. 6r); peasant reaping (Jul.; f. 7r); peasant threshing (Aug.; f. 8r); man stomping grapes in vat (Sept.; f. 9r); man with apron sowing fields (Oct.; f. 10r); woman feeding acorns to pigs (Nov.; f. 11r); man with axe slaughtering pig (Dec.; f. 12r).

Twenty-two large miniatures in arch-topped and square frames introduce the canonical hours and major texts: Peter Martyr (f. 47r; arch-topped), Francis receiving stigmata (f. 48r; square), John the Apostle (f. 49r; square), Nativity (f. 50r; arch-topped), Christ before Pilate (f. 50r; arch-topped), Mocking of Christ (f. 57r; arch-topped), Annunciation to shepherds (f. 59r; square), Flagellation (f. 63r; arch-topped), Christ carrying the Cross (f. 67v; square), Christ nailed to the Cross (f. 67v; square), Flight into Egypt (f. 69v; square), Crucifixion (f. 73v; square), expiration on the Cross (f. 74v; square), Three Living and Three Dead (f. 75v; square), Presentation in the temple (f. 76r; square), Deposition (f. 79v; square), Pietà (f. 80v; square), Entombment (f. 87r; square), kneeling figure (Christ?) with three others (f. 88r; square), Mary Magdalene (f. 89r; square), two saints (f. 111r; square), praying the Office of the Dead (f. 114r; square). Miniatures depicting the Visitation, Betrayal, Pentecost, Mass of St. Gregory, Crowning of Thorns, Adoration of the Magi, Coronation, and King David are known but still at large [see OWNERS & PROVENANCE].

CALENDAR: Two pages per month; recto/verso; historiated with monthly labors; dominical letter a in red or blue ink; Roman time marked in red and blue ink alternating in color; production contains many anomalies [see MINIATURES and CONTENTS 1].

CONTENTS:

1. Calendar (Vannes)—ff. 1r–12v.

Composite calendar with graded feasts in blue ink. The calendar is haphazardly copied and imitates deluxe specimens by alternating feast days in red and black ink with graded feasts in blue on ff. 1r, 4v (partial), 5r–8v, 10v, and 11v. All feasts on ff. 1v–4r, 9r–10r, and 11r are written in red ink and graded feasts in blue. Liturgical remnants from the calendar's exemplar were copied on ff. 2v (partial), 3v, 9v (partial), and 10r (partial) which specify nine or three *lectiones*, or a *commemoratio*.

Significant feasts include: Deposition of Gildas (Jan. 30), Angulus (Feb. 7), Albinus of Angers (Mar. 1), Winwaloe (Mar. 3), Deposition of Padarn (Apr. 16; blue), Gildas (May 11), Karanteg (May 16), Ivo of Kermartin (May 19; blue), ordination of Padarn (May 21), Gudwal (Jun. 6), Meriadeg (Jun. 7), Meven (Jun. 21), Bili (Jun. 23), Turiaw (Jul. 13), Samson (Jul. 28), William of Saint-Brieuc (Jul. 29), Melaine (Oct. 11), translation of Ivo (Oct. 20; blue), Gwenhael (Nov. 3; blue), Clarus (Nov. 3), Melaine (Nov. 6), Malo (Nov. 15), Columbanus (Nov. 21), Corentin (Dec. 12), and Guigner (Dec. 14). Another calendar for the use of Vannes found in København, Kongelige Bibliothek, Thott 114 8° is nearly identical.

2. *Obsecro te* (feminine forms; incomplete)—ff. 13r–16v.

INC.: [f. 13r] <ar>changelum annunciatus et conceptus est filius dei . . . mihi famule tue . . .; EXPL.: [f. 16v] . . . audi et exaudi me miseram peccatricem dulcissima domina mater dei et misericordie amen. salue regina misercordie. concede nos famulos [cf. LEROQUAIS 2:346–347].

3. Hours of the Virgin, use of Rennes; commemorations (*ad laudes*); Hours of the Cross (intercalated); Hours of the Holy Spirit (intercalated)—ff. 18r–21v, 24r–29v, 31r–34v, 36r–v, 47r–58v, 63r–v, 66r–76v, 78r–80v, 84r–88v.

3.1. Hours of the Virgin, use of Rennes [incomplete]—ff. 18r–21v, 24r–29v, 31r–34v, 36r–v, 50r–55v, 58r–v, 66r–67r, 69v–73r, 76r–69r, 84r–86v.

3.1.1. Matins—ff. 18r–21v, 24r–29v. HYM.: quem terra ponthus . . .; ANT. PS. 8: benedicta tu; LECT. I.: sancta maria uirgo . . .; R. I.: sancta et inmaculata . . .

3.1.2. Lauds [incomplete]—ff. 31r–34v, 36r–v. PSS.: 92 (incomplete), 99, 62, 66, Benedicite, 149.

3.1.3. Prime—ff. 50r–55v. PSS.: 53, 116, 117; HYM.: ueni creator spiritus . . .; ANT.: o admirabile; CAP.: gaude maria uirgo . . .; R.: ihesu christe fili dei uiui . . .; V.: qui de uirgine maria . . .

3.1.4. Terce [incomplete]—f. 58r–v. PSS.: 119; HYM.: pater [*sic*] dei sanctissima atque uirgo perpetua . . .; ANT.: quando natus.

3.1.5. Sext [incomplete]—ff. 66r–67r. PSS.: 123 (incomplete), 124; ANT. rubum quem uiderat . . .; CAP.: ego flos campi lilium . . .; R.: sancta dei genitrix . . .; V.: intercede pro nobis . . .

3.1.6. None—ff. 69v–73r. RUB.: [f. 69r] ad nonam; PSS.: 125, 126, 127; HYM.: enixa est puerpera . . .; ANT.: ecce maria; CAP. sicut cynamomum et balsamum . . .; R.: ora pro nobis sancta dei genitrix; V.: ut digni efficiamur . . .; V.: speciosa facta es . . .

3.1.7. Vespers [incomplete]—ff. 76r–79r. RUB.: [f. 75r] ad uesperas; PSS.: 121, 122, 123, 124, 125; ANT.: beata mater . . .; CAP.: beata es uirgo maria . . .;

3.1.8. Compline [incomplete]—ff. 84r–86v. PSS.: 128 (incomplete), 130; CAP.: maria uirgo semper lectare [*sic*] . . .; HYM.: uirgo dei genitrix . . .; ANT. POST NUNC DIM.: tota pulchra es amica mea . . .

3.2. Commemorations (*ad laudes*) [incomplete]—ff. 47r–49v.

3.2.1. Peter Martyr—f. 47r–v. INC.: hic est uere martiri qui pro christi nomine sanguinem suum fudit . . .; OR.: presta quesumus omnipotens deus ut qui beati petri martiris in natalicia . . . in tui nominis amore roboremur per [cf. *CO* 4518].

3.2.2. Francis—f. 48r–v. INC.: iste cognouit iusticiam et uidit mirabilia magna et exorauit . . .; OR.: deus qui ecclesiam tuam beati francisci meritis fetu . . . donorum semper participacione gaudere per [*CO* 1561].

3.2.3. John—f. 49r–v. INC.: iste est discipulus qui dignus fuit esse inter secreta dei . . .; OR.: ecclesiam tuam quesumus domine benignus infunde illustra ut beati iohannis apostoli tui et euuangeliste . . . ad dona perueniat sempiterna qui [cf. *CO* 2416b, 2416c].

3.3. Hours of the Cross (intercalated) [incomplete]—ff. 56r–v, 67v–68r, 73v–74r, 79r–80r, 87r–v.

Prime (f. 56r–v), Sext (ff. 67v–68r), None (ff. 73v–74r), Vespers (ff. 79v–80r), Compline (f. 87r–v).

3.4. Hours of the Holy Spirit (intercalated) [incomplete]—ff. 57r–v, 63r–v, 68v–69r, 74v–75r, 80v, 88r–v.

Prime (f. 57r–v). Terce (f. 63r–v), Sext (ff. 68v–69r), None (ff. 74v–75r), Vespers (f. 80v; incomplete), Compline (f. 88r–v).

4. Unfinished leaf—f. 89r–v.

Recto contains a miniature of Mary Magdalene, borders, and two blank lines; verso blank but ruled.

5. Penitential Psalms, Litany, and Collects—ff. 91r–96v, 98r–v, 101r–102v, 105r–110v.

5.1. Penitential Psalms [incomplete]—ff. 91r–96v, 98r–v, 101r–102v.

5.2. Litany [incomplete]—ff. 105r–110r.

Features Corentin among the martyrs; Maude, Ivo of Kermartin, Padarn, Malo, Albinus of Angers, William of St.-Brieuc, and Gildas among the confessors.

5.3. Collects—f. 110r–v.

5.3.1. f. 110r. INC.: deus cui proprium est misereri semper et parcere . . . miseracio tue pietatis absoluat per [*CO* 1143].

5.3.2. f. 110r–v. INC.: ure igne sancti spiritus renes nostros . . . et mundo corde placeamus per [*CO* 6025].

5.3.3. f. 110v. INC.: pretende domine famulis et famulabus tuis dexteram celestis . . . que tibi digne postulant assequantur qui ui(uis) [*CO* 4587a].

5.3.4. f. 110v. INC.: fidelium deus omnium [*CO* 2684b].

6. Unfinished leaf—f. 111r–v.

Recto contains a miniature of two saints, border, and two blank lines; verso blank but ruled.

7. Office of the Dead (Short Office Five)—ff. 114r–v, 117r–118v, 121r–129v.

OTTOSEN nos. 14-72-38.

Owners & Provenance: The parent manuscript was acquired by Joseph Pope (1921–2010) from H. & M. Fletcher (London) in January 1981 and formed part of his Bergendal Collection (Toronto, Ontario). After Pope's death in 2010, many of his manuscripts were sold by his children at Sotheby's in 2011. The parent manuscript was broken by a German firm soon after auction in July 2011 and was disseminated through eBay and various auction houses. The ninety-two leaves were acquired by the university through a series of acquisitions from private collectors, dealers, and auctions in Germany, France, and the United States between February 2012 and April 2015.

The parent manuscript (*olim* Bergendal MS 8) contained 129 folios of which three were blank before it was broken. To date there are thirty-seven leaves at large; unless specified the last known location/reference is London, Sotheby's, 5 July 2011, lot 113:

f. 17	Blank leaf	
ff. 22–23	Matins *BMV*	
f. 30	Visitation (Lauds *BMV*)	
f. 35	Lauds *BMV* (Dn 3.84–88+56; Ps 148.1–5)	Private Collection, USA
ff. 37–41	Lauds *BMV* (Ps 148.5 ff.)	
f. 42	Betrayal (Matins *SC*)	
f. 43	Pentecost (Matins *SS*)	
f. 44–45	Matins *SS*	
f. 46	Mass of St. Gregory (Suffrage).	Königstein im Taunus, Reiss & Sohn, Auction 146, lot 1239 (plate in Taffel 3)
ff. 59–61	Terce *BMV*	
f. 62	Crowning of Thorns (Terce *SC*)	
f. 64	Adoration of the Magi (Sext *BMV*)	
f. 65	Sext *BMV*	
f. 77	Vespers *BMV*	
f. 81	Coronation (Vespers/Compline *BMV*)	
f. 82	Compline *BMV* (Pss12.1–6, 42.1)	Private Collection, Netherlands
f. 83	Compline *BMV* (Pss 42.1–5, 128.2–3)	Private Collection, Netherlands
f. 90	King David (Penitential Psalms: Ps 6.1–6)	
f. 97	Penitential Psalms (Ps 50.7–5)	
ff. 99–100	Penitential Psalms (Ps 101.3–27)	
f. 103	Penitential Psalms (Ps 142.5 ff.)	
f. 104	Penitential Psalms/Litany (Ps 142; Litany before John the Baptist)	
ff. 112–113	Blank leaves	
ff. 115–116	Office of the Dead (Ps 114.8 to verse before Ps 145)	
ff. 119–120	Office of the Dead (Ps 94.1 to Ps 7.2)	

Sales & Catalogues: Sotheby's, 5 July 2011, lot 113 (parent manuscript). Leaves sold at auction (excluding eBay) or by booksellers: Reiss & Sohn, 1–2 November 2011 (Auction 146), lots 1236 (ff. 1–12), 1237 (f. 50), 1238 (f. 48), 1239 (f. 46), 1240 (f. 49), 1241 (f. 47), 1242 (ff. 51–55), 1243 (ff. 13–16, 28–29); Reiss & Sohn 2012, lots 677 (f. 67), 678 (f. 68), 679 (f. 73), 680 (f. 87), 681 (f. 89), 682 (f. 111); Griffon #52203 (f. 49); Pirages, Cat. 65, nos. 77 (f. 58), 78 (f. 76), 79 (f. 69), 80 (f. 56), 81 (f. 79); Auctionata, 23 March 2015, lot 4 (f. 88).

Former Shelfmark: Bergendal MS 8 (parent manuscript).

Bibliography: Stoneman 1997, 168; Pope 1999, no. 8.

Frag. V. 1

Origin: Italy, s. xvi^{in}.
Content Overview: Antiphonary, Sanctorale (leaf).

In Latin, on parchment; 1 f.; 576 x 353 mm (page) [see Layout for ruling].

Layout:

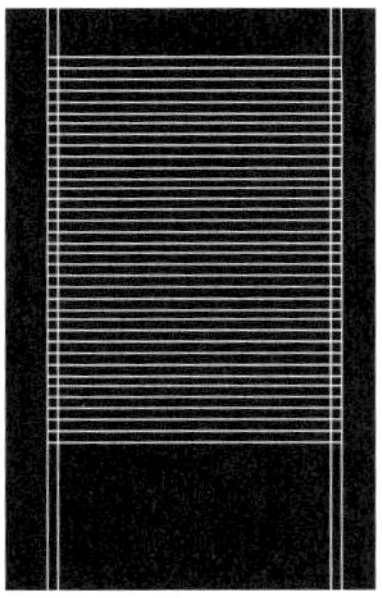

A

A Combined technique; 392 x 280 mm; 6 four-line staves, 6 text lines.

Pattern **A** is traced using a combined technique of red ink (staves and vertical bounding lines) and lead (text lines); single column/full-music layout; no prickings are visible.

Script: A single hand (M1) writes all text in Southern Textualis Formata (Rotunda).

Decoration:

I. Rubrication: Rubrics in red ink; letter heightening of cadels and majuscules in yellow ink.

II. Initials: Flourished and cadel initials occur in hierarchy.

a. Flourished initials (4 staves, one text line) alternate in red with brown penwork and blue with red penwork.

b. Cadels in black ink and penwork with yellow wash are used in second position following flourished initials and divisions within a verse or response.

Music & Staves: Four-line staves traced in red ink with a rake; 33 mm; square neumes in black ink.

Contents:

1. Antiphonal, Sanctorale [1 leaf].

inc.: [recto] mea dedit odorem suum . . .; **expl.:** [verso] . . . uirgo parens christi pa<ritura>.

Contains part of the Office of the Assumption or a Marian votive office.

Owners & Provenance: Library records indicate the fragment was donated by St. Mary's Hospital (Gallup, NM) in April 1933. The hospital was founded in 1916 by the Poor Sisters of St. Francis of the Perpetual Adoration as an infirmary for railroad workers. The hospital has been part of Rehoboth McKinley Christian Health Care Services since 1983; see also Frag. II. 3.

Former Shelfmark: MSE/MR 17f (Notre Dame).

Frag. V. 2

Origin: Spain, s. xvi.
Content Overview: Gradual, Sanctorale (leaf).

In Latin, on parchment; 1 f.; generally 581 x 395 mm (page) [see Layout for ruling].

Foliation: Contemporary foliation in red ink with Roman numerals is visible above the top staff line on the recto; other folio numbers are written above cues on the recto.

Layout: Ruled using a combined technique of red ink (staves) and lead (vertical bounding lines and text lines); 435 x 258 mm (ruling); single column/full-music layout; no prickings are visible; leaf is ripped and has fire damage in the lower margin.

Script: A single hand (M1) writes all text in a large Southern Textualis Formata displaying Spanish features.

Decoration:
I. Rubrication: Rubrics in red ink.
II. Initials: Flourished and cadel initials occur in hierarchy.
a. One flourished initial (1 staff and 1 text line) in red ink with blue penwork begins the introit on the recto.
b. One cadel (1 staff and 1 text line) in black ink begins the verse on the verso; smaller cadels are used as majuscules and follow flourished initials in second positions.

Music & Staves: Five-line staves traced in red ink; 37 mm; square neumes in black ink.

Contents:
1. Gradual, Sanctorale [leaf].
inc.: [recto] <interio>ra mea nomen sanctum eius . . .; **expl.**: [verso] . . . est et ego mundo. uersus uoce mea.

Contains portions of the masses for Michael (Sept. 29), Jerome (Sept. 30), and Francis (Oct. 4).

Owners & Provenance: Date and source of acquisition by the university are unknown.

Former Shelfmark: MSE/MR 18f (Notre Dame).

Frag. V. 3

Origin: Italy, s. xiii[1].
Content Overview: Antiphonary, Temporale (binding fragment).

In Latin, on parchment; 1 piece; generally 378 x 536 mm (piece) [see Layout for ruling].

Quires: The fragment was at one time a bifolium; flesh side is in very poor condition.

Layout: Ruled using hard-point technique and yellow and red ink [see Music & Staves]; single column/full-music layout; approx. 280 x 200 mm; 14–16 text lines with four-line staves between each.

Script: A single hand (M1) writes all text in Southern Textualis Formata (Rotunda) with transitional features; **e** caudata persists, frequent **st** ligatures, fusions are rare, but biting occurs more frequently; abbreviations are those of Rotunda.

Decoration:
I. Rubrication: Rubrics in red ink; letter heightening of majuscules in red ink.
II. Initials: Plain initials occur in hierarchy.
a. Plain initials (2 staff lines, 1 text line) in red ink begin antiphons, verses, and responses; when in the outer margin, initials are hanging placement; vestiges of Romanesque stylization apparent in some forms.

Music & Staves: Four-line staves traced using hard-point technique; C and F traced in yellow and red ink; 10 mm; square neumes in black ink.

Contents:

1. Antiphonary, Temporale [binding fragment].

inc.: [f. 1r] ***[*mutil. 1 ln.*] lux <perpetua lucebit sanctis tuis domine> et eternitas temporum alelluia alleluia ***[*uersus mutil.*] responsum de ore prudentis procedit mel alleluia dulcedo mellis est lingua eius . . .; expl.: [f. 1v] . . . sancti spiritus et anime iustorum hymnum dicite deo alleluia euoue. inc.: [f. 2r] alleluia alleuia uersus et unus de senioribus dixit . . .; expl.: [f. 2v] . . . in primum nocturnum antiphona alleluia alleluia ***[*mutil.*].

The fragment is very damaged on the flesh side and much text is illegible even under ultraviolet light; f. 1r–v contains portions of the Office for the common of saints during Eastertide; f. 2r–v contains portions of the Office for Easter Wednesday (Fer. 4 p. Pascha), Easter Thursday (Fer. 5 p. Pascha), Easter Friday (Fer. 6 p. Pascha), Saturday after Easter (Sabbato in Albis), Octave of Easter (Octaua Paschae).

Owners & Provenance: Acquired from Mackus Co. (Springfield, IL) by the university in May 2014; the book from which the fragment was extracted is unknown.

Constable MS 1

Origin: Low Countries, s. xv^{2} (Bruges).
Content Overview: Book of Hours, use of Rome (leaf).

In Latin, on parchment; 1 f.; generally 92 x 66 mm (page) [see Layout for ruling].

Layout:

A

A Rose ink; 48 x 36 mm; 12 lines.

Pattern **A** is traced in rose ink; single column; writing below top line; no prickings are visible.

Script: A single hand (M1) writes all text in Southern Textualis Formata of the Flemish variety.

Decoration:
I. Rubrication: Rubrics in red ink; letter heightening of majuscules in yellow ink.
II. Initials: Dentelle and flourished initials occur in hierarchy.
a. Dentelle initials (2 line square inset; hanging **i**) begin major sections of text.
b. Flourished initials (1 line versals) in blue ink with red penwork and gold with blue penwork alternate on the verso.

Contents:

1. Book of Hours, use of Rome [leaf].

inc.: [recto] <la>teribus domus tue filii tui sicut nouelle oliuarum . . .; **expl.**: [verso] . . . famulorum tuorum quesumus domine delictis ignosce ut.

1.1. None—recto–verso. **ant.**: pulcra est [*sic*] . . .; **cap.**: in plateis sicut cynamomum et balsamum . . .; **v.**: post partum uirgo . . .

Owners & Provenance: Donated to the university in August 2015 by Giles Constable in memory of his daughter, Olivia Remie Constable (1960–2014).

Constable MS 2

Origin: Low Countries, s. xv^2 (Bruges).
Content Overview: Book of Hours (leaf).

In Latin, on parchment; 1 f.; generally 134 x 97 mm (page) [see Layout for ruling].

Layout:

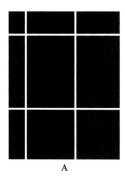

A

A Ink; 67 x 43 mm; 17 lines.

Pattern **A** is traced lightly in diluted ink; single column; writing below top line; no prickings are visible.

Script: A single hand (M1) writes all text in Southern Textualis Formata of the Flemish variety.

Decoration:
I. Rubrication: Rubrics in red ink.
II. Initials: Flourished and dentelle initials occur in hierarchy.
a. Flourished initials (2 line square inset) begin the first and second lessons.
b. A dentelle initial (1 line versal) begins the responsory on the verso.

III. Borders & Frames:

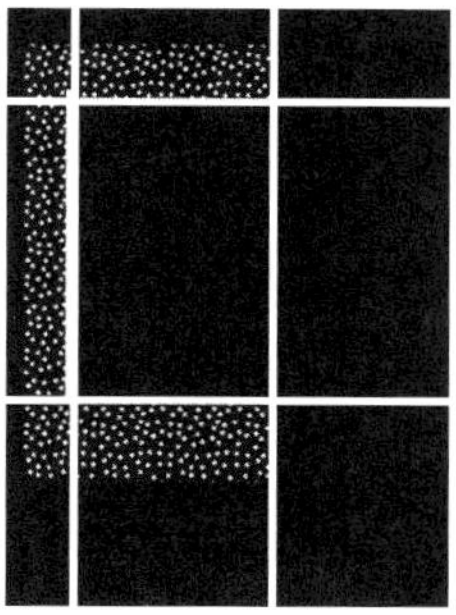

B

Bracket-left borders of black and gold rinceaux with orange, blue, and green acanthus and vegetal motifs are painted on the recto and verso (**B**); area to be decorated defined either by lead or hard-point (worn); frames in the outer margin of gold and white baguettes.

Contents:

1. Book of Hours [leaf].

inc.: [recto] <salua>torem meum. uersiculus. quem uisurus sum ego ipse et non alius . . .; expl.: [verso] manus tue domine fecerunt me et plas<mauerunt>.

Contains portions of the first responsory, first versicle, second reading, second responsory and versicle, and the beginning of the third reading for the Office of the Dead; responsories of the first nocturn are Ottosen nos. 14-72-x.

Owners & Provenance: Donated to the university in August 2015 by Giles Constable in memory of his daughter, Olivia Remie Constable (1960–2014).

Constable MS 3

ORIGIN: France, s. xiv^{1}.
CONTENT OVERVIEW: Bible (leaf).

In Latin, on parchment; 1 f.; generally 185 x 124 mm (page) [see LAYOUT for ruling].

LAYOUT:

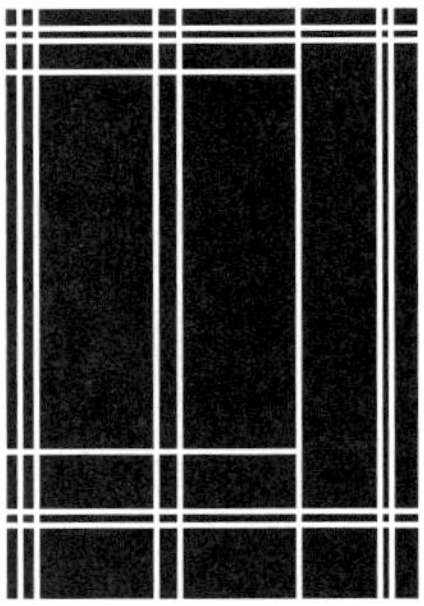

A

A Ink; 119 x 80 mm; intercol. 7 mm; 32 lines.

Pattern **A** is traced in black ink; two columns (intercol. 7 mm); writing below top line; prickings visible in the upper and lower margin for vertical bounding lines; leaf has been trimmed.

SCRIPT: A single hand (M1) writes all text in Northern Textualis Formata of the early fourteenth century.

DECORATION:
I. RUBRICATION: Letter heightening in red ink.
II. INITIALS: Flourished initials occur in hierarchy.
A. Flourished initials (1–2 line square inset) in red and blue ink with contrasting penwork begin the chapter and chapter number; flourished initials also mark the book in the upper margin.

III. Borders & Frames: Flourished border of red and blue ink with blue and red penwork sprays from the initial in the outer margin of the verso.

Contents:

1. Bible [leaf].

inc.: [recto] uir et nubes et impleuit atrium interius . . . [Ez 10.3]; expl.: [verso] . . . fili hominis fratres tui uiri propinqui tui et omnis domus [Ez 11.15].

Contains Ez 10.3–11.15.

Owners & Provenance: Donated to the university in August 2015 by Giles Constable in memory of his daughter, Olivia Remie Constable (1960–2014). The parent manuscript was broken by Otto F. Ege (1888–1951) and included in two of his portfolios, both entitled *Original Leaves from Famous Bibles, Nine Centuries, 1121 A.D.–1935 A.D.* Known leaves in institutional collections (including those from Gwara 2013, *Handlist* no. 61) are:

Austin, Univ. Texas, Harry Ransom Center, MS Leaf B10
Berea, Berea College, Hutchins Library, s.n.
Corning, Corning Community College, Arthur A. Houghton, Jr., Library, s.n.
Dallas, Southern Methodist Univ., Bridwell Library, MS 56
Oberlin, Oberlin College, Mudd Center, MS B3
Notre Dame, Univ. Notre Dame, Hesburgh Library, Constable MS 3
Providence, Providence Public Library, MS Ege 2

Locations of both *Original Leaves from Famous Bibles* portfolios are listed in Gwara 2013, 95–99, to which may be added:

Richmond (IN), Earlham College, Lilly Library, Z239 . O7

Bibliography: Gwara 2013, 95–99; Gwara 2013, *Handlist* no. 61.

Constable MS 4

Origin: England, s. xiii^{1}.
Content Overview: Processional (leaf).

In Latin, on parchment; 1 f.; generally 180 x 118 mm (page) [see Layout for ruling].

Layout:

A

A Combined technique; 132 x 80 mm; 9 four-line staves, 9 text lines.

Pattern **A** is traced using a combined technique of lead (verticals and text lines) and red ink (staves); single column/full-music layout; writing below top line; prickings visible in the outer margin for upper horizontal and all text lines.

Script: A single hand (M1) writes all text in Northern Textualis Formata, but transitional features remain; consistent use of half-uncial **d**, **st**, and **ct** ligatures, and the ampersand.

Decoration:
I. Rubrication: Rubrics in red ink.
II. Initials: Flourished initials occur in hierarchy.
a. Flourished initials (4 staves and 1 text line square inset) in blue with red penwork begin the chants after each rubric.

Music & Staves: Four-line staves traced in red ink; 7 mm; square neumes in black ink.

Contents:

1. Processional [leaf].

inc.: [recto] facio pascha cum discipulis meis et fecerunt discipuli sicut preseperat [*sic*] eis dominus . . .; **expl.**: [verso] . . . hic est qui de edom uenit tinctis bosra.

Owners & Provenance: Donated to the university in August 2015 by Giles Constable in memory of his daughter, Olivia Remie Constable (1960–2014). The parent manuscript was broken by Otto F. Ege (1888–1951), and leaves were included as Leaf no. 8 in his portfolio, *Fifty Original Leaves from Medieval Manuscripts.* The parent manuscript was at Wilton Abbey until ca. 1860 according to Altstatt 2016. Known leaves in institutional collections with individual shelfmarks (including those from Gwara 2013, *Handlist* no. 8) are:

Columbia, Univ. South Carolina, Thomas Cooper Library, Early MS 8 (Ege 8)
Greensboro, Univ. North Carolina, Jackson Library, Z6605. L3 E44_08
Iowa City, Univ. Iowa, Main Library, xfMMs. Gr3
Minneapolis, Univ. Minnesota, Elmer L. Anderson Library, Ege MS 8
New York City, Pierpont Morgan Library, MS M.1021.8
Notre Dame, Univ. Notre Dame, Hesburgh Library, Constable MS 4
Rochester, RIT, Wallace Center, Cary Collection, Portfolio Box 1–8
Toledo, Toledo Museum of Art, Acc. 1953.129H
Urbana, Univ. Illinois, William R. and Clarice V. Spurlock Museum, Acc. 1948.6.4

The shelfmarks of known *Fifty Original Leaves* portfolios in institutional collections containing leaves (see Gwara 2013, 106–107 for a list of portfolio numbers and locations) are:

Albany, New York State Library, 091 xE29m
Amherst, Univ. Massachusetts, W. E. B. Du Bois Library, MS 570
Athens, Ohio Univ., Vernon R. Alden Library, ND2920 . E45 1950x
Bloomington, Indiana Univ., Lilly Library, Z118 . A3 E28 (Ege mss.)
Boulder, Univ. Colorado, Norlin Library, ND2950 E38 1900
Buffalo, Buffalo and Erie County Public Library, RBR MSS. F54 1100
Cleveland, Case Western Reserve Univ., Kelvin Smith Library, Z109 . F54 1900z
Cleveland, Cleveland Public Library, Z109 . E34 1900z
Cleveland, Cleveland Institute of Art, Jessica R. Gund Library, ND2920 . E33
Cincinnati, Public Lib. of Cincinnati and Hamilton County, 096.1 ffF459
Columbus, Ohio State Univ., Thompson Memorial Library, MS Lat. 7
Gambier, Kenyon College, Olin Library, Z113 . F5
Granville, Denison Univ., William Howard Doane Library, Z113 . F5
Hartford, Wadsworth Atheneum Museum of Art (unaccounted for)
Kent, Kent State Univ., University Library, s.n.

Lima, Lima Public Library, Main Library, F-MEM 91 E Lufkin
Newark, Newark Public Library, Main Library (unaccounted for)
Northampton, Smith College, Neilson Library, MS 35
Saskatoon, Univ. Saskatchewan, Murray Library, MSS 14
Stony Brook, Stony Brook Univ., Frank Melville Jr. Memorial Library, Z109 . E4
Toronto, Art Gallery of Ontario (unaccounted for)
Toronto, Massey College, Robertson Davies Library, Gurney FF 0001
Toronto, Ontario College of Art and Design Univ., Dorothy H. Hoover Library, ND2920 E44 R.B.C. oversize

Bibliography: Gwara 2013, 106–107; Gwara 2013, *Handlist* no. 8; Altstatt 2016.

Constable MS 5

Origin: Italy, s. xii^2.
Content Overview: Gregory the Great, *Dialogi* (binding fragment).

In Latin, on parchment; 1 piece; generally 340 x 215 mm (piece) [see Layout for ruling].

Layout: Ruled using hard-point technique; indentations on hair side; single column; writing above top line; 246 x 137 mm.

Script: A single hand (M1) writes all text in Praegothica displaying several transitional features.

Contents:

1. Gregory the Great, *Dialogi* [binding fragment].

inc.: [recto] hic namque uenerabilis uir cum uitam multis plenam uirtutibus duceret . . .; **expl.:** [verso] . . . cuius ruinae et uerecundiae isdem iudaeus consulens qualiter hoc cognouisset uel quae in conuentu.

Contains 3.7.11–70 [*CPL* 1713].

Edition: De Vogüé 1978–1980; Simonetti and Pricoco 2005–2006.

Owners & Provenance: Donated to the university in August 2015 by Giles Constable in memory of his daughter, Olivia Remie Constable (1960–2014).

Constable MS 6

Origin: Italy, s. xiv[1].
Content Overview: *Authenticum* (leaf).

In Latin, on parchment; 1 piece; approx. 396 x 290 mm (page unfolded); approx. 215 x 150 mm (folded as document folio) [see Layout for ruling].

Layout: Ruled in lead; ruling 250 x 148 mm; two columns (intercol. 11 mm); writing below top line.

Script: A single hand (M1) writes all text in Southern Textualis Formata (Rotunda).

Decoration:
I. Rubrication: Rubrics in red ink; majuscules stylized with black penwork.
II. Initials: Decorated and flourished initials occur in hierarchy.
a. Historiated initials (7 lines square inset) in blue, orange, white, and grays feature a bearded man with acanthus sprays to the bottom of the page.
b. One flourished initial (1 line versal) in red ink with blue penwork begins the *praefatio* of *collatio* 9, *titulus* 9 following the rubric.
III. Borders & Frames: Flourished borders in red and blue ink with contrasting penwork occupy the outer margin of the recto and the outer margin and intercolumnium of the verso.

Contents:

1. *Authenticum* [leaf].

inc.: [recto[a]] humilitatis cognitionem in aliis quidem rebus quas constantinus gloriose memorie hyerio seniori . . .; expl.: [verso[b]] . . . quam nostris largitionibus et comitti [*sic*] priuatarum pro inferendis pecuniis unicuique predictarum.

Contains portions of Auth. coll. 9.8. = Nov. 159; and Auth. coll. 9.9 = Nov. 134. The leaf has been refolded and trimmed to create a document folio; leather cord attached to front flap.

Owners & Provenance: Donated to the university in August 2015 by Giles Constable in memory of his daughter, Olivia Remie Constable (1960–2014).

Constable MS 7

Origin: Spain, s. xiii^{in}.
Content Overview: Lectionary or Breviary (binding fragment).

In Latin, on parchment; generally 331 x 235 mm (piece) [see Layout for ruling].

Layout: Ruled in lead; two columns (intercol. 23 mm); prickings visible in the lower margin for intercolumnium.

Script: A single hand (M1) writes all text in an early phase of Southern Textualis using distinctive forms of Iberian Peninsula; transitional features still present, notably the use of the ampersand alongside Tironian **et**.

Decoration:
I. Rubrication: Rubrics in red ink; letter heightening of majuscules in red ink.
II. Initials: Flourished initials occur in hierarchy.
a. Flourished initials (6 line square inset) in Romanesque style are drawn in red ink with blue and green penwork.

Contents:

1. Lectionary or Breviary [binding fragment].

inc.: [recto] <fu>giendi audiuit autem ionathas sermones appollini et motus est animo . . . [1 Mcc 73/74]; **expl.:** [verso] . . . et ipse tamquam sponsus procedens de thalamo suo tanquam sponsus [*CPL* 1711, 2.38.3]

Owners & Provenance: Donated to the university in August 2015 by Giles Constable in memory of his daughter, Olivia Remie Constable (1960–2014).

Constable MS 8

ORIGIN: Low Countries, s. xiv^{in}.
CONTENT OVERVIEW: Bible, *Interpretation of Hebrew Names* (leaf).

In Latin, on parchment; 1 f.; generally 404 x 270 mm (page) [see LAYOUT for ruling].

SIGNATURES: An *ad hoc* signature (.iiij.) written in brown ink is visible in the lower margin of the recto.

LAYOUT:

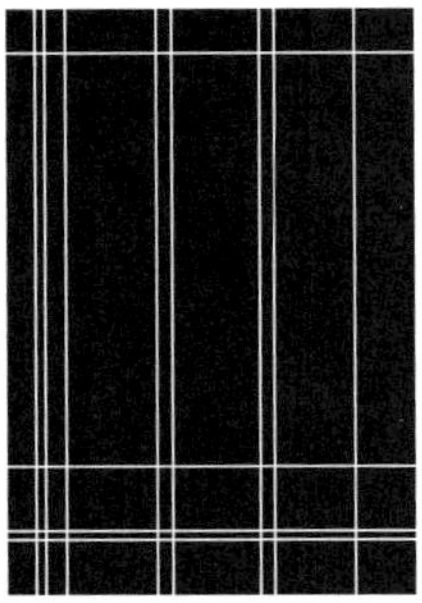

A

A Lead; 286 x 191 mm; intercol. 10 mm; 50 lines.

Pattern **A** is traced in lead; three columns (intercol. 10 mm); writing below top line; prickings visible in upper and lower margins for horizontal through lines and one vertical bounding line.

SCRIPT: A single hand (M1) writes all text in Northern Textualis Formata.

DECORATION:
I. INITIALS: Plain initials occur in hierarchy.
A. Plain initials (1 line versals) alternating in red and blue ink begin each Hebrew name.

Contents:

1. Bible [leaf].

INC.: [recto] alchath sculpsit . . .; EXPL.: [verso] . . . ananias donum gratie domini uel donata.

Contains a portion of the *Interpretation of Hebrew Names* from Alcath to Ananias.

Owners & Provenance: Donated to the university in August 2015 by Giles Constable in memory of his daughter, Olivia Remie Constable (1960–2014). The leaf likely formed part of the Lectern Bible broken by Otto F. Ege (1888–1951), of which leaves were included as Leaf no. 14 in his portfolio, *Fifty Original Leaves from Medieval Manuscripts* (see Gwara 2013, *Handlist* no. 14).

Constable MS 9

Origin: Italy, s. xii[1].
Content Overview: Atlantic Bible (binding fragments).

In Latin, on parchment; 2 pieces; generally 305 x 376 mm (piece) [see Layout for ruling].

Layout: Ruled using hard-point technique; two columns (intercol. 28 mm).

Script: A single hand (M1) writes all text in Praegothica. Artificialized capitals are used in the rubric and incipit; Uncial is used as a display script in the explicit of the *capitula* and in the incipit of Lc following the capitals.

Decoration:
I. Rubrication: Rubric in red ink.
II. Initials: Decorated and plain initials occur in hierarchy.
a. Decorated initial followed by initial matter occupies a column-wide space of 15 lines.
b. Plain initials (hanging) in red ink are painted in Romanesque style.

Contents:
1. Bible [binding fragments].
inc.: [piece 1, recto[a]] nec credunt discipuli euntes duo ad castellum . . .; expl.: [piece 2, recto[b]] . . . et ait angelus ei ne timeas maria inue<nisti>.

Text on versos has been obliterated; verso of piece 1 contains later heraldic markings and a drawing of saint.

1.1. *Capitula super Lucam* [incomplete]—piece 1, recto[a]. inc.: nec credunt discipuli euntes duo ad castellum . . .; expl.: . . . laudantes deo in templo [Stegmüller 11016].
1.2. Lc 1.1–30 [incomplete]—piece 1, recto[a]-piece 2, recto[b]. rub.: incipit euangelium secundum lucam; inc.: quoniam quidem multi conati sunt ordinare . . .; expl.: . . . et ait angelus ei ne timeas maria inue<nisti>.

Owners & Provenance: Donated to the university in August 2015 by Giles Constable in memory of his daughter, Olivia Remie Constable (1960–2014).

Catalogue

University of Notre Dame, Snite Museum of Art

Acc. 1967.19

Origin: Low Countries, s. xv^{2}.

Content Overview: Book of Hours, Geert Groote, trans. (leaf).
In Dutch, on parchment; 1 f.; 131 x 96 mm (page) [see Layout for ruling].

Layout:

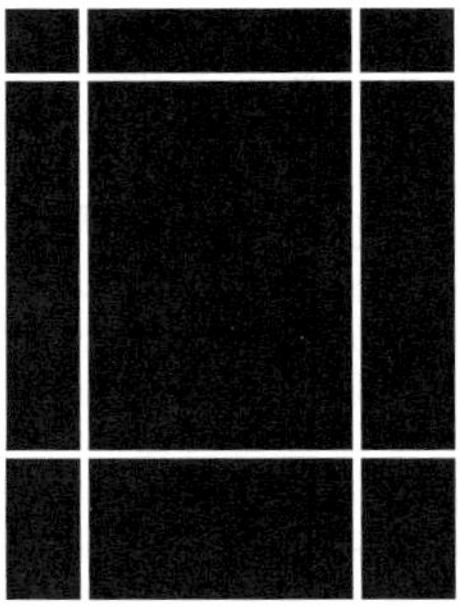

A

A Ink; 85 x 58 mm; 19 lines.

Pattern **A** is traced in brown ink; single column; writing below top line; prickings visible in the lower margin for vertical bounding lines.

Script: A single hand (M1) writes all text in Northern Textualis Formata in brown ink.

Decoration:
I. Rubrication: Rubrics in red ink; letter heightening of majuscules in red ink.
II. Initials: Dentelle and plain initials occur in hierarchy.
a. One dentelle initial (4 line square inset) begins compline on the verso.
b. Plain initials (2 line square inset; 1 line versals) alternate in the red and blue ink. Those 2 lines in size begin the psalms and collect.

CONTENTS:

1. Book of Hours, Geert Groote, trans. [leaf].

INC.: [recto] onsen vaderen abraham ende sinen geslechte van beghinne glorie alst . . .; EXPL.: [verso] . . . ic op dat bedde dat onder mi gespreit is of gheue ic slaep minen ogen.

1.1. Vespers [incomplete]—recto. ANT.: heilige maria coem te hulpen den ongeualligen . . .; OR.: verleen ons here god dinen dienres des bid den wi di dat wi verbilden van gesontheit . . . benedien wi den heren gode seg wi danck alle gelouighe sielen moten rusten in vreden amen [VAN WIJK 1940, 66–67].

1.2. Compline [incomplete]—verso. RUB.: compleet; INC.: bekeer ons god onse heilgheuer . . .; PS.: ghebendeke here davids ende alle sijnre sachtmoedicheit . . . [VAN WIJK 1940, 67].

Contains the end of vespers and beginning of compline.

EDITION: VAN WIJK 1940.

OWNERS & PROVENANCE: Purchased from London Grafica Arts, Inc. (Detroit, MI) in November 1966 by Rev. Anthony J. Lauck, C.S.C., for the University Art Gallery (now Snite Museum of Art).

Acc. 1967.20.4

Origin: Italy, s. xv^{2}.
Content Overview: Book of Hours (leaf).

In Latin, on parchment; 1 f.; 168 x 121 mm (page) [see Layout for ruling].

Layout:

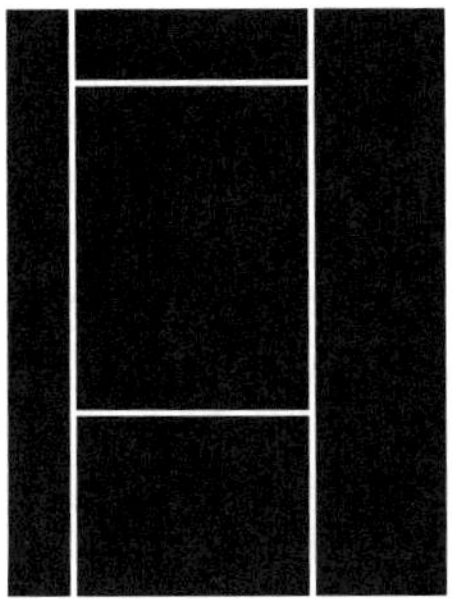

A

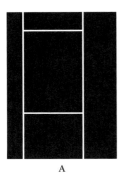

A Combined technique; 94 x 66 mm; 16 lines.

Pattern **A** is traced using lead for vertical bounding lines and purple ink for text lines; single column; writing below top line; prickings visible in margins for vertical bounding lines and horizontal through lines.

Script: All text is written by a single hand (M1) in Southern Textualis Formata (Rotunda).

Decoration:
I. Rubrication: Rubrics in red ink.
II. Initials: Dentelle and flourished initials occur in hierarchy.
a. One dentelle initial (2 line square inset) begins Ps 55 on the verso; black and gold rinceaux sprays into the inner margin.
b. Flourished initials (1 line versals) in gold with blue penwork and blue with red penwork alternate on the recto and verso.

Contents:

1. Book of Hours [leaf].

inc.: [recto] non enim est illis comutatio et non timuerunt deum [Ps 54.20] . . .; expl.: [verso] . . . sic sustinuerunt animam meam pro nichilo saluos [Ps 55.8].

Contains Pss 54.20–55.8.

Owners & Provenance: Purchased from Ferdinand Roten Gallery (Baltimore, MD) in 1967 by the University Art Gallery (now Snite Museum of Art); FRG inventory number written in pencil on the verso. Known leaves from the parent manuscript are:

Akron, Charles Edwin Puckett (firm), IM-10849
Columbia, Columbia Museum of Art, Acc. 1965.15.14
Columbia, Columbia Museum of Art, Acc. 1965.15.15
Roanoke, Hollins Univ., Wyndham Robertson Library, MS 8

Sales & Catalogues: Ferdinand Roten Gallery no. 124-74-84.

Acc. 1972.34

Origin: Low Countries, s. xv^{2} (Arnhem?).
Content Overview: Book of Hours, Geert Groote, trans. (leaf).

In Dutch, on parchment; 1 f.; 123 x 83 mm (page) [see Layout for ruling].

Foliation: Foliated in modern pencil with Arabic numerals in the upper right corner (f. 106).

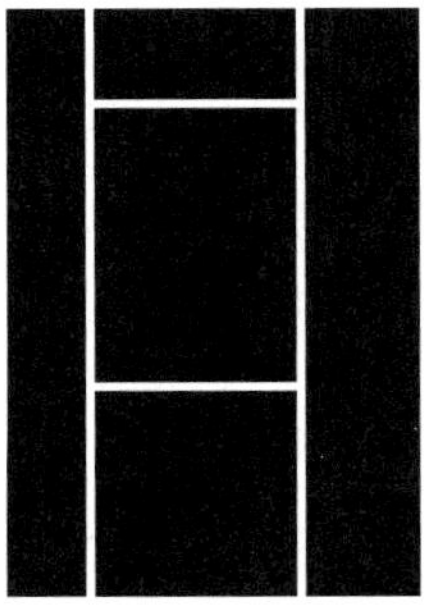

A

Layout:

A Ink; 59 x 42 mm; 15 lines.

Pattern A is traced in brown ink; single column; writing below top line; no prickings are visible.

Script: A single hand (M1) writes all text in Northern Textualis Formata.

Decoration:

I. Rubrication: Rubrics in red ink; letter heightening of majuscules in red ink.

II. Initials: Historiated, dentelle, and flourished initials occur in hierarchy.

a. One historiated initial (8 line square inset) in blue on gold grounds begins the text of none on the recto; the initial depicts a bearded saint holding book.

b. Dentelle initials (2 line square inset) begin the hymns on the verso.

c. Flourished initials (1 line versals) in blue ink with red penwork and gold with blue penwork alternate on the recto and verso.

III. Borders & Frames:

B

One four-margins border (**B**) is painted on the recto; comprised of black and gold rinceaux and blue florals on gold grounds. A gold bar with no outline frames the upper, outer, and lower margin; a nude male figure interrupts the frame and inhabits the outer margin. The style of border is similar to that attributed to the so-called Masters of Margriet Uutenham.

Contents:

1. Book of Hours, Geert Groote, trans. [leaf].

rub.: toe none tijt; **inc.**: [recto] uui aenbeden di criste ende benedien dy want ouermids dinen heilighen cruce heustu die werlt verlosset . . . [van Wijk 1940, 131]; **expl.**: [verso] . . . sonder sake voer tfolc in die versinade galghe amen here ic heb in di gheho<pet> [van Wijk 1940, 131].

1.1. None [incomplete]. **hym.**: dat salighe liden cristi moet sijn onse verlossinghe ende ouermids dat liden . . .; **hym.**: here ic heb in di gheho<pet> . . . [van Wijk 1940, 131].

Contains the beginning of none of the Hours of the Cross.

Edition: van Wijk 1940.

Owners & Provenance: Purchased from Mathias Komor (New York, NY) by the University Art Gallery (now Snite Museum of Art) in December 1972.

Sales & Catalogues: Lot 535 from an unidentified sale (catalogue description pasted to matte); Komor no. I 331.

Acc. 1973.51

Origin: France, s. xiii^{ex}.
Content Overview: Psalter (leaf).

In Latin, on parchment; 1 f.; 238 x 177 mm (page) [see Layout for ruling].

Foliation: Foliated in modern pencil with Arabic numerals in the lower right corner (f. 38).

Layout:

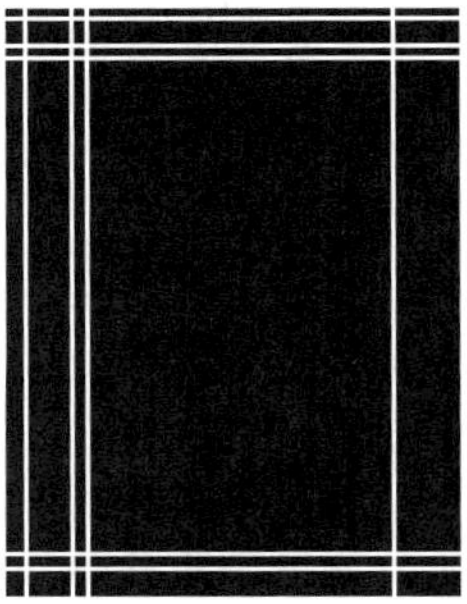

A

A Lead; 207 x 119 mm; 19 lines.

Pattern **A** is traced in lead; single column; writing below top line; no prickings remain; single verticals used to align initials; superfluous through lines in the upper margin.

Script: A single hand (M1) writes all text in Northern Textualis Formata.

Decoration:
I. Initials: Decorated and flourished initials occur in hierarchy.
a. One decorated initial (2 lines square inset) with deep red, blue, and green begins Ps 64; a bird in red and brown wash perches on the crossbar of the **t** in the inner margin.
b. Flourished initials (1 line versals) alternate in blue ink with red penwork and gold with blue penwork for the verses.
II. Line Fillers: Line fillers in red and blue ink with gold dots, and gold with blue penwork are drawn in a variety of arabesque patterns on the recto and verso.

CONTENTS:

1. Psalter [leaf].

INC.: [recto] dixerunt quis uidebit eos scrutati sunt iniquitates defecerunt . . . [Ps 63.6–7];
EXPL.: [verso] . . . benedices corone anni benignitatis tue [Ps 64.12].

Contains Pss 63.6–64.12

OWNERS & PROVENANCE: Museum records indicate purchase in 1973 from a Richard Conyers in Scotland by the University Art Gallery (now Snite Museum of Art). The parent manuscript is the so-called Whitby Psalter or Bird Psalter. The psalter was formerly thought to be from the Benedictine Abbey of Sts. Peter and Hilda in Whitby, England (TAKAMIYA 2010, 435), but this provenance is no longer accepted (see MORGAN 2013b, 28–29). Thirty-three folios, which were owned by a K. B. Starkie and then Lt.-Col. William E. Moss (1875–1953), are now Cambridge, Harvard Univ., Houghton Library, MS Lat 394. Four other leaves were in the Esther Rosenbaum Collection and sold at Sotheby's on 25 April 1983, lot 70. Known leaves are:

Ann Arbor, Univ. of Michigan, Museum of Art, 1986/2.87
Cambridge (MA), Harvard Univ., Houghton Library, MS Lat 394 (33 leaves)
London, Stephen Keynes Collection (4 leaves)
Notre Dame, Univ. Notre Dame, Snite Museum of Art, Acc. 1973.51
Tokyo, Toshiyuki Takamiya Collection, MS 80 (1 bifolium)

SALES & CATALOGUES: Leighton, Cat. 19, no. 259 (parent manuscript); Sotheby's, 2 March 1937, lot 1172 (parent manuscript); ibid., 25 April 1983, lot 70 (f. 47 and three other leaves).

Acc. 1973.55

Origin: Low Countries, s. xv (Flanders; for English market).
Content Overview: Book of Hours, use of Sarum (leaf).

In Latin, on 1 f. parchment; 180 x 128 mm (page) [see Layout for ruling].

Layout:

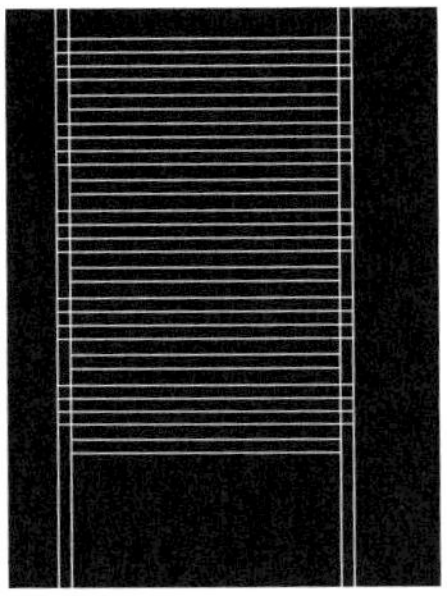

A

A Rose ink; 105 x 72 mm; 23 lines.

Pattern **A** is traced in rose ink; single column; writing below top line; no prickings are visible.

Script: A single hand (M1) writes all text in Northern Textualis Formata.

Decoration:
I. Rubrication: Rubrics in red ink; letter heightening of majuscules in red ink.
II. Initials: Dentelle and flourished initials occur in hierarchy.
a. Dentelle initials (2 line square inset) begin chapters, hymns, and psalms on the recto and verso.
b. Flourished initials (1 line versals) in gold with blue penwork and blue with red penwork alternate on the recto and verso.

CONTENTS:

1. Book of Hours, use of Sarum [leaf].

INC.: [recto] eum in tympano et choro laudate eum in cordis et organo . . . [Ps 150.4]; EXPL.: [verso] . . . o gloriosa dei genitrix uirgo semper maria que dominum omnium meruisti portare et re<gem>.

1.1. Lauds. ANT. o admirabile . . .; CAP.: maria uirgo semper letare . . .; HYM.: o gloriosa domina . . .; ANT. SUP. BEN.: o gloriosa dei.

The fragment contains the end of Ps 150 and Benedictus along with antiphons, chapter, and hymn, all of which are consistent with the use of Sarum. The leaf is likely from a Flemish manuscript prepared for the English market.

OWNERS & PROVENANCE: Purchased from Ferdinand Roten Gallery (Baltimore, MD) in 1973 by the University Art Gallery (now Snite Museum of Art); FRG inventory number written in pencil on the verso.

SALES & CATALOGUES: Ferdinand Roten Gallery no. 43-57-23.

Acc. 1974.28

Origin: Italy, s. xv.
Content Overview: Antiphonary, Temporale (leaf).

In Latin, on parchment; generally 553 x 397 mm (page) [see Layout for ruling].

Layout:

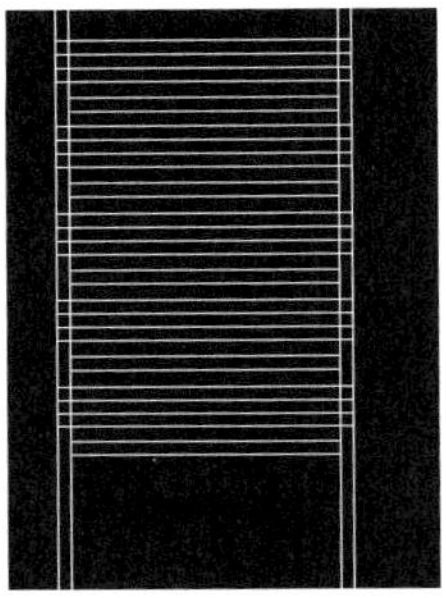

A

A Ink; 402 x 273 mm; 5 four-line staves, 5 text lines.

Pattern A is traced in red ink; single column/full-music layout; no prickings are visible.

Script: A single hand (M1) writes all text in a large Southern Textualis Formata (Rotunda).

Decoration:
I. Rubrication: Rubrics in red ink.
II. Initials: Foliate initials occur in hierarchy.
a. Two Italian style foliate initials (4 staves and 1 text line square inset) are painted in pink, blue, red, and green with marginal sprays.

Music & Staves: Four-line staves traced in red ink; 42 mm; square neumes in black ink.

CONTENTS:

1. Antiphonary, Temporale [leaf].

INC.: [recto] ad illam celestem patriam quamtotius [*sic*] properate . . .; EXPL.: [verso] . . . tentauit deus habraam et dixit ad eum.

Contains the chants *Si culmen ueri honoris* (recto; incomplete), *Vobis datum est* (recto–verso), and *Tentauit Deus Abraham* (verso; incomplete) for Sexagesima Sunday and Quinquagesima Sunday (rubricated for *sabbato in quinquegesima*).

OWNERS & PROVENANCE: Purchased from Walter Schatzki (New York, NY) by the University Art Gallery (now Snite Museum of Art) with the Charles A. Wightman Purchase Fund in 1974.

Acc. 1974.29

Origin: Italy, s. xv².
Content Overview: Antiphonary, Sanctorale (leaf).

In Latin, on parchment; 1 f.; 397 x 330 mm (page) [see Layout for ruling].

Layout:

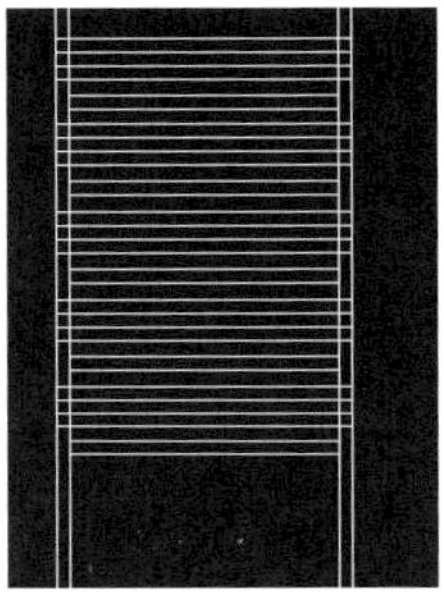

A

A Combined technique; 371 x 272 mm; 6 four-line staves, 6 text lines.

Pattern **A** is traced in red ink (staves) and lead (initial guides) and diluted black ink (verticals and text lines); single column/full-music; prickings are not visible.

Script: A single hand (M1) writes all texts in Southern Textualis Formata (Rotunda).

Decoration:
I. Rubrication: Rubrics in red ink.
II. Initials: Foliate and flourished initials occur in hierarchy.
a. An Italian style foliate initial (4 staves and 1 text line square inset) is painted on the recto in blue, violet, green, and red with white penwork.
b. Flourished initials (2 staves and 1 text line square inset) alternate in blue and red ink with contrasting penwork and are used as versals.

Music & Staves: Four-line staves traced in red ink; 32 mm; square neumes in black ink.

CONTENTS:

1. Antiphonary, Sanctorale [leaf].

INC.: [recto] gaude maria uirgo cunctas hereses sola interemisti. uersus. que gabrielis . . .;
EXPL.: [verso] . . . et post partum uirgo inuiolata permansisti uersus dei.

Gaude Maria uirgo cunctas . . . intermisti with *Quae Gabrielis archangeli* and *Dum uirgo Deum* and *Dei* <genetrix intercede> as verses; Purification (Feb. 2).

OWNERS & PROVENANCE: Purchased from Walter Schatzki (New York, NY) by the University Art Gallery (now Snite Museum of Art) with the Charles A. Wightman Purchase Fund in 1974.

Acc. 1974.30

Origin: France, s. xv^{2}.
Content Overview: Book of Hours (leaf).

In Latin, on parchment; 1 f.; 180 x 115 mm (page) [see Layout for ruling].

Foliation: Foliated in modern pencil with Arabic numerals in the upper right corner (f. 157).

Layout:

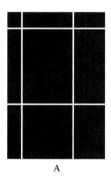

A

A Red ink; 93 x 60 mm; 20 lines.

Pattern A is traced in red ink; single column; writing below top line; no prickings are visible.

Script: A single hand (M1) writes all text in Cursiva Formata (Bastarda).

Decoration:
I. Rubrication: Rubrics in red ink; letter heightening of majuscules in yellow ink.
II. Initials: Trompe l'oeil and decorated initials occur in hierarchy.
a. Trompe l'oeil initials (2 line square inset) in white and red with blue, orange, and green floral motifs on gold grounds begin the readings on the recto and verso.
b. Decorated initials (1 line versals) in gold alternate on red and blue grounds.
III. Line Fillers: Line fillers painted in the same style as versals occur on the recto.

IV. Borders & Frames:

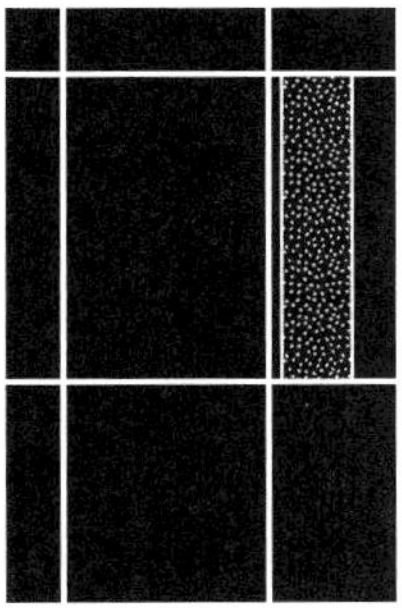

B

Outer borders (**B**) of large floral motifs in blue, orange, and green on gold grounds; borders correspond to initials in style; outlined in black ink; mirrored on verso.

Contents:

1. Book of Hours [leaf].

inc.: [recto] dum confringuntur ossa mea exprobauerunt michi . . . [Ps 41.11]; **expl.**: [verso] . . . pelli mee consumptis carnibus adhesit os meum et derelicta sunt tantummodo labia cir<ca> [Iob 19.20].

Contains the seventh reading and the beginning of the eighth reading (third nocturn) of the Office of the Dead; Ottosen nos. x-x-x , 32-57-x, 68-x-x (with Acc. 1974.32); use undetermined.

Owners & Provenance: Purchased from Walter Schatzki (New York, NY) by the University Art Gallery (now Snite Museum of Art) with the Charles A. Wightman Purchase Fund in 1974. Known leaves from the parent manuscript are:

Notre Dame, Univ. Notre Dame, Snite Museum of Art, Acc. 1974.30
Notre Dame, Univ. Notre Dame, Snite Museum of Art, Acc. 1974.32

Acc. 1974.31

Origin: Low Countries, s. xv^{2}.
Content Overview: Book of Hours (leaf).

In Dutch, on parchment; 1 f.; 161 x 113 mm (page) [see Layout for ruling].

Layout:

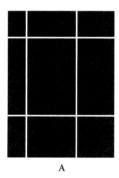

A

A Ink; 84 x 53 mm; 19 lines.

Pattern A is traced in brown ink; single column; writing below top line; prickings visible in the upper and lower margins for vertical bounding lines.

Script: A single hand (M1) writes all text in Northern Textualis Formata; corrections via rasura are visible on the verso.

Decoration:
I. Rubrication: Rubrics in red ink; letter heightening of majuscules in red ink.
II. Initials: Plain initials occur in hierarchy.
a. Plain initials (2 line square inset; 1 line versals) alternate in red and blue ink beginning the chapter and psalm; 1 line versals alternate similarly.

CONTENTS:

1. Book of Hours [leaf].

INC.: [recto] te gader mitten heilighen gheest ende ons moet die sone senden aenname gauen des . . .; EXPL.: [verso] me des dodes te leiden onse voeten inden wech des vreden glorie siden vader.

1.1. HYM.: te gader mitten heilighen gheest ende ons moet die sone . . .; CAP.: doe petrus sprac totten volke quam die heilighe gheest op hem die . . .; V.: die gheest des heren . . .; PS.: ghebenedijt si die here god van israhel want hi heuet sijn . . .

OWNERS & PROVENANCE: Purchased from Walter Schatzki (New York, NY) by the University Art Gallery (now Snite Museum of Art) with the Charles A. Wightman Purchase Fund in 1974.

Acc. 1974.32

Origin: France, s. xv^{2}.
Content Overview: Book of Hours (leaf).

In Latin, on parchment; 1 f.; 180 x 115 mm (page) [see Layout for ruling].

Foliation: Foliated in modern pencil with Arabic numerals in the upper right corner (f. 159).

Layout:

A

A Red ink; 93 x 60 mm; 20 lines.

Pattern A is traced in red ink; single column; writing below top line; no prickings are visible.

Script: A single hand (M1) writes all text in Cursiva Formata (Bastarda).

Decoration:
I. Rubrication: Rubrics in red ink; letter heightening of majuscules in yellow ink.
II. Initials: Trompe l'oeil initials occur in hierarchy.
a. Trompe l'oeil initials (2 line square inset) in white and red with blue, orange, and green floral motifs on gold grounds begin the readings on the recto and verso.

III. Borders & Frames:

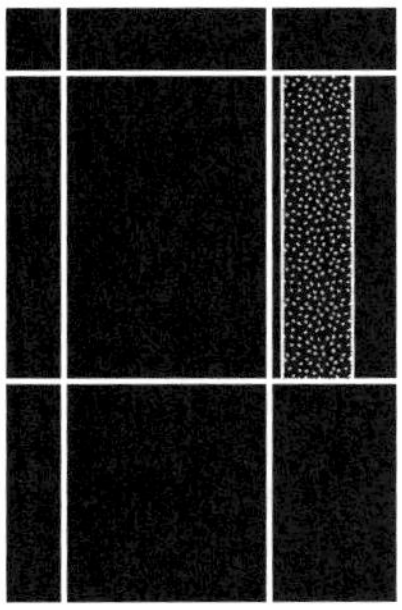

B

Outer borders (**B**) of white acanthus (trompe l'oeil) with blue, orange, and green floral motifs are on gold grounds; borders correspond to initials in style; outlined in black ink; mirrored on verso.

Contents:

1. Book of Hours [leaf].

inc.: [recto] quantas habeo iniquitates et peccata scelera mea . . . [Iob 13.23]; **expl.**: [verso] . . . donec optata ueniat et sicut mercennarii dies eius [Iob 14.6] responsorium ne re<corderis>.

Contains the fourth reading and ends with the responsory for the fifth reading (second nocturn) of the Office of the Dead; Ottosen nos. x-x-x , 32-57-x, 68-x-x (with Acc. 1974.30); use undetermined.

Owners & Provenance: Purchased from Walter Schatzki (New York, NY) by the University Art Gallery (now Snite Museum of Art) with the Charles A. Wightman Purchase Fund in 1974. Known leaves from the parent manuscript are:

Notre Dame, Univ. Notre Dame, Snite Museum of Art, Acc. 1974.30
Notre Dame, Univ. Notre Dame, Snite Museum of Art, Acc. 1974.32

Acc. 1974.33

Origin: France, s. xv^{2}.
Content Overview: Book of Hours (leaf).

In Latin, on parchment; 1 f.; 177 x 117 mm (page) [see Layout for ruling].

Layout:

A

A Rose ink; 114 x 64 mm; 20 lines.

Pattern A is traced in rose ink; single column; writing below top line; prickings not visible.

Script: A single hand (M1) writes all text in Cursiva Formata (Bastarda); opening line painted in an artificial capitalis.

Decoration:
I. Rubrication: Rubrics in red ink.
II. Initials: Decorated initials occur in hierarchy.
a. Decorated initials (2 line square inset; 1 line versals) in gold alternate on red and blue grounds; those 2 lines in height begin psalms.
III. Line Fillers: Line fillers in red and blue with gold penwork occur in the same style as the initials.

Contents:

1. Book of Hours [leaf].

inc.: [recto] domine ne in furore tuo arguas me . . . miserere mei domine quoniam . . . [Ps 6.2–3]; expl.: [verso] . . . ut dominus peccatum nec est in spiritu eius dolus [Ps 31.2].

Contains a portion of the Penitential Psalms: Ps 6 and the beginning of Ps 31.

Owners & Provenance: Purchased from Walter Schatzki (New York, NY) by the University Art Gallery (now Snite Museum of Art) with the Charles A. Wightman Purchase Fund in 1974.

Acc. 1975.43

Origin: Southern France, s. xiii^{ex} (Bordeaux?).
Content Overview: Bible (leaf).

In Latin, on parchment; 1 f.; 330 x 229 mm (page) [see Layout for ruling].

Catchwords: A horizontal catchword is written in the lower right margin of the verso; stylized.

Layout:

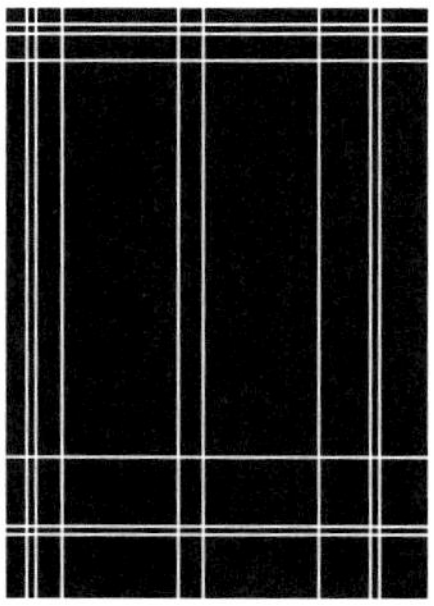

A

A Lead; 221 x 142 mm; intercol. 13 mm; 40 lines.

Pattern A is traced in lead; two columns (intercol. 13 mm); writing below top line; prickings visible for vertical bounding lines and horizontal through lines.

Script: A single hand (M1) writes all text in Southern Textualis Formata (Rotunda) with a strong Northern influence.

Decoration:
I. Rubrication: Rubrics in red ink; letter heightening of majuscules in red ink.
II. Initials: Historiated and decorated initials occur in hierarchy.
a. One historiated initial (9+23 lines stepped) depicting the Tree of Jesse begins Mt 1 on the verso; palette uses blue, pink, green, gold, yellow, red, orange, and white; marginal spray creates a border in the inner intercolumnium.

B. Decorated initials (6 lines square inset) in pink, blue, gold, red, and green with inner vegetal motifs and white penwork throughout begin the prologues on the recto and verso; initials have marginal spray forming piece borders.

III. LINE FILLERS: A single line filler in red ink is painted on the verso.

IV. BORDERS & FRAMES: see II. A–B.

CONTENTS:

1. Bible [leaf].

INC.: [recto^{a}] <best>ie equitesque in loco oportuno positi considerans machabeus . . . [2 Mcc 15.20–21]; EXPL.: [verso^{b}] . . . ezechias autem genuit manassem a. manasses [Mt 1.10].

1.1. 2 Mcc 15.20–40—recto^{a-b}. INC.: <bes>tie equitesque in loco oportuno positi; EXPL.: [recto^{b}] . . . hic ergo erit consummatus.

1.2. Prologue to Mt—recto^{b}–verso^{a}. RUB.: explicit liber machabeorum secundus incipit prologus in matheum euangelistam; INC.: matheus ex iudea sicut in ordine primus ponitur ita . . .; EXPL.: . . . et operantis dei intelligendam dilligenter esse dispositionem querentibus non tacere [STEGMÜLLER 590, cf. 591].

1.3. Prologue to Mt—verso^{a-b}. RUB.: item alius prologus; INC.: matheus cum primo predicasset euangelium in iudea . . .; EXPL.: in leone regnum in aquila exprimitur diuinitatis sacramentum [STEGMÜLLER 589].

1.4. Mt 1.1.10—verso^{b}. RUB.: expliciunt prologi incipit matheus euangelista; INC.: liber generationis ihesu christi filii dauid . . .; EXPL.: . . . ezechias autem genuit manassem a. manasses.

Contains 2 Mcc. 15.20–40, prologues to Mt. [STEGMÜLLER 590 and 589], and Mt. 1.10.

OWNERS & PROVENANCE: Purchased from Philip Duschnes (New York, NY) by the University Art Gallery (now Snite Museum of Art) with the Samuel S. Schatz Purchase Fund in 1975. The parent manuscript, W.173, was one of the so-called Chester Beatty Bibles. The manuscript was acquired by Sir Thomas Phillipps (1792–1872) from Thomas Thorpe (MUNBY 3:149); Sir Alfred Chester Beatty (1875–1968) purchased the manuscript (*olim* Phillipps MS 2506) in 1921 from Phillipps' heirs (see MANION, VINES, & DE HAMEL 1989, 105); lot 57 in Sotheby's Beatty Sale on 24 June 1969; purchased by Alan Thomas; sold to Philip Duschnes (New York, NY), who broke it; see also Acc. 1975.57.

A list of identifiable leaves with recognizable parts of the text and their locations is provided in the description of Dunedin, Public Library, Reed Fragment 41 by MANION, VINES, & DE HAMEL 1989, 105–106. Updates to MANION, VINES, & DE HAMEL 1989, 105–106 are:

Is 29–30	Dublin, Chester Beatty Library, W 173.2
Lam 1–2.16	Notre Dame, Univ. Notre Dame, Snite Museum of Art, Acc. 1975.57
Bar 2–3	Dublin, Chester Beatty Library, W 173.1

1 Mcc–2 Mcc	McMinnville (OR), Pirages, Cat. 65, no. 49
2 Mcc 15.20–Mt 1.10	Notre Dame, Univ. Notre Dame, Snite Museum of Art, Acc. 1975.43
Mc 16.5–Lc 1.26	McMinnville (OR), Pirages, Cat. 65, no. 50
1 Pt 4.15–2 Pt 3.1	Dublin, Chester Beatty Library, W 173.3

Sales & Catalogues: Sotheby's, 24 June 1969, lot 57 (parent manuscript); Thomas, Cat. 23, no. 5 (parent manuscript); Duschnes, Cat. 209, no. 172; see Manion, Vines, & De Hamel 1989, 105–106 for sale information of other leaves.

Former Shelfmarks: Phillipps MS 2506 (parent manuscript); MS W.173 (parent manuscript).

Bibliography: Phillipps no. 2506; Munby 3:149; Manion, Vines, & De Hamel 1989, 105–106.

Acc. 1975.56

Origin: France, s. xv² (Rouen).
Content Overview: Book of Hours (leaf).

In French, on parchment; 1 f.; 162 x 111 mm (page) [see Layout for ruling].

Layout:

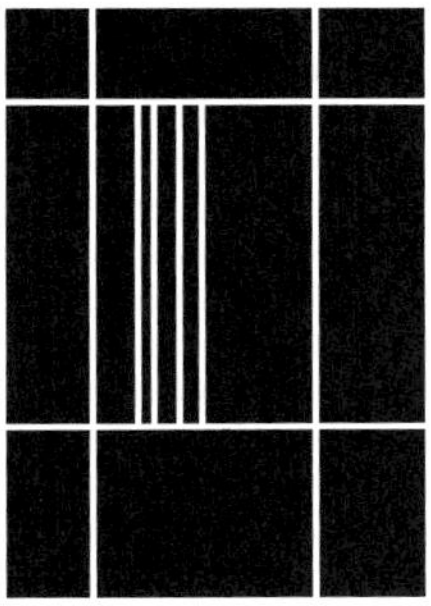

A

A Rose ink; 90 x 56 mm; 12/4/7/6/30 mm (cols.); 17 lines.

Pattern **A** is traced in rose ink; five columns (12/4/7/6/30 mm); writing below top line; one pricking is visible in the lower margin for the inner vertical bounding line.

Script: All text is written by a single hand (M1) in Northern Textualis Formata.

Decoration:
I. Rubrication: Rubric for days and moons of the month in gold.
II. Initials: Foliate and dentelle initials occur in hierarchy.
a. Foliate initials (2 line square inset) begin the calendar (**kl**) on the recto.
b. Dentelle initials (1 line versals) mark the dominical letter **a** throughout the calendar.

III. Borders & Frames:

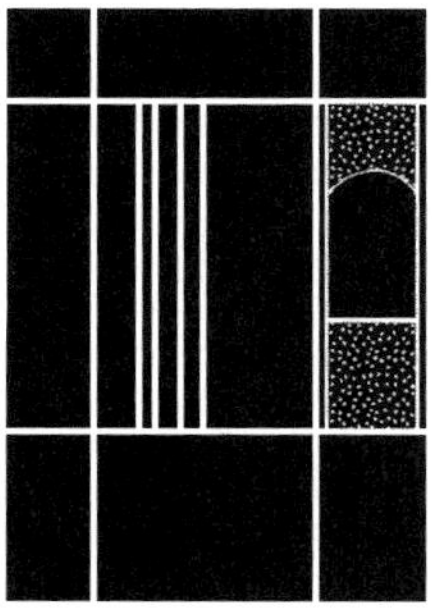

B

Outer borders comprised of acanthus in blues and yellows, strawberries in red and green, floral motifs in blues and green, and black and gold rinceaux are painted on the recto and verso; area to be decorated is defined in rose ink; an arch-topped miniature frame in black ink is inset into the border (**B**).

Miniatures: Two arch-topped miniatures are painted in the borders for the monthly labor and zodiac sign; man warming by the fire (recto); Pisces (verso).

Calendar: Two pages per month; recto/verso; historiated with monthly labor and zodiac sign; Roman time without numerals alternates in red and blue ink; dominical letter **a** in dentelle style.

Contents:

1. Book of Hours, Calendar [leaf].

Composite calendar for February in deluxe double-graded presentation; graded feasts in gold; normal feasts alternate in red and blue ink. Calendar is representative of the Parisian model; notable variants of the P group include Theodore (Feb. 7), Lucien (Feb. 15), and Cloust (Feb. 20).

Owners & Provenance: Purchased from Philip Duschnes (New York, NY) by the University Art Gallery (now Snite Museum of Art) with the Samuel S. Schatz Purchase Fund in 1975.

Acc. 1975.57

Origin: Southern France, s. xiii^{ex} (Bordeaux?).
Content Overview: Bible (leaf).

In Latin, on parchment; 1 f.; 330 x 229 mm (page) [see Layout for ruling].

Layout:

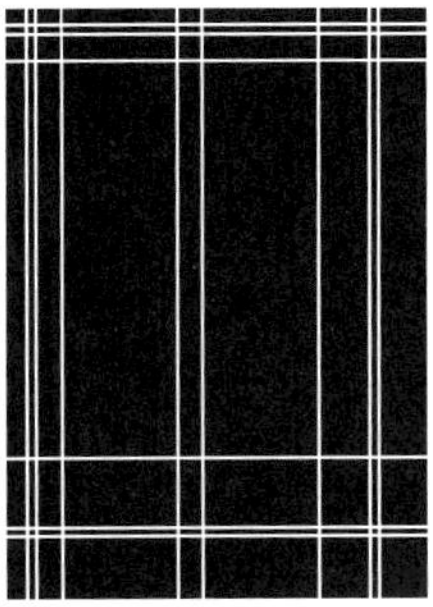

A

A   Lead; 224 x 142 mm; intercol. 13 mm; 40 lines.

Pattern **A** is traced in lead; two columns (intercol. 13 mm); writing below top line; prickings visible for vertical bounding lines and horizontal through lines.

Script: A single hand (M1) writes all text in Southern Textualis Formata (Rotunda) with a strong Northern influence.

Decoration:

I. Rubrication: Rubrics in red ink; letter heightening of majuscules in red ink.

II. Initials: Historiated and flourished initials occur in hierarchy.

a. One historiated initial (7 lines square inset) depicting Jeremiah in lamentation is painted on the recto in blue, gold, pink, red, and gray; a grotesque stands on the initial in the upper margin; tail of **q** hangs through the bottom of the page.

b. One flourished initial (2 lines square inset) in red ink with blue penwork incorporating a flourished border begins the second chapter on the verso.

CONTENTS:

1. Bible [leaf].

INC.: [recto[a]] aleph quomodo sedet sola ciuitas plena populo . . . [Lam 1.1.]; EXPL.: [verso[b]] . . . aperuerunt super te os suum os inimici tui [Lam 2.16].

Contains Lam 1.1–2.16.

OWNERS & PROVENANCE: Purchased from Philip Duschnes (New York, NY) by the University Art Gallery (now Snite Museum of Art) with the Samuel S. Schatz Purchase Fund in 1975. The parent manuscript, W.173, was one of the so-called Chester Beatty Bibles. The manuscript was acquired by Sir Thomas Phillipps (1792–1872) from Thomas Thorpe (MUNBY 3:149); Sir Alfred Chester Beatty (1875–1968) purchased the manuscript (*olim* Phillipps MS 2506) in 1921 from Phillipps' heirs (see MANION, VINES, & DE HAMEL 1989, 105); lot 57 in Sotheby's Beatty Sale on 24 June 1969; purchased by Alan Thomas; sold to Philip Duschnes (New York, NY), who broke it; see also Acc. 1975.43.

A list of identifiable leaves with recognizable parts of the text and their locations is provided in the description of Dunedin, Public Library, Reed Fragment 41 by MANION, VINES, & DE HAMEL 1989, 105–106. Updates to MANION, VINES, & DE HAMEL 1989, 105–106 are:

Is 29–30	Dublin, Chester Beatty Library, W 173.2
Lam 1–2.16	Notre Dame, Univ. Notre Dame, Snite Museum of Art, Acc. 1975.57
Bar 2–3	Dublin, Chester Beatty Library, W 173.1
1 Mcc–2 Mcc	McMinnville (OR), Pirages, Cat. 65, no. 49
2 Mcc 15.20–Mt 1.10	Notre Dame, Univ. Notre Dame, Snite Museum of Art, Acc. 1975.43
Mc 16.5–Lc 1.26	McMinnville (OR), Pirages, Cat. 65, no. 50
1 Pt 4.15–2 Pt 3.1	Dublin, Chester Beatty Library, W 173.3

SALES & CATALOGUES: Sotheby's, 24 June 1969, lot 57 (parent manuscript); Thomas, Cat. 23, no. 5 (parent manuscript); Duschnes, Cat. 209, no. 173; see MANION, VINES, & DE HAMEL 1989, 105–106 for sale information of other leaves.

FORMER SHELFMARKS: Phillipps MS 2506 (parent manuscript); MS W.173 (parent manuscript).

BIBLIOGRAPHY: PHILLIPPS no. 2506; MUNBY 3:149; MANION, VINES, & DE HAMEL 1989, 105–106.

Acc. 1978.28

Origin: France, s. xv^{ex} (1490–1500).
Content Overview: Calendar (Parisian; use of Rome) (6 leaves).

In French, on parchment; 6 ff.; generally 208 x 146 mm (page) [see Layout for ruling]; unfoliated.

Layout:

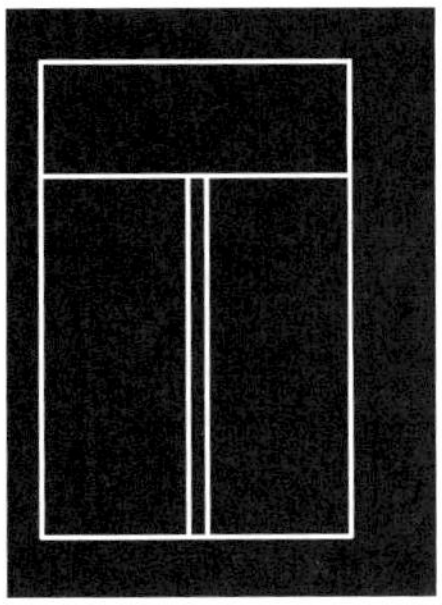

A

A Combined technique; 149 x 117 mm; intercol. 6 mm; 16 lines.

Pattern A is painted on each folio in various pigments (see Borders & Frames); lead is faintly visible for text lines; two columns (intercol. 6 mm).

Script: A single hand (M1) writes all text in Cursiva Formata (Bastarda).

Decoration:
I. Initials: Decorated initials occur in hierarchy.
A. Decorated initials (2 line square inset; 1 line versals) in gold on blue and pink grounds alternate throughout the calendar; those of the 2 line size mark begin each month (**kl**); dominical letter **a** marked with initials 1 line in size.

II. Borders & Frames: Borders are painted as columns in blue, pink, and green with gold; various patterns (fleur-de-lys, flowers, leaves, and other shapes) are incorporated into each column. Miniatures are painted above the text.

Miniatures: Twelve miniatures depict the monthly labors and signs of the zodiac in a single illustration: man and woman warming by the fire, nude Aquarius bathing outdoors (January); peasant breaking ground with shovel and man warming by fire outdoors, Pisces in stream (February); three peasants pruning vines, Ares entering right of frame (March); nude figure with branch on horse back, Taurus sitting (April); man and two women in the garden, Gemini as nude male and female in embrace (May); two peasants mowing and one drinking, Cancer in water (June); three peasants reaping, Leo on grass (July); two peasants threshing, Virgo with branch sitting (August); peasant sowing seeds from apron, Libra hanging in window (September); peasant in vat, other peasants bringing grapes, Scorpio on ground (October); two peasants shaking trees for acorns and pigs eating, Sagittarius as a centaur shooting a bow (November); man baking bread and two women at table, Capricorn on ground (December).

Calendar: One page per month; Roman time not marked; dominical letter **a** in gold on blue or pink grounds; historiated with monthly labors and zodiac signs.

Contents:

1. Calendar (Parisian, use of Rome) [6 leaves].

Composite calendar in red and blue ink with graded feasts in gold; calendar is very representative of Drigsdahl's T-Group of du Pré and then Verard. Principal variants of the T-Group contained are: Silvain (Feb. 15), Cloust (Feb. 18), Front (Feb. 20), Gencien (Feb. 21), Paulin (Feb. 25), Felix (Feb. 26), Aubert [*sic*] (Feb. 27), Fortunat (Mar. 3), Victorin (Mar. 6), Pantaleon (Mar. 8), Viron (Mar. 9), Gorgon (Mar. 11), Leon (Mar. 14), Theodoire (Mar. 19), Urbain (Mar. 20), Saturnin (Mar. 22), Victorian (Mar. 23), Maxime (Mar. 26), Iehan hermite (Mar. 27), Rogat (Mar. 28), Sabine (Mar. 31), Helene (Apr. 5), Timothe (Apr. 7), Perpetin (Apr. 8), Appollinaire (Apr. 9), Aubert [*sic*] (Apr. 10), Just (Apr. 12), Calixte (Apr. 16), Fremin (Apr. 18), Leon (Apr. 19), Urbain (Apr. 20), Robert (Apr. 21), Avit (Apr. 24), Spire (Apr. 26), Aquillain (May 2), Hylaire (May 5), Juvenal (May 7), Sixte (May 8), Achile (May 12), Victor (May 14), Richier (Jun. 3), Quirin (Jun. 4), Tyrin (Jun. 12), Bernard (Jun. 20), Fuscien (Jun. 27), Victorin (Jul. 8), Felix (Jul. 12), Vaast (Jul. 15), Quirin (Aug. 4), Aresme (Aug. 6), Prive (Aug. 22), Apollinaire (Aug. 23), Bernard (Aug. 26), Eleuthere (Sept. 6), Maclou (Sept. 7), Turin (Sept. 12), Apollinaire (Oct. 5), Theophile (Oct. 13), Faron (Oct. 29), Hubert (Nov. 4), Cler (Nov. 5), Martin (Nov. 10), Ogin (Nov. 14), Maclou (Nov. 15), Lin (Nov. 28), Cancian (Dec. 3).

Owners & Provenance: Jean-Bénigne Lucotte (1668–1750), seigneur du Tilliot; the upper margin of the first leaf contains the ownership mark *ex musaeo du Tilliot anno 1700*); János Scholz (1903–1993) acquired the calendar from Herbert E. Feist Gallery (New York, NY); donated by János Scholz to the University Art Gallery (now Snite Museum of Art) in 1978.

Acc. 1980.58.4

Origin: Southern France, s. xv^{ex}.
Content Overview: Antiphonary, Temporale (leaf).

In Latin, on parchment; 1 f.; 560 x 402 mm (page) [see Layout for ruling].

Layout:

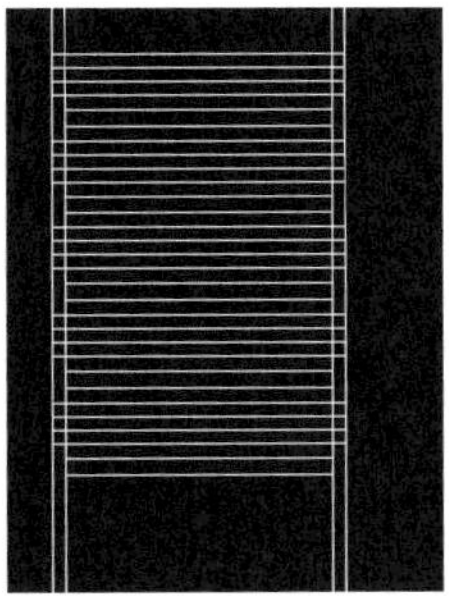

A

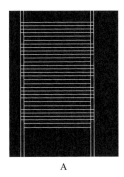

A Combined technique; 405 x 246 mm; 5 four-line staves, 5 text lines.

Pattern **A** is traced using a combined technique of red ink (verticals and staves) and lead (text lines); single column/full-music layout; no prickings are visible.

Script: A single hand (M1) writes all text in a large Southern Textualis Formata; script is under Italian influence, but decoration is Northern.

Decoration:
I. Rubrication: Rubrics in red ink.
II. Initials: Foliate initials occur in hierarchy.
a. Foliate initials (3 staves and 1 text line square inset) in Northern style (French or Flemish) begin the antiphons on the recto and verso.

Music & Staves: Four-line staves are traced with a rake in red ink; 40 mm; square neumes in black ink.

CONTENTS:

1. Antiphonary, Temporale [leaf].

INC.: [recto] <an>nos nondum habes et habraam uidisti . . .; EXPL.: [verso] . . . de ore leonis libe<ra>.

Antiphons (*Quinquaginta annos, Tulerunt lapides Iudei*) and response (*De ore leonis libera*) for the Fifth Sunday of Lent (Dom. de Passione); the leaf was previously used as a wrapper.

OWNERS & PROVENANCE: From the collection of Everett McNear (1904–1984) of Chicago, IL; donated by Everett McNear to the Snite Museum of Art in 1980.

Acc. 1980.58.5

Origin: Italy, s. xv^2.
Content Overview: Antiphonary, Temporale (leaf).

In Latin, on parchment; 1 f.; 631 x 450 mm (page) [see Layout for ruling].

Foliation: Contemporary foliation in red ink with Arabic numerals is centered in the upper margin.

Layout:

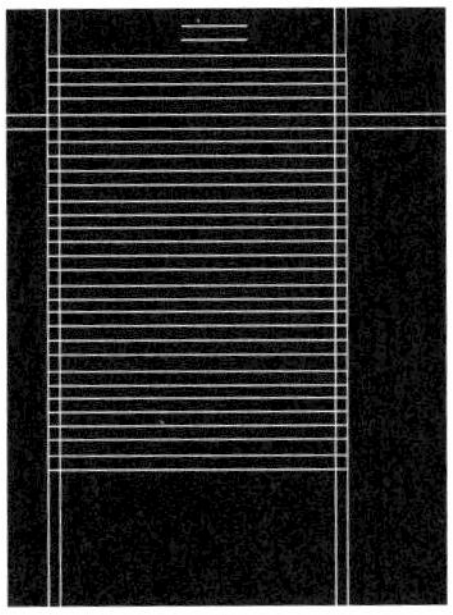

A

A Combined technique; 437 x 308 mm; 5 four-line staves, 5 text lines.

Pattern A is traced using a combined technique of red ink (staves) and lead (verticals and text lines); single column/full-music layout; prickings visible in the lower margin for vertical bounding lines.

Script: A single hand (M1) writes all text in Southern Textualis Formata (Rotunda).

Decoration:
I. Rubrication: Rubrics in red ink.
II. Initials: Foliate initials occurs in hierarchy.
a. One foliate initial (1 staff, 1 text line) in Italian style is painted on the recto; palette comprised of purples, blues, greens, gold, and white.

Music & Staves: Four-line staves traced in red ink; 45 mm; square neumes in black ink.

Contents:

1. Antiphonary, Temporale [leaf].

inc.: [recto] <in>troibo ad altare dei ad deum qui letificat . . .; expl.: [verso] . . . et refugium meum es tu et propter nomen tuum.

Contains the chants *Introibo ad altare Dei* (recto) and *Esto mihi Deum protectorem* (recto–verso) for Sexagesima Sunday and Quinquegesima Sunday.

Owners & Provenance: From the collection of Everett McNear (1904–1984) of Chicago, IL; donated by Everett McNear to the Snite Museum of Art in 1980.

Bibliography: Lauck 1974, no. 28.

Acc. 1984.3.1

ORIGIN: Spain, s. xvi.
CONTENT OVERVIEW: Gradual, Temporale (leaf).

In Latin, on parchment; 1 f.; 572 x 412 mm (page) [see LAYOUT for ruling].

FOLIATION: Contemporary foliation with Roman numerals in red ink appears in the upper right margin (f. lxxxvj).

LAYOUT:

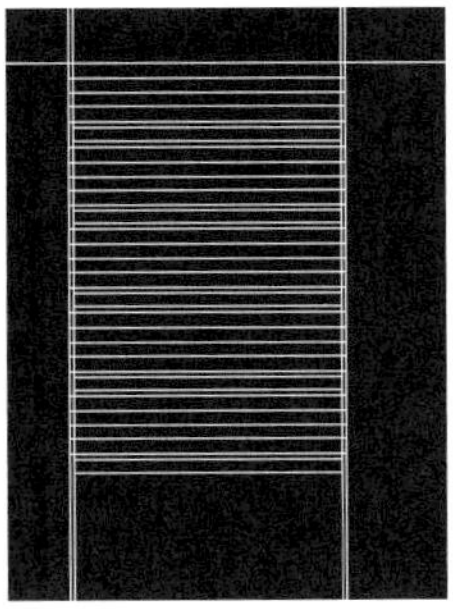

A

A Combined technique; 385 x 260 mm; 5 five-line staves, 5 text lines.

Pattern A is traced using a combined technique of red ink (staves) and lead (verticals and text lines); single column/full-music layout.

SCRIPT: A single hand (M1) writes all text in a Southern Textualis Formata with Spanish forms.

DECORATION:
I. RUBRICATION: Rubrics in red ink; letter heightening of cadels in green ink.
II. INITIALS: A single cadel with heightening in green begins the verse on the recto.
III. LINE FILLERS: Line fillers in red ink join the syllables of each word as a unit in each text line.

Music & Staves: Five-line staves traced in red ink; 61 mm; square neumes in black ink.

Contents:

1. Gradual, Temporale [leaf].

inc.: [recto] quoniam nomen tibi deus tu solus . . .; **expl.:** [verso] . . . et sicut stipulam ante faciem uenti tractus.

Contains the gradual (*Sciant gentes quoniam nomen*; incomplete) and verse (*Deus meus pone illos*; incomplete) for Sexagesima Sunday.

Owners & Provenance: From the collection of Everett McNear (1904–1984) of Chicago, IL; donated by Everett McNear to the Snite Museum of Art in 1984.

Acc. 1984.3.2

Origin: Italy, s. xiv.
Content Overview: Antiphonary, Sanctorale (leaf).

In Latin, on parchment; 1 f.; 485 x 330 mm (page) [see Layout for ruling].

Layout:

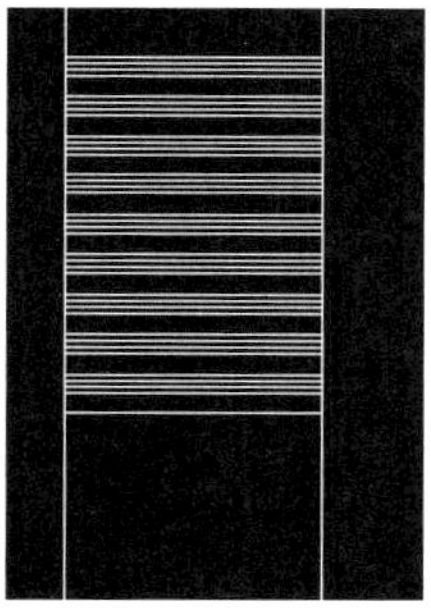

A

A Combined technique; approx. 315 x 203 mm; 9 staves and text lines.

Pattern **A** is traced using a combined technique of lead and red ink (staves); verticals traced very lightly; single column/full-music layout; prickings visible in the inner and outer margins for text lines.

Script: Two scribal bookhands are discernable (M1–M2). M1 writes the text below the staves in Southern Textualis Formata (Rotunda). M2 writes directive rubrics and other text in Semitextualis Libraria incorporating documentary features on the recto.

Decoration:

I. Rubrication: Rubrics in red and brown ink; red ink occurs only below staves; letter heightening of majuscules in red ink on the verso.

II. Initials: Littera duplex and plain initials occur in hierarchy.

a. Littera duplex initial (3 staves and 3 text lines square inset) is drawn on the verso with plentiful red penwork spraying into the upper and outer margin.

b. Plain initials (1 line versals; square inset and hanging) are drawn in red ink.

Music & Staves: Four-line staves traced in red ink; uniformity in hesitation marks indicate rake-ruling; 17 mm; square neumes in black ink.

Contents:

1. Antiphonary, Sanctorale [leaf].

rub.: antiphona; inc.: [recto] stephanus uidit celos apertos uidit et introiuit beatus homo . . .; expl.: [verso] . . . et scimus quia uerum est testimonium eius.

Chants for Offices of Stephen and John the Evangelist (incomplete).

Owners & Provenance: From the collection of Everett McNear (1904–1984) of Chicago, IL; donated by Everett McNear to the Snite Museum of Art in 1984.

Acc. 1984.3.3

Origin: Germany or Low Countries, s. xvi^{in}.
Content Overview: Antiphonary, Sanctorale (leaf).

In Latin, on parchment; 1 f.; 484 x 343 mm (page) [see Layout for ruling].

Foliation: Contemporary foliation in red ink with Roman numerals centered in the upper margin (f. ccxvj).

Layout:

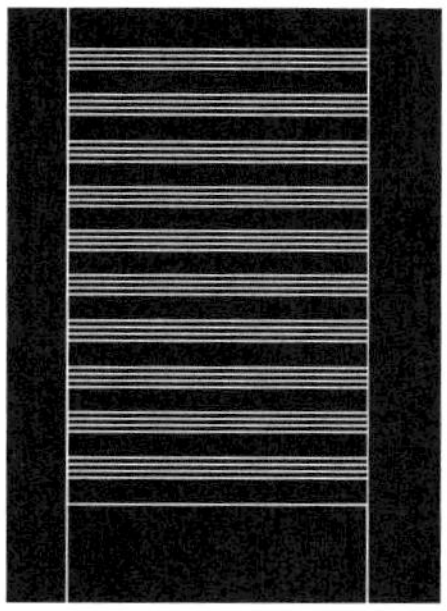

A

A Combined technique; 360 x 237 mm; 10 four-line staves, 10 text lines.

Pattern **A** is traced using a combined technique of red ink (staves) and black crayon (text lines); verticals untraced; prickings in the inner margin.

Script: Three scribal book hands can be distinguished (M1–M3). M1 writes the uncorrected text in a dark Northern Textualis Formata; M2 writes rubrics and cues in Northern Textualis Formata on a parchment strip pasted over previous text on the verso; M3 writes directives in Semihybrida Libraria on the recto. All hands use Germanic forms.

Decoration:

I. Rubrication: Rubrics in red ink; letter heightening of cadels and majuscules in red ink.

II. Initials: Decorated and plain initials occur in hierarchy.

a. One decorated initial (1 staff and 2 text lines square inset) begins the feast of Mary Magdalene on the verso; initial depicts Mary Magdalene in faceted style with brown hues on orange grounds.

b. Plain initials (1 staff and 1 text line square inset) alternate in blue and red ink and begin antiphons.

Music & Staves: Four-line staves traced in red ink; 16 mm; square neumes in black ink.

Contents:

1. Antiphonary, Sanctorale [leaf].

rub.: canticum; **inc.**: [recto] magnificat. sequitur commendatio de sancto iohanne . . .; **expl.** [verso] . . . stans retro secus pedes domini ihesu lacrimis cepit rigare pedes eius et capillis.

Recto contains the Offices for octave of John the Baptist and the Visitation; the verso contains the Offices for octave of Peter and Paul (pasted onto parchment) and the solemnity of Mary Magdalene.

Owners & Provenance: From the collection of Everett McNear (1904–1984) of Chicago, IL; donated by Everett McNear to the Snite Museum of Art in 1984.

Sales & Catalogues: Maggs Bros., Bulletin 6, no. 21.

Former Shelfmark: MS 2784 (unknown).

Bibliography: Lauck 1974, no. 31.

Acc. 1984.3.4

Origin: Spain, s. xvi^{2}.
Content Overview: Antiphonary, Sanctorale (6 leaves).

In Latin, on parchment; 6 ff.; generally 507 x 340 mm (page) [see Layout for ruling].

Collation: 1^{8-2}

Quires: The fragment is comprised of a single parchment quaternion, H/H; does not obey Gregory's Rule; the third bifolium is lacking (third and sixth leaves).

Signatures: Signatures are written within the quire on the rectos (hh i, hh ij, hh iiij) in brown ink.

Foliation: Contemporary foliation in red ink with Roman numerals is written in the upper right corner (ff. clxiiij, clxvj, clxvij, etc.).

Layout:

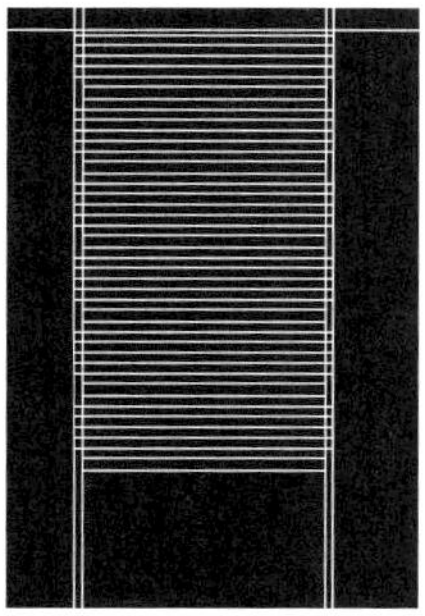

A

A Combined technique; 401 x 215 mm; 6 five-line staves, 6 text lines.

Pattern **A** is traced using a combined technique of red ink (staves) and lead (vertical bounding lines and text lines); single column/full-music layout; prickings are not visible.

Script: A single hand (M1) writes all text in a late Southern Textualis Formata with Spanish features.

Decoration:

I. Rubrication: Rubrics in red ink.

II. Initials: Littera duplex, plain, and cadel initials occur in hierarchy.

a. Littera duplex initials (2 staves and two text lines square inset; 1 staff and 1 text line) begin the major divisions on ff. 163v and 170r.

b. Plain initials (1 line versals) in red ink begin verses throughout the fragment.

c. Cadels (1 staff and 1 text line) begin antiphons throughout the fragment.

Music & Staves: Five-line staves traced in red ink; 39 mm; square neumes in black ink.

Contents:

1. Antiphonary, Sanctorale [6 leaves].

rub. [f. 163r] commune sanctoum [*sic*] in natali apostolorum ad uesperas antiphona; **inc.**: [f. 163v] hoc est praeceptum meum ut diligatis . . .; **expl.**: [f. 170v] . . . in caelestibus regnis sanctorum habitatio est alleluia.

The quire contains the common of saints; apostles (ff. 163v–170r), apostles and evangelists (f. 170r–v).

Owners & Provenance: From the collection of Everett McNear (1904–1984) of Chicago, IL; donated by Everett McNear to the Snite Museum of Art in 1984.

Acc. 1984.3.6

Origin: Italy, s. xv^{2}.
Content Overview: Confessional.

In Italian, on paper; i +11 ff. +i; generally 211 x 140 mm (page) [see Layout for ruling]; parchment flyleaves (ruled); foliated in modern pencil with Arabic numerals; f. 11v blank.

Collation: i +1^{10+1} +i

Bibliographical Format: 4°.

Quires: A paper quinion folded in quarto comprises the manuscript; f. 11 is pasted to f. 10v; the manuscript has been trimmed.

Watermarks: Four occurrences of three different watermarks: (**A**) Scales; occurs on ff. 1/10 and 3/8; cf. Piccard 116140 (Venice, 1451). (**B**) Uncial M with cross above; occurs on ff. 4/7; cf. Briquet 8354 (Lucca, 1436). (**C**) Scissors (partial); occurs on f. 11; cf. Piccard 122494 (Gemona, 1471).

Layout:

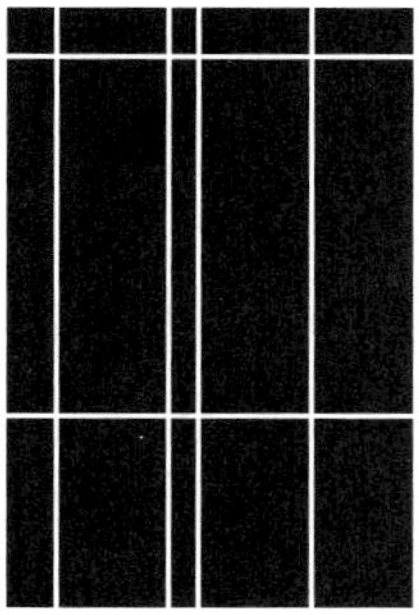

A

A ff. 1r–11r. Lead; 131 x 87.5 mm; intercol. 9 mm; 32 lines.

Pattern A is traced in lead on ff. 1r–11r; two columns (intercol. 9 mm); writing below top line; prickings visible in upper and lower margins for vertical bounding lines and in the outer margins for horizontals.

SCRIPT: Single hand (M1) writes Southern Textualis Libraria (Rotunda), quickly becoming Semitextualis Libraria; the influence of Hybrida is noticeable as rapidity increases, but most letter forms are those of Rotunda.

DECORATION:
I. RUBRICATION: Rubrics in red ink; letter heightening in red ink.
II. INITIALS: A decorated initial and flourished initials occur in hierarchy.
A. One gold painted initial with bianchi girari (3 line square inset) begins the text on f. 1r.
B. Flourished initials (2 line square inset) in red and blue ink with contrasting penwork are painted throughout the manuscript.
III. BORDERS & FRAMES: Bianchi girari border with blue, green, and purple on f. 1r.

CONTENTS:

1. Confessional—ff. 1r[a]–11r[b].

RUB.: incomenza el tractato dela confessione deli peccati; INC.: [f. 1r[a]] con cio sia cosa che de sopra sia dicto de doy parte principale de questa opera cioe dela fede et dele opere de essa fede . . .; EXPL.: [f. 11r[b]] . . . cioe che contucto el cuore perdoniamo al proximo. prestante domino nostro yhesu christo qui cum patre et spiritu sancto uiuit et regnat per infinita secula seculorum. amen.

BINDING: s. xix?; green silk with florals over pasteboards.

OWNERS & PROVENANCE: Rev. Monsignor David McRoberts (1912–1978); Everett McNear (1904–1984) of Chicago, IL; donated by Everett McNear to the Snite Museum of Art in 1984.

SALES & CATALOGUES: Sotheby's, 3 June 1929, lot 548; ibid., 10 December 1973, lot 48; ibid., 24 June 1980, lot 78.

Acc. 1984.3.7

Origin: Spain, s. xvi^{2}.
Content Overview: Antiphonary, Temporale (leaf).

In Latin, on parchment; 1 f.; 783 x 581 mm (page) [see Layout for ruling].

Layout:

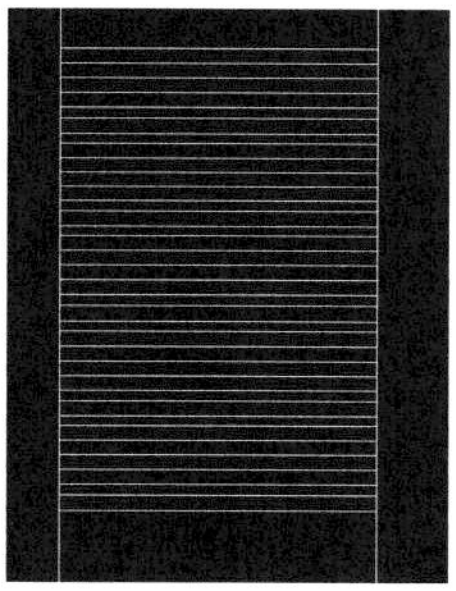

A

A Combined technique; 620 x 422 mm; 5 five-line staves, 5 text lines.

Pattern **A** is traced using a combined technique of red ink (staves) and lead (verticals and text lines); single column/full-music layout; prickings are not visible.

Script: A single hand (M1) writes all text in a large, sixteenth-century Southern Textualis Formata with clear Spanish forms.

Decoration:
I. Rubrication: Rubrics in red ink.
II. Initials: Littera duplex and cadel initials occur in hierarchy.
a. One littera duplex initial (2 staves and 2 text lines square inset) with "mudejar" motifs on the grounds is painted on the verso.
b. Cadels in black ink without heightening occur on the recto and verso.

Music & Staves: Five-line staves are traced in red ink; 80 mm; square neumes in black ink.

Contents:

1. Antiphonary, Temporale [leaf].

inc.: [recto] <mo>mentum orto iam sole . . .; **expl.**: [verso] . . . et accedens reuoluit lapidem et.

Contains the end of matins and beginning of Laudes (*Angleus autem Domini*) for Easter Sunday.

Owners & Provenance: From the collection of Everett McNear (1904–1984) of Chicago, IL; donated by Everett McNear to the Snite Museum of Art in 1984.

Acc. 1985.25

Origin: Italy, s. xiv^2 (Bologna).
Content Overview: *Meditationes uitae Christi* (Italian; 'short version').

In Italian, on parchment; ii + 121 ff. +ii; generally 180 x 125 mm (page) [see Layout for ruling]; flyleaves modern parchment; foliated in modern pencil with Arabic numerals.

Collation: ii $+1^{8-2}$ $+2^{8-2}$ $+3–5^{8}$ $+6^{8-1}$ $+7–11^{8}$ $+12^{8-2}$ $+13–16^{8}$ +ii

Quires: Parchment quaternions, F/F, are the normal quire forms. Quire 1 lacks the inner bifolium; obeys Gregory's Rule. Quire 2 lacks the third bifolium; does not obey Gregory's Rule; the missing bifolium between ff. 8–9 and 10–11 is also confirmed by the incongruous *ad hoc* signature [see Signatures]. Quire 6 (H/F) lacks the fifth leaf; does not obey Gregory's Rule; f. 37 may have been reversed when reattached; the first word of f. 37v corresponds to catchword of quire 5 on f. 36v; Phillips 2006, 271 n. 30 locates f. 37 as the missing conjugate of f. 40. Quire 12 lacks the inner bifolium; obeys Gregory's Rule. The manuscript has been trimmed.

Catchwords: Horizontal catchwords are written in the lower center margin; stylized for quires 1–15. All catchwords correspond, except for quire 5, which corresponds to f. 37v [see Quires].

Signatures: Signatures of the *ad hoc* type are written in the lower right corner for most quires; most are alphanumeric combinations (e.g., a i, a ii, a iii, etc.); signatures for quires 7, 8, 12, lost from trimming; remnants in quires 1 and 9.

Layout:

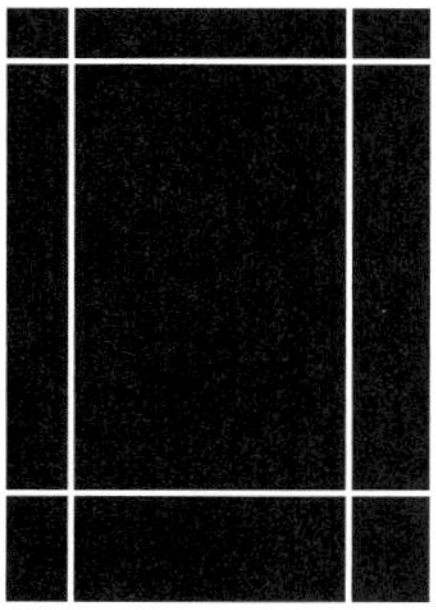

A

A ff. 1r–121v. Lead; 131 x 82 mm; 26 lines.

Pattern **A** is traced in lead on ff. 1r–121v; single column; writing below top line; prickings for vertical bounding lines visible in the upper and lower margins; pricking for upper horizontal visible in outer margin. Dimensions of **A** are subject to some variability. When miniatures occur, three sets of double prickings are added in the upper and lower margins for justification of the square frame [see Miniatures].

Script: A single hand (M1) writes all text in Southern Textualis Formata (Rotunda); instructions to the rubricator and illuminator are written in the margins in Cursiva. A later hand (s. xvi) adds Justinian, *Dig.* 39.1.5.12–13 on f. 121v.

Decoration:
I. Rubrication: Rubrics and paraph marks in red ink.
II. Initials: Decorated and flourished initials occur in hierarchy.
a. Decorated initials (3–7 line square inset) in typical Bolognese style are painted throughout the manuscript with marginal spray and gold dots; the 7 line initial occurs on f. 1r.
b. Flourished initials (2 line square inset; 1 line versals) alternate in red and blue ink with contrasting penwork on ff. 119v–121r.
III. Borders & Frames: Miniature frames in black ink and gold; frames vary in size depending on miniature.

Miniatures: Forty-eight square miniatures remain: Christ enthroned (f. 1r); Presentation of the Virgin (f. 5v); Annunciation (f. 8r); Visitation (f. 10v); Joseph thinking of leaving Mary (f. 12r); Nativity (f. 13v); Bathing the Christ Child (f. 15r); Annunciation to the shepherds (f. 16v); Circumcision (f. 18r); Adoration of the Magi (f. 20r); Presentation in the temple (f. 23v); Flight into Egypt (f. 26r); Return from Egypt (f. 33r); God the Father (f. 37r); Baptism of Christ (f. 45v); Temptation (f. 49r); Entry into Jerusalem (f. 54v); Meal at the house of Magdalene (f. 57v); Christ washes feet of disciples (f. 59r); Last Supper (f. 59v); Christ's Sermon to the Disciples (f. 65r); Agony in the garden (f. 67v); Mocking of Christ (f. 72v); Christ before Pilate (f. 74v); Flagellation (f. 76r); Second Mocking of Christ (f. 77v); Road to Calvary (f. 78r); Lamentation (f. 80r); Christ nailed to cross (f. 80v); Crucifixion (f. 85r); Entombment (f. 87r); Lamentation and return of Peter (f. 91v); Descent into Limbo (f. 93r); Apparition to Mary (f. 94r); Three Marys at the sepulcher (f. 95v); Noli me tangere (f. 97v); Apparition to three Marys (f. 99v); Apparition to Joseph of Arimathea (f. 100r); Apparition to James Minor (f. 100v); Apparition to Peter (f. 101r); Road to Emmaus (f. 102v); Apparition to disciples (f. 104r); Doubting Thomas (f. 106r); Apparition to disciples in Galilee (f. 107v); Apparition to more than five hundred (f. 108v); Ascension (f. 110r); Ascendant Christ (f. 112v); Pentecost (f. 117r).

Contents:

1. *Meditationes uitae Christi* (Italian; 'short version')—ff. 1r–121r.

inc.: [f. 1r] intra lli altre grandi uertudi chessi legano di santa cicilia uergine sie questa una grandissima coe chella portaua sempre el uangelio de christo . . .; expl.: [f. 121r] . . . persone bone possano conuersare in lo mio santo seruixio .c.xij. desuiati possano tornare in la mia uia. amen.

edition: cf. Sarri 1933.

Binding: s. xx; brown goatskin; bound at the Newberry Library bindery in 1965 (gilt binder's stamp); gilt title on spine.

Owners & Provenance: The manuscript was the property of "The Mount Vernon Street Warrens" of Boston, MA (see Green 1989) until it was sold at Sotheby's on 9 December 1963; Susan Cornelia Clarke Warren [Mrs. Samuel Dennis Warren] (1825–1901); Cornelia Lyman Warren (1857–1921); Gretchen Osgood Warren [Mrs. Fiske Warren] (1871–1961); from the collection of Everett McNear (1904–1984) of Chicago, IL; purchased by Everett McNear from Maggs Bros. on 24 January 1964; donated by Ann Katherine McNear (1902?–1994) of Chicago, IL, to the Snite Museum of Art in 1985 in memory of her husband, Everett.

Sales & Catalogues: Sotheby's, 9 December 1963, lot 123.

Bibliography: Lauck 1974, no. 14; Porter 1975, 98 (no. 97); Porter 1987, 11, 61; Flora 2003, 64 nn. 10, 11 [incorrectly cited as "Snite 95"]; Nolan 2006, 7; Phillips 2006; Flora 2009, 33, 50–51, 53–58, 64, 66; McNamer 2009, 905 n. 1; Bartal 2014, 156 n. 5; Phillips 2016.

Acc. 1989.20.1

Origin: Low Countries, s. xv^2 (Bruges?).
Content Overview: Miniature of St. Agatha (cutting).

Miniature (cutting), on parchment; 91 x 62 mm.

Decoration:
I. Borders & Frames: The miniature is enclosed in an arch-topped frame in gold (91 x 62 mm), which has been cut from its folio.

Miniatures: An arch-topped miniature depicting St. Agatha holding pliers with breast and a book with a chemise binding is painted on the verso; the recto is blank as is common with imported Flemish miniatures.

Owners & Provenance: Sir Bruce Ingram (1877–1963); Clifford Maggs (of Maggs Bros.) bid on behalf of Everett McNear (1904–1984) in the Ingram sale of July 1964; donated by Ann Katherine McNear (1902?–1994) of Chicago, IL, to the Snite Museum of Art in 1989 in memory of her husband, Everett.

Sales & Catalogues: Sotheby's, 6 July 1964, lot 214.

Bibliography: Kessler 1969, no. 12; Lauck 1974, no. 29.

Acc. 1989.20.2

Origin: France, s. xiii[2] (Paris).
Content Overview: Bible (leaf).

In Latin, on parchment; 1 f.; 230 x 160 mm (page) [see Layout for ruling].

Layout:

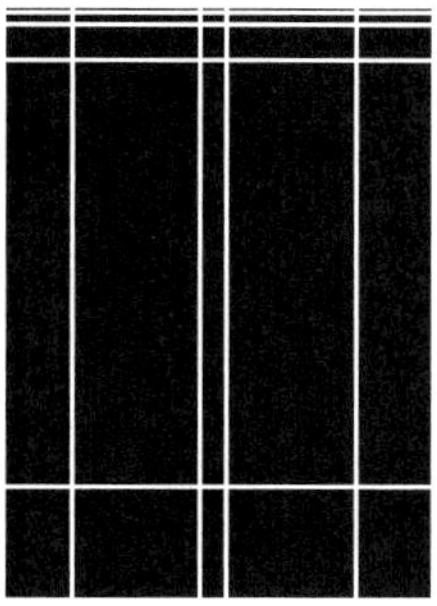

A

A Lead; 167 x 107 mm; intercol. 10 mm; 51 lines.

Pattern **A** is traced in lead; two columns (intercol. 10 mm); writing below top line; no prickings remain.

Script: A single hand (M1) writes all text in Northern Textualis Formata.

Decoration:
I. Rubrication: Rubric in red ink.
II. Initials: Historiated and decorated initials occur in hierarchy.
a. One historiated initial P (10+4 lines stepped) is painted on the recto in Parisian style; depicts Head of God and Gideon in mail. The historiated initial is attributed to the Dominican Painter (Branner 1977, 118–122).
b. One decorated initial (2 lines square inset) begins the chapter on the verso; same style as above.
III. Line Fillers: A line filler comprised of circles in red ink follows the rubric for Idc.

CONTENTS:

1. Bible [leaf].

INC.: [recto[a]] ei responderuntque testes nunc ergo ait auferte deos alienos de medio uestri . . . [Ios 24.22–33; EXPL.: [verso[b]] . . . feceruntque filii israel malum in conspectu domini et seruierunt baalim et astaroth ac dimi<serunt> [Idc 2.12].

Contains Ios 24.22–33 and Idc 1.1–2.12.

1.1. Ios 24.22–33—recto[a]. INC.: ei responderuntque testes nunc ergo ait auferte deos alienos de medio uestri . . .; EXPL.: . . . in gabaa phinees et filii eius que data est ei in monte effraum.

1.2. Idc 1.1–2.12—recto[a]–verso[b]. RUB.: incipit liber iudicum; INC.: post mortem iosue consuluerunt filii israel dominum . . .; EXPL.: . . . feceruntque filii israel malum in conspectu domini et seruierunt baalim et astaroth ac dimi-.

OWNERS & PROVENANCE: Purchased from Maggs Bros. by Everett McNear (1904–1984) ca. 1969; donated by Ann Katherine McNear (1902?–1994) of Chicago, IL, to the Snite Museum of Art in 1989 in memory of her husband, Everett. The parent manuscript, W.116, was one of the so-called Chester Beatty Bibles. W.116 was broken by Folio Fine Art (London) in 1969 after Sotheby's Beatty sale of December 1968. Known leaves are:

Gn 49.13–Ex 2.7	Notre Dame, Univ. Notre Dame, Hesburgh Library, Frag. I. 34
Ios 24.22–Idc 2.11	Notre Dame, Univ. Notre Dame, Snite Museum of Art, Acc. 1989.20.2
2 Rg 24.21–3 Rg 1.53	Notre Dame, Univ. Notre Dame, Snite Museum of Art, Acc. 1989.20.3
Ps 144.21–Prv 1	Boulder, Univ. Colorado, Norlin Library, MS 320
Prv 31.5–Ecc 2.17	Dublin, Chester Beatty Library, W 116 f. 54
12 leaves from Io	San Francisco, John Windle, March List 2014, no. 12

SALES & CATALOGUES: Sotheby's, 3 December 1968, lot 14 (parent manuscript); Maggs Bros., Bulletin 6, no. 2 (leaf).

FORMER SHELFMARK: MS 3679 (unknown); MS W.116 (Chester Beatty).

BIBLIOGRAPHY: ARTS CLUB OF CHICAGO 1970, no. 14; LAUCK 1974, no. 7.

Acc. 1989.20.3

Origin: France, s. xiii^{2} (Paris).
Content Overview: Bible (leaf).

In Latin, on parchment; 1 f.; 230 x 160 mm (page) [see Layout for ruling].

Foliation: The recto is marked in modern pencil with two sets of Arabic numerals, 14 and 139.

Layout:

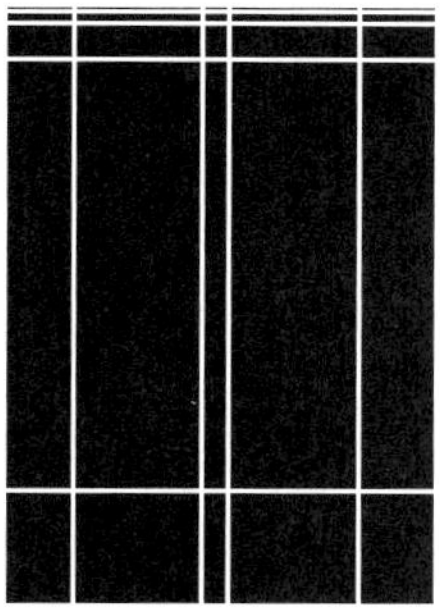

A

A Lead; 167 x 107 mm; intercol. 10 mm; 51 lines.

Pattern **A** is traced in lead; two columns (intercol. 10 mm); writing below top line; no prickings remain.

Script: A single hand (M1) writes all text in Northern Textualis Formata.

Decoration:
I. Rubrication: Rubrics in red ink; letter heightening of majuscules in red ink.
II. Initials: Historiated and plain initials occur in hierarchy.
a. Historiated initial (10 line square inset) is painted on the recto in Parisian style; scene depicts an attendant bringing Abishag to David. The historiated initial is attributed to the Dominican Painter (Branner 1977, 118–122).
b. Plain initials in blue and red ink alternate in the upper margin for the book title.

CONTENTS:

1. Bible [leaf].

INC.: [recto[a]] <alta>re domino ut cesset interfectio que grassatur in populo . . . [2 Rg 24.21]; EXPL.: [verso[b]] . . . et ingressus adorauit regem salomonem dixitque ei salo<mon> [3 Rg 1.53].

1.1. 2 Rg 24.21–25—recto[a]. INC.: <alta>re domino ut cesset interfectio que grassatur in populo . . .; EXPL.: . . . et repropiciatus est dominus terre et cohibita est plaga ab israel.

1.2. 3 Rg 1.1–53.—recto[a]–verso[b]. RUB.: incipit liber tertius regum; INC.: et rex dauid senuerat habebatque etatis plurimos dies . . .; EXPL.: . . . et ingressus adorauit regem salomonem dixitque ei salo<mon>.

Contains 2 Rg 24.21–3 Rg 1.53.

OWNERS & PROVENANCE: Purchased from Maggs Bros. by Everett McNear (1904–1984); donated by Ann Katherine McNear (1902?–1994) of Chicago, IL, to the Snite Museum of Art in 1989 in memory of her husband, Everett. The parent manuscript, W.116, was one of the so-called Chester Beatty Bibles. W.116 was broken by Folio Fine Art (London) in 1969 after Sotheby's Beatty sale of December 1968. Known leaves are:

Gn 49.13–Ex 2.7	Notre Dame, Univ. Notre Dame, Hesburgh Library, Frag. I. 34
Ios 24.22–Idc 2.11	Notre Dame, Univ. Notre Dame, Snite Museum of Art, Acc. 1989.20.2
2 Rg 24.21–3 Rg 1.53	Notre Dame, Univ. Notre Dame, Snite Museum of Art, Acc. 1989.20.3
Ps 144.21–Prv 1	Boulder, Univ. Colorado, Norlin Library, MS 320
Prv 31.5–Ecc 2.17	Dublin, Chester Beatty Library, W 116 f. 54
12 leaves from Io	San Francisco, John Windle, March List 2014, no. 12

SALES & CATALOGUES: Sotheby's, 3 December 1968, lot 14 (parent manuscript).

FORMER SHELFMARK: MS 3684 (unknown); MS W.116 (Chester Beatty).

BIBLIOGRAPHY: ARTS CLUB OF CHICAGO 1970, no. 14; LAUCK 1974, no. 8; PORTER 1992, 22.

Acc. 1989.20.4

Origin: Low Countries, s. xiv^{in} (Flanders).
Content Overview: Book of Hours, Ghistelles Hours (leaf).

In Latin, on parchment; 1 f.; 118 x 81 mm (page) [see Layout for ruling].

Layout:

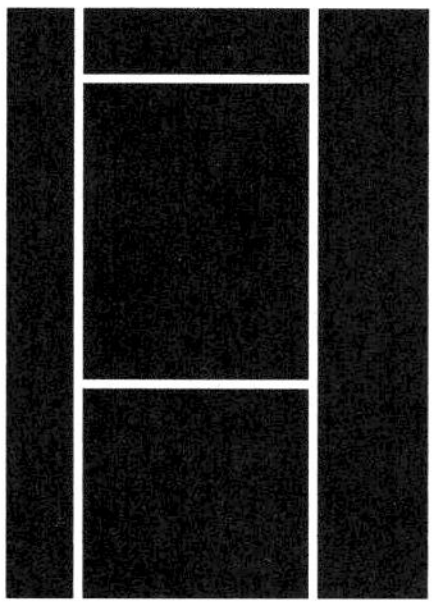

A

A Ink; 61 x 45 mm; 11 lines.

Pattern **A** is traced in brown ink; single column; writing below top line; prickings visible in the upper and lower margin for vertical bounding lines.

Script: A single hand (M1) writes all text in Northern Textualis Formata.

Decoration:
I. Rubrication: Rubrics in red ink.
II. Initials: Dentelle and cadels initials occur in hierarchy.
a. One dentelle initial (2 line square inset) begins the first reading on the recto; borders emerge from initial.
b. Cadels are used as 1 line versals.
III. Line Fillers: Blue floral with red penwork serves as a line filler on the verso.
IV. Borders & Frames: Dentelle style bar border is painted on the recto; the border frames the upper, inner, and lower margins terminating in grotesque and lion faces in gold; figure in blue hose and orange tunic with bird perched on left hand emerges from the lion's mouth into the outer margin.

Contents:

1. Book of Hours [leaf].

inc.: [recto] benedicere sancta uirgo uirginum intercede pro nobis ad dominum . . .; expl.: [verso] . . . oret uoce pia pro nobis uirgo maria amen lectio secunda.

1.1. Matins—recto–verso. lect. i.: sancta maria uirgo . . .; r. i.: sancta et immaculata . . .

The recto contains the first reading for matins; verso contains response, verse, and rubric for the second reading.

Owners & Provenance: Acquired by Clifford Maggs for Everett McNear (1904–1984) in 1971; donated by Ann Katherine McNear (1902?–1994) of Chicago, IL, to the Snite Museum of Art in 1989 in memory of her husband, Everett. The parent manuscript was the so-called Ghistelles Hours. The manuscript is thought to be associated with John III Ghistelles, lord of Ghistelles and Ingelmuster, or his household (de Hamel 2010, 82); the manuscript was broken by Heinrich Eisemann (1890–1972) in the 1940s and dispersed (de Hamel 2010, 82). Manion, Vines, & de Hamel 1989, 91–92 lists known leaves, which is updated by de Hamel 2010, 82. Manion, Vines, & de Hamel 1989, 92 identifies f. 24, the end of *Nunc Dimittis*, with the sale information for this leaf incorrectly. Leaves in institutional collections are:

Baltimore, Walters Art Museum, W 851 (calendar)
Bloomington, Indiana Univ., Lilly Library, MS 47
Cambridge, Harvard Univ., Houghton Library, MS Lat 446
Dunedin, Public Library, Reed Fragment 9
Notre Dame, Snite Museum of Art, Acc. 1989.20.4

Sales & Catalogues: Sotheby's 12 July 1971, lot 1.

Bibliography: Lauck 1974, no. 11; Manion, Vines, & de Hamel 1989, 92 (sale information misattributed).

Acc. 1989.20.5

Origin: England, s. xiii².
Content Overview: Bible (binding fragment).

In Latin, on parchment; 1 piece (2 ff., conjugate leaves); generally 230 x 369 mm (fragment) [see Layout for ruling]; unfoliated.

Collation: 1^{2}

Quires: The fragment is a single bifolium which has been trimmed significantly and used as a wrapper.

Layout: Ruled in lead; two columns (intercol. 7 mm; cols. with trimming approx. 213 x 61); approx. 66 lines.

Script: A single hand (M1) writes all text in Northern Textualis Formata.

Decoration:
I. Rubrication: Rubrics in red ink.
II. Initials: Littera duplex, flourished, and plain initials occur in broken hierarchy.
a. One littera duplex initial (12 lines standing) begins Sir.
b. Flourished initials (12 lines standing; 4 lines square inset; 4–5 lines hanging) divide the text.
c. One plain initial (hanging) in blue ink occurs as an anomaly; flourishing never added.
III. Line Fillers: Line fillers in red and blue ink are painted throughout the fragment.

Contents:

1. Bible [binding fragment].

inc.: [second leaf, recto[a]] uocat et pro itinere petit ab eo qui ambulare non potest . . . [Sap 13.19]; expl. [second leaf, verso[a]] . . . sed uerbo illum qui se uexabat subiecit iuramenta parentum [Sap 18.22]. inc.: [first leaf, recto[a]] illam que ad uiuos ducebat uiuam *** [*mutil.*] poderis quam habebat totus erat orbis terrarum . . . [Sap 18. 23–24]; expl.: [first leaf, verso[b]] . . . et miserebitur tui magis quam mater [Sir 4.11].

The former binding fragment is unfoliated and folded in reverse; the first leaf is the second in order of texts; contains Sap 13.19–19.20, and Sir 1.1–4.11 with preface and prologue [Stegmüller 472].

1.1. Sap 13.19–19.20—second leaf, recto[a]–first leaf, recto[a]. INC.: uocat et pro itinere petit ab eo qui ambulare non potest . . .; EXPL.: . . . et in omni tempore et in omni loco assistens eis.

1.2. Sir with preface and prologue—first leaf, recto[a]–first leaf, verso[b].

1.2.1. Preface, Sir—first leaf, recto[a–b]. RUB.: explicit liber sapientie habet uersus .i.dcc. incipit prephatium in libro ihesu filii syrach; INC.: multorum nobis et magnorum per legem et prophetas . . .; EXPL.: . . . qui secundum legem domini proposuerint uitam agere.

1.2.2. Prologue—first leaf, recto[b]. RUB.: explicit prephatium. incipit prologus; INC.: hic ihesus filius syrach ante .cclxxij. annos hunc librum scripsit . . .; EXPL.: . . . autem saluator noster natus est olimpia fuit .cxcij. [STEGMÜLLER 472].

1.2.3. Sir 1.1–4.11—first leaf, recto[b]–first leaf, verso[b]. RUB.: incipit liber ihesu filii syrach id est ecclesiasticus salomonis; INC.: omnis sapientia a domino deo est et cum illo fuit semper et est ante euum . . .; EXPL.: . . . et miserebitur tui magis quam mater.

OWNERS & PROVENANCE: Purchased by Everett McNear (1904–1984) of Chicago, IL, from Maggs Bros. in August 1979; donated by Ann Katherine McNear (1902?–1994) of Chicago, IL, to the Snite Museum of Art in 1989 in memory of her husband, Everett.

Acc. 1989.20.6

Origin: France or Flanders, s. xiv^{2} (ca. 1350).
Content Overview: Book of Hours (leaf).

In Latin, on parchment; 1 f.; 135 x 96 mm (page) [see Layout for ruling].

Foliation: Foliated in modern ink with Arabic numerals in the lower right margin (f. 102).

Layout:

A

A Lead; 96 x 55 mm; 12 lines.

Pattern **A** is traced in lead (very faded); single column; writing below top line; no prickings visible.

Script: A single hand (M1) writes all text in Northern Textualis Formata.

Decoration:
I. Initials: Foliate, dentelle, and flourished initials occur in hierarchy.
a. One foliate initial (4 line square inset) with inner zoomorphic motifs begins the hour on the recto.
b. One dentelle initial (2 line square inset) begins the psalm on the verso.
c. Flourished initials (1 line versals) in gold with blue penwork and blue with red penwork alternate throughout the recto and verso.
II. Line Fillers: Line fillers in gold with blue, white, and red penwork occur on the recto and verso.

Contents:

1. Book of Hours [leaf].

inc.: [recto] domine exaudi orationem meam benedicamus domino deus in adiutorium . . .; expl.: [verso] . . . sicut oculi ancille in manibus domine sue ita oculi nostri.

1.1 Terce or Sext [incomplete]–recto–verso. hym.: memento salutis auctor; ant.: ecce tu pulcra es et decora; ps.: ad te leuaui oculos meos qui habitat in celis ecce sicut oculi . . . [Ps 122].

One of the little hours, either Terce or Sext.

Owners & Provenance: According to the matte, the leaf was owned by Ernst Detterer (1888–1947), then Rodney Chirpe of Chicago, IL. Detterer must have acquired the leaf from his former classmate, Otto F. Ege (1888–1951), who broke the parent manuscript and sold the leaves as part of an "Augustinian Book of Hours, ca. 1310." Everett McNear (1904–1984) acquired the leaf from an unspecified private collector in June 1975; donated by Ann Katherine McNear (1902?–1994) of Chicago, IL, to the Snite Museum of Art in 1989 in memory of her husband, Everett.

Other known leaves (including those in Gwara 2013, *Handlist*, no. 325 with additions) are:

Buffalo, Albright-Knox Art Gallery, 1940:355.25
Notre Dame, Univ. Notre Dame, Snite Museum of Art, Acc. 1989.20.6
Phoenix, Phoenix Public Library, Manuscript Frag. 71
Roanoke, Hollins Univ., Wyndham Robertson Library, MS 13

Bibliography: Gwara 2013, *Handlist*, no. 325 (Snite leaf unrecorded); Arts Club of Chicago 1970, no. 16 (Snite, Acc. 1989.20.6); Porter 1975, no. 96 (Snite, Acc. 1989.20.6); Shailor 2009, 21; Gwara 2013, 37 n. 96, 69; images of other leaves are Shailor 2009, color plate 2c (Phoenix, PL, MS Frag. 71), and Gwara 2013, fig. 65 (Roanoke, Hollins Univ., WRL, MS 13).

Acc. 1989.20.7

Origin: Italy, s. xiii^2.
Content Overview: Iacobus de Voragine, *Legenda aurea;* Master of Monza (attr.), Sts. Prothus, Hyacinthus, and Eugenia (cutting).

In Latin, on parchment; 96 x 76 mm.

Script: A single hand (M1) writes Southern Textualis Formata (Rotunda).

Decoration:
I. Rubrication: Rubric in red ink.

Contents:
1. Iacobus de Voragine, *Legenda aurea.*
inc.: [recto] <colloca>uit. de sanctis proto et h<yacintho>.

The text and rubric above the illustration correspond to the end of cap. 129 and beginning of 130 of the *Legenda aurea* [see Maggioni 1998, 2:924–925]. Text on the verso is mutilated, even with ultraviolet light.

Miniatures: Three saints with tonsure and habits; two hold books. The painter of the miniature was identified as the Master of Monza by Valagussa 1997 on the basis of Kraków, Biblioteka Jagiellońska, MS Rps. Akc. 20/1951. The three figures are likely Sts. Protus, Hyacinthus, and Eugenia. On the depiction of St. Eugenia as a man, see Grayson 2009, 147–148; cf. Acc. 1989.20.7 with the miniature on Paris, Bibliothèque nationale de France, MS Fr. 185, f. 254v.

Owners & Provenance: Robert Forrer (1866–1947); purchased from Maggs Bros. by Everett McNear (1904–1984) in June 1974; donated by Ann Katherine McNear (1902?–1994) of Chicago, IL, to the Snite Museum of Art in 1989 in memory of her husband, Everett.

This cutting was one of ten from the same parent manuscript in the collection of Robert Forrer in Strasbourg ca. 1902, which was dispersed in the 1920s. Twenty-nine cuttings from the parent manuscript have been verified with images. The list below in alphabetical order supplements, updates, and corrects those of Valagussa 1997 and Freuler 2013:

1. Agatha	London, Maggs Bros., Bulletin 8, no. 4 (June 1974)
2. Baptism of Christ	Providence, RISD, Museum of Art, 2010.19.1
3. Baptism of Paul	Paris, Les Enluminures, Cat. 1, no. 18a (1992)
4. Barbara	London, Christie's, 6 July 2011, lot 2
5. Benedict	London, Sotheby's, 8 December 1975, lot 7
6. Boniface	London, Christie's, 6 July 2011, lot 3
7. Catherine of Alexandria	Paris, Musée national du Moyen Age
8. Cecilia	(Freuler 2013, 426, no. 40)
9. Christ's descent into Limbo	Zurich, Koller Auctions, 18 September 2015, lot 157
10. Christ's entry to Jerusalem	Unknown (Freuler 2013, 426)
11. Chrysanthus	London, Sotheby's, 23 June 1992, lot 28.
12. Clement	Private Collection (Freuler 2013, 430, fig. c)
13. Felicity	Milano, Collezione Longari (Valagussa 1997)
14. Francis	ex-Strölin Collection (Freuler 2013, 429, fig. b)
15. Giles or Eustace	Paris, Les Enluminures, Cat. 1, no. 18b (1992)
16. John and Paul	Paris, Les Enluminures, Cat. 3, no. 16b (1994)
17. John(?), bishop at altar	Unknown (Forrer 1902, 1: Tafel VI)
18. Josaphat	Private Collection (Freuler 2013, 431, fig. d)
19. Mary Magdalene	London, Sotheby's, 18 June 1991, lot 9
20. Massacre of Innocents	La Spezia, Museo Amedeo Lia, Inv. 523
21. Nativity	Paris, Les Enluminures, Cat. 7, no. 10 (1998)
22. Peter on *cathedra*	London, Maggs Bros. Bulletin 8, no. 1 (June 1974)
23. Protus, Hyacinthus, Eugenia	Notre Dame, Snite Museum of Art, Acc. 1989.20.7
24. Remigius	La Spezia, Museo Amedeo Lia, Inv. 522
25. Silvester	Private Collection (according to Valagussa 1997)
26. Thomas, apostle	London, Maggs Bros. Bulletin 8, no. 3 (June 1974)
27. Unidentified saint, bishop, initial T	London, Maggs Bros. Bulletin 8, no. 5 (June 1974)
28. Unidentified saint, female, tower	London, Sotheby's, 22 June 2004, lot 20
29. Unidentified saint, initial M	London, Sotheby's, 8 December 1975, lot 8

Freuler 2013, 426 lists "St. Paul the Hermit (?)" as sold at Sotheby's 8 December 1975 without a lot number; the same miniature is possibly the "Unidentified saint, bishop initial T" of the above list. Likewise, Freuler 2013, 426 also lists a Thomas of Canterbury sold by Les Enluminures, though no sale information is provided.

Sales & Catalogues: Maggs Bros., Bulletin 8, no. 6.

Bibliography: Forrer 1902, 1:15, Tafel VIII; Porter 1975, no. 95; Porter 1992, 22; Todini 1996, 291–294; Valagussa 1997; Freuler 2013, 427–431.

Acc. 1996.48

ORIGIN: Low Countries, s. xv^{2}.
CONTENT OVERVIEW: Antiphonary, Sanctorale (leaf).

In Latin, on parchment; 1 f.; 480 x 360 mm (page) [see LAYOUT for ruling].

LAYOUT:

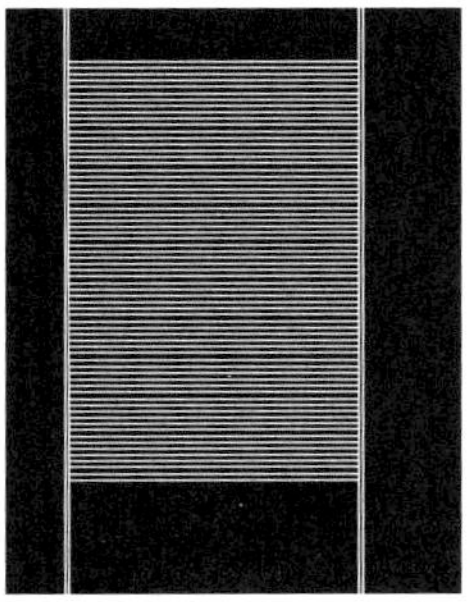

A

A Ink; 345 x 232 mm; 11 four-line staves, 11 text lines.

Pattern **A** is traced in red ink (staves); no ink or lead is visible for text lines; single column/full-music layout; double prickings for vertical bounding lines are visible in the lower margin, but verticals are not traced.

SCRIPT: A single hand (M1) writes all text in Northern Textualis Formata.

DECORATION:
I. RUBRICATION: Rubrics in red ink.
II. INITIALS: Flourished and cadel initials occur in hierarchy.
A. Flourished initials (4 staff lines and 1 text line) in red and blue ink with contrasting penwork begin the antiphons on the recto and verso.
B. Cadels (4 staff lines and 1 text line) with red and black penwork begin the verses on the verso.

Music & Staves: Four-line staves traced in red ink; 15 mm; square neumes in black ink.

Contents:

1. Antiphonary, Sanctorale [leaf].

inc.: [recto] <li>bera. uersus. seuit hostis innocentes perimens atrociter sed tyranni . . .;
expl.: [verso] . . . suo sponso pro quo tulit aspera mundi euouae antiphona or-.

Contains matins (incomplete) for the Office of St. Katherine (Nov. 25); the fragment ends imperfectly in the second nocturn.

Owners & Provenance: Dean A. Porter; donated by Dr. and Mrs. Dean A. Porter to the Snite Museum of Art in 1996.

Acc. 2015.37

Origin: Low Countries, s. xv^{2}.
Content Overview: Psalter (leaf).

In Latin, on parchment; 1 f.; 149 x 112 mm (page) [see Layout for ruling].

Layout:

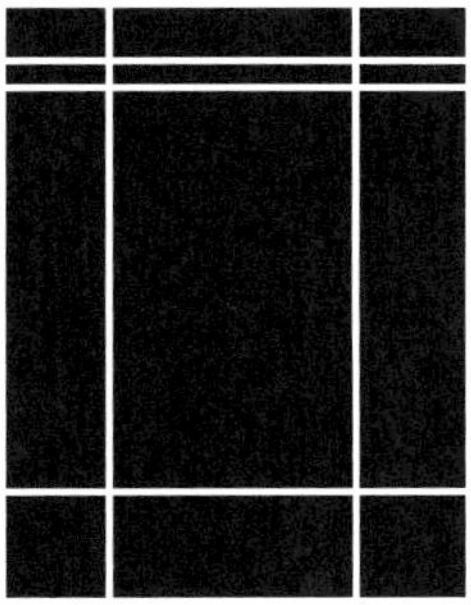

A

A Ink; 109 x 60 mm; 16 lines.

Pattern **A** is traced in black ink; single column; writing below top line; prickings visible in the outer margin for text lines.

Script: A single hand (M1) writes all text in Northern Textualis Formata; script is Quadrata with frequent superfluous hairlines; very Northern features, likely of Germanic origin.

Decoration:
I. Initials: Plain initials occur as versals.
a. Plain initials (1 line versals) alternate in blue and red ink.

CONTENTS:

1. Psalter [leaf].

INC. [recto] inuocaui dominum et exaudiuit me in latitudine dominus . . . [Ps 117. 5]; EXPL.: [verso] . . . hec est dies quam fecit [Ps 117. 24].

Contains Ps 117.5–24; fragment from either a psalter or breviary.

OWNERS & PROVENANCE: The leaf formed part of the Snite Museum of Art's "teaching collection" and was thus undocumented until it was rediscovered and accessioned in May 2015.

Catalogue

Saint Mary's College, Cushwa-Leighton Library

MS 1

Origin: Germany, s. xii^{ex}–xiii^{2}.
Content Overview: Peter Lombard, *Sentences* (Lib. IV; incomplete); excerpts of Rather of Verona, *Synodica*; excerpts of Adalgerus, *De studio uirtutum*; substantial selections of Burchard of Worms, *Decretum.*

In Latin, on parchment; i +38 ff. +i; 203 x 144 mm (page) [see Layout for ruling]; flyleaves and pastedowns are early modern paper; foliated in modern pencil with Arabic numerals.

Collation: i +1^{10} +2^{8} +3^{4} +4–5^{8} +i

Quires: Parchment quaternions, H/H, are the predominant quire forms; quire 1 is a quinion, H/H; quire 3 is a binion, H/H. The manuscript has been trimmed, resulting in a loss of marginal text.

Layout:

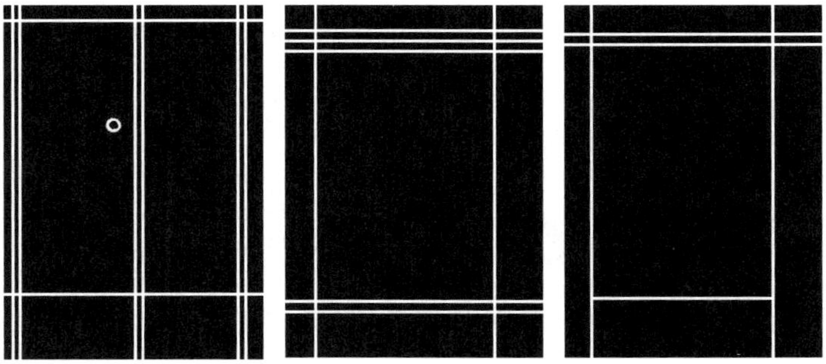

AB C D

- A ff. 1r–10v. Lead; 157 x 124 mm; intercol. 4 mm; 45 lines.
- B ff. 11r–18v. Lead; 166 x 103 mm; intercol. 4 mm; 46 lines.
- C ff. 19r–22v. Ink; 156–159 x 100 mm; 30 lines.
- D ff. 23r–38v. Ink; 152–159 x 101 mm; 19 lines.

Pattern **A** is traced in lead on ff. 1r–10v; two columns (intercol. 4 mm); writing above top line; prickings visible in the upper and lower margins for vertical bounding lines; prickings in outer margin for horizontals. Pattern **B** is traced in lead on ff. 11r–18v; two columns (intercol. 4 mm); writing above top line; presentation and pricking pattern identical to **A**, but **B** has smaller lateral dimensions. Pattern **C** is traced in brown ink on ff. 19r–22v; single column; writing above top line; prickings visible for vertical bounding lines in the upper and lower margins. Pattern **D** is traced in brown ink on ff. 23r–38v; single column; writing above top line; prickings visible as in **C**.

Script: Two scribal bookhands (M1–M2) write all texts. M1 writes a small, well-executed Northern Textualis Libraria of the early thirteenth century on ff. 1r–18v; rapid execution resulting in appearance of single compartment **a**. M2 writes Northern Textualis displaying many transitional features of Praegothica at the end of the twelfth or beginning of the thirteenth century on ff. 19r–38v. Two hands (M3–M4, s. xiii) have made additions on f. 38v.

Decoration:
I. Rubrication: Rubrics in red ink; letter heightening of majuscules in red ink.
II. Initials: Plain initials occur throughout the manuscript.
a. Plain initials (1–4 line square inset) in red on ff. 1r–18v; plain initials (1–2 line square inset; most are hanging) on ff. 19r–38v in red and black ink.

Contents:

1. Peter Lombard, *Sentences*, Book IV [incomplete]—ff. 1r[a]–18v[b].

rub.: de sacramentis ubi quattuor prius consideranda sunt; inc.: [f. 1r[a]] samaritanus enim uulnerato approprians curationi[-s] eius sacramentorum alligamenta adhibuit . . .; expl.: [f. 18v[b]] . . . symoniacos uero non symoniace a symoniacis ordinatos miseri-.

The first portion begins on f. 1r[a] with Lib. IV. Dist. 1. Cap. 1. n. 1 to Dist. 14. Cap. 2. n. 5, in which M1 adds rubrics within the text and in all margins. The second portion of the text begins on f. 11r[a] mid-sentence at Lib. IV. Dist. 18. Cap. 4. n. 4, and breaks off on f. 18v[b] at Lib. IV. Dist. 25. Cap. 5 (line 5); spaces for rubrics within the text remain.

Edition: Grottaferrata 1971–1981.

2. Rather of Verona, *Synodica* [incomplete]—f. 19r–v.

inc.: [f. 19r] uulgus nocturnis horis celebrare solet contradicite et cachinnos quos exercent . . . [*PL* 136.563]; expl.: [f. 19v] . . . ut idonei uideantur ecclesiastice dignitati [*PL* 136.564] uidete si absque horum que premisimus scientia ministerium nostrum facere potestis et plebes uobis conmissas ad uitam ducere et christo presentare [*PL* 136.568].

The text begins imperfectly in chapter 11, continues through chapter 13, and includes the final sentence of chapter 15.

Edition: *PL* 136.563–564, 568.

3. *Vniuscuiusque Christi minister*—f. 19v.

INC.: [f. 19v] uniuscuiusque christi minister cum barrochiam sibi conmissam causa reguminis [*sic*] adeat nulli pre multitudine grauis existat . . .; EXPL.: [f. 19v] . . . modii auaenae [*sic*] ad eius seruicium peragendum semper sit paratum.

EDITION: KRAUSE 1894, 110.

4. Burchard of Worms, *Decretum* (Lib. 19.3)—ff. 19v–20r.

INC.: [f. 19v] domine deus omnipotens propicius esto michi peccatori ut digne tibi possim gratias agere . . .; EXPL.: [f. 20r] . . . a quibus constricti tenentur et ad te per condignam satisfactionem reuertantur per.

The prayer is found in chapter 3 under the rubric *Oratio sacerdotis dicenda ad poenitentiam uenientibus.*

EDITION: *PL* 140.950.

5. Adalgerus (attr.), *De studio uirtutum*, cap. 14.—ff. 20r–22r.

INC.: [f. 20r] hortor igitur ut uel infirmitas uel alia contrarietas tibi acccidert [*sic*] quatenus ualeas scire . . .; EXPL.: [f. 22r] . . . argumenta et machinamenta omnia antiqui hostis destruxit.

EDITION: *PL* 134.932–934.

6. *Adam de octo partibus est creatus*—f. 22r

INC.: [f. 22r] adam de octo partibus est creatus primam partem habens de limo terre secundam de mari terciam de sole quartam de uento . . .; EXPL.: [f. 22r] . . . et dixit dominus ad oriel [*sic*] adam et dixit uocatur nomen eius adam.

EDITION: FÖRSTER 1908, 479–480; see also K. FISCHER 1996, 226.

7. Burchard of Worms, *Decretum* [selections]—ff. 22r–38v.

INC.: [f. 22r] augustinus de occultis incestis si quis incestum occulte conmiserit et sacerdoti occulte confessionem egerit [Lib. 19.36] . . .; EXPL.: [f. 38v] . . . si nulla peccati delectatio sequatur peccatum omni modo perpetratum <non> est [*sic*] [Lib. 5.43].

EDITION: *PL* 140.537–1058.

8. Additions—f. 38v.

8.1. [cf. CONTENTS 6]. **INC.**: archangelus michael abiit et uidit stellam que . . .; **EXPL.**: . . . huius hominis angelis ***.

8.2. Ps. 17.26. **INC.**: cum sancto sanctus eris et uiro innocente innocens eris.

BINDING: s. xvii–xx (repaired); stiff vellum binding.

OWNERS & PROVENANCE: Acquired by Saint Mary's College in October 1962 according to the note written on flyleaf I verso; sticker of "Cosmopolitan Science & Art Service Co. Inc. 638 Lexington Avenue, New York, NY" on rear pastedown [see MS 2].

SALES & CATALOGUES: Hirsch, *Valuable Manuscripts*, no. 21.

FORMER SHELFMARK: B 765 . P47 S4 1200 (Saint Mary's College).

MS 2

ORIGIN: France and England, s. xiii^{ex}–xiv^{in} (section dated 10 December 1299).
CONTENT OVERVIEW: Thomas Aquinas, *De ente et essentia*; Aristoteles Latinus, *De longitudine*, and *Analytica priora*; sermon collection; fragment of Deuteronomy 15–17.

In Latin, on parchment; i +31 ff. +i; generally 204 x 144 mm (page) [see LAYOUT for ruling]; foliated in modern pencil with Arabic numerals; flyleaf early modern paper.

COLLATION: i $+1^{6+1} +2^{10-2} +3^{6+1} +4^{12\text{-}4+1}$ +i

QUIRES: Parchment quires of various forms are used throughout the manuscript. Quire 1 is a ternion, F/F, with a leaf added (f. 6; text continuous); quire 2 is a quinion, H/H, lacking the ninth and tenth leaves (writing visible on stubs). Quire 3 is a ternion, H/H, with an added leaf (f. 20; text continuous); does not obey Gregory's Rule. Quire 4 is a sexternion, F/F, with the last four leaves canceled and one added (f. 31). Assembly is typical of scholastic manuscript; parchment well scraped, but flawed; endcuts present. The manuscript has been trimmed.

LAYOUT:

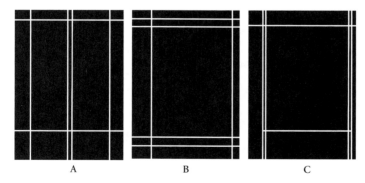

A B C

A ff. 1r–7v. Ink; 154 x 105 mm; intercol. 5.5 mm; 32 lines.
B ff. 8r–15v. Ink; 162 x 113 mm; 43 lines.
C ff. 16r–31v. Ink; 145 x 111 mm; 30 lines.

Pattern A is traced in brown ink on ff. 1r–7v; two columns (intercol. 5.5 mm); writing below top line; prickings visible in the upper and lower margins for vertical bounding lines;

scholastic presentation for glossing evidenced by occasional inner vertical. Pattern **B** is traced in brown ink on ff. 8r–15v; single column; writing below top line; prickings visible for vertical bounding lines. Pattern **C** is traced in brown ink on ff. 15r–31v; single column; writing below top line; prickings visible for vertical bounding lines; scholastic presentation for glossing as **A** (inner vertical sometimes visible). The binding fragment from a large Bible [see CONTENTS 5] is ruled in lead using a two-column layout.

SCRIPT: Four scribal bookhands (M1–M4) write all texts. M1 writes Northern Textualis Libraria on ff. 1r–7v. M2 writes Northern Textualis Libraria on ff. 8r–14v. M3 writes a similar script on ff. 14v–15v which begins to admit looped ascenders and a straight **s** that descends below the line, but exclusive use of two compartment **a**; when the script presents the features of Cursiva Antiquior, it also admits Anglicana forms (e.g., **d** on f. 15r; **r** form). M4 writes Northern Textualis Libraria on ff. 16r–31v. All scripts are typically scholastic and highly abbreviated. The binding fragment from a large Bible [see CONTENTS 5] is written in Northern Textualis Formata by M5.

DECORATION:

I. RUBRICATION: Rubrics, paraph marks, and letter heightening in red ink on ff. 8r–14v. Letter heightening in red ink on binding fragment, and a paraph mark in blue ink.

II. INITIALS: Plain initials were executed on ff. 8r–14r and f. 16r; several 2–3 line square insets remain throughout the manuscript; no guide letters present.

A. Flourished initials (2 line square inset) in red and blue ink with contrasting penwork occur in the Bible fragment used as the front and rear cover [see CONTENTS 5].

B. Plain initials (2–3 line square inset; hanging **i**) are drawn in red ink on ff. 8r–14r; a 3 line square inset initial is traced in black ink on f. 16r, but not painted.

DIAGRAMS: Three syllogisms for the *Analytica priora* are drawn in black and brownish ink in the margins of ff. 23r, 24r, 28r.

CONTENTS:

1. Thomas Aquinas, *De ente et essentia* (with glosses)—ff. 1r^{a}–6r^{b}.

INC.: [f. 1r^{a}] <q>uia paruus error in principio magnus in fine . . .; EXPL.: [f. 6r^{b}] . . . propter suam simplicitatem in quo finis et consumatio huius operis. explicit de ente et essencia thome de monte aquino; SCRIBAL COLOPHON [*in det. marg.*]: anno domini millesimo ducento nonagesimo nono quarto ydus decembris indictione non[-e]a.

Glosses were added by the text hand subsequently. According to the colophon, the glossing was completed 10 December 1299.

EDITION: LEON. 1976, 315–381.

2. Aristoteles Latinus, *De longitudine*—ff. 6v[a]–7v[b].

INC.: [f. 6v[a]] <d>e eo autem quidem [*sic*] quod est esse animalium alia quidem longe uite alia uero breuis uite . . .; EXPL.: [f. 7v[b]] . . . parum autem est aliqua alia dicitur in eo quod est superesse longioris uite. finit liber de longitudine et breuitate uite.

EDITION: *AL* 16.2 (ed. DE LEEMANS, *AL* database).

3. Sermon Collection—ff. 8r–15v.

Item 3.9 is also found in Budapest, Egyetemi Könyvtár, Cod. 42, f. 26 (*olim* Cod. Lat. 42), and Wien, Schottenstift, Stiftsbibliothek, Cod. 336, ff. 252r–253r (*olim* 54.d.3; HÜBL no. 296).

3.1. f. 8r–v. RUB.: incipit commune sanctorum et primo de dedicacione; INC.: habitabit cum eis et ipsi populus eius erunt et ipse deus cum eis erit eorum deus apocalypsis iohannis ewangelista [Apc 21.3] raptus per speciem in suo spiritu uidit ciuitatem nouam de celo descendentem . . .; EXPL.: . . . et tunc pone solum uerbum pro principio.

3.2. f. 9r–v. RUB.: [f. 8v] de secundo sermo; INC.: ipsi populus eius erunt [Apc 21.3] scriptum est numeri .xx. quod dixit dominus ad moysen tolle inquid uirgam et congrega populum [Nm 20.8] quemadmodum enim pastor ouium cum uirga et baculo congregat gregem suum ut reducat eum ad domum . . .; EXPL.: . . . uide igitur quid opereris ut propere mercedem recipiens uicam [*sic*] sine grauamine recipere merearis et hoc habeas pro secundo sermone.

3.3. ff. 9v–10v. RUB.: de tercio; INC.: ipse deus cum eis erit eorum deus [Apc 21.3] hic nota inmensitas habitalitatis [*sic*] diuine quia ipse erit eorum deus . . .; EXPL.: . . . rogemus et nos dominum ut sic eo influente simus dispositi quod consumemus uitam in bono ut ex hoc uitam mereamur eternam.

3.4. ff. 10v–11r. RUB.: de apostolis; INC.: hoc est preceptum meum ut diligatis inuicem sicut dilexi uos io. [Io 15.12] scitis karissimi et uidemus ad sensum quod quanto carior est dominus . . .; EXPL.: . . . quam hodie orandis de uocatione quacum eo adiuuante ab ista mortali uita ad eternam ualeas peruenire rogemus.

3.5. ff. 11r–12r. RUB.: de uno martyre; INC.: gloriosam mortem magis quam odibilem uitam amplectens uoluntarie ibat ad supplicium .i. machabei .vj. [2 Mcc 6.19] iste fidelissimus elazarus etate grandeuus moribus et honestate . . .; EXPL.: . . . tyrannum superauit moriens uitam promeruit quam et nobis ipsius meritis prestare dignetur pater et filius et spiritus sanctus amen.

3.6. ff. 12r–13r. RUB.: de martyribus; INC.: in paucis uexati in multis bene disponentur quoniam deus temptauit illos et inuenit eos dignos se sap. .ij. [Sap 3.5] responsum legitur numeri .xviij. quod dixerunt filii israhel cum intrarent terram egypti ad explorand[–a]um . . .; EXPL.: . . . rogemus et nos ipsos ut pro nobis ad dominum intercedant ut ad eorum mereamur peruenire societatem amen.

3.7. ff. 13r–14r. RUB.: de confessoribus sermo; INC.: dilectus deo et hominibus cuius memoria in benedictione est sap. [Sir 45.1] dicunt sancti quod caritas est uirtus qua unaquemque res tanta habeatur quanta habundantia est . . .; EXPL.: . . . regnum dei pro merito et scientiam quam sancti habent in congnoscendo [*sic*] deo rogantes christum ut hoc nobis suis obtineat orationibus amen.

3.8. f. 14r–v. RUB.: de uirginibus; INC.: simile est regnum celorum thezauro [Mt 13.31] iterum margarite iterum sagene misse in mare mt. [Mt 13.47] responsum istud ewangelium de uirginibus eo quod tota uita qua peruenitur ad regnum . . .; EXPL.: . . . ut patet in ista gloriosa uirgine quod et nobis suo adiutorio donare dignetur benedictus in secula amen. deo laus et gloria sit per.

3.9. ff. 14v–15v. INC.: <s>uscipiens ehsus [*sic*] uidit illum et cetera usque ma<nere> luc. .xix. [Lc 19.5] ewangelium istud in quo agitur de commisione magni peccatoris . . .; EXPL.: . . . parui operis qui deo preparat donum mentis rogemus ergo et cetera cetera [*sic*].

3.10. f. 15v [incomplete]. INC.: <i>n domo tua oportet me manere luce [Lc 19.5] in solempnitate dedicationis in qua legitur presens ewangelium ubi plures conueniunt de peccatore zacheo narratur . . .; EXPL.: . . . primum propter quod zacheus dignus fuit recipere dominum fuit sollicitudo.

4. Aristoteles Latinus, *Analytica priora* [incomplete]—ff. 16r–31v.

INC.: [f. 16r] primum oportet dici [*sic*] circa quod et de quo est intentio quoniam circa demonstracionem quia de disciplina . . .; EXPL.: [f. 31v] . . . per impossibile autem sillogismis ostendetur [*sic*] quidem quoniam [*sic*] contradictio supponitur conclusionis assumitur [2.11].

EDITION: *AL* 3.1–4 (ed. MINIO-PALUELLO 1962, 5–115).

5. Dt 15.11–17.4 [binding fragment]—front and rear covers.

INC. [rear cover]: dominus deus tuus in cunctis operibus que agis [Dt 15.11] . . .; EXPL. [front cover]: . . . et hoc tibi fuerit nuntiatum audiensque inquisieris diligenter et uerum esse repp- [Dt 17.4].

Leaf used in binding is French.

BINDING: s. xvii–xx (repaired); stiff vellum binding; cover made from fragment [see CONTENTS 5].

OWNERS & PROVENANCE: Acquired by Saint Mary's College in 1962 [see MS 1]; sticker of "Cosmopolitan Science & Art Service Co. Inc. 638 Lexington Avenue, New York, NY" on rear pastedown [see MS 1].

SALES & CATALOGUES: Hirsch, *Valuable Manuscripts*, no. 24.

FORMER SHELFMARK: B 765 . T5 1500 (Saint Mary's College).

MS 3

Origin: Northern France, s. xv^{2} (*Amiénois, ante* 1478); with additions s. xv^{2}–xvi^{2}.
Content Overview: Book of Hours, use of Amiens.

In Latin and French (Picard), on parchment; ii +129 ff. +iv; generally 204 x 140 mm (page) [see Layout for ruling]; flyleaves i, ii, iv, v modern paper; a fifteenth-century parchment document was previously a pastedown (now f. 1r) that functioned as a flyleaf; ff. 53v, 70v, 121v blank but ruled; foliated in modern pencil with Arabic numerals.

Collation: iii +1–3^{6} +4–5^{8} +6^{8-2} +7^{8-5} +8^{8-1} +9^{8-4} +10–12^{8} +13^{1+1+1} +14–15^{8} +16^{2+3} +17–18^{4} +19^{8-1} +20^{2+1} +21^{6} +22^{2} +iv

Quires: Parchment quaternions, F/F, are the predominant quire forms. Ternions are used for quires 1–3 and quire 21. Quire 6 lacks the second and sixth leaves. Quire 7 lacks five leaves. Quire 8 lacks the fifth leaf. Quire 9 lacks four leaves. Quire 13 is comprised of two singletons with stubs (ff. 80 and 82) with another singleton (f. 81) pasted together. Quire 16 is a bifolium with three singletons added (ff. 101–103). Quires 17 and 18 were originally one quaternion but were split into two binions and reversed [see Contents 9, 10, and 10.6]. Quire 19 lacks the eighth leaf. Quire 20 is a bifolium with an added singleton (f. 121). Quire 22 is a bifolium. Several leaves have been excised; stubs and the resultant singletons were glued together subsequently in an effort to conceal the mutilation of the manuscript. The well-scraped parchment has been damaged by water (heavily) and fire (slightly) and is very rigid. The manuscript has been trimmed and much adhesive was applied in the modern era.

Catchwords: Horizontal catchwords remain in lower right margin of f. 63v and in the center lower margin of f. 90v (stylized); both correspond. Markings appear in the lower right corners on the rectos of ff. 101–105 and 112–116 in extremely light brown ink and are faded severely; perhaps *ad hoc* signatures were used for this section.

Layout:

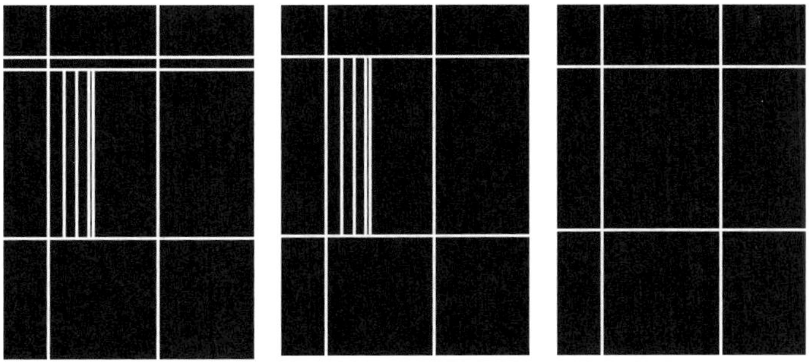

A B CDEFG

A ff. 2r–7v. Rose ink; 9/7/6.5/2/39 mm (cols.); 101–104 x 63 mm; 17 lines.
B ff. 8r–13v. Rose ink; 9/7/6.5/2/39 mm (cols.); 101–104 x 63 mm; 17 lines.
C ff. 14r–51v, 56r–82v, 99r–111v. Rose ink; 93–96 x 63 mm; 16 lines.
D ff. 52r–55v, 83r–98v, 128r–129v. Rose ink; 104 x 60–63 mm; 17 lines.
E ff. 112r–118v. Brown ink; 105 x 63 mm; 17 lines.
F ff. 119r–121v. Rose ink; 104 x 60 mm; 17 lines.
G ff. 122r–127v. Rose ink; 102–103 x 60–62 mm; 17 lines.

Prickings are visible for each pattern in the right, upper, and lower margins for single vertical bounding lines and horizontal through lines (double upper for **A**). Pattern **A** is traced in rose ink for the calendar (January–June) in five columns; writing below top line; Pattern **B** (used for July–December) is traced identically to **A**, but with a single upper horizontal through line. Patterns **C**, **D**, **E**, **F**, and **G** vary in dimensions but maintain a similar appearance; **C**, **D**, **F**, and **G** traced in rose ink; **E** in brown ink; all single column; writing below top line. The various patterns correspond to the division of labor, quire structure, and additional content [see Script].

Script: A total of eight hands are present: one documentary hand (s. xv^2, 146*) on f. 1r (former pastedown); five distinguishable scribal bookhands (M1–M5) write all texts and rubrics in Northern Textualis Formata at varying abilities. M1 writes the bulk of the text (ff. 14r–18v, 28v–51v, 64v–79v, 99r–111v) with substantial contributions from M3 (ff. 2r–13v, 22v, 52r–55v, 82v–98v, 112r–118v), and M2 (ff. 20r–22r, 23v–28r, 56r–64r); M4 (ff. 119r–121v) and M5 (ff. 19r–v, 122r–126v) have written additional content. M3 is the predominant rubricator, but M4 and M5 write their respective rubrics. Two separate hands supply ownership information: an unidentified cursive hand (s. xv^2) records the birth of Jehenne Le Féron (f. 127v); the sixteenth-century autograph of François Grisel (ff. 127v–128r) writes all details pertaining to the Grisel family. Gura 2012, 268 contains a synoptical table of the distribution of scribal labor.

Decoration:

I. Rubrication: Rubrics in red ink by M3, M4, M5 [see Script]; letter heightening of majuscules and cadels in yellow ink; heightening in red and red over yellow occurs sparsely, and usually only in association with M5 (e.g., f. 122r).

II. Initials: Initials of the foliate and dentelle types occur in hierarchy.

a. Foliate initials (3–6 line square inset) begin the major sections of each text. The initials were executed by at least two separate painters (P1 and P2). P1 is responsible for the initial on f. 20r (6 line square inset) and P2 for all others (4 line square inset) and likely those beginning *O intemerata* and *Obsecro te* (ff. 112r and 115r; 3 line square inset each).

b. Dentelle initials (2 line square indent) occur throughout the manuscript with contrasting backgrounds mimicking a littera duplex style with various motifs in white penwork (vegetation, fleur-de-lys, etc.). Dentelles are also used as 1 line versals with normal grounds. The dentelles present on ff. 122r–127r (especially 2 lines in size) have a distinctly different style than those throughout the rest of the manuscript.

III. Line Fillers: Dentelle type line fillers occur in the Litany; all others are predominantly red, or red and blue ink; rarely, brown ink heightened in red like a cadel (e.g., f. 122r), or only blue (e.g., f. 106v).

IV. Borders & Frames:

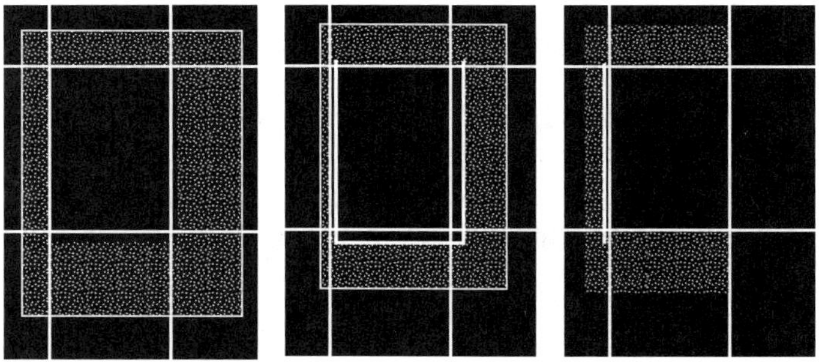

H I J

Six borders painted by at least two individuals remain on text folios. Four-margins border by the first painter (H) on f. 20r (cf. Nash 1999, type 3), and by the second (I) on ff. 28v, 56r, 71r (cf. Nash 1999, types 2–3); general vegetal motifs in all; border **H** on f. 20r lacks a frame, and is inhabited with pheasants, drolleries, and a peacock. The palettes of the painters differ: the first (f. 20r) uses mainly dark and light blues, orange, and light green; few instances of golden yellow and purple; red is generally avoided except for minimal shading of orange leaves. The second (ff. 28v, 56r, 71v) favors a lighter palette of light blues and white, light green, and light pinks; the use of orange and red shading is minimal; second set of borders **I** are uninhabited; area to be decorated defined in lead; dentelle style frames. Three-margins-left borders (**J**) on ff. 112r and 115r; palette is predominantly blues, orange, and dark red with very minimal pink, green, and yellow. The borders are mainly acanthus and floral motifs in addition to the rinceaux; dentelle style frame.

Miniatures: No miniatures are present; paint transfer visible on most leaves which faced those now excised.

Calendar: Two pages per month; recto/verso; dominical letters a are dentelles; Roman time with ordinals marked in black and red ink.

Contents:

1. Fragmentary document from Amiens—f. 1r–v.

inc.: [f. 1r] uicarii generales in spiritualibus et temporalibus reuerendi in christo patris et domini . . .; expl.: [f. 1r] . . . datum ambianensis sub sigillo uicariatus officii anno domini 146*.

Former pastedown in mutilated condition; fragmentary due to trimming of the right edge, and some text is obscured by the glue. The document is dated 146* at Amiens and is a request to fill a vacancy of (presumably) a parish priest. The document also names the Benedictine Abbey of Saint-Fuscien-aux-Bois [see Cottineau, col. 2683]; for a diplomatic edition see Gura 2012, 259.

2. Calendar (Amiens)—ff. 2r–13v.

Composite calendar in French (Picard) in black ink with graded feasts in red; three days unfilled; April 30 does not appear at all. The calendar contains few deviations from the Amiens Model calendar in Nash 1999, 405–408; Gura 2012, 238–241 contains a detailed analysis of this calendar. Important feasts for Amiens in red ink include: Firmin the Martyr (Sept. 25; Jan. 13), Firmin the Confessor (Sept. 1), Honeré (May 16), Fuscian (Dec. 11), decollation of John the Baptist (Aug. 29), Eloi (Jun. 25; Dec.1), Martin (Nov. 11), Thomas Becket (Dec. 29). Other significant feasts in black ink: vigil of Firmin the Martyr (Sept. 24), invention of Fuscian (Jun. 27), Ulphia (Jan. 31), Quentin (Oct. 31), Waleric (Apr. 1; Dec. 12), translation of Wulfram (Oct. 15), translation of Vedast (Jul. 15), Olimpe (Apr. 15), Hildevert (May 27), Maxime (Nov. 27), Oswald (Aug. 5), Grimabauld (July 8), Elphege (Apr. 19), Theodore (Mar. 23), Edmund (Nov. 16), Augustine (May 26).

3. Gospel Lessons—ff. 14r–18v.

Rubrics for both Matthew and Mark are labeled incorrectly as Luke [rub.: *secundum lucam*], though the texts are correctly those of the respective evangelist.

4. Suffrages to St. Adrian (French and Latin)—f. 19r–v.

4.1. rub.: [f. 18v] memore de saint adrian martire; inc.: [f. 19r] saint adrian dut de nichomedie . . .

4.2. rub.: anthaimie; inc.: [f. 19r] aue sancte adriane qui martirium inmane passus es in corpore . . .

The Latin version is datable to ca. 1450; see Mone 3: no. 758.

5. Hours of the Virgin, use of Amiens [incomplete]—ff. 20r–51v.

5.1. Matins—ff. 20r–28v. INV.: aue maria . . .; HYM.: quem terra ponthus . . .; ANT. PS. 8: benedicta tu; LECT. I: sancta maria uirgo . . .; R. I.: sancta et immaculata . . .

5.2. Laudes—ff. 28v–36v. RUB.: laudes; PSS.: 92, 99, 62, 66, Benedicite, 148, 149, 150; ANT.: o admirabile; CAP.: in omnibus requiem . . .; HYM.: o gloriosa domina . . .; ANT. SUP. BEN.: o gloriosa.

5.3. Prime [incomplete]—ff. 37r–39v. PSS.:1 [incomplete], 2, 5; ANT.: o admirabile . . .; CAP.: hec est uirgo sancta . . .; R.: aue maria . . . benedicta tu . . .

5.4. Terce [incomplete]—ff. 40r–41v. PSS.: 119, 120, 121; HYM.: ueni creator; ANT.: quando natus . . .; CAP.: paradysi porta . . .; R.: post partum uirgo . . .

5.5. Sext [incomplete]—ff. 42r–43v. PSS.: 122, 123, 124; ANT.: rubum quem; CAP.: gaude maria uirgo . . .; R.: sancta dei genitrix . . .; V.: intercede pro nobis . . .

5.6. None [incomplete]—f. 44r–v. PSS.: 125, 126, 127; ANT.: ger<minauit> [*mutil.*].

5.7. Vespers [incomplete]—ff. 45r–48v. PSS.: 109, 112, 121, 126, 147; ANT.: beata mater; CAP.: beata es maria que . . .; HYM.: aue maris stella . . .; ANT. SUP. MAGNIF.: sancta maria.

5.8. Compline [incomplete]—ff. 49r–51v. PSS.: 12, 42, 128, 130; ANT.: cum iocunditate; CAP.: sicut cynamonum [*sic*] . . .; HYM.: uirgo singularis; ANT. SUP. NUNC DIM.: sub tuum.

6. Hours of the Cross [incomplete]—ff. 52r–53r.

Incomplete; three leaves missing. Extant rubric for Prime (f. 52r), Terce (f. 52v), and Compline (f. 53r).

7. Hours of the Holy Spirit [incomplete]—ff. 54r–55v.

Incomplete; one leaf missing. Extant rubrics for Prime (f. 54r), None (f. 54v), Vespers (f. 55r), Compline (f. 55r); Terce and Sext are the reverse of MONE 1: no. 191.

8. Penitential Psalms, Litany, & Collects—ff. 56r–70r.

8.1. Penitential Psalms—ff. 56r–66r.

8.2. Litany (Amiens)—ff. 66r–69v.

Martyrs: Stephen, Laurence, Vincent, Fabian, Sebastian, Clement, Cornelius, Denis (*cum soc.*), Fuscian (*cum soc.*), Firmin, Quentin, George, Christopher, Blaise. *Confessors*: Silvester, Nicholas, Firmin, Gregory, Giles, Lupus, Anthony, Maturunus [*sic*], Eloi. *Virgins*: Mary Magdalene, Mary of Egypt, Katherine, Margaret, Agatha, Lucia, Petronilla, Anastacia, Juliana, Spes, Caritas.

8.3. Collects—ff. 69v–70r.

8.3.1. f. 69v. RUB.: oracio; INC.: deus cui proprium est misereri semper et parcere . . . miseratio tue pietatis absoluat. per [*CO* 1143].

8.3.2. ff. 69v–70r. RUB.: oracio; INC.: fidelium deus omnium conditor et redemptor . . . piis supplicationibus consequantur [*CO* 2684b]. qui uiuis et regnas deus per omnia omnia secula seculorum amen. benedicamus domino. deo gratias. fidelium anime per misericordiam dei requiescant in pace amen.

9. Office of the Dead, use of Amiens—ff. 71r–104v, 108r–109v.

Ottosen nos. 72-14-56, 24-32-57, 68-40-38. Due to rebinding, ff. 108r–109v, which contain part of the Office of the Dead, are out of order; textually, ff. 108r–109v should be placed between ff. 103 and 104 [see Quires].

10. Suffrages—ff. 104v–111v.

Ten suffrages: Trinity, John the Baptist, Peter and Paul, Sebastian, Christopher, Laurence, Nicholas, Anthony abb., Mary Magdalene, and Katherine. As with the Office of the Dead, rebinding has disturbed the order of the text: ff. 110–111 should follow f. 107, thus the *oratio* in the suffrage to Laurence begins on f. 107v and is completed on f. 110r [see Quires].

10.1. Trinity—ff. 104v–105r. **rub.**: idiy ensuit memore de le trinite; **ant.**: te deum patrem . . .; **or.**: omnipotens sempiterne deus qui dedisti famulis tuis in confessione . . . firmitate ab omnibus semper muniamur aduersis qui uiuis et regnas deus per omnia secula seculorum amen [*CO* 3920] .

10.2. John the Baptist—f. 105r–v. **rub.**: memore de saint iehan baptiste; **ant.**: inter natos mulierum . . .; **or.**: perpetuis nos quesumus domine sancti . . . necessariis attolle suffragiis per christum dominum nostrum amen [*CO* 4222b].

10.3. Peter and Paul—ff. 105v–106r. **rub.**: memore de saint pierre; **ant.**: isti sunt due oliue et duo candelabra lucentia ante dominum habent . . .; **or.**: deus cuius dextera beatum petrum . . . ut amborum meritis eternitatis gloriam consequamur [*CO* 1158b].

10.4. Sebastian—f. 106r–v. **rub.**: de saint sebastian; **ant.**: o quam mira refulsit gratia sebastianus . . .; **or.**: deus qui beatum sebastianum gloriosum martyrem tuum in tua fide et dilectione . . . que a te iussa sunt recta intentione perficere per christum [cf. Leroquais 1:354; 2:33, 49, 118].

10.5. Christopher—f. 107r–v. **rub.**: memore de saint christofle; **ant.**: christofori sancti speciem quicumque . . .; **or.**: omnipotens sempiterne qui famulo tuo beato christoforo martiri tuo uictoriam martirii contulisti . . . et lumen oculorum meorum tam corporis quam anime quamdiu uixero uellis custodire per uirtutem sancte trinitatis et unitatis patris et filii et spiritus sancti amen.

10.6. Laurence—ff. 107v, 110r. **rub.**: memore de saint laurens; **ant.**: beatus laurentius bonum opus . . .; **or.**: da quesumus omnipotens deus uitiorum nostrorum flammas . . . [f. 110r] tribuisti tormentorum suorum incendia superare per christum dominum nostrum amen [*CO* 960].

10.7. Nicholas—f. 110r. **rub.**: memore de saint nicholay; **ant.**: beatus nicholaus adhuc puerulus . . .; **or.**: deus qui beatum nicholaum pontificem tuum . . . a gehenne incendiis liberemur per christum dominum nostrum amen [*CO* 1463].

10.8. Anthony—ff. 110r–110v. **rub.**: memore de saint anthoine; **ant.**: uox de celo ad anthonium . . .; **or.**: deus qui concedis obtentu beati antonii . . . tibi feliciter in gloria presentari per christum dominum nostram amen [*CO* 1486].

10.9. Mary Magdalene—ff. 110v–111r. rub.: de le magdalene; ant.: maria ergo unxit pedes . . .; or.: largire nobis clementissime pater . . . impetret beatitudinem per christum [*CO* 3231].

10.10. Katherine—f. 111r–v. rub.: memore de saintte katherine; ant.: katherina mirabilis atque deo amabilis per omnia laudabilis . . .; or.: deus qui dedisti legem moysi . . . et intercessione ualeamus peruenire per christum dominum nostrum amen [*CO* 1521].

11. *O intemerata* (masculine forms)—ff. 112r–115r.

inc.: [f. 112r] o intemerata . . . mihi miserrimo peccatori . . .; expl.: [f. 115r] . . . ita ut parcat mihi in alia uita concedens mihi misericorditer cum sanctis et electis suis uitam et requiem sempiternam amen [cf. Wilmart, 494–495].

12. *Obsecro te* (masculine forms)—ff. 115r–118r.

rub.: oracio; inc.: [f. 115r] obsecro te domina . . . ego sum facturus locuturus aut cogitaturus . . . famulo tuo . . .; expl.: [f. 118r] . . . audi et exaudi me dulcissima maria mater dei et misericordie amen [cf. Leroquais 2:346–347].

13. Suffrage to St. Barbara—f. 118v.

rub.: memore de saintte barbe; ant.: o pulcra precipuum rosa dans odorem . . .; v.: martirum preconium uirgoque decora; r.: nobis in auxilium assis mortis hora; or.: deus qui beatissimam uirginem barbaram roseo . . . claritati humilli<ma> deuocione congaudent per christum [*CO* 1398].

14. Additional Prayers—ff. 119r–122r.

14.1. Memore du Saint Sacrement de l'autel—ff. 119r–121r. rub.: deuote salutacion a notre seir [*ut uid.*].; inc.: <j>e te salue tres saint et precieulx corps de mon createur et redempteur ihesucrist qui es parfaittement en ce saint sacrement cy . . . [Sonet/Sinclair/Rézeau 901].

14.2. Indulgence attributed to Pope John XII (apocryphal)—f. 122r. rub.: pape jehan .xij^{e}. a donne a tous passans par quelconque chimentiere deuotement disans ceste oroison qui sensient autant de jours de indulgences qui il y a de corps** enterres; inc.: auete omnes christifideles anime det uobis requiem ille . . .

15. Hours of the Conception—ff. 122v–126r.

rub.: [f. 122r] chi sensieuent heures de lassumpcion de la uierge marie.

15.1. Matins—ff. 122v–123r. hym.: erubuscant incensati qui . . . [*RH* 5225]; or.: deus qui beatissimam annam sterilem prole gloriosa atque humane generi salutifera absque orginali macula fetum absque dare uoluisti presta quesumus . . . in sue mortis articulo patrocinia eius percipere in celis per christum dominum nostrum.

15.2. Prime—f. 123r–v. RUB.: prime; HYM.: conceptio laudabilis ab angelo . . . [*RH* 3700]; OR.: deus qui pro salute humani generis carnem gloriose uirginis marie assumere dignatus es . . . interuentione ad eterne consolacionis concepcione [*sic*] perducamur per christum.

15.3. Terce—ff. 123v–124r. RUB.: tierche; HYM.: beata sit concepcio matris . . .; OR.: omnipotens sempiterne deus qui per admirabilem concepcionem beate marie hominem perditum . . . et ipsius materne [*sic*] consolatione ad eterne consolacionis premia perduci per christum.

15.4. Sext—f. 124r–v. RUB.: mydy; HYM.: tuum corpus et uiscera . . . [*RH* 34184]; OR.: ineffabilis clementie tue deus qui corpus et animam beate et gloriose uirginis marie . . . da ut cuius concepcione letamur eius benigna intercessione a morsu eterne dampnacionis liberemur per christum.

15.5. None—ff. 124v–125r. RUB.: nonne; HYM.: aue regina celorum . . . [*RH* 2071]; OR.: deus qui hunc sacratissimum honorabilem diem nobis in beate marie uirginis et matris tue piissima concepione signis ac miraculis . . . uenerari conceptum quem religionis sumpsit exordium qui uiuis et regnas deus per christum.

15.6. Vespers—f. 125r–v. RUB.: uesprez; HYM.: salue mater redemptoris . . . [*RH* 33135]; OR.: omnipotens sempiterne deus qui in utero beatissime anne gloriosam uirginem . . . et filie peruenire ualeamus parte [*sic*] ihesu christe saluator mundi rex glorie qui unus et regnas deus per omnia secula. [cf. San Marino, Huntington Library, HM 1088].

15.7. Compline—ff. 125v–126r. HYM.: matris dei concepcio nostre erat . . . [*RH* 29552]; OR.: deus qui uirginalem aulam beate marie uirginis in qua habitares . . . iocundos faciat sue interesse concepcioni qui uiuis et regis. [cf. *CO* 2167].

15.8. Recommendatio—f. 126r. INC.: concepcionis honore has propter christe horas diximus . . .; EXPL.: . . . ut in celis tecum sumus amen [*RH* 3702].

16. Suffrage to Mary Magdalene—ff. 126r–127r.

RUB.: memore de saintte marie magdalene; INC.: [f. 126r] gaudia pia magdalena . . . [*RH* 6895]; OR.: [f. 127r] dulcissime domine ihesu christe qui beatissime marie magdalene penitenciam ita gratam acceptamque fecisti ut non solum ei peccata dimitteres nam etiam cor eius amoris tui dulcedine intentissime perlustrares da nobis quesumus eius sic flere mala que commisimus sanctis precibus ut cum uenerit hora mortis sanctam indulgenciam consequi ualeamus qui uiuis et regis deus per omnia secula seculorum. amen [cf. *CO* 1370].

17. Ownership Annotations (*livre de raison*)—ff. 127v–128r.

INC.:[f. 127v] le .vj. jour de juillet .m.l.cccc.lxxviij. fut nee jehenne le feron; [*in alia manu*] quy fut femme de jean grisel escuyer seigner du fay lez hornoy . . .; EXPL.: [f. 128r] . . . et pour marines damoiselle marie du bos, femme de monseigneur des blymond mon oncle et damoiselle jenne de belloy, fille du seigneur de catillon et de la damme de francieres. f. grisel. il mourut au bout .xj. moys.

Births, deaths, etc. written in the autograph (s. xvi²) of a François Grisel of Fay-lès-Hornoy [see SCRIPT; OWNERS & PROVENANCE].

Bibliography: Gura 2012, 252–254.

Binding: s. xix/xx; brown leather over binder's board; tooled; gilt tooled turn-ins; marbled flyleaves; binding detached and in poor shape. The original or earlier binding had a single clasp [see f. 1 for clasp marks; also Contents 1].

Owners & Provenance: Early ownership can be ascribed to two families in Haute Picardie. The birth of a Jehenne Le Féron on 6 July 1478 is recorded by a contemporary hand on f. 127v. The sixteenth-century autograph of François Grisel adds more information on the Grisel family (ff. 127v–128r) until 1586. From at least 1507 to the early seventeenth century, the manuscript was in Fay-lès-Hornoy (now Thieulloy-l'Abbaye); Gura 2012, 252–254 discusses the persons and their identities. How the manuscript came to Saint Mary's College is unknown; dealer marks and a price code present on flyleaves.

Former Shelfmark: ND 3363 . H8 1561 (Saint Mary's College).

Bibliography: Gura 2012.

MS 4

Origin: Italy, s. xiv².
Content Overview: Antiphonary, Temporale (2 leaves).

In Latin, on parchment; 2 ff. (framed); generally 370 x 555 mm (conjugate leaves); [see Layout for ruling]; unfoliated.

Layout: Ruled using a combined technique of lead (verticals and horizontals) and red ink (staves); single column/full-music layout; writing below top line; no prickings visible; six four-line staves, six text lines per page [see Music & Staves]; dimensions of the ruling approx. 261 x 180 mm (per page); fragment is framed in double-sided glass.

Script: A single hand (M1) writes all text in Southern Textualis Formata (Rotunda).

Decoration:
I. Rubrication: Rubrics in red ink.
II. Initials: Flourished initials occur in hierarchy.
a. Flourished initials (approx. 4 lines square inset and half inset) in red and blue ink with contrasting penwork alternate and begin antiphons on the recto and verso.

Music & Staves: Four-line staves traced in red ink; approx. 22 mm; square neumes in black ink.

Contents:

1. Antiphonary, Temporale [2 leaves].

inc.: [flesh side, right leaf] et exultabor in te psallam nomini tuo altissime deus . . .; **expl.**: [flesh side, left leaf] . . . propitius esto peccatis nostris domine ps. deus uenerit.

The conjugate was the inner bifolium of a quire; contains the Office for Wednesdays and Thursdays for the year (Fer. 4, Fer. 5 per totum annum); the flesh sides are the first and last leaves of the fragment (hair sides sequential).

Owners & Provenance: Unrecorded gift to Saint Mary's College.

MS 5

Origin: Italy, s. xv^2.
Content Overview: Gradual, Temporale (2 leaves).

In Latin, on parchment; 2 ff. (framed); generally 555 x 795 mm (conjugate leaves) [see Layout for ruling].

Foliation: Contemporary foliation in blue and red ink with Roman numerals is centered in the upper margins (ff. 43 and 48).

Layout: Ruled using a combined technique of brown ink (verticals) and red ink (staves); single column/full-music layout; writing below top line; no prickings visible; six four-lines staves and six text lines per page [see Music & Staves]; dimensions of the ruling approx. 393 x 290 mm (per page); fragment is framed in double-sided glass.

Script: A single hand (M1) writes all text in Southern Textualis Formata (Rotunda).

Decoration:
I. Rubrication: Rubrics in red ink.
II. Initials: Flourished initials occur in hierarchy.
a. Flourished initials (2 staves, 1 text line square inset) in red and blue ink with contrasting penwork alternate and begin major divisions of the text.

Music & Staves: Four-line staves traced in red ink; 44 mm; square neumes in black ink.

Contents:
1. Gradual, Temporale [2 leaves].
inc.: [f. 43r] <labi>is tuis. uersus. eructauit cor meum uerbum bonum dico . . .; **expl.** [f. 43v] . . . qui querebant animam pueri. in sancti siluestri pape et confessoris. introitus. sacerdo<tes>; **inc.**: [f. 48r] et uenimus cum muneribus adorare dominum . . .; **expl.**: [f. 48v] . . . in excelso throno uidi se<dere>.

As is common in some manuscripts, portions of the Sanctorale near Christmas are included. Contains in fragmentary form: f. 43r: gradual and gradual verse for Sunday after Christmas (Dom. p. Nat. Dom.); f. 43v: verse, offertory, *postcommunio* for the Sunday after Christmas (Dom. p. Nat. Dom.), introit for feast of St. Silvester (Dec. 31); f. 48r: *communio* and offertory for Epiphany (Jan. 6); f. 48v: introit for Sunday in Octave of the Epiphany.

Owners & Provenance: Unrecorded gift to Saint Mary's College.

MS 6

Origin: Spain, s. xvi.
Content Overview: Gradual, Temporale (leaf).

In Latin, on parchment; 1 f. (framed); generally 394 x 255 mm; unfoliated.

Layout: Ruled using a combined technique of lead (verticals) and red ink (staves); single column/full music layout; writing below top line; six five-line staves and six text lines per page [see Music & Staves); matted and framed.

Script: A single hand (M1) writes all text in Southern Textualis Formata; letter forms are Iberian.

Decoration:
I. Rubrication: Rubrics in red ink.
II. Initials: Flourished initials occur in hierarchy.
a. One Flourished initial (5 staves, 1 text line square inset) in blue ink with red penwork begins the *communio*.

Music & Staves: Five-line staves traced in red ink; 42 mm; square neumes in black ink.

Contents:
1. Gradual, Temporale [leaf].
inc.: [recto] dextris est mihi ne commouear . . .; expl.: [recto] . . . qua in admirabile est nomen tu<um>.

Contains in fragmentary form: part of the offertory (*Benedicam Dominum qui mihi tribuit*) and *communio* (*Domine Dominus noster*) for Monday of the second week of Lent (Fer. 2 Hebd. 2 Quad.); only one side of the fragment is visible due to framing.

Owners & Provenance: Unrecorded gift to Saint Mary's College.

MS 7

Origin: Spain, s. xvi^{in}.
Content Overview: Antiphonary, Sanctorale [leaf].

In Latin, on parchment; 1 f.; generally 553 x 372 mm (page) [see Layout for ruling].

Foliation: Contemporary foliation in black ink with Roman numerals is written in the upper right margin (f. 121).

Layout:

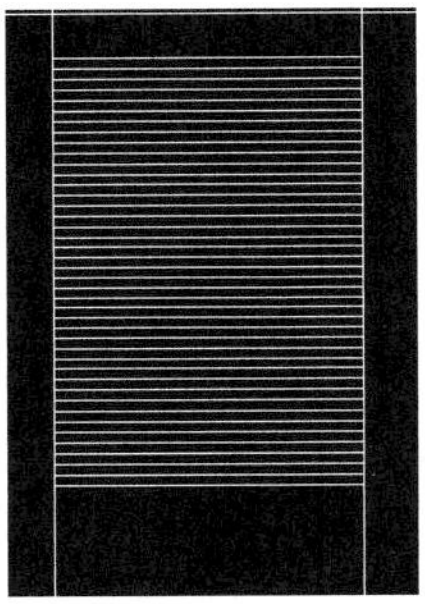

A

A Combined technique; 457 x 280 mm; 7 four-line staves, 7 text lines.

Pattern **A** is traced using a combined technique of hard-point (bounding lines), brown ink (text lines), and red ink (staves); single column/full-music layout; writing below top line; no prickings visible.

Script: A single hand (M1) writes all text in Southern Textualis Formata; letter forms are Iberian.

Decoration:
I. Rubrication: Rubrics in red ink.
II. Initials: Flourished and cadel initials occur in hierarchy.
a. Flourished initials (4 staves, 1 text line square inset) in red and blue ink with contrasting penwork alternate and begin antiphons.
b. Cadels initials (1 line versals) in black ink with black penwork follow flourished initials, and begin the differentia.

Music & Staves: Four-line staves traced in red ink; 42 mm; square neumes in black ink.

Contents:

1. Antiphonary, Sanctorale [leaf].

inc.: [recto] oremus omnes ad dominum iesum christum ut confessoribus suis fontis uenam aperiat . . .; **expl.:** [verso] . . . omnes gentes per girum crediderunt christo domino. euouae.

Contains portions of the Office for St. Clement (Nov. 23).

Owners & Provenance: Unrecorded gift to Saint Mary's College.

MS 8

Origin: Spain, s. xvi.
Content Overview: Gradual, Common of saints (leaf).

In Latin, on parchment; 1 f.; generally 530 x 375 mm (page) [see Layout for ruling].

Signatures: A signature written in black ink remains on the lower corner of the recto [t .iiij.°].

Foliation: Contemporary foliation in red ink with Roman numerals is written in the upper right margin (f. cxxxv).

Layout:

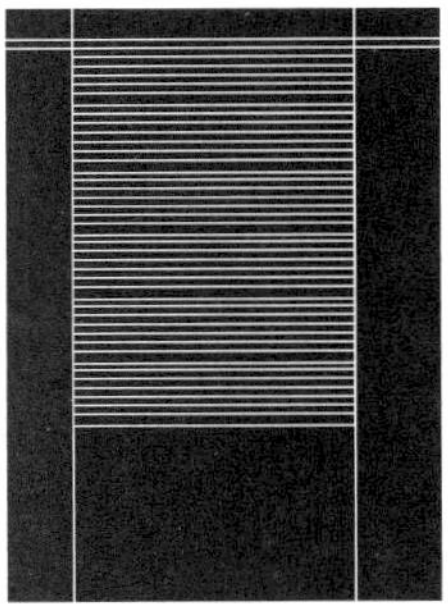

A

A Combined technique; 425 x 243 mm; 6 five-line staves, 6 text lines.

Pattern **A** is traced using a combined technique of lead (bounding lines) and red ink (staves); single column/full-music layout; writing below top line; no prickings visible.

Script: A single hand (M1) writes all text in Southern Textualis Formata; letter forms are Iberian.

Decoration:

I. Rubrication: Rubrics in red ink.

II. Initials: Flourished and cadel initials occur in hierarchy.

a. Flourished initials (5 staves, 1 text line) in red ink with blue penwork begin the *Alleluia* on the recto and the tract on the verso.

b. One cadel in black ink (5 staves, 1 text line) begins the verse on the recto.

Music & Staves: Five-line staves traced in red ink; 43 mm; square neumes in black ink.

Contents:

1. Gradual, Common of saints [leaf].

inc.: [recto] -rum domine alleluia. uersus. hic est sacerdos quem coronauit . . .; expl.: [verso] . . . beatus uir qui timet dominum in mandatis eius cupit nimis.

Contains part of the Common of saints for a martyr and bishop.

Owners & Provenance: Unrecorded gift to Saint Mary's College.

MS 9

Origin: Spain, s. xvi.
Content Overview: Gradual, Sanctorale (leaf).

In Latin, on parchment; 1 f. (framed); generally 750 x 490 mm (page) [see Layout for ruling]; unfoliated; verso blank.

Layout: Ruled using a combined technique of lead (verticals) and red ink (staves); single column/full-music layout; writing below top line; six five-line staves, six text lines per page [see Music & Staves]; no prickings visible; dimensions of the ruling approx. 645 x 395 mm; framed in double-sided glass.

Script: A single hand (M1) writes all text in Southern Textualis Formata; letter forms are Iberian.

Decoration:
I. Initials: Flourished initials occur in hierarchy.
a. One flourished initial (4 staves, 1 text line square inset) in red ink with black penwork and yellow wash framed in blue ink begins the fragment.

Music & Staves: Five-line staves traced in red ink; 70 mm; square neumes in black ink.

Contents:
1. Gradual, Sanctorale [leaf]
inc.: [recto] domine probasti me et cognouisti me . . .; **expl.**: [recto] . . . sessionem meam et resurrectionem meam. seculorum.

Contains the invitatory *Domine probasti me et.*

Owners & Provenance: Unrecorded gift to Saint Mary's College.

MS 10

Origin: Spain, s. xvi.
Content Overview: Gradual, Common of saints (leaf).

In Latin, on parchment; 1 f. (framed); generally 800 x 545 mm (page); [see Layout for ruling].

Foliation: Contemporary foliation in red ink with Roman numerals is written in the upper right margin (f. cxxx).

Layout: Ruled using a combined technique of lead (verticals), black ink (horizontals), and red ink (staves); single column/full-music layout; writing below top line; no prickings visible; five five-line staves, five text lines [see Music & Staves]; dimensions of the ruling approx. 655 x 413 mm; framed in double-sided glass.

Script: A single hand (M1) writes all text in Southern Textualis Formata; letter forms are Iberian.

Decoration:
I. Rubrication: Rubrics in red ink.
II. Initials: Flourished initials occur in hierarchy.
a. Flourished initials (5 staves, 1 text line square inset with overflow) begins the gradual on the verso.
III. Line Fillers: Line fillers in red ink comprised of polygons occur on the verso.

Music & Staves: Five-line staves traced in red ink; 78 mm; square neumes in black ink.

Contents:
1. Gradual, Common of saints [leaf].
inc.: [recto] manebit et sedes eius sicut sol in conspectu meo et sicut luna perfecta in eternum . . .; expl.: [verso] . . . domine preuenisti eum in benedictionibus dulcedinis posuisti in capite eius coronam.

Contains the common for a martyr and bishop, confessors not bishops, confessor and abbot; many chants are given in cue form.

Owners & Provenance: Unrecorded gift to Saint Mary's College.

Appendix 1

Former and Permanent Hesburgh Library Shelfmarks

Former Shelfmark	*Permanent Shelfmark*
MS 1	cod. Lat. b. 1
MS 2	cod. Lat. b. 2
MS 3	cod. Lat. d. 1
MS 4	cod. Lat. a. 1
MS 5	cod. Lat. a. 5
MS 6	cod. Lat. b. 3
MS 7	cod. Lat. b. 7
MS 8	cod. Lat. c. 6
MS 9	cod. Lat. b. 11
MS 11	cod. Lat. b. 6
MS 12	cod. Lat. b. 9
MS 13	cod. Lat. c. 4
MS 15	cod. Lat. b. 5
MS 17	MS Ital. b. 1
MS 18	MS Ital. b. 2
MS 19	cod. Lat. d. 4
MS 22	cod. Lat. e. 2
MS 25	cod. Lat. a. 4
MS 27	cod. Lat. c. 1
MS 28	cod. Lat. c. 10
MS 29	cod. Lat. c. 5
MS 30	cod. Lat. d. 6
MS 31	cod. Lat. c. 7
MS 33	cod. Lat. c. 9

Former Shelfmark (*cont.*)	*Permanent Shelfmark* (*cont.*)
MS 34	MS Fr. d. 1
MS 35	cod. Lat. a. 2
MS 37	MS Fr. c. 1
MS 40	cod. Lat. d. 3
MS 42	cod. Lat. c. 8
MS 43	cod. Lat. c. 11
MS 44	cod. Lat. d. 2
MS 45	cod. Lat. e. 1
MS 46	cod. Lat. e. 3
MS 50	MS Ital. d. 1
MS 51	MS Fr. c. 2
MS 53	cod. Lat. d. 5
MS 55	cod. Lat. b. 8
MS 56	cod. Lat. b. 12
MS 58	cod. Lat. b. 10
MS 65	cod. Lat. e. 4
MS 66	cod. Lat. a. 3
MS 67	MS Eng. d. 1
MSE/MR 9	Frag. I. 2
MSE/MR 11	Frag. I. 4
MSE/MR 12	Frag. I. 5
MSE/MR 13	Frag. I. 6
MSE/MR 14	Frag. I. 7
MSE/MR 15	Frag. I. 8
MSE/MR 16f	Frag. II. 3
MSE/MR 17f	Frag. V. 1
MSE/MR 18f	Frag. V. 2
MSE/MR 52	Frag. I. 11

Appendix 2

North American Manuscripts by State or Province

The purpose of the following list is to faciliate easy browsing of North American manuscripts mentioned in this catalogue by larger geographical region, excluding those of Notre Dame, Indiana. The citations are given in the Index of Manuscripts Cited, where each manuscript will appear alphabetically by city.

Alabama
Auburn, Auburn University, Ralph Brown Draughon Library, Z 105.5 . S56 S4 1434

Arizona
Phoenix, Phoenix Public Library, 091 B471TC
Phoenix, Phoenix Public Library, MS Fragment 69
Phoenix, Phoenix Public Library, MS Fragment 71
Phoenix, Phoenix Public Library, MS Fragment 79

California
Claremont, Claremont Colleges Honnold/Mudd Library, Crispin 8
Claremont, Claremont Colleges Honnold/Mudd Library, Crispin 9
Los Angeles, Loyola Marymount University, William H. Hannon Library, Coll. 25, 14
Orange, Chapman University, Leatherby Libraries, Z 105.5 . S56 S4 1434
San Francisco, John Windle (firm), March List 2014, no. 12
San Marino, Huntington Library, HM 1088
San Marino, Huntington Library, HM 1180
San Marino, Huntington Library, HM 25771

Colorado
Boulder, University of Colorado, Norlin Library, MS 320
Boulder, University of Colorado, Norlin Library, ND2950 E38 1900

Connecticut
New Haven, Yale University, Beinecke Library, Marston MS 130
New Haven, Yale University, Beinecke Library, MS 3.12
New Haven, Yale University, Beinecke Library, MS 535

Delaware
Newark, University of Delaware, Hugh M. Morris Library, Liturgical Text Collection, 14

Florida
Tampa, Tampa-Hillsborough County Public Library, MS 2

Georgia
Atlanta, Emory University, Pitts Theological Library, RG 020-2, Box 1, Folder 2
Atlanta, Emory University, Pitts Theological Library, RG 020-2, Box 1, Folder 3
Atlanta, Emory University, Pitts Theological Library, RG 020-2, Box 1, Folder 5
Atlanta, Emory University, Pitts Theological Library, RG 020-2, Box 2, Folder 2

Illinois
Evanston, Collection of Charles S. Jenson, VL 93 (F6-18)
Urbana, University of Illinois, William R. and Clarice V. Spurlock Museum, Acc. 1948.6.4

Indiana
Bloomington, Indiana University, Lilly Library, MS 47
Bloomington, Indiana University, Lilly Library, Z118 . A3 E28 (Ege mss.)
Richmond, Earlham College, Lilly Library, Z239 . O7

Iowa
Iowa City, University of Iowa, Main Library, xfMMs. Gr3

Kansas
Lawrence, University of Kansas, Kenneth Spencer Research Library, Pryce MS P4

Kentucky
Berea, Berea College, Hutchins Library, s.n.

Maryland
Baltimore, Walters Art Museum, W 851

Massachusetts
Amherst, University of Massachusetts, W. E. B. Du Bois Library, MS 570
Boston, Boston University, School of Theology Library, MS Leaf 18
Cambridge, Harvard University, Houghton Library, MS Lat 394
Cambridge, Harvard University, Houghton Library, MS Lat 446
Cambridge, Harvard University, Houghton Library, MS Lat 447
Cambridge, Harvard University, Houghton Library, MS Lat 448
Cambridge, Harvard University, Houghton Library, MS Lat 449
Northampton, Smith College, Neilson Library, MS 35

Michigan
Ann Arbor, University of Michigan, Hatcher Graduate Library, Mich. MS 290
Ann Arbor, University of Michigan, Museum of Art, 1986/2.87
Kalamazoo, Western Michigan University, Waldo Library, Pages from the Past, Box 2, folder 3, item 3

Minnesota
Minneapolis, University of Minnesota, Elmer L. Andersen Library, Ege MS 8
Minneapolis, University of Minnesota, Elmer L. Andersen Library, MS 44

Missouri
Columbia, University of Missouri, Ellis Library, Rare Folio Z113 . P3, item 9

New York
Albany, New York State Library, 091 xE29m
Buffalo, New York, Albright-Knox Art Gallery, 1940:355.25
Buffalo, Buffalo and Erie County Public Library, RBR MSS. F54 1100
Corning, Corning Community College, Arthur A. Houghton, Jr. Library, s.n.
New York City, Pierpont Morgan Library, MS M.1021.8
Rochester, Rochester Institute of Technology, Wallace Center, Cary Collection, Portfolio Box 1–8
Stony Brook, Stony Brook University, Frank Melville Jr. Memorial Library, Z109 . E4

North Carolina
Chapel Hill, University of North Carolina, Wilson Library, MS 258
Greensboro, University of North Carolina, Jackson Library, Z6605. L3 E44_08

Ohio
Akron, Charles Edwin Puckett (firm), IM-10849
Athens, Ohio University, Vernon R. Alden Library, ND2920 . E45 1950x
Cleveland, Case Western Reserve University, Kelvin Smith Library, Z109 . F54 1900z
Cleveland, Cleveland Institute of Art, Jessica R. Gund Library, ND2920 . E33
Cleveland, Cleveland Museum of Art, Ege deposit, TR 12828/50
Cleveland, Cleveland Public Library, f 091.97 EG121M vol. 2
Cleveland, Cleveland Public Library, Z109 . E34 1900z
Columbus, The Ohio State University, Thompson Memorial Library, MS Lat. 7
Columbus, The Ohio State University, Thompson Memorial Library, MS. MR. Frag.197
Columbus, The Ohio State University, Thompson Memorial Library, MS. MR. Frag.59.1
Columbus, The Ohio State University, Thompson Memorial Library, MS. MR. Frag.59.2
Cincinnati, Public Library of Cincinnati and Hamilton County, 096.1 ffF469
Gambier, Kenyon College, Olin Library, Z113 . F5
Granville, Denison University, William Howard Doane Library, Z113 . F5
Kent, Kent State University, University Library, s.n.
Lima, Lima Public Library, Main Library, F-MEM 91 E Lufkin
Oberlin, Oberlin College, Harvey Mudd Center, MS B2
Oberlin, Oberlin College, Harvey Mudd Center, MS B3
Oberlin, Oberlin College, Harvey Mudd Center, MS P4
Toledo, Toledo Museum of Art, Acc. 1953.129H
Westerville, Otterbein University, Courtright Memorial Library, Archives, Clements Rare Manuscripts Collection, s.n.

Ontario
Toronto, Massey College, Robertson Davies Library, Gurney FF 0001
Toronto, Ontario College of Art and Design University, Dorothy H. Hoover Library, ND2920 E44 R.B.C. oversize

Oregon
McMinnville, Phillip Pirages (firm), Catalogue 65, no. 49
McMinnville, Phillip Pirages (firm), Catalogue 65, no. 50

Pennsylvania
Beaver Falls, Geneva College, McCartney Library, MS 1 (missing)

Québec
Montréal, McGill University, McLennan Library, Rare Books and Special Collections, MS 122

Rhode Island
Providence, Providence Public Library, MS Ege 2
Providence, Rhode Island School of Design, Museum of Art, 1943.433
Providence, Rhode Island School of Design, Museum of Art, 2010.19.1

Saskatchewan
Saskatoon, University of Saskatchewan, Murray Library, MSS 14

South Carolina
Cayce, King Alfred's Notebook (firm), *Enchiridion* 17, no. 3
Columbia, Columbia Museum of Art, Acc. 1965.15.14
Columbia, Columbia Museum of Art, Acc. 1965.15.15
Columbia, University of South Carolina, Thomas Cooper Library, Early MS 8 (Ege 8)
Columbia, University of South Carolina, Thomas Cooper Library, Early MS 54

Texas
Austin, University of Texas, Harry Ransom Center, MS Leaf B2
Austin, University of Texas, Harry Ransom Center, MS Leaf B10
Austin, University of Texas, Harry Ransom Center, MS Leaf M3
Dallas, Southern Methodist University, Bridwell Library, MS 56
Houston, University of Houston, M. D. Anderson Library, s.n.

Virginia
Roanoke, Hollins University, Wyndham Robertson Library, MS 8
Roanoke, Hollins University, Wyndham Robertson Library, MS 13

Appendix 3

Tables of Distribution of Watermarks

Tables are provided only for manuscripts containing more than two distinct watermarks. Locations and dates are drawn from bibliographical references and are approximate except in the case of an exact match.

List of Tables

Table 1. Distribution of Watermarks: Hesburgh Library, cod. Lat. b. 10

Quire	*Watermark*	*Motif*	*Folio(s)*	*Reference*	*Location*	*Date*
Flyleaf	A (partial)	Circle	flyleaf iv	—	—	—
1	B	Bird	1/16	Piccard 42381	Rome	1563
1	C	Stag	3/14	—	—	—
1	C	Stag	5/12	—	—	—
1	C	Stag	7/10	—	—	—
2	C	Stag	19/28	—	—	—
2	C	Stag	21/26	—	—	—
2	C	Stag	23/24	—	—	—
3	C	Stag	30/41	—	—	—
3	C	Stag	33/38	—	—	—
3	C	Stag	35/36	—	—	—
4	C	Stag	42/43	—	—	—
4	C	Stag	44/51	—	—	—
4	C	Stag	46/49	—	—	—
5	D	Bird	54/65	Briquet 12152	Naples	1495
5	D	Bird	56/63	Briquet 12152	Naples	1495
5	D	Bird	59/60	Briquet 12152	Naples	1495
6	D	Bird	67/76	Briquet 12152	Naples	1495
6	D	Bird	68/75	Briquet 12152	Naples	1495
6	D	Bird	70/73	Briquet 12152	Naples	1495
7	E	Crown	79/88	Piccard 51694	Ravenna	1500
7	E	Crown	80/87	Piccard 51694	Ravenna	1500
7	E	Crown	83/84	Piccard 51694	Ravenna	1500
8	F	Bird	91/108	Piccard 52388	Ellwangen	1495
8	F	Bird	93/106	Piccard 52388	Ellwangen	1495
8	F	Bird	95/104	Piccard 52388	Ellwangen	1495
8	F	Bird	97/102	Piccard 52388	Ellwangen	1495
8	F	Bird	99/100	Piccard 52388	Ellwangen	1495
9	F	Bird	110/129	Piccard 52388	Ellwangen	1495
9	F	Bird	113/126	Piccard 52388	Ellwangen	1495
9	F	Bird	115/124	Piccard 52388	Ellwangen	1495
9	F	Bird	117/122	Piccard 52388	Ellwangen	1495
9	F	Bird	119/120	Piccard 52388	Ellwangen	1495
10	E	Crown	132/137	Piccard 51694	Ravenna	1500
10	E	Crown	134/135	Piccard 51694	Ravenna	1500
11	F	Bird	141/150	Piccard 52388	Ellwangen	1495
11	F	Bird	142/149	Piccard 52388	Ellwangen	1495
11	F	Bird	145/146	Piccard 52388	Ellwangen	1495
12	B	Bird	153/160	Piccard 42381	Rome	1563
12	B	Bird	155/158	Piccard 42381	Rome	1563

Table 1. Distribution of Watermarks: Hesburgh Library, cod. Lat. b. 10 (*cont.*)

Quire	*Watermark*	*Motif*	*Folio(s)*	*Reference*	*Location*	*Date*
13	G	Bird	162/181	Briquet 12205	Florence	1497
13	G	Bird	165/178	Briquet 12205	Florence	1497
13	G	Bird	167/176	Briquet 12205	Florence	1497
13	C	Stag	168/175	—	—	—
13	C	Stag	171/172	—	—	—
14	H	Crown	pp. 1/23	Piccard 51068	Florence	1486
14	I	Crown	pp. 7/17	Piccard 51004	Rome	1486
14	I	Crown	pp. 9/15	Piccard 51004	Rome	1486
15	I	Crown	p. 33	Piccard 51004	Rome	1486
15	I	Crown	42	Piccard 51004	Rome	1486
15	I	Crown	44	Piccard 51004	Rome	1486
16	J	Scissors	45/56	Piccard 122549	Genova	1485
16	H	Crown	47/54	Piccard 51068	Florence	1486
16	I	Crown	51	Piccard 51004	Rome	1486
17	I	Crown	58/67	Piccard 51004	Rome	1486
17	I	Crown	59/66	Piccard 51004	Rome	1486
17	H	Crown	62/63	Piccard 51068	Florence	1486
18	H	Crown	70/79	Piccard 51068	Florence	1486
18	I	Crown	71/78	Piccard 51004	Rome	1486
18	H	Crown	73/76	Piccard 51068	Florence	1486
19	K	Letter P	81/92	Briquet 8492	Rome	1484
19	K	Letter P	84/89	Briquet 8492	Rome	1484
19	K	Letter P	86/87	Briquet 8492	Rome	1484
20	K	Letter P	94/103	Briquet 8492	Rome	1484
20	L	Anchor	95/102	Briquet 429	Udine	1489
20	L	Anchor	98/99	Briquet 429	Udine	1489
21	M	Crown	107/114	Piccard 51049	Quinzano	1483
21	M	Crown	110/111	Piccard 51049	Quinzano	1483
21	N (partial)	Bull's Head	116	—	—	—
22	O	Bird	118/139	Piccard 42386	Rome	1490
22	O	Bird	119/138	Piccard 42386	Rome	1490
22	O	Bird	121/136	Piccard 42386	Rome	1490
22	O	Bird	124/133	Piccard 42386	Rome	1490
22	O	Bird	126/131	Piccard 42386	Rome	1490
22	O	Bird	127/130	Piccard 42386	Rome	1490
23	P	Sun/Star	142/143	Piccard 41202	Rome	1530
24	Q	Tower	150/151	—	—	—

Table 2. Distribution of Watermarks: Hesburgh Library, cod. Lat. b. 14

Quire	*Watermark*	*Motif*	*Folio(s)*	*Reference*	*Location*	*Date*
1	A	Letter P	3/8	Piccard 109359	Arnhem	1499
1	B	Letter P	4/7	Piccard 110465	Straßburg	1505
2	A	Letter P	11/20	Piccard 109359	Arnhem	1499
2	C	Letter P	12/19	Piccard 110122	Mecheln	1505
2	B	Letter P	14/17	Piccard 110465	Straßburg	1505
3	D	Hand	21/30	Piccard 154597	Düsseldorf	1506
3	D	Hand	24/27	Piccard 154597	Düsseldorf	1506
4	E	Letter P	31/40	Piccard 110365	—	1513
4	F	Letter P	34/37	Piccard 109713	Löwen	1486
5	E	Letter P	42/49	Piccard 110365	—	1513
5	G	Letter P	43/48	Piccard 111394	Middelburg, Zeeland	1493

Table 3. Distribution of Watermarks: Hesburgh Library, cod. Lat. d. 1

Quire	*Watermark*	*Motif*	*Folio(s)*	*Reference*	*Location*	*Date*
1	A	Scale	4	Piccard 117475	Bavaria	1461
1	A	Scale	6	Piccard 117475	Bavaria	1461
1	A	Scale	8	Piccard 117475	Bavaria	1461
1	A	Scale	10	Piccard 117475	Bavaria	1461
1	A	Scale	11	Piccard 117475	Bavaria	1461
1	A	Scale	12	Piccard 117475	Bavaria	1461
2	B	Scale	13	Piccard 116697	Triest	1498
2	B	Scale	14	Piccard 116697	Triest	1498
2	B	Scale	15	Piccard 116697	Triest	1498
2	B	Scale	18	Piccard 116697	Triest	1498
2	B	Scale	20	Piccard 116697	Triest	1498
2	B	Scale	21	Piccard 116697	Triest	1498
3	B	Scale	25	Piccard 116697	Triest	1498
3	B	Scale	28	Piccard 116697	Triest	1498
3	B	Scale	29	Piccard 116697	Triest	1498
3	C	Bull's Head	30	Piccard 65246	Nuremberg	1430
3	B	Scale	31	Piccard 116697	Triest	1498
3	C	Bull's Head	33	Piccard 65246	Nuremberg	1430
3	C	Bull's Head	36	Piccard 65246	Nuremberg	1430
3	C	Bull's Head	38	Piccard 65246	Nuremberg	1430
4	B	Scale	44	Piccard 116697	Triest	1498
4	B	Scale	45	Piccard 116697	Triest	1498
4	B	Scale	48	Piccard 116697	Triest	1498
4	B	Scale	49	Piccard 116697	Triest	1498
4	B	Scale	50	Piccard 116697	Triest	1498

Table 3. Distribution of Watermarks: Hesburgh Library, cod. Lat. d. 1 (*cont.*)

Quire	*Watermark*	*Motif*	*Folio(s)*	*Reference*	*Location*	*Date*
4	B	Scale	51	Piccard 116697	Triest	1498
5	B	Scale	52	Piccard 116697	Triest	1498
5	B	Scale	54	Piccard 116697	Triest	1498
5	B	Scale	55	Piccard 116697	Triest	1498
5	B	Scale	58	Piccard 116697	Triest	1498
5	B	Scale	59	Piccard 116697	Triest	1498
5	B	Scale	62	Piccard 116697	Triest	1498
6	B	Scale	64	Piccard 116697	Triest	1498
6	B	Scale	66	Piccard 116697	Triest	1498
6	B	Scale	67	Piccard 116697	Triest	1498
6	B	Scale	69	Piccard 116697	Triest	1498
6	B	Scale	71	Piccard 116697	Triest	1498
6	B	Scale	74	Piccard 116697	Triest	1498
7	B	Scale	76	Piccard 116697	Triest	1498
7	B	Scale	77	Piccard 116697	Triest	1498
7	B	Scale	79	Piccard 116697	Triest	1498
7	B	Scale	81	Piccard 116697	Triest	1498
7	B	Scale	83	Piccard 116697	Triest	1498
7	B	Scale	85	Piccard 116697	Triest	1498
8	B	Scale	93	Piccard 116697	Triest	1498
8	B	Scale	95	Piccard 116697	Triest	1498
8	B	Scale	96	Piccard 116697	Triest	1498
8	B	Scale	97	Piccard 116697	Triest	1498
8	B	Scale	98	Piccard 116697	Triest	1498
8	B	Scale	99	Piccard 116697	Triest	1498
9	B	Scale	101	Piccard 116697	Triest	1498
9	B	Scale	104	Piccard 116697	Triest	1498
9	B	Scale	105	Piccard 116697	Triest	1498
9	B	Scale	108	Piccard 116697	Triest	1498
9	B	Scale	109	Piccard 116697	Triest	1498
9	B	Scale	112	Piccard 116697	Triest	1498
10	D	Anvil	115	Piccard 122666	Grätz	1457
10	D	Anvil	116	Piccard 122666	Grätz	1457
10	D	Anvil	118	Piccard 122666	Grätz	1457
10	D	Anvil	119	Piccard 122666	Grätz	1457
10	D	Anvil	122	Piccard 122666	Grätz	1457
10	D	Anvil	125	Piccard 122666	Grätz	1457
11	D	Anvil	126	Piccard 122666	Grätz	1457
11	D	Anvil	128	Piccard 122666	Grätz	1457
11	D	Anvil	130	Piccard 122666	Grätz	1457
11	D	Anvil	132	Piccard 122666	Grätz	1457

Table 3. Distribution of Watermarks: Hesburgh Library, cod. Lat. d. 1 (*cont.*)

Quire	*Watermark*	*Motif*	*Folio(s)*	*Reference*	*Location*	*Date*
11	D	Anvil	134	Piccard 122666	Grätz	1457
11	D	Anvil	136	Piccard 122666	Grätz	1457
12	E	Scale	139	Piccard 116755	Wiener Neustadt	1450
12	E	Scale	142	Piccard 116755	Wiener Neustadt	1450
12	E	Scale	143	Piccard 116755	Wiener Neustadt	1450
12	E	Scale	146	Piccard 116755	Wiener Neustadt	1450
12	E	Scale	147	Piccard 116755	Wiener Neustadt	1450
12	E	Scale	149	Piccard 116755	Wiener Neustadt	1450
13	E	Scale	151	Piccard 116755	Wiener Neustadt	1450
13	E	Scale	154	Piccard 116755	Wiener Neustadt	1450
13	E	Scale	156	Piccard 116755	Wiener Neustadt	1450
13	E	Scale	158	Piccard 116755	Wiener Neustadt	1450
13	E	Scale	159	Piccard 116755	Wiener Neustadt	1450
13	E	Scale	161	Piccard 116755	Wiener Neustadt	1450
14	E	Scale	166	Piccard 116755	Wiener Neustadt	1450
14	E	Scale	168	Piccard 116755	Wiener Neustadt	1450
14	E	Scale	170	Piccard 116755	Wiener Neustadt	1450
14	E	Scale	171	Piccard 116755	Wiener Neustadt	1450
14	E	Scale	172	Piccard 116755	Wiener Neustadt	1450
14	E	Scale	173	Piccard 116755	Wiener Neustadt	1450
15	E	Scale	176	Piccard 116755	Wiener Neustadt	1450
15	E	Scale	179	Piccard 116755	Wiener Neustadt	1450
15	E	Scale	181	Piccard 116755	Wiener Neustadt	1450
15	E	Scale	182	Piccard 116755	Wiener Neustadt	1450
15	E	Scale	184	Piccard 116755	Wiener Neustadt	1450
15	E	Scale	185	Piccard 116755	Wiener Neustadt	1450
16	A	Scale	188	Piccard 117475	Bavaria	1461
16	A	Scale	190	Piccard 117475	Bavaria	1461
16	A	Scale	192	Piccard 117475	Bavaria	1461
16	A	Scale	194	Piccard 117475	Bavaria	1461
16	A	Scale	196	Piccard 117475	Bavaria	1461
16	A	Scale	197	Piccard 117475	Bavaria	1461
16	A	Scale	198	Piccard 117475	Bavaria	1461
17	E	Scale	200	Piccard 116755	Wiener Neustadt	1450
17	E	Scale	201	Piccard 116755	Wiener Neustadt	1450
17	E	Scale	204	Piccard 116755	Wiener Neustadt	1450
17	E	Scale	206	Piccard 116755	Wiener Neustadt	1450
17	E	Scale	207	Piccard 116755	Wiener Neustadt	1450
17	E	Scale	210	Piccard 116755	Wiener Neustadt	1450
18	E	Scale	212	Piccard 116755	Wiener Neustadt	1450
18	E	Scale	213	Piccard 116755	Wiener Neustadt	1450

Table 3. Distribution of Watermarks: Hesburgh Library, cod. Lat. d. 1 (*cont.*)

Quire	*Watermark*	*Motif*	*Folio(s)*	*Reference*	*Location*	*Date*
18	E	Scale	215	Piccard 116755	Wiener Neustadt	1450
18	E	Scale	217	Piccard 116755	Wiener Neustadt	1450
18	E	Scale	219	Piccard 116755	Wiener Neustadt	1450
18	E	Scale	222	Piccard 116755	Wiener Neustadt	1450
19	E	Scale	223	Piccard 116755	Wiener Neustadt	1450
19	E	Scale	225	Piccard 116755	Wiener Neustadt	1450
19	E	Scale	226	Piccard 116755	Wiener Neustadt	1450
19	E	Scale	229	Piccard 116755	Wiener Neustadt	1450
19	E	Scale	230	Piccard 116755	Wiener Neustadt	1450
19	E	Scale	233	Piccard 116755	Wiener Neustadt	1450
19	E	Scale	236	Piccard 116755	Wiener Neustadt	1450
20	F	Anvil	239	Piccard 122662	Vienna	1455
20	F	Anvil	240	Piccard 122662	Vienna	1455
20	F	Anvil	241	Piccard 122662	Vienna	1455
20	F	Anvil	243	Piccard 122662	Vienna	1455
20	F	Anvil	247	Piccard 122662	Vienna	1455
20	F	Anvil	248	Piccard 122662	Vienna	1455
21	A	Scale	252	Piccard 117475	Bavaria	1461
21	A	Scale	253	Piccard 117475	Bavaria	1461
21	A	Scale	254	Piccard 117475	Bavaria	1461
21	A	Scale	255	Piccard 117475	Bavaria	1461
21	A	Scale	260	Piccard 117475	Bavaria	1461
21	A	Scale	262	Piccard 117475	Bavaria	1461
22	A	Scale	263	Piccard 117475	Bavaria	1461
22	A	Scale	266	Piccard 117475	Bavaria	1461
22	A	Scale	267	Piccard 117475	Bavaria	1461
22	A	Scale	269	Piccard 117475	Bavaria	1461
22	A	Scale	272	Piccard 117475	Bavaria	1461
22	A	Scale	273	Piccard 117475	Bavaria	1461
23	D	Anvil	281	Piccard 122666	Grätz	1457
23	D	Anvil	282	Piccard 122666	Grätz	1457

Table 4. Distribution of Watermarks: Hesburgh Library, cod. Lat. d. 4

Quire	*Watermark*	*Motif*	*Folio(s)*	*Reference*	*Location*	*Date*
1	A	Hat	2	Briquet 3387	Florence	1465
1	A	Hat	4	Briquet 3387	Florence	1465
1	A	Hat	6	Briquet 3387	Florence	1465
1	A	Hat	8	Briquet 3387	Florence	1465
2	B	Griffon	12	Piccard 123882	Padua	1461

Table 4. Distribution of Watermarks: Hesburgh Library, cod. Lat. d. 4 (*cont.*)

Quire	*Watermark*	*Motif*	*Folio(s)*	*Reference*	*Location*	*Date*
2	B	Griffon	16	Piccard 123882	Padua	1461
2	B	Griffon	17	Piccard 123882	Padua	1461
2	B	Griffon	18	Piccard 123882	Padua	1461
2	B	Griffon	20	Piccard 123882	Padua	1461
3	B	Griffon	21	Piccard 123882	Padua	1461
3	B	Griffon	26	Piccard 123882	Padua	1461
3	B	Griffon	27	Piccard 123882	Padua	1461
3	B	Griffon	28	Piccard 123882	Padua	1461
3	B	Griffon	29	Piccard 123882	Padua	1461
4	B	Griffon	33	Piccard 123882	Padua	1461
4	B	Griffon	34	Piccard 123882	Padua	1461
4	B	Griffon	36	Piccard 123882	Padua	1461
4	B	Griffon	39	Piccard 123882	Padua	1461
4	C	Griffon-Semi	40	Piccard 123874	Florence	1385
5	D	Horn	42	Briquet 7684	Padua	1416
5	D	Horn	46	Briquet 7684	Padua	1416
5	D	Horn	47	Briquet 7684	Padua	1416
5	D	Horn	48	Briquet 7684	Padua	1416
5	D	Horn	50	Briquet 7684	Padua	1416
6	D	Horn	51	Briquet 7684	Padua	1416
6	D	Horn	52	Briquet 7684	Padua	1416
6	D	Horn	56	Briquet 7684	Padua	1416
6	D	Horn	57	Briquet 7684	Padua	1416
6	D	Horn	58	Briquet 7684	Padua	1416
7	C	Griffon-Semi	63	Piccard 123874	Florence	1385
7	C	Griffon-Semi	66	Piccard 123874	Florence	1385
7	C	Griffon-Semi	67	Piccard 123874	Florence	1385
7	C	Griffon-Semi	69	Piccard 123874	Florence	1385
7	C	Griffon-Semi	70	Piccard 123874	Florence	1385
8	E	Bird	72	Piccard 42178	Naples	1476
8	E	Bird	73	Piccard 42178	Naples	1476
8	E	Bird	76	Piccard 42178	Naples	1476
8	E	Bird	77	Piccard 42178	Naples	1476
8	E	Bird	80	Piccard 42178	Naples	1476
9	D	Horn	83	Briquet 7684	Padua	1416
9	F	Crown	85	Briquet 4689	Venice	1482
9	E	Bird	87	Piccard 42178	Naples	1476
9	E	Bird	89	Piccard 42178	Naples	1476
9	E	Bird	90	Piccard 42178	Naples	1476
10	D	Horn	93	Briquet 7684	Padua	1416
10	B	Griffon	96	Piccard 123882	Padua	1461

Table 4. Distribution of Watermarks: Hesburgh Library, cod. Lat. d. 4 (*cont.*)

Quire	*Watermark*	*Motif*	*Folio(s)*	*Reference*	*Location*	*Date*
10	B	Griffon	97	Piccard 123882	Padua	1461
10	B	Griffon	99	Piccard 123882	Padua	1461
10	B	Griffon	100	Piccard 123882	Padua	1461
11	B	Griffon	101	Piccard 123882	Padua	1461
11	B	Griffon	102	Piccard 123882	Padua	1461
11	B	Griffon	105	Piccard 123882	Padua	1461
11	B	Griffon	106	Piccard 123882	Padua	1461

Table 5. Distribution of Watermarks: Hesburgh Library, cod. Lat. d. 6

Quire	*Watermark*	*Motif*	*Folio(s)*	*Reference*	*Location*	*Date*
1	A	Bull's Head	1	Piccard 65964	Schwabach	1466
1	A	Bull's Head	3	Piccard 65964	Schwabach	1466
1	A	Bull's Head	6	Piccard 65964	Schwabach	1466
1	A	Bull's Head	8	Piccard 65964	Schwabach	1466
1	A	Bull's Head	9	Piccard 65964	Schwabach	1466
1	A	Bull's Head	11	Piccard 65964	Schwabach	1466
2	A	Bull's Head	14	Piccard 65964	Schwabach	1466
2	A	Bull's Head	18	Piccard 65964	Schwabach	1466
2	A	Bull's Head	20	Piccard 65964	Schwabach	1466
2	A	Bull's Head	21	Piccard 65964	Schwabach	1466
2	A	Bull's Head	22	Piccard 65964	Schwabach	1466
2	A	Bull's Head	24	Piccard 65964	Schwabach	1466
3	A	Bull's Head	25	Piccard 65964	Schwabach	1466
3	A	Bull's Head	29	Piccard 65964	Schwabach	1466
3	A	Bull's Head	30	Piccard 65964	Schwabach	1466
3	A	Bull's Head	33	Piccard 65964	Schwabach	1466
3	A	Bull's Head	34	Piccard 65964	Schwabach	1466
3	A	Bull's Head	35	Piccard 65964	Schwabach	1466
4	A	Bull's Head	38	Piccard 65964	Schwabach	1466
4	A	Bull's Head	40	Piccard 65964	Schwabach	1466
4	A	Bull's Head	42	Piccard 65964	Schwabach	1466
4	A	Bull's Head	44	Piccard 65964	Schwabach	1466
4	A	Bull's Head	46	Piccard 65964	Schwabach	1466
4	A	Bull's Head	48	Piccard 65964	Schwabach	1466
5	A	Bull's Head	49	Piccard 65964	Schwabach	1466
5	A	Bull's Head	51	Piccard 65964	Schwabach	1466
5	A	Bull's Head	52	Piccard 65964	Schwabach	1466
5	A	Bull's Head	54	Piccard 65964	Schwabach	1466
5	A	Bull's Head	56	Piccard 65964	Schwabach	1466

Table 5. Distribution of Watermarks: Hesburgh Library, cod. Lat. d. 6 (*cont.*)

Quire	*Watermark*	*Motif*	*Folio(s)*	*Reference*	*Location*	*Date*
5	A	Bull's Head	59	Piccard 65964	Schwabach	1466
6	A	Bull's Head	62	Piccard 65964	Schwabach	1466
6	A	Bull's Head	66	Piccard 65964	Schwabach	1466
6	A	Bull's Head	68	Piccard 65964	Schwabach	1466
6	A	Bull's Head	69	Piccard 65964	Schwabach	1466
6	A	Bull's Head	70	Piccard 65964	Schwabach	1466
6	A	Bull's Head	72	Piccard 65964	Schwabach	1466
7	B	Bull's Head	73	Piccard 65181	Różan	1475
7	B	Bull's Head	74	Piccard 65181	Różan	1475
8	C	Triple Mount	79	Piccard 153457	Vicenza	1452
8	C	Triple Mount	80	Piccard 153457	Vicenza	1452
8	C	Triple Mount	81	Piccard 153457	Vicenza	1452
8	C	Triple Mount	83	Piccard 153457	Vicenza	1452
8	C	Triple Mount	87	Piccard 153457	Vicenza	1452
8	C	Triple Mount	88	Piccard 153457	Vicenza	1452
9	C	Triple Mount	95	Piccard 153457	Vicenza	1452
9	C	Triple Mount	96	Piccard 153457	Vicenza	1452
9	C	Triple Mount	97	Piccard 153457	Vicenza	1452
9	C	Triple Mount	98	Piccard 153457	Vicenza	1452
9	C	Triple Mount	99	Piccard 153457	Vicenza	1452
9	C	Triple Mount	100	Piccard 153457	Vicenza	1452
10	C	Triple Mount	101	Piccard 153457	Vicenza	1452
10	C	Triple Mount	105	Piccard 153457	Vicenza	1452
10	C	Triple Mount	107	Piccard 153457	Vicenza	1452
10	C	Triple Mount	109	Piccard 153457	Vicenza	1452
10	C	Triple Mount	110	Piccard 153457	Vicenza	1452
10	C	Triple Mount	111	Piccard 153457	Vicenza	1452
11	C	Triple Mount	114	Piccard 153457	Vicenza	1452
11	C	Triple Mount	119	Piccard 153457	Vicenza	1452
11	C	Triple Mount	120	Piccard 153457	Vicenza	1452
11	C	Triple Mount	121	Piccard 153457	Vicenza	1452
11	C	Triple Mount	122	Piccard 153457	Vicenza	1452
11	C	Triple Mount	124	Piccard 153457	Vicenza	1452
12	D	Scales	125	Piccard 116205	—	1457
12	D	Scales	126	Piccard 116205	—	1457
13	C	Triple Mount	128	Piccard 153457	Vicenza	1452
13	C	Triple Mount	132	Piccard 153457	Vicenza	1452
13	C	Triple Mount	133	Piccard 153457	Vicenza	1452
13	C	Triple Mount	136	Piccard 153457	Vicenza	1452
13	C	Triple Mount	137	Piccard 153457	Vicenza	1452
13	C	Triple Mount	138	Piccard 153457	Vicenza	1452

Table 5. Distribution of Watermarks: Hesburgh Library, cod. Lat. d. 6 (*cont.*)

Quire	*Watermark*	*Motif*	*Folio(s)*	*Reference*	*Location*	*Date*
13	C	Triple Mount	140	Piccard 153457	Vicenza	1452
14	C	Triple Mount	142	Piccard 153457	Vicenza	1452
14	C	Triple Mount	143	Piccard 153457	Vicenza	1452
14	C	Triple Mount	145	Piccard 153457	Vicenza	1452
14	C	Triple Mount	148	Piccard 153457	Vicenza	1452
14	C	Triple Mount	149	Piccard 153457	Vicenza	1452
14	C	Triple Mount	152	Piccard 153457	Vicenza	1452
15	E	Bull's Head	155	Piccard 65641	Könitz	1459
15	E	Bull's Head	158	Piccard 65641	Könitz	1459
15	E	Bull's Head	159	Piccard 65641	Könitz	1459
15	E	Bull's Head	162	Piccard 65641	Könitz	1459
15	E	Bull's Head	163	Piccard 65641	Könitz	1459
15	D	Scales	164	Piccard 116205	—	1457
16	E	Bull's Head	169	Piccard 65641	Könitz	1459
16	E	Bull's Head	171	Piccard 65641	Könitz	1459
16	E	Bull's Head	173	Piccard 65641	Könitz	1459
16	E	Bull's Head	174	Piccard 65641	Könitz	1459
17	E	Bull's Head	175	Piccard 65641	Könitz	1459
17	E	Bull's Head	177	Piccard 65641	Könitz	1459
17	E	Bull's Head	180	Piccard 65641	Könitz	1459
17	E	Bull's Head	181	Piccard 65641	Könitz	1459
17	E	Bull's Head	182	Piccard 65641	Könitz	1459
17	E	Bull's Head	184	Piccard 65641	Könitz	1459
18	E	Bull's Head	185	Piccard 65641	Könitz	1459
18	E	Bull's Head	186	Piccard 65641	Könitz	1459
18	E	Bull's Head	191	Piccard 65641	Könitz	1459
18	E	Bull's Head	192	Piccard 65641	Könitz	1459
18	E	Bull's Head	193	Piccard 65641	Könitz	1459
18	E	Bull's Head	194	Piccard 65641	Könitz	1459
19	F	Head w/ diadem	197	Piccard 20368	Innsbruck	1436
19	F	Head w/ diadem	199	Piccard 20368	Innsbruck	1436
19	G	Bull's Head	200	Piccard 70359	Königsberg	1440

Table 6. Distribution of Watermarks: Hesburgh Library, MS Fr. c. 2

Quire	*Watermark*	*Motif*	*Folio(s)*	*Reference*	*Location*	*Date*
Flyleaf I	A	Posts/Pillars	i	Heawood 3514	Paris	1667
1	B	Unicorn	1	Piccard 124423	Wesel	1460
1	B	Unicorn	4	Piccard 124423	Wesel	1460
1	B	Unicorn	5	Piccard 124423	Wesel	1460

Table 6. Distribution of Watermarks: Hesburgh Library, MS Fr. c. 2 (*cont.*)

Quire	*Watermark*	*Motif*	*Folio(s)*	*Reference*	*Location*	*Date*
1	B	Unicorn	6	Piccard 124423	Wesel	1460
1	B	Unicorn	9	Piccard 124423	Wesel	1460
1	B	Unicorn	10	Piccard 124423	Wesel	1460
1	B	Unicorn	14	Piccard 124423	Wesel	1460
1	B	Unicorn	15	Piccard 124423	Wesel	1460
2	B	Unicorn	19	Piccard 124423	Wesel	1460
2	B	Unicorn	21	Piccard 124423	Wesel	1460
2	B	Unicorn	23	Piccard 124423	Wesel	1460
2	B	Unicorn	25	Piccard 124423	Wesel	1460
2	B	Unicorn	27	Piccard 124423	Wesel	1460
2	B	Unicorn	29	Piccard 124423	Wesel	1460
2	B	Unicorn	31	Piccard 124423	Wesel	1460
2	B	Unicorn	32	Piccard 124423	Wesel	1460
2	B	Unicorn	33	Piccard 124423	Wesel	1460
3	B	Unicorn	34	Piccard 124423	Wesel	1460
3	B	Unicorn	36	Piccard 124423	Wesel	1460
3	B	Unicorn	38	Piccard 124423	Wesel	1460
3	B	Unicorn	39	Piccard 124423	Wesel	1460
3	B	Unicorn	42	Piccard 124423	Wesel	1460
3	B	Unicorn	44	Piccard 124423	Wesel	1460
3	B	Unicorn	45	Piccard 124423	Wesel	1460
3	B	Unicorn	48	Piccard 124423	Wesel	1460
4	B	Unicorn	55	Piccard 124423	Wesel	1460
4	B	Unicorn	56	Piccard 124423	Wesel	1460
4	B	Unicorn	57	Piccard 124423	Wesel	1460
4	B	Unicorn	58	Piccard 124423	Wesel	1460
4	B	Unicorn	63	Piccard 124423	Wesel	1460
4	B	Unicorn	64	Piccard 124423	Wesel	1460
4	B	Unicorn	65	Piccard 124423	Wesel	1460
4	B	Unicorn	66	Piccard 124423	Wesel	1460
5	B	Unicorn	67	Piccard 124423	Wesel	1460
5	B	Unicorn	69	Piccard 124423	Wesel	1460
5	B	Unicorn	70	Piccard 124423	Wesel	1460
5	B	Unicorn	72	Piccard 124423	Wesel	1460
5	B	Unicorn	74	Piccard 124423	Wesel	1460
5	B	Unicorn	76	Piccard 124423	Wesel	1460
5	B	Unicorn	78	Piccard 124423	Wesel	1460
5	B	Unicorn	81	Piccard 124423	Wesel	1460
6	B	Unicorn	83	Piccard 124423	Wesel	1460
6	B	Unicorn	86	Piccard 124423	Wesel	1460
6	B	Unicorn	87	Piccard 124423	Wesel	1460

Table 6. Distribution of Watermarks: Hesburgh Library, MS Fr. c. 2 (*cont.*)

Quire	*Watermark*	*Motif*	*Folio(s)*	*Reference*	*Location*	*Date*
6	B	Unicorn	90	Piccard 124423	Wesel	1460
6	B	Unicorn	92	Piccard 124423	Wesel	1460
6	B	Unicorn	94	Piccard 124423	Wesel	1460
6	B	Unicorn	95	Piccard 124423	Wesel	1460
6	B	Unicorn	98	Piccard 124423	Wesel	1460
6	B	Unicorn	99	Piccard 124423	Wesel	1460
7	C	Anchor	101	Piccard 118220	Düsseldorf	1463
7	C	Anchor	102	Piccard 118220	Düsseldorf	1463
7	C	Anchor	104	Piccard 118220	Düsseldorf	1463
7	C	Anchor	105	Piccard 118220	Düsseldorf	1463
7	C	Anchor	107	Piccard 118220	Düsseldorf	1463
7	C	Anchor	109	Piccard 118220	Düsseldorf	1463
7	C	Anchor	111	Piccard 118220	Düsseldorf	1463
7	C	Anchor	114	Piccard 118220	Düsseldorf	1463
8	C	Anchor	118	Piccard 118220	Düsseldorf	1463
8	C	Anchor	119	Piccard 118220	Düsseldorf	1463
8	C	Anchor	120	Piccard 118220	Düsseldorf	1463
8	C	Anchor	122	Piccard 118220	Düsseldorf	1463
8	C	Anchor	123	Piccard 118220	Düsseldorf	1463
8	C	Anchor	125	Piccard 118220	Düsseldorf	1463
8	C	Anchor	128	Piccard 118220	Düsseldorf	1463
8	C	Anchor	132	Piccard 118220	Düsseldorf	1463
9	C	Anchor	133	Piccard 118220	Düsseldorf	1463
9	C	Anchor	134	Piccard 118220	Düsseldorf	1463
9	C	Anchor	136	Piccard 118220	Düsseldorf	1463
9	C	Anchor	139	Piccard 118220	Düsseldorf	1463
9	C	Anchor	140	Piccard 118220	Düsseldorf	1463
9	C	Anchor	143	Piccard 118220	Düsseldorf	1463
9	C	Anchor	144	Piccard 118220	Düsseldorf	1463
9	C	Anchor	146	Piccard 118220	Düsseldorf	1463
10	D	Letter P	150	Piccard 112407	Baden-Baden	1469
10	D	Letter P	151	Piccard 112407	Baden-Baden	1469
10	B	Unicorn	152	Piccard 124423	Wesel	1460
10	D	Letter P	154	Piccard 112407	Baden-Baden	1469
10	D	Letter P	156	Piccard 112407	Baden-Baden	1469
10	C	Anchor	158	Piccard 118220	Düsseldorf	1463
10	D	Letter P	160	Piccard 112407	Baden-Baden	1469
10	D	Letter P	162	Piccard 112407	Baden-Baden	1469
10	D	Letter P	166	Piccard 112407	Baden-Baden	1469
11	D	Letter P	167	Piccard 112407	Baden-Baden	1469
11	D	Letter P	168	Piccard 112407	Baden-Baden	1469

Table 6. Distribution of Watermarks: Hesburgh Library, MS Fr. c. 2 (*cont.*)

Quire	*Watermark*	*Motif*	*Folio(s)*	*Reference*	*Location*	*Date*
11	D	Letter P	170	Piccard 112407	Baden-Baden	1469
11	D	Letter P	171	Piccard 112407	Baden-Baden	1469
11	D	Letter P	175	Piccard 112407	Baden-Baden	1469
11	D	Letter P	176	Piccard 112407	Baden-Baden	1469
11	D	Letter P	177	Piccard 112407	Baden-Baden	1469
11	D	Letter P	180	Piccard 112407	Baden-Baden	1469
12	D	Letter P	184	Piccard 112407	Baden-Baden	1469
12	D	Letter P	185	Piccard 112407	Baden-Baden	1469
12	D	Letter P	187	Piccard 112407	Baden-Baden	1469
12	D	Letter P	189	Piccard 112407	Baden-Baden	1469
12	D	Letter P	191	Piccard 112407	Baden-Baden	1469
12	D	Letter P	193	Piccard 112407	Baden-Baden	1469
12	D	Letter P	195	Piccard 112407	Baden-Baden	1469
12	D	Letter P	198	Piccard 112407	Baden-Baden	1469
13	B	Unicorn	202	Piccard 124423	Wesel	1460
13	B	Unicorn	205	Piccard 124423	Wesel	1460
13	B	Unicorn	207	Piccard 124423	Wesel	1460
13	B	Unicorn	209	Piccard 124423	Wesel	1460
13	B	Unicorn	210	Piccard 124423	Wesel	1460
13	B	Unicorn	212	Piccard 124423	Wesel	1460
13	D	Letter P	213	Piccard 112407	Baden-Baden	1469
13	D	Letter P	214	Piccard 112407	Baden-Baden	1469
14	B	Unicorn	215	Piccard 124423	Wesel	1460
14	B	Unicorn	216	Piccard 124423	Wesel	1460
14	B	Unicorn	218	Piccard 124423	Wesel	1460
14	B	Unicorn	219	Piccard 124423	Wesel	1460
14	B	Unicorn	222	Piccard 124423	Wesel	1460
14	B	Unicorn	224	Piccard 124423	Wesel	1460
14	B	Unicorn	225	Piccard 124423	Wesel	1460
14	B	Unicorn	228	Piccard 124423	Wesel	1460
15	B	Unicorn	231	Piccard 124423	Wesel	1460
15	B	Unicorn	232	Piccard 124423	Wesel	1460
15	B	Unicorn	234	Piccard 124423	Wesel	1460
15	B	Unicorn	237	Piccard 124423	Wesel	1460
15	B	Unicorn	238	Piccard 124423	Wesel	1460
15	B	Unicorn	240	Piccard 124423	Wesel	1460
16	B	Unicorn	247	Piccard 124423	Wesel	1460
16	B	Unicorn	249	Piccard 124423	Wesel	1460
16	B	Unicorn	251	Piccard 124423	Wesel	1460
16	B	Unicorn	252	Piccard 124423	Wesel	1460
16	B	Unicorn	253	Piccard 124423	Wesel	1460

Table 6. Distribution of Watermarks: Hesburgh Library, MS Fr. c. 2 (*cont.*)

Quire	*Watermark*	*Motif*	*Folio(s)*	*Reference*	*Location*	*Date*
16	B	Unicorn	254	Piccard 124423	Wesel	1460
17	B	Unicorn	255	Piccard 124423	Wesel	1460
17	B	Unicorn	256	Piccard 124423	Wesel	1460
17	B	Unicorn	259	Piccard 124423	Wesel	1460
17	B	Unicorn	260	Piccard 124423	Wesel	1460
17	B	Unicorn	263	Piccard 124423	Wesel	1460
17	B	Unicorn	264	Piccard 124423	Wesel	1460
18	B	Unicorn	267	Piccard 124423	Wesel	1460
18	B	Unicorn	269	Piccard 124423	Wesel	1460
18	B	Unicorn	270	Piccard 124423	Wesel	1460
18	B	Unicorn	271	Piccard 124423	Wesel	1460
18	B	Unicorn	273	Piccard 124423	Wesel	1460
18	B	Unicorn	277	Piccard 124423	Wesel	1460
19	B	Unicorn	279	Piccard 124423	Wesel	1460
19	B	Unicorn	281	Piccard 124423	Wesel	1460
19	B	Unicorn	283	Piccard 124423	Wesel	1460
19	B	Unicorn	284	Piccard 124423	Wesel	1460
19	B	Unicorn	287	Piccard 124423	Wesel	1460
19	B	Unicorn	289	Piccard 124423	Wesel	1460
20	B	Unicorn	291	Piccard 124423	Wesel	1460
20	B	Unicorn	292	Piccard 124423	Wesel	1460
20	B	Unicorn	295	Piccard 124423	Wesel	1460
20	B	Unicorn	296	Piccard 124423	Wesel	1460
Flyleaf IV	A	Posts/Pillars	iv	Heawood 3514	Paris	1667
Flyleaf VI	E	Pot	vi	Heawood 3679	—	—

Table 7. Distribution of Watermarks: Hesburgh Library, MS Ital. b. 2

Quire	*Watermark*	*Motif*	*Folio(s)*	*Reference*	*Location*	*Date*
1	A	Ladder	2/9	Piccard 122760	Milan	1477
1	B	Ladder	4/7	Piccard 122751	Venice	1463
1	A	Ladder	5/6	Piccard 122760	Milan	1477
2	B	Ladder	11/20	Piccard 122751	Venice	1463
2	B	Ladder	13/18	Piccard 122751	Venice	1463
3	A	Ladder	24/27	Piccard 122760	Milan	1477
3	A	Ladder	25/26	Piccard 122760	Milan	1477
4	A (partial)	Ladder	31/-	Piccard 122760	Milan	1477
5	B (partial)	Ladder	33/-	Piccard 122751	Venice	1463
5	B (partial)	Ladder	34/-	Piccard 122751	Venice	1463
5	C (partial)	Hat	40/-	Piccard 31981	Como	1483

Table 7. Distribution of Watermarks: Hesburgh Library, MS Ital. b. 2 (*cont.*)

Quire	*Watermark*	*Motif*	*Folio(s)*	*Reference*	*Location*	*Date*
5	C (partial)	Hat	42/-			
6	C	Hat	43/52	Piccard 31981	Como	1483
6	C	Hat	45/50	Piccard 31981	Como	1483
7	C	Hat	53/62	Piccard 31981	Como	1483
7	C	Hat	55/60	Piccard 31981	Como	1483
7	C	Hat	57/58	Piccard 31981	Como	1483
8	C	Hat	63/71	Piccard 31981	Como	1483
8	C	Hat	64/70A	Piccard 31981	Como	1483
8	C	Hat	65/70	Piccard 31981	Como	1483
9	C	Hat	74/79	Piccard 31981	Como	1483
9	C	Hat	76/77	Piccard 31981	Como	1483
10	C	Hat	82/95	Piccard 31981	Como	1483
10	C	Hat	83/94	Piccard 31981	Como	1483
10	C	Hat	87/90	Piccard 31981	Como	1483
11	D	Eagle	96/108	Piccard 42605	Ravenna	1500
11	D	Eagle	100/104	Piccard 42605	Ravenna	1500
11	D	Eagle	101/103	Piccard 42605	Ravenna	1500
Flyleaf II	E (partial)	Triple Mount	ii	—	—	—
Rear	pastedown	F	(partial)	Circle	—	—

Table 8. Distribution of Watermarks: Hesburgh Library, MS Ital. d. 1

Quire	*Watermark*	*Motif*	*Folio(s)*	*Reference*	*Location*	*Date*
1	A	Hat	1	Piccard 31981	Como	1483
1	A	Hat	3	Piccard 31981	Como	1483
1	A	Hat	4	Piccard 31981	Como	1483
1	A	Hat	5	Piccard 31981	Como	1483
1	A	Hat	9	Piccard 31981	Como	1483
2	A	Hat	13	Piccard 31981	Como	1483
2	A	Hat	15	Piccard 31981	Como	1483
2	A	Hat	17	Piccard 31981	Como	1483
2	A	Hat	19	Piccard 31981	Como	1483
2	A	Hat	20	Piccard 31981	Como	1483
3	A	Hat	21	Piccard 31981	Como	1483
3	A	Hat	24	Piccard 31981	Como	1483
3	A	Hat	25	Piccard 31981	Como	1483
3	A	Hat	28	Piccard 31981	Como	1483
3	A	Hat	29	Piccard 31981	Como	1483
4	A	Hat	33	Piccard 31981	Como	1483
4	A	Hat	36	Piccard 31981	Como	1483

Table 8. Distribution of Watermarks: Hesburgh Library, MS Ital. d. 1 (*cont.*)

Quire	*Watermark*	*Motif*	*Folio(s)*	*Reference*	*Location*	*Date*
4	A	Hat	37	Piccard 31981	Como	1483
4	A	Hat	39	Piccard 31981	Como	1483
4	A	Hat	40	Piccard 31981	Como	1483
5	A	Hat	41	Piccard 31981	Como	1483
5	A	Hat	42	Piccard 31981	Como	1483
5	A	Hat	45	Piccard 31981	Como	1483
5	A	Hat	47	Piccard 31981	Como	1483
5	A	Hat	48	Piccard 31981	Como	1483
6	A	Hat	53	Piccard 31981	Como	1483
6	A	Hat	55	Piccard 31981	Como	1483
6	A	Hat	57	Piccard 31981	Como	1483
6	A	Hat	59	Piccard 31981	Como	1483
6	A	Hat	60	Piccard 31981	Como	1483
7	A	Hat	63	Piccard 31981	Como	1483
7	A	Hat	64	Piccard 31981	Como	1483
7	A	Hat	65	Piccard 31981	Como	1483
7	A	Hat	69	Piccard 31981	Como	1483
7	A	Hat	70	Piccard 31981	Como	1483
8	A	Hat	73	Piccard 31981	Como	1483
8	A	Hat	76	Piccard 31981	Como	1483
8	A	Hat	77	Piccard 31981	Como	1483
8	A	Hat	79	Piccard 31981	Como	1483
8	A	Hat	80	Piccard 31981	Como	1483
9	A	Hat	81	Piccard 31981	Como	1483
9	A	Hat	82	Piccard 31981	Como	1483
9	A	Hat	83	Piccard 31981	Como	1483
9	A	Hat	84	Piccard 31981	Como	1483
9	A	Hat	85	Piccard 31981	Como	1483
10	A	Hat	91	Piccard 31981	Como	1483
10	A	Hat	92	Piccard 31981	Como	1483
10	A	Hat	93	Piccard 31981	Como	1483
10	A	Hat	96	Piccard 31981	Como	1483
10	A	Hat	97	Piccard 31981	Como	1483
11	A	Hat	101	Piccard 31981	Como	1483
11	A	Hat	102	Piccard 31981	Como	1483
11	A	Hat	104	Piccard 31981	Como	1483
11	A	Hat	106	Piccard 31981	Como	1483
11	A	Hat	108	Piccard 31981	Como	1483
12	A	Hat	111	Piccard 31981	Como	1483
12	A	Hat	116	Piccard 31981	Como	1483
12	A	Hat	117	Piccard 31981	Como	1483

Table 8. Distribution of Watermarks: Hesburgh Library, MS Ital. d. 1 (*cont.*)

Quire	*Watermark*	*Motif*	*Folio(s)*	*Reference*	*Location*	*Date*
12	A	Hat	118	Piccard 31981	Como	1483
12	A	Hat	119	Piccard 31981	Como	1483
13	A	Hat	121	Piccard 31981	Como	1483
13	A	Hat	123	Piccard 31981	Como	1483
13	A	Hat	124	Piccard 31981	Como	1483
13	A	Hat	126	Piccard 31981	Como	1483
13	A	Hat	129	Piccard 31981	Como	1483
14	A	Hat	131	Piccard 31981	Como	1483
14	A	Hat	132	Piccard 31981	Como	1483
14	A	Hat	135	Piccard 31981	Como	1483
14	A	Hat	137	Piccard 31981	Como	1483
14	A	Hat	138	Piccard 31981	Como	1483
15	A	Hat	141	Piccard 31981	Como	1483
15	A	Hat	143	Piccard 31981	Como	1483
15	A	Hat	144	Piccard 31981	Como	1483
15	A	Hat	146	Piccard 31981	Como	1483
15	A	Hat	149	Piccard 31981	Como	1483
16	A	Hat	151	Piccard 31981	Como	1483
16	A	Hat	152	Piccard 31981	Como	1483
16	A	Hat	154	Piccard 31981	Como	1483
16	A	Hat	155	Piccard 31981	Como	1483
16	B	Crown	158	Piccard 51114	Piacenza	1480
17	A	Hat	161	Piccard 31981	Como	1483
17	A	Hat	163	Piccard 31981	Como	1483
17	A	Hat	164	Piccard 31981	Como	1483
17	C	Horn	166	Piccard 119351	Urbino	1496
17	A	Hat	169	Piccard 31981	Como	1483
18	A	Hat	171	Piccard 31981	Como	1483
18	B	Crown	173	Piccard 51114	Piacenza	1480
18	A	Hat	175	Piccard 31981	Como	1483
18	A	Hat	177	Piccard 31981	Como	1483
18	A	Hat	179	Piccard 31981	Como	1483

Table 9. Distribution of Watermarks: Snite Museum of Art, Acc. 1984.3.6

Quire	*Watermark*	*Motif*	*Folio(s)*	*Reference*	*Location*	*Date*
1	A	Scales	1/10	Piccard 116140	Venice	1451
1	A	Scales	3/8	Piccard 116140	Venice	1451
1	B	Uncial M	4/7	Briquet 8354	Lucca	1436
1	C (partial)	Scissors	11	Piccard 122494	Gemona	1471

Bibliography

ABBAMONTE 2015: Giancarlo Abbamonte, "Naples—A Poets' City: Attitudes towards Statius and Virgil in the Fifteenth Century." In *Remembering Parthenope: The Reception of Classical Naples from Antiquity to the Present*, edited by Jessica Hughes and Claudio Buongiovanni, 170–188. Oxford: Oxford University Press, 2015.

ADRIAEN 1958: Marcus Adriaen, *Magni Aurelii Cassiodori Expositio Psalmorum I–LXX*. Corpus Christianorum Series Latina 97, pt. 2.1. Turnhout: Brepols, 1958.

AERTS and KORTEKAAS 1998: W. J. Aerts and G. A. A. Kortekaas, *Die Apokalypse des Pseudo-Methodius: Die ältesten griechischen und lateinischen Übersetzungen*. Corpus Scriptorum Christianorum Orientalium 569. Leuven: Peeters, 1998.

AKERBOOM 2003: Dick Akerboom, "'. . . Only the Image of Christ in Us': Continuity and Discontinuity between the Late Medieval *ars moriendi* and Luther's *Sermon von der Bereitung zum Sterben*." In *Spirituality Renewed: Studies on Significant Representatives of the Modern Devotion*, edited by Hein Blommestijn, Charles Caspers, and Rijcklof Hofman, 209–272. Leuven: Peeters, 2003.

ALBERIGO ET AL. 2006–2013: Giuseppe Alberigo, Adolf Martin Ritter, et al., eds. *Conciliorum oecumenicorum generaliumque decreta: Editio critica*. Corpus Christianorum 1–3. Turnhout: Brepols, 2006–2013.

ALTSTATT 2016: Alison Altstatt, "Re-membering the Wilton Processional." *Notes: The Quarterly Journal of the Music Library Association* 72.4 (June 2016): 690–732.

ANDERSON, H. 2009: Harald Anderson, *The Manuscripts of Statius* 1–3. Arlington, VA: s.n., 2009.

ANDERSON, R., ET AL. 1979: R. D. Anderson, P. J. Parsons, and R. G. M. Nisbet, "Elegaics by Gallus from Qasr Ibrîm." *Journal of Roman Studies* 69 (1979): 125–155.

ANDRIEU 1940: Michel Andrieu, *Le Pontifical Romain au Moyen-Age III: Le Pontifical de Guillaume Durand*. Studi e Testi 88. Vatican City: Biblioteca Apostolica Vaticana, 1940.

ANTWERP 1588: Guilielmus Peraldus, *Summae virtutum ac vitiorum*. Antwerp: Martin Nutius, 1588.

ARTS CLUB OF CHICAGO 1970: Arts Club of Chicago, *The Calligraphic Statement: An Exhibition of Western and Eastern Calligraphy and Painting from the 8th to the 20th Century*. Chicago: Arts Club of Chicago, 1970.

AUSTIN 2009: Greta Austin, *Shaping Church Law around the Year 1000: The Decretum of Burchard of Worms*. Burlington, VT: Ashgate, 2009.

BAIN 2001: David Bain, "Grelot and the *Compendium aureum*." *Eikasmos* 12 (2001): 346–352.

BAKER 1985: J. H. Baker, *English Legal Manuscripts in the United States of America: A Descriptive List. Part I: Medieval and Renaissance Period (to 1558)*. London: Selden Society, 1985.

BALDZUHN 2009: Michael Baldzuhn, *Schulbücher im Trivium des Mittelalters und der Frühen Neuzeit* 1–2. Berlin: De Gruyter, 2009.

BALLAIRA 1993: Guglielmo Ballaira, *Esempi di scrittura latina dell' età romana* 1. Turin: Edizioni dell' Orso, 1993.

BANDINI 1774–1777: Angelo Maria Bandini, *Catalogus codicum latinorum Bibliothecae Mediceae Laurentianae*. Florence: s.n., 1774–1777.

BANKS 1959: John Patrick Banks, "Speculum Devotorum: An Edition with Commentary." Ph. D diss., Fordham University, 1959.

BARON 1928: Hans Baron, *Leonardo Bruni Aretino. Humanistisch-Philosophische Schriften mit einer Chronologie seiner Werke und Briefe*. Quellen zur Geistesgeschichte des Mittelalters und der Renaissance 1. Leipzig: Teubner, 1928.

BARROW ET AL. 1984–1985: J. Barrow, C. Burnett, and D. Luscombe, "A Checklist of the Manuscripts Containing the Writings of Peter Abelard and Heloise and Other Works Closely Associated with Abelard and His School." *Revue d'histoire des textes* 14–15 (1984–1985): 183–302.

BARTAL 2014: Renana Bartal, "Repetition, Opposition, and Invention in an Illuminated *Meditationes vitae Christi*: Oxford, Corpus Christi College, MS 410." *Gesta* 53 (2014): 155–174.

BARTOLA 2010: Alberto Bartola, "Per la fortuna di Enrico Suso nell'Italia del Quattrocento. Prime ricerche sulla tradizione manoscritta dell'Oriuolo della sapientia." *Archivio italiano per la storia della pietà* 23 (2010): 19–72.

BARTOŠ 1919: František Michálek Bartoš, "Postila Mikuláš Biskupce na evangelní harmonii." *Časopis Musea Království českého* 93 (1919): 174–176.

BASEL 1481: *Quaestiones Evangeliorum de tempore et de sanctis. Add: Nicolaus de Byard [Dictionarius pauperum] Flos theologiae*. Basel: Johann Amerbach, 1481.

——— 1551: *Aeneae Sylvii Piccolominei Senensis qui post adeptum pontificatum Pius eius nominis secundus appellatus est : opera quae extant omnia nunc demum post corruptissimas aeditiones summa diligentia castigata & in unum corpus redacta, quorum elenchum versa pagella indicabit*. Basel: ex officina Henricpetrina, 1551; repr. Frankfurt-am-Main: Minerva, 1967.

——— 1597: *Ioannis de Rupescissa, qui vixit ante CCCXX annos, de consideratione quintae essentiae rerum omnium, opus sane egregium: Accessere Arnaldi de Villanova Epistola de Sanguine humano distillato. Raymundi Lullii Ars operativa, et alia quaedam. Michaelis Savanarolae libellus optimus de Aqua Vitae, nunc valde correctior quam ante annos LXX editus*. Basel: Conrad Waldkrich, 1597.

BASWELL 2009: Christopher Baswell, "England's Antiquities: Middle English Literature and the Classical Past." In *A Companion to Medieval English Literature and Culture, c.1350–c.1500*, edited by Peter Brown, 231–246. Chichester: Wiley-Blackwell, 2009.

BATAILLON 1994: Louis Jacque Bataillon, "The Tradition of Nicholas of Biard's Distinctiones." *Viator* 25 (1994): 245–288.

BEICHNER 1956: Paul E. Beichner, "Non Alleluia Ructare." *Mediaeval Studies* 18 (1956): 135–144.

——— 1965: Paul E. Beichner, *Aurora Petri Rigae Biblia Versificata: A Verse Commentary on the Bible* 1–2. Notre Dame, IN: University of Notre Dame Press, 1965.

——— 1969: Paul E. Beichner, "The *Floridus Aspectus* of Peter Riga and Some Relationships to the *Aurora*." *Classica et Mediaevalia* 30 (1969): 451–481.

Bénedictins de Bouveret 1965–1982: Saint-Benoît de Port-Valais (Bénedictins de Bouveret), *Colophons de manuscrits occidentaux des origines au XVIe siècle* 1–6. Fribourg: Suisse, Editions universitaires, 1965–1982.

Bertalot 1985–2004. Ludwig Bertalot and Ursula Jaitner-Hahner, *Initia humanistica Latina: Initienverzeichnis lateinicher Prosa und Poesie aus der Zeit des 14 bis 16* 1–2.2. Tübingen: M. Niemeyer, 1985–2004.

Bertram 2013: Martin Bertram, *Kanonisten und ihre Texte (1234 bis Mitte 14. Jh.): 18 Aufsätze und 14 Exkurse*. Education and Society in the Middle Ages and Renaissance 43. Leiden: Brill, 2013.

Bestul 1996: Thomas H. Bestul, *Texts of the Passion: Latin Devotional Literature and Medieval Society*. Philadelphia: University of Pennsylvania Press, 1996.

Bévenot 1972: Maurice Bévenot, *Sancti Cypriani episcopi opera. Pars 1, De ecclesiae Catholice unitate.* Corpus Christianorum Series Latina 3. Turnhout: Brepols, 1972.

Bipontine 1789: *Historiae Romanae scriptores minores. Sex. Aur. Victor, Sex. Rufus, Eutropius, Messala Corvinus; ad optimas editiones collati praemittitur notitia literaria accedit index studiis Societatis Bipontinae*. Biponti: ex typographica Societatis, 1789.

Bloomfield et al. 1979: Morton W. Bloomfield, Bertrand Georges Guyot, Donald Roy Howard, and Thyra B. Kabelao, *Incipits of Latin Works on the Virtues and Vices, 1100–1500 A.D., Including a Section of Incipits of Works on the Pater Noster*. Cambridge, MA: Mediaeval Academy of America, 1979.

Boccini 2006: Fabiana Boccini, "La *Vita beati Benedicti abbatis (BHL 1102) in alcuni omeliari e leggendari medievali*," in *I Dialogi di Gregorio Magno: Tradizione del testo e antichie traduszioni*, edited by Paolo Chiesa, 57–81. Florence: SISMEL Edizioni del Galluzzo, 2006.

Bollandists 1898–1986: [Bollandists], *Bibliotheca Hagiographica Latina* 1–2. Brussels: Socii Bollandiani, 1898–1901. *Novum supplementum* by Henryk Fros. Brussels: Société des Bollandistes, 1986.

Bonanno 2008: Francesca Bonanno, *Plutarco Parallela minora: Traduzione latina di Guarino Veronese*. Messina: Centro interdipartimentale di studi umanistici, 2008.

Booton 2010: Diane E. Booton, *Manuscripts, Market, and the Transition to Print in Late Medieval Brittany*. Burlington, VT: Ashgate, 2010.

Boulton 2003: Maureen Boulton, "*Nous deffens de feu, . . . de pestilence, de guerres*: Christine de Pizan's Religious Works." In *Christine de Pizan: A Casebook*, edited by Barbara K. Altmann and Deborah L. McGrady, 215–228. New York: Routledge, 2003.

——— 2006: Maureen Boulton, "The Knight and the Rose: French Manuscripts in the Notre Dame Library." In *The Text in the Community: Essays on Medieval Works, Manuscripts, Authors, and Readers*, edited by Jill Mann and Maura Nolan, 217–236. Notre Dame, IN: University of Notre Dame Press, 2006.

Boyer 2008: Christine Boyer, *Humberti de Romanis De dono timoris*. Corpus Christianorum, Continuatio Mediaevalis 218. Turnhout: Brepols, 2008.

Braekman 1990: Willy L. Braekman, "A Treatise on the Planetary Herbs Found by Alexius Africanus in the Tomb of Kyranos." *Würzburger medizinhistorische Mitteilungen* 8 (1990): 161–192.

Branner 1977: Robert Branner, *Manuscript Painting in Paris during the Reign of Saint Louis: A Study of Styles*. Berkeley: University of California Press, 1977.

Brantley 2006: Jessica Brantley, "The Visual Environments of Carthusian Texts: Decoration and Illustration in Notre Dame 67." In *The Text in the Community: Essays on Medieval Works, Manuscripts, Authors, and Readers*, edited by Jill Mann and Maura Nolan, 173–216. Notre Dame, IN: University of Notre Dame Press, 2006.

——— 2007: Jessica Brantley, *Reading in the Wilderness: Private Devotion and Public Performance in Late Medieval England.* Chicago: University of Chicago Press, 2007.

Breen 2002: Aidan Breen, "*De XII abusiuis*: Text and Transmission." In *Ireland and Europe in the Early Middle Ages: Texts and Transmission*, edited by Próinséas Ní Chatháin and Michael Richter, 78–94. Dublin: Four Courts Press, 2002.

Briquet 1968: Charles-Moïse Briquet, *Les filigranes: Dictionnaire historique des marques du papier dès leur apparition vers 1282 jusqu'en 1600; A Facsimile of the 1907 Edition with Supplementary Material* 1–4, edited by Alan Stevenson. 3rd ed. Amsterdam: Paper Publications Society, 1968.

Brown, C. 2005: Cynthia J. Brown, *Pierre Gringoire, Les Entrées Royales a Paris de Marie d'Angleterre (1514) et Claude de France (1517).* Textes Littéraires Francais. Geneva: Libraire Droz, 2005.

——— 2011: Cynthia J. Brown, *The Queen's Library: Image-Making at the Court of Anne of Brittany, 1477–1514.* Material Texts. Philadelphia: University of Pennsylvania Press, 2011.

Brown, M. 1994: Michelle P. Brown, *Understanding Illuminated Manuscripts: A Guide to Technical Terms.* Los Angeles: Getty Publications, 1994.

Brown, V. 2008: Virginia Brown, "A Second New List of Beneventan Manuscripts (V)." *Mediaeval Studies* 70 (2008): 275–355.

——— 2012: Virginia Brown, *Beneventan Discoveries: Collected Manuscript Catalogues, 1978–2008*, edited by Roger E. Reynolds. Toronto: Pontifical Institute of Mediaeval Studies, 2012.

Brundage 1996: James A. Brundage, *Medieval Canon Law.* New York: Routledge, 1995.

Brunhölzl 1984: Franz Brunhölzl, "Der sogenannte Galluspapyrus von Kasr Ibrim." *Codices Manuscripti* 10 (1984): 33–40.

Bruylants 1952: Placide Bruylants, *Les Oraisons du Missel Romain: Texte et Histoire* 1–2. Louvain: Centre de Documentation et d'information Liturgiques, 1952; repr. 1965.

Budde and Krischel 2001: Rainer Budde and Roland Krischel, eds. *Das Stundenbuch der Sophia van Bylant.* Cologne: Wallraf Richartz Museum, 2001.

Busard 1971: Hubertus Lambertus Ludovicus Busard, *Der Tractatus proportionum von Albert von Sachsen.* Österreichische Akademie der Wissenschaften, Mathematisch–naturwissenschaftliche Klasse, Denkschriften 116.2. Vienna: Springer in Komm., 1971.

Cacciatore 2006: Paola Volpe Cacciatore, "Guarino Guarini traduttore di Plutarco." In *Ecos de Plutarco en Europa: De Fortuna Plutarchi Studia Selecta*, edited by Rosa M. Aguilar and Ignacio R. Alfageme, 261–268. Madrid: Servicio de Publicaciones de la Universidad Complutense, 2006.

Callu 1972: Jean-Pierre Callu, *Lettres [de] Symmaque: Livres I–II.* Paris: Les Belles Lettres, 1972.

Capasso 2003: Mario Capasso, *Il ritorno di Cornelio Gallo: Il papiro di Qaṣr Ibrîm venticinque anni dopi.* Naples: Graus, 2003.

Carley and Crick 1995: James P. Carley and Julia Crick, "Constructing Albion's Past: An Annotated Edition of *De Origine Gigantum*." *Arthurian Literature* 13 (1995): 41–114.

Carlvant 2012: Kerstin Carlvant, *Manuscript Painting in Thirteenth-Century Flanders.* Turnhout: Harvey Miller, 2012.

Carmody 1956: Francis J. Carmody, *Arabic Astronomical and Astrological Sciences in Latin Translation: A Critical Bibliography.* Berkeley: University of California Press, 1956.

Carthusian monk 2006: A Carthusian monk, *Carthusian Saints.* Carthusian Booklets Series, no. 8. Arlington, VT: Charterhouse of the Transfiguration, 2006.

Castaldi 2003: Lucia Castaldi, "Per un'edizione critica dei 'Dialogi' di Gregorio Magno: Ricognizione preliminari." *Filologia mediolatina* 10 (2003): 1–39.

Castan 1889: Auguste Castan, "Le Bibliothèque de l'Abbaye de Saint-Claude du Jura: Esquisse de son Histoire." *Bibliothèque de l'École des chartes* 50 (1889): 301–354.

Cervigni 1979: Dino S. Cervigni, "Inediti di Jacopo Corsi e del Sannazaro in un ms. della University of Notre Dame." *Studi e problemi di critica testuale* 19 (1979): 25–31.

Chavasse 2003: Ruth Chavasse, "The *studia humanitatis* and the Making of a Humanist Career: Marcantonio Sabellico's Exploitation of the Humanist Literary Genres." *Renaissance Studies* 17 (2003): 27–38.

Chevalier 1892–1921: Ulysse Chevalier, *Repertorium hymnologicum* 1–6. Subsidia hagiographica 4. Louvain: Lefever, 1892–1912; Brussels: s.n., 1920–1921.

Ciccolini 2011: Laetitia Ciccolini, "Un florilège biblique mis sous le nom de Cyprien de Carthage: L'*Exhortatio de paenitentia* (*CPL* 65)." *Recherches Augustiniennes et Patristiques* 36 (2011): 89–138.

Clayton 2012: Mary Clayton, "*De Duodecim abusiuis*, Lordship and Kingship in Anglo-Saxon England." In *Saints and Scholars: New Perspectives on Anglo-Saxon Literature and Culture in Honour of Hugh Magennis*, edited by Stuart McWilliams, 141–163. Woodbridge: Boydell and Brewer, 2012.

Cohen 1999: Jeffrey Jerome Cohen, *Of Giants: Sex, Monsters, and the Middle Ages.* Minneapolis: University of Minnesota Press, 1999.

Cole and Turville-Petre 2010: Gavin Cole and Thorlac Turville-Petre, "Sir Thomas Chaworth's Books." In *The Wollaton Medieval Manuscripts: Texts, Owners and Readers*, edited by Ralph Hanna and Thorlac Turville-Petre, 20–29. Woodbridge: Boydell and Brewer, 2010.

Colgrave and Mynors 1969: Bertram Colgrave and R. A. B. Mynors, *Bede's Ecclesiastical History of the English People.* Oxford: Clarendon Press, 1969.

Colker 1983: Marvin L. Colker, "Two Manuscripts of Suetonius' *De Grammaticis et Rhetoribus.*" *Manuscripta* 27 (1983): 165–169.

Comper 1917: Frances M. M. Comper, *The Book of the Craft of Dying and Other Early English Tracts Concerning Death Taken from Manuscripts and Printed Books in the British Museum and Bodleian Libraries.* London: Longmans, Green, and Co., 1917.

Corbett 1951: James A. Corbett, "Two German Dominican Psalters." *Mediaeval Studies* 13 (1951): 247–252.

——— 1957: James A. Corbett, "A Fifteenth Century Book of Hours of Salisbury." *Ephemerides Liturgicae* 71 (1957): 293–307.

——— 1978: James A. Corbett, *Catalogue of the Medieval & Renaissance Manuscripts of the University of Notre Dame.* Notre Dame, IN: University of Notre Dame Press, 1978.

Cortesi 1995: Mariarosa Cortesi, "La tecnica di tradurre presso gli umanisti." In *The Classical Tradition in the Middle Ages and the Renaissance*, Proceedings of the First European Science Foundation Workshop on "The Reception of Classical Texts," edited by Claudio Leonardi and Birger Munk Olsen, 143–168. Collana della "Società internazionale per lo studio del medioevo latino" 15. Spoleto: Centro italiano di studi sull'alto Medioevo, 1995.

——— 1997: Mariarosa Cortesi, "Lettura di Plutarco alla scuola di Vittorino da Feltre." In *Filologia umanistica per Gianvito Resta* 1, edited by Vincenzo Fera and Giacomo Ferraù, 429–451. Medioevo e Umanesimo 94. Padova: Antenore, 1997.

Cottineau 1934–1970: Laurent Henri Cottineau, *Répertoire topo-bibliographique des abbayes et prieurés* 1–3. Mâcon: Protat frères, 1934–1970.

Courtney 1993: Edward Courtney, *The Fragmentary Latin Poets.* Oxford: Clarendon Press, 1993.

Cremonini 2006: Stefano Cremonini, "Per l'edizione delle laude di Feo Belcari." Ph.D. diss., Università degli Studi di Bologna, 2006.

Crick 1986: Julia C. Crick, "The Manuscripts of the Works of Geoffrey of Monmouth: A New Supplement." *Arthurian Literature* 6 (1986): 157–162.

——— 1989: Julia C. Crick, *The Historia Regum Britannie of Geoffrey of Monmouth III: A Summary Catalogue of the Manuscripts.* Cambridge: D. S. Brewer, 1989.

——— 1991: Julia C. Crick, *The Historia Regum Britannie of Geoffrey of Monmouth IV: Dissemination and Reception in the Later Middle Ages.* Cambridge: D. S. Brewer, 1991.

d'Alverny 1965: Marie-Thérèse d'Alverny, *Alain de Lille: Textes Inédits.* Études de philosophie médiévale 52. Paris: Librairie philosophique J. Vrin, 1965.

——— 1981: Marie-Thérèse d'Alverny, "Review of *Catalogue of the Medieval and Renaissance Manuscripts of the University of Notre Dame*, by James A. Corbett." *Scriptorium* 35 (1981): 106–108.

Daniel 1855–1856: Hermann Adalbert Daniel, *Thesaurus Hymnologicus sive hymnorum canticorum sequentiarum circa annum MD usitatarum collectio amplissima.* Leipzig: J. T. Loeschke, 1855–1856.

Davidson 2002: Ivor J. Davidson, *Ambrose: De officiis* 1–2. Oxford: Oxford University Press, 2002.

Deér 1959: József Deér, *The Dynastic Porphyry Tombs of the Norman Period in Sicily.* Dumbarton Oaks Studies 5. Cambridge, MA: Harvard University Press, 1959.

Defoer 1990: Henri L. M. Defoer, "The Artists of the East Netherlands, ca. 1460–1480." In *The Golden Age of Dutch Manuscript Painting*, edited by James H. Marrow, Henri L. M. Defoer, Anne S. Korteweg, and Wilhemina C. M. Wüstefeld, 244–252. New York: G. Braziller, 1990.

de Hamel 2010: Christopher de Hamel, *Gilding the Lilly: A Hundred Medieval and Illuminated Manuscripts in the Lilly Library.* Bloomington, IN: Lilly Library, 2010.

Dekkers and Gaar 1995: Eligius Dekkers and Emil Gaar, eds., *Clavis patrum latinorum: Qua in corpus christianorum edendum optimas quasque scriptorum recensiones a Tertulliano ad Bedam.* Corpus Christianorum Series Latina. 3rd ed. Steenbrugge: In Abbatia Sancti Petri, 1995.

de Lagarde 1959: P. de Lagarde, *Liber interpretationis hebraicorum nominum.* In *S. Hieronymi Presbyteri Opera. Pars 1, Opera Exegetica* 1. *Corpus* Christianorum 72. 57–161. Turnhout: Brepols, 1959.

de la Mare 1971: Albinia C. de la Mare, *Catalogue of the Collection of Medieval Manuscripts Bequeathed to the Bodleian Library Oxford by James P. R. Lyell.* Oxford: Clarendon Press, 1971.

——— 1976: Albinia C. de la Mare, "The Return of Petronius to Italy." In *Medieval Learning and Literature: Essays Presented to Richard William Hunt*, edited by Jonathan James Graham Alexander and Margaret T. Gibson, 220–254. Oxford: Clarendon Press, 1976.

Delatte 1942: Louis Delatte, *Textes Latins et vieux Français relatifs aux Cyranides: La traduction latine du XIIe siècle. Le Compendium aureum. Le de XV stellis d'Hermes. Le Livre de secrez de nature.* Bibliothèque de la Faculté de Philosophie et Lettres de l'Université de Liège 93. Paris: Faculté de philosophie et lettres, 1942.

D'Elia 2002: Anthony F. D'Elia, "Marriage, Sexual Pleasure, and Learned Brides in the Wedding Orations of Fifteenth-Century Italy." *Renaissance Quarterly* 55 (2002): 379–433.

——— 2003: Anthony F. D'Elia, "Genealogy and the Limits of Panegyric: Turks and Huns in Fifteenth-Century Epithalamia." *The Sixteenth Century Journal* 34 (2003): 973–991.

——— 2006: Anthony F. D'Elia, "Heroic Insubordination in the Army of Sigismundo Malatesta: Petrus Parleo's *Pro Milite*, Machiavelli and the Uses of Cicero and Livy." In *Humanism and Creativity in the Renaissance: Essays in Honor of Ronald G. Witt*, edited by Christopher S.

Celenza and Kenneth Gouwens, 31–60. Brill's Studies in Intellectual History 136. Leiden: Brill, 2006.

Dell'Oso 2013: Lorenzo Dell'Oso, "Tra le carte del MS. Lat. D 5 della Hesburgh Library *(U. Of Notre Dame)*: Una silloge quattrocentesca inedita di versi volgari. Ricognizione filologica, edizione fototipica, diplomatico-interpretativa e critica." Tesi di Laurea magistrale, Università degli Studi di Pavia, 2013.

——— 2014: Lorenzo Dell'Oso, "Un domenicano contra la stampa: Nuove acquisizioni al *corpus* di Filippo da Strada." *Tipofilologia* 7 (2014): 69–99.

——— 2015: Lorenzo Del'Oso, "Litre De Stampa Son Caliginose: The Role of Filippo Da Strada (1450–1505) in the Debate of Printing in Renaissance Italy." M.A. thesis, University of Notre Dame, 2015.

Delmas 2014: Sophie Delmas, "La *Summa de abstinentia* attribuée à Nicolas de Biard: Circulation et réception." In *Entre stabilité et itinérance: Livres et culture des ordres mendiants XIIIe–XVe* siècle, edited by Nicole Bérou, Martin Mordard, and Donatella Nebbiai, 303–327. Bibliologia 37. Turnhout: Brepols, 2014.

de Ricci 1930: Seymour de Ricci, *English Collectors of Books and Manuscripts (1530–1930) and Their Marks of Ownership*. Cambridge: Cambridge University Press, 1930.

de Ricci and Wilson 1935–1940: Seymour de Ricci and William Jerome Wilson, *Census of Medieval and Renaissance Manuscripts in the United States and Canada* 1–3. New York: H.W. Wilson, 1935, 1937, 1940.

Derolez 1984: Albert Derolez, *Codicologie des manuscrits en écriture humanistique sur parchemin* 1–2. Mitteilung-Kommission für Humanismusforschung 4. Turnhout: Brepols, 1984.

——— 2003a: Albert Derolez. "Masters and Measures: A Codicological Approach to Books of Hours." *Quaerendo* 33 (2003): 83–95.

——— 2003b: Albert Derolez, *The Palaeography of Gothic Manuscript Books from the Twelfth to the Early Sixteenth Century*. Cambridge: Cambridge University Press, 2003.

——— 2011: Albert Derolez, "The Codicology of Late Medieval Music Manuscripts: Some Preliminary Observations." In *The Calligraphy of Medieval Music*, edited by John Haines, 23–35. Musicalia Medii Aevi 1. Turnhout: Brepols, 2011.

de Sceaux 1955: Raoul de Sceaux, "Étude sur la chartreuse de Vauvert-lès-Paris." *Le amis de saint François* 71 (1955): 14–32.

Deschamps 1975: J. Deschamps, "De verspreiding van Johan Scutkens vertaling van het Niewe Testament en de Oudtestamentische perikopen." *Nederlands Archeif voor Kergeschiedenis* n.s. 51 (1975/1976): 159–179.

Deventer 1484: *Quaestiones evangeliorum de tempore et de sanctis Add. Nicolaus de Byard: [Dictionarius pauperum] Flos theologiae*. Deventer: Richard Paffraet, 1484.

de Vogüé 1978–1980. Adalbert de Vogüé, *Grégoire le Grand. Dialogues*. Sources chrétiennes 251, 260, 265. Paris: Éditions du Cerf, 1978–1980.

di Ciaccia 1996–1999: Giuseppe di Ciaccia, *Le Lettere di Santa Caterina da Siena: Versione in Italiano Corrente* 1–3. Collana Attendite Ad Petram 14–16. Bologna: ESD, 1996–1999.

Dickmann 2001: Ines Dickmann, "Das Stundenbuch der Sophia van Bylant und die Meister der Margriet Uutenham." In *Das Stundenbuch der Sophia van Bylant*, edited by Rainer Budde and Roland Krischeleds, 177–186. Cologne: Wallraf Richartz Museum, 2001.

Diercks 1972: G. F. Diercks, *Novatiani opera*. Corpus Christianorum Series Latina 4. Turnhout: Brepols, 1972.

——— 1994: G. F. Diercks, *Sancti Cypriani episcopi opera. Pars 3.2, Epistularium. Epistulae 1–57 (Cyprianus)*. Corpus Christianorum Series Latina 3B. Turnhout: Brepols, 1994.

——— 1996: G. F. Diercks, *Sancti Cypriani episcopi opera. Pars 3.3, Epistularium. Epistulae 58–81 (Cyprianus)*. Corpus Christianorum Series Latina 3C. Turnhout: Brepols, 1996.

Dinkova-Bruun 2006: Greti Dinkova-Bruun, "Peter Riga's *Aurora* and Its Gloss from Salzburg, Stiftsbibliothek Sankt Peter, MS a.VII.6." In *Insignis Sophiae Arcator: Essays in Honour of Michael W. Herren on his 65th Birthday*, edited by Gernot R. Wieland, Carin Ruff, and Ross G. Arthur, 237–260. Publications of the Journal of Medieval Latin 6. Turnhout: Brepols, 2006.

——— 2007: Greti Dinkova-Bruun, "Additions to Peter Riga's *Aurora* in Paris, Bibliothèque nationale de France Lat. 13050." *Mediaeval Studies* 69 (2007): 1–57.

——— 2008: Greti Dinkova-Bruun, "*Proverbia Salomonis*: An Anonymous Accretion to Peter Riga's *Aurora*." In *Classica et Beneventana: Essays Presented to Virginia Brown on the Occasion of her 65th Birthday*, edited by Frank T. Coulson and Anna A. Grotans, 9–44. Fédération Internationale des Instituts d'Études Médiévales, Textes et Études du Moyen Âge 36. Turnhout: Brepols, 2008.

——— 2011: Greti Dinkova-Bruun, "Aegidius of Paris and the Seven Seals: A Prose Prologue to the Gospels in Peter Riga's *Aurora*." *Mediaeval Studies* 73 (2011): 119–145.

——— 2012: Greti Dinkova-Bruun, "*Corrector Ultimus*: Aegidius of Paris and Peter Riga's *Aurora*." In *Modes of Authorship in the Middle Ages*, edited by Slavica Rancovi , 172–189. Papers in Mediaeval Studies 22. Toronto: Pontifical Institute of Mediaeval Studies, 2012.

Dionisotti 1968: Carlo Dionisotti, *Gli umanisti e il volgare fra quattro e cinquecento*. Florence: Le Monnier, 1968.

Drigsdahl 1997–2013: Erik Drigsdahl, CHD: Center for Håndskriftstudier i Danmark. 1997–2013. http://manuscripts.org.uk/chd.dk.

Dumont, forthcoming: Stephen Dumont, "New Questions by Giles of Rome (I): The Intention and Remission of Forms." Forthcoming.

Dusch 1975: Marieluise Dusch, *De veer utersten: Das "Cordiale de quatuor novissimis" von Gerhard von Vliederhoven in mittelniederdeutscher Überlieferung*. Niederdeutsche Studien 20. Cologne: Böhlau, 1975.

Dutschke et al. 1986: Consuelo W. Dutschke and Richard Hunter Rouse, with the assistance of Mirella Ferrari, *Medieval and Renaissance Manuscripts in the Claremont Libraries*. Berkeley: University of California Press, 1986.

Edwards 2006: A. S. G. Edwards, "The Contexts of Notre Dame 67." In *The Text in the Community: Essays on Medieval Works, Manuscripts, Authors, and Readers*, edited by Jill Mann and Maura Nolan, 107–128. Notre Dame, IN: University of Notre Dame Press, 2006.

Ehrenschwendtner 1996: Marie-Luise Ehrenschwendtner, "A Library Collected by and for the Use of Nuns: St. Catherine's Convent, Nuremberg." In *Women and the Book: Assessing the Visual Evidence*, edited by Jane H. M. Taylor and Lesley Smith, 123–132. Toronto: British Library and University of Toronto Press, 1996.

Embree 1993: Dan Embree, "The Fragmentary Chronicle in British Library, Additional MS 37049." *Manuscripta* 37 (1993): 193–200.

——— 1999: Dan Embree, *The Chronicles of Rome: An Edition of the Middle English "Chronicle of Popes and Emperors" and "The Lollard Chronicle."* Medieval Chronicles 1. Woodbridge: Boydell Press, 1999.

Emery, Jr. and L. Jordan 1998: Kent Emery, Jr., and Louis E. Jordan, "*Familia Praedicatoria* in the University of Notre Dame Library: Manuscripts, Incunables and the Sixteenth-Century Books Containing Text and Images of the Order of Preachers." In *Christ among the Medieval Dominicans: Representations of Christ in the Texts and Images of the Order of Preachers*, ed. Kent Emery, Jr., and Joseph Wawrykow, 493–541. Notre Dame, IN: University of Notre Dame Press, 1998.

Ewald and Hartmann 1992: Paul Ewald and Ludo Moritz Hartmann, *Gregorii I Papae Registrum Epistolarum Libri VIII–XIV. Epistolae 2.* Munich: Monumenta Germaniae historica, 1992.

Faral 1946: Edmond Faral, "Jean Buridan: Notes sur le manuscrits les editions, et le contenu de ses ouvrages." *Archives d'histoire doctrinale et littéraire du moyan âge* 15 (1946): 1–53.

——— 1950: Edmond Faral, *Jean Buridan, maître des arts de l'Université de Paris.* Paris: Imprimerie nationale, 1950.

Farquhar 1977: James Douglas Farquhar, "The Manuscript as a Book." In Sandra Hindman and James Douglas Farquhar, *Pen to Press: Illustrated Manuscripts and Printed Books in the First Century of Printing*, 11–99. College Park, MD: Art Department, University of Maryland, 1977.

Faucon 1990–1991: Jean-Claude Faucon, *Le chanson de Bertrand du Guesclin de Cuevelier* 1–3. Toulouse: Éditions universitaires du Sud, 1990–1991.

Faye and Bond 1962: Christopher Urdahl Faye and William Henry Bond, *Supplement to the Census of Medieval and Renaissance Manuscripts in the United States and Canada.* New York: Bibliographical Society of America, 1962.

Finzi 1893: Vittorio Finzi, "Il Pianto della B. Vergine attribuito a fratre Enselmino da Treviso, una laude di Leonardo Guistiniani, alcune orazioni di S. Gregorio Magno, ed altri componimenti tratti dal codice Lucchese, 1302." *Il Propugnatore* n.s. 6.2 (1893): 168–194.

Fischer, E. 2011: Ernst Fischer, *Verleger Buchhändler & Antiquare aus Deutschland und Österreich in der Emigration nach 1933: Ein biographisches Handbuch.* Stuttgart: Verband Deutscher Antiquare e.V., 2011.

Fischer, K. 1996: Klaus-Dietrich Fischer, "*De coelo vita—de terra mors.* Zwei Zeugnisse zur physischen Anthropologie aus dem frühen Mittelalter." In *Worte, Bilder, Töne: Studien zur Antike und Antikerezeption*, edited by Richard Faber and Bernd Seidensticker, 213–230. Würzburg: Königshausen und Neumann, 1996.

Flora 2003: Holly Flora, "A Book of Poverty's Daughters: Gender and Devotion in Paris Bibliothèque Nationale Ital. 115." In *Varieties of Devotion in the Middle Ages and Renaissance*, edited by Susan C. Karant-Nunn, 61–97. Arizona Studies in the Middle Ages and the Renaissance 7. Turnhout: Brepols, 2006.

——— 2009: Holly Flora, *The Devout Belief of the Imagination: The Paris 'Meditationes Vitae Christi' and Female Franciscan Spirituality in Trecento Italy.* Disciplina Monastica 6. Turnhout: Brepols, 2009.

Florence 1492: *Incominciano alchuni singulari tractati di Vgho Pantiera da Prato dellordine de Frati minori.* Florence: Lorenzo de Morgiani and Giovanni da Maganza, 1492.

Fohlen 1980: J. Fohlen, "Un apocryphe de Sénèque mal connu: Le *De verborum copia.*" *Mediaeval Studies* 42 (1980): 139–211.

Folkard 1900: Henry Tennyson Folkard, *Catalogue of Books* 4. Wigan: R. Platt, 1900.

——— 1902: Henry Tennyson Folkard, *Catalogue of Books* 5. Wigan: James Starr, 1902.

Forrer 1902: Robert Forrer, *Unedierte Federzeichnungen Miniaturen und Initialen des Mittelalters* 1. Strassburg: Schlesier and Schweikhardt, 1902.

Förster 1908: Max Förster, "Adams Erschaffung und Namengebung." *Archiv für Religionswissenschaft* 11 (1908): 477–589.

Franz 1902: Adolph Franz, *Die Messe im deutschen Mittelalter.* Freiburg-im-Breisgau: Herder, 1902.

——— 1909: Adolph Franz, *Die Kirchlichen Benediktionen im Mittelalter* 1–2. Freiburg-im-Breisgau: Herder, 1909; repr. Graz: Akademische Druck- und Verlagsanstalt, 1960.

Freckmann 2006: Anja Freckmann, *Die Bibliothek des Klosters Bursfelde im Spämittelalter.* Gottingen: V & R unipress, 2006.

Freuler 2013: Gaudenz Freuler, *Italian Miniatures from the Twelfth to the Sixteenth Centuries.* Cinisello Balsamo: Silvana editoriale, 2013.

Friedberg 1959: Emil Friedberg, *Corpus Iuris Canonici* 1–2. Graz: Akademische Druck- und Verlagsanstalt, 1959.

Friedrich 1968: Hans-Veit Friedrich, *Thessalos von Tralles griechisch und lateinisch.* Meisenheim: Hain, 1965.

Fries 1924: Walter Fries, "Kirche und Kloster zu St. Katharina in Nürnberg." *Mitteilungen des Vereins für Geschichte der Stadt Nürnberg* 25 (1924): 1–143.

Fuderer 1994: Laura Fuderer, "Rare Books and Special Collections at the University of Notre Dame." In *What Is Written Remains: Historical Essays on the Libraries of Notre Dame*, edited by Maureen Gleason and Katharina J. Blackstead, 171–188. Notre Dame, IN: University of Notre Dame Press, 1994.

Fudge 2000: Thomas A. Fudge, "Crime, Punishment and Pacifism in the Thought of Bishop Mikuláš of Pelhřimov, 1420–1452." *Bohemian Reformation and Religious Practice* 3 (2000): 69–103.

Gagliardi 2011: Paolo Gagliardi, "Plakato iudice te: Per la lettura dei vv. 8–9 del papiro di Gallo." *Zeitschrift für Papyrologie und Epigraphik* 176 (2011): 82–95.

Galletti 1863: Gustavo C. Galletti, *Laude spirituali di Feo Belcari, di Lorenzo de' Medici, di Francesco d'Albizzo, di Castellan Castellani e di altri, compresse nelle quarto più antiche raccolte.* Florence: Molini e Cechhi, 1863.

Gelsomino 1967: Remo Gelsomino, *Vibius Sequester.* Leipzig: Teubner, 1967.

Gibson 1993: Margaret T. Gibson, *The Bible in the Latin West.* Notre Dame, IN: University of Notre Dame Press, 1993.

Gilbert 1973: Felix Gilbert, "Biondo, Sabellico, and the Beginnings of Venetian Official Historiography." In *Florilegium Historiale: Essays Presented to Wallace K. Ferguson*, edited by J. G. Rowe and W. H. Stockdale, 275–293. Toronto: University of Toronto Press, 1971.

Gillespie 2006: Vincent Gillespie, "The Haunted Text: Reflections in *A Mirror to Devout People*." In *The Text in the Community: Essays on Medieval Works, Manuscripts, Authors, and Readers*, edited by Jill Mann and Maura Nolan, 129–172. Notre Dame, IN: University of Notre Dame Press, 2006.

——— 2008: Vincent Gillespie, "The Haunted Text: Reflections in *The Mirror to Devout People*." In *Medieval Texts in Context*, edited by Graham D. Caie and Denis Renevey, 136–166. London: Routledge, 2008. [A revised version of Gillespie 2006.]

——— 2011: Vincent Gillespie, "1412–1524: Culture and History." In *The Cambridge Companion to Medieval English Mysticism*, edited by Samuel Fanous and Vincent Gillespie, 163–194. Cambridge: Cambridge University Press, 2011.

Giovanazzi 2009: Barbara Giovanazzi, "Per l'edizione degli *Amori* e di *Argo* di Giovan Francesco Caracciolo." Tesi Dott., Università degli Studi di Trento, 2009.

Girgensohn 1964: Dieter Girgensohn, *Peter von Pulkau und die Wiedereinführung des Laienkelches.* Göttingen: Vandenhoeck and Ruprecht, 1964.

Godefroy 1649: Théodore Godefroy, *Le ceremonies observées en France aux sacres & couronnemens de roys, & reynes, & de quelques anciens ducs de Normandie, d'Aquitaine, & de Bretagne: comme aussi à leurs entrées solennelles: et à celles d'aucuns dauphins, gouuerneurs de prouinces, & autres seigneurs, dans diuerses villes du royaume* 1. Paris: Sébastien Cramoisy and Gabriel Cramoisy, 1649.

Goering 1995: Joseph Goering, "The Summa '*Qui bene presunt*' and Its Author." In *Literature and Religion in the Later Middle Ages: Philological Studies in Honor of Siegfried Wenzel*, edited by Richard G. Newhauser and John A. Alford, 143–159. Medieval and Renaissance Texts and Studies 118. Binghamton, NY: Medieval and Renaissance Texts and Studies, 1995.

Grafton 2001: Anthony Grafton, *Bring out Your Dead: The Past as Revelation.* Cambridge, MA: Harvard University Press, 2001.

Gras 1918: Norman Gras, *The Early English Customs System.* Cambridge, MA: Harvard University Press, 1918.

Grayson 2009: Saisha Grayson, "Disruptive Disguises: The Problem of Transvestite Saints for Medieval Art, Identity, and Identification." *Medieval Feminist Forum* 45 (2009): 138–174.

Great Britain, Royal Commission on Historical Manuscripts 1874: *Fourth Report of the Royal Commission on Historical Manuscripts* 1–2. London: Eyre and Spottiswoode, 1874.

Green 1989: Martin Green, *The Mount Vernon Street Warrens: A Boston Story, 1860–1910.* New York: Charles Scribner's Sons, 1989.

Greenfield 1998: Jane Greenfield, *ABC of Bookbinding: A Unique Glossary with Over 700 Illustrations for Collectors and Librarians.* New Castle, DE: Oak Knoll Press, 1998.

Grottaferrata 1971–1981: P. P. Collegii S. Bonventurae ad Claras Aquas, ed., *Magistri Petri Lombardi Parisiensis episcopi Sententiae in IV libris distinctae* 1–2. Spicilegium Bonaventurianum 4–5. Grottaferrata: Editiones Collegii S. Bonaventurae ad Claras Aquas, 1971–1981.

Gualdo Rosa 1972–1973: Lucia Gualdo Rosa, "Niccolò Loschi e Pietro Perleone e le traduzioni dell'orazione pseudo isocrata 'A Demonico.'" *Atti dell'istituto veneto di scienze lettere e arti* 131 (1972–73): 825–856.

Gumbert 2009: J. P. Gumbert, "Times and Places for Initials." *Quaerendo* 39 (2009): 304–327.

Gura 2010: David T. Gura, "From the *Orléanais* to Pistoia: The Survival of the *Catena* Commentary." *Manuscripta* 54 (2010): 171–188.

——— 2012: David T. Gura, "A Hitherto Unknown Fifteenth-Century Book of Hours from the *Amiénois*: Notre Dame, Saint Mary's College, Cushwa-Leighton Library, MS 3 (or the Le Féron-Grisel Hours." *Manuscripta* 56 (2012): 227–268.

Gutiérrez Cuadrado 1992: Juan Gutiérrez Cuadrado, "El vaso de vino de Berceo." In *Estudios filológicos en homenaje a Eugenio de Bustos Tovar*, edited by José Antonio Bartol Hernández et al., 1:423–432. Salamanca: Ediciones Universidad de Salamanca, 1992.

Gwara 2013: Scott Gwara, *Otto Ege's Manuscripts.* Cayce, SC: De Brailes, 2013.

Hägele 1996: Günter Hägele, *Lateinische mittelalterliche Handschriften in Folio der Universitätsbibliothek Augsburg* 1. Wiesbaden: Harrassowitz, 1996.

Hagenau 1498: *Sermones Pomerii fratris Pelbarti de Themeswar diui ordinis Francisci de tempore.* Hagenau: Heinrich Gran, 1498.

Haines 2008: John Haines, "The Origins of the Musical Staff." The *Musical Quarterly* 91 (2008): 327–378.

HALM ET AL. 1894: Karl Halm, Georg von Laubmann, and Wilhelm Meyer, *Catalogus Codicum Latinorum Bibliothecae Regiae Monacensis* 1.2. Munich: Bibliotecae Regiae, 1894.

HAMMOND BAMMEL 2010: Caroline P. Hammond Bammel, Michel Fédou, and Luc Brésard, *Origène. Commentaire sur L'Épître au Romains. Tome II, Livres III–V.* Sources Chrétiennes 539. Paris: Editions du Cerf, 2010.

HANKINS 1990: James Hankins, *Plato in the Italian Renaissance* 1–2. Columbia Studies in the Classical Tradition 17. Leiden: Brill, 1990; repr. 1992.

——— 1991: James Hankins, "Bruni Manuscripts in North America. A Handlist." In *Per il censimento dei codici dell'epistolario di Leonardo Bruni,* edited by L. Gualdo Rosa and P. Viti, 55–90. Istituto storico italiano per il Medio Evo. Nuovi studi storici 10. Rome: Nella sede dell'Istituto, 1991.

——— 1997: James Hankins, *Repertorium Brunianum: A Critical Guide to the Writings of Leonardo Bruni.* Vol. 1, *A Handlist of Manuscripts.* Istituto storico italiano per il Medio Evo. Storia dell'Italia medievale subsidia 5. Rome: Istituto storico italiano per il Medio Evo, 1997.

HARWOOD 1866: Alfred J. Harwood, ed., *Year Books of the Reign of King Edward the First.* Vol. 1, *Years XX and XXI.* London: Longmans, Green, Reader, and Dyker, 1866.

HAURÉAU 1890: Barthélemy Hauréau, *Poèmes Latins attribués a Saint Bernard.* Paris: C. Klincksieck, 1890.

HEAWOOD 2003: Edward Heawood, *Watermarks Mainly of the 17th and 18th Centuries.* Monumenta chartae papyraceae historiam illustrantia 1. Culver City: Krown and Spellman, 2003.

HEJNIC and ROTHE 2005: Joseph Hejnic and Hans Rothe, *Aeneas Silvius Piccolomini. Historia Bohemica 1: Historisch-kritische Ausgabe des lateinischen Textes.* Cologne: Böhlau, 2005.

HELLMANN 1909: Sigmund Hellmann, *Pseudo-Cyprianus, De XII abusivis saeculi.* Texte und Untersuchungen zur Geschichte der altchristlichen Literatur 34.1. Leipzig: Hinrichs, 1909.

HERRE and QUIDDE 1928: Hermann Herre and Ludwig Quidde, *Deutsche Reichstagsakten unter Kaiser Friedrich III. Abt. 1441–1442* 1–2. Deutsche Reichstagsakten 16. Stuttgart: Perthes, 1928.

HERVIEUX 1884-1899: Léopold Hervieux, *Les Fabulistes latins: Depuis le siécle d'Auguste jusqu'à la fin du moyen âge* 1–5. Paris: Firmin-Didot, 1884–1899.

HEYNE 1819: Christian Gottlob Heyne, *P. Virgilii Maronis opera omnia ex editione heyniana cum notis interpretatione in usum delphini variis lectionibus notis variorum excursibus heynianis recensu editionum et codicum et indice locupletissimo accurate recensita* 1–8. London: A. J. Valpy, 1819.

HILMO 2012: Maidie Hilmo, "The Power of Images in the Auchinleck, Vernon, Pearl, and Two *Piers Plowman* Manuscripts." In *Opening Up Middle English Manuscripts: Literary and Visual Approaches,* edited by Kathryn Kerby-Fulton, Maidie Hilmo, and Linda Olson, 153–205. Ithaca, NY: Cornell University Press, 2012.

HOGG 1973-1974: James Hogg, *The 'Speculum Devotorum' of an Anonymous Carthusian of Sheen, Edited from the Manuscripts Cambridge University Library Gg. 1.6 and Foyle, with an Introduction and a Glossary.* Analecta Cartusiana 12–13. Salzburg: Institut für englische Sprache und Literatur, 1973–1974.

——— 2009: James Hogg, "A Vauvert Liturgical Manuscript on Sale at Paris." *Analecta cartusiana* 278 (2009): 77–86.

HOLLIS 2007: Adrian S. Hollis, *Fragments of Roman Poetry, c.60 BC–AD 20.* Oxford: Oxford University Press, 2007.

HORVÁTH 1932: Konstantin Horváth, *Johannis Lemovicensis abbatis de Zirc 1208–1218 opera omnia* 1–3. Veszprém: Egyházmegyei Könyvnyomda, 1932.

HOSKINS 1901: Edgar Hoskins, *Horae Beatae Mariae Virginis or Sarum and York Primers with Kindred Books and the Primers of the Reformed Roman Use Together with an Introduction.* London: Longmans, Green, and Co., 1901.

HOURLIER and MOUSTIER 1957: Jacques Hourlier and Benoît du Moustier, "Le Calendrier cartusien." *Études grégoriennes* 2 (1957): 151–161.

HÜBL 1899: Albert Hübl, *Catalogus codicum manuscriptorum qui in bibliotheca Monasterii B. M. V. ad Scotos Vindonbonae servantur.* Vienna: W. Braumüller, 1899.

HUNT 1991: Tony Hunt, *Teaching and Learning Latin in Thirteenth-Century England* 1–3. Cambridge: D. S. Brewer, 1991.

——— 2005: Tony Hunt, *Les paraboles Maistre Alain en françoys.* Modern Humanities Research Association Critical Texts 2. London: Modern Humanities Research Association, 2005.

——— 2007: Tony Hunt, *Les proverbez d'Alain.* Classiques français du moyen âge 151. Paris: Champion, 2007.

IKAS 2000: Wolfgang-Valentin Ikas, "Martinus Polonus' Chronicle of the Popes and Emporers: A Medieval Best-Seller and Its Neglected Influence on Medieval English Chroniclers." *The English Historical Review* 116 (2001): 327–341.

——— 2002: Wolfgang-Valentin Ikas, *Martin von Troppau (Martinus Polonus), O.P. (1278) in England: Überlieferungs- und wirkungsgeschichtliche Studien zu dessen Papst- und Kaiserchronik.* Wissensliteratur im Mittelalter 40. Wiesbaden: Reichert, 2002.

——— 2004: Wolfgang-Valentin Ikas, *Fortsetzungen zur Papst- und Kaiserchronik Martins von Troppau aus England.* Monumenta Germaniae historica. Scriptores rerum Germanicarum 19. Hannover: Hahnsche Buchhandlung, 2004.

ITER 1963–1993: Paul Oskar Kristeller, *Iter Italicum: A Finding List of Uncatalogued or Incompletely Catalogued Humanist Manuscripts of the Renaissance in Italian and Other Libraries* 1–6. London: Warburg Institute; Leiden: Brill, 1963–1993.

IVES 1943: Samuel A. Ives, *Philippus Iadrensis, a Hitherto Unknown Poet of the Renaissance: A Contribution to Italian Literary History.* Rare Books: Notes on the History of Old Books and Manuscripts 2.2. Published for the Friends and Clients of H. P. Kraus. New York: H. P. Kraus, 1943.

JOHNSON, I. 1999: Ian R. Johnson, "Speculum Devotorum." In *The Idea of the Vernacular: An Anthology of Middle English Literary Theory, 1280–1520*, edited by Jocelyn Wogan-Browne, Nicholas Watson, Andrew Taylor, and Ruth Evans, 73–78. University Park: Pennsylvania State University Press, 1999.

——— 2013: Ian R. Johnson, *The Middle English Life of Christ: Academic Discourse, Translation, and Vernacular Theology.* Medieval Church Studies 30. Turnhout: Brepols, 2013.

JOHNSON, L. 1995: Lesley Johnson, "Return to Albion." *Arthurian Literature* 13 (1995): 19–40.

JOLLIFFE 1974: Peter S. Jolliffe, *A Check-List of Middle English Prose Writings of Spiritual Guidance.* Toronto: Pontifical Institute of Mediaeval Studies, 1974.

JORDAN, H. 1869: Henri Jordan, "Über das Buch Origo Gentis Romanae." *Hermes* 3 (1869): 389–428.

——— 1871–1907: Henri Jordan, *Topographie der Stadt Rom im Alterthum* 1–2. Berlin: Weidmannsche Buchhandlung, 1871–1907.

JORDAN, L. 1993: Louis Jordan, "Problems of Interpreting Dated Colophons Based on the Examples from the Biblioteca Ambrosiana." In *Scribi e colofoni: Le sottoscrizioni di copisti dalle orgini all'avvento dalla stampa. Atti del seminario di Erice. X Colloquio del Comité international de paléographie latine (23–28 ottobre 1993)*, edited by Ema Condello and Giuseppe De Gregorio, 367–384. Spoleto: Centro italiano di studi sull'alto Medioevo, 1993.

JORDAN, M. 1998: Mark D. Jordan, *The Invention of Sodomy in Christian Theology.* Chicago: University of Chicago Press, 1998.

KAEPPELI and PANELLA 1970–1993: Thomas Kaeppeli and Emilio Panella, *Scriptores Ordinis Praedicatorum Medii Aevi* 1–4. Rome: Ad. S. Sabinae; Istituto storico domenicano, 1970–1993.

KASKE 1988: Robert Kaske with Arthur Groos and Michael W. Twomey, *Medieval Christian Literary Imagery: A Guide to Interpretation.* Toronto: University of Toronto Press, 1988.

KASTER 1992: Robert A. Kaster, *Studies on the Text of Suetonius "De Grammaticis et Rhetoribus."* Atlanta: Scholar's Press, 1992.

——— 1995: Robert A. Kaster, *C. Suetonius Tranquillus: De Grammaticis et Rhetoribus.* Oxford: Clarendon Press, 1995.

KER 1960: Neil R. Ker. "From 'Above Top Line' to 'Below Top Line': A Change in Scribal Practice." *Celtica* 5 (1960): 13–16.

——— 1969-2002: Neil R. Ker, *Medieval Manuscripts in British Libraries* 1–5. Oxford: Clarendon Press, 1969–2002.

KER and WATSON 1987: Neil R. Ker and Andrew G. Watson, eds., *Medieval Libraries of Great Britain, A List of Surviving Books: Supplement to the Second Edition.* Royal Historical Society Guides and Handbooks 15. London: Royal Historical Society, 1987.

KERBY-FULTON ET AL. 2012: Kathryn Kerby-Fulton, Maidie Hilmo, and Linda Olson, eds., *Opening Up Middle English Manuscripts: Literary and Visual Approaches.* Ithaca, NY: Cornell University Press, 2012.

KESSLER 1969: Herbert L. Kessler, *French and Flemish Illuminated Manuscripts from Chicago Collections.* Chicago: Division of the Humanities of the University of Chicago, 1969.

KING 1986: Margaret L. King, *Venetian Humanism in an Age of Patrician Dominance.* Princeton, NJ: Princeton University Press, 1986.

——— 1994: Margaret L. King, *The Death of the Child Valerio Marcello.* Chicago: University of Chicago Press, 1994.

KIPLING 1998: Gordon Kipling, *Enter the King: Theatre, Liturgy, and Ritual in the Medieval Civic Triumph.* Oxford: Clarendon Press, 1998.

KLIMA 2009: Gyula Klima, *John Buridan.* Oxford: Oxford University Press, 2009.

KÖRNTGEN 2006: Ludger Körntgen, "Canon Law and the Practice of Penance: Burchard of Worms's Penitential." *Early Medieval Europe* 14 (2006): 103–117.

KRAUSE 1894: Victor Krause, "Die Münchener Handschriften 3851. 3853 mit einer Compilation von 181 Wormser Schlüssen." *Neues Archiv der Gesellschaft für ältere deutsche Geschichtkunde zur Beförderung einer Gesammtausgabe der Quellenschriften deutscher Geschichten des Mittelalters* 19 (1894): 85–139.

KRISTELLER 1985: Paul Oskar Kristeller, *Studies in Renaissance Thought and Letters II.* Storia e letteratura 166. Rome: Edizioni di Storia e Letteratura, 1985.

KÜNZLE 1977: Pius Künzle, *Heinrich Seuses Horologium sapientiae.* Freiburg: Universitätsverlag, 1977.

LABALME 1969: Patricia H. Labalme, *Bernardo Giustiniani: A Venetian of the Quattrocentro.* Uomini e Dottrine 13. Rome: Edizioni di Storia e Letteratura, 1969.

LAPIDGE 2006: Michael Lapidge, "Versifying the Bible in the Middle Ages." In *The Text in the Community: Essays on Medieval Works, Manuscripts, Authors, and Readers,* edited by Jill Mann and Maura Nolan, 11–40. Notre Dame, IN: University of Notre Dame Press, 2006.

Larson 2014: Atria A. Larson, *Masters of Penance: Gratian and the Development of Penitential Thought and Law in the Twelfth Century*. Washington, DC: Catholic University of America Press, 2014.

Lauck 1974: Anthony J. Lauck, *Medieval Art: 1060–1550. Dorothy Miner Memorial*. Notre Dame, IN: University of Notre Dame, Art Gallery, 1974.

Leclercq et al. 1957–1977: Jean Leclercq, Charles H. Talbot, and Henri Rochais, *Sancti Bernardi Opera* 1–9. Rome: Editiones Cistercienses, 1957–1977.

Lecoy 1965–1970: Félix Lecoy, *Le Roman de la Rose* 1–3. Classiques français du moyen âge 92, 95, 98. Paris: Champion, 1965–1970.

Lemaitre 2006: Jean-Loup Lemaitre, "Amans-Alexis Monteil (1769–1850) et les manuscrits." *Bibliotèque de l'École de chartres* 164 (2006): 227–249.

Leon. [Leonine Commission] 1976: *Sancti Thomae de Aquino Opera omnia iussu Leonis XIII P. M. edita, Tomus 43: De principiis natura; De aeternitate mundi; De motu cordis; De mixtione elementorum; De operationibus occultis naturae; De iudiciis astrorum; De sortibus; De unitate intellectus; De ente et essentia; De fallaciis; De propositionibus modalibus. cura et studio Fratrum Praedicatorum*. Rome: Editori di San Tommaso, 1976.

Leroquais 1927: Victor Leroquais, *Les Livres d'heures manuscrits de la Bibliothèque Nationale* 1–2. Paris: Protat frères, 1927.

——— 1940–1941: Victor Leroquais, *Les Psautiers manuscrits des bibliothèques publiques de France* 1–2. Mâcon: Protat frères, 1940–1941.

——— 1943: Victor Leroquais, *Supplement aux Livres d'heures manuscrits de la Bibliothèque Nationale*. Mâcon: Protat frères, 1943.

Lewis et al. 1985: Robert E. Lewis, N. F. Blake, and A. S. G. Edwards, *Index of Printed Middle English Prose*. New York: Garland, 1985.

Lhotsky 1957: Alphons Lhotsky, *Thomas Ebendorfer: Ein österreichischer Geschichtsschreiber, Theologe und Diplomat des 15 Jahrhunderts*. Schriften der Monumenta Germaniae historica 15. Stuttgart: Anton Hiersemann, 1957.

Limone 1993: Oronzo Limone, *Liber parabolarum: Una raccolta di aforismi*. Galatina: Congedo, 1993.

Lindsay 1911: Wallace M. Lindsay, *Isidori Hispalensis Episcopi Etymologiarum siue Originum libri XX*. Oxford: Clarendon Press, 1911.

Lippe 1889: Robert Lippe, *Missale Romanum Mediolani, 1474*. Henry Bradshaw Society 17. London: Harrison and Sons, 1899.

Littlehales 1897: Henry Littlehales, *The Prymer or Lay Folks' Prayer Book*. Early English Text Society, o.s. 109. London: Kegan Paul, Trench, Trübner and Co., 1897.

Lohr 1968: Charles H. Lohr, "Medieval Latin Aristotle Commentaries: Authors G–I." *Traditio* 24 (1968): 149–245.

——— 1970: Charles H. Lohr, "Medieval Latin Aristotle Commentaries: Johannes Buridanus." *Traditio* 26 (1970): 161–183.

Luscombe 1983: David E. Luscombe, "Excerpts from the Letter Collection of Heloise and Abelard in Notre Dame (Indiana) MS 30." In *Pascua Mediaevalia*, edited by R. Lievens, E. Van Mingroot, and W. Verbeke, 529–544. Leuven: Leuven University Press, 1983.

——— 2013: David E. Luscombe, ed. and trans., after the translation of Betty Radice, *The Letter Collection of Peter Abelard and Heloise*. Oxford: Oxford University Press, 2013.

Luttikhuizen 2011: Henry Luttikhuizen, "Still Walking: Spiritual Pilgrimage, Early Dutch Painting and the Dynamics of Faith." In *Push Me, Pull You: Imaginative and Emotional Interaction in Late Medieval and Renaissance Art*, edited by Sarah Blick and Laura D. Gelfand, 199–226. Leiden: Brill, 2011.

Luxford 2009: Julian M. Luxford, "The Commemoration of Foundation at English Charterhouses." In *Self-Representation of Medieval Religious Communities*, edited by Anne Müller and Karen Stöber, 275–306. Berlin: LIT, 2009.

Lyon 1549: Aegidius de Bellamera, *Aegidii Bellemerae, Ivris Pontificii Doctoris Mvlto Celeberrimi . . . In . . . Decre. Lib. parte[m] Prælectiones vltra fide[m] doctae ac luculentae . . . nu[n]c tandem desyderatae diu . . . typis . . . excussae . . . 5 Aegidii Bellemeræ, Ivris Pontificii Doctoris Praestantissimi audientiarum olim palatii, ac deinde contradictarum auditoris prudentissimi in Secundam Secundi Decret. Lib. partem Praelectiones non minùs doctae, quàm elegantes: in quibus non antiquitatem modò, uerum totius antiquitatis autores facilè principes agnoscere licet: iamdiu desyderatae, nunc uerò tandem summa diligentia, ac fide doctissimorum uirorum opera emendatae, & typis pulcherrimis excusae.* Lyon: Senneton, 1549.

Madre 1965: Alois Madre, *Nikolaus von Dinkelsbühl: Leben und Schriften. Ein Beitrag zur theologischen Literaturgeschichte.* Beiträge zur Geschichte der Philosophie und Theologie des Mittelalters 40.4. Münster: Äschendorffsche Verlagsbuchhandlung, 1965.

Maggioni 1998: Giovanni Paolo Maggioni, *Iacopo da Varazze. Legenda Aurea* 1–2. Florence: SISMEL Edizioni del Galluzzo, 1998.

Manion, Vines, & de Hamel 1989: Margaret M. Manion, Vera F. Vines, and Christopher de Hamel, *Medieval and Renaissance Manuscripts in New Zealand Collections.* Melbourne: Thames and Hudson, 1989.

Mann 2006: Jill Mann, "'He Knew Nat Catoun': Medieval School-Texts and Middle English Literature." In *The Text in the Community: Essays on Medieval Works, Manuscripts, Authors, and Readers*, edited by Jill Mann and Maura Nolan, 41–74. Notre Dame, IN: University of Notre Dame Press, 2006.

Mansi 1901-1927: Giovan Domenico Mansi et al., *Sacrorum conciliorum nova et amplissima collectio* 1–54. Paris: H. Welter, 1901–1927.

Marrow et al. 1990: James H. Marrow, Henri L. M. Defoer, Anne S. Korteweg, and Wilhelmina C. M. Wüstefeld, eds., *The Golden Age of Dutch Manuscript Painting.* New York: G. Braziller, 1990.

Martin 1962: Joseph Martin, *Sancti Aurelii Augustini de doctrina christiana, de vera religione.* Corpus Christianorum Series Latina 32. Turnhout: Brepols, 1962.

Mauro 1961: Alfredo Mauro, *Iacobo Sannazaro: Opere Volgari.* Scrittori d'Italia 220. Bari: Laterza, 1961.

McDonald 2013: Anthony P. McDonald, "Between Philosophy and the Muse: A Fifteenth Century Versification of Boethius's *Consolatio Philosophiae.*" M.A. thesis, University of Notre Dame, 2013.

McNamer 2009: Sarah McNamer, "The Origins of the *Meditationes uitae Christi.*" *Speculum* 84 (2009): 905–955.

McVaugh 2005: Michael McVaugh, "Chemical Medicine in the Medical Writings of Arnau de Vilanova." In *Actes de la II Trobada Internacional d'estudis sobre Arnau de Vilanova*, edited by Josep Perarnau, 239–267. Trebalis de la Secció de Filosofia i Ciències Socials 30. Barcelona: Institut d'Estudis Catalans, 2005.

Mearns 1914: James Mearns, *The Canticles of the Christian Church, Eastern and Western, in Early and Medieval Times.* Cambridge: Cambridge University Press, 1914.

MEERMAN 1824: Gerard Meerman and Johan Meerman, *Bibliotheca Meermanniana; sive, Catalogus librorum impressorum et codicum manuscriptorum, quos maximam partem collegerunt viri nobilissimi Gerardus et Joannes Meerman; morte dereliquit Joannes Meerman, toparcha in Dalem et Vuren, etc. etc. Quorum publica fiet auctio die VIII sqq. junii, anni MDCCCXXIV Hagae Comitum in aedibus defuncti . . . Per bibliopolas S. et J. Luchtmans, Lugduno-Batavos, fratres Van Cleef, Haganos et Amstelodamenses, et B. Scheurleer, Haganum* 1–4. Hagae Comitum, 1824.

MEISTER 1991: Ferdinand Meister, *Daretis Phrygii de excidio Troiae historia*. Leipzig: Teubner, 1991.

MERRILL 1906: Elmer Truesdell Merrill, "The Date of *Notitia* and *Curiosum*." *Classical Philology* 1 (1906): 133–144.

MICHAUD-QUANTIN 1962: Pierre Michaud-Quantin, *Sommes de casuistique et manuels de confession au Moyen Âge (XII–XVI siècles)*. Louvain: Nauwelaerts, 1962.

MOELLER ET AL. 1992–2004: Edmund Eugène Moeller, Jean-Marie Clément, and Bertrand Coppieters 't Wallant, eds., *Corpus orationum*. Corpus Christianorum Series Latina 160 et al. Turnhout: Brepols, 1992–2004.

MOHAN 1975: Gaudens Eugene Mohan, "Initia operum Franciscalium." *Franciscan Studies* 35 (1975): i, iii, v–ix, 1–92.

——— 1976: Gaudens Eugene Mohan, "Initia operum Franciscalium (XIII–XV S.) D–H." *Franciscan Studies* 36 (1976): 92–177.

——— 1977: Gaudens Eugene Mohan, "Initia operum Franciscalium (XIII–XV S.) I–Q." *Franciscan Studies* 37 (1977): 178–375.

——— 1978: Gaudens Eugene Mohan, "Initia operum Franciscalium (XIII–XV S.) R–Z." *Franciscan Studies* 38 (1978): 375–498.

MOLNÁR 1970: Amedeo Molnár, "De divisione Scripture sacre multiplici Nicolaus Biskupec de Pelhřimov." *Communio Viatorum* 13 (1970): 154–170.

MONE 1964. Franz Joseph Mone, *Lateinische Hymnen des Mittelalters* 1–3. Aalen: Scientia, 1964.

MOORMAN 1983: John Richard Humpidge Moorman, *Medieval Franciscan Houses*. Franciscan Institute Publications, History Series 4. St. Bonaventure, NY: The Franciscan Institute, 1983.

MORAWSKI 1923: Joseph Morawski, *Le Facet en françoys: Edition critique des cinq traductions des deux Facetus latins avec introduction, notes et glossaire*. Poznan: Gebethnera i Wolffa, 1923.

MOREL-FATIO 1896: Alfred Morel-Fatio, "Les deux Omero Castillans," *Romania* 25 (1896): 111–129.

MORESCHINI 1976: Claudio Moreschini, *Sancti Cypriani episcopi opera. Pars 2, De dominica oratione; De bono patientiae*. Corpus Christianorum Series Latina 3A. Turnhout: Brepols, 1976.

——— 2000: Claudio Moreschini, *Boethius, De consolatione philosophiae; Opuscula theologica*. Munich: K. G. Saur, 2000.

MORGAN 2001: Nigel Morgan, "The Introduction of the Sarum Calendar into the Dioceses of England in the Thirteenth Century." In *Thirteenth Century England VIII: Proceedings of the Durham Conference 1999*, edited by Michael Prestwich, Richard Britnell, and Robin Frame, 179–206. Woodbridge: Boydell Press, 2001.

——— 2013a: Nigel Morgan, "English Books of Hours." In *Books of Hours Reconsidered*, edited by Sandra Hindman and James H. Marrow, 65–95. Turnhout: Harvey Miller, 2013.

——— 2013b: Nigel Morgan, ed., *English Monastic Litanies of the Saints after 1100*. Vol. 2, *Pontefract-York*. Henry Bradshaw Society 120. London: Boydell Press, 2013.

Morlet 1967: Marie-Thérèse Morlet, *Étude d'Anthroponymie Picarde: Les noms de persone en Haute Picardie aux XIIIe, XIVe, Xve siècles.* Collection de la Société de Linguistique Picarde 6. Amiens: Musée de Picardie, 1967.

Morton 2015: Jonathan Morton, "Le Roman de la rose." *French Studies* 69 (2015): 79–86.

Mosin 1973: Vladimir Mosin, *Anchor Watermarks.* Chartae Papyraceae Historiam Illustrata XIII. Amsterdam: Paper Publications Society Labarre Foundation, 1973.

Mulchahey 1998: Marian Michèle Mulchahey, *"First the Bow Is Bent in Study": Dominican Education before 1350.* Toronto: Pontifical Institute of Mediaeval Studies, 1998.

Müller 1995: Konrad Müller, *Petronius. Satyricon Reliquiae.* Leipzig: Teubner, 1995.

Munby 1951: Alan Noel Latimer Munby, *The Catalogues of Manuscripts & Printed Books of Sir Thomas Phillipps, Their Composition and Distribution.* Phillipps Studies 1. Cambridge: Cambridge University Press, 1951.

——— 1952: Alan Noel Latimer Munby, *The Family Affairs of Sir Thomas Phillipps.* Phillipps Studies 2. Cambridge: Cambridge University Press, 1952.

——— 1954: Alan Noel Latimer Munby, *The Formation of the Phillipps Library up to the Year 1840.* Phillipps Studies 3. Cambridge: Cambridge University Press, 1954.

——— 1956: Alan Noel Latimer Munby, *The Formation of the Phillipps Library from 1841 to 1872.* Phillipps Studies 4. Cambridge: Cambridge University Press, 1956.

——— 1960: Alan Noel Latimer Munby, *The Dispersal of the Phillipps Library.* Phillipps Studies 5. Cambridge: Cambridge University Press,1960.

Mutzenbecher 1984: Almut Mutzenbecher, *Sancti Augustini Rectractationum libri II.* Corpus Christianorum Series Latina 57. Turnhout: Brepols, 1984.

Nash 1999: Susie Nash, *Between France and Flanders: Manuscript Illumination in Amiens.* London: The British Library and University of Toronto Press, 1999.

Newhauser 1993: Richard Newhauser, *The Treatise on Vices and Virtues in Latin and the Vernacular.* Typologie des Sources du Moyen Âge Occidental 68. Turnhout: Brepols, 1993.

Newhauser and Bejczy 2008: Richard Newhauser and István Pieter Bejczy, *A Supplement to Morton W. Bloomfield et al., 'Incipits of Latin Works on the Virtues and Vices, 1100–1500 A.D.'* Instrumenta Patristica et Mediaevalia 50. Turnhout: Brepols, 2008.

Nighman 2001–2013: Craig L. Nighman, The Electronic *Manipulus florum* Project. http://web.wlu.ca/history/cnighman/index.html. 2001–2013.

Noffke 2000–2008: Suzanne Noffke, *The Letters of Catherine of Siena* 1–4. Medieval and Renaissance Textual Studies 202, 203, 329, 355. Tempe: Arizona Center for Medieval and Renaissance Studies, 2000–2008.

Nolan 2006: Maura Nolan, "Introduction." In *The Text in the Community: Essays on Medieval Works, Manuscripts, Authors, and Readers,* edited by Jill Mann and Maura Nolan, 1–7. Notre Dame, IN: University of Notre Dame Press, 2006.

Nordh 1949: Arvast Nordh, *Libellus de regionibus urbis Romae; Notitia urbis Romae regionum XIV.* Skrifter utgivna av Svenska institut i Rom 8. Lund: C. W. K. Gleerup, 1949.

Northeast 2001: Peter Northeast, *Wills of the Archdeaconry of Sudbury, 1439–1474. Wills from the Register 'Baldwyne', Part I: 1439–1461.* Suffolk Records Society 44. Woodbridge: Boydell Press, 2001.

Northeast and Falvey 2010: Peter Northeast and Heather Falvey, *Wills of the Archdeaconry of Sudbury, 1439–1474. Wills from the Register 'Baldwyne', Part II: 1461–1474.* Suffolk Records Society 53. Woodbridge: Boydell Press, 2010.

Novati 1887: F. Novati, "I codici Trivulzio-Trotti." *Giornale storico della letteratura italiana* 9 (1887): 137–185.

Ogilvie 1974: Robert Maxwell Ogilvie, *Titi Livi Ab Vrbe Condita. Tomus I. Libri I–V.* Oxford: Clarendon Press, 1974.

Oliver 1985: Judith Oliver, *Manuscripts, Sacred and Secular.* Boston: Endowment for Biblical Research, 1985.

Omont 1889: Henri Auguste Omont, *Manuscrits relatifs a l'histoire de Frances conservés dans la bibliothèque de Sir Thomas Phillipps a Cheltenham.* Paris: A. Picard, 1889.

Onelli 2014: Corinna Onelli, "Freedom and Censorship: Petronius' *Satyricon* in Seventeenth-Century Italy." *Classical Receptions Journal* 6 (2014): 104–130.

Orme 2006: Nicholas Orme, *Medieval Schools: From Roman Britain to Renaissance England.* New Haven: Yale University Press, 2006.

Ottosen 1993: Knud Ottosen, *The Responsories and Versicles of the Latin Office of the Dead.* Aarhus: Aarhus University Press, 1993.

Ouy 1998: Gilbert Ouy, *Gerson Bilingue: Les deux rédactions, latine et françaíse, de quelques oeuvres du chancelier parisien.* Paris: H. Champion, 1998.

Pace 2006: Giovanna Pace, "Osservazioni sulla tecnica versoria di Guarino Guarini: Il caso dei *Parallela minora.*" In *Ecos de Plutarco en Europa: De Fortuna Plutarchi Studia Selecta*, edited by Rosa Maria Aguilar and Ignacio R. Alfageme, 207–232. Madrid: Servicio de Publicaciones de la Universidad Complutense, 2006.

Pacetti 1967: Dionisio Pacetti, "La tradizione dei trattati spritiuali di Ugo Panziera." *Studi Francescani* 64 (1967): 30–77.

Pade 2007: Marianne Pade, *The Reception of Plutarch's Lives in Fifteenth-Century Italy* 1–2. Renaessance studier 14. Copenhagen: Museum Tusculanum Press, University of Copenhagen, 2007.

Palmer 1993: Nigel F. Palmer, "Ars moriendi und Totentanz: Zur Verbildlichung des Todes im Spätmittelalter, mit einer Bibliographie zur 'Ars moriendi.'" In *Tod im Mittelalter*, edited by Arno Borst, 313–334. Constance: Universitätsverlag Konstanz, 1993.

Paris 1498: *Dictionarius paupe[rum] : omnibus predicatoribus verbi diuini [per]necessarius in quo multu[m] succincte co[n]tine[n]tur materie singulis festiuitatibus totius anni ta[m] de t[empor]e [quam] de sanctis acco[m]moda[n]de vt in tabula huius operis facile et lucide cognoscetur.* Paris: André Bocard, 1498.

——— 1500: *Incipit tractatus de vinis editus a Magistro arnaldo de vila nova.* Paris: Félix Baligualt, Claude Jaumar, and Thomas Julian, ca. 1500.

——— 1512: *Vetus editio Ecclesiastae Olympiodorus in Ecclesiasten inserta noua tralatione* [sic] *interprete Zenobio Acciaiolo Florentino. Aristeas de lxxij legis hebraice interpretatione interprete Matthia Plamerio Vincentino.* Paris: Henri Estienne, 1512.

——— 1513: *Questiones Ioannis buridani super decem libros ethicorum aristotelis ad nicomachum.* Paris, 1513; repr. as *Super decem libros ethicorum.* Frankfurt-am-Main: Minerva, 1968.

——— 1515: Antonius Parmensis, *Medulla seromonum super singulas dominicas totius anni necnon et singulas ferias et dominicas totius quadragesime exquisitos sermones cotinens* [sic]. Paris: Regnaldus Chaudier, 1515.

——— 1523: Philippus Cancellarius, *In Psalterium Davidicum CCCXXX sermones.* Paris: J. Badius, 1523.

——— 1535: *Johannes Monacus Picardus Cisterciensis Glossa aurea nobis priori loco super Sexto Decretalium libro addita.* Neudruck der Ausgabe Paris, 1535; repr. Aalen: Scientia Verlag, 1968.

Parker 1959: Bruce Robert Parker, "Tractatus Proportionum. Edited, Translated into English and with a Commentary by B. R. Parker." A. B. honors thesis, Harvard University, 1959.

Parroni 1965: Piergiorgio Parroni, *Vibii Sequestris De fluminibus, fontibus, lacubus, etc.* Testi e documenti per lo studio dell'antichita 11. Milan: Istituto Editoriale Cisalpino, 1965.

Patar 2001: Benoît Patar, *La Physique de Bruges de Buridan et Le Traité du Ciel d'Albert de Saxe* 1–2. Longueuil: Presses philosophiques, 2001.

Patterson 2006: Paul J. Patterson, "Myrror to Devout People (*Speculum devotorum*): An Edition with Commentary." Ph.D. diss., University of Notre Dame, 2006.

——— 2011: Paul J. Patterson, "Preaching with Hands: Carthusian Book Production and the *Speculum devotorum*." In *Medieval Latin and Middle English Literature: Essays in Honour of Jill Mann*, edited by Christopher Cannon and Maura Nolan, 136–151. Cambridge: D. S. Brewer, 2011.

——— 2016: Paul J. Patterson, *A Mirror to Devout People (Speculum devotorum)*. Early English Text Society, o.s. 346. Oxford: Oxford University Press, 2016.

Pelaez 1935: Mario Pelaez, "Un nuovo ritmo latino sui mesi ed altri carmi latini medievali." *Studi Medievali* 8 (1935): 56–71.

Pelle 2009: Stephen Pelle, "The *Revelationes* of Pseudo-Methodius and 'Concerning the Coming of Antichrist' in British Library MS Cotton Vespasian D. XIV." *Notes and Queries* 56 (2009): 324–330.

Pennington 1996: Kenneth Pennington, "Roman and Secular Law." In *Medieval Latin: An Introduction and Bibliographical Guide*, edited by Frank Anthony, Carl Mantello, and A. G. Rigg, 254–266. Washington, DC: Catholic University of America Press, 1996.

Pereira 1989: Michela Pereira, *The Alchemical Corpus Attributed to Raymond Lull.* Warburg Institute Surveys and Texts 18. London: The Warburg Institute, University of London, 1989.

——— 2004: Michela Pereira, "Maestro di segreti caposcuola contestato? Presenza di Arnaldo da Villanova e di temi della medicina arnaldiana in alcuni testi alchemici pseudo-lulliani." In *Actes de la II Trobada Internacional d'estudis sobre Arnau de Vilanova*, edited by Josep Perarnau, 381–412. Trebalis de la Secció de Filosofia i Ciències Socials 30. Barcelona: Institut d'Estudis Catalans, 2005.

Pfaff 1974: Richard W. Pfaff, "The English Devotion of St Gregory's Trental." *Speculum* 49 (1974): 75–90.

——— 2009: Richard W. Pfaff, *The Liturgy in Medieval England: A History*. Cambridge: Cambridge University Press, 2009.

Phillipps 1968: Thomas Phillipps, *Catalogus librorum manuscriptorum in bibliotheca D. Thomae Phillipps, BT. impressum Typis Moedio-Montanis 1837–1871*. Reprinted as *The Phillipps Manuscripts* with an introduction by A. N. L. Munby. London: Holland Press, 1968.

Phillips 2016: Dianne Tisdale Phillips, "The Illustration of the *Meditations on the Life of Christ*: A Study of an Illuminated Fourteenth-Century Italian Manuscript at the University of Notre Dame (Snite Museum of Art, Acc. No. 85.25)." Ph.D. diss., Yale University, 2016.

——— 2006: Dianne Phillips, "The *Meditations on the Life of Christ*: An Illuminated Fourteenth-Century Italian Manuscript at the University of Notre Dame." In *The Text in the Community: Essays on Medieval Works, Manuscripts, Authors, and Readers*, edited by Jill Mann and Maura Nolan, 237–281. Notre Dame, IN: University of Notre Dame Press, 2006.

Piccard 1961–1997: Gerhard Piccard, *Wasserzeichenkartei im Hauptstaatsarchiv Stuttgart*. Stuttgart: Kohlhammer, 1961–1997.

PICCIAFUOCO 1980: Umberto Picciafuoco, *Fr. Nicolò da Osimo, 1370?–1453: Vita, opere, spiritualità.* Monteprandone: Officine Grafiche Anxanum, 1980.

PINGREE 1976: David Pingree, "Thessalus Astrologus." In *Catalogus translationum et commentariorum: Mediaeval and Renaissance Latin Translations and Commentaries: Annotated Lists and Guides* 3, edited by F. Edward Cranz, assoc. ed. Paul Oskar Kristeller, 83–85. Washington, DC: Catholic University of America Press, 1976.

——— 1992: David Pingree, "Thessalus Astrologus: Addenda." In *Catalogus translationum et commentariorum: Mediaeval and Renaissance Latin Translations and Commentaries; Annotated Lists and Guides* 7, edited by Virginia Brown, assoc. eds. Paul Oskar Kristeller and F. Edward Cranz, 330–332. Washington, DC: Catholic University of America Press, 1992.

PLATELLE 2004: Henri Platelle, *Présence de l'au-delà: Une vision médiévale du monde.* Villeneuve d'Acqu: Presses universitaires du Septentrion, 2004.

POIRION 1974: Daniel Poirion, *Le Roman de la Rose.* Texte intégral 270. Paris: Garnier-Flammarion, 1974.

POPE 1999: Joseph Pope, *One Hundred and Twenty-five Manuscripts: Bergendal Collection Catalogue.* Toronto: Brabant Holdings, 1999.

PORTER 1975: Dean A. Porter, *Everett McNear: Painter, Designer, Collector.* Chicago: American Publishers Press, 1975.

——— 1987: Dean A. Porter, *Selected Works from the Snite Museum of Art, the University of Notre Dame, Notre Dame, Indiana.* South Bend, IN: Mossberg and Company, 1987.

——— 1992: Dean A. Porter, *The University of Notre Dame Friends and Alumni Collect; A Sesquicentennial Celebration: June 7–September 20, 1992.* Notre Dame, IN: Snite Museum of Art, University of Notre Dame, 1992.

PRIBRAM 1890: Alfred Francis Pribram, *Thomas Ebendorfers Chronica regum Romanorum.* Innsbruck: Wagner, 1890.

PROCHASKA 1882: Antoni Prochaska, *Codex epistolaris Vitoldi Magni Ducis Lithuaniae 1376–1430.* Wydawnictwa Komisji Historycznej Akademii Umiej tno ci w Krakowie 23; Monumenta Medii Aevi Historica Res Gestas Poloniae Illustrantia 6. Krakow: Acad. Literarum, 1882.

PROCTER and WORDSWORTH 1879–1886: Francis Procter and Christopher Wordsworth, *Breviarium ad usum insignis ecclesiae Sarum* 1–3. Cambridge, 1879–1886; repr. Farnborough, Hants: Gregg, 1970.

QUARACCHI 1898: *Bonaventurae Opera omnia*, edited by PP. Colegii S. Bonaventurae, 1–11. Quaracchi: ex typographia Colegii S. Bonaventurae, 1882–1902.

RAGEY 1892: Philibert Ragey, *Hynmarum Quotidianum B.M.V.: Ex hymnis medii aevii comparatum.* Paris: P. Lethielleux, 1892.

RAYMOND 2013: Emmanuelle Raymond, "Caius Cornelius Gallus: 'The inventor of Latin love elegy.'" In *The Cambridge Companion to Latin Love Elegy*, edited by Thea S. Thorsen, 59–67. Cambridge: Cambridge University Press, 2013.

RAYNAUD DE LAGE 1951: Guy Raynaud de Lage, *Alain de Lille: Poete du XIIe siècle.* Publications de l'Institut d'études médiévales 12. Montréal: Institut d'études médiévales, 1951.

REEVE 1991a: Michael D. Reeve, "The Rediscovery of Classical Texts in the Renaissance." In *Itinerari dei Testi Antichi*, edited by Oronzo Pecere, 115–157. Saggi di Storia Antica 3. Rome: "L'Erma" di Bretschneider, 1991.

——— 1991b: Michael D. Reeve, "The Transmission of the *Historia regum Britanniae*." *Journal of Medieval Latin* 1 (1991): 73–117.

Reeve and Wright 2007: Michael D. Reeve and Neil Wright, *Geoffrey of Monmouth: The History of the Kings of Britain. An Edition and Translation of De gestis Britonum [Historia regum Britannie].* Arthurian Studies 69. Woodbridge: Boydell Press, 2007.

Reinburg 2012: Virginia Reinburg, *French Books of Hours: Making an Archive of Prayer, c. 1400–1600.* Cambridge: Cambridge University Press, 2012.

Reutlingen 1484: *Postilla super Evangeliis; et, Epistolis dominiis.* Reutlingen: Johann Otmar, 1484.

Reynolds 1983: L. D. Reynolds, ed., *Texts and Transmission: A Survey of the Latin Classics.* Oxford: Clarendon Press, 1983.

Rézeau 1986: Pierre Rézeau, *Répertoire d'incipit des prières français à la fin du moyen âge. Addenda et corrigenda aux répertoires de Sonet et Sinclair nouveaux incipit.* Geneva: Librairie Droz, 1986.

Rice 1972: Eugene F. Rice, Jr., *The Prefatory Epistles of Jacques Lefèvre d'Etaples and Related Texts.* New York: Columbia University Press, 1972.

Richardson, L. 1992: Lawrence Richardson, *A New Topographical Dictionary of Ancient Rome.* Baltimore: Johns Hopkins University Press, 1992.

Richardson, T. 1984: T. Wade Richardson, "A New Renaissance Petronius Manuscript: Indiana Notre Dame 58." *Scriptorium* 38 (1984): 89–100.

Rigollot 1870: Louis-Marie Rigollot, *Ludolphus de Saxonia, Vita Jesu Christi: Ex Evangelio et approbatis ab ecclesia catholica doctoribus sedule collecta* 1–4. Paris: V. Palmé, 1870.

Rose 1893–1919: Valentin Rose, *Verzeichniss der lateinischen handschriften der Königlichen bibliothek zu Berlin* 1–3. Berlin: A. Asher & Co., 1893–1919.

Rossi, A. 2005: Antonio Rossi, *Serafino Aquilano: Sonetti e altre rime.* Biblioteca del Cinquecento 119. Rome: Bulzoni, 2005.

Rossi, G. 1886: Girolamo Rossi, *Storia della città di Ventimiglia.* Oneglia: G. Ghilini, 1886.

Rossi-Casè 1889: Luigi Rossi-Casè, *Di maestro Benvenuto da Imola, commentatore Dantesco, studio.* Pergola: Gasperini Editori, 1889.

Rouse and Rouse 1979: Richard H. Rouse and Mary A. Rouse, *Preachers, Florilegia, and Sermons: Studies on the Manipulus florum of Thomas of Ireland.* Toronto: Pontifical Institute of Mediaeval Studies, 1979.

Rudolf 1957: Rainer Rudolf, *Ars Moriendi von der Kunst de Heilsamen Lebens und Sterbens.* Cologne: Böhlau, 1957.

Rudy 2012: Kathryn M. Rudy, "Images, Rubrics and Indulgences on the Eve of the Reformation." In *The Authority of the Word: Reflecting on Image and Text in Northern Europe, 1400–1700,* edited by Celeste Brusati, Karl A. E. Enenkel, and Walter S. Melion, 443–479. Intersections: Interdisciplinary Studies in Early Modern Culture 20-2011. Leiden: Brill, 2012.

Saenger 1989: Paul Henry Saenger, *A Catalogue of the Pre-1500 Western Manuscript Books at the Newberry Library.* Chicago: University of Chicago Press, 1989.

Salembier 1886: Louis Salembier, *Petrus de Alliaco. Dissertatio inauguralis.* Lille: ex typis J. Lefort, 1886.

Salter 1964: Elizabeth Salter, "Ludolphus of Saxony and His English Translators." *Medium Aevum* 32 (1964): 26–35.

Salzman 2011: Michele R. Salzman, *The Letters of Symmachus. Book I.* Atlanta: Society of Biblical Literature, 2011.

SANTAGATA 1980: Marco Santagata, "Nota su un sonetto attribuito al Sannazaro." *Studi e problemi di crictica testuale* 20 (1980): 25–27.

SARGENT 1994: Michael G. Sargent, "Versions of the Life of Christ: Nicholas Love's *Mirror* and Related Works." *Poetica* 42 (1994): 39–70.

SARRI 1933: Francesco Sarri, *Le "Meditazioni della vita di Cristo" di un Frate Minore del secolo XIV.* Biblioteca ascetica 9. Milan: Vita e pensiero, 1933.

SAUGRAIN 1764: Antoine-Claude Saugrain and Laurent-François Le Clerc, *Catalogus manuscriptorum codicum Collegii Claromontani: Quem excipit catalogus manuscriptorum domus professae Parisiensis.* Parisiis in Palatio: Saugrain and Le Clerc, 1764.

SCHMIDT 1938: Wieland Schmidt, *Die vierundzwanzig alten Ottos von Passau.* Palaestra 212. Leipzig: Akademische Verlagsgesellschaft m. b. h., 1938.

SCHNEIDER 1967: Karin Schneider, *Die Handschriften der Stadtbibliothek Nürnberg* 2.1. Wiesbaden: Harrassowitz, 1967.

——— 1983: Karin Schneider, "Die Bibliothek des Katharinenklosters in Nürnberg und die städtische Gesellschaft." In *Studien zum städtischen Bildungswesen des späten Mittelalters und der frühen Neuzeit*, edited by Bernd Moeller, Hans Patze, and Karl Stackmann, 70–82. Göttingen: Vandenhoeck and Ruprecht, 1983.

——— 1989: Karin Schneider, "Petrus de Alliaco (Pieree d'Ailly)." In *Die deutsche Literatur des Mittelalters. Verfasserlexikon Begründet von Wolfgang Stammler, fortgeführt von Karl Langosch* 7, 496–499. Berlin: De Gruyter, 1989.

SCHNEYER 1973–1990: Johannes Baptist Schneyer, *Repertorium der lateinischen Sermones des Mittelalters für die Zeit von 1150–1350* 1–11. Beiträge zur Geschichte der Philosophie und Theologie des Mittelalters 43. Münster: Aschendorffsche Verlagsbuchhandlung, 1973–1990.

SCHROEDER 1911: Carl Schroeder, "Der deutsche Facetus." *Palaestra* 6 (1911): 1–30.

SCOTT 1897: Temple Scott, *Book Sales of 1896: A Record of the Most Important Books Sold at Auction and the Prices Realized with Introduction, Notes and Index by Temple Scott.* London: P. Cockram, 1897.

SEDLÁK 1914: Jan Sedlák, *Tractatus causam Magistri Joannis Hus e parte catholica illustrantes.* Brno: Typ. et Sumptibus Pont. Typ. Benedictinorum Rajhradiensium, 1914.

SELMAN 2000: Rebecca Selman, "Spirituality and Sex Change: *Horologium sapientiae* and *Speculum devotorum*," in *Writing Religious Women: Female Spiritual and Textual Practices in Late Medieval England*, edited by Denis Renevey and Christiana Whitehead, 63–79. Toronto: University of Toronto Press, 2000.

SHAILOR 1992: Barbara A. Shailor, *Catalogue of Medieval and Renaissance Manuscripts in the Beinecke Rare Book and Manuscript Library, Yale University.* Vol. 3, *Marston Manuscripts.* Binghamton, NY: Medieval and Renaissance Texts and Studies, 1992.

——— 2009: Barbara A. Shailor, "Otto Ege: Portfolios vs. Leaves." *Manuscripta* 53 (2009): 13–27.

SHARPE 2001: Richard Sharpe, *A Handlist of the Latin Writers of Great Britain and Ireland before 1540, with Additions and Corrections.* Publications of the *Journal of Medieval Latin* 1. Turnhout: Brepols, 2001.

SILVA 1811: Ercole Silva, *Catalogo de' libri della Biblioteca Silva in Cinisello.* Monza: dalla stamperia di Luca Corbetta, 1811.

SIMON, A. 2012: Anne Simon, *The Cult of Saint Katherine of Alexandria in Late-Medieval Nuremberg.* Burlington, VT: Ashgate, 2012.

Simon, W. 2003: Wolfgang Simon, *Die Messopfertheologie Martin Luthers: Voraussetzungen, Genese, Gestalt und Rezeption.* Spätmittelalter und Reformation; neue Reihe 22. Tübingen: Mohr Siebeck, 2003.

Simonetti 1976: Manlio Simonetti, *Sancti Cyrpiani episcopi opera. Pars 2, Ad Donatum; De mortalitate; Ad Demetrianum; De opere eleemosynis; De zelo et livore.* Corpus Christianorum Series Latina 3A. Turnhout: Brepols, 1976.

Simonetti and Pricoco 2005–2006: Manlio Simonetti and Salvatore Pricoco, *Gregorio Magno. Storie di Santi e di Diavoli (Dialoghi)* 1–2. Rome: Fondazione Lorenzo Valla, 2005–2006.

Simó Santonja 2007: Vicent Lluís Simó Santonja, *De Vinis (A propòsit dels vins). Arnau de Vilanova prosa. Introducció, Transcriptió, Traducció i Notes.* Col·lecció Clàssics Valencians 28. Valéncia: L'Ornella, 2007.

Sinclair 1978: Keith Val Sinclair, *Prières en ancien français. Nouvelles réferences, renseignements complémentaires, indications bibliographiques, corrections et tables des articles du 'Répertoire' de Sonet.* Hamden, CT: Archon Books, 1978.

——— 1987: Keith Val Sinclair, *Prières en ancien français. Additions et corrections aux articles 1–2374 du 'Répertoire de Sonet.* Capricornia 7. Townsville, Queensland: Department of Modern Languages, James Cook University of North Queensland, 1987.

Singer 1931: Dorothea Waley Singer, *Catalogue of Latin and Vernacular Alchemical Manuscripts in Great Britain and Ireland Dating from before the XVI Century* 3. Brussels: M. Lamertin, 1931.

Smyth 1994: Marina Smyth, "The Medieval Institute Library: A Brief History." In *What Is Written Remains: Historical Essays on the Libraries of Notre Dame*, edited by Maureen Gleason and Katharina J. Blackstead, 211–229. Notre Dame, IN: University of Notre Dame Press, 1994.

Sonet 1956: Jean Sonet, *Répertoire d'incipit de prières en ancien français.* Geneva: Librairie Droz, 1956.

Spunar 1995: Pavel Spunar, *Repertorium auctorum Bohemorum provectum idearum post Universitatem Pragensem conditam illustrans. Tomus II.* Studia Copernicana 35. Wrocław: Institutum Ossolinianum, 1995.

Staubach 1997: Nikolaus Staubach, "*Memores Pristinae Perfectionis:* The Importance of the Church Fathers for the Devotio Moderna." In *The Reception of the Church Fathers in the West: From the Carolingians to the Maurists* 1, edited by Irena Dorota Backus, 405–471. Leiden: Brill, 1997.

Stegmüller 1950–1980: Friedrich Stegmüller (8–11 with N. Reinhardt), *Repertorium Biblicum Medii Aevi* 1–11. Madrid: s.n., 1950–1980.

Stillwell 1923: Margaret Bingham Stillwell, "General Hawkins as He Revealed Himself to His Librarian." *Bibliographical Society of America, Papers* 16 (1923): 69–97.

Stoneman 1997: William P. Stoneman, "A Summary Guide to the Medieval and Later Manuscripts in the Bergendal Collection, Toronto." In *A Distinct Voice: Medieval Studies in Honor of Leonard Boyle, O.P.*, edited by Jacqueline Brown and William P. Stoneman, 163–206. Notre Dame, IN: University of Notre Dame Press, 1997.

Stoppacci 2012: Patrizia Stoppacci, *Cassiodoro. Expositio Psalmorum. Tradizione manoscritta, fortuna, edizione critica* 1. Edizione nazionale dei testi mediolatini 28.1. Serie 1.17/1. Florence: SISMEL Edizioni del Galluzzo, 2012.

Strasbourg 1490: *Tractatus et sermones.* Strasbourg: Georg Husner, 1490.

Strubel 1992: Armand Strubel, *Le Roman de la rose.* Paris: Librairie générale française-Livre de poche, 1992.

SUÁREZ-SOMONTE 1988: Pilar Saquero Suárez-Somonte and Tomas Gonazalez Rolan, "Sobre la prexencia en España de la version latina de la 'Ilíada' de Pier Candido Decembrio. Edición de la 'Vita Homeri' y de su traducción castellana." *Cuadernos de Filología Clásica* 21 (1988): 319–344.

SUTHERLAND 1963: Donald W. Sutherland, *Quo Warranto Proceedings in the Reign of Edward I, 1278–1294*. Oxford: Clarendon Press, 1963.

SWANSON 2007: Robert Norman Swanson, *Indulgences in Late Medieval England: Passports to Paradise?* Cambridge: Cambridge University Press, 2007.

SYLWAN 2005: Agneta Sylwan, *Petri Comestoris Scolastica historia liber Genesis*. Corpus Christianorum Continuatio Mediaevalis 191. Turnhout: Brepols, 2005.

TABARRONI 1984: Andrea Tabarroni, "A Note on a Short Treatise Attributed to Ockham: The 'Super terminos naturales.'" *Franciscan Studies* 44 (1984): 329–349.

TAKAMIYA 2010: Toshiyuki Takamiya, "A Handlist of Western Medieval Manuscripts in the Takamiya Collection." In *The Medieval Book: Glosses from Friends and Colleagues of Christopher De Hamel*, edited by James H. Marrow, Richard A. Linenthal, and William Noel, 421–440. 't Goy-Houten: Hes & De Graaf, 2010.

TATARZYŃSKI 1997: Ryszard Tatarzyński, *Peregrini de Opole Sermones de tempore et de sanctis*. Studia Przegladu tomistycznego 1. Warsaw: Institutum Thomisticum PP. Dominicanorum Varsaviensium, 1997.

TENTLER 1977: Thomas N. Tentler, *Sin and Confession on the Eve of the Reformation*. Princeton, NJ: Princeton University Press, 1977.

THOMAS 2010: Alfred Thomas, *Prague Palimpsest: Writing, Memory, and the City*. Chicago: University of Chicago Press, 2010.

THORNDIKE 1955: Lynn Thorndike, "Unde Versus." *Traditio* 11 (1955): 163–193.

——— 1958: Lynn Thorndike, "De Complexionibus." *Isis* 49 (1958): 398–408.

TKACZ 2004: Catherine Brown Tkacz, "Women a[s] Types of Christ: Susanna and Jephthah's Daughter." *Gregorianum* 85.2 (2004): 278–311.

TODINI 1996: Filippo Todini, ed., *Miniature: La Spezia, Museo civico Amedeo Lia*. Cinisello Balsamo: Silvana editoriale, 1996.

VACHER 1993: Marie-Claude Vacher, *Suétone. Grammairiens et Rhéteurs*. Paris: Les Belles Lettres, 1993.

VALAGUSSA 1997: Giovanni Valagussa, "Santi lombardi di fine Duecento." In *Scritti per l'Istituto Germanico di Storia dell'Arte de Firenze*, edited by Cristina Acidini Luchinat et al., 23–34. Florence: Casa Editrice Le Lettre, 1997.

VALENTINI and ZUCCHETTI 1940–1953: Roberto Valentini and Giuseppe Zucchetti, *Codice Topografico della città di Roma*. 4 vols. Rome: Tipografia del Senato, 1940–1953.

VAN AELST 2005: José van Aelst, *Passie voor het Lijden: De Hundert Betrachtungen und Begehrungen van Henricus Suso en de oudste drie bewerkingen uit de Nederlanden*. Miscellanea Neerlandica 23. Leuven: Peeters, 2005.

——— 2011: José van Aelst, *Vruchten van de passie: De laatmiddeleeuwse passieliteratuur verkend aan de hand van Suso's Honderd artikelen*. Middeleeuwse studies en bronnen 129. Hilversum: Verloren, 2011.

VAN DEN BERG ET AL. 2005: Marinus K. A. van den Berg, Amand Berteloot, Thom Mertens, and Hans Kienhorst, *Het Gaesdonckse-traktatenhandschrift: Olim hs. Gaesdonck, Collegium Augustinianum, ms. 16*. Middeleeuwse verzamelhandschriften uit de Nederlanden 9. Hilversum: Verloren, 2005.

VAN DIJK 1963: S. J. P. van Dijk, *Sources of the Modern Roman Liturgy*. Studia et documenta franciscana 1–2. Leiden: Brill, 1963.

VAN HECK 2007: Adrian van Heck, *Enee Silvii Piccolominei Epistolarium Seculare complectens De duobus amantibus de naturis equorum, de curialium miseriis*. Studi e Testi 439. Vatican City: Biblioteca Apostolica Vaticana, 2007.

VANNINI 2010: Giulio Vannini, *Petronii Arbitri Satyricon 100–115: Edizione critica e commento*. Beiträge zur Altertumskunde 281. Berlin: De Gruyter, 2010.

VAN WIJK 1940: Nicolaas van Wijk, *Het getijdenboek van Geert Grote*. Leiden: Brill, 1940.

VECCHIO 2005: Silvana Vecchio, trans. Helen Took, "The Seven Deadly Sins between Pastoral Care and Scholastic Theology: The *Summa de vitiis* by John of Rupella." In *In the Garden of Evil: The Vices and Culture in the Middle Ages*, edited by Richard Newhauser, 104–127. Toronto: Pontifical Institute of Mediaeval Studies, 2005.

VENICE 1474: *Supplementum summae pisanellae*. Venice: Per Franciscum de Hailbrun et Nicolaus de Frankfordia socios, 1474.

——— 1496: *Repetitiones domini Joannis Calderini. : Repetitio. super prohemio decretalium. Repetitio. c. in nostra de rescriptis. Repetitio. Mandatum de rescriptis. Repetitio. c. ab. exco[m]municato de rescriptis. Repetitio. c. super eo. de electione. Repetitio. c. cum in iure de electione. Repetitio Rubrice de ordi. cogniti. Repetitio. c. cum intellexim[us]. de ordi. cogniti. Repetitio. c. cum spoliatione de ordi. cogniti. Repetitio. c. cum dilectus. de causa poss. [et] p[ro]prietatis. Repetitio. c. post cessionem de probationibus. Repetitio. c. dilectorum de testibus cogendis. Repetitio. c. vestra de coha. cleri. [et] mulierem. Repetitio. c. cu[m] nostris de concessione prebende. Repetitio. c. siquis presbyterorum. de reb[us] eccl[es]ie no[n] alie. Repetitio. c. propter eius de donationibus. Repetitio. c. de illis de raptoribus. Repetitio. c. naviganti de usuris. Gaspar. Calderinus. Repetitio super. c. postulati de peni. [et] remis. Repetitio Alexandri de Antilla super. c. tibi qui de rescriptis in. vi. Repetitio Francisci Zabarelle. c. ut a[n]i[m]a[rum] de co[n]stitut. li. vi.* Venice: per Joannem [et] Gregorius de Gregorijs fratres, 1496.

——— 1497: *Burlei super artem veterem Porphirii et Aristotelis*. Venice: Otinus de Luna, Papiensis, 1497; repr. Frankfurt-am-Main: Minerva, 1967.

——— 1511: *Horologio della sapientia et meditationi sopra la passione del nostro signore Iesu Christo vulgare*. Venice: Simon de Luere, 1511.

VERNIER 2007: Richard Vernier, "The Afterlife of a Hero: Bertrand du Guesclin Imagined." In *The Hundred Years War (Part II): Different Vistas*, edited by L. J. Andrew Villalon and Donald J. Kagay, 329–345. Leiden: Brill, 2007.

VOIGTS 2008: Linda Ehrsam Voigts, "Plants and Planets: Linking the Vegetable with the Celestial in Late Medieval Texts." In *Health and Healing from the Medieval Garden*, edited by Peter Dendle and Alain Touwaide, 29–59. Woodbridge: Boydell Press, 2008.

VOLPATO 2002: Antonio Volpato, *Recensione critica di testi: Letture in Santa Caterina: Opera omnia. Testi e concordanze*, edited by Fausto Sbaffoni. [CD-ROM]. Pistoia: Provincia Romana dei Frati Predicatori Centro Riviste, 2002.

VON HARTEL 1868–1871: Wilhelm von Hartel, *Opera Omnia Cypriani* 1–3. Corpus Scriptorum Ecclesiasticorum Latinorum 3. Vienna: Apud C. Geroldi filium, 1868–1871.

VON PERGER 2001: Mischa von Perger, "Walter Burley's *Expositio vetus super librum Porphyrii*: An Edition." *Franciscan Studies* 59 (2001): 237–269.

WALTHER 1963–1967: Hans Walther, *Proverbia sententiaeque latinitatis medii aevi. Lateinische Sprichworter und Sentenzen des Mittelalters in alphabetischer Anordnung.* Carmina medii aevi posterioris latina 2. Göttingen: Vandenhoeck and Ruprecht, 1963–1967.

——— 1969: Hans Walther, *Initia carminum ac versuum medii aevi posterioris latinorum.* Carmina medii aevi posterioris latina 1. Göttingen: Vandenhoeck and Ruprecht, 1969.

WARD 1996: John O. Ward, "From Marginal Gloss to *Catena* Commentary: The Eleventh-Century Origins of a Rhetorical Teaching Tradition in the Medieval West." *Parergon* 13 (1996): 109–120.

WEBER 1972: Robert Weber, *Sancti Cypriani opera omnia. Pars 1, Ad Quirinum; Ad Fortunatum.* Corpus Christianorum Series Latina 3. Turnhout: Brepols, 1972.

WEILAND 1872: Ludwig Weiland, "Martini Oppaviensis chronicon pontificum et imperatorum." *Monumenta Germaniae Historica Scriptores* 22 (1872): 377–475.

WEISHEIPL 1968: James A. Weisheipl, "Ockham and Some Mertonians." *Mediaeval Studies* 30 (1968): 163–213.

——— 1969: James A. Weisheipl, "Repertorium Mertonense." *Mediaeval Studies* 31 (1969): 174–224.

WENZEL 1992: Siegfried Wenzel, "The Continuing Life of William Peraldus's 'Summa vitiorum.'" In *Ad litteram: Authoritative Texts and Their Medieval Readers*, edited by Mark D. Jordan and Kent Emery, Jr., 135–163. Notre Dame, IN: University of Notre Dame Press, 1992.

WIECK 1988: Roger S. Wieck, *The Book of Hours in Medieval Art and Life.* London: Sotheby's, 1988.

——— 2007: Roger S. Wieck with Sandra Hindman and Ariane Bergeron-Foote, *Picturing Piety: The Book of Hours.* Les Enluminures Catalogue 13. London: Paul Holberton Pub. for Les Enluminures, 2007.

WIESNER 1970: William Theodore Wiesner, "S. Ambrosii *De Bono Mortis* A Revised Text with an Introduction, Translation, and Commentary." Ph. D diss., Catholic University of America, 1970.

WILLMEUMIER-SCHALIJ 1979: J. M. Willmeumier-Schalij, "De LXV artikelen van de Passie van Jordanus van Quedlinburg in middelnederlandse handschriften." *Ons Geestelijk Erf* 53 (1979): 15–35.

WILMART 1932: André Wilmart, *Auteurs spirituels et textes dévots du moyen âge latin: Études d'histoire littéraire.* Paris: Bloud and Gay, 1932.

WILSHER 1956: Bridget Ann Wilsher, "An Edition of 'Speculum Devotorum,' a Fifteenth Century English Meditation on the Life and Passion of Christ, with an Introduction and Notes." Ph. D diss., University of London, 1956.

WOELKI 2011: Thomas Woelki, *Lodovico Pontano (ca. 1409–1439). Eine Juristenkarriere an Universität, Fürstenhof, Kurie und Konzil.* Education and Society in the Middle Ages and Renaissance 38. Leiden: Brill, 2011.

WOGAN-BROWNE 2011: Jocelyn Wogan-Browne, "Mother or Stepmother to History? Joan de Mohun and Her Chronicle." In *Motherhood, Religion, and Society in Medieval Europe, 400–1400: Essays Presented to Henrietta Leyser*, edited by Conrad Leyser and Lesley Smith, 297–316. Burlington, VT: Ashgate, 2011.

WOLKAN 1909: Rudolf Wolkan, *Der Briefwechsel des Eneas Silvius Piccolomini.* Fontes Rerum Austriacarum. Österreichische Geschichts-Quellen 62. Vienna: A. Hölder, 1909.

——— 1912: Rudolf Wolkan, *Der Briefwechsel des Eneas Silvius Piccolomini.* Fontes Rerum Austriacarum. Österreichische Geschichts-Quellen 67. Vienna: A. Hölder, 1912.

Wordsworth 1920: Christopher Wordsworth, *Horae Eboracenses: The Prymer or Hours of the Blessed Virgin Mary According to the Use of the Illustrious Church of York; with Other Devotions as They Were Used by the Lay-Folk in the Northern Province in the XVth and XVIth Centuries.* Publications of the Surtees Society 132. Durham: Andrews and Co., 1920.

Ziolkowski 2007: Jan M. Ziolkowski, "Mastering Authors and Authoring Masters in the Long Twelfh Century." In *Latinitas Perennis I: The Continuity of Latin Literature*, edited by Wim Verbaal, Yanick Maes, and Jan Papy, 93–118. Leiden: Brill, 2007.

Zumkeller 1966: Adolar Zumkeller, *Manuskripst von Werken der Autoren des Augustiner-Eremitenordens in mitteleuropäischen Bibliotheken.* Cassiciacum 20. Würzburg: Augustinus-Verlag, 1966.

Zupko 2003: Jack Zupko, *John Buridan: Portrait of a Fourteenth-Century Arts Master.* Notre Dame, IN: University of Notre Dame Press, 2003.

Online Resources:

Cantus Database. http://cantusdatabase.org

Cantus Index: Catalogue for Mass and Office Chants. www.cantusindex.org

CHD: Center for Håndskriftstudier i Danmark. Erik Drigsdahl. http://manuscripts.org.uk/chd.dk

DIAMM: Digital Image Archive of Medieval Music. http://www.diamm.ac.uk/

Global Chant Database. Jan Koláček. globalchant.org Piccard Online. www.piccard-online.de

Repertorium operum antihussiticorum. Pavel Soukup. www.antihus.eu

Repertorium pomponianum. http://www.repertoriumpomponianum.it/

Schoenberg Database of Manuscripts. http://dla.library.upenn.edu/dla/schoenberg/index.html

Trismegistos: An interdisciplinary portal of papyrological and epigraphical resources, formerly Egypt and the Nile valley (800 BC–AD 800), now expanding to the Ancient World in general. http://www.trismegistos.org

Index of Manuscripts Cited

Index of Incipits

General Index

DAVID T. GURA
is Curator of Ancient and Medieval Manuscripts
in the Hesburgh Library and concurrent assistant professor
in the Medieval Institute at the
University of Notre Dame.